T0304306

Our Uncommon Heritage

Biodiversity change is the biggest environmental problem of our time. It leads to much more than species extinctions, affecting the food we eat, the diseases we face, our vulnerability to fire and flood, and our ability to adapt to climate change. *Our Uncommon Heritage* explores the many dimensions of human-driven biodiversity change. It integrates ecology, economics, and policy to examine the causes and consequences of changes in ecosystems, species and genes, and to identify better ways to manage those changes. It explores the place of biodiversity in the wealth of nations, the rights and responsibilities people have for natural resources at local, regional, national, and international levels, and the challenges faced in protecting the common good at the global level. This is an important book for students and researchers in the fields of conservation and sustainability science, ecology, natural resource economics and management. It also has much to say to those engaged in international conservation, health, agriculture, forestry, and fisheries policy.

CHARLES PERRINGS is Professor of Environmental Economics at Arizona State University, where he directs the Ecoservices Group – a research (and research training) group that focuses on ecosystem services. He was for several years vice-chair of the international biodiversity science research program, DIVERSITAS, and more recently represented the International Council of Science in negotiations with national governments to establish the Intergovernmental Science-Policy Platform on Biodiversity and Ecosystem Services (IPBES).

Our Uncommon Heritage

Biodiversity Change, Ecosystem Services, and Human Wellbeing

CHARLES PERRINGS

CAMBRIDGE
UNIVERSITY PRESS

32 Avenue of the Americas, New York NY 10013-2473, USA

Cambridge University Press is part of the University of Cambridge.

It furthers the University's mission by disseminating knowledge in the pursuit of education, learning and research at the highest international levels of excellence.

www.cambridge.org
Information on this title: www.cambridge.org/9781107043732

First published 2014

A catalogue record for this publication is available from the British Library

Library of Congress Cataloguing in Publication data
Perrings, Charles.
Our uncommon heritage : biodiversity change, ecosystem services, and human wellbeing / Charles Perrings.
    pages   cm
Includes bibliographical references and index.
ISBN 978-1-107-04373-2 (hardback)
1. Ecology – Economic aspects.   2. Biodiversity – Economic aspects.
3. Ecosystem services.   4. Environmental economics.   I. Title.
QH541.15.E25P47   2014
577–dc23

                                                              2014006079

ISBN 978-1-107-04373-2 Hardback
ISBN 978-1-107-61898-5 Paperback

To Ann, for bringing more than just light into my life

Contents

Figures

Tables

Foreword

PARTHA DASGUPTA* AND GEORGINA MACE**

The economic development that was initiated by the Industrial Revolution has been self-consciously intensive in the use of natural resources. The pace has not slowed. Since the end of the Second World War, even as world population and average income per person have grown at unprecedented rates, humanity's reliance on natural resources in large measure has increased correspondingly. During the twentieth century world population grew by a factor of four (to more than six billion) and world output by fourteen, industrial output increased by a multiple of forty, and the use of energy by sixteen. Methane-producing cattle population grew in pace with human population, fish catch increased by a multiple of thirty-five, and carbon and sulfur dioxide emissions rose by a factor exceeding ten. Vitousek *et al.* (1986) estimated that some 40 percent of the 45–60 billion metric tons of carbon that was then being harnessed annually by terrestrial photosynthesis (net primary production of the biosphere) was being appropriated for human use.

In this century the pace has accelerated. The release of nitrogen to the terrestrial environment from the use of fertilizers, fossil fuels, and leguminous crops now well exceeds that from all natural sources combined. Carbon concentration in the atmosphere is currently rising at a rate of 1 part per million a year, the concentration having just passed 400 parts per million, a level not reached since more than two million years ago. The scale of the human enterprise is so influencing global environmental change now, that as Ehrlich and Ehrlich (2008)

* Chairman, Scientific Advisory Committee, International Human Dimensions Programme; Faculty of Economics, University of Cambridge
** Chairman, Scientific Advisory Committee, DIVERSITAS; Faculty of Life Sciences, University College London

documented, we should recognize humankind as earth's dominant species. Humanity would appear to have ushered in a new geological epoch in which our activities are influencing not only local landscapes but also the global processes driving the earth system. Appropriately enough, the present era has recently been christened Anthropocene (Steffen *et al.* 2011).

Nature as an asset

Nature is a mosaic of capital assets. It comprises assets of intrinsic value (sacred groves, for example), those that are direct sources of human wellbeing (the air we breathe and the water we drink), and many others that have indirect value as inputs in the production of goods and services (crops providing food, and trees providing timber and energy). In fact nature's services are inputs in everything we do. The problem is that nature is degradable. Agricultural land, forests, watersheds, fisheries, freshwater sources, estuaries, the atmosphere – more generally, ecosystems – are assets that are self-regenerative, but suffer from depletion or deterioration if exploited without care.[1] The term "self-regenerative" should not be taken to mean that natural resources regenerate in isolation when left untouched by humans; for nature's capital – or natural capital – consists of an interconnected body of assets undergoing change over time in size and character. The potential regenerative capacity of one depends on the mosaic of which it is a part. The processes driving those changes differ in spatial scales, operate at different speeds, interact with each other, and are almost invariably non-linear. It should be no cause for surprise that nature is complex.

Human activities affect nature's processes just as nature's processes influence the choices we humans make. The mutual influence is so powerful today that, for many scientists, talk of "nature's processes" makes little sense. To them "socio-environmental" is a more appropriate way to describe the intertwined processes. A few broad principles underlying the processes are understood; but the devil lies in the details, and the details affect the daily lives of households everywhere.

Stresses in the system are often described as "environmental problems." They are problems of the environment, largely resulting from humans' influences on them; they are rarely also problems due to the

---

[1] We are ignoring subsoil resources in this account.

environment. Some are global while many are spatially localized, some occur slowly and may therefore miss detection until it is too late, while others are all too noticeable and a cause of persistent societal difficulties. That may be why there is frequently a tension in the sense of urgency people are known to express about carbon emissions and acid rains that sweep across regions, nations, and continents; about the stresses communities face when, say, grasslands transform into shrublands; and about declines in firewood and water sources that are specific to the needs and concerns of the poor in small, village communities. Moreover, socio-environmental processes are very poorly understood. For these reasons environmental problems present themselves differently to different people. Some identify environmental problems with population growth while others identify them with the wrong sorts of economic growth. Then there are those who view the problems through the spectacle of poverty in poor countries. Each of those visions is correct. There is no single environmental problem; there is an innumerable collection of them.

Economics and the environment

These observations may appear as obvious empirical truths, but twentieth-century economics saw them as neither obvious nor, more importantly, truths. Macro-economists, who are in the business of studying production and consumption in the aggregate, went further by building theories of economic growth and development that almost invariably took the inputs necessary in economic activities to be restricted to manufactured capital (roads, building, machinery, equipment), human capital (education, skills, health), and knowledge (arts, humanities, and the sciences). Nature was left out of the account. If the lacuna was mentioned, a typical response from growth economists would be that it was in the character of development processes that technological progress overrides the effects of diminished and degraded natural capital.

To be sure, *micro*-economists have long noted the presence of natural capital. A large, informative body of work in the field of environmental and resource economics has pointed to the need for public policy in the form of taxes and regulations to correct for humanity's excessive use of natural resources. (Economists uncovered reasons why, in terms of human interest, our use of nature is almost always excessive, rarely insufficient.) Nevertheless, even environmental and resource economists have mostly studied natural resources in isolation. Their account could give the impression that in the world we inhabit it is possible to pluck one resource at a time. The interconnectedness of the constituents of natural capital and the mutual (non-linear) influences among the socio-environmental processes that come allied to it are rarely probed.

It could be that growth and development economists have neglected nature because the services it provides are taken to be luxury consumption goods, as in the view expressed some years ago in two prominent newspapers that "economic growth is good for the environment because countries need to put poverty behind them in order to care," and that "trade improves the environment, because it raises incomes, and the richer people are, the more willing they are to devote resources to cleaning up their living space." The idea here is that environmental degradation is a mere irritant.

The idea is a deep, cosmopolitan misconception. It is a misconception because nature's services are critical inputs in consumption, production, and leisure, a fact that is self-evident to any agrarian person.

Wealth and wellbeing

That mistaken viewpoint has infected the public understanding of economic development. Macro-economic forecasts routinely exclude nature as an input in economic activity. Accounting for nature, if it comes into the calculus of forecasts at all, is an afterthought to the real business of doing economics. That most commonly used economic statistic for judging the progress or regress of nations, gross domestic product (GDP), does not record the use to which nature is put in economic activities. If a wetland is drained to make way for a shopping mall, the construction of the latter (including expenditures incurred for drainage) is deemed to contribute to GDP, but the destruction of the former goes unrecorded. If the social value of the former in absolute terms exceeds the social value of the latter, the economy will have become poorer (wealth will have declined), but GDP will tell us otherwise. The popular and seemingly more humane Human Development Index (HDI) of the United Nations (UN) adopts the same point of view: by neglecting to account for environmental changes, it misleads in the same way.

The rogue word in gross domestic product is "gross." Depreciation of capital is not deducted from final output and this is a reason why the index misleads when used as a reflection of human wellbeing. The point is that an economy's GDP could be made to grow simply by mining its assets. So GDP could grow even as the economy was becoming poorer. The moral is simple, even banal: if we are to study the sustainability of development processes, we should be estimating movements in wealth and its distribution relative to population, not per capita GDP, not the HDI. By a near-identical reasoning it can be shown that the coin with which changes in public policy (such as expenditure on new investment projects) should be evaluated is also wealth and its distribution relative to population.

Ecosystems as assets

An economy's wealth is the societal worth of its assets. It follows that economic problems are asset management problems. Of immediate and direct interest to human populations are ecosystems, which range in spatial extent from biomes, to lakes, to spoonfuls of rainwater collected on leaves of tropical plants and trees. In an important publication, the Millennium Ecosystem Assessment (2005) reported that fifteen of the twenty-four large ecosystems that had been studied in detail were found to be either degraded or subject to unsustainable use.

The character of ecosystems, for example their capacity to supply goods and services of use to humanity, can change relatively fast. Such flips share three important characteristics: (1) they are frequently irreversible (or at best they take a long time to recover from); (2) except in a very limited sense, it is not possible to replace degraded ecosystems by new ones; and (3) ecosystems can collapse abruptly, without much prior warning. Imagine what would happen to a city's inhabitants if the infrastructure connecting it to the outside world were to break down without notice. Vanishing water sources, deteriorating grazing fields, barren slopes, wasting mangroves, and bleached coral reefs are spatially confined instances of a corresponding breakdown among the rural poor in poor countries. Ecological collapse, such as has been experienced in recent years in Rwanda, the Horn of Africa, and the Darfur region of Sudan, can also come about in tandem with rapid civic decline.

A feature of significance of any ecosystem is the diversity of species. In a magisterial treatise on the diversity of life, Wilson (1992) reviewed

evidence on current species extinction rates to conclude that humanity
has triggered a process that compares with the five great global extinctions that have taken place over geological time. Recent syntheses of
data and trends suggest that indeed current extinction rates are on the
brink of what would formally count as a mass extinction (Barnosky
et al. 2011).

Determining the functional value of biological diversity – biodiversity
for short – is a deep and difficult matter but the consensus now is that
diversity of species and biological forms contributes positively to many
ecosystems and functions and to their resilience under changing pressures (Cardinale *et al.* 2012). When ecologists speak favorably of biodiversity, which they do in unison and with regularity, there is an
implicit assumption that the diverse species have co-evolved under
selection and represent more than a simple headcount of species.
When the Nile perch was introduced into Lake Victoria, the diversity
of species increased, but did not last for long. The lake, as a fishery, was
devastated.

Biodiversity is a key to ecosystem productivity and the resilience (that
is, stability) of that productivity. By "productivity" is meant the production of biomass. The total productivity of a population of species is
greater than the sum of the productivities of the individual species
grown in isolation. This reflects the non-linearity of environmental
processes and owes itself in part to the fact that species' populations
in an ecosystem play complementary roles; they cannot all be substitutes
for one another. This has the corollary that to invoke the idea of
substitutability among natural resources in order to play down the
usefulness of biodiversity, as is not infrequently done by growth economists, is a wrong intellectual move. For if biodiversity is necessary for
an ecosystem to continue providing services, the importance of that
same biodiversity cannot be downplayed by the mere hope that for
every species there are substitute species lying in wait within that same
ecosystem. Here it is useful to recall the analogy in Ehrlich and Ehrlich
(1981) relating species populations in an ecosystem to rivets in an airplane. One by one, perhaps, species may disappear and not be missed,
for there is spare capacity (in part "species substitutability").
Eventually, though, the cumulative effect of biodiversity loss will lead
to the crash of ecosystem functioning ("species complementarity" will
kick in), just as the cumulative loss of redundant rivets will lead to the
crash of an airplane. In a recent symposium Barrett, Travis and Dasgupta

(2011) reported that biodiversity loss has been closely connected to the persistence of rural poverty in Africa.

It remains a popular belief that the utilitarian value of biodiversity is located primarily in the potential uses of the genetic material it harbors (e.g. for pharmaceutical purposes). Preserving biodiversity is seen as a way of holding a diverse portfolio of assets with uncertain payoff. But biodiversity is vastly more valuable: it is essential for the maintenance of a wide variety of services on which humans depend for survival both now and for the future.

The economics of ecosystems

As ecosystems are assets, why can they not be adequately managed by the kinds of institutions that oversee the production and use of such assets as machinery and equipment? In particular, why can markets not suffice? One reason stands out (there are other reasons): natural capital is often mobile. The wind blows, rivers flow, fish swim, birds and insects fly, and even earthworms are known to move. That means that property rights to prominent classes of natural capital are not just difficult to enforce; worse, they are difficult to define. As no one is responsible for their management, their use gives rise to "externalities," which are the unaccounted for consequences for others – including future people – of decisions made by each of us.

What kinds of institutional arrangements should we seek to create for the management of natural capital? In which ways are they likely to depend on the specific nature of the ecosystem in question? Do institutions governing the management of local ecosystems that have proved to be relatively successful in traditional societies offer hints on how global resources such as the atmosphere as a carbon sink could be governed? If not, why not? Do simulated markets offer humanity a possible mode of governance? If so, which kinds of ecological capital would be most appropriate for them? Why can societies not rely simply on environmental taxes, subsidies, and regulations? Most importantly, who should govern the assets?

Our uncommon heritage

Although environmental and resource economists in recent years have studied many of these questions and have offered tentative answers, they have done so in a case-by-case manner. We do not have a treatise-length account which traces the answers to the socio-environmental processes that are shaping our lives and defining our hopes and anxieties for the future. In his classic work, Wilson (1992) did not offer a study of the human institutions that have permitted, even encouraged, the extinction process to which he was at pains to alert the world. Nor did he seek to identify the kinds of public policy that are now required. But then, neither of these was his goal, which required someone expert both in the science of biodiversity and ecosystem services and in economic analysis.

It is against this background that Charles Perrings's work at the interface of ecology, economics, and environmental policy has been so significant. In this book he has put together the ideas that he and others have developed over the years to present the full breadth and depth of this important science. His book is the natural successor to Wilson's treatise. Perrings offers an account that is lucid throughout and presents analyses that are never beyond the reach of the engaged reader. We write this foreword as chairs of two global environmental change programs, one focusing on biodiversity science, the other on human dimensions. The time has come for these two closely linked streams of science to come together to solve environmental problems for the benefit of current and future generations. Doing this effectively will rest on the foundations, insights, and future directions laid down in this book.

References

Barnosky, A. D., Matzke, N., Tomiya, S., Wogan, G. O. U., Swartz, B., Quental, T. B., Marshall, C., McGuire, J. L., Lindsey, E. L., Maguire, K. C., Mersey, B. and Ferrer, E. A. (2011) Has the Earth's sixth mass extinction already arrived? *Nature*, 471, 51–57.

Barrett, C. B., Travis, A. J. and Dasgupta, P. (2011) On biodiversity conservation and poverty traps. *Proceedings of the National Academy of Sciences*, 108, 13907–13912.

Cardinale, B. J., Duffy, J. E., Gonzalez, A., Hooper, D. U., Perrings, C., Venail, P., Narwani, A., Mace, G. M., Tilman, D., Wardle, D. A., Kinzig, A. P., Daily, G. C., Loreau, M., Grace, J. B., Larigauderie, A., Srivastava, D. S. and Naeem, S. (2012) Biodiversity loss and its impact on humanity. *Nature*, 486, 59–67.

Ehrlich, P. R. and Ehrlich, A. H. (1981) *Extinction: The Causes and Consequences of the Disappearance of Species*. Random House, New York.

(2008) *The Dominant Animal: Human Evolution and the Environment*. Island Press, Washington, DC.

Millennium Ecosystem Assessment (2005) *Ecosystems and Human Well-Being: Biodiversity Synthesis*. World Resources Institute, Washington, DC.

Steffen, W., Grinevald, J., Crutzen, P. and McNeill, A. J. (2011) The Anthropocene: conceptual and historical perspectives. *Philosophical Transactions of the Royal Society A: Mathematical, Physical and Engineering Sciences*, 369, 842–867.

Vitousek, P. M., Ehrlich, P. R., Ehrlich, A. H. and Matson, P. (1986) Human appropriation of the product of photosynthesis. *Bioscience*, 36, 368–373.

Wilson, E. O. (1992) *The Diversity of Life*. Harvard University Press, Cambridge, MA.

Preface

This book marks the end of a journey that began twenty-two years ago when I accepted an invitation from Karl-Göran Mäler, the newly appointed Director of the re-formed Beijer Institute at the Royal Swedish Academy of Sciences, to lead an interdisciplinary research program on biodiversity. That program brought together around forty social and natural scientists, and charged them with exploring the anthropogenic dimensions of biodiversity change. The results were summarized in three volumes (Barbier, Burgess and Folke 1994; Perrings *et al*. 1994, 1995).

They were heady times. The 1992 UN Conference on Environment and Development (UNCED) had concluded with a declaration of the intention of the governments represented there to achieve "a new and equitable global partnership through the creation of new levels of cooperation among States, key sectors of societies and people . . .which respect the interests of all and protect the integrity of the global environmental and developmental system." The Conventions on Biodiversity, Climate Change, and Desertification were opened for signature at the conference.

They were also momentous times. The principles that had guided human attitudes to the resources of the common environment since the time of Hugo Grotius[1] were being unraveled. The Rio Declaration endorsed a set of principles that included the following:

States have, in accordance with the Charter of the United Nations and the principles of international law, the sovereign right to exploit their own resources pursuant to their own environmental and developmental policies, and the responsibility to ensure that activities within their jurisdiction or control do not cause damage to the environment of other States or of areas beyond the limits of national jurisdiction. (United Nations Conference on Environment and Development 1992)

---

[1] Grotius enunciated the freedom of the high seas as a fundamental principle of international law in 1608.

That principle was embodied in the Convention on Biological Diversity (CBD), which was opened for signature at the conference.

When the first Global Biodiversity Assessment was initiated a year later, 1,500 scientists contributed to what we hoped would be the start of a constructive relationship with the international policy community. When the report of the Global Biodiversity Assessment was published in 1995 (Heywood and Watson 1995) we discovered just how wrong we were. To borrow the words of Dorothy Parker, the report was not tossed aside lightly by many governments of the day, it was thrown with great force.

The next seventeen years saw repeated efforts to build a science–policy interface that would inform both national governments and multilateral agreements. Whereas the Global Biodiversity Assessment had been sponsored by the UN Environment Programme (UNEP) alone, by the time the Millennium Ecosystem Assessment (MA) was launched in 2000 it had the backing of four UN agencies: the International Council for Science, the Consultative Group on International Agricultural Research (CGIAR), the World Bank, the World Resources Institute (WRI), the World Business Council for Sustainable Development, and the World Conservation Union. Its reports (Millennium Ecosystem Assessment 2005a, 2005b, 2005c), often referred to in this book, were more favorably received than the reports of the Global Biodiversity Assessment. However, the lack of direct engagement of national governments still compromised its effectiveness as a vehicle for bringing international biodiversity science to the policy community.

In a similar attempt to enhance its relevance to the policy community the international biodiversity science program, DIVERSITAS, had reformed itself at the turn of the century around an agenda that was directed to understanding the causes and human consequences of global biodiversity change. I joined the Science Committee of the program at that moment (and later co-directed the ecoSERVICES core project with Shahid Naeem). In 2005, the year the MA reported, DIVERSITAS was asked to carry forward an initiative of Jacques Chirac, then President of France, to test the international community's interest in the establishment of a permanent science-policy body. For two years the initiative, under the name of International Mechanism of Scientific Expertise on Biodiversity, conducted consultative meetings around the world. Once it had been demonstrated that there was at least some appetite for such a mechanism, the effort was adopted by UNEP and merged with a separate effort to follow up the MA and the consultative meetings gave way to formal intergovernmental conferences to explore the establishment of an Intergovernmental Science-Policy Platform for Biodiversity and Ecosystem Services (IPBES). In 2010, at the third such conference, governments agreed to recommend establishment of the body and before the end of that year – the International Year of Biodiversity – the General Assembly of the UN had asked UNEP to initiate the body. In April 2012 IPBES was formally launched.

What has happened to the science in the meantime? The one clear trend has been the rise of ecosystem services: a concept introduced to natural scientists by Westman's 1977 review of the implications of the way that economists approached the valuation of the benefits of ecosystems (Westman 1977). But the concept of ecosystem services has been far from unifying, and has not affected all. Taxonomists and systematists, for example, find little that they can use in the concept. Conservation biology had been developing as a subdiscipline since the late 1970s with a focus on habitat loss, species extinctions, and genetic erosion. It connected ecology and population biology to conservation practice and hence to the non-governmental organizations most directly involved in the conservation effort. Despite the fact that some of these organizations had already embraced a conservation and development agenda, however, conservation biology typically focused only on wild-living species. During the 1990s conservation biologists began to include ecosystem services among the reasons advanced for conservation, but the services considered were only those generated by wild species. Within ecology, the 1990s saw the development of a field of inquiry focused on the relationship between biodiversity and ecosystem functioning that has laid the foundations for a systematic analysis of the linkages between biodiversity and ecosystem services, but this too has largely focused on experimental manipulation of natural systems (Cardinale *et al.* 2012).

The science of managed systems has been just as resistant to change. Before the 1990s, biodiversity in agro-ecosystems largely meant crop genetic diversity and the diversity of pests and pathogens. Since that time there has been growing interest in agro-biodiversity *sensu largo*. DIVERSITAS added a crosscutting network on agro-biodiversity in the early years of this century. Yet interactions between agronomists, pest management scientists, and ecologists have been minimal. The same can be said of human, animal, and plant health science. The science has been caught in stubborn silos.

Within economics, the discipline that spurred interest in ecosystem services in the first place, the 1990s saw the establishment of the field of ecological economics. This was an attempt to create a science of the interactions between human production and exchange and the processes of the biophysical environment. It required collaboration between economists and ecologists (at a minimum) and sought to build new ways of understanding the dynamics of coupled systems. Indeed, the Beijer biodiversity program was an early foray into the field. The reformed Beijer International Institute of Ecological Economics, the International Society for Ecological Economics, and the biodiversity program were all launched in the same year. Much has been achieved. The work of Gretchen Daily and colleagues in the Natural Capital Project is one of the better-known examples, but there are many others. The existence of the field has itself been an irritant to many economists working on problems of the environment precisely because it encourages work across traditional disciplinary boundaries, but it has also changed the way that natural resource economics is done.

Nevertheless, if one has to ask whether the science is ready to contribute policy-relevant knowledge to the new IPBES, the answer has to be "no." The scientists working within particular disciplines and sub-disciplines may well be ready to contribute data and analysis from their own fields. However, our capacity to put the information together in meaningful ways, to undertake meta-analyses across fields, to model the feedbacks between social and biophysical systems well enough to be able to make conditional projections of the consequences of particular policy options, is extremely limited. Biodiversity science may be more challenging than other areas of science in this respect, simply because it covers so many dimensions of both social and biophysical systems. But the fact is that we still have extreme difficulty in working across disciplines. Nor do we have the models of coupled systems needed to undertake the kind of policy experiments called for by the new body.

The problems posed by global biodiversity change demand that we do better. The two decades since the first Rio conference have seen a decline in almost every indicator we have for the diversity of wild-living species. The MA reported that we are currently experiencing extinction rates up to a thousand times the background rate. We now know that these rates are still increasing. There are, however, other similarly pressing dimensions to the process. While growth in the production of foods, fuels, fibers, and pharmaceuticals is still positive, for example, the rate of increase has slowed to the point where per capita consumption growth is threatened. This may not be an issue for all people in all places, but it is for the more than 50 percent of the Sub-Saharan African population still surviving on less than $1.25 a day. The associated biodiversity change problem is nothing if not complex. It spans the effects of changes in crop genetic diversity, the diversity of wild crop relatives (and the genetic diversity within particular wild crop relatives), the impact of crop intensification not just on crop competitors and predators, but on other species both on and off farm. It includes the effects of the extensive growth of agriculture on habitat, and the services which that provides. It includes the impact of reactive nitrogen depositions in sites far removed from the source of nitrogen emissions.

This book is about the process of anthropogenic biodiversity change – what that process involves, why it is occurring, and what its consequences are. It is about the science needed to understand the process and the levers available to those who would manage it. It is about the many dimensions of the process, from the conversion of habitat for the production of foods, fuels, and fibers, to the dispersal of pathogens through trade and travel. It is about the knowledge required to determine when enough is enough in each case: when the change in biodiversity associated with an expansion of trade along some route, say, harms more than it helps. Understanding the process requires understanding of what people believe they are getting by the actions they take, but it also requires an understanding of what impacts their actions have on others, now and in the future. It requires, for example, that we embed the mechanisms that link biodiversity, ecological functioning, and the production of ecosystem services in models of system dynamics. It requires that we project the consequences of governance structures and incentive systems for the difference between outcomes that are "best" from a private perspective, and those that are "best" from the perspective of wider society.

For the managers of biodiversity change it is important to understand the trade-offs and synergies involved in alternative actions, and the way these play out at different scales. For national policy-makers it is important to understand both the leverage points on national biodiversity conservation and the payoffs to national action in different areas. For those responsible for the implementation of multilateral environmental agreements (MEAs) it is important to understand when national governments have an incentive to comply with the terms of the agreement, and how that incentive relates to the nature of the ecosystem services at stake. For biodiversity scientists it is important to understand how the different pieces of the puzzle fit together. The book is written with all of these people in mind. In identifying the elements of an integrated biodiversity science it shows what is gained by focusing on a particular aspect of the problem, but also what is left out of account.

The IPBES does not start with a blank page scientifically. The legacy of the Global Biodiversity Assessment and the MA matters, as does the legacy of the many other international environmental assessments that have already been concluded. Much of that legacy will be helpful, but some will not. A cost of the very strong natural science bias of past assessments, for example, is that none has successfully grappled with the problem of developing sufficiently integrated models to conduct realistic social policy experiments on the time frames relevant to decision-makers. It will be important for the new body to move beyond the scenarios used as a substitute for such models in other assessments, and to explore the future consequences of policy experiments framed by national governments rather than scientists.

There are several dominant trends that are likely to play out over the next two or three decades that limit both the range of policy options worth considering, and the responsiveness of the system to new information. As in any path-dependent system, future options for the conservation of biodiversity in both production and natural landscapes are constrained by past decisions. The title of this book, *Our Uncommon Heritage*, reflects two things. One is the uniqueness of the components of biodiversity that collectively contribute to a global public good, the gene pool. The other is the trend since the 1980s to renounce what had previously been recognized as our common heritage in genetic resources, and to substitute sovereign control. Just as the UN Convention on the Law of the Sea (UNCLOS) legitimated national appropriation of the exclusive economic zones (EEZs), so the Convention on Biological Diversity and the International Treaty on Plant Genetic Resources for Food and Agriculture (ITPGRFA) legitimated national appropriation of rights to genetic resources within areas of national jurisdiction. Understanding the degree to which societies are locked into particular patterns of use or particular solutions is critical to the development of realistic alternatives.

Since the path to this book has been long I have naturally accumulated many intellectual debts along the way. Karl-Göran Mäler started me on the path, but others in the Beijer family have also been important – especially Sara Aniyar, Kenneth Arrow, Partha Dasgupta, Paul Ehrlich, Carl Folke, Buzz Holling, Anne-Marie Janssen, Bengt-Owe and Simon Levin and, in a different way, Christina Leijonhufvud. The Beijer bio-diversity program itself left me with many debts, especially to my co-editors, co-authors, and the authors of the science-policy report of the program, *Paradise Lost: The Ecological Economics of Biodiversity*, Ed Barbier, Jo Burgess, and Carl Folke (Barbier *et al.* 1994). I was also involved in two follow-up activities from the program – the Resilience Network, later Resilience Alliance, and the establishment of the Cambridge University Press journal *Environment and Development Economics*. The Resilience Network provided both a generally stimulat-ing environment in which to explore interdisciplinary collaboration in what the English historian, Hugh Trevor-Roper, would have called "picturesque but irrelevant corners of the globe." It also introduced me to Buz Brock, to whom my many debts will be apparent. The journal left me owing much to my associate editors, Ed Barbier, Scott Barrett, Kanchan Chopra, Rashid Hassan, Ramon Lopez, and Jeff Vincent.

Scientifically, the Global Biodiversity Assessment was the first assess-ment to draw together findings from the many disciplines concerned with anthropogenic biodiversity change, and I learned much from Vernon Heywood and my co-authors.[2] My relation with the MA was more arm's length, but along with many others worldwide I share a debt to Walter Reid and the final drafting team for formulating the problem of biodiversity change in a way that created a natural bridge between the ecology and economics of the problem.

My association with DIVERSITAS has finally ended, but for more than ten years it provided an opportunity to engage with a wide range of scientists in ways that have profoundly influenced my approach to the problem of biodiversity change. Between 2001 and 2006 I was Vice Chair to the DIVERSITAS Science Committee, then led by Michel Loreau. To Michel, Rodolfo Dirzo, Michael Donoghue, and Peter Daszak, and to the Executive Director of DIVERSITAS, Anne

---

[2] Ed Barbier, Gardener Brown, Silvana Dalmazzone, Carl Folke, Madhav Gadgil, Nick Hanley, Buzz Holling, Karl-Göran Mäler, Pam Mason, Theo Panayotou, and Kerry Turner.

Larigauderie, I owe much. In a second life with the program, between 2006 and 2012 I co-chaired the DIVERSITAS ecoSERVICES core project with Shahid Naeem. To the co-editors of the volumes produced during my tenure (Naeem *et al.* 2009, Perrings, Mooney and Williamson 2010),[3] to the ecoSERVICES Scientific Committee,[4] and to successive Chairs of the DIVERSITAS Science Committee, Michel Loreau, Hal Mooney, and, now, Georgina Mace, I owe a great deal.

It will be apparent to every reader that this book builds on numerous collaborative papers with others. The list of my co-authors on papers cited in this book is long.[5] I am, however, particularly in debt to a few, especially Ed Barbier, Buz Brock, George Halkos, Unai Pascual, Julia Touza, Silvio Simonit, as well as younger colleagues Rodrigo Arriagada, Terry Iverson and Reuben Keller. I am also indebted to

[3] Dan Bunker, Andy Hector, Michel Loreau, Hal Mooney, Shahid Naeem, and Mark Williamson.

[4] Peter Burkill, Graciela Canziani, Jed Fuhrman, Fabian Jaksic, Zenichiro Kawabata, Daniel Rondeau, David Tilman, John Tschirhart, Wolfgang Weisser, and Tasos Xepapadeas.

[5] J. Agard, F. Ahrestani, S. Aniyar, A. Ansuategi, F. J. Areal, C. W. Armstrong, J. L. Aronson, K. Arrow, M. T. K. Arroyo, D. Babin, R. Barbault, E. B. Barbier, T. Barker, S. Barrett, M. Bartlett, S. Baumgärtner, W. Baumol, K. Bawa, C. Bliss, B. Bolin, G. Brown, L. Brussaard, E. H. Bulte, D. Bunker, S. Burgiel, P. Burkill, G. Canziani, D. Capistrano, B. J. Cardinale, S. R. Carpenter, C. Castillo-Chavez, M. G. Ceddia, F. S. Chapin, K. Chopra, G. Chowell, C. J. Cleveland, R. Costanza, C. Costello, W. Cramer, G. C. Daily, S. Dalmazzone, P. Dasgupta, R. de Groot, P. C. de Ruiter, R. S. DeFries, K. Dehnen-Schmutz, D. Delfino, S. di Falco, S. Díaz, T. Dietz, M. Donoghue, M. Drechsler, J. E. Duffy, A. K. Duraiappah, P. Ehrlich, T. Elmqvist, D. P. Faith, E. Fenichel, R. Ferrati, A. Fitter, C. Folke, J. Fuhrman, M. Gadgil, P. A. Gonzalez Parra, A. Gonzalez, J. B. Grace, I.-M. Gren, V. Grimm, G. Halkos, N. Hanley, B. Hannon, R. Hassan, A. Hector, C. Heip, G. J. Hickling, C. S. Holling, G. Holloway, D. U. Hooper, R. D. Horan, A. Huth, T. Iverson, L. E. Jackson, F. Jaksic, A.-M. Jansson, B.-O. Jansson, V. Kasulo, Z. Kawabata, R. P. Keller, A. Kinzig, A. Larigauderie, P. Le Prestre, M. Lehman, S. A. Levin, W. M. Lonsdale, M. Loreau, F. Lupi, K. Ma, G. Mace, A. MacLeod, K.-G. Mäler, E. Maltby, D. Martin, P. Mason, F. Milano, H. A. Mooney, B. Morin, M. Mortimer, S. Naeem, A. Narwani, J. Norberg, J. B. Opschoor, A. Oteng-Yeboah, M. R. Palmer, M. G. Palmieri, T. Panayotou, D. W. Pearce, H. M. Pereira, D. Pimentel, S. Polasky, H. Possingham, A.-H. Prieur-Richard, P. Raven, W. V. Reid, I. Ring, J. Sarukhan, P. Schei, R. J. Scholes, E. Shenshinski, J. Shogren, P. Simmons, S. Simonit, A. Skonhoft, M. Smale, V. K. Smith, I. Sousa Pinto, N. J. Spence, M. Springborn, D. S. Srivastava, M. Termansen, D. Tilman, J. Touza, J. Tschirhart, R. K. Turner, B. L. Turner, L. Velazquez, P. Venail, J. Verboom-Vasiljev, C. Villalobos, J. R. Vincent, B. H. Walker, M. Walpole, B. A. Walther, D. A. Wardle, A. Watkinson, J. E. Watson, R. T. Watson, F. Wätzold, W. Weisser, A. Whyte, and C. Wissel.

Anantha Duraiappah who made collaborative work with these younger colleagues possible, and who encouraged me to consider the steps required to develop wealth accounts. For long-standing collaboration on the problems of invasive pests and pathogens I am indebted to Hal Mooney and Mark Williamson. More recently I have benefitted from participation in the National Institute for Mathematical and Biological Synthesis (NIMBioS) Spider Working Group organized by Eli Fenichel, and from collaborators on the grant we share from the National Institute of General Medical Sciences at the National Institutes of Health (1R01GM100471–01), especially Carlos Castillo-Chavez, Peter Daszak, Rick Horan, Marm Kilpatrick, Simon Levin, Ben Morin, and Mike Springborn.

The book was started during a sabbatical from Arizona State University. I am also indebted to ASU for seed funding of the ecoSERVICES group, and to colleagues and students in the group for providing a stimulating and collegial environment in which to explore the synergies to be had from cross-disciplinary exploration of a common problem. I thank the Campus do Mar program at the University of Vigo for the invitation to contribute to their program that brought me to Galicia, and to Julia Touza for making that possible. The book can also be thought of as the final product of a Research Coordination Network funded by the National Science Foundation, the Biodiversity and Ecosystem Services Training Network (BESTNet) (NSF 0639252). Many of the people listed here have engaged in BESTNet workshops and so have contributed directly or indirectly, but I am especially indebted to Louise Jackson and Rodolfo Dirzo.

Finally, I owe thanks to the various people who provided valuable feedback on all or part of the draft manuscript: Terry Chapin, Jim Collins, Terry Iverson, Julia Touza, and Mark Williamson. Four students in the Honors/Recitation section of my undergraduate course, Sean Reed, Sarah Schimpp, Amanda Wolf, and Nicole Zeig, provided a good test of the accessibility of the material. I thank Mike Hoffmann and Silvio Simonit for their help in securing high resolution maps for various figures. Vernon Heywood and Patricia Balvanera read the draft manuscript for Cambridge University Press. Their reports helped improve the manuscript substantially. Most of all, I am in debt to Ann Kinzig. She is not only a co-author on many of the papers cited in the book, but she willingly read and commented on every chapter. She also lived through their making in Baiona, Chicago, and Tempe, and made sure that these were the very best of times. She heard the arguments of the book as they developed, and discussed their strengths and weaknesses – not always patiently, because that is not her way, but always insightfully. The book is much better for it.

References

Barbier, E. B., Burgess, J. C. and Folke, C. (1994) *Paradise Lost? The Ecological Economics of Biodiversity*. Earthscan, London.
Cardinale, B. J., Duffy, J. E., Gonzalez, A., Hooper, D. U., Perrings, C., Venail, P., Narwani, A., Mace, G. M., Tilman, D., Wardle, D. A., Kinzig, A. P., Daily, G. C., Loreau, M., Grace, J. B., Larigauderie, A., Srivastava, D. S. and Naeem, S. (2012) Biodiversity loss and its impact on humanity. *Nature*, 486, 59–67.
Heywood, V. and Watson, R. (eds.) (1995) *Global Biodiversity Assessment*. Cambridge University Press.
Millennium Ecosystem Assessment (2005a) *Ecosystems and Human Well-Being: Biodiversity Synthesis*. World Resources Institute, Washington, DC.
  (2005b) *Ecosystems and Human Well-being: General Synthesis*. Island Press, Washington, DC.
  (2005c) *Ecosystems and Human Well-Being: Current State and Trends*. Island Press, Washington, DC.
Naeem, S., Bunker, D., Hector, A., Loreau, M. and Perrings, C. (eds.) (2009) *Biodiversity, Ecosystem Functioning, and Human Wellbeing: An Ecological and Economic Perspective*. Oxford University Press.
Perrings, C., Mooney, H. A. and Williamson, M. H. (eds.) (2010) *Bioinvasions and Globalization: Ecology, Economics, Management, and Policy*. Oxford University Press.
Perrings, C., Mäler, K.-G., Folke, C., Holling, C. S. and Jansson, B.-O. (eds.) (1994) *Biodiversity Conservation: Problems and Policies*. Kluwer Academic Press, Dordrecht.
  (1995) *Biodiversity Loss: Economic and Ecological Issues*. Cambridge University Press.
United Nations Conference on Environment and Development (1992) *Rio Declaration on Environment and Development*. United Nations Environment Programme, Nairobi.
Westman, W. E. (1977) How much are nature's services worth? *Science*, 197, 960–964.

Acronyms

ACC	auctioned conservation contracts
ASEAN	Association of Southeast Asian Nations
BSE	bovine spongiform encephalopathy
CARICOM	Caribbean Community
CBD	Convention on Biological Diversity
CDC	United States Centers for Disease Control
CFC	chlorofluorocarbon
CGIAR	Consultative Group on International Agricultural Research
CI	Conservation International
CIMMYT	Centro Internacional de Mejoramiento de Maíz y Trigo (International Maize and Wheat Improvement Center)
CITES	Convention on International Trade in Endangered Species of Wild Fauna and Flora
CMS	(Bonn) Convention on Migratory Species of Wild Animals
CO_2	carbon dioxide
COMESA	Common Market for Eastern and Southern Africa
EEZ	exclusive economic zone
EPA	United States Environmental Protection Agency
FAO	Food and Agriculture Organization of the United Nations
GATT	General Agreement on Tariffs and Trade
GBO2/3	Global Biodiversity Outlook 2/3
GDP	gross domestic product
GEF	Global Environment Facility
GEO BON	Group on Earth Observations Biodiversity Observation Network
HDI	Human Development Index
HIPC	Heavily indebted poor countries

HIV/AIDS	human immunodeficiency virus/acquired immune deficiency syndrome
IAASTD	International Assessment for Agricultural Science, Technology and Development
IATA	International Air Transport Association
ICAO	International Civil Aviation Organization
IFAD	International Fund for Agricultural Development
IHDP	International Human Dimensions Programme
IHR	International Health Regulations
IMF	International Monetary Fund
IMO	International Maritime Organization
IPBES	International Science-Policy Platform on Biodiversity and Ecosystem Services
IPCC	Intergovernmental Panel on Climate Change
IPPC	International Plant Protection Convention
ITPGRFA	International Treaty on Plant Genetic Resources for Food and Agriculture
IUCN	International Union for Conservation of Nature
LME	large marine ecosystem
MA	Millennium Ecosystem Assessment
MEA	multilateral environmental agreement
MERCOSUR	Southern American Common Market
NAFTA	North American Free Trade Agreement
NGO	non-governmental organization
NNI	net national income
OAU	Organization of African Unity
OECD	Organization for Economic Cooperation and Development
OIE	World Animal Health Organization
OLS	ordinary least squares
OTA	United States Office of Technology Assessment
PES	payment for environmental services
REDD	Reduced Emissions from Deforestation and Forest Degradation
RFMO	Regional Fishery Management Organization
SADC	Southern African Development Community
SARS	severe acute respiratory syndrome
SEEA	system of environmental-economic accounts

SNA	system of national accounts
SO$_2$	sulfur dioxide
SPS	Sanitary and Phytosanitary
TBT	Agreement on Technical Barriers to Trade
TDR	transferable development right
TEEB	The Economics of Ecosystems and Biodiversity
TNC	The Nature Conservancy
TRIPS	Trade-Related Aspects of Intellectual Property Rights
UN	United Nations
UNCCD	United Nations Convention to Combat Desertification
UNCED	United Nations Conference on Environment and Development
UNCLOS	United Nations Convention on the Law of the Sea
UNDP	United Nations Development Programme
UNEP	United Nations Environment Programme
UNESCO	United Nations Educational, Scientific and Cultural Organization
UNFCCC	United Nations Framework Convention on Climate Change
UNU	United Nations University
UNWTO	United Nations World Tourism Organization
UPOV	International Convention for Protection on New Plant Varieties
USDA	United States Department of Agriculture
WCMC	World Conservation Monitoring Centre
WHC	UNESCO World Heritage Convention
WHO	World Health Organization
WTO	World Trade Organization
WWF	World Wildlife Fund

1 | *Biodiversity change*

1.1 Biodiversity

At the beginning of the Holocene, around 12,000 years ago, the vast majority of terrestrial and marine systems were barely impacted by humans. Today, there is arguably no ecosystem on earth that is not impacted by humans to some degree. All ecosystems are affected by anthropogenic climate change. Most have been altered by changes in land use and land cover, or have been impacted by the off-site effects of such changes. Of the fourteen major terrestrial biomes only tundra and boreal forests have been left relatively intact. All others have been transformed to some degree, and in six (temperate grasslands, Mediterranean forests, tropical dry forests, temperate broadleaf forests, tropical grassland, and flooded grasslands) the area converted to agriculture, forestry, or urban industrial, commercial, domestic, or other activities currently lies somewhere between a half and two-thirds (Millennium Ecosystem Assessment 2005a). Much of the earth's biodiversity now lies outside natural systems, in systems created or at least heavily impacted by people.

The term biodiversity refers to the diversity of genes, species, and ecosystems (Wilson 1988). Many people use the term in a more restricted way to mean the diversity of species in wildlands, but it goes far beyond that. It encompasses the variety of species used in human production and consumption activities: the food we eat, the biologically derived fuels and fibers that support production of a wide range of commodities, and the varying landscapes that we access for inspiration, recreation, and learning. It encompasses the genetic diversity of cultivated crops, of crop pests, of wild crop relatives, and of weedy species. It encompasses the range of diseases that affect humans, animals, and plants, and the species used to counter those diseases – traditional medicinal plants and the plants used as the source of modern pharmaceuticals. It encompasses the species that underpin biotechnology-based industries as well as those that support more traditional forestry and fisheries.

Biodiversity change reflects the fact that we have redesigned the world around us. During the Holocene the human population is thought to have grown from around one million to around seven billion. It is expected to stabilize at something below ten billion towards the end of this century. That growth has been possible both because we have appropriated an increasing share of the earth's ecosystems for our own use, and because we have changed the species in ecosystems converted for our use in ways that have dramatically improved both the quality and quantity of biomass we have been able to extract. The process has not been smooth. Moments of innovation have punctuated periods of stasis. Whether population growth was caused by or caused such moments of innovation is a matter of debate, but during the Holocene there has been a strong association between the two. The second half of the twentieth century was such a moment of innovation. The MA concluded that within the last four decades of the century, wheat yields in developing countries rose by 208 percent, rice yields by 109 percent, and maize yields by 157 percent (Millennium Ecosystem Assessment 2005a). While there is increasing concern that agricultural productivity growth has not been maintained at levels that will allow this to continue (Fuglie 2008; Piesse and Thirtle 2010), the transformation of crop genetic diversity has been hugely important in accommodating the pressures that led Paul Ehrlich to warn that the world population growth was outpacing the production of food (Ehrlich 1968).

In much the same way, the parasites, fungi, bacteria, and viruses to which people are exposed reflect the choices they make about where to live, whom to conquer, and whom to engage in commerce, how to structure their biophysical environment, and so on. Of course not all illnesses are due to microorganisms, and not all disease controllers are biotic, but many are. This makes the choices that affect our exposure to diseases or that harness disease controllers a part of the biodiversity change problem. Anthropogenic biodiversity change is a "directed" process. It is not random. People choose the species they wish to associate with. They deliberately simplify ecosystems to make them more "productive" or less "harmful." People have transformed many of the earth's ecosystems to increase the abundance of domesticated species – the source of foods, fuels, and fibers – and to reduce the risks posed by pests and pathogens. In so doing they have destroyed habitat for other species, and extirpated competitor species such as weeds, pest species such as bird or insect predators, and disease vectors (Scherr and McNeely 2008). In their place people have introduced cultivated crops, livestock strains, and a host of commensals (Williamson 1996).

People have also created entirely new ecosystems with new combinations of species. The Holocene is the age of agriculture, but it is also the age of urbanization. When the first Levantine cities were established – around 7000 BC – most of the people on earth were still nomadic. Today, a majority of the earth's human population lives in cities: constructed ecosystems with a completely different mix of species than occur anywhere else. Moreover, every city is a node in a communications web that is increasingly tightly connected globally. The net result is what Jeff McNeely has termed "The Great Reshuffling" (McNeely 2001). Species have been moved around the world in ways and at levels that are wholly unprecedented. Sometimes deliberately, sometimes not: sometimes harmfully, sometimes not.

I write these lines from the small coastal town of Baiona in Galicia, in northwestern Spain. The town celebrates the fact that this is where the first of Columbus's vessels to return to Europe, the *Pinta*, made landfall on March 1, 1493. For the townspeople this made them the first in Europe to learn of the existence of the New World. But it also marked the completion of the first move in what has come to be called the Columbian exchange: the transmission of a range of species across the Atlantic first through explorers, then through the conquistadores, and later through trade (Crosby 1972).

The Columbian exchange involved a wide range of species including livestock, crops, ornamental and medicinal plants. Some have transformed agriculture around the world. Crops introduced from the New World include, for example, maize (*Zea mays*), potato (*Solanum tuberosum*), tomato (*Solanum lycopersicum*), rubber (*Hevea brasiliensis*), cacao (*Theobroma cacao*), and tobacco (*Nicotiana rustica*). Crops introduced to the New World include wheat (*Triticum spp.*), rice (*Oryza sativa*), coffee (*Coffea*), and fruit such as oranges (*Citrus sinensis*), banana (*Musa*), and mango (*Mangifera*) (Crosby 1972, 1986). The Columbian exchange also involved an exchange of diseases between the Old and the New Worlds that has had a lasting impact on both. Common Old World diseases that had devastating effects on the human populations of the New World included the bubonic plague, cholera, influenza, leprosy, measles, scarlet fever, smallpox, typhoid, typhus, and yellow fever. In the century after Columbus's first voyage, the population of central Mexico, for example, was reduced to little more than 5 percent of its pre-Columbian levels by the effects of small-pox, influenza, measles, and typhus. Many of the social and political systems of the Americas were effectively destroyed as populations collapsed. In exchange, the Old World was introduced to syphilis and its close relatives, bejel and pinta, as well as Chagas disease (Crosby 1972; McNeill 1977).

The Columbian exchange may have transformed the world, but it was also just one step in a longer, punctuated process of directed biodiversity change. The Columbian exchange was not the first time species had been dispersed by human agency. The bubonic plague, the suspected cause of the Black Death in Europe in the fourteenth century, had been introduced along the silk route – the main trade route between China and Europe. It led to recurrent outbreaks of plague for the next three centuries that resulted in the deaths of up to half the population of affected cities (Herlihy 1997). Indeed, by the time of Columbus's first journey to the Americas, Europe had experienced three waves of biological exchange. The first was associated with the arrival of the Neolithic complex from southwest Asia, the second came with the expansion of the Roman empire, and the third with contacts between Europe and the Islamic world between 1000 and 1350 (McNeill 2003). In more recent times the introduction of mass air travel has sharply reduced the time it takes for emerging diseases such as HIV/AIDS and severe acute respiratory syndrome (SARS) to spread, dramatically increasing the number of people who are susceptible (Tatem, Rogers and Hay 2006a; Tatem, Hay and Rogers 2006b).

The dispersal of species has had profound effects on human wellbeing, but it has had equally profound effects on ecosystems. A recent study of the level of plant invasion in different regions, for example, calculated the proportion of the most widely distributed plant species that had been introduced. It found that aliens accounted for 51.3 percent of the 120 most widely distributed plant species in North America, 34.2 percent in Chile, and 29.7 percent in Argentina. The result has been the homogenization of the floras of these regions (Stohlgren *et al.* 2011), and the transformation of the functioning of affected ecosystems.

The common threads in the process of directed biodiversity change are the search for foods, fuels, fibers, and other products deriving from living species; protection against pests, pathogens, and predators; and the dispersal of species as a byproduct of the progressive integration of human societies. The search for foods, fuels, and fibers is what has led to the fragmentation and loss of habitat, to the pollution of both aquatic and terrestrial ecosystems, and to the harvesting of wild-living species. Protection against pests and pathogens is what has led to the use of pesticides and antibiotics, the elimination of "nuisance" species and the disruption of species mobility through "cordons sanitaires." The dispersal of species as trade goods themselves, or as passengers on trade goods, is what has led to the problem of biological invasions.

Anthropogenic biodiversity change is driven by our interest in altering the mix of species around us to produce the goods and services we want, to reduce our exposure to pests and pathogens, to foster domesticates, and to counter wild predators or competitors. It is not enough to lament this process. We need to understand why people make the choices they do, what they think they are gaining and losing, and what gains and losses they ignore in the process. We need to acknowledge that much is at stake: the food people eat, the fuels they burn, the fibers they use to clothe and shelter themselves, their vulnerability to storms, floods, drought, fire, and disease. We need to recognize that if the choice is to clear land to grow crops or to starve people will clear land to grow crops. We should not sit in judgment of that choice. It follows that the problem of biodiversity change is about the way that people's choices are structured by the biophysical world and the society in which they find themselves. What people do and do not know matters. The technologies available to them limit both their production and consumption possibilities. Their understanding of the wider and longer-term consequences of their actions limits their ability to take these into account. But so do the social rules and norms that guide their behavior, and the income, wealth, rights, and obligations that constrain their options.

The biodiversity at issue is the mix of all genes, species, and ecosystems that affect our wellbeing. It is the mix of species used to generate foods, fuels, fibers, and other commodities, or harnessed as inputs in biotechnology industries. It is the variety of pathogens behind diseases of humans, animals, and plants and the species used to counter diseases. It is the range of complementary species that insure us against the effects of environmental change, or the impact of extreme events. It is the genetic blueprint for future evolution on the planet. Biodiversity in all these senses affects human wellbeing. Sometimes the effect is quite localized and immediate. Sometimes it is global in reach and means more for the wellbeing of future generations than it does for the wellbeing of the present generation.

In every case, though, we can ask how human wellbeing is affected by a change in the variety of genes, species, or ecosystems. Few generalizations are possible. Two, however, stand out. First, more biodiversity is not always and everywhere better than less biodiversity. The progressive simplification of the world's ecosystems since Neolithic times to increase the production of foods, fuels, and fibers has underpinned every other mark of progress we have. It has enabled the specialization that lies behind productivity increases in every sector of the modern economy. At the beginning of the Neolithic revolution close to 100 percent of the population would have been involved in food production through hunting, gathering, or the beginnings of agriculture. At the beginning of the twenty-first century less than 1 percent of the population is engaged in these activities in many countries. In the same interval, control of the abundance of pests and pathogens along with enhanced nutrition has increased life expectancy at birth from around age twenty to age sixty-seven (ranging, in 2012, from forty-eight to forty-nine in a number of Sub-Saharan African countries to nearly ninety in Monaco) (World Bank 2012).

It is true that not every ecosystem service requires the simplification of ecosystems. A recent review of the evidence on the relation between biodiversity, ecological functioning, and ecosystem services found that biodiversity has a positive but saturating effect on ecosystem services that depend on biomass alone, such as carbon sequestration (Cardinale *et al.* 2012). For most services of interest to people, however, the optimal level of species diversity will be strictly less than the level of species diversity expected in a natural system. Indeed, that is the motivation for the simplification of ecosystems. Wherever people are interested in specific traits of plants or animals, they will eliminate species that do not have those traits, or that do not support species having those traits. The question to ask of modified systems is whether the extent to which they have been simplified is in the best interests of society, given its goals and resources. Within simplified systems intraspecific diversity may matter more than species diversity. Crop yields, for example, are generally increasing in intraspecific genetic diversity (Cardinale *et al.* 2012).

A second generalization we can make is that one of the main reasons for being concerned about biodiversity trends is the fact that we live in a risky world. This is not the only reason that biodiversity matters, of course. The myriad of life forms encountered in both terrestrial and marine environments have individual traits that we value for many different reasons. But the composition of species, and the genetic variation within species, matters because we live in a fluctuating environment. The diversity of species, like the diversity of financial assets in a portfolio, helps us negotiate a risky world. And how much diversity is needed within a portfolio of species depends both on the expected range of environmental conditions, and on the covariance in the response of distinct species to differences in environmental conditions. The greater the expected variation in conditions, and the less the covariance in species' responses, the greater will be the required diversity (Elmqvist *et al.* 2003). So, for example, yield stability increases with species diversity in fisheries, and resistance to invasive species and pathogens increases with species richness in plant communities (Cardinale *et al.* 2012).

There are, or course, very good reasons why people might not choose a portfolio of species, or of genes within species, that is in the collective interest. Much of this book is concerned with the factors that compromise decisions people make about the simplification of production systems and the conservation of protected areas: the incompleteness of markets (externalities), the public good nature of the benefits of biodiversity, and the effects of poverty and poverty alleviation. Because many of the benefits generated by the diversity of genes or species are jointly produced ecosystem services, and because many of these are not marketed, we may expect that decisions driven by markets for foods, fuels, and fibers will have unanticipated effects on co-produced services. Moreover, these effects will be widespread wherever co-produced services have the characteristics of public goods.

Since people's decisions are made in a social context, they are also hostage to the institutions constructed at many different levels. The social context includes our collective understanding of the world and of the consequences of biodiversity change. It includes our culturally formed preferences over states of nature, along with the social mores and norms that structure our behavior. It includes the legal and regulatory environment and the property regime that determine our rights and responsibilities. It includes the institutions we have created at local, national, and international levels to govern resources that lie in the public domain, and to address the consequences of the failure of markets to signal the true value of those resources.

This book is about the biodiversity change that has been one of the main consequences of the increasing dominance of humankind. People have altered their environment in ways that have been directly responsible for dramatic changes in the relative abundance of many species, including the local extirpation of many and the global extinction of some. For the most part these changes have been purposeful. People have deliberately chosen to convert habitat, to drive out pests and predators, to control harmful microorganisms, to promote domesticates and their symbionts, and to protect landscapes of special appeal. They have accepted that the growth of agriculture, forestry, fisheries, mining, and industry, the spread of cities, the development of roads, railways, dams, oil pipelines, and power transmission lines have had consequences for other species by reducing and fragmenting habitat, by diverting water, and by polluting air, soils, and water. Their choices may not always have been well informed. Sometimes decision-makers have ignored the costs of actions taken to alter the mix of species in some landscape. Sometimes they have simply misunderstood the consequences of their actions. But they have made choices nonetheless.

This is the real nature of the problem of anthropogenic biodiversity change. It is by far the most significant environmental problem confronting humanity. It dwarfs climate change, freshwater scarcity, particulate pollution, or any other of the environmental issues currently attracting attention. All biologically based production, all human, animal, and plant health management, and all biotic environmental regulation are affected by biodiversity change. More than that, since the global gene pool offers the blueprint for all future evolution on the planet, its erosion has consequences that potentially compromise all future generations.

1.2 The Holocene extinction

The MA reached many alarming conclusions, but none more so than this:

Over the past few hundred years, humans have increased the species extinction rate by as much as 1,000 times over background rates typical over the planet's history ... Some 10–30% of mammal, bird, and amphibian species are currently threatened with extinction. (Millennium Ecosystem Assessment 2005a)

Current rates of extinction are comparable to the most significant of the extinction events observed in the fossil record over the last 540 million years (Raup and Sepkoski 1986). Of these, the Cretaceous-Tertiary extinction event 65 million years ago saw 50 percent of all genera go extinct. The Triassic-Jurassic and Devonian-Carboniferous transition extinction events 205 and 360–375 million years ago respectively were of similar magnitude. Larger events at the Ordovician-Silurian transition between 400 and 450 million years ago, and the Permian-Triassic transition 251 million years ago, accounted for more genera – 57 percent and 83 percent respectively. Current rates of change in the numbers of species identified as being at risk of extinction may partly be an artifact of improvements in measurement and monitoring, but if they are anywhere close to reality, and if they are sustained in the centuries ahead, the final outcome of the Holocene extinction could be as severe as any of these.

Two things characterize the current extinction event. The first is its suddenness. All past events (including those induced by asteroid impacts) occurred over much longer periods of time. The second is that it is caused by a single species. It is due to human agency. The only species to have increased in either range or abundance are those that are valued by people, those that thrive in human-modified landscapes, and those benefitting from the establishment of protected areas. The stark result is that 12 percent of bird species, 23 percent of mammals, 25 percent of conifers, 32 percent of amphibians, and 52 percent of cycads are currently threatened with extinction (International Union for Conservation of Nature (IUCN) 2004; Millennium Ecosystem Assessment 2005a).

In recent years two papers have reviewed the status of vertebrates (Hoffmann *et al.* 2010) and selected other groups of species (Butchart *et al.* 2010). Motivated by an interest in checking progress towards the CBD's 2010 target to reduce the rate of biodiversity loss, both provide evidence that the extinction risks faced by these species are growing on very short timescales. Using the updated IUCN Red List of threatened species, Hoffman *et al.* evaluated changes in population trends and threat status since 1984 for 25,780 vertebrate species (all mammals, birds, amphibians, cartilaginous fishes, along with representative samples of reptiles and bony fishes) (Table 1.1).

They found that for every class of vertebrate assessed the net expected rate of species extinctions had increased in the period since the MA was undertaken (Figure 1.1). Over the whole period assessed they concluded that an average of fifty-two species of mammals, birds, and

Table 1.1 *Percentage of species in each IUCN Red List category threatened for all vertebrates and all completely or randomly assessed non-vertebrate and plant groups*

	Mammals (5,489)	Birds (10,027)	Amphibians (6,284)	Cartilaginous fishes (1,044)	Reptiles* (1,500)	Bony fishes* (1,436)	Dragonflies* (1,498)	Freshwater crabs (1,280)	Freshwater crayfish (589)	Corals (845)	Conifers (619)	Cycads (303)	Seagrasses (72)
Threatened/ extant assessed	21	13	30	17	18	12	8	16	24	27	28	62	14
Threatened/ extant assessed-DD	25	13	41	33	22	15	13	31	32	33	29	63	16
Threatened + DD/extant assessed	36	13	56	64	37	33	43	65	47	44	32	63	26
Proportion of extant assessed as DD	15	1	26	47	19	21	35	49	23	17	4	1	13

Notes: DD = data deficient. Threatened includes species in categories vulnerable, endangered, and critically endangered; asterisks indicate those groups in which estimates are derived from a randomized sampling approach.

Source: Supplementary on-line material (Hoffmann *et al.* 2010).

	0.00
	−0.37
	−0.90
	−2.63
	−4.55
	−6.15

Figure 1.1 Global patterns of net change in overall extinction risk across birds (1988 to 2008), and amphibians (1980 to 2004), mapped as the average number of genuine Red List category changes per cell per year. Shades of grey correspond to a net increase in extinction risk in that cell. White indicates no change. Cells are units within a hexagonal grid that retain their shape and area (approximately 23,322 km^2) throughout the globe.

Source: supplementary on-line material (Hoffmann *et al.* 2010).

amphibians had moved one IUCN risk category closer to extinction each year (Table 1.1). The approach adopted by Butchart *et al.* was different, but reached very similar conclusions (Butchart *et al.* 2010). Within a pressure–state–response framework they considered ten state indicators: the Living Planet index, the wild bird index, the waterbird population status index, the Red List index, the water quality index, and the marine trophic index, together with measures of forest, mangrove, and seagrass extent, and the condition of coral reefs. They found that since 1970 eight of the ten indicators had declined (only the water quality and marine trophic indices had improved in the period). Moreover, the decline had accelerated during the period since the CBD came into force.

All of the mass extinctions in the fossil record were followed by a recovery, and there is no reason to believe that the Holocene extinction will be any different. But this is cold comfort. Past recoveries have taken up to 20 million years, and the species that have dominated at the end of the recovery period have always been different from the species that dominated prior to the extinction event. The problem for humankind is to manage the changes now being visited on the planet in ways that secure the future for our own species, that respect both the current and future costs of genetic erosion among many other species, and that avoid the irreversible genetic losses caused by the extinction of some. What is ultimately at stake in the changes recorded in aggregate species richness is the global gene pool. On shorter time-scales, however, genetic erosion of existing species may be the greater problem for the effect it has on our capacity to adapt those systems to environmental change.

1.3 The challenge for biodiversity science

Securing our common future poses many challenges both for the science and management of biodiversity. The origins of an integrated biodiversity science lie in the eighteenth century, and in the work of someone more closely associated with economics and demography than with biology. In his *Principles of Population*, Thomas Robert Malthus famously argued that since human population had a tendency to increase at a faster rate than the means of subsistence, population growth would eventually collapse to zero in ways that would impose significant strains on society (Malthus 1999). This is exactly the idea behind the theory of density-dependent growth that underpins much of population biology (see, for example, Lotka 1925). More importantly, it is the idea that lies behind Darwin's theory of natural selection. Darwin freely acknowledged his debt to Malthus, noting in his autobiography that:

In October 1838 ... I happened to read ... Malthus on Population, and being well prepared to appreciate the struggle for existence which everywhere goes on, from long-continued observation of the habits of animals and plants, it at once struck me that under these circumstances favourable variations would tend to be preserved and unfavourable ones to be destroyed. Here, then, I had at last got a theory by which to work. (Darwin 1958)

Darwin's theory of evolution by natural selection applied Malthusian insights to an explanation of the success or failure of particular species, given competition between species. But he was also interested in anthropogenic selection:

we have evidence that variability, when it has once come into play, does not cease under domestication for a very long period; nor do we know that it ever ceases, for new varieties are still occasionally produced by our oldest domesticated productions. Variability is not actually caused by man; he only unintentionally exposes organic beings to new conditions of life, and then nature acts on the organization and causes it to vary. But man can and does select the variations given to him by nature, and thus accumulates them in any desired manner. He thus adapts animals and plants for his own benefit or pleasure. He may do this methodically, or he may do it unconsciously by preserving the individuals most useful or pleasing to him without any intention of altering the breed. It is certain that he can largely influence the character of a breed by selecting, in each successive generation, individual differences so slight as to be inappreciable except by an educated eye. This unconscious process of selection has been the great agency in the formation of the most distinct and useful domestic breeds. That many breeds produced by man have to a large extent the character of natural species is shown by the inextricable doubts whether many of them are varieties or aboriginally distinct species. (Darwin 1859, p. 286)

By transforming the landscape through land-use change, land-cover manipulation, or by animal or plant breeding programs, humans have altered not just the survival and growth possibilities of particular species, but the evolutionary potential of the system itself. Darwin's approach to the role of human agency in the evolution of the natural system has subsequently fed back into economic science – through Norgaard's notion of the co-evolution of coupled social-ecological systems (Norgaard 1984). But it is also present in the literature on agricultural innovation and the now very substantial body of work on feedbacks between ecological and economic systems (see, for example, Clark 1973; Dasgupta and Heal 1979; Tschirhart 2000; Bulte and Damania 2003; Clark 2010). At the same time, ecologists interested in the links between biodiversity and ecosystem functioning have explored the impact of anthropogenic changes in biodiversity for ecological functioning at population, community, and ecosystem levels (see, for example, Kinzig, Pacala and Tilman 2002, Loreau, Naeem and Inchausti 2002, and Naeem *et al.* 2009a).

At the core of the socio-economic contribution to the development of an integrated biodiversity science are three sets of results. The first deals with the necessary and sufficient conditions for the efficient exploitation of both private and public environmental assets over space and time. These results explain the socially optimal allocation of resources, and hence the socially optimal mix of species in any given system. The second deals with the role of institutions (interpreted broadly to include markets, market-like instruments, property rights, governance systems, cultural and religious restrictions, and so on) in structuring people's choices. These explain why the actual allocation of resources, and hence the actual mix of species in a system, may differ from the social optimum. The third deals with the options for closing the gap between the actual mix of species and the socially optimal mix of species in some system.

Foundational contributions to the first set of results include Hotelling's original theory of the optimal exploitation of exhaustible environmental resources (Hotelling 1931), and the general development of that theory (Dasgupta and Heal 1979). Other foundational contributions include the extension of the results obtained for exhaustible resources to biological systems (Clark 1973, 1976), to the relationship between economic growth and environmental change (Mäler 1974), and to the conditions for the sustainable exploitation of environmental resources (Hartwick 1977, 1978). This set of results identified the conditions in which it is efficient to reduce the abundance of particular species (deplete "renewable" resources), and the conditions in which it is efficient to leave them intact. Given the public good nature of many environmental assets, also foundational are Samuelson's results on the efficient allocation of public goods (Samuelson 1954).

Foundational contributions to the second set of results include the effects of common property on optimal resource extraction (Gordon 1954), the theory of externality (Meade 1973), the effect of governance systems on the efficiency of common pool resource use (Ostrom 1990), and the impact of property rights systems more generally on the rate at which resources are extracted (Dasgupta 1982). These works, among others, identified many of the conditions that compromise efficient exploitation of biodiversity: the problem of open access and weakly regulated common pool resources, missing markets for ecosystem services, and the interdependence of economic activities founded on exploitation of a common environment. Gordon, for example, showed that particular institutional conditions – open access or weakly regulated common property – could lead to levels of exploitation of particular fish stocks that, while privately optimal, would be excessive from a social perspective (Gordon 1954).

The third set of critical results concern the options for closing the gap when institutional conditions have led to a divergence between private and social optima – the difference between outcomes that are best from the perspective of the private decision-maker and those that are best from the perspective of society. Many of the later chapters in this book will be concerned with this problem, implicitly or explicitly building on the insights provided by contributions in two main areas: the design of corrective policies to achieve the social optimum (Brock and Xepapadeas 2003, 2004; Brock, Kinzig and Perrings 2010), and the impact of uncertainty, hysteresis, and irreversibility on the choice of policy (Weitzman 1974; Dasgupta 1982; Brock and Xepapadeas 2002; Dasgupta and Mäler 2004).

From an ecological perspective the critical element in an integrated biodiversity science is the relationship between biodiversity, ecosystem functioning, and the production of ecosystem services over a range of conditions. The assets from which people extract services are functioning ecosystems. These comprise both abiotic and biotic components, and a set of biogeochemical processes that underpin system functioning. The biological organisms in the system affect its geochemical processes. The stocks of the system are functioning ecosystems (or components of functioning ecosystems) and flows are the services those systems yield. So stocks include the atmospheric, lithospheric, and hydrospheric pools of carbon, nutrients, and water, together with the plants, animals, and microorganisms that move carbon, nutrients, and water into and out of the ecosystem, and that move pools of carbon, nutrients, and water back into biomass, and flows include the services secured from those stocks (Naeem *et al.* 2009b). At the core of the ecological contribution to biodiversity science are four key results on the relation between biodiversity, ecosystem functioning, and ecosystem services.

The first is that functional specialization between species enhances the functioning of communities and ecosystems regardless of the state of nature. Any positive diversity-functioning relationship that enhances the efficiency of resource exploitation through niche partitioning and does not rely on sampling effects implies complementarity between species. So too does any obligate or symbiotic relationship between species. The complementarity between species, like the complementarity between factors of production in economic activities, enhances the productivity and hence value of ecosystems (Loreau and Hector 2001; Schmid *et al.* 2009; Loreau 2010). More recently, a review of both experimental and field research on the relationship between biodiversity, ecosystem functions, and ecosystem services concluded that any reduction in the number of genes, species, or functional groups reduces the efficiency with which nutrients, water, sunlight, or prey are captured and converted into biomass. Moreover, these effects are consistent across groups of organisms, trophic levels, and ecosystems (Cardinale *et al.* 2012).

The second is that the apparent "redundancy" of particular species within some functional group provides insurance against changes in conditions that compromise other species in the same group. That is, species that apparently play a minor role within a functional group under one set of environmental conditions can play a major role if environmental conditions change (Walker, Kinzig and Langridge 1999; Kinzig *et al.* 2002). One foundational contribution in this area is Holling's argument that the appropriate measure of performance over long periods of time is a measure of the capacity of the system to respond to external stresses and shocks without losing function (Holling 1973, 1986). Indeed, Holling's concept of resilience has since been adapted by scientists working on the sustainable use of natural resources in a wide range of disciplines (see, for example, Levin *et al.* 1998; Carpenter, Ludwig and Brock 1999; Scheffer *et al.* 2001; Folke *et al.* 2004; Walker *et al.* 2004; Chapin *et al.* 2005; Brock and Carpenter 2006; Carpenter *et al.* 2009).

In this sense, biodiversity is like a portfolio of assets. The value of the portfolio depends on both the range of conditions that is expected to occur, and the performance of each asset in the portfolio over that range of conditions. From an ecological perspective this amounts to the proposition that increasing diversity within functional groups will enhance the intertemporal stability of ecosystem functioning (Griffin *et al.* 2009; Loreau 2010). There is considerable empirical support for this proposition. A number of experiments that have manipulated diversity both in the field and in microcosms have found that increasing species richness increases the stability of ecosystem functions (Hooper and Vitousek 1997; Hooper *et al.* 2005) through one of three mechanisms: overyielding, statistical averaging, and compensatory dynamics (Cardinale *et al.* 2012).[1] This underlines the connection between sustainability or intertemporal stability and biodiversity – at least at some level.

Third, a counterpart to the finding that increasing species richness enhances functioning at the community and ecosystem level is that increasing species richness also reduces the average contributions of individual species. The ecological reasons for this are quite intuitive and have been understood for fifty years (Macarthur and Levins 1967). If total resource inputs from the environment determine the community or ecosystem response, and if these resource inputs are distributed among the species in the system, then the average response must decrease as the number of species in the system rises. The evidence for this effect from biodiversity-ecosystem functioning experiments is also very strong (Schmid *et al.* 2009).

The fourth result is that the evolutionary potential of the system is an increasing function of the gene combinations that enable species to exploit novel conditions. Indeed, this is the point that most strongly connects modern biodiversity-ecosystem functioning research with the inferences Darwin drew from his reading of Malthus (Naeem *et al.* 2009b). There is no consensus on whether the appropriate measure of biodiversity is phylogenetic (the length of evolutionary pathways that connect distinct taxa) (Forest *et al.* 2007), taxon richness, or something else (Brooks *et al.* 2006). However, there is consensus that the loss of genetic diversity restricts evolutionary options (Levin 1999).

---

[1] Overyielding implies that mean biomass production increases with diversity more rapidly than does its standard deviation. Statistical averaging implies that random variation in the abundance of different species reduces variability in aggregate ecosystem variables. Compensatory dynamics occur when competitive interactions lead to asynchronous environmental responses (Cardinale *et al.* 2012).

The development of an integrated biodiversity science has roots in both biology and political economy. The social system and its environment are both evolving, and the evolutionary potential of each is integrally linked (Norgaard 1984). The evolution of the social system is reflected in the transformation of technology (and knowledge more generally), institutions (including markets), and culture, as well as the human demographics that worried Malthus. These all have the effect of changing the mix of ecosystems and of the species within ecosystems. So while the evolution of the natural system depends on the selective pressures identified by Darwin, these are structured by the evolution of the social system. Moreover, the strength of the social impact on evolution of the natural system increases with both demographic and economic growth. More particularly, the greater the impact of demographic and economic growth on the gene pool, the greater the constraint it places on the evolutionary potential of the natural system.

The nature of biodiversity change reflects the independent decisions of the billions of people who impact the environment through their resource use. This is what the statement that "biodiversity change is a directed process" means. Understanding the process requires that we understand people's decisions, and the way that those decisions are made. This includes the economic, institutional, political, cultural, religious, and ethical context in which decisions are made, and the ecological context within which they have effect. Much of this book addresses the way that decisions at different levels affecting the mix of species are made, in order to be able to project the biodiversity effects of changes in context.

While it is recognized that the social system and its environment are integrally linked, the ways in which the environment is constrained by or constrains the social system are not. Nor are environmental changes necessarily reflected in existing social institutions. In fact this is a recurrent theme since Malthus. Of course the environmental constraints on economic or population growth are not as straightforward as Malthus claimed. The carrying capacity of the environment depends on much more than the means of subsistence. The capacity to assimilate waste or to provide an aesthetically pleasing or spiritually nourishing environment may be as important as the capacity to generate biomass to satisfy human wants. What this means is that choices that alter the mix of species may be blind to many of the consequences this has for the wellbeing of other people, or other species.

The principal challenge of an integrated biodiversity science is thus both to understand the socially optimal mix of species, and to find ways to change the independent decisions of resource users to achieve it. Integrated biodiversity science embeds traditional biodiversity science and the disciplines involved in that – population, community, and ecosystem ecology, taxonomy and systematics, biological evolution and development – but goes beyond traditional biodiversity science to include the sciences concerned with human behavior and institutions, technology, and the dynamics of complex systems (Levin 1999).

1.4 Science and policy at the crossroads

The context in which this book is being written is the development of novel institutions for bringing international biodiversity science and international biodiversity policy together. In 2005 the then President of France, Jacques Chirac, initiated a process to establish an intergovernmental science-policy body for biodiversity and ecosystem services. During the time this book has been written that process has finally come to fruition. On December 20, 2010, the UN General Assembly effectively approved creation of an intergovernmental platform on biodiversity and ecosystem services IPBES to track and interpret changes in biodiversity for policy-makers by calling on UNEP to convene a meeting to finalize the form and functions of the new body. On April 21, 2012, the new body was formally established in Panama with the support of ninety-four governments. It has four key functions:

1 to identify and prioritize key scientific information needed for policy-makers;
2 to perform regular and timely assessments of knowledge on biodiversity and ecosystem services;
3 to support policy formulation and implementation by identifying policy-relevant tools and methodologies; and
4 to prioritize key capacity-building needs to improve the science-policy interface.

While all standing assessments undertake the second of these functions, the others are more novel. They ask scientists to support policy in ways that go well beyond those adopted by earlier assessments. They imply that assessments be undertaken at a scale, frequency, and with a time horizon appropriate to the phenomena being assessed; that assessments include quantitative projections of the consequences of a range of policy actions; that these projections be based on policies and programs specified by the plenary of the new body and not on arbitrary future scenarios; and that the new body catalyze efforts to build the scientific capacity to do this (Perrings *et al.* 2011).

There is a distinction between assessment and research. The role of research is to uncover the mechanisms that explain how biosphere change impacts ecological processes and functions, the delivery of ecosystem services, and human wellbeing. The role of assessment in the same domain is to synthesize and report the evidence of change, and to evaluate options for mitigation, adaptation, or stabilization identified by policy-makers. For assessments to be useful from a policy perspective they should provide sufficient information on the future consequences of alternative policies to make it possible to select between these alternatives. But this requires that the underpinning science is capable of evaluating the future consequences of current actions taking account of the many varied feedbacks between the social and biophysical components of the general system.

This requires a different approach to the projection of future change than that used by the MA, or by the Intergovernmental Panel for Climate Change (IPCC). IPCC assessments have tended to evaluate the future consequences of human behavior through non-probabilistic scenarios in which arbitrary human behaviors are treated as exogenous forcing functions that remain insensitive to the projected state of the system over long periods of time (IPCC 2000). The MA's look forward similarly rested on the development of four arbitrary storylines. "Global orchestration" focused on the implications of failure to deal with large-scale processes, including abrupt, often catastrophic change. "Order from strength" focused on the implications of patchy failure of ecosystem services and the effect that has on poverty. "Adapting mosaic" considered local adaptation to changing conditions, and "Techno garden" addressed the capacity of technological change to manage losses of ecosystem services. None considered business as usual (Millennium Ecosystem Assessment 2005b). The approach adopted in both assessments poses three rather obvious difficulties. First, it makes it difficult to incorporate human responses in projections of environmental change. Second, it restricts the set of policy options evaluated to an arbitrary set that may have little relation to the policies being evaluated by either national governments or MEAs. Third, it precludes evaluation of current actions designed to mitigate future risks, rather than to adapt to those risks.

What will be needed for IPBES to do its work are conditional predictive models of the consequences of options under consideration by national and international decision-makers – probabilistic projections of the consequences of policy options based on models of the feedbacks between the social and biophysical systems (Perrings *et al.* 2011). The science needed to make this happen is still in development. However, even if IPBES had not been formed there would be strong incentives to accelerate the process. The CBD has recently agreed a ten-year strategic plan, supported by twenty targets: the Aichi targets (Perrings *et al.* 2010; Convention on Biological Diversity 2012). It needs to know what actions are feasible to implement the plan, and what probability of success those actions will have. A key element in the future science of biodiversity change will therefore be the development of a new generation of predictive models. While there has been a substantial improvement in quantitative projections of biodiversity change (Pereira *et al.* 2010), more work needs to be done if we want to improve understanding of the future consequences of anthropogenic impacts on biodiversity and ecosystem services. In particular, we need integrated models of social and environmental change that are capable of providing conditional predictions of the consequences of real policy options. The establishment of a global science-policy platform for the understanding of biosphere change is an important step towards the effective governance of the biosphere. Knowing when the effects of biosphere change are contained within a decision-maker's jurisdiction, and when they are not, is critical to the development of coordinated or cooperative management of the problem across jurisdictions. Understanding the likely consequences of alternative policy options is critical to the choice of the best management strategy.

The central point here is that the projection of directed anthropogenic environmental change – any directed anthropogenic environmental change – requires an understanding of the human decisions driving that change. It also requires an understanding of the way that future decisions will respond to environmental change. We need to know how and why people make decisions about the mix of species around them, and with what consequences. Managing directed biodiversity change then requires that we understand the socially optimal mix of species, and that we are able to influence private decisions to close the gap between what is socially and what is privately desirable. It is not enough to be able to measure changes in a range of indices for biodiversity in relatively intact ecosystems. We need to be able to gauge the direction of change sought by private individuals, to relate this to the socially optimal direction of change, and to find ways to align one with the other.

A future in which scientists simply berate policy-makers for ignoring the consequences of the Holocene extinction, without understanding the choices those policy-makers face, will be as unproductive as a past in which biodiversity science and policy have lived in different worlds. The MA was a step in the right general direction: but *only* a step and only in the right *general* direction. The establishment of IPBES offers an opportunity to build a much more productive relation between science and policy, grounded in an integrated science of anthropogenic biodiversity change. This book indicates at least some of the elements of such an integrated science.

1.5 The challenge for conservation

The book is not about biodiversity conservation in the traditional sense of the preservation of wild-living species in protected areas and remnant wild lands, but it is about conservation nonetheless. Directed biodiversity change is the result of decisions about which species to promote, and which to control, which gene stocks to build, and which to run down. One of the most significant papers in the economics of natural resources investigated the conditions in which the owner of a non-renewable resource, such as a mineral deposit, would be indifferent between extracting the resource and leaving it in place. It found that the owner of the resource would be indifferent between extracting it and leaving it in place when the value of the resource in place was expected to grow at the same rate as the return on alternative assets (Hotelling 1931). It has been shown that the argument extends naturally to the case of renewable resources, in which the growth in value of the resource in place reflects not just a change in its price but also a change in its physical magnitude. In fact it gives us a general theory of conservation (Perrings and Halkos 2012). For any environmental asset, it will be optimal to conserve that asset if and only if the value of the asset in the conserved state is expected to grow at a rate at least equal to the rate of return on the asset when converted to an alternative state.

While it might be thought that this condition requires explicit calculation of the monetary value of conserved habitat, it really requires only
that the decision-maker consider the opportunity cost of conservation
or development decisions. Since conservation will only be optimal if the
growth in value of the resource exceeds the opportunity cost, a decision
to conserve taken in the knowledge of the opportunity cost implies that
the expected growth in the value of the conserved resource is above the
yield on alternative assets. A decision to convert implies the opposite. It
follows that conservation and conversion decisions should both be
informed by an understanding of what has to be given up in the process.
Another implication of this is that conservation decisions are not limited
to protected areas or remnant wildlands. There are conservation decisions to be made about simplified or modified landscapes just as there
are for natural landscapes.

The general challenge is to ensure that biodiversity conservation
options are given appropriate weight everywhere – not only in areas
under protection, or covered by integrated conservation and development projects. An important rider here is that the biodiversity to be
conserved is likely to be specific not only to the ecosystem involved,
but also to the use that is made of it. It makes little sense to have the
same conservation objectives in agro-ecosystems, production forests,
wildlands, and exclusive (marine) economic zones. This book offers a
common way to approach the conservation problem in different systems, but recognizes that the conservation problem itself will differ
from ecosystem to ecosystem.

1.6 A roadmap

The book is divided into two parts. Part I considers the nature and
extent of the problem posed by biodiversity change. It is a diagnosis of
sorts. Part II then considers the options for managing biodiversity
change. Part I asks what the decisions were that led to the main biodiversity changes observed in the later part of the Holocene, what
people have gained from biodiversity change, and what they have lost.
Gains and losses are described in terms of the ecosystem services that
have become familiar since publication of the MA, using the range of
metrics available. Some gains or losses map into the categories of the
national income accounts, and so have dollar values attached to them or
at least can be measured as a share of GDP or gross national income.

Others do not. For these our measures are at best indicative, and are intended to give some sense of the magnitude of effects that are ignored in routine resource use decisions. Often the best that can be done is to indicate a lower or upper bound. Part I also asks about the context within which resource use decisions are made, and what affects the size of the wedge between privately and socially optimal biodiversity. Part II then takes what is known about the mechanisms connecting biodiversity, ecosystem functioning, ecosystem services, and the goods and services that enter into final demand (the goods and services that people consume), and uses this to evaluate the various measures being taken to address the problem of biodiversity change.

Part I comprises six chapters. In the first of these I sketch the significance of biodiversity in the modern world, focusing on three areas of activity: agriculture, health, and the conservation of wild-living species. I consider the choices confronting decision-makers in each area, while at the same time initiating a discussion of the main drivers of biodiversity change. In every case the decision problem has common features. Agriculture involves the promotion of particular crop and livestock varieties and the control of pests. Health is about protection against the negative effects of protozoa, helminthes, viruses, and bacteria. Both clearly involve the simplification of ecosystems – the deliberate extirpation of some species, and control over the abundance of others. The conservation of wild-living species is less selective but it is also motivated by the promotion of particular species – those that are rare and endangered. It also involves the extirpation or control of others, especially invasive alien species.

In Chapter 3, I consider the benefits yielded by biodiversity change, exploring the services secured from both managed and natural landscapes. Building on the findings of the MA, I first describe the ecosystem services reported in the assessment, and then discuss the way in which different services are supported by biodiversity. Emphasis is given to those services that depend on the diversity of species *per se*. In the language of the MA these are the regulating services. However, it turns out that variability in the production of ecosystem services depends on the diversity of the species responsible for the ecological functions on which those services are based. I conclude by examining what is known about the value and valuation of ecosystem services that lie outside the market, emphasizing the central fact that the value of any ecosystem service derives from the value the goods and services it supports.

Chapters 4 and 5 address three concepts that are central to our understanding of the choices people make about the diversity of life around them. The first of these, the concept of biodiversity as a portfolio of natural assets, is introduced in the context of the indices most frequently used by biologists to characterize different types of biodiversity. I consider the relationship between the decision-makers' objectives and the combination of species they select as a problem of portfolio choice. I then discuss the reasons why people's private choices might not coincide with the choices that would best serve society. Along the way I explore two other critical concepts: externality and public goods. More particularly, I investigate the distinction between the decision problems faced by private resource users and the society to which they belong, and show how the lack of markets for particular ecosystem services drives a wedge between the outcome favored by private decision-makers and the outcome that best serves society. I also explore the public good nature of many ecosystem services, showing both how public goods relate to the institutional, political, and cultural conditions in society, and how they give rise to free-riding behavior. The effect of the type of public good on the incentive to contribute to its provision is discussed in some detail.

These two chapters are the core of Part I. They show both how decision-makers will approach the choice of one combination of species over another, and the factors that lead private decisions to diverge from those that would be best for society. The basic decision model used in these and later chapters helps clarify both the logical structure of private and social decision-problems and the way that changes in conditions affect the outcome. Since the structure and results of the models are described verbally, however, the book can be read without necessarily exploring them in detail.

In the final two chapters in Part II consider the importance of two phenomena that are frequently claimed to cause biodiversity loss: poverty and globalization. Chapter 6 focuses on the problem of poverty. While all the evidence indicates that poverty is declining, it is still very high in particular regions. In Sub-Saharan Africa, for example, the proportion of the population surviving on less than $1.25 a day is still above 50 percent. The chapter reconsiders a central point in the Brundtland Report: that poverty induces people to overexploit environmental resources, increasing environmental degradation in the process (World Commission on Environment and Development 1987). Since the same point is what lies behind the claim that poverty alleviation is environmentally beneficial, I consider the relationship between income growth and threats to biodiversity. Although income growth in middle- and high-income countries is associated with a reduction in the number of threatened species, the opposite relation is found in low-income countries. The chapter then considers the broader implications of this finding.

Chapter 7 addresses the last of the major drivers of biodiversity change – globalization. The growth and closer integration of the global economy has two main implications for biodiversity. One is a dramatic increase in the rate at which species are dispersed across the world as either objects of trade, or as the incidental byproducts of trade and travel. The second is closely related. It is the increasing homogeneity of ecosystems, especially in bioclimatically similar zones. Ecosystems converted to agriculture typically focus on a small number of crops and livestock strains. Similarly, the dispersal of species through trade leads to the establishment and spread of a relatively small number of invasive species. A third effect of the closer integration of the global system is an increase in the speed with which environmental effects propagate through the system.

Part II comprises eight chapters the first of which, Chapter 8, addresses what I have identified as the central challenge of an integrated biodiversity science: the conditional prediction of biodiversity change and its consequences for human wellbeing. This depends on the development of models of biodiversity change, and the feedbacks between biodiversity change, the biophysical system, and the socio-economic system. Although modeling methods have improved in recent years, this is the area where we are currently least well served by science. Most assessments rely on the use of non-probabilistic scenarios to make forward projections. They neglect feedbacks between the social and other components of the system, and hold human behavior constant in the face of far-reaching environmental change. The chapter explores what is needed to do better.

Chapter 9 addresses another side of the same problem. It considers what is currently known about the effect of biodiversity change on human wellbeing, and what is being done to measure this at the national level, especially through the national income accounts. It also considers what steps are being taken to improve these measures. These are then assessed through the lens of the theory of inclusive wealth developed by Dasgupta, and reflected in the recent Inclusive Wealth Report (Dasgupta 2009; Arrow *et al.* 2012; UNU-IHDP and UNEP 2012).

The chapter identifies what has yet to be done to generate indicators of wellbeing that national governments can evaluate alongside the indicators conventionally used to select between policy options. It also points to the need for indicators of wellbeing that relate to environmental assets that lie beyond national jurisdiction.

Chapter 10 then turns to a group of problems that – beyond our capacity to model the system, or to generate measures of wellbeing – bedevil prognosis. These are the related problems of risk, uncertainty, and irreversibility. The chapter first returns to the basic portfolio problem discussed in Chapter 4. It shows how attitudes to risk shape the choice of portfolio of species and how attitudes may be expected to differ in rich and poor countries. It then addresses the complications brought by fundamental uncertainty and the irreversibility of biodiversity loss, and considers what this means for policy. The chapter discusses how the precautionary principle may be operationalized in such cases.

The next two chapters consider the currently available options for dealing with the problems posed by biodiversity-related externalities and public goods identified in Chapter 5. Chapter 11 focuses on the instruments currently in use around the world to change the incentives faced by private landholders. It asks what instruments are available at different scales, how they can be deployed and with what potential effect. It focuses on the important differences between problems at the local or national scale, and problems at the international scale. Particular attention is paid to systems of payments for ecosystem services. These are increasingly popular for encouraging developing country landholders to adopt management practices that provide the global community with ecosystem services that would otherwise be underprovided because of their public good nature. Examples considered include the Reduced Emissions from Deforestation and Forest Degradation (REDD) scheme. Since an additional motivation for this is the advantage such instruments offer in terms of poverty alleviation, this is also considered.

Chapter 12 then focuses on the demand side of the same problem. It considers the institutions established by the international community to generate the resources needed to operationalize payment schemes of the kind discussed in Chapter 11. Differences in the governance structures that operate at various scales turn out to be critical for the policy options available at those scales, just as differences in the nature of the public good being supported turn out to be critical for the choice between incentive systems (e.g. systems of payments for ecosystem services, taxes, or access fees), and direct public investment (e.g. through parks or protected areas, public health, or scientific research support). The chapter considers three different funding sources: the Global Environment Facility (GEF), national governments, and private foundations. It draws particular attention to the discrepancy in the level of international funding for environmental public goods and the scale of the problem addressed in this way.

Part II closes with two chapters on the role of international institutions in the solution of the transboundary dimensions of the biodiversity change problem. Just as the book began with a focus on agriculture, health, and conservation, these chapters distinguish between agreements that are concerned with production systems (both marine and terrestrial), with trade-related human, animal, and plant health risks, and with conservation. Chapter 13 begins with the most important of the international biodiversity conventions – the CBD – and discusses the steps that have been taken to enhance its effectiveness since it came into force, including the identification of the recently agreed Aichi targets and accompanying strategic plan. It identifies the stringent conditions that need to be satisfied for the targets to be met. These include coordination between multilateral agreements addressing different dimensions of the same problem.

The chapter then considers the agreements concerned with two other dimensions of the problem of biodiversity change. The first is the set of agreements concerned with the regulation of the trade-related dispersal of pests and pathogens, especially the General Agreement on Tariffs and Trade (GATT), the International Health Regulations (IHR), and the Sanitary and Phytosanitary (SPS) Measures Agreement. It analyzes the capacity of agreements of this kind to internalize the transboundary externalities of international trade. The second set of agreements deals with the exploitation of marine areas lying beyond national jurisdiction, and includes the UNCLOS and related fishery agreements. It flags the role assigned to the extension of national sovereignty and control over resources defined under the Law of the Sea to be the common heritage of humankind.

The penultimate chapter in Part II, Chapter 14, considers a similar problem: the development of rights to the genetic resources contained in both production and natural landscapes. As in the Law of the Sea there has been a major shift away from the perception that the genetic resources of the world are the common heritage of humankind. There has been a significant extension of national sovereignty over these resources, along with the formalization of intellectual property regimes. The chapter describes the process, and analyzes its implications for the efficiency, equity, and sustainability of genetic resource use.

The book closes with a review of the main implications for biodiversity science and policy, particularly at the international scale. Biodiversity change is a many-faceted problem. Just as biodiversity science has been divided many ways – between evolution, ecology, conservation biology and genetics, political science, sociology, law and economics – so has the development of governance structures and policy. Chapter 15 draws conclusions for both science and policy, and identifies the principal challenges yet to be addressed in developing an integrated approach to this, the most significant environmental problem of our time.

References

Arrow, K. J., Dasgupta, P., Goulder, L. H., Mumford, K. J. and Oleson, K. (2012) Sustainability and the measurement of wealth. *Environment and Development Economics*, 17, 317–353.

Brock, W. A. and Carpenter, S. (2006) Rising variance: a leading indicator of ecological transition. *Ecology Letters*, 9, 311–318.

Brock, W. A. and Xepapadeas, A. (2002) Biodiversity management under uncertainty: species selection and harvesting rules. *Economic Theory for the Environment: Essays in Honour of Karl-Goran Maler* (ed. B. Kristrom, P. Dasgupta and K. Lofgren), pp. 62–97. Edward Elgar, Cheltenham.

(2003) Valuing biodiversity from an economic perspective: a unified economic, ecological, and genetic approach. *American Economic Review*, 93, 1597–1614.

(2004) Optimal management when species compete for limited resources. *Journal of Environmental and Economic Management*, 44, 189–220.

Brock, W. A., Kinzig, A. P. and Perrings, C. (2010) Modeling the economics of biodiversity and environmental heterogeneity. *Environmental and Resource Economics*, 46, 43–58.

Brooks, T. M., Mittermeier, R. A., da Fonseca, G. A. B., Gerlach, J., Hoffmann, M., Lamoreux, J. F., Mittermeier, C. G., Pilgrim, J. D. and Rodrigues, A. S. L. (2006) Global biodiversity conservation priorities. *Science*, 313, 58–61.

Bulte, E. H. and Damania, R. (2003) Managing ecologically interdependent species. *Natural Resource Modeling*, 16, 21–38.

Butchart, S., Walpole, M., Collen, B., van Strien, A., Scharlemann, J. P. W., Almond, R. E. A., Baillie, J. E. M., Bomhard, B., Brown, C., Bruno, J.,

Carpenter, K. E., Carr, G. M., Chanson, J., Chenery, A. M., Csirke, J., Davidson, N. C., Dentener, F., Foster, M., Galli, A., Galloway, J. N., Genovesi, P., Gregory, R. D., Hockings, M., Kapos, V., Lamarque, J.-F., Leverington, F., Loh, J., McGeoch, M. A., McRae, L., Minasyan, A., Morcillo, M. H., Oldfield, T. E. E., Pauly, D., Quader, S., Revenga, C., Sauer, J. R., Skolnik, B., Spear, D., Stanwell-Smith, D., Stuart, S. N., Symes, A., Tierney, M., Tyrrell, T. D., Vie, J.-C. and Watson, R. (2010) Global biodiversity: indicators of recent declines. *Science*, 328, 1164–1168.

Cardinale, B. J., Duffy, J. E., Gonzalez, A., Hooper, D. U., Perrings, C., Venail, P., Narwani, A., Mace, G. M., Tilman, D., Wardle, D. A., Kinzig, A. P., Daily, G. C., Loreau, M., Grace, J. B., Larigauderie, A., Srivastava, D. S. and Naeem, S. (2012) Biodiversity loss and its impact on humanity. *Nature*, 486, 59–67.

Carpenter, S., Ludwig, D. and Brock, W. (1999) Management of eutrophication for lakes subject to potentially irreversible change. *Ecological Applications*, 9, 751–771.

Carpenter, S. R., Mooney, H. A., Agard, J., Capistrano, D., DeFries, R. S., Díaz, S., Dietz, T., Duraiappah, A. K., Oteng-Yeboah, A., Pereira, H. M., Perrings, C., Reid, W. V., Sarukhanm, J., Scholes, R. J. and Whyte, A. (2009) Science for managing ecosystem services: beyond the Millennium Ecosystem Assessment. *Proceedings of the National Academy of Sciences*, 106, 1305–1312.

Chapin, F. S., Hoel, M., Carpenter, S. R., Lubchenco, J., Walker, B., Callaghan, T. V., Folke, C., Levin, S., Mäler, G., Nilsson, C., Barrett, S., Crépin, A.-S., Danell, K., Rosswall, T., Starrett, D. and Xepapadeas, A. (2005) Building resilience and adaptation to manage arctic change. Beijer Institute Working Papers, Stockholm.

Clark, C. W. (1973) The economics of overexploitation. *Science*, 181, 630–634.
  (1976) *Mathematical Bioeconomics: The Optimal Management of Renewable Resources*. John Wiley, New York.
  (2010) *Mathematical Bioeconomics: The Mathematics of Conservation*. John Wiley & Sons, Hoboken, NJ.

Convention on Biological Diversity (2012) *Conference of the Parties to the Convention on Biological Diversity, Tenth meeting, Nagoya, Japan, 18–29 October 2010*. Agenda item 4.2, Updating and revision of the strategic plan for the post-2010 period, Decision as adopted. Available at www.cbd.int/nagoya/outcomes/ (accessed 2010).

Crosby, A. W. (1972) *The Columbian Exchange: The Biological and Cultural Consequences of 1492*. Greenwood Press, Westport, CT.
  (1986) *Ecological Imperialism: The Biological Expansion of Europe, 900–1900*. Cambridge University Press, New York.

Darwin, C. (1859) *On the Origin of Species by Means of Natural Selection.* John Murray, London.

(1958) *Autobiography.* Collins, London.

Dasgupta, P. (1982) *The Control of Resources.* Blackwell, Oxford.

(2009) The welfare economic theory of green national accounts. *Environmental and Resource Economics*, 42, 3–38.

Dasgupta, P. and Heal, G. M. (1979) *Economic Theory and Exhaustible Resources.* Cambridge University Press.

Dasgupta, P. and Mäler, K.-G. (eds.) (2004) *The Economics of Non-Convex Ecosystems.* Kluwer Academic Publishers, Dordrecht, Boston, London.

Ehrlich, P. (1968) *The Population Bomb.* Buccaneer Books, New York.

Elmqvist, T., Folke, C., Nystrom, M., Peterson, G., Bengtsson, J., Walker, B. and Norberg, J. (2003) Response diversity, ecosystem change, and resilience. *Frontiers in Ecology and the Environment*, 1, 488–494.

Folke, C., Carpenter, S., Walker, B., Scheffer, M., Elmqvist, T., Gunderson, L. and Holling, C. S. (2004) Regime shifts, resilience, and biodiversity in ecosystem management. *Annual Review of Ecology, Evolution and Systematics*, 35, 557–581.

Forest, F., Grenyer, R., Rouget, M., Davies, T. J., Cowling, R. M., Faith, D. P., Balmford, A., Manning, J. C., Proches, S., van der Bank, M., Reeves, G., Hedderson, T. A. J. and Savolainen, V. (2007) Preserving the evolutionary potential of floras in biodiversity hotspots. *Nature*, 445, 757–760.

Fuglie, K. O. (2008) Is a slowdown in agricultural productivity growth contributing to the rise in commodity prices? *Agricultural Economics*, 39, 431–441.

Gordon, H. S. (1954) The economic theory of common-property resources. *Journal of Political Economy*, 62, 124–142.

Griffin, J. N., O'Gorman, E. J., Emmerson, M. C., Jenkins, S. R., Klein, A.-M., Loreau, M. and Symstad, A. (2009) Biodiversity and the stability of ecosystem functioning. *Biodiversity, Ecosystem Functioning, and Human Wellbeing: An Ecological and Economic Perspective* (ed. D. B. S. Naeem, A. Hector, M. Loreau and C. Perrings), pp. 78–93. Oxford University Press.

Hartwick, J. (1977) Intergenerational equity and the investing of rents from exhaustible resources. *American Economic Review*, 66, 972–974.

(1978) Substitution among exhaustible resources and intergenerational equity. *Review of Economic Studies*, 45, 347–354.

Herlihy, D. (1997) *The Black Death and the Transformation of the West.* Harvard University Press, Cambridge, MA.

Hoffmann, M., Hilton-Taylor, C., Angulo, A., Böhm, M., Brooks, T. M., Butchart, S. H. M., Carpenter, K. E., Chanson, J., Collen, B., Cox, N. A., Darwall, W. R. T., Dulvy, N. K., Harrison, L. R., Katariya, V., Pollock, C. M., Quader, S., Richman, N. I., Rodrigues, A. S. L.,

Tognelli, M. F., Vié, J.-C., Aguiar, J. M., Allen, D. J., Allen, G. R., Amori, G., Ananjeva, N. B., Andreone, F., Andrew, P., Ortiz, A. L. A., Baillie, J. E. M., Baldi, R., Bell, B. D., Biju, S. D., Bird, J. P., Black-Decima, P., Blanc, J. J., Bolaños, F., Bolivar, G., W., Burfield, I. J., Burton, J. A., Capper, D. R., Castro, F., Catullo, G., Cavanagh, R. D., Channing, A., Chao, N. L., Chenery, A. M., Chiozza, F., Clausnitzer, V., Collar, N. J., Collett, L. C., Collette, B. B., Fernandez, C. F. C., Craig, M. T., Crosby, M. J., Cumberlidge, N., Cuttelod, A., Derocher, A. E., Diesmos, A. C., Donaldson, J. S., Duckworth, J. W., Dutson, G., Dutta, S. K., Emslie, R. H., Farjon, A., Fowler, S., Freyhof, J., Garshelis, D. L., Gerlach, J., Gower, D. J., Grant, T. D., Hammerson, G. A., Harris, R. B., Heaney, L. R., Hedges, S. B., Hero, J.-M., Hughes, B., Hussain, S. A., Icochea M., J., Inger, R. F., Ishii, N., Iskandar, D. T., Jenkins, R. K. B., Kaneko, Y., Kottelat, M., Kovacs, K. M., Kuzmin, S. L., La Marca, E., Lamoreux, J. F., Lau, M. W. N., Lavilla, E. O., Leus, K., Lewison, R. L., Lichtenstein, G., Livingstone, S. R., Lukoschek, V., Mallon, D. P., McGowan, P. J. K., McIvor, A., Moehlman, P. D., Molur, S., Alonso, A. M., Musick, J. A., Nowell, K., Nussbaum, R. A., Olech, W., Orlov, N. L., Papenfuss, T. J., Parra-Olea, G., Perrin, W. F., Polidoro, B. A., Pourkazemi, M., Racey, P. A., Ragle, J. S., Ram, M., Rathbun, G., Reynolds, R. P., Rhodin, A. G. J., Richards, S. J., Rodriguez, L. O., Ron, S. R., Rondinini, C., Rylands, A. B., Sadovy de Mitcheson, Y., Sanciangco, J. C., Sanders, K. L., Santos-Barrera, G., Schipper, J., Self-Sullivan, C., Shi, Y., Shoemaker, A., Short, F. T., Sillero-Zubiri, C., Silvano, D. B. L., Smith, K. G., Smith, A. T., Snoeks, J., Stattersfield, A. J., Symes, A. J., Taber, A. B., Talukdar, B. K., Temple, H. J., Timmins, R., Tobias, J. A., Tsytsulina, K., Tweddle, D., Ubeda, C., Valenti, S. V., Paul van Dijk, P., Veiga, L. M., Veloso, A., Wege, D. C., Wilkinson, M., Williamson, E. A., Xie, F., Young, B. E., Akçakaya, H. R., Bennun, L., Blackburn, T. M., Boitani, L., Dublin, H. T., da Fonseca, G. A. B., Gascon, C., Lacher, T. E., Mace, G. M., Mainka, S. A., McNeely, J. A., Mittermeier, R. A., Reid, G. M., Rodriguez, J. P., Rosenberg, A. A., Samways, M. J., Smart, J., Stein, B. A. and Stuart, S. N. (2010) The impact of conservation on the status of the world's vertebrates. *Science*, 330, 1503–1509.

Holling, C. (1973) Resilience and stability of ecological systems. *Annual Review Ecology and Systematics*, 4, 1–23.

   (1986) The resilience of terrestrial ecosystems: local surprise and global change. *Sustainable Development of the Biosphere* (ed. W. C. Clark and R. E. Munn), pp. 292–317. Cambridge University Press.

Hooper, D. U. and Vitousek, P. M. (1997) The effects of plant composition and diversity on ecosystem processes. *Science*, 277, 1302–1305.

Hooper, D. U., Chapin, F. S., Ewel, J. J., Hector, A., Inchausti, P., Lavorel, S., Lawton, J. H., Lodge, D. M., Loreau, M., Naeem, S., Schmid, B., Setälä, H., Symstad, A. J., Vandermeer, J. and Wardle, D. A. (2005) Effects of biodiversity on ecosystem functioning: a consensus of current knowledge. *Ecological Monographs*, 75, 3–35.

Hotelling, H. (1931) The economics of exhaustible resources. *Journal of Political Economy*, 39, 137–175.

IPCC (2000) *Emissions Scenarios: A Special Report of IPCC Working Group III*. IPCC, Geneva.

IUCN (2004) *The IUCN Red List of Threatened Species*. Available at www.iucnredlist.org/ (accessed 2012).

Kinzig, A. P., Pacala, S. and Tilman, D. (eds.) (2002) *Functional Consequences of Biodiversity: Empirical Progess and Theoretical Extensions*. Princeton University Press.

Levin, S. (1999) *Fragile Dominion: Complexity and the Commons*. Perseus Books, Reading, MA.

Levin, S., Barrett, S., Aniyar, S., Baumol, W., Bliss, C., Bolin, B., Dasgupta, P., Ehrlich, P., Folke, C., Gren, I.-M., Holling, C. S., Jansson, A., Jansson, B.-O., Mäler, K.-G., Martin, D., Perrings, C. and Shenshinski, E. (1998) Resilience in natural and socioeconomic systems. *Environment and Development Economics*, 3, 222–262.

Loreau, M. (2010) *The Challenges of Biodiversity Science*. International Ecology Institute, Oldendorf.

Loreau, M. and Hector, A. (2001) Partitioning, selection and complementarity in biodiversity experiments. *Nature*, 412, 72–76.

Loreau, M., Naeem, S. and Inchausti, P. (2002) *Biodiversity and Ecosystem Functioning: Synthesis and Perspectives*. Oxford University Press.

Lotka, A. J. (1925) *Elements of Physical Biology*. Williams & Wilkins Co., Baltimore, MD.

Macarthur, R. and Levins, R. (1967) The limiting similarity, convergence, and divergence of coexisting species. *The American Naturalist*, 101, 377–385.

Mäler, K.-G. (1974) *Environmental Economics: A Theoretical Inquiry*. Johns Hopkins University Press, Baltimore, MD.

Malthus, T. R. (1999[1798]) *An Essay on the Principle of Population*. Oxford University Press.

McNeely, J. A. (2001) An introduction to human dimensions of invasive alien species. *The Great Reshuffling: Human Dimensions of Invasive Alien Species* (ed. J. A. McNeely), pp. 5–20. IUCN, Gland.

McNeill, J. R. (2003) Europe's place in the global history of biological exchange. *Landscape Research*, 28, 33–39.

McNeill, W. H. (1977) *Plagues and People*. Anchor Books, New York.

Meade, J. E. (1973) *The Theory of Externalities*. Institute Universitaire de Hautes Etudes Internationales, Geneva.

Millennium Ecosystem Assessment (2005a) *Ecosystems and Human Well-being: General Synthesis*. Island Press, Washington, DC.

  (2005b) *Ecosystems and Human Well-being: Scenarios*, Vol. 2. Island Press, Washington, DC.

Naeem, S., Bunker, D., Hector, A., Loreau, M. and Perrings, C. (2009a) Can we predict the effects of global change on biodiversity loss and ecosystem functioning? *Biodiversity, Ecosystem Functioning, and Human Wellbeing: An Ecological and Economic Perspective* (ed. S. Naeem, D. Bunker, A. Hector, M. Loreau and C. Perrings), pp. 290–298. Oxford University Press.

Naeem, S., Bunker, D., Hector, A., Loreau, M. and Perrings, C. (eds.) (2009b) *Biodiversity, Ecosystem Functioning, and Human Wellbeing: An Ecological and Economic Perspective*. Oxford University Press.

Norgaard, R. (1984) Coevolutionary development potential. *Land Economics*, 60, 160–173.

Ostrom, E. (1990) *Governing the Commons: The Evolution of Institutions for Collective Action*. Cambridge University Press.

Pereira, H. M., Leadley, P. W., Proença, V., Alkemade, R., Scharlemann, J. P. W., Fernandez-Manjarrés, J. F., Araújo, M. B., Balvanera, P., Biggs, R., Cheung, W. W. L., Chini, L., Cooper, H. D., Gilman, E. L., Guénette, S., Hurtt, G. C., Huntington, H. P., Mace, G. M., Oberdorff, T., Revenga, C., Rodrigues, P., Scholes, R. J., Sumaila, U. R. and Walpole, M. (2010) Scenarios for global biodiversity in the 21st century. *Science*, 330, 1496–1501.

Perrings, C. and Halkos, G. (2012) Who cares about biodiversity? Optimal conservation and transboundary biodiversity externalities. *Environmental and Resource Economics*, 52, 585–608.

Perrings, C., Duraiappah, A., Larigauderie, A. and Mooney, H. (2011) The biodiversity and ecosystem services science-policy interface. *Science*, 331, 1139–1140.

Perrings, C., Naeem, S., Ahrestani, F., Bunker, D. E., Burkill, P., Canziani, G., Elmqvist, T., Ferrati, R., Fuhrman, J., Jaksic, F., Kawabata, Z., Kinzig, A., Mace, G. M., Milano, F., Mooney, H., Prieur-Richard, A.-H., Tschirhart, J. and Weisser, W. (2010) Ecosystem services for 2020. *Science*, 330, 323–324.

Piesse, J. and Thirtle, C. (2010) Agricultural R&D, technology and productivity. *Philosophical Transactions of the Royal Society B: Biological Sciences*, 365, 3035–3047.

Raup, D. and Sepkoski, J. (1986) Periodic extinction of families and genera. *Science*, 231, 833–836.

Samuelson, P. A. (1954) The pure theory of public expenditure. *Review of Economics and Statistics*, 36, 387–389.

Scheffer, M., Carpenter, S. Foley, J. A., Folke, C. and Walker, B. (2001) Catastrophic shifts in ecosystems. *Nature*, 413, 591–596.

Scherr, S. J. and McNeely, J. A. (2008) Biodiversity conservation and agricultural sustainability: towards a new paradigm of "ecoagriculture" landscapes. *Philosophical Transactions of the Royal Society B: Biological Sciences*, 363, 477–494.

Schmid, B., Balvanera, P., Cardinale, B. J., Godbold, J., Pfisterer, A. B., Raffaelli, D., Solan, M. and Srivastava, D. S. (2009) Consequences of species loss for ecosystem functioning: meta-analyses of data from biodiversity experiments. *Biodiversity, Ecosystem Functioning, and Human Wellbeing: An Ecological and Economic Perspective* (ed. S. Naeem, D. Bunker, A. Hector, M. Loreau and C. Perrings), pp. 14–29. Oxford University Press.

Stohlgren, T. J., Pyšek, P., Kartesz, J., Nishino, M., Pauchard, A., Winter, M., Pino, J., Richardson, D. M., Wilson, J. R. U., Murray, B. R., Phillips, M. L., Li, M.-Y., Celesti-Grapow, L. and Font, X. (2011) Widespread plant species: natives versus aliens in our changing world. *Biological Invasions*, 13, 1931–1944.

Tatem, A. J., Rogers, D. J. and Hay, S. I. (2006a) Global transport networks and infectious disease spread. *Advances in Parasitology*, 62, 293–343.

Tatem, A. J., Hay, S. S. and Rogers, D. J. (2006b) Global traffic and disease vector dispersal. *Proceedings of the National Academy of Sciences*, 103, 6242–6247.

Tschirhart, J. (2000) General equilibrium of an ecosystem. *Journal of Theoretical Biology*, 203, 13–32.

UNU-IHDP and UNEP (2012) *Inclusive Wealth Report 2012: Measuring Progress toward Sustainability*. Cambridge University Press.

Walker, B. H., Kinzig, A. P. and Langridge, J. (1999) Plant attribute diversity, resilience, and ecosystem function: the nature and significance of dominant and minor species. *Ecosystems*, 2, 95–113.

Walker, B. H., Holling, C. S., Carpenter, S. R. and Kinzig, A. P. (2004) Resilience, adaptability, and transformability. *Ecology and Society*, 9, 5.

Weitzman, M. L. (1974) Prices vs. quantities. *Review of Economic Studies*, 41, 477–491.

Williamson, M. (1996) *Biological Invasions*. Chapman and Hall, London.

Wilson, E. O. (ed.) (1988) *Biodiversity*. National Academy Press, Washington, DC.

World Bank (2012) *Life Expectancy at Birth, Total (Years)*. Available at http://data.worldbank.org/indicator/SP.DYN.LE00.IN (accessed 2012).

World Commission on Environment and Development (1987) *Our Common Future*. Island Press, Washington, DC.

PART I

Diagnosing the biodiversity change problem

Everyone in the world depends completely on earth's ecosystems and the services they provide, such as food, water, disease management, climate regulation, spiritual fulfillment, and aesthetic enjoyment. Over the past fifty years, humans have changed these ecosystems more rapidly and extensively than in any comparable period of time in human history, largely to meet rapidly growing demands for food, freshwater, timber, fiber, and fuel. This transformation of the planet has contributed to substantial net gains in human wellbeing and economic development. But not all regions and groups of people have benefitted from this process – in fact, many have been harmed. Moreover, the full costs associated with these gains are only now becoming apparent (Millennium Ecosystem Assessment 2005c).

2 | *Biodiversity in the modern world*

2.1 Widening horizons

What do we know about the role of biodiversity in the modern world? What are the effects of biodiversity change on the two-fifths of the terrestrial system that have been fundamentally transformed by humankind? While the shape of the Holocene extinction is familiar to many – certainly to all those who work in the biological sciences – the way in which changes in species abundance and richness affect human activities is not. Most biodiversity research has focused on natural systems, and not on the role of biodiversity in supporting the production of goods and services of value to people. Research on agro-biodiversity, for example, is a vanishingly small proportion of total agricultural and forestry research. There are relatively few studies of the biodiversity in urban ecosystems, and almost no studies of the impact of changes in species diversity on ecosystem services in urban areas. The literature on biodiversity and health is primarily concerned with the role of species diversity in affecting disease transmission in natural ecosystems. The literature on invasive species is more broadly concerned with the impact of invaders on both managed and unmanaged systems, but it too focuses on the role of invaders in disrupting existing, functioning systems. The result is that we understand much about the ecology of biodiversity change, but little about its consequences for the production and consumption processes at the core of all human activity. Yet these are the things we need to understand if we are to understand directed biodiversity change.

To get a sense of the role of biodiversity in the modern world this chapter considers the evidence on the effects of biodiversity change in three areas of human activity that are highly sensitive to the mix of genes, species, and ecosystems: agriculture, health, and wildlife conservation. Two of these, agriculture and health, involve the deliberate simplification of ecosystems. The third, wildlife conservation, involves the protection of species threatened by demographic and economic growth. This is not intended to be an exhaustive description. There are a number of assessments that offer overviews of biodiversity change at a sectoral level (Millennium Ecosystem Assessment 2005a, 2005b, 2005c; International Assessment of Agricultural Knowledge Science and Technology for Development 2008; Convention on Biological Diversity 2010; Food and Agriculture Organization 2010). There is also the second edition of the *Encyclopedia of Biodiversity*, which summarizes many different aspects of biodiversity science (Levin 2013). My aim, instead, is to give a sense of the commonalities and the differences in the conservation problem addressed in each of these three areas. In every case there is a level or range of biodiversity that is, in some sense, optimal – given the objectives of the people involved. Discussion of the specific ecosystem services at issue, and the way that decisions on the optimal level of biodiversity are made, is deferred until later. At this point I wish to illustrate the broad characteristics of directed biodiversity change in terms of the different roles that species play in production landscapes and wildlands.

2.2 Agriculture and biodiversity

The primary driver of biodiversity change in the Holocene has been the conversion of habitat for the production of foods, fuels, and fibers, for industrial activity and for human habitation. The pollution of soils, air, and water and the dispersal of species beyond their natural ranges have also had a significant impact on biodiversity, but are dominated by the alteration of habitat. There are four main effects at work.

First, the conversion of habitat leads to the destruction of directly affected sessile species. The extensive growth of agriculture – growth that depends on expanding the area of land committed to agriculture – generally involves clearance of all existing vegetation and the species that depend on that vegetation. This is widely recognized to be the primary cause of biodiversity loss during the Holocene (Millennium Ecosystem Assessment 2005c).

Second, conversion of particular pieces of land leads to the fragmentation of habitat. As the habitat remnants become smaller, the size of the populations of plants and animals that can be supported falls. This in turn makes them more vulnerable to variation in climatic conditions, resource availability, and the introduction of new species. Moreover, the greater the distance between remnants the lower is the likelihood that the sub-populations will mix, and the greater is the likelihood that each will experience genetic erosion. Indeed, habitat fragmentation is recognized to be a significant cause of biodiversity change, with the effect of fragmentation depending both on the size and remoteness of habitat fragments (Rosenzweig 1995; Reed 2004) and the nature of the habitat itself (see, for example, Fagan 2002).

Third, interactions between converted and unconverted land lead to off-site effects on biodiversity. These include the effects of nutrient flows, pesticide applications, and the diversion of available water. Largely as a result of agriculture, the global flux of nitrogen has roughly doubled, and the global flux of phosphorus has roughly tripled over background levels (Kinzig and Socolow 1994; Millennium Ecosystem Assessment 2005b; Childers *et al.* 2011; Elser 2011). The dead zone in the Gulf of Mexico, for example, is an off-site effect of excess nutrient applications on farms in the Mississippi basin (Dodds 2006; Turner *et al.* 2008). Similar effects can be observed in many other parts of the world (Diaz and Rosenberg 2008).

Fourth, the introduction of domesticated species in agriculture, and the accidental introduction of pests and pathogens along with traded agricultural inputs and outputs, have led to establishment and spread of many invasive species, frequently with negative effects on native biodiversity (Williamson 1996; Perrings, Fenichel and Kinzig 2010).

All of these processes continue to accelerate. The MA reported the extent to which the extensive growth of agriculture had led to the transformation of all but two of the world's major biomes, and noted that while the loss of some biomes was expected to slow, conversion of land in the most species-rich parts of the world – the tropics – was still increasing (Figure 2.1).

In 2001, David Tilman and colleagues projected the consequences of the growth of agriculture as a function of population and economic growth (Tilman *et al.* 2001). Their conclusions were both sobering and instructive. In the absence of significant technical change, they projected that land committed to raising livestock would increase by 5.4×10^6 million hectares by 2050, and that lands committed to raising crops would increase by 3.5×10^6 million hectares. This implies an overall increase in agricultural land of around 18 percent in the first half of the century, most of which would occur in developing countries. This is

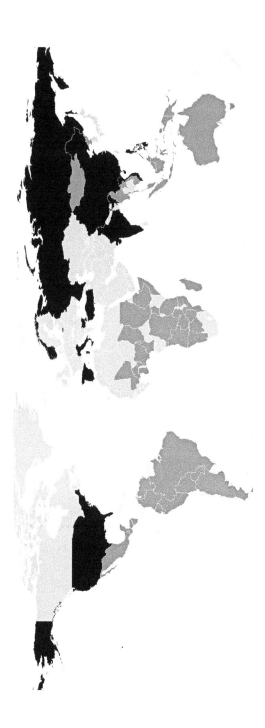

Figure 2.1 Change in forest area by country, 2005–2010. Countries experiencing continuing deforestation or net loss in forest area are shaded dark grey. Countries experiencing a net gain in forest area are shaded black. Countries where there was no significant change in forest area are shaded light grey.

Source: data derive from Food and Agriculture Organization (2010).

an area equivalent to around one-third of remaining tropical and temperate forests, savannas, and grasslands. In addition they projected that global application of nitrogen would increase by 2.7 times 2001 levels by 2050 (equivalent to 236×10^6 million tons of nitrogen relative to 140×10^6 million tons from natural sources), and that the global application of phosphorus would increase by 2.4 times 2001 levels. The consequences include eutrophication of surface waters (freshwater lakes and streams in the case of phosphorus, estuaries and coastal seas in the case of nitrogen), along with changes in species composition in both terrestrial and aquatic ecosystems.

There is necessarily considerable uncertainty attaching to projections that assume constant preferences and technology. The projections above assumed a 50 percent increase in global population, the generalization of Western meat-based diets, and a continuation of agricultural intensification by means of fertilization, irrigation, pesticide application, and crop breeding, leading to growth in yields at the rate that has occurred since the Green Revolution. If yield increases were not to be maintained, they argued that the land that would need to be committed to agriculture would be even greater.

What is particularly sobering about Tilman *et al.*'s estimates is that all the evidence is that yield growth rates are declining, largely because of a secular decline in public funding of agricultural research (Pardey *et al.* 2006; Alston, Beddow and Pardey 2009; Alston *et al.* 2010). Globally, while the pattern of public spending on agricultural R&D is mixed, aggregate spending has been declining in real per capita terms (Nin Pratt and Fan 2010). Since private sector investment in agricultural R&D accounts for only 6 percent in developing countries, a decline in public sector spending is critical (Piesse and Thirtle 2010). In some regions (Sub-Saharan Africa) per capita yields have been declining for some time. In others the per capita yield growth is still positive, but slowing – and that is the problem. Unless population increases at much lower rates than forecast, a likely result is that the land converted to food production in the next few decades will be well above the 10^9 hectares estimated in Tilman *et al.* (2001). At the same time, the projected growth in biofuels production has added another dimension to the demand for agricultural land that is expected to add to the pressure on biodiversity (Tilman, Hill and Lehman 2006).

The off-farm biodiversity consequences of agricultural growth are one half of the biodiversity change story. The other half concerns biodiversity change on farm. The question to ask of the biodiversity change associated with the growth of agriculture is what it has given us. Against the biodiversity costs of land conversion, habitat fragmentation, nutrient and pesticide use, and invasive species are a set of benefits from specializing ecosystems for the production of foods, fuels, fibers, pharmaceuticals, and other products. From the first attempts to protect naturally occurring food and fiber plants, farmers have chosen to increase the relative abundance of species with more desirable traits, often by protecting them against pests and predators, and to decrease the relative abundance of species with less desirable traits. They have directed biodiversity change to realize the gains from exploiting particular traits in particular species.

There is evidence that wild grains have been used for at least 20,000 years, but domestication is a more recent phenomenon. The domestication of wheat, barley, peas, lentils, bitter vetch, chickpeas, and flax in the Middle East dates from around 9400 BC. Rice, millet and mung, soy, and azuki beans were cultivated in China from around 8000 BC; wheat, barley, and jujube in India from the same period, sorghum in Africa from around 5000 BC; and maize in Central and South America from around 3000 BC (Tauger 2009). In all cases the motivation was the same: to increase the abundance of species whose particular traits made them favored sources of food or fiber. The results fundamentally transformed human society and the scope for engaging in activities beyond hunting and gathering. Agriculture is associated with two critically important processes: sedentism and specialization. Agriculture requires people to settle near to croplands, and generates the surplus that allows them to specialize in non-agricultural activities. These two processes underpin the development of cities, trade and markets, and military capacity. In other words, the city states that were both the dominant political form up until the emergence of nation states, and the engines of economic development, have their origins in the Neolithic agricultural revolution (Bairoch 1988).

The role of agricultural surpluses in stimulating industrial growth in agrarian economies was in fact the central feature of the dual-economy models developed in the 1950s (Lewis 1954; Fei and Ranis 1964). These models assume that the economy comprises two distinct sectors: a traditional agricultural sector on the one side, and a modern industrial sector on the other. While labor and products flow freely between the sectors, capital does not. Thus, while there is a tendency for wages/average rural incomes and prices to equalize across the economy, the rate of return on assets in the two sectors can differ. The agricultural sector is characterized by the existence of a labor surplus. This creates a pool that is available to the industrial sector at no cost – at least in terms of forgone output. Industrial labor is supplied at a constant real wage greater than the average rural income (the opportunity cost of industrial labor), and employment in the industrial sector expands up to the point at which the marginal revenue product of industrial labor is equated with the marginal cost of that labor. The main inference of the model follows directly. Until such time as the labor surplus is exhausted, the expansion of the industrial sector leads to a rising profit share in national income, a rising savings ratio, increasing levels of investment, and hence an accelerating rate of growth (Lewis 1979; Perrings 1997).

The dual-economy models are alone among economic growth models in assigning agricultural labor surplus a role in driving growth elsewhere in the economy. They offer a plausible explanation of the initiation of economic growth over a wide range of conditions. Indeed, the models describe the fifth millennium BC growth of city economies such as Eridu and Ur (Bairoch 1988; Oates *et al.* 2007) just as well as they describe the twentieth-century industrialization of agrarian economies in the developing world. In both cases a labor surplus in the agricultural sector fueled the development of non-agricultural activities.

A number of competing explanations have been offered for the origin of a labor surplus in agriculture. Among the most compelling of these, offered by Esther Boserup, is that population increase itself stimulated technical change, and with it the agricultural productivity growth that released labor for non-agricultural activities (Boserup 1965; Binswanger and Ruttan 1978; Boserup 1981). Others, Jarad Diamond and Paul Ehrlich among them, have seen population growth as a source of collapse in agrarian systems (Ehrlich 1968; Diamond 2005). However, an exhaustive review of the archeological evidence on early agrarian societies indicates that while some societies did indeed significantly overshoot the carrying capacity of the land at their disposal, most responded positively to population stress: increasing output by applying capital, adopting new technologies, making production more knowledge intensive (Tainter 2006).

The dual-economy models themselves largely ignored technological change. Specifically, they assumed that an increasing labor force applied to a fixed area of land with a fixed technology would lead the marginal physical product of labor to fall to zero, creating a redundant work force that could be redeployed to the industrial sector (Fei and Ranis 1964). It turns out, however, that the origin of the labor surplus is largely irrelevant to the insights of the model. What drives the growth of non-agricultural activities is a flow of labor from the agricultural to the non-agricultural sector and, in a closed economy, this implies that the agricultural sector is able to satisfy aggregate demand for food when the share of the population engaged in agriculture is less than 100 percent. It also implies that the benefits of agricultural productivity growth extend beyond value added in the agricultural sector, or the wellbeing of the direct consumers of agricultural products. The existence of agricultural surpluses is what has made possible all advances beyond the subsistence economy.

To obtain a measure of the benefits of agriculture in a closed economy (i.e. where the goods and services consumed in an economy are also produced in that economy) we need something other than agricultural income. The share of non-agricultural income in aggregate income is an indirect measure of the benefits generated by enhanced agricultural productivity. Prior to the Neolithic agricultural revolution the share of what we would now refer to as the economically active population engaged in producing food would have been very close to 100 percent, and food production would have accounted for almost all of what we would now refer to as income. Today, the agricultural labor force in the most advanced economies is less than 2 percent, and the share of agriculture in GDP is less than 1 percent. But across the world the size of both the agricultural labor force and its contribution to GDP vary widely. Figure 2.2 shows the share of non-agricultural income in GDP and the share of the labor force engaged in agriculture for a sample of countries (ranked by the share of the labor force engaged in agriculture).

As one might expect it shows a negative relation[1] between the two – the smaller the share of the labor force engaged in agriculture, the larger the share of non-agricultural activities in GDP. It gives us an alternative measure of the value added by agricultural productivity growth: the value added by the labor force freed up to engage in other activities. There are certainly diminishing returns to the diversion of labor from agriculture. In countries where 30 percent or more of the economically

---

[1] Denoting the share of non-agricultural income in GDP by X, and the share of the labor force engaged in agriculture by Y, the relation between the two (t statistics in parentheses) is: $X = 0.987 (187.6) - 0.348Y (- 13.1)$, adjusted $R^2 = 0.68$.

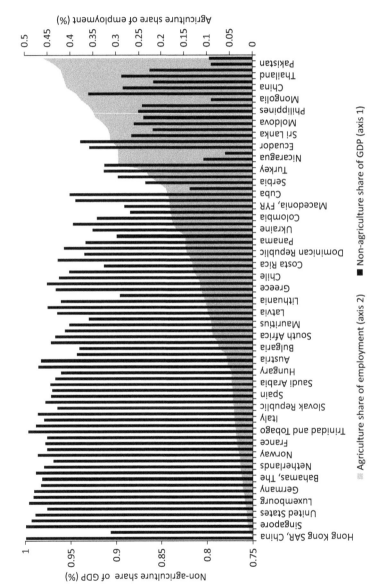

Figure 2.2 The share of non-agricultural activities in GDP and share of total labor force in agriculture, 2007. Countries are ordered by share of agriculture in GDP. The figure shows the inverse relation between that and the proportion of the labor force engaged in agriculture. Some of the countries evaluated are listed on the horizontal axis.
Source: data derive from World Bank (2012a, 2012b).

active population are engaged in agriculture, non-agricultural activities account for around 87 percent of GDP. In countries where less than 3 percent are engaged in agriculture, non-agricultural activities account for around 98 percent of GDP. There are also external costs to agriculture that increase with intensification, and that should ideally be captured in any measure of agricultural GDP. But that said, the specialization of agro-ecosystems for the production of foods, fuels, and fibers has enabled the growth of productivity in all other areas of economic activity, and the value added outside agriculture is the measure of that.

The increase in agricultural productivity that has made growth elsewhere possible may have its roots in the Neolithic revolution, but it has accelerated dramatically in the last one hundred years. In the United States, for example, agriculture accounted for 41 percent of the labor force at the turn of the twentieth century – much the same as Indonesia, Thailand, or Pakistan today. By 1930 the share of agriculture in total employment had halved, and agriculture accounted for some 7 percent of GDP – not very different from Turkey today. Between 1930 and 1970, the share of agriculture in total employment had fallen to 4 percent, and agriculture accounted for only 2.3 percent of GDP (Dimitri, Effland and Conklin 2005). That is similar to Italy today. By 2007 the numbers were 1.4 percent and 1.14 percent respectively (Figure 2.2)(Alston *et al.* 2010).

What has driven productivity growth in this period is what can only be described as the massive simplification of agro-ecosystems. This has had two aspects. One is the stripping out of crop and livestock competitors, predators, pests, and pathogens through the application of herbicides, fungicides, insecticides, biological control agents, microbial pesticides, and antibiotics. The other is the elimination of "inferior" crops, crop varieties, and livestock strains through the diffusion and adoption of high-yielding crop varieties and more productive livestock strains. Plant and animal breeding programs have narrowed the genetic base of agriculture to the point where more than 90 percent of global food supply derives from only eleven species: wheat, rice, corn, oats, tomato, potato, cattle, sheep, pigs, chickens, and ducks. Moreover, within each of these species there has been substantial loss of intraspecific genetic diversity. To take one example, the adoption of high-yielding rice varieties has led to the abandonment of traditional varieties bred to meet local conditions over millennia. In India, ten varieties currently account for around 75 percent of production.

Before the Green Revolution there were something like 30,000 varieties in cultivation, with no dominant varieties. A similar concentration of production in a small number of varieties has been observed in Sri Lanka, Bangladesh, and Indonesia (Cervigni 2001).

While a reduction in intraspecific genetic diversity has been associated with increased average yields, it also has the potential to increase the variance of yields (Conway and Barbier 1988; Smale *et al.* 1998; Widawsky and Rozelle 1998; Carew, Smith and Grant 2009). But this effect also depends on the genetic variability within the varieties selected for cultivation, and there is no evidence that genetic variability within the crop varieties selected for in-plant breeding programs has declined. For example, a study of 105 Argentine bread wheat (*Triticum aestivum L.*) cultivars released between 1932 and 1995 found no significant differences in genetic diversity between cultivars released before 1960 and those released in the 1970s, 1980s, and 1990s (Manifesto *et al.* 2001). Similarly, a study of 511 widely grown winter wheat varieties of central and northern Europe over a similar period found that plant breeding had not induced any genetic erosion within the species selected (Huang *et al.* 2007).

This is not surprising. Genetic erosion within a species is measured by the reduction in richness of common local alleles, or combinations of alleles.[2] It is generally caused by the declining abundance of that species. It follows that it is more likely to be observed in the landraces and wild crop relatives left behind in the plant breeding process than it is in widely distributed high-yielding varieties. Genetic erosion has, for example, been reported in a number of wild relatives of oats (*Avena spp.*) (Loskutov and Rines 2011). The genetic erosion of landraces and wild crop relatives matters more in some places than in others. There are eight major centers of origin for crops (Figure 2.3). These are the areas in which crops first emerged, and were enhanced through the incorporation of wild relatives in traditional plant breeding programs. The cost of the local loss of wild crop relatives in these areas is the lost opportunity to use their genetic material to breed or engineer desirable traits in future crops. Most cultivated crop varieties and many livestock strains already contain genetic material from wild crop relatives, landraces, or traditional livestock strains. Indeed, it was estimated that at least half

---

[2] Alleles are alternative forms of the same gene. They are the source of distinct traits passed from parents to offspring.

Figure 2.3 Vavilov centers of origin. (1) Mexico–Guatemala, (2A) Peru–Ecuador–Bolivia, (2B) southern Chile, (2C) southern Brazil, (3) Mediterranean, (4) Middle East, (5) Ethiopia, (6) Central Asia, (7A) Indo–Burma, (7B) Siam–Malaya–Java, (8) China. *Source:* constructed from Vavilov (1935).

of the increase in agricultural productivity during the twentieth century was directly attributable to artificial selection, recombination, and intraspecific gene transfer procedures. For example, Mexican beans have been used to improve resistance to the Mexican bean weevil that destroys or damages as much as 25 percent of stored beans in Africa and 15 percent in South America. Similarly, traditional wheat varieties from Turkey have been used to improve genetic resistance to a range of diseases. Indian landraces have been used to strengthen resistance to grassy stunt virus in rice. Ethiopian barley has been used to combat yellow dwarf virus in Californian crops (Heywood and Watson 1995; Millennium Ecosystem Assessment 2005c). The loss of wild crop relatives and their contribution to future plant breeding activities therefore has potentially high global costs.

The choice of which crop cultivars or livestock strains to employ on farm has historically depended on a range of factors, but in the last fifty years at least it has been primarily driven by the economic return that different crop combinations offer to the landholder. In other words it is the set of relative prices (net of taxes and subsidies) that drives the farmer's choice of crop genetic diversity. Two aspects of this choice that will be explored in more detail in later chapters are important to keep in mind. The first is that unless the goods and services generated by land management practices are priced in the market, they will not be factored into farmers' decisions. Markets exist for the products of agriculture, aquaculture, and forestry. Markets do not exist for many of the benefits of watershed protection (Heal 2000), habitat provision (Bulte and Horan 2003; Barbier, Burgess and Grainger 2010), pest and disease regulation (Ostfeld, Keesing and Eviner 2008), micro- and macro-climatic regulation (Canadell and Raupach 2008), and hazard protection (Barbier 2008).

A second important aspect of the problem is that engagement in the market has changed the nature of agricultural risks, and with it the combination of species planted. The introduction of agricultural subsidies, agricultural tariffs, agricultural income support, crop insurance, and the like has changed the risks faced by farmers, as has the closer integration of global agricultural markets. In the past, farmers have managed the risks posed by weather, disease, and pest infestations through their choice of crop varieties. By selecting crops and cultivars that were vulnerable to different stressors, they reduced the likelihood that they would experience total crop failure in "bad" years. Where alternative means of insuring against such risks exist, planting patterns change, and farmers tend to select the varieties that perform best in average conditions. Studies of the relation between crop genetic diversity and agricultural support have shown that crop genetic diversity is lower the higher the level (and predictability) of agricultural support (di Falco, Smale and Perrings 2008).

I return to these issues in later chapters. What is important to note here is that by simplifying ecosystems to make them more productive in terms of foods, fuels, or fibers, agriculture has both transformed the world's biodiversity and released the resources that have underpinned all development beyond the subsistence economy. The social payoff to the growth of agriculture has been huge. This is what needs to be set on the scales when we assess the negative impacts of agriculture on habitat, soil water and air quality, and the like. It is also what needs to be set on the scales when we evaluate the genetic erosion of both wild crop relatives and other species. At the same time, because farmers have not been faced by the true social cost of their use of resources, or been compensated for the social benefits conferred by their use of the land, they have typically ignored the effects they have on others. So while the directed biodiversity change induced by the growth of agriculture has resulted in very substantial benefits, there is good reason to believe that it is far from optimal. We collectively could do much better.

2.3 Biodiversity and disease

The second issue I want to consider is the relation between biodiversity and health – human, animal, and plant health. More particularly, I want to consider the problem of diseases caused by biological agents: prions, viruses, bacteria, fungi, protozoa, helminths, and arthropods. As with agriculture, the protection of human, animal, and plant health has involved the simplification of ecosystems. The Neolithic revolution initiated a process of land-use change that has transformed the structure and function of many of the world's ecosystems, destroyed the habitat of many of the world's species, and underpinned the Holocene mass extinction. Coincidentally, it initiated a process of demographic concentration (the clustering of people in villages, towns, and cities) and economic integration (the development of linkages between peoples and ecosystems through war, tribute, and trade). Both processes exposed humans, their crops and livestock to repeated assaults from novel parasites. The concentration of people, animals, or plant communities turns out to be a necessary condition for the successful replication of parasites, since that is what allows the parasites to spread – to achieve a basic reproductive rate greater than one. Interactions between populations, both within and across species, turns out to be a necessary condition for the transmission of disease. The earliest examples of communicable human diseases included influenza, measles, and smallpox, all of which are thought to have evolved from animal diseases – avian influenza, rinderpest, and monkeypox (Daily and Ehrlich 1996).

Like agriculture, this is a process that has continued for around twelve thousand years. It has proceeded in fits and starts as people in one part of the world have discovered people in other parts of the world, and set out either to defeat and enslave them, or to trade with them. Nowadays we refer to the process as globalization, implying that the integration it refers to is at the global scale. But it is the same process that started with trade and other interactions between the first towns and villages. It is a process that has given humankind a very particular perspective on microbial biodiversity and its management. Like agriculture, this is a perspective that has led people to control the abundance of harmful species, and in two cases (smallpox and rinderpest) to drive harmful organisms to extinction. Like agriculture too, it has yielded extraordinary benefits to humankind but without always confronting people with the true cost of their actions.

The diseases of humans, plants, and animals before the Neolithic revolution were, in some sense, self regulating. Pre-Neolithic people tended towards a balance in their relation to parasites in their home range depending on the virulence of those species. The virulence of both macroparasites (protozoa and helminthes) and microparasites (viruses and bacteria) evolves over time to maximize the fitness of the organism. While this leads to the reduction of virulence in some cases, it does not always do so. For example, trypanosomiasis – sleeping sickness in Africa (*Trypanosoma brucei spp.*) or Chagas disease in Latin America (*Trypanosoma cruzi*) – is a parasitic protozoon transmitted, respectively, by tsetse fly in Africa and the assassin bug in Latin America. In Africa it is a normal parasite in a number of herbivores, but is frequently fatal when transmitted to humans. This has been advanced as the main reason for the persistence of ungulate herds in Africa, since people were unable to survive in tsetse fly areas (McNeill 1977). However, it is also the reason why there has been no evolution in the virulence of the disease in humans. Whether the optimal virulence of pathogens is high or low depends, in part, on the conditions in which transmission occurs. So waterborne or vector-borne diseases such as cholera or dengue tend to remain highly virulent, whereas respiratory diseases that require their hosts to remain capable of making contact with others do not (Ewald 1995). In most cases, the virulence of pathogens would be expected to change if environmental conditions changed, which is why the process of integrating first local, then regional, then global communities is such an important part of the health story. The virulence of pathogens evolves not just with environmental conditions, but also with social conditions and land management regimes.

Both macroparasites and microparasites are part of the community of species within which people live and work. While the cost of contracting different diseases varies with their virulence, almost all negatively affect human wellbeing. The effect may not be linear. Exposure to less virulent forms of a disease can confer immunity against more virulent forms. However, at some scale people have an interest in reducing the harm done by pathogens. They have an interest, that is, in reducing both the number and abundance of parasites. As in the case of agriculture, there are compelling reasons why people seek to reduce the richness and abundance of these types of species.

It has already been remarked that there have, historically, been occasions when the cost of human diseases has been particularly high. The bubonic plague that literally decimated the populations of Europe in the fourteenth century is one. The effect of smallpox, influenza, measles, and typhus on the populations of Central America in the sixteenth century is another. In the last century the Spanish influenza of 1918–1920 and the HIV/AIDS epidemic are a third (McNeill 1977). When Malthus developed his theory of population in the late eighteenth century, war and disease were the two main checks on population growth in most parts of the world. Indeed, his *Essay on the Principles of Human Population* is primarily about the role of the environmental constraints, including disease, in limiting human population growth (Malthus 1999). Just as the growth of agricultural productivity freed people to engage in other activities, so the growth of our capacity to control diseases removed the primary check on growth of the human population.

The relation between the two processes is reflected in the demographic transition hypothesis (Caldwell 1976). This followed observations by the demographer Warren Thompson that decreases in birth rates typically followed decreases in death rates with a lag (Thompson 1929). In the first

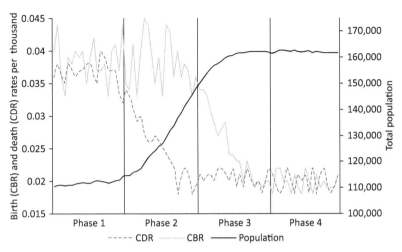

Figure 2.4 The demographic transition. In the first phase, birth (CBR) and death (CDR) rates are both highly variable, but balanced. In the second phase death rates fall, while birth rates remain high. In the third phase death rates fall, and in the fourth phase both are again in equilibrium balance. Total population increases at an increasing rate in the second phase and at a decreasing rate in the third phase. In the fourth phase total population is again stable.

phase of the demographic transition, birth and death rates are argued to be high and variable, but in balance, implying stable population levels. In fact, average population growth rates for much of the period since the Neolithic revolution have been less than 0.05 percent. In the second phase, death rates fall due to advances in controlling diseases but birth rates remain high. In the third phase, birth rates fall and stabilize at replacement rates, leading to a fourth phase in which total population is once again stable (Figure 2.4).

Different countries are typically at different stages in the demographic transition. The factors that drive the second phase of the transition are frequently argued to include improvements in nutrition due to increasing food supply, but the critical factor everywhere has been a reduction in mortality through the control of disease. In most cases this has been due to the development of public health programs that have targeted the waterborne, food-borne, and vector-borne diseases most implicated in child mortality. In Europe, this phase of the transition began around the time that Malthus developed his notions of population growth, but its progress was far from straightforward. The industrialization of western

European countries was associated with a number of trends that increased both the risk of infection and the virulence of diseases, the most important being overcrowding in newly industrializing cities. In Britain this meant that life expectancy at birth remained constant for much of the nineteenth century, in part due to the interactive effects between tuberculosis, other respiratory diseases, waterborne diseases such as typhus and typhoid fever, and food-borne diseases such as cholera and diarrhea that accounted for much child mortality. It was only when municipal public health programs in the 1870s made serious progress against typhoid and cholera that death rates declined significantly (Szreter 1997).

The increase in life expectancy experienced by most countries in the twentieth century was led by the introduction of vaccination programs and the control of infectious diseases such as polio, diphtheria, yellow fever, and smallpox. Public health programs were initially highly localized efforts on water and sanitation. Increasingly, however, the realization that the health of people in any one place depends on the health of people elsewhere has led to the internationalization of public health efforts. The establishment of the World Health Organization (WHO) after the Second World War was a critical step in the development of global campaigns against particular diseases. Smallpox was driven to extinction in 1979. As I write, polio is close to being eliminated as well. Currently only Afghanistan, India, Nigeria, and Pakistan are still polio endemic – just 4 out of the 125 countries that were polio endemic when the eradication initiative was launched in 1988. Other human diseases targeted for eradication include rubella, mumps, measles, lymphatic filariasis, and taeniasis. The benefits of such campaigns are potentially substantial. In the century before smallpox was driven extinct, for example, the disease had been responsible for something like 500 million deaths worldwide. Although polio epidemics were unknown before the twentieth century, at their height in the 1940s and 1950s they were responsible for around 500,000 deaths a year (Paul 1971). Among the diseases currently targeted for eradication, measles is still responsible for the deaths of nearly 800,000 children a year (Quadros 2006).

Although human diseases have had the most profound effects on human wellbeing, diseases of other species are not far behind. Human pathogens were not the only species involved in the Columbian exchange, for example. The introduction of a variety of European plants and animals, along with their pathogens, transformed many

Mesoamerican landscapes and displaced many native Mesoamerican species. Pathogens that affect the production of crops or livestock have been particularly costly. Rinderpest (cattle plague) is now the second disease to have been driven to extinction (Normile 2008), but historically it was especially destructive. In Europe, three major epidemics in the eighteenth century involved mortality rates approaching 100 percent in immunologically naive cattle populations. In Africa, an epidemic in the 1890s is thought to have killed up to 90 percent of all cattle as well as a number of other ruminants in southern Africa and the Horn of Africa (Spinage 2003).

Among crop pests, phylloxera (*Daktulosphaira vitifoliae*), an insect similar to the aphid and of North American origin, destroyed most of the vineyards of Europe in the late nineteenth century. While most crop diseases are less lethal, invasive pests and pathogens still impact agriculture in all parts of the world, and have especially severe effects in areas where control systems are weak. A number of crop pests and pathogens continue to have severe effects on crop yields in the world's poorest region, Sub-Saharan Africa: witchweed (*Striga hermonthica*), grey leaf spot (*Circosporda zeae-maydis*), the large grain borer (*Prostephanus truncatus*), cassava mealybug (*Phenacoccus manihoti*), and the cassava green mite (*Mononychellus tanajoa*) (Rangi 2004).

Military campaigns may not have the inadvertent role in the transmission of human diseases that they once did, but disease is still a recognized part of the armory of combatants. The use of biological weapons by nation states is banned under the Biological Weapons Convention (1972). However, a number of biological agents are recognized to be weapons of non-state (terrorist) aggression. These include several bacterial diseases of humans and other animals, including anthrax, brucellosis, cholera, and plague, and some viral diseases including encephalitis and smallpox (Rotz *et al.* 2002). For the most part, however, disease transmission depends on the movement of people and goods. Trade, transport, and travel are the mechanisms that drive most species introductions today (Perrings *et al.* 2005).

The causes and consequences of the dramatic acceleration in the number of species introductions for human livelihoods and wellbeing are discussed later in this book, but the primary driver is the growth of world trade. While climate change alters the natural range of species, and while the disturbance of habitats that follows land-use change affects the vulnerability of ecosystems to invasion, the growth of trade is what affects the number and frequency of new introductions and hence the likelihood that species will establish and spread. The global-ization of the world economy has dramatically increased the rate at which new introductions are occurring: initiating a series of more or less uncontrolled experiments in Jeff McNeeley's "great reshuffling" of species (McNeely 2001).

Of course, just as improvements in human, animal, and plant health have enhanced human wellbeing, so has the closer integration of world markets. While the development of an agricultural surplus is what freed up labor for use in non-agricultural pursuits, the development of markets is what made the specialization that has underwritten most productivity gains since. The growth and closer integration of markets has allowed specialization between producers at every scale from the village to the globe. At the international scale it has allowed countries to specialize in the production of goods and services in which they have a comparative advantage – in which their relative costs are lowest. The result has been lower costs, increased choice, and the diffusion of productivity-enhancing technologies across the globe.

Although it is impossible to estimate the magnitude of the benefits from the growth and integration of international markets, every effort to calculate the welfare effects of particular integration-enhancing events has a similar story to tell. Integration adds value through its effects on costs, productivity, and growth. For example, a recent estimate of the contribution of the North American Free Trade Agreement (NAFTA) to the participating countries showed that all gained from the agreement, though the gains differed among countries. In Mexico, 93 percent of the change in imports and exports over the period 1993–2005 was due to tariff reductions secured under the agreement. The corresponding figures for Canada and the USA are 58 percent and 55 percent respectively. NAFTA had significant positive effects on real wages in all three coun-tries, although once again the gain was largest in Mexico (Caliendo and Parro 2011).

Not all countries gain from closer integration, though, and not all countries that gain do so equally. The measures agreed under the Uruguay Round of the GATT, for example, were found to yield global gains equivalent to $171 billion per annum in the 1990s. However, a number of developing countries were found to have lost by the tariff changes in that round (Harrison, Rutherford and Tarr 1997). Moreover, where closer integration of markets increases the volume of trade without addressing the externalities of trade, such as the transmission of human, animal, and plant diseases, the social costs of trade growth may mount in ways that are not at all transparent to those involved.

The persistence of the disease externalities of trade and travel, like the persistence of the biodiversity externalities of trade more generally, has much to do with the way that international markets and the rules of international trade are structured. There is some evidence that environmental and health policies have been used in place of trade policies to protect local industry. Environmental standards below those of the trading partner have been used in place of subsidies to increase exports. Standards above those of the trading partner have been used in place of tariffs to reduce imports (Copeland 2000). Nevertheless, the SPS Measures Agreement and the IHR both formally allow countries to impose restrictions on trade in order to protect human, animal, and plant life – such restrictions being authorized by Article 20 of the GATT.

2.4 Wildlife conservation

Agriculture and the management of human, animal, and plant health are both examples of activities that have yielded immense benefits to humankind, but only at the cost of reducing particular types of bio-diversity. There are many other activities that similarly yield benefits only at the cost of reduced diversity. Most industrial activity, infra-structural development, and urban development belong in this cate-gory. All involve the conversion of habitat to alternative uses, and so lead to the loss of the species that occupied the converted habitat. Industrial development frequently has off-site effects involving the pollution of air, water, and soils that reduce the abundance or richness of species in affected areas. The development of roads, railways, power transmission corridors, and canals also fragments the habitats through which they pass, with similar effects on species richness and abundance. Urban development typically transforms existing habitat, sometimes leaving fragments intact, but always introducing new communities of microorganisms, insects, plants, and animals. In some cases, the biodiversity in urban systems is much greater than the biodiversity in the habitats displaced by urban development. This is almost always true of microorganisms, but is frequently true of plants as well (Crane and Kinzig 2005). In others, little is added beyond the human commensals and micro- and macroparasites that accompany dense human populations.

There are, however, activities that depend much more strongly on maintaining biodiversity, and these are the focus of my third illustration of the role of biodiversity in modern society. Such activities include conservation itself, an activity that spans both the science and practice of the preservation of species. Within the sciences the field of conservation biology is defined as the study of biodiversity, the factors leading to its loss, and the measures required for its protection. Unlike most scientific fields its goal is not just the pursuit of knowledge. It is the realization of a specific outcome: the preservation of species richness. Unlike most scientific fields of inquiry, it espouses a particular ethic. In the words of the scientist most directly responsible for founding the field, Michael Soulé,

Biotic diversity has intrinsic value, irrespective of its instrumental or utilitarian value. This normative postulate is the most fundamental. In emphasizing the inherent value of nonhuman life, it distinguishes the dualistic, exploitive world view from a more unitary perspective: Species have value in themselves, a value neither conferred nor revocable, but springing from a species' long evolutionary heritage and potential or even from the mere fact of its existence. (Soulé 1986)

The content of this ethical position will be considered later. All that matters at this juncture is that there exists a body of science whose *raison d'être* is the preservation of species.

That body of science serves a large and growing set of activities in the practice of conservation. Such activities exist at every scale, from local to global. They involve every kind of human institution including households, firms, government agencies at scales ranging from the municipality to international federations such as the European Community. They also involve non-governmental organizations (NGOs) such as the IUCN, the World Wildlife Fund (WWF), The Nature Conservancy (TNC), Conservation International (CI), and many others. In addition, they involve multilateral agreements such as the CBD, the Convention on International Trade in Endangered Species of Wild Fauna and Flora (CITES), the Convention on Migratory Species of Wild Animals (CMS), the Ramsar Convention on Wetlands of International Importance especially as Waterfowl Habitat, and the Convention concerning the Protection of World

Cultural and Natural Heritage (WHC). The activities they support include not just the designation and implementation of protected areas, but the restoration of degraded ecosystems, the design and implementation of conservation-compatible development projects, and the establishment of a regulatory framework designed to limit the impact of other activities on biodiversity outside protected areas.

Like agriculture and health, wildlife conservation is not a new concern. But like agriculture and health too, its scale and focus have changed as the global system has become more and more integrated. Conservation activities in hunter-gatherer societies and the earliest shifting cultivator societies were probably grounded in nature worship. They included protection of sacred species such as lemurs in Madagascar or ficus trees in India, and protection of sacred groves, ponds, or river stretches. Such protection could be flexible; thus spotbilled pelicans and painted storks were protected at their breeding colony on trees in the middle of the village of Kokre-Bellur in Karnataka, but could be hunted outside the breeding season. Similarly, regulations governing removal of plant biomass from sacred groves in India range from taboos over removal even of fallen fruit or leaves to permission to take away any plant material that could be removed by hand. The very extensive system of sacred groves called orans from the state of Rajasthan supported the fuel and fodder needs of local communities while guarding tree growth (Gadgil, Berkes and Folke 1993; Gokhale *et al.* 1998).

The earliest protected areas on a larger scale were probably hunting reserves that may have extended over tens of square kilometers. Many modern wildlife sanctuaries and national parks have their origin in such hunting reserves. In some instances, the designation of hunting reserves was accompanied by the development of menageries and zoos that included both indigenous and exotic animals. For example, a painting from the court of the seventeenth-century Mughal emperor Jehangir shows that he had in his collection the now extinct dodo from Madagascar. While conservation may not have been the primary aim of such *ex situ* collections, they sometimes had that effect. The Père David's deer from China, for example, survived extinction only because it had been included in the Duke of Bedford's private collection in Britain. The colonial powers added botanical gardens that systematically maintained collections drawn from large parts of the world (Perrings and Gadgil 2003).

In certain respects, the pattern of protection in modern times has changed markedly. Following the hunting reserves and private parks, the next phase in the development of global conservation efforts was the designation of wilderness areas of outstanding natural beauty or landscapes of special cultural significance as national parks within nation states. In the USA, much of the impetus came from the conservation-minded President Theodore Roosevelt. Roosevelt not only designated the first national parks in the country, including Mesa Verde in Colorado and Crater Lake in Oregon, but also secured the right, under the 1906 Antiquities Act, to proclaim historic landmarks, structures, or objects of scientific interest as national monuments. The Grand Canyon was designated as a national monument, under the authority of this Act, in 1908.

Since that time, the designation of protected areas across the world has followed a similar pattern, focusing on landscapes of special significance, reserves dedicated to the protection of mega-vertebrates, or sites of special scientific interest. Indeed, the designation of protected areas has become entrenched as the main mechanism for conservation of all biological resources. It was the cornerstone of the 1992 Caracas Action Plan of the World Parks Congress, which set a goal of protecting at least 10 percent of each of the world's major biomes. Since that time the proportion of the area designated as protected has increased sharply in some regions (e.g. Latin America) but has remained more or less constant in others (e.g. Sub-Saharan Africa). Overall, the proportion of the world's land surface under some form of protection has increased in the period since the Caracas Action Plan by around 44 percent (see Table 2.1(a)).

A much smaller proportion of the oceans under territorial jurisdiction are protected as of now, but the rate at which new sea areas within national jurisdiction are being brought under some form of protection is much greater than on land. In the period since the Caracas Action Plan, protected national waters have increased by more than 130 percent. The current share, 7.2 percent, is still a vanishingly small proportion of the world's oceans as a whole, but is expected to continue to grow rapidly (Table 2.1(b)).

In Latin America, Eastern, Southeastern, and Western Asia, the selection of new areas for protection increasingly targets densely populated areas having high conservation value. These are the areas named by Norman Myers as biodiversity hotspots (Myers 1988). Indeed, the

Table 2.1(a) *Proportion of terrestrial area nominally protected (percentage of terrestrial area)*

	1990	2000	2010
World (outside Antarctica)	8.8	11.3	12.7
Developed regions	8.7	10.7	11.6
Developing regions	8.8	11.7	13.3
Northern Africa	3.3	3.7	4.0
Sub-Saharan Africa	11.1	11.3	11.8
Latin America and the Caribbean	9.7	15.3	20.3
Caucasus and Central Asia	2.7	3.0	3.0
Eastern Asia	12.0	14.9	15.9
Southern Asia	5.3	5.9	6.2
Southeastern Asia	8.7	13.1	13.8
Western Asia	3.8	15.3	15.4
Oceania	2.0	3.0	4.9
Small island developing states (SIDS)	4.0	6.3	7.6

Source: UNEP–WCMC and the IUCN World Commission on Protected Areas (2012).

notion of biodiversity hotspots fits naturally and neatly into the conservation through protected areas approach, and has been adopted by major conservation NGOs (especially CI) as the guiding principle behind their conservation investments.

Biodiversity hotspots are areas high in species richness and endemism (the species exist nowhere else) that are also acutely threatened by human activity (Figure 2.5). Although they account for only 2.3 percent of the earth's land surface, they contain a very high proportion of endemic species, accounting for over 50 percent of all plant species and 42 percent of all terrestrial vertebrates. They are also areas that are subject to high and increasing pressure. It is estimated that something like 1.3 billion people (about 19 percent of the world's population) live in hotspots. The hotspots have already lost at least 70 percent of their original vegetation, and 86 percent of the area has been converted from natural habitat to alternative land cover.

Although biodiversity hotspots have been important in the designation of protected areas they remain just one of many reasons for protection. There is some correlation between hotspot status and the density of protected areas, but the relationship is relatively weak. This

Table 2.1(b) *Proportion of territorial waters protected (percentage of waters < 12 nautical miles from shore)*

	1990	2000	2010
World (outside Antarctica)	3.1	5.2	7.2
Developed regions	5.9	8.5	11.5
Developing regions	1.0	2.9	4.0
Northern Africa	3.1	3.6	4.6
Sub-Saharan Africa	1.4	3.1	4.0
Latin America and the Caribbean	2.7	8.9	10.8
Caucasus and Central Asia	0.2	0.4	0.4
Eastern Asia	0.8	1.4	1.6
Southern Asia	0.9	1.1	1.2
Southeastern Asia	0.6	1.3	2.1
Western Asia	0.7	2.0	2.2
Oceania	0.2	0.6	2.8
Small island developing states (SIDS)	0.4	1.2	2.8

Source: UNEP–WCMC and the IUCN World Commission on Protected Areas (2012).

partly reflects the changing relationship between conservation through protected areas and other activities. The establishment of areas that privilege landscapes of great natural beauty, or that protect "naturally" occurring species of animals, birds, and plants, have many advantages to offer beyond conservation. Conservation is increasingly being paired with sustainable use.

The CBD, the main biodiversity-related multilateral agreement, is one of three major conventions to have been concluded at the Rio Summit in 1992. Its goals (Article 1) are: "the conservation of biological diversity, the sustainable use of its components, and the fair and equitable sharing of the benefits arising out of the use of genetic resources" (United Nations 1993). The combination of these three goals has encouraged the development of multiple-use protected areas in which the different objectives are traded off against one another. Protected areas are increasingly promoted as the source of a number of ecosystem services, some of which – ecotourism, bioprospecting, and scientific inquiry – have found ready markets.

Since many hotspot habitats have already been converted to alternative uses, both the CBD and the main conservation NGOs have attempted

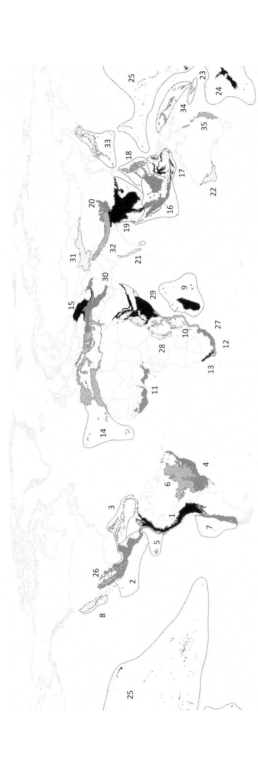

Figure 2.5 Biodiversity hotspots. These comprise the set of twenty-five hotspots identified in (Myers 2000): (1) the tropical Andes; (2) Mesoamerica; (3) the Caribbean Islands; (4) the Atlantic forest; (5) Tumbes–Chocó–Magdalena; (6) the Cerrado; (7) Chilean winter rainfall–Valdivian forests; (8) the California floristic province; (9) Madagascar and the Indian Ocean Islands; (10) the coastal forests of Eastern Africa; (11) the Guinean forests of West Africa; (12) the Cape floristic region; (13) the succulent Karoo; (14) the Mediterranean basin; (15) the Caucasus; (16) Sundaland; (17) Wallacea; (18) the Philippines; (19) Indo-Burma; (20) the mountains of southwest China; (21) western Ghats and Sri Lanka; (22) southwest Australia; (23) New Caledonia; (24) New Zealand; (25) Polynesia and Micronesia. The figure also includes another ten hotspots identified later: (26) the Madrean pine-oak woodlands; (27) Maputaland–Pondoland–Albany; (28) the eastern Afromontane; (29) the Horn of Africa; (30) the Irano-Anatolian; (31) the mountains of central Asia; (32) eastern Himalaya; (33) Japan; (34) East Melanesian Islands; (35) forests of eastern Australia.
Source: Conservation International (2013).

to ensure that protected areas in hotspots are able to deliver benefits aside from the conservation of endangered endemic species. One constituency is the people living in or directly affected by the establishment of protected areas. Benefits to this constituency include the creation of jobs in protected area management, ecosystem restoration, and projects designed to generate support for protected areas. The most important of these have been ecotourism projects that seek to take advantage of one of the fastest-growing segments of the global market for recreation and tourism. A second constituency comprises those living elsewhere who benefit from the environmental public goods provided by protected areas. Co-benefits of conservation include carbon sequestration, watershed protection, protection against natural hazards, and the mitigation of emergent zoonotic disease risks (Brandon and Bruner 2008).

The nature and significance of ecosystem services, and particularly of ecosystem services for which there are no functioning markets, is discussed in the next chapter. To give a sense of the importance of at least the marketed services associated with conservation, however, consider ecotourism. Ecotourism markets are a subset of the markets for all forms of tourism. Taking all tourism markets together, the global industry accounts for approximately 9 percent of global GDP and employs some 235 million people directly or indirectly. It has been one of the fastest growing sectors of the global economy for some time. Using international tourist arrivals as a measure of the physical growth of tourism the global industry has grown by just under 4 percent a year, on average, since the Caracas Action Plan (Table 2.2).

The decade of the 1990s saw faster rates of growth than the decade of the 2000s, in part due to the recession, but tourism is still one of the most robust sectors of the global economy (World Tourism Organization 2011). Tourism is of particular importance to developing countries. In the world's forty poorest countries, for example, it is second only to oil as a source of foreign exchange. In some countries – Ethiopia, Mexico, Nepal, Mali, Kenya, Egypt, El Salvador, Thailand, and Costa Rica – it accounts for 20 percent or more of export receipts. The bias is even more marked in the case of biodiversity-based ecotourism (Roe *et al.* 2004).

This is a form of tourism of growing importance that is also more closely tied to the outcome of conservation activities than other forms of tourism. Whereas tourist arrivals in general grew by 3.4 percent per year on average in the last decade, for example, tourist arrivals in twenty-three

Table 2.2 *World tourism growth, 1990–2010*

	International tourist arrivals (million)					Average annual growth (%)	
	1990	1995	2000	2005	2010	1990–2000	2001–2010
World	435	528	675	798	940	4.5	3.4
Advanced economies	296	334	417	453	498	3.5	1.8
Emerging economies	139	193	257	345	442	6.3	5.6
Europe	261.5	304.1	385.6	439.4	476.6	4.0	2.1
Northern Europe	28.6	35.8	43.7	57.3	58.1	4.3	2.9
Western Europe	108.6	112.2	139.7	141.7	153.7	2.6	1
Central/Eastern Europe	33.9	58.1	69.3	8.5	95.1	7.4	3.2
Southern/ Mediteranean/ Europe	90.3	98	133	153	169.7	3.9	2.5
Asia and the Pacific	55.8	82	110.1	153.6	203.8	7.0	6.3
Northeast Asia	26.4	41.3	58.3	85.9	111.6	8.2	6.7
Southeast Asia	21.2	28.4	36.1	48.5	69.6	5.5	6.8
Oceania	5.2	8.1	9.6	11	11.6	6.3	1.9
South Asia	3.2	4.2	6.1	8.1	11.1	6.7	6.2
Americas	92.8	109	128.2	133.3	149.8	3.3	1.6
North America	71.7	80.7	91.5	89.9	98.2	2.5	0.7
Caribbean	11.4	14	17.1	18.8	20.1	4.1	1.6
Central America	1.9	2.6	4.3	6.3	7.9	8.5	6.2
South America	7.7	11.7	15.3	18.3	23.5	7.1	4.4
Africa	14.8	18.9	26.5	35.4	49.4	6.0	6.4
North Africa	8.4	7.3	10.2	13.9	18.7	2.0	6.2
Sub-Saharan Africa	6.4	11.6	16.2	21.5	30.7	9.7	6.6
Middle East	9.6	13.7	24.1	36.3	60.3	9.6	9.6

Source: World Tourism Organization (2011).

of thirty-four biodiversity hotspots are argued to have grown at annual rates above 7.5 percent (Hall 2006). Moreover, although tourist arrivals fell during the recession in almost every region, they continued to grow in the region where tourism is most directly biodiversity-based, Sub-Saharan Africa (World Tourism Organization 2011).

There is no one criterion for the establishment of protected areas. Indeed, a 2006 review of global conservation priorities identified eight biodiversity conservation criteria aside from biodiversity hotspots: crisis ecoregions, endemic bird areas, centers of plant diversity, megadiversity countries, global 200 ecoregions, high-biodiversity wilderness areas, frontier forests, and the last of the wild. All, however, are focused on species, and all balance species "irreplaceability" and "vulnerability" in some way. Irreplaceability tends to be proxied by endemism, although other metrics suggested have included taxonomic uniqueness and the global rarity of habitat types. Vulnerability is typically measured in one of four ways: the proportion of habitat lost, the proportion of habitat protected, the number of threatened species, and expert opinion. The balance between the two then identifies sites of importance for wildlife conservation both in terms of the representation of species, and the connectivity and spatial structures of protected area networks (Brooks *et al.* 2006). As we will later see, there is good reason to think that a conservation strategy that focuses only on the preservation of vulnerable wild species in protected areas is far too limited, but it is a reasonable description of the dominant approach to managing the loss of those species. It also helps to highlight the essential similarities between the conservation problem addressed in each of the three areas of activity discussed in this chapter.

2.5 Finding the balance

Agriculture, public health, and wild species protection are not, of course, the whole story. Human lives and livelihoods depend on biodiversity in a myriad of other ways: some positive, some negative. But these activities illustrate the most central features of directed biodiversity change, and the essential similarity of the conservation problem in areas that – on the surface – are very dissimilar. Many of the most severe stresses on wild-living species derive from activities that are, at the same time, a source of wellbeing. The positive feedbacks between agricultural productivity, improvements in human health, and human population growth have also driven the conversion of natural habitats. In some cases human interests have been served by direct attacks on the abundance – sometimes the existence – of other species. In others they have been served by land-use change that indirectly or incidentally harms other species.

There is always an optimal mix of species involved. Sometimes the mix is sparse, sometimes not. The positive gains to be had from protected areas in places of high conservation value provide incentives to preserve a richer array of species than in the world's agro-ecosystems, but there is still a balance to be struck between the efforts made to conserve ecosystems, to produce food, to protect health, and to undertake all the other activities that affect biodiversity. Directed biodiversity change is a consequence of the ways in which people approach that problem. We need to understand the interests that lie behind biodiversity change, and then we need to ask if the balance currently being struck is the right one.

In sum, many of the activities that most directly enhance human well-being involve selecting for species with desirable traits, and against species with undesirable traits. Selecting for the species that support production of foods, fuels, and fibers and against their competitors and predators has led to the conversion and fragmentation of habitat – with both on-site and off-site effects on other species. The introduction of domesticated plants and livestock has transformed the mix of species in agro-ecosystems. It has at once replaced the competitive dominants of the natural system with domesticated plants or animals, changed the niche structure of that system in ways that have compromised many other species, and selected plant and livestock competitors and predators for eradication or control. The biodiversity that is the focus of attention in agro-ecosystems is not the diversity of wild-living species, but the interspecific diversity of cultivated plants and livestock strains along with their predators, competitors, and symbionts, and the intraspecific genetic diversity of particular cultivated species, landraces, and wild crop relatives.

While there is a cost to the transformation of agro-ecosystems, there are also benefits. In fact it is hard to overstate the benefits. Everything else that humankind has achieved has been made possible because of the growth in agricultural productivity. That we have collectively been able to divert resources from the production of food to warfare, trade, industry, commerce, science and learning, religion, and the arts is because we have had to commit fewer resources to feeding ourselves. The dramatic differences between the most and least developed countries are first and foremost differences in the proportion of the population that is engaged in agriculture, and the proportion of output that is accounted for by agriculture. The gains we have secured from the growth in agricultural output are what have to be put in the balance when we consider the negative effects of agriculture on other species. Implicitly, that is what is being done in the drive to intensify agriculture in the developing world, as we shall see in later chapters. But two things are important to underline now. The first is that agriculture is the basis on which all else has been built. The second is that the conversion of ecosystems to the production of foods, fuels, and fibers still involves a biodiversity problem – albeit one specific to agriculture. People still need to determine the mix of species, and the genetic diversity within domesticated species in agro-ecosystems, that best serves their interests.

The control of disease due to biological agents in humans, and the plants and other animals that humans care about, has also involved the deliberate simplification of systems through the extirpation of disease vectors, macroparasites, and microparasites. As in agriculture, the control of diseases reduces the diversity of species (and biological entities like viruses that fit less neatly into conventional species classifications), but also offers immense benefits to humankind that need to be set in the balance when we assess its negative effects on the controlled species, and collateral effects on other species. As in agriculture, too, the biodiversity change problem in the management of human, animal, and plant health is specific to those activities. The steps taken by people to control diseases themselves alter the epidemiological environment, often in ways that are not anticipated by those making control decisions, and often in ways that are quite perverse. Every control measure induces a self-protective response on the part of disease vectors or agents that potentially has negative consequences for other people and other species.

The best known of these responses is the effect of antibiotic use on antibiotic resistance – in part because the phenomenon has been documented since the middle of the last century, and in part because its effects are so widely felt. But it is not the only example. Daily and Ehrlich cite the effects of agricultural spraying of cotton and rice on the evolution of pesticide resistance in the Anopheles mosquito, the vector for malaria (Daily and Ehrlich 1996), an effect observed since the 1980s (Chapin and Wasserstrom 1981). They also note the effects of changes in habitat. A change in grass species associated with intensification of agriculture in the Argentinian pampas, for example, is argued to have favored a mouse that is the reservoir for the Junin virus, the cause of Argentine hemorrhagic fever (Daily and Ehrlich 1996). In fact, the interactions between human health and the control of animal and plant diseases in agriculture are a critically important part of the biodiversity problem. Getting the balance right involves trading off the benefits of disease control in one dimension against costs of increased disease risk in another. As with climate change the science is not uncontested. While the use of streptomycin to control plant diseases has long been linked to antibiotic resistance in humans (Levy 1992), for example, studies have raised doubts about the transmission mechanisms (Rezzonico, Stockwell and Duffy 2009). Similarly, while sub-therapeutic doses of a range of antibiotics in animal feed has also been linked to increased antibiotic resistance in people (Witte 1998), there are some who claim that the greater threat is human antibiotic use and that the evidence for a direct link between antibiotics in animal feed and human clinical outcomes is weak (Phillips *et al.* 2004). As we shall see in later chapters the existence of uncertainty may complicate the decision problem, but it does not change the fact that decisions have to be made.

In wildlife conservation, as in agriculture and disease control, there are choices to be made about the optimal diversity of species – the balance between species richness and abundance that best meets society's interests. It is no more possible to preserve all species in wildlands in their current state than it is to eliminate all pests and pathogens. There is a balance to be struck between the resources devoted to the production of foods, fuels, and fibers, the promotion of human, animal, and plant health, and the conservation of threatened species. That balance depends on the value to society of what is gained and what is lost by actions in each arena. It is not always easy to translate the conservation value of species, landscapes, or ecosystems into terms that can be directly compared to the benefits of agriculture or disease control, but that is the task we face.

Much of this book is an attempt to answer the question: is the balance currently being struck the right one? It is an attempt to understand the pathology of choice and to identify its consequences. If we wish to know how different societies should manage biodiversity change, we need to understand both their goals and the set of constraints under which they operate. We need to understand the ways in which they interact with others and the consequences for all of the choices of each. From the Neolithic revolution forward, human history can be told as the story of closer integration. It is a halting story, containing many twists and turns, and many dead ends. But it is also a consistent one. This book is not about the story itself, but it is about its implications for the choices we make in our interactions with the other species of our world.

References

Alston, J. M., Beddow, J. M. and Pardey, P. G. (2009) Agricultural research, productivity, and food prices in the long run. *Science*, 325, 1209–1210.

Alston, J. M., Andersen, M. A., James, J. J. and Pardey, P. G. (2010) *Persistence Pays: US Agricultural Productivity Growth and the Benefits from Public R&D Spending*. Springer, Dordrecht.

Bairoch, P. (1988) *Cities and Economic Development: From the Dawn of History to the Present*. University of Chicago Press.

Barbier, E. B. (2008) In the wake of tsunami: lessons learned from the household decision to replant mangroves in Thailand. *Resource and Energy Economics*, 30, 229–249.

Barbier, E. B., Burgess, J. C. and Grainger, A. (2010) The forest transition: towards a more comprehensive theoretical framework. *Land Use Policy*, 27, 98–107.

Binswanger, H. P. and Ruttan, V. W. (1978) *Induced Innovation: Technology, Institutions and Development*. Johns Hopkins University Press, Baltimore, MD.

Boserup, E. (1965) *The Conditions of Agricultural Growth: The Economics of Agrarian Change under Population Pressure*. George Allen and Unwin, London.

  (1981) *Population and Technological Change: A Study of Long Term Trends*. University of Chicago Press.

Brandon, K. and Bruner, A. (2008) Benefits of protected areas: perspectives and experiences of Conservation International. *Protected Areas in Today's World: Their Values and Benefits for the Welfare of the Planet* (ed. Secretariat of the Convention on Biological Diversity), pp. 29–36. Convention on Biological Diversity, Montreal.

Brooks, T. M., Mittermeier, R. A., da Fonseca, G. A. B., Gerlach, J., Hoffmann, M., Lamoreux, J. F., Mittermeier, C. G., Pilgrim, J. D. and Rodrigues, A. S. L. (2006) Global biodiversity conservation priorities. *Science*, 313, 58 61.

Bulte, E. H. and Horan, R. D. (2003) Habitat conservation, wildlife extraction and agricultural expansion. *Journal of Environmental Economics and Management*, 45, 109–127.

Caldwell, J. C. (1976) Toward a restatement of demographic transition theory. *Population and Development Review*, 2, 321–366.

Caliendo, L. and Parro, F. (2011) Estimates of the trade and welfare effects of NAFTA. Working Paper, Princeton University.

Canadell, J. G. and Raupach, M. R. (2008) Managing forests for climate change mitigation. *Science*, 320, 1456–1457.

Carew, R., Smith, E. G. and Grant, C. (2009) Factors influencing wheat yield and variability: evidence from Manitoba, Canada. *Journal of Agricultural and Applied Economics*, 41, 625–639.

Cervigni, R. (2001) *Biodiversity in the Balance: Land Use, National Development and Global Welfare*. Edward Elgar, Cheltenham.

Chapin, G. and Wasserstrom, R. (1981) Agricultural production and malaria resurgence in Central America and India. *Nature*, 293, 181–185.

Childers, D. L., Corman, J., Edwards, M. and Elser, J. J. (2011) Sustainability challenges of phosphorus and food: solutions from closing the human phosphorus cycle. *Bioscience*, 61, 117–123.

Conservation International (2010) *Global Biodiversity Outlook 3*. Convention on Biological Diversity, Montreal.

(2013) *The Biodiversity Hotspots*. Available at www.conservation.org/where/priority_areas/hotspots/Pages/hotspots_main.aspx (accessed 2013).

Conway, G. R. and Barbier, E. B. (1988) After the Green-Revolution – sustainable and equitable agricultural-development. *Futures*, 20, 651–670.

Copeland, B. R. (2000) Trade and environment: policy linkages. *Environment and Development Economics*, 5, 405–432.

Crane, P. and Kinzig, A. (2005) Nature in the metropolis. *Science*, 308, 1225.

Daily, G. and Ehrlich, P. (1996) Global change and human susceptibility to disease. *Annual Review of Energy and the Environment*, 21, 125–144.

di Falco, S., Smale, M. and Perrings, C. (2008) The role of agricultural cooperatives in sustaining the wheat diversity and productivity: the case of southern Italy. *Environmental & Resource Economics*, 39, 161–174.

Diamond, J. (2005) *Collapse*. Penguin Books, New York.

Diaz, R. J. and Rosenberg, R. (2008) Spreading dead zones and consequences for marine ecosystems. *Science*, 321, 926–929.

Dimitri, C., Effland, A. and Conklin, N. (2005) The 20th century transformation of US agriculture and farm policy. USDA Economic Research Service, Washington, DC.

Dodds, W. K. (2006) Nutrients and the dead zone: the link between nutrient ratios and dissolved oxygen in the northern Gulf of Mexico. *Frontiers in Ecology and the Environment*, 4, 211–217.

Ehrlich, P. (1968) *The Population Bomb*. Buccaneer Books, New York.

Elser, J. J. (2011) A world awash with nitrogen. *Science*, 334, 1504–1505.

Ewald, P. (1995) The evolution of virulence: a unifying link between ecology and parasitology. *Journal of Parasitology*, 81, 659–669.

Fagan, W. F. (2002) Connectivity, fragmentation, and extinction risk in dendritic metapopulations. *Ecology*, 83, 3243–3249.

Fei, J. C. H. and Ranis, G. (1964) *Development of the Labor Surplus Economy: Theory and Policy*. R.D. Irwin, Holmewood, IL.

Food and Agriculture Organization (2010a) *Global Forest Resources Assessment 2010, Main Report*. FAO, Rome.

(2010b) *The State of the World Fisheries and Aquaculture*. FAO, Rome.

Gadgil, M., Berkes, F. and Folke, C. (1993) Indigenous knowledge for biodiversity conservation. *Ambio*, 22, 151–156.

Gokhale, Y., Velankar, R., Chandran, M. D. S. and Gadgil, M. (1998) Sacred woods, grasslands and waterbodies as self-organized systems of conservation. *Conserving the Sacred for Biodiversity Management* (ed. P. S. Ramakrishnan, K. G. Saxena and U. M. Chandrashekara), pp. 366–396. Oxford University Press, New Delhi.

Hall, C. M. (2006) Tourism, biodiversity and global environmental change. *Tourism and Global Environmental Change: Ecological, Social, Economic and Political Interrelationships* (ed. S. Gossling and C. M. Hall), pp. 211–228. Routledge, New York.

Harrison, G. W., Rutherford, T. F. and Tarr, D. G. (1997) Quantifying the Uruguay Round. *Economic Journal*, 107, 1405–1430.

Heal, G. (2000) Valuing ecosystem services. *Ecosystems*, 3, 24–30.

Heywood, V. and Watson, R. (eds.) (1995) *Global Biodiversity Assessment*. Cambridge University Press.

Huang, X.-Q., Wolf, M., Ganal, M. W., Orford, S., Koebner, R. M. D. and Röder, M. S. (2007) Did modern plant breeding lead to genetic erosion in European winter wheat varieties? *Crop Science*, 47, 343–349.

International Assessment of Agricultural Knowledge Science and Technology for Development (2008) *Agriculture at a Crossroads: Synthesis Report*. Island Press, Washington, DC.

Kinzig, A. P. and Socolow, R. H. (1994) Human impacts on the nitrogen cycle. *Physics Today*, 47, 24–32.

Levin, S. A. (2013) *Encylopedia of Biodiversity*, 2nd edn. Elsevier, New York.

Levy, S. B. (1992) *The Antibiotic Paradox*. Plenum, New York.

Lewis, W. A. (1954) Economic development with unlimited supplies of labour. *The Manchester School of Economic and Social Studies*, 22, 139–191.

(1979) The dual economy revisited. *The Manchester School of Economic and Social Studies*, 47, 211–229.

Loskutov, I. G. and Rines, H. R. (2011) *Avena*. *Wild Crop Relatives: Genomic and Breeding Resources (Cereals)* (ed. C. Kole), pp. 109–184. Springer, Berlin.

Malthus, T. R. (1999[1798]) *An Essay on the Principle of Population*. Oxford University Press.

Manifesto, M. M., Schlatter, A. R., Hopp, H. E., Suárez, E. Y. and Dubcovsky, J. (2001) Quantitative evaluation of genetic diversity in wheat germplasm using molecular markers. *Crop Science*, 41, 682–690.

McNeely, J. A. (2001) An introduction to human dimensions of invasive alien species. *The Great Reshuffling: Human Dimensions of Invasive Alien Species* (ed. J. A. McNeely), pp. 5–20. IUCN, Gland.

McNeill, W. H. (1977) *Plagues and People.* Anchor Books, New York.

Millennium Ecosystem Assessment (2005a) *Ecosystems and Human Well-being: General Synthesis.* Island Press, Washington, DC.

(2005b) *Ecosystems and Human Well-Being: Biodiversity Synthesis.* World Resources Institute, Washington, DC.

(2005c) *Ecosystems and Human Well-Being: Current State and Trends.* Island Press, Washington, DC.

Myers, N. (1988) Threatened biotas: "hot spots" in tropical forests. *Environmentalist*, 8, 187–208.

Myers, N., Mittermeier, R. A. Mittermeier, C. G., da Fonseca, G. A. B. and Kent, J. (2000) Biodiversity hotspots for conservation priorities. *Nature*, 403, 853–858.

Nin Pratt, A. and Fan, S. (2010) R&D investment in national and international agricultural research. International Food Policy Research Institute (IFPRI), IFPRI discussion papers.

Normile, D. (2008) Rinderpest: driven to extinction. *Science*, 319, 1606–1609.

Oates, J., McMahon, A., Karsgaard, P., Al Quntar, S. and Ur, J. (2007) *Antiquity*, 81, 585–600.

Ostfeld, R. S., Keesing, F. and Eviner, V. T. (2008) *Infectious Disease Ecology: Effects of Ecosystems on Disease and of Disease on Ecosystems.* Princeton University Press.

Pardey, P., Beintema, N., Dehmer, S. and Wood, S. (2006) Agricultural research a growing global divide? IFPRI, Washington, DC.

Paul, J. R. (1971) *A History of Poliomyelitis.* Yale University Press, New Haven, CT.

Perrings, C. (1997) Industrial growth, rural income, and the overexploitation of land in the dual economy. *Economics of Ecological Resources: Selected Essays.* Edward Elgar, Cheltenham.

Perrings, C. and Gadgil, M. (2003) Conserving biodiversity: reconciling local and global public benefits. *Providing Global Public Goods: Managing Globalization* (ed. I. Kaul, P. Conceicao, K. Le Goulven and R. L. Mendoza), pp. 532–555. Oxford University Press.

Perrings, C., Fenichel, E. and Kinzig, A. (2010) Globalization and invasive alien species: trade, pests and pathogens. *Globalization and Bioinvasions: Ecology, Economics, Management and Policy* (ed. C. Perrings, H. A. Mooney and M. Williamson), pp. 42–55. Oxford University Press.

Perrings, C., Dehnen-Schmutz, K., Touza, J. and Williamson, M. (2005) How to manage biological invasions under globalization. *Trends in Ecology and Evolution*, 20, 212–215.

Phillips, I., Casewell, M., Cox, T., De Groot, B., Friis, C., Jones, R., Nightingale, C., Preston, R. and Waddell, J. (2004) Does the use of antibiotics in food animals pose a risk to human health? A critical review of published data. *Journal of Antimicrobial Chemotherapy*, 53, 28–52.

Piesse, J. and Thirtle, C. (2010) Agricultural R&D, technology and productivity. *Philosophical Transactions of the Royal Society B: Biological Sciences*, 365, 3035–3047.

Quadros, C. A. (2006) Is global measles eradication feasible? *Mass Vaccination: Global Aspects – Progress and Obstacles* (ed. S. Plotkin), pp. 153–163. Springer, Berlin and Heidelberg.

Rangi, D. K. (2004) *Invasive Alien Species: Agriculture and Development.* UNEP, Nairobi.

Reed, D. H. (2004) Extinction risk in fragmented habitats. *Animal Conservation*, 7, 181–191.

Rezzonico, F., Stockwell, V. O. and Duffy, B. (2009) Plant agricultural streptomycin formulations do not carry antibiotic resistance genes. *Antimicrobial Agents and Chemotherapy*, 53, 3173–3177.

Roe, D., Ashley, C., Page, S. and Meyer, D. (2004) *Tourism and the Poor: Analysing and Interpreting Tourism Statistics from a Poverty Perspective.* PPT Partnership, London.

Rosenzweig, M. L. (1995) *Species Diversity in Space and Time.* Cambridge University Press.

Rotz, L. D., Khan, A. S., Lillibridge, S. R., Ostroff, S. M. and Hughes, J. M. (2002) Public health assessment of potential biological terrorism agents. *Emerging Infectious Diseases*, 8, 225–230.

Smale, M., Hartell, J., Heisey, P. W. and Senauer, B. (1998) The contribution of genetic resources and diversity to wheat production in the Punjab of Pakistan. *American Journal of Agricultural Economics*, 80, 482–493.

Soulé, M. E. (1986) What is conservation biology? *Bioscience*, 35, 727–734.

Spinage, C. A. (2003) *Cattle Plague: A History.* Kluwer, Dordrecht.

Szreter, S. (1997) Economic growth, disruption, deprivation, disease, and death: on the importance of the politics of public health for development. *Population and Development Review*, 23, 698–728.

Tainter, J. A. (2006) Archaeology of overshoot and collapse. *Annual Review of Anthropology*, 35, 59–74.

Tauger, M. (2009) *Agriculture in World History.* Taylor and Francis, New York.

Thompson, W. S. (1929) Population. *American Journal of Sociology*, 34, 959–975.

Tilman, D., Hill, J. and Lehman, C. (2006) Carbon-negative biofuels from low-input high-diversity grassland biomass. *Science*, 314, 1598–1600.

Tilman, D., Fargione, J., Wolff, B., D'Antonio, C., Dobson, A., Howarth, R., Schindler, D., Schlesinger, W. H., Simberloff, D. and Swackhamer, D. (2001) Forecasting agriculturally driven global environmental change. *Science*, 292, 281–284.

Turner, R. E., Rabalais, N. N. and Justic, D. (2008) Gulf of Mexico hypoxia: alternate states and a legacy. *Environmental Science & Technology*, 42, 2323–2327.

UNEP–WCMC and the IUCN World Commission on Protected Areas (2012) *World Database on Protected Areas*: Available at www.wdpa.org/ (accessed 2012).

United Nations (1993) *Convention on Biological Diversity*. United Nations, New York.

Vavilov, N. I. (1935) *Botanical-Geographic Principles of Selection*. Lenin Academy of Agricultural Sciences, Leningrad.

Widawsky, D. and Rozelle, S. (1998) Varietal diversity and yield variability in Chinese rice production. *Farmers, Gene Banks, and Crop Breeding* (ed. M. Smale), pp. 159–172. Kluwer, Norwell, MA.

Williamson, M. (1996) *Biological Invasions*. Chapman and Hall, London.

Witte, W. (1998) Medical consequences of antibiotic use in agriculture. *Science*, 279, 996–997.

World Bank (2012a) *Agriculture, Value Added (% of GDP)*. Available at http://data.worldbank.org/indicator/NV.AGR.TOTL.ZS/countries?page=3 (accessed 2012).

(2012b) *Employment in Agriculture (% of Total Employment)*. Available at http://data.worldbank.org/indicator/SL.AGR.EMPL.ZS (accessed 2012).

World Tourism Organization (2011) *World Tourism Highlights*. UNWTO, Madrid.

3 | *Biodiversity and ecosystem services*

3.1 Biodiversity, ecosystem services, and the market

For many readers of this book their first encounter with the concept of ecosystem services will have been the 2005 report of the MA (Millennium Ecosystem Assessment 2005b), and their first reaction may well have been as instinctively cautious as that expressed in 2006 by Douglas McCauley, then a graduate student at Stanford University. Writing in *Nature*, he characterized the approach taken by the MA as "selling out on nature":

> The underlying assumption is that if scientists can identify ecosystem services, quantify their economic value, and ultimately bring conservation more in synchrony with market ideologies, then the decision-makers will recognize the folly of environmental destruction and work to safeguard nature. But market-based mechanisms for conservation are not a panacea for our current conservation ills. If we mean to make significant and long-lasting gains in conservation, we must strongly assert the primacy of ethics and aesthetics in conservation. We must act quickly to redirect much of the effort now being devoted to the commodification of nature back towards instilling a love for nature in more people. (McCauley 2006)

McCauley's reaction was not wholly surprising. After all, the conviction that other species have infinite intrinsic value had been defined by Michael Soulé as a quintessential feature of the field of conservation biology (Soulé 1986). That conviction is one that is shared by many in the ecological sciences, and finds ready echoes in the works of the most important precursors of the field, Aldo Leopold (1949) and Alexander von Humboldt (1850).

Yet the concept of ecosystem services has nothing to do with market ideologies. Nor does it imply the commodification of nature. Some ecosystem services that are important today are certainly provided through markets. Many foods, fuels, and fibers are in this category. Other services will surely be provided through markets in the future. The identification of new pharmacologically active compounds, for example, is likely to lead to the emergence of markets for the species that are the source of those compounds. But there are many ecosystem services that are not now, and never will be, provided through markets. What the concept of ecosystem services does is to give us a way of characterizing the interests that people have in their environment. Whether an ecosystem service can be provided through the market depends on its properties, and not on the fact that it is important to people.

This chapter explains how the concept of ecosystem services helps us understand what we gain – and what we lose – from the conservation (*sensu lato*) of biodiversity. By distinguishing services whose benefits can be captured by private individuals from those whose benefits accrue to all, it explains why some services are at risk, and why others are not. By distinguishing between the price and value of marketed ecosystem services, it explains where markets are likely to succeed in signaling the importance of biodiversity and where they are likely to fail. By identifying the value of services for which no price exists, it indicates what we lose when we allow those services to erode. The concept of ecosystem services has its roots in the discipline of economics – the science of the allocation of scarce resources – but this does not imply that all ecosystem services may be bought and sold as commodities in the market. In some cases markets can and should be used to promote the socially optimal level of biodiversity conservation, in others not. Knowing when this is so is key to the development of socially responsible biodiversity management strategies.

Markets exist for foods, fuels, and fibers for two main reasons. One is that they are scarce. This does not imply that they are rare. It implies that their production has an opportunity cost. Something has to be given up in order to get them. The other is that they can be privately produced and consumed. Whether foods are produced by agriculture, aquaculture, or wild capture, those who sell them and those who buy them are both able to capture the benefits of doing so. The products of agriculture, aquaculture, forestry, and fisheries are said to be "rival" and "exclusive" in consumption. They are rival in the sense that consumption by one person precludes their consumption by others. Two people cannot eat the same morsel of food. They are exclusive in the sense that the owner is able to exclude others. The person who purchases food is able to deny others access to that food.

By contrast, markets do not and cannot exist for many ecosystem services that have the characteristics of public goods. An example of this would be the contribution of oceanic phytoplankton to the regulation of a number of important gases. Marine biogeochemical pathways are responsible for as much climate regulation through carbon sequestration as all terrestrial contributions combined. Something like 92.2 Gt per year of atmospheric carbon enters the ocean, and something like 90.6 Gt of carbon exits the ocean to the atmosphere (Denman *et al.* 2007). Similarly, the oxygen in one out of every two breaths we take is produced directly by microscopic marine phytoplankton (Behrenfeld *et al.* 2006). Such services are hugely important to humankind, but because they are not exclusive, none can capture the benefits of their production. They are global public goods. If they are threatened, all are affected and collective action will be needed to protect them.

Some environmental public goods, to be sure, are only non-exclusive because people have chosen to make them so. Most protected areas, for example, are in public ownership. Though not intrinsically non-exclusive, they are held in trust for the collectivity, and are open access by law. Others are inherently public. None can be excluded from the benefits of climate regulation through carbon sequestration, for example. Yet even public goods of this kind may be privately produced. Carbon sequestration depends on land cover everywhere, whether in public or private ownership. In such circumstances society may collectively choose to contract with individual landholders for its provision. The important point here is that wherever people have an interest in their environment they will find ways of securing that interest. So societies interested in the conservation of resources have historically used, *inter alia*, traditional taboos, potlatch consumption, religious injunctions, appropriation through war or insurrection, development of common pool management rules, social norms, and protective legislation. They have also used the price mechanism. Later chapters will consider the options open to societies interested in ecosystem services characterized by different degrees of publicness, and will show that markets are part of the story, but only part. In this chapter I consider the interests that people have in their environment, and the way that these interests are related to biodiversity.

3.2 Origins of ecosystem services

The MA shifted attention from the conservation of endangered species for the sake of conservation to the role of biodiversity in the production of a much wider range of benefits obtained from the environment. This includes the benefits people get from the moral stewardship of other species, the essence of traditional conservation, but it also includes the production of foods, fuels, fibers, water, genetic resources, and chemical compounds. It includes human, animal, and plant health, recreation, renewal, aesthetic and spiritual satisfaction, and the buffering of many ecological processes and functions against the effects of environmental variation. The approach has its roots in the way that economists think about the choices people make. The term ecosystem services was introduced to natural scientists by Walter Westman, in a paper that examined the strengths and weaknesses of the way that economists then incorporated the value of the non-marketed benefits of nature (Westman 1977). Westman focused on the relationship between the functioning of ecosystems and the benefits they provide to humans. He argued that ecosystem functioning, defined as the flow of materials and energy in biotic communities, underpinned the production of all services valued by humankind. This reflected the approach then being developed by economists to embed ecological processes in the functions describing the production of environmentally based goods and services (Mäler 1974).

Subsequent efforts to develop the notion of ecological production functions built on research linking biodiversity and ecological functioning (Schulze and Mooney 1993). This led to the extension of the concept of ecological production functions to include the biotic and abiotic environmental stocks that supported such functions. It was argued that the value of species, like that of other inputs to the production of the goods and services people want, derives from the value of those goods and services. For particular services, the production of timber or paper for example, the value of individual tree species derives from the value of timber or paper products. But trees also have a role in providing a number of other services, including the supply of water, water quality, habitat, non-timber forest products, micro- and macro-climatic regulation, soil erosion control, and so on. And trees also depend on a range of other species. The value of the mix of species derives from the bundle of services generated by the whole community of species, from the functional complementarity/substitutability between them, and from their effect on the variability in the supply of services. In particular, it was argued that a major part of the value of biodiversity lies in its role in assuring the resilience of ecological systems – their capacity to function over a range of environmental conditions (Perrings, Folke and Mäler 1992).

The relationship between biodiversity and variability in the production of goods and services will be explored in more detail in the next chapter. What is important to note now is that the concept of ecosystem services captures the role of ecosystem components – the species and the landscapes they inhabit – in supporting ecological functions that are used by people to produce goods and services. Some of these services have long been priced in the market, others not. But the fact that many have not been priced in the market does not mean they are unimportant. As Ehrlich and Ehrlich put it:

plants, animals, and microorganisms help to supply human beings with an array of free ecosystem services, without which civilization could not persist. These include such things as controlling the gaseous mix of the atmosphere, generating and maintaining soils, controlling pests, and running biogeochemical cycles. The present extinction episode caused by human activity seriously jeopardizes the ethical, aesthetic, direct economic and life-support values of biodiversity; it may be the single most important externality associated with human economic activity. (Ehrlich and Ehrlich 1992)

The Global Biodiversity Assessment, which reported in 1995, offered the first broad review of what was then understood about the value of biodiversity deriving from its role in the provision of ecosystem services. It noted that while there was considerable information on the value of the species most directly concerned in the production of individual commodities, much less was known about the value of the mix of species. While it was known, for example, that the value of the mix of species stemmed from the capacity of ecosystems to maintain a flow of services over a range of environmental conditions, the Global Biodiversity Assessment was able to report few reliable estimates of what this implied in any given ecosystem or for any given ecosystem service. The basis for valuing biodiversity in this approach is straightforward. If an ecosystem service depends on one set of organisms in one possible state of nature, and another set of organisms in a different state of nature, then the value of both sets of organisms depends on the likelihood that each state of nature will occur. At that time, however, little had been done to identify the value of the portfolio of species involved in the production of anything beyond a limited set of foods, fuels, and fibers (Heywood and Watson 1995).

During the later 1990s the nature of ecosystem services was further explored by scientists interested in identifying both the set of benefits offered by ecosystems (Myers 1996; Daily 1997b) and the value of these benefits to humankind (Costanza *et al.* 1997). The paper by Myers (1996) is a landmark. Written from within conservation biology, it nevertheless considered the relative importance of multiple services, only some of which involve market transactions. Like Ehrlich and Ehrlich (1992) it anticipated many of the ecosystem services evaluated by the MA, but paid special attention to what the MA was later to term the regulating services: micro-climatic regulation through water cycling, macro-climatic regulation through the attenuation of carbon and other greenhouse gas emissions, the regulation of both the quality and quantity of water supplies, and soil protection through erosion control. More importantly, it connected such services with the resilience of ecosystems – their capacity to function over a range of environmental conditions.

As Westman had earlier noted, understanding the links between eco-system services and ecological functioning is critical. Myers observed that while the relation between biodiversity and ecological functioning was clear in some cases, it was not in many others. More importantly, he noted that in cases where the links were understood, increasing biodiver-sity did not necessarily enhance ecological functioning (Myers 1996). A decade later an exhaustive review of the ecological literature was able to report consensus on five things. First, the functional characteristics of species have a strong effect on ecosystem properties. Second, anthro-pogenic biodiversity change has altered the functioning of many ecosys-tems. Third, changes in the composition of species have different effects on different ecosystem properties. Fourth, ecosystem properties are initially insensitive to species loss in part because multiple species carry out similar functional roles. Fifth, more species are needed to underpin ecological functioning as spatial and temporal variability increases, and as longer time periods and larger areas are considered (Hooper *et al.* 2005).

The same review concluded that changes in biodiversity would be expected to have greater effects on the properties of ecosystems that affect human wellbeing than changes in abiotic conditions – climate, for example. In more recent years this has led ecologists interested in the relationship between biodiversity and ecological functioning to focus on the diversity within functional groups rather than species richness *per se* (Naeem *et al.* 2009). This makes it possible to identify the species needed to maintain particular functions and therefore ecosystem services. Because the effect of species diversity on ecosystem functions tends to saturate – adding species after some point does not add functionality – the question is which species have the greatest effect in the conditions expected to occur.

Of course, identifying which services we need to keep requires a different calculus. Since we cannot have them all, it is important to understand the relative value of different services to humankind. The exercise by Costanza and others (Costanza *et al.* 1997) to value global ecosystem services by extrapolating from a limited set of country-specific studies to the whole world was roundly criticized by economists on methodological grounds. However, it did mark a first – albeit flawed – attempt to pose the question about the relative importance of different types of ecosystem services. The vehemence of the criticisms of that paper may have been the reason that the MA shied away from the valuation of the services it identified. It may also have been the reason why the first UNEP-sponsored assessment of the value of ecosystem services, *The Economics of Ecosystems and Biodiversity* (TEEB), reports only the range of assessed values and not the mean (Kumar 2010). Although it remains the case that the valuation of ecosystem services is unfinished business, we can say much about which ecosystem services are important to people, why, and how their valuation differs by region, culture, and income. I return to the question later in this chapter.

3.3 Ecosystem services in the Millennium Ecosystem Assessment

Ecosystem services were defined in the MA as the benefits people obtain from ecosystems (Millennium Ecosystem Assessment 2005b). While we might, strictly, want to define the benefits delivered by ecosystems to be the social utility conferred by the goods and services they provide, this is a useful first approximation. The services described in the MA include not only the provision of foods, fuels, and fibers (the provisioning services), but also a range of non-consumptive benefits such as recreation, amenity, and spiritual renewal (the cultural services). These in turn depend on a set of basic ecosystem processes such as photosynthesis and nutrient cycling (the supporting services), buffered by the diversity of genes, species, and ecosystems (the regulating services).

From an economic perspective, the provisioning and cultural services together describe the environmentally derived goods and services that enter final demand, i.e. that directly satisfy people's wants and needs (Table 3.1). The supporting and regulating services describe the ecosystem processes and functions that underpin production of the provisioning and cultural services.

Table 3.1 *Ecosystem services identified by the MA*

Provisioning services	*Food p*roducts derived from plants, animals, and microbes
	Fiber such as wood, jute, cotton, hemp, silk, and wool
	Fuel such as wood, dung, and other combustible biological materials
	Genetic resources used for animal and plant breeding and biotechnology
	Biochemicals, natural medicines, and pharmaceuticals obtained from wild species
	Ornamental resources such as plants used for landscaping and ornaments
	Freshwater obtained from ecosystems
Cultural services	*Cultural diversity* as affected by the diversity of ecosystems
	Spiritual and religious values of ecosystems or ecosystem components
	Knowledge traditional and formal knowledge of ecosystems
	Educational values of ecosystems and their components
	Inspiration for art, folklore, national symbols, architecture, and advertising
	Aesthetic values of ecosystems affecting parks, housing locations, etc.
	Social relations determined by ecosystem characteristics
	Sense of place associated with the natural environment
	Cultural heritage values of landscapes or totemic species
	Recreation and ecotourism in natural or cultivated landscapes
Regulating services	*Air quality regulation* through emissions to and extractions from the atmosphere
	Climate regulation through temperature and precipitation control, or carbon sequestration
	Water regulation through control of runoff, flooding, and aquifer recharge
	Erosion regulation effects of land cover on soil retention

Table 3.1 (*cont.*)

	Water purification and waste treatment through waste decomposition and detoxification
	Disease regulation through control of pathogens and disease vectors
	Pest regulation through impacts on crop and livestock pests
	Pollination through the distribution and abundance of pollinators
	Natural hazard regulation including effects of mangroves and coral reefs on storm damage
Supporting services	*Soil formation* and effects on soil fertility
	Photosynthesis
	Primary production through conversion of energy and nutrients by organisms
	Nutrient cycling effects on nitrogen, phosphorus, and other essential nutrients
	Water cycling, delivery of water essential for living organisms

Source: adapted from Millennium Ecosystem Assessment (2005b).

More particularly, the provisioning services are the processes that supply plant and animal products: foods, fibers, fuels, water, biochemicals, medicines, pharmaceuticals, genetic material, and so on. Many of these products are directly consumed, are subject to reasonably well-defined property rights, and are supplied through more or less well-functioning markets. There are certainly important externalities involved in their production or consumption. The impacts of agriculture and forestry on, for example, watershed protection (Heal 2000), habitat provision (Bulte and Horan 2003; Barbier, Burgess and Grainger 2010), pest and disease regulation (Ostfeld, Keesing and Eviner 2008), micro- and macro-climatic regulation (Canadell and Raupach 2008), and hazard protection (Barbier 2008) are generally not priced in the market. We will later consider the implications of such externalities, but even though they exist the prices of many plant and animal products bear some relation to their scarcity.

The cultural services, by contrast, describe people's non-consumptive uses of the environment such as recreation, tourism, education, science, and learning. They include, for example, the spiritual, religious, aesthetic, and inspirational wellbeing that people derive from the natural world (which may include human-modified landscapes). They include the attachment that people have to particular places or environmental attributes – their sense of place and the cultural importance of particular landscapes and species. They also include the traditional and scientific environmental information, awareness, and understanding offered by functioning ecosystems. Finally, they include the moral satisfaction generated by the preservation of threatened or endangered species for those who hold a conservationist ethic.

One modern expression of cultural services – ecotourism – involves well-developed markets (see Chapter 2). Others do not. Although intellectual property rights in biochemical and genetic material drawn from ecosystems are increasingly well defined, many cultural services are still regulated by custom and usage, or by traditional taboos, rights, and obligations. Many of these services depend on traditional ways of knowing and using the natural world. They privilege different components of ecosystems and are measured by different indicators (Gadgil, Berkes and Folke 1993; Berkes, Colding and Folke 2000).

The remaining categories of ecosystem services identified in the MA, the supporting and regulating services, describe the properties of ecosystems that, respectively, enable production of the provisioning and cultural services, and moderate the impact of environmental stresses and shocks on the variability of production.

The supporting services describe the ecosystem processes and ecological functions that underpin production of the things that people care about. Examples include soil formation, photosynthesis, primary production, nutrient, carbon, and water cycling. These services typically play out at different spatial and temporal scales. For example, nutrient cycling involves the maintenance of the roughly twenty nutrients essential for life, in different concentrations in different parts of the system. It is often localized and is frequently captured in the price of land or of marketed animal and plant products. Carbon cycling, on the other hand, operates at a global scale, and is very poorly captured in any set of prices. In both cases, though, since the supporting services are embedded in the other services, their value derives from the value of those others services, whether or not that value is expressed in market prices (Millennium Ecosystem Assessment 2005b).

The regulating services were described in the MA as comprising air quality regulation, climate regulation, water regulation, erosion regulation, water purification and waste treatment, disease regulation, pest regulation, natural hazard regulation, and pollination. Aside from the last of these (which is better thought of as a supporting service), all affect the impact of environmental stresses and shocks on variability in the production of plant and animal products or the non-consumptive benefits of ecosystems – the provisioning and cultural services. That is, they moderate the impact of perturbations on the provisioning or cultural services. By changing the potential cost associated with a given stress or shock, they mitigate the environmental risks people face and enhance adaptive capacity. The value of the regulating services, like the value of the supporting services, derives from the value of the provisioning and cultural services and depends both on the regime of stresses and shocks experienced, and on people's aversion to risk.

Human modification of hydrological systems, such as the damming of rivers, drainage of wetlands, and construction of canals, was reported to have stabilized river flows and enhanced the supply of freshwater for human use and for power generation. Yet many water supply systems were far from sustainable. Between 5 percent and 25 percent of global freshwater use exceeded long-term accessible supply, necessitating either inter-basin water transfers or overdraft of groundwater supplies. On water quality regulation, the MA reported that while pathogen and organic pollution of water had decreased in many countries, globally water quality had continued to decline. Nitrate concentrations, for example, had increased substantially in the second half of the twentieth century. In many cases, the problem had been exacerbated by land-use change, and in particular by the loss of wetlands. More generally, the diversion of water for human use had substantially reduced the amount of water available to the wider ecosystem.

On climate regulation, the MA noted that the ability of the atmosphere to cleanse itself of pollutants had declined slightly since preindustrial times but likely not by more than 10 percent. Ecosystems were known to be a sink for tropospheric ozone, ammonia, NO_X, SO_2, particulates, and CH_4, but it was not known how these sinks had changed. Terrestrial ecosystems had been, on average, a net source of CO_2 during the nineteenth and early twentieth centuries, but became a net sink sometime in the mid-twentieth century. Land-cover changes since 1750 were thought to have contributed to a net cooling at the global scale due to increased albedo. On the other hand, the microclimatic impacts of land-cover change were largely negative. The effect of tropical deforestation and desertification, for example, had both been to reduce local rainfall. The effect of ecosystem change on the timing and magnitude of runoff, flooding, and aquifer recharge depends on the ecosystem involved and on the specific modifications made to the ecosystem (Millennium Ecosystem Assessment 2005b).

Disease regulation had been affected by the modification of ecosystems. In agro-ecosystems, for example, the increased use of pesticides had degraded the capacity of ecosystems to provide pest control and to support a number of other important ecosystem processes and functions. The MA reported a global decline in the abundance of pollinators, with adverse implications for the production of seeds and fruit. It also noted that losses in populations of specialized pollinators had compromised the reproductive ability of some rare plants. Finally, it reported that the tendency for people to locate in places exposed to extreme events, together with a decline in the capacity of ecosystems to buffer extreme events, had led to the increasing human and economic cost of "natural disasters" (Millennium Ecosystem Assessment 2005b).

The MA was concerned less with the value of ecosystem services than with their physical status. Its objective was to record changes in the physical magnitude of different services in the second half of the twentieth century (see Table 3.2). So it reported that the production of food had grown at a faster rate than human population, and that while there had been increases in yields per hectare, this reflected a significant expansion in cropland. Marine fish harvest had increased until the late 1980s but had been declining since then, the gap in demand being made up from aquaculture which had grown from virtually nothing in the mid twentieth century to 27 percent of world fish production at the end of the century. Timber production had increased by 60 percent, and while forests continued to be depleted in many regions they were expanding in a number of temperate countries. In fiber production, as in food production, some crops (e.g. cotton, silk) had expanded while others (e.g. jute, hemp) had declined. Demand for biochemicals, pharmaceuticals, cosmetics, and bioremediation was reported to be growing, but also that species extinction and overharvesting of medicinal plants had negatively affected the supply of these resources (Millennium Ecosystem Assessment 2005b).

On the cultural services, the MA reported that land-use and land-cover change had adversely affected landscapes of special significance for people at various scales. At the smallest scale it noted that there had been a decline in the numbers of sacred groves and similar protected

Table 3.2 *Changes in ecosystem services, 1950–2000*

Ecosystem service		Change	Market
Provisioning services	Crops	⇑	YY
	Livestock	⇑	YY
	Capture fisheries	⇓	YN
	Aquaculture	⇑	YY
	Wild foods	⇓	NN
	Timber	+/–	YY
	Cotton, silk	+/–	YY
	Wood fuel	⇓	YN
	Genetic resources	⇓	YN
	Biochemicals, medicines	⇓	YN
	Freshwater	⇓	YN
Cultural services	Spiritual and religious values	⇓	NN
	Aesthetic values	⇓	NN
	Recreation and ecotourism	+/–	YY
Regulating services	Air quality regulation	⇓	YN
	Climate regulation – global	⇑	YN
	Climate regulation – regional	⇓	YN
	Water regulation	+/–	YN
	Erosion regulation	⇓	NN
	Water purification and waste treatment	⇓	NN
	Disease regulation	+/–	NN
	Pest regulation	⇓	NN
	Pollination	⇓	YN
	Natural hazard regulation	⇓	NN

Note: the table is adapted from the MA. Arrows facing upwards indicate an increase in the physical availability of a service. Arrows facing down indicate a decrease. +/– indicates that the direction of change is uncertain. The final column has been added, and indicates whether or not the services concerned are secured through market transaction. A double YY indicates that almost all services are transacted through markets. A double NN indicates that almost no services are transacted through markets. YN indicates that only some services are transacted through markets. *Source*: Millennium Ecosystem Assessment (2005b) with author's additions.

areas of traditional significance, and conjectured that this had weakened the spiritual benefits people obtained from ecosystems. It also reported that there had been a decline in the quantity and quality of landscapes available for recreation, renewal, aesthetic, spiritual, educational, and

scientific activities. At the same time, increased urbanization and continued population growth had increased demand for such landscapes.
As a result, even though land was increasingly being converted from
other uses towards recreation and other cultural services, the congestion
of such sites had led to their degradation, coral reefs being cited as a
leading example (Millennium Ecosystem Assessment 2005b).

In all, fifteen out of twenty-four ecosystem services evaluated (including 70 percent of the regulating and cultural services) had been degraded
or used unsustainably in the second half of the twentieth century. Since
the value of these services was not considered, the MA was unable to
indicate how much the recorded changes mattered, but the implication
is that every negative change in a service represents the degradation of
the ecosystems generating that service. This may be true in some cases,
but is clearly not true in others. The fact that production of some plant-
derived fibers has fallen over the last fifty years, for example, is an
indicator that demand for the fibers has fallen, and not that the agro-
ecosystems involved in their production have been degraded. There is a
relation between the relative scarcity of ecosystem services and their
value to humankind, but it is a complex one and reflects much more
than the availability of the service. A change in the value that something
has for people can indeed be driven by a change in its availability, but it
can also be driven by a change in preferences or technologies, by a change
in the number of people making use of the service, or by a combination
of these things. We will return to the question of value later.

What can be said, at this stage, is that the services most affected by
human action have been those generated in biomes converted to agriculture. The MA reported that in eleven of thirteen terrestrial biomes
considered,[1] between 20 percent and 75 percent of the area had been
converted, generally to agriculture. Only biomes relatively unsuited
to agriculture, such as boreal forests and tundra, had remained intact.
Since many of the provisioning, cultural, and regulating services provided by different biomes are distinct, the impact of land-use change
in terms of the displacement of services differs by biome. The study by

---

[1] Tundra; boreal forests; temperate coniferous forests; montane grasslands and
shrublands; tropical and sub-tropical moist broadleaf forests; deserts; tropical and
sub-tropical coniferous forests; temperate broadleaf and mixed forests;
Mediterranean forests, woodlands, and scrub; tropical and sub-tropical dry
broadleaf forests; tropical and sub-tropical grasslands, savannas, and shrublands;
flooded grasslands and savannas; temperate forest, steppe, and woodland.

Costanza *et al.* for example, distinguished seventeen services deriving-from sixteen biomes.[2] The authors found that the balance between the services corresponding to each biome was markedly different. Tropical forests, for example, were argued to be sources of foods, fuels, and fibers, but the more important services generated by biomes of that type were climate regulation, erosion control, and nutrient recycling. Temperate and boreal forests were similarly important for climate regulation, but not for erosion control or nutrient recycling. Among aquatic systems, they found that the greater part of the value to human-kind of tidal marshes and mangroves lay in the regulation of disturban-ces and waste treatment. Swamps and floodplains also have that role, but were argued to be primarily important as sources of water. Estuaries and seagrass beds were argued to be important more for their role in nutrient cycling than for anything else (Costanza *et al.* 1997). Improvements in our understanding of the relation between ecological functioning and ecosystem services has since clarified both the services delivered by distinct biomes, and the sensitivity of those services to environmental and anthropogenic stress. But the central point remains that ecosystem services vary by biome, and hence by the set of species they contain.

3.4 Ecosystem services and biodiversity

The connection between ecosystem services and biodiversity is still a con-tested area. David Tilman's early grassland experiments in Minnesota showed a positive relation between the diversity of grassland species and the stability of primary productivity (Tilman and Downing 1994). While the experimental design of the Minnesota grassland studies was criticized (Huston 1997), other large-scale grassland experiments in Europe showed similar results (Hector *et al.* 1999; Loreau, Naeem and Inchausti 2002). What became progressively clearer, though, is that the type of diversity matters. A study of grass species in California, for exam-ple, considered the relative effects of plant richness and the composition

---

[2] Biomes: open ocean, estuaries, seagrass/algae beds, coral reefs, shelf, tropical forest, temperate/boreal forest, grass/rangelands, tidal marsh/mangroves, swamps/floodplains, lakes/river, desert, tundra, ice/rock, cropland, urban.

   Services: gas regulation, climate regulation, disturbance regulation, water regulation, water supply, erosion control and sediment retention, soil formation, nutrient cycling, waste treatment, pollination, biological control, refugia, food production, raw materials, genetic resources, recreation, cultural.

of plant functional groups on primary productivity and soil nitrogen. It found that differences in plant composition had a greater impact on the variation in production than did the number of functional groups (Hooper and Vitousek 1997). Since that time, ecological research on the linkages between biodiversity and ecological functioning has continued to explore the relationship between biodiversity and ecosystem stability, focusing on the linkages between functional diversity, trophic complexity, and ecosystem functions (Naeem *et al.* 2009). While there are still points of dispute, this work has clarified a number of things. If we are interested in ecosystem services then we are interested in the diversity of species associated with the production of those services. One immediate implication of this is that simple species counts may be relatively unimportant. In other words, taxonomic diversity, or species richness, may not be the most appropriate measure of diversity in the system. A better measure of the biodiversity needed to produce ecosystem services may be diversity within the functional groups responsible for the service: the species of plants, animals, and microorganisms that support the ecological functions behind the service (Solan *et al.* 2004; Bunker *et al.* 2005; McIntyre *et al.* 2007; Bracken *et al.* 2008; Perrings *et al.* 2011).

A recent survey of the field as it has developed over the last two decades has clarified what can (and cannot) be said about the way that biodiversity – the variety of genes, species, or functional traits in an ecosystem – affects the functioning of ecosystems and the services they deliver (Cardinale *et al.* 2012). It concludes that there are at least six things that can be said with confidence. First, biodiversity loss reduces the efficiency with which ecological communities capture resources, produce biomass, and decompose and recycle nutrients. Second, biodiversity increases the stability of ecosystem functions through time. Third, the impact of biodiversity on particular functions is increasing but at a decreasing rate (it saturates). An implication of this is that the effect of biodiversity loss on the function may be expected to accelerate as biodiversity loss increases. Fourth, more diverse communities may be more productive than less diverse communities both because they may contain species that have a disproportionate influence on productivity, and because differences in functional traits among organisms increase total resource capture. Fifth, loss of diversity across trophic levels has a greater effect on productivity than loss of diversity within trophic levels. Finally, the effect of the extinction or extirpation of species on ecosystem function depends heavily on the functional traits of the lost organisms (Cardinale *et al.* 2012).

One implication of these statements is that the value of diversity to the production of particular services depends on the range of environmental conditions expected. The greater the variation in environmental conditions, the greater will be the value of diversity. That is, the value of biodiversity derives from the complementarity/substitutability between species in the supply of ecosystem services over a range of environmental conditions. In subsequent chapters, this is interpreted to mean that biodiversity has a portfolio effect on the risks attaching to the supply of ecosystem services. It leads to lower variation in the functionality of the combination of species, relative to the average of the variations in the functionality of the individual species.

From an ecological perspective, the mechanisms linking diversity and stability are generally stated rather differently. They include overyielding, statistical averaging, and compensatory dynamics. Overyielding implies that mean biomass production increases with diversity more rapidly than its standard deviation. Statistical averaging means that random variation in the population abundances of different species allows stability of aggregate ecosystem variables. Compensatory dynamics, driven either by competitive interactions or differential reactions to environmental fluctuations, occur when responses to environmental change are asynchronous (Cardinale *et al.* 2012). These effectively amount to the same thing as the portfolio effect. They all smooth out the variability of ecological functioning, and hence the production of ecosystem services.

The approach accordingly requires specification of production functions that embed the ecosystem processes and ecological functions that connect biodiversity and ecosystem services. Species are related through functional traits that make them more or less redundant in executing particular ecological functions. Individual species are highly redundant (near perfect functional substitutes for other species) if they share a full set of traits with those other species. Conversely, they are singular if they possess a unique set of traits (Naeem 1998). Species are also related through ecological interactions – trophic relationships, competition, parasitism, facilitation, and so on – that make them more or less complementary in executing ecological functions (Thébault and Loreau 2006).

It follows that to build an understanding of the value of species that support particular ecological functions requires an understanding of both their substitutability and complementarity in the performance of those functions over a range of environmental conditions. It also requires an understanding of the way that directed biodiversity change affects both the functions they perform and the interactions between functions. The simplification of an ecosystem affects the array of services that system delivers, partly because the number of functions performed decreases as the number of species declines (Hector and Bagchi 2007), and partly because each species in a system typically performs multiple functions (Díaz, Hector and Wardle 2009). To understand what species are needed, we need first to understand how different species respond to changing environmental conditions.

3.5 Changing environmental conditions: a digression on climate

Consider the most frequently cited example of environmental change – climate. There is considerable evidence that climate change is already inducing an adaptive response on the part of the world's biota, including changes in species distributions and abundance, changes in the timing of reproduction in animals and plants, changes in animal and bird migration patterns, and changes in the frequency and severity of pest and disease outbreaks (Peters and Lovejoy 1994; Gitay *et al.* 2002; Millennium Ecosystem Assessment 2005a, 2005b; Lovejoy and Hannah 2006; Karl, Melillo and Peterson 2009; Willis and Bhagwat 2009; Steffen *et al.* 2010). Some of these effects are the direct result of changes in temperature, precipitation, sea level, or storm surges. Others are the indirect effect of changes in, for example, the frequency of fire. In general, species are moving from lower to higher elevations, and from lower to higher latitudes, although the rapidity of the response among species varies very considerably. In any given ecosystem, changes in the frequency and intensity of disturbances determine the rate at which plant and animal assemblages will change.

From a conservation perspective, the main feature of climate change is that it differentially affects the probability that species will be driven to extinction. It has been argued that the risk of extinction is likely to increase for many species that are already vulnerable (Thomas *et al.* 2004), in part because of the time it takes for many species to adjust to climate change (Menéndez *et al.* 2006). While the impact of climate change on extinction probabilities remains contentious (Willis and

Bhagwat 2009), this is the effect that motivates the conservation community most strongly. Among marine systems, coral reefs are thought to be particularly vulnerable to climate change. Temperature increases and ocean acidification are expected to compromise carbonate accretion, putting corals increasingly at risk. They are also expected to exacerbate the effects of other anthropogenic stresses (from pollution and over-exploitation) (Hoegh-Guldberg *et al.* 2007). Nor are coral reefs the only marine ecosystems likely to be affected by climate change. The poster child of the effects of climate change in the Arctic, the polar bear, is just one of many species with limited distributions that depend on ice for foraging, reproduction, and the avoidance of predators. Others include the ivory gull (*Pagophila eburnean*), Pacific walrus (*Odobenus rosmarus divergens*), the hooded seal (*Cystophora cristata*), and the narwhal (*Monodon monoceros*) (Post *et al.* 2009). Less charismatic species are also at risk. Experimental work combined with climate-linked models of ocean acidification suggests that significant changes in pterapod communities could occur in high latitudes within decades (Orr *et al.* 2005).

Aside from the conservation implications of climate change, there is concern over the potential impacts of climate change on the species that most directly affect the production of foods, fuels, and fibers, and human, animal, and plant health. Climate change is expected to have a number of direct effects on agro-ecosystems. In the USA, for example, although a number of crops are expected to respond positively to higher levels of carbon dioxide and moderate increases in mean temperature, so too will weeds, diseases, and insect pests. More extreme increases both in mean temperature and rainfall variability are expected to reduce crop growth and yields. Forage quality in rangelands is expected to decline with increasing carbon dioxide concentration because of its effects on plant nitrogen and protein content. Livestock are expected to be adversely affected by increased temperatures, disease risks, and weather extremes (Karl *et al.* 2009).

In many other parts of the world the effect of climate change on agriculture is expected to be more severe. One attempt to simulate the consequences of two scenarios of climate change using a model of global agriculture concluded that, under both scenarios, the net effects of climate change on agriculture would generally be negative, and would be strongly negative in many developing countries (Nelson *et al.* 2009). In developing countries, climate change is expected to induce yield declines for the most important crops, especially in South Asia. It is, for example, expected that irrigated yields for all crops will fall; that price increases for rice, wheat, maize, soybeans, and meat prices will reduce the growth in meat consumption slightly and cereals consumption significantly; and that calorie availability in 2050 will have declined relative to 2000 levels in all developing countries. Since around half of all economically active people in developing countries are dependent on agriculture, and since 75 percent of the world's poor live in rural areas, this suggests that the effects of climate change on agriculture are likely to have a disproportionate effect in developing countries.

The impacts of climate-induced biodiversity change on human, animal, and plant health are of concern because of the potentially high cost associated with both emerging zoonotic diseases, and changes in the distribution of existing disease vectors. Changes in agricultural practices have been strongly implicated in the emergence of a number of zoonotic diseases (Daszak *et al.* 2004, 2006). The IPCC's fourth assessment report highlighted the impact of climate change on the distribution of a number of infectious disease vectors, and the seasonal distribution of some allergenic pollen species (Confalonieri *et al.* 2007). For example, the climatic basis for changes in the distribution of the main dengue fever vector *Stegomyia* has been modeled, and turns out to map well into observed changes in disease distribution (Hopp and Foley 2003). Diseases that were previously limited to low latitudes have spread to higher latitudes. Insect-borne diseases such as trypanosomosis and anaplasmosis are now found in parts of the world where their vectors have never been found in the past. Climate, in association with land-use change, has been associated with global increases in morbidity and mortality from emergent parasitic diseases. Other diseases affected by climate change include leishmaniasis, cryptosporidiosis, giardiasis, schistosomiasis, lariasis, onchocerciasis, and loiasis (Patz *et al.* 2000; Jones *et al.* 2008).

Climate change is also expected to increase the frequency with which species across a wide range of taxa are able to spread outside their home range. A study of the implications of climate change for the potential invasibility of all terrestrial ecosystems concluded that a high proportion of existing ecosystems are likely to become vulnerable to invasion by species from elsewhere under even moderate climate change scenarios. Using the Hadley HadCM3, B1 scenario, Thomas and Ohlemüller identified the areas of the world sharing a common climate but not sharing the same pest controllers (being more than 1,000 km distant) in

1945 and 2045. They found that under climate change of this kind, virtually all ecosystems would be vulnerable to invasion (Thomas and Ohlemüller 2010).

3.6 The valuation of ecosystem services

To approach the value of both individual species and the variation among species, we need first to understand the value of the services they provide. This is because the value of species to people derives from the value of those services. The value of individual species is not an inherent property of those species. It reflects the fact that people are willing to pay (either monetarily or in other ways) for the services they yield. What people are willing to pay depends partly on the character- istics of the species concerned, and partly on people's preferences, institutions, culture, and technology. It also depends on the distribution of income and wealth among people. Rich people are able to pay more for the services they want than poor people. So even if the relative weight given to some service by the poor is greater than that given to the same service by the rich, the preferences of the rich may still dom- inate. This is not to justify a distribution of income and assets that gives more purchasing power to some than to others. It is to recognize that private expressions of value reflect private wealth, just as social expres- sions of value reflect social wealth. All this implies that the derived value of biodiversity is instrumental, anthropocentric, and context dependent (Goulder and Kennedy 1997; Baumgärtner *et al.* 2006).

It is the derived value of species that gives direction to biodiversity change, precisely because it is the derived value of species that informs people's actions. It is worth emphasizing that derived value bears no relationship to any intrinsic value that species may have. Intrinsic value is normally thought of as a measure of the inherent worth of a species, and is independent of any instrumental value the species may have. It is frequently taken to be the primary motivation for species conserva- tion (Soulé 1986). Yet precisely because it is independent of human- kind's interest in other species, intrinsic value is also irrelevant to human decisions. Whenever the intrinsic value of species is used as an argument for guiding conservation decisions, the value being referred to is an instrumental anthropocentric value. Indeed, the fact that conservation decisions demand that people weigh the value of conservation against other social objectives means that the values put in the balance have to be anthropocentric. They have to be instrumental. And they cannot be infinite. While the point has been acknowledged – and cogently argued – by at least some ethicists, philosophers, and ecologists (Justus *et al.* 2009), it remains a point of tension between conservation biologists and others who work on the management of environmental resources.

Ecosystem services can only have derived value if they are scarce – if obtaining an additional unit of the service implies that something else must be given up. If something is not scarce, the supply of oxygen in the atmosphere for example, then acquiring an additional unit has no opportunity cost. Nothing has to be given up to get it. If it is scarce, the supply of freshwater or habitat for endangered species for example, then people have to forgo other things in order acquire more of it. In many cases, the prices struck in market transactions between the buyers and sellers of scarce services offer a reasonable approximation of their opportunity cost to society. But this is not always true. Wherever there are effects of the production or consumption of the service that are not reflected in its price – that are external to the transaction – then the market price will be an imperfect measure of its scarcity. The management problems posed by externalities are considered in the next chapter. What is important here is that if the aggregate willingness to pay for the benefits of ecosystem services is not revealed through market outcomes, efficient management of such ecosystem services requires separate estimates of their social value (Heal *et al.* 2005).

A number of studies prior to the MA drew attention to the importance of quantifying the value of non-marketed ecosystem services to human societies in terrestrial (Daily *et al.* 1997), marine (Duarte 2000), and agro-ecosystems (Heywood and Watson 1995; Björkland, Limburg and Rydberg 1999). However the MA itself had great difficulty in attaching values to the observed changes in physical magnitudes. One reason for this is that ecosystem services tend to be the result of a complex interaction between natural cycles operating over a wide range of space and timescales (Barbier *et al.* 2009). Even where the relationship between biodiversity and ecosystem functioning is well understood, the current state of knowledge may not be sufficient to link ecosystem functioning to the provision of ecosystem services, or specific benefit streams. In other words, we may not understand the ecological production functions well enough to quantify how changes in ecosystem condition or function affect the ecosystem services produced – a point made by Daily in the 1990s (Daily 1997), but still true.

Ecosystem services are typically intermediate inputs – they are used to produce the things that lead directly to economically valued goods or services. Initially, economists distinguished between use value (benefits deriving from consumptive or non-consumptive use by the individual) and non-use value (benefits from consumptive or non-consumptive use by others) (Weisbrod 1964; Krutilla 1967). So the benefits stemming from the ethical, spiritual, or religious desire to conserve biodiversity for future generations would be styled a non-use value. Use values were described as either direct (e.g. most provisioning and many cultural services) or indirect (e.g. the regulating services). They were further described as being either *consumptive* (e.g. foods, fuels, and fibers) or *non-consumptive use* (e.g. recreation, tourism, science, and education).

Among non-use values, two categories of value were initially identified as important: *bequest value* and *existence value* (Krutilla 1967). The first is a measure of altruistic willingness to forgo benefits to ensure that future generations can enjoy the benefits from ecosystems. The second, existence value, was originally defined as people's willingness to pay to ensure the continued existence of biodiversity irrespective of any actual or potential use. That is, it was seen as a form of altruism towards non-human species or nature in general, motivated by ethical or religious concerns. This is the category of value that most naturally maps into the conservationist ethic.

It is clear that direct and indirect non-consumptive use values both link to the MA's cultural services, whereas direct and indirect consumptive use values link to the provisioning services. Non-use values may link to either category. They refer to use by other people or other species, and that use may be either consumptive or non-consumptive. The timing of use is also important. This is partly because consumption in the future is less valuable to people than consumption today (we typically discount future consumption at a positive rate), and partly because the future is uncertain. Ecosystem services of species that are not important today might be important in the future. It follows that today's biodiversity has an *option value* in the sense that it might contain a cure for future diseases, the biological control of future pests, or the basis for a new technology (Simpson, Sedjo and Reid 1996; Goeschl and Swanson 2003). So one interpretation of the option value of biodiversity conservation is that it is equivalent to an insurance premium against future pests or diseases (Baumgärtner 2007; Quaas and Baumgartner 2007).

The value of ecosystems derives from the flow of services they yield over time – the discounted stream of benefits they produce. Over the last fifty years economists have developed a number of methods for valuing what we would now call non-marketed ecosystem services. Table 3.3 summarizes the methods most commonly used. The detail of such

Table 3.3 *Valuation methods applied to ecosystem services*

Valuation method[a]	Types of value estimated[b]	Common types of applications	Ecosystem services valued
Travel cost	Direct use	Recreation	Maintenance of beneficial species, productive ecosystems, and biodiversity
Averting behavior	Direct use	Environmental impacts on human health	Pollution control and detoxification
Hedonic price	Direct and indirect use	Environmental impacts on residential property and human morbidity and mortality	Storm protection; flood mitigation; maintenance of air quality
Production function	Indirect use	Commercial and recreational fishing; agricultural systems; control of invasive species; watershed protection; damage costs avoided	Maintenance of beneficial species; maintenance of arable land and agricultural productivity; prevention of damage from erosion and siltation; groundwater recharge; drainage and natural irrigation; storm protection; flood mitigation
Replacement cost	Indirect use	Damage costs avoided; freshwater supply	Drainage and natural irrigation; storm protection; flood mitigation

Table 3.3 (*cont.*)

Valuation method[a]	Types of value estimated[b]	Common types of applications	Ecosystem services valued
Stated preference	Use and non-use	Recreation; environmental impacts on human health and residential property; damage costs avoided; existence and bequest values of preserving ecosystems	All of the above

Notes:

[a] See Freeman (2003), Pagiola, von Ritter and Bishop (2004), and Heal *et al.* (2005) for more discussion of these various valuation methods and their application to valuing ecosystem goods and services.

[b] Typically, use values involve some human "interaction" with the environment whereas non-use values do not, as they represent an individual valuing the pure "existence" of a natural habitat or ecosystem or wanting to "bequest" it to future generations. Direct use values refer to both consumptive and non-consumptive uses that involve some form of direct physical interaction with environmental goods and services, such as recreational activities, resource harvesting, drinking clean water, breathing unpolluted air, and so forth. Indirect use values refer to those ecosystem services whose values can only be measured indirectly, since they are derived from supporting and protecting activities that have directly measurable values.

Source: Barbier (2007b).

methods is covered in Freeman (2003), Heal *et al.* (2005), and Hanley and Barbier (2009). Here I am interested in how such methods relate to the estimation of the derived demand for ecosystem services, individual species, and biodiversity.

Some of the cultural services and many of the products of the provisioning services are bought and sold in the marketplace, and hence have prices that signal their scarcity at any moment in time and under any given set of conditions. Of course those prices may not be very good measures of the scarcity of ecosystem services for reasons to be discussed in the next chapter, but they nevertheless indicate what members of society are willing to pay. Such prices can be used to derive the implied willingness to pay for the ecosystem components needed to supply them (Barbier 2007b; Barbier *et al.* 2009), but only as long as the ecological production functions are known.

For example, a study of the derived value of pollination services in the production of coffee in Costa Rica found that the value of these services was equivalent to 7 percent of average farm income (Ricketts *et al.* 2004). The same method has been used to derive the value of the effect of coastal habitat loss on Thai fisheries (Barbier 2007b). The latter study found that the estimated value of habitat loss to the fishery depended heavily on whether or not the long-run effects of habitat change on fish abundance were taken into account. So the method can be used to distinguish between the ecological short run (no stock effects of habitat change) and the ecological long run (where habitat change has positive stock effects).

If the goods and services produced using ecosystem services are not priced in the market (or if the market contains serious imperfections that make derived values suspect), it is still possible to estimate their value, but in this case a first step is to estimate the value of the goods and services that do enter final demand. There are a number of now well-established methods to elicit people's preferences for such goods and services, most relying on direct surveys or choice experiments. As in standard market research, such methods survey individuals who benefit from some non-marketed good or service to elicit their willingness to pay for those services. In contingent valuation methods, respondents are either invited to state their willingness to pay or select from willingness to pay options. In choice experiments and conjoint analysis, they are asked to rank, rate, or choose among various environmental outcomes (Freeman 2003; Heal *et al.* 2005).

To illustrate, Allen and Loomis used stated preference methods to obtain a willingness to pay for the conservation of a charismatic species – golden eagles in the Snake River basin of Idaho – and then, following Goulder and Kennedy (1997), used production functions to derive the value of species at lower trophic levels (Allen and Loomis 2006). Specifically, they derived the implicit willingness to pay for the conservation of prey species from direct estimates of willingness to pay for top predators. They argued that it was not necessary for people to understand the trophic structure of the ecosystem, since their willingness to pay for top predators effectively captured their willingness to pay for the top predator's habitat and prey.

In the language of ecological production functions, prey species are intermediate inputs in the production of predators (Crocker and Tschirhart 1992). Their value depends both on the marginal contribution to the maintenance of the predator, and on the state of the environment. So, for example, the derived value of members of a functional group of species, each of which performs differently in different environmental conditions, will depend on the likelihood that conditions in which they perform relatively well occur. Species that appear to be redundant in some conditions will still have value, depending on the likelihood that the conditions in which they do have value will occur in the future (Loreau *et al.* 2002).

Other cases will be different. For example, *in situ* conservation of charismatic megafauna like the tiger requires conservation of all the species and other ecosystem components that constitute suitable tiger habitat – all components of the tiger's dependent trophic levels (Srivastava and Vellend 2005). To understand the derived value of individual species or the composition of species in each case requires that we understand two sets of production functions: economic production functions that describe the relationship between ecosystem services as inputs and the goods and services entering final demand as outputs, and ecological production functions that describe the ecosystem functions through which the biotic and abiotic components of ecosystems support the set of ecosystem services (Perrings *et al.* 2011).

Other methods exist for valuing charismatic landscapes. Indeed, the oldest non-market valuation method, the travel cost method, takes the cost of travel and travel-time to a site to be a first approximation of the value of access to that site to the traveler. It has most frequently been applied to the valuation of sites visited for aesthetic, recreational, or spiritual reasons (Freeman 2003). As in the case of the study by Allen and Loomis, such estimates can then be used to infer the value of the biotic and abiotic components of the landscape.

Economic production functions reflect both prevailing technological possibilities, and people's preferences. It follows that changes in technology or preferences can both lead to changes in the derived value of biodiversity. So, for example, the abundance of sperm whales only became economically important in the eighteenth century when spermaceti replaced tallow as the candle wax of choice, and disappeared when other materials became available (Whitehead, Christal and Dufault 1997). Similarly, the salt tolerance of rice varieties only became important in the twentieth century when irrigation led to the increasing salinization of farmlands (Maas and Hoffman 1977).

Ecological production functions are, in a sense, no less sensitive to technology, although the effect is less on the mechanisms involved than on the conditions in which ecological functions are carried out. For example, in the early 1900s the Haber-Bosch process to convert atmospheric dinitrogen to ammonium on industrial scales was developed. Since that time, use of the nitrogen-bearing fertilizers that result from this process has risen steadily, until humans now rival microorganisms in their capacity to fix nitrogen (Kinzig and Socolow 1994). Galloway and Cowling estimate that humans fixed just under 150 Tg(N) in 1990 – appoximately 78 Tg(N) per year from fertilizer production, another 13 Tg from other products, appoximately 40 Tg(N) per year from the expansion of nitrogen-fixing crops, and 21 Tg(N) per year from fossil fuel consumption (Galloway and Cowling 2002). Only a small proportion of the nitrogen applied in fertilizers to agricultural systems finds its way into the crop – the rest is leached into groundwater, carried away in surface run off, volatilized to the atmosphere, or converted to other gaseous forms that escape to the atmosphere (Vitousek *et al.* 1997). This has major effects on ecological functioning, in the most extreme cases leading to dead zones – areas so depleted of oxygen they are incapable of supporting any ecological functions.

The production function approach can also be used to derive the value of the ecosystem services that are least well reflected in market prices: the regulating services. We have already seen that the early grassland experiments showed that diversity of functional groups increased ecological stability and resilience (Griffin *et al.* 2009). Experiments in grassland plots (Tilman, Wedin and Knops 1996; Tilman *et al.* 2005) and in controlled environments (Naeem and Li 1997) both showed that increasing the number of species in the system tended to increase system productivity and stability. In heterogeneous environments, greater diversity within functional groups allows the group to be more productive (the niche differentiation effect) (Tilman *et al.* 1996). If the value of stability in the supply of goods or services entering final demand can be identified, then the value of the contribution of each in a portfolio of species within a functional group can be derived as a function of the expected range of environmental conditions.

While there are a very large number of valuation studies investigating willingness to pay for non-marketed goods and services entering final

Table 3.4 *TEEB estimates of the maximum value of twenty-two ecosystem services in eleven biomes (in 2007 dollars per hectare per year)*

	Open oceans	Coral reefs	Coastal systems	Coastal wetlands	Inland wetlands	Lakes and rivers	Tropical forests	Temperate and boreal forests	Woodlands	Grasslands
Provisioning services	22	20,892	7,549	8,289	9,709	5,776	9,384	1,736	862	715
Food	22	3,752	7,517	2,600	2,090	196	1,204	1,204	203	82
Freshwater supply				4,240	5,189	5,580	875	455		602
Raw materials		16,792	32	1,414	2,430		3,273	54	659	31
Genetic resources							1,799			
Medicinal resources		348					1,782	23		
Ornamental resources				35						
Regulating services	62	33,640	30,451	135,361	23,018	4,978	7,135	456	1,088	2,067
Influence on air quality							957			
Climate regulation	55			4,677	351		761	376	387	1,661
Moderating extreme events		33,556		9,729	4,430		340			
Regulation of water flows					9,369		36	3		
Waste treatment/ water purification		77		120,200	4,280	4,978	665	77	701	358
Nutrient cycling			30,451	755	4,588		3,211			47
Pollination		7					99			
Biological control	7									

Habitat services	56,137	164	68,795	3,471		5,277	2,575	293
Lifecycle maintenance		164	59,645	917				
Gene pool protection	56,137		9,150	2,554		5,277	2,575	293
Cultural services	1,084,809	41,416	2,904	8,399	2,733	1,426	96	11
Aesthetic information	27,317			3,906				
Recreation and tourism	1,057,492	41,416	2,904	3,700	2,733	1,426	96	11
Culture, art, design				793				
Spiritual experience								
Education and science								

Note: not all services were valued.
Source: Kumar (2010).

demand, there are relatively few studies of the value of the regulating services. Barbier has used the expected storm damage of a change in coastal wetland area to estimate the value of the wetland (Barbier 2007a). The approach involves estimating the impact of a change in coastal mangroves on the probability of damage in the event of a storm, and the cost of damage if it does occur. While the same approach has been used in other fields, there are few other examples of its application in the economics of the environment. Most studies of the regulating services estimate the mean value of the instrument of regulation – carbon sequestration in the case of climate regulation – and use that as a proxy for the value of regulation. The TEEB assessment, for example, used existing studies to estimate the mean value of both the macroclimatic regulation offered by terrestrial carbon sequestration, and the change in provisioning and cultural services offered by forest systems. In its pre-liminary findings, TEEB suggested that the mean values of forest ecosys-tem services, in US$/ha/year were dominated by regulatory functions: specifically regulation of climate ($1965), water flows ($1360), and soil erosion ($694). The mean value of all other services combined comprising timber and non-timber forest products, food, water, genetic information, and pharmaceuticals ($1313) was found to be less than the value of water flow regulation alone (TEEB 2009).

The final TEEB report reviewed estimates, obtained from the wider literature, of the value of twenty-two ecosystem services in eleven biomes. It reported the range of estimates in the literature for each service and each biome, but did not report either the mean or variance in those estimates (Kumar 2010). Since the lower bound on the value any service is at or close to zero, the interesting number in the TEEB report is the maximum value. These maximum values are contained in Table 3.4, and are 2007 dollar values per hectare per year. As the upper bound of the estimates contained in the studies reviewed in the assessment these numbers tell us little about the distribution of those estimates, but they still provide some useful information. In particular, they tell us something about which services are sufficiently well recognized as products of particular ecosystem types estimates of their value to exist. For example, medicinal and genetic resources are recognized to be associated with tropical and temperate forests, ornamental resources are associated with coral reefs and wetlands, and freshwater supplies are associated with wetlands, lakes and rivers, and forested watersheds. By contrast every biome is recognized to be a source of food. The numbers do not tell us very much about the relative value of services or biomes. They do, however, indicate that coral reefs and coastal systems potentially generate more tourism revenue than other biomes, and that for such systems tourism and recreation can dominate other ecosystem services. Coral reefs and coastal wetlands (mangroves) are similarly recognized to play a greater role in the moderation of the impact of extreme events than other systems.

Since the value of many ecosystem services is contingent on local conditions, however, there are few useful generalizations to be made. For services that affect the quality of real estate, the value of those services should be capitalized into land prices. The recreational or storm buffering value of coral reefs, for example, should be reflected in the price of coastal land. The quality of each service will therefore be taken into account by landholders, at least in part. For services offering public benefits that lie outside the market, however, this will not be true, and there will be a greater role for non-market valuation.

3.7 Scratching the surface

While progress in the identification and valuation of non-marketed ecosystem services has been substantial, we have barely scratched the surface of the problem. But in scratching the surface we have uncovered both how large a problem it is, and how great is the gulf that divides those who would measure the value of biodiversity and those who would assert it. I began this discussion by recalling McCauley's plea to scientists to treat the concept of ecosystem services with caution, and to reassert the "primacy of ethics and aesthetics in conservation" (McCauley 2006). The same ethic is what prompts many to assert not just that species have infinite intrinsic value, but also that this should somehow guide conservation decisions. Yet this cannot be. If all species have infinite intrinsic value they all have no value, for it is impossible to distinguish among them. Moreover, if all species have infinite intrinsic value, all else has no value. It is impossible to sanction any action that increases the extinction probability of any species by any amount, yet almost every action we take collectively or as individuals has some impact on the extinction probabilities of some species. The intrinsic value of species, whatever that value, cannot guide human decisions.

This is not to say that ethics and aesthetics are unimportant. They are major factors in the value of species for some people. So too are religious convictions, cultural traditions, and social norms. The non-use values identified by economists include the value of assuring the continued existence of species, not only for the enjoyment of the individual who expresses that value, but also for the benefit of future generations, of people elsewhere on the planet, and of other species. It is the willingness of people to commit resources towards some end that enables us to derive the value of the ecosystem components needed to meet that end. If people are not willing to commit the resources required to conserve some species, then they will not be willing to commit the resources required to conserve the habitat on which that species depends.

People's willingness to commit resources is ultimately constrained by the availability of resources: i.e. willingness to pay is ultimately constrained by ability to pay. Within that constraint, however, if the relevant production functions are understood it is possible to determine both the relative and absolute value of each species needed to generate goods and services people are willing to pay for. Even the things that people declare to be priceless, if obtained at a cost, have a price. By observing what people are prepared to give up to secure endangered species, for example, it is possible to calculate the value of the habitats needed for the purpose.

There is, of course, uncertainty about many of the ecological functions needed to produce the things that people care about, and about how those functions are affected by environmental and social change. The complexity and evolutionary character of social-ecological systems means that we have limited capacity to predict their future course, and hence limited capacity to estimate the value of biodiversity in different environmental conditions. But we do have some capacity to do so. Though the state of a complex system may be unknowable in advance, the bounds within which it operates are often quite well understood. In such cases the derived value of species and species richness is still knowable within bounds.

The problem of uncertainty (and irreversibility) is considered in more detail in Chapter 10. For now what is important to note is that understanding the derived value of biodiversity is not an insurmountable task. Both revealed and stated preference methods of valuation are capable of giving reasonable first-order approximations of individual and collective willingness to pay for the goods and services entering final demand, while economic and ecological science are frequently capable of giving reasonable first-order approximations of the functions that connect those goods and services to species and species richness. So while we may have done little more than scratch the surface of the problem in the research that has been done to date, we have some capacity to improve the decisions that direct biodiversity change.

References

Allen, B. P. and Loomis, J. B. (2006) Deriving values for the ecological support function of wildlife: an indirect valuation approach. *Ecological Economics*, 56, 49–57.

Barbier, E. B. (2007a) Valuing ecosystem services as productive inputs. *Economic Policy*, January, 178–229.

(2007b) Frontiers and sustainable economic development. *Environmental & Resource Economics*, 37, 271–295.

(2008) In the wake of tsunami: lessons learned from the household decision to replant mangroves in Thailand. *Resource and Energy Economics*, 30, 229–249.

Barbier, E. B., Burgess, J. C. and Grainger, A. (2010) The forest transition: Towards a more comprehensive theoretical framework. *Land Use Policy*, 27, 98–107.

Barbier, E. B., Baumgärtner, S., Chopra, K., Costello, C., Duraiappah, A., Hassan, R., Kinzig, A., Lehman, M., Pascual, U., Polasky, S. and Perrings, C. (2009) The valuation of ecosystem services. *Biodiversity, Ecosystem Functioning, and Human Wellbeing: An Ecological and Economic Perspective* (ed. S. Naeem, D. Bunker, A. Hector, M. Loreau and C. Perrings), pp. 248–262. Oxford University Press.

Baumgärtner, S. (2007) The insurance value of biodiversity in the provision of ecosystem services. *Natural Resources Modeling*, 20, 87–127.

Baumgärtner, S., Becker, C., Manstetten, R. and Faber, M. (2006) Relative and absolute scarcity of nature: assessing the roles of economics and ecology for biodiversity conservation. *Ecological Economics*, 59, 487–498.

Behrenfeld, M. J., O'Malley, R. T., Siegel, D. A., McClain, C. R., Sarmiento, J. L., Feldman, G. C., Milligan, A. J., Falkowski, P. G., Letelier, R. M. and Boss, E. S. (2006) Climate-driven trends in contemporary ocean productivity. *Nature*, 444, 752–755.

Berkes, F., Colding, J. and Folke, C. (2000) Rediscovery of traditional ecological knowledge as adaptive management. *Ecological Applications*, 10, 1251–1262.

Björkland, J., Limburg, K. E. and Rydberg, T. (1999) Impact of production intensity on the ability of the agricultural landscape to generate ecosystem services: an example from Sweden. *Ecological Economics*, 29, 269–291.

Bracken, M. E., Friberg, S. E., Gonzales-Dorantes, C. A. and Williams, S. L. (2008) Functional consequences of realistic biodiversity changes in a marine ecosystem. *Proceedings of the National Academy of Sciences*, 105, 924–928.

Bulte, E. H. and Horan, R. D. (2003) Habitat conservation, wildlife extraction and agricultural expansion. *Journal of Environmental Economics and Management*, 45, 109–127.

Bunker, D. E., DeClerck, F., Bradford, J. C., Colwell, R. K., Perfecto, I., Phillips, O. L., Sankaran, M. and Naeem, S. (2005) Species loss and aboveground carbon storage in a tropical forest. *Science*, 310, 1029–1031.

Canadell, J. G. and Raupach, M. R. (2008) Managing forests for climate change mitigation. *Science*, 320, 1456–1457.

Cardinale, B. J., Duffy, J. E., Gonzalez, A., Hooper, D. U., Perrings, C., Venail, P., Narwani, A., Mace, G. M., Tilman, D., Wardle, D. A., Kinzig, A. P., Daily, G. C., Loreau, M., Grace, J. B., Larigauderie, A., Srivastava, D. S. and Naeem, S. (2012) Biodiversity loss and its impact on humanity. *Nature*, 486, 59–67.

Confalonieri, U., Menne, B., Akhtar, R., Ebi, K. L., Hauengue, M., Kovats, R. S., Revich, B. and Woodward, A. (2007) Human health. Climate Change 2007: impacts, adaptation and vulnerability. Contribution of Working Group II. *Fourth Assessment Report of the Intergovernmental Panel on Climate Change* (ed. M. L. Parry, O. F. Canziani, J. P. Palutikof, P. J. Van Der Linden and C. E. Hanson), pp. 391–431. Cambridge University Press.

Costanza, R., d'Arge, R., de Groot, R., Farber, S., Grasso, M., Hannon, B., Limburg, K., Naeem, S., O'Neill, R. V., Paruelo, J., Raskin, R. G., Sutton, P. and van den Belt, M. (1997) The value of the world's ecosystem services and natural capital. *Nature*, 387, 253–260.

Crocker, T. D. and Tschirhart, J. (1992) Ecosystems, externalities, and economics. *Environmental Resource Economics*, 2, 551–567.

Daily, G. (ed.) (1997) *Nature's Services: Societal Dependence on Natural Ecosystems*. Island Press, Washington, DC.

Daily, G. C., Alexander, S., Ehrlich, P. R., Goulder, L., Lubchenco, J., Matson, P. A., Mooney, H. A., Postel, S., Schneider, S. H., Tilman, D. and Woodwell, G. M. (1997) Ecosystems services: benefits supplied to human societies by natural ecosystems. *Issues in Ecology*, 1, 1–18.

Daszak, P., Tabor, G. M., Kilpatrick, A. M., Epstein, J. and Plowright, R. (2004) Conservation medicine and a new agenda for emerging diseases. *Impact of Ecological Changes on Tropical Animal Health and Disease Control*, 1026, 1–11.

Daszak, P., Plowright, R., Epstein, J. H., Pulliam, J., Rahman, S. A., Field, H. E., Smith, C. S., Olival, K. J., Luby, S., Halpin, K., Hyatt, A. D. and Cunningham, A. A. (2006) The emergence of Nipah and Hendra virus: pathogen dynamics across a wildlife-livestock-human continuum. *Disease Ecology: Community Structure and Pathogen Dynamics* (ed. S. Collinge and C. Ray), pp. 186–201. Oxford University Press.

Denman, K. L., Brasseur, G., Chidthaisong, A., Ciais, P., Cox, P. M., Dickinson, R. E., Hauglustaine, D., Heinze, C., Holland, E., Jacob, D., Lohmann, U., Ramachandran, S., da Silva Dias, P. L., Wofsy, S. C. and Zhang, X. (2007) Couplings between changes in the climate system and biogeochemistry. *Climate Change 2007: The Physical Science Basis. Contribution of Working Group I to the Fourth Assessment Report of the Intergovernmental Panel on Climate Change* (ed. S. Solomon, D. Qin, M. Manning, Z. Chen, M. Marquis, K. B. Averyt, M. Tignor and H. L. Miller). Cambridge University Press.

Diaz, S., Hector, A. and Wardle, O. A. (2009) Biodiversity in forest carbon sequestration initiatives: not just a side benefit. *Current Opinion in Environmental Sustainability*, 1, 55–60.

Duarte, C. M. (2000) Marine biodiversity and ecosystem services: an elusive link. *Journal of Experimental Marine Biology and Ecology*, 250, 117–131.

Ehrlich, P. R. and Ehrlich, A. H. (1992) The value of biodiversity. *Ambio*, 21, 219–226.

Freeman, A. M. I. (2003) *The Measurement of Environmental and Resource Values: Theory and Methods*, 2nd edn. Resources for the Future, Washington, DC.

Gadgil, M., Berkes, F. and Folke, C. (1993) Indigenous knowledge for biodiversity conservation. *Ambio*, 22, 151–156.

Galloway, J. N. and Cowling, E. B. (2002) Reactive nitrogen and the world: 200 years of change. *Ambio*, 31, 64–71.

Gitay, H., Suarez, A., Watson, R. T. and Dokken, D. J. (2002) Climate change and biodiversity. *IPCC Technical Paper*. Intergovernmental Panel on Climate Change.

Goeschl, T. and Swanson, T. (2003) Pests, plagues, and patents. *Journal of the European Economic Association*, 1, 561–575.

Goulder, L. H. and Kennedy, D. (1997) Valuing ecosystem services: philosophical bases and empirical methods. *Nature's Services: Societal Dependence on Natural Ecosystems* (ed. G. C. Daily), pp. 23–47. Island Press, Washington, DC.

Griffin, J. N., O'Gorman, E. J., Emmerson, M. C., Jenkins, S. R., Klein, A.-M., Loreau, M. and Symstad, A. (2009) Biodiversity and the stability of ecosystem functioning. *Biodiversity, Ecosystem Functioning, and*

Human Wellbeing: An Ecological and Economic Perspective (ed. D. B. S. Naeem, A. Hector, M. Loreau and C. Perrings), pp. 78–93. Oxford University Press.

Hanley, N. and Barbier, E. B. (2009) *Pricing Nature: Cost-Benefit Analysis and Environmental Policy*. Edward Elgar, Cheltenham.

Heal, G. (2000) Valuing ecosystem services. *Ecosystems*, 3, 24–30.

Heal, G. M., Barbier, E. B., Boyle, K. J., Covich, A. P., Gloss, S. P., Hershner, C. H., Hoehn, J. P., Pringle, C. M., Polasky, S., Segerson, K. and Shrader-Frechette, K. (2005) *Valuing Ecosystem Services: Toward Better Environmental Decision Making*. The National Academies Press, Washington, DC.

Hector, A. and Bagchi, R. (2007) Biodiversity and ecosystem multifunctionality. *Nature*, 448, 188–190.

Hector, A., Schmid, B., Beierkuhnlein, C., Caldeira, M. C., Diemer, M., Dimitrakopoulos, P. G., Finn, J. A., Freitas, H., Giller, P. S., Good, J., Harris, R., Högberg, P., Huss-Danell, K., Joshi, J., Jumpponen, A., Körner, C., Leadley, P. W., Loreau, M., Minns, A., Mulder, C. P. H., O'Donovan, G., Otway, S. J., Pereira, J. S., Prinz, A., Read, D. J., Scherer-Lorenzen, M., Schulze, E.-D., Siamantziouras, A.-S. D., Spehn, E. M., Terry, A. C., Troumbis, A. Y., Woodward, F. I., Yachi, S. and Lawton, J. H. (1999) Plant diversity and productivity experiments in European grasslands. *Science*, 286, 1123–1127.

Heywood, V. and Watson, R. (eds.) (1995) *Global Biodiversity Assessment*. Cambridge University Press.

Hoegh-Guldberg, O., Mumby, P. J., Hooten, A. J., Steneck, R. S., Greenfield, P., Gomez, E., Harvell, C. D., Sale, P. F., Edwards, A. J., Caldeira, K., Knowlton, N., Eakin, C. M., Iglesias-Prieto, R., Muthiga, N., Bradbury, R. H., Dubi, A. and Hatziolos, M. E. (2007) Coral reefs under rapid climate change and ocean acidification. *Science*, 318, 1737–1742.

Hooper, D. U. and Vitousek, P. M. (1997) The effects of plant composition and diversity on ecosystem processes. *Science*, 277, 1302–1305.

Hooper, D. U., Chapin, F. S., Ewel, J. J., Hector, A., Inchausti, P., Lavorel, S., Lawton, J. H., Lodge, D. M., Loreau, M., Naeem, S., Schmid, B., Setälä, H., Symstad, A. J., Vandermeer, J. and Wardle, D. A. (2005) Effects of biodiversity on ecosystem functioning: a consensus of current knowledge. *Ecological Monographs*, 75, 3–35.

Hopp, M. J. and Foley, J. A. (2003) Worldwide fluctuations in dengue fever cases related to climate variability. *Climate Research*, 25, 85–94.

Huston, M. A. (1997) Hidden treatments in ecological experiments: re-evaluating the ecosystem function of biodiversity. *Oecologia*, 110, 449–460.

Jones, K. E., Patel, N. G., Levy, M. A., Storeygard, A., Balk, D., Gittleman, J. L. and Daszak, P. (2008) Global trends in emerging infectious diseases. *Nature*, 451, 990–993.

Justus, J., Colyvan, M., Regan, H. and Maguire, L. (2009) Buying into conservation: intrinsic versus instrumental value. *Trends in Ecology and Evolution*, 24, 187–191.

Karl, T. R., Melillo, J. M. and Peterson, T. C. (eds.) (2009) *Global Climate Change Impacts in the United States.* Cambridge University Press.

Kinzig, A. P. and Socolow, R. H. (1994) Human impacts on the nitrogen cycle. *Physics Today*, 47, 24–32.

Krutilla, J. V. (1967) Conservation reconsidered. *The American Economic Review*, 57, 777–786.

Kumar, P. (ed.) (2010) *The Economics of Ecosystems and Biodiversity.* Earthscan, London.

Leopold, A. (1949) *A Sand County Almanac: And Sketches Here and There.* Oxford University Press.

Loreau, M., Naeem, S. and Inchausti, P. (2002) *Biodiversity and Ecosystem Functioning: Synthesis and Perspectives.* Oxford University Press.

Lovejoy, T. E. and Hannah, L. J. (eds.) (2006) *Climate Change and Biodiversity.* Yale University Press, New Haven, CT.

Maas, E. V. and Hoffman, G. J. (1977) Crop salt tolerance: current assessment. *ASCE Journal of Irrigation and Drainage*, 103, 115–124.

Mäler, K.-G. (1974) *Environmental Economics: A Theoretical Enquiry.* Johns Hopkins University Press, Baltimore, MD.

McCauley, D. J. (2006) Selling out on nature. *Nature*, 443, 27–28.

McIntyre, P. B., Jones, L. E., Flecker, A. S. and Vanni, M. J. (2007) Fish extinctions alter nutrient recycling in tropical freshwaters. *PNAS*, 104, 4461–4466.

Menéndez, R., González Megías, A., Hill, J. K., Braschler, B., Willis, S. G., Collingham, Y. C., Fox, R., Roy, D. B. and Thomas, C. D. (2006) Species richness changes lag behind climate change. *Proceedings of the Royal Society B: Biological Sciences*, 273, 1465–1470.

Millennium Ecosystem Assessment (2005a) *Ecosystems and Human Well-being: General Synthesis.* Island Press, Washington, DC.

   (2005b) *Ecosystems and Human Well-Being: Current State and Trends.* Island Press, Washington, DC.

Myers, N. (1996) Environmental services of biodiversity. *Proceedings of the National Academy of Sciences of the United States of America*, 93, 2764–2769.

Naeem, S. (1998) Species redundancy and ecosystem reliability. *Conservation Biology*, 12, 39–45.

Naeem, S. and Li, S. (1997) Biodiversity enhances ecosystem reliability. *Nature*, 390, 507–509.

Naeem, S., Bunker, D., Hector, A., Loreau, M. and Perrings, C. (eds.) (2009) *Biodiversity, Ecosystem Functioning, and Human Wellbeing: An Ecological and Economic Perspective.* Oxford University Press.

Nelson, G. C., Rosegrant, M. W., Koo, J., Robertson, R., Sulser, T., Zhu, T., Ringler, C., Msangi, S., Palazzo, A., Batka, M., Magalhaes, M., Valmonte-Santos, R., Ewing, M. and Lee, D. (2009) *Climate Change Impact on Agriculture and Costs of Adaptation.* International Food Policy Research Institute, Washington, DC.

Orr, J. C., Fabry, V. J., Aumont, O., Bopp, L., Doney, S. C., Feely, R. A., Gnanadesikan, A., Gruber, N., Ishida, A., Joos, F., Key, R. M., Lindsay, K., Maier-Reimer, E., Matear, R., Monfray, P., Mouchet, A., Najjar, R. G., Plattner, G.-K., Rodgers, K. B., Sabine, C. L., Sarmiento, J. L., Schlitzer, R., Slater, R. D., Totterdell, I. J., Weirig, M.-F., Yamanaka, Y. and Yool, A. (2005) Anthropogenic ocean acidification over the twenty-first century and its impact on calcifying organisms. *Nature*, 437, 681–686.

Ostfeld, R. S., Keesing, F. and Eviner, V. T. (2008) *Infectious Disease Ecology: Effects of Ecosystems on Disease and of Disease on Ecosystems.* Princeton University Press.

Pagiola, S., von Ritter, K. and Bishop, J. (2004) *How Much Is an Ecosystem Worth? Assessing the Economic Value of Conservation.* The World Bank, Washington, DC.

Patz, J. A., Graczyk, T. K., Gellera, N. and Vittor, A. Y. (2000) Effects of environmental change on emerging parasitic diseases. *International Journal for Parasitology*, 30, 1395–1405.

Perrings, C., Folke, C. and Mäler, K. H. G. (1992) The ecology and economics of biodiversity loss: the research agenda. *Ambio*, 21, 201–211.

Perrings, C., Naeem, S., Ahrestani, F., Bunker, D. E., Burkill, P., Canziani, G., Elmqvist, T., Ferrati, R., Fuhrman, J., Jaksic, F., Kawabata, Z., Kinzig, A., Mace, G. M., Milano, F., Mooncy, H., Prieur-Richard, A.-H., Tschirhart, J. and Weisser, W. (2011) Ecosystem services, targets, and indicators for the conservation and sustainable use of biodiversity. *Frontiers in Ecology and the Environment*, 9, 512–520.

Peters, R. L. and Lovejoy, T. E. (eds.) (1994) *Global Warming and Biological Diversity.* Yale University Press, New Haven, CT.

Post, E., Forchhammer, M. C., Bret-Harte, M. S., Callaghan, T. V., Christensen, T. R., Elberling, B., Fox, A. D., Gilg, O., Hik, D. S., Høye, T. T., Ims, R. A., Jeppesen, E., Klein, D. R., Madsen, J., McGuire, A. D., Rysgaard, S., Schindler, D. E., Stirling, I., Tamstorf, M. P., Tyler, N. J. C., van der Wal, R., Welker, J.,

Wookey, P. A., Schmidt, N. M. and Aastrup, P. (2009) Ecological dynamics across the Arctic associated with recent climate change. *Science*, 325, 1355–1358.

Quaas, M. and Baumgartner, S. (2007) Natural vs. financial insurance in the management of public good ecosystems. *Ecological Economics*, 65, 397–406.

Ricketts, T. H., Daily, G. C., Ehrlich, P. R. and Michener, C. D. (2004) Economic value of tropical forest to coffee production. *Proceedings of the National Academy of Sceinces*, 101, 12579–12582.

Schulze, E. D. and Mooney, H. A. (1993) *Biodiversity and Ecosystem Function*. Springer-Verlag, Berlin.

Simpson, R. D., Sedjo, R. A. and Reid, J. W. (1996) Valuing biodiversity for use in pharmaceutical research. *Journal of Political Economy*, 104, 163–185.

Solan, M., Cardinale, B. J., Downing, A. L., Engelhardt, K. A. M., Ruesink, J. L. and Srivastava, D. S. (2004) Extinction and ecosystem function in the marine benthos. *Science*, 306, 1177–1180.

Soulé, M. E. (1986) What is conservation biology? *Bioscience*, 35, 727–734.

Srivastava, D. S. and Vellend, M. (2005) Biodiversity–ecosystem function research: is it relevant to conservation? *Annual Review of Ecology, Evolution and Systematics*, 36, 267–294.

Steffen, W., Burbidge, A. A., Hughes, L., Kitching, R., Lindenmayer, D., Musgrave, W., Stafford Smith, M. and Werner, P. A. (2010) *Australia's Biodiversity and Climate Change*. CSIRO, Canberra.

TEEB (2009) *TEEB Climate Issues Update*. UNEP, Nairobi.

Thébault, E. and Loreau, M. (2006) The relationship between biodiversity and ecosystem functioning in food webs. *Ecological Research*, 21, 17–25.

Thomas, C. and Ohlemüller, R. (2010) Climate change and species distributions: an alien future? *Bioinvasions and Globalization: Ecology, Economics, Management, and Policy* (ed. C. Perrings, H. Mooney and M. Williamson), pp. 19–29. Oxford University Press.

Thomas, C. D., Cameron, A., Green, R. E., Bakkenes, M., Beaumont, L. J., Collingham, Y. C., Erasmus, B. F. N., de Siqueira, M. F., Grainger, A., Hannah, L., Hughes, L., Huntley, B., van Jaarsveld, A. S., Midgley, G. F., Miles, L., Ortega-Huerta, M. A., Townsend Peterson, A., Phillips, O. L. and Williams, S. E. (2004) Extinction risk from climate change. *Nature*, 427, 145–148.

Tilman, D. and Downing, J. A. (1994) Biodiversity and stability in grasslands. *Nature*, 367, 363–365.

Tilman, D., Wedin, D. and Knops, J. (1996) Productivity and sustainability influenced by biodiversity in grassland ecosystems. *Nature*, 379, 718–720.

Tilman, D., May, R. M., Polasky, S. and Lehman, C. L. (2005) Diversity, productivity and temporal stability in the economies of humans and nature. *Journal of Environmental Economics and Management*, 49, 405–426.

Vitousek, P. M., Mooney, H. A., Lubchenco, J. and Melillo, J. M. (1997) Human domination of Earth's ecosystem. *Science*, 277, 494–499.

von Humboldt, A. (1850) *Views of nature, or, Contemplations on the sublime phenomena of creation: with scientific illustrations*. Henry G. Bohn, London.

Weisbrod, B. A. (1964) Collective-consumption services of individualized-consumption goods. *Quarterly Journal of Economics*, 78, 471–477.

Westman, W. E. (1977) How much are nature's services worth? *Science*, 197, 960–964.

Whitehead, H., Christal, J. and Dufault, S. (1997) Past and distant whaling and the rapid decline of sperm whales off the Galápagos Islands. *Conservation Biology*, 11, 1387–1396.

Willis, K. J. and Bhagwat, S. A. (2009) Biodiversity and climate change. *Science*, 326, 806–807.

4 | Biodiversity loss, sustainability, and stability

4.1 Sustainability and stability

There has been a burgeoning interest in the sustainability of many current trends – consumption, economic and demographic growth, and environmental change among them.[1] While the origin of the term sustainable development is usually given as the report of the Brundtland Commission, *Our Common Future* (World Commission on Environment and Development 1987), its roots lie much deeper than that. One of the main precursors to the Brundtland Report, Herman Daly's *Towards a Steady State Economy* (Daly 1973), directly appealed to John Stuart Mill's mid-nineteenth-century thoughts on the stationary state. Mill saw a less growth-oriented strategy as the key to preserving at least some part of the natural environment (Mill 1909). Yet to do no more than maintain average incomes in many developing countries aggregate income is required to grow at rates up to 3.5 percent a year (i.e. to match the population growth rate), and increasing average incomes requires aggregate income to grow at rates above that. As Malthus had observed at the close of the eighteenth century, the consequences of failure to maintain average incomes have historically been severe (Malthus 1999). The challenge given to the global community by the Brundtland Commission was not just to avoid Malthusian crisis through the degradation of the resource base, but also to eliminate poverty worldwide.

The Brundtland definition of sustainable development – "development that meets the needs of the present without compromising

---

[1] At the time I write these lines there is a popular cartoon depicting a time trend for the use of the word "sustainable." It plots the frequency with which the word appears in US English text as a percentage of all words produced in a given year. By 2036 the cartoon claims that the word sustainable will appear, on average, once a page. By 2061 it will occur once a sentence. And by 2109 all sentences will comprise only the word sustainable repeated over and over and over again!

the ability of future generations to meet their own needs" – refers to the capacity of a system to maintain a flow of services over time (World Commission on Environment and Development 1987). This is a systems-level property that implies something both about system stability and about the value of system assets over time. What matters for the Brundtland definition is the capacity of the system to continue to deliver benefits over the expected range of environmental conditions.

Economists have typically approached this problem from its implications for the value of the assets (the produced, natural, and human capital) that generate services, and have established the conditions for the value of assets to be non-declining (Hotelling 1931; Hartwick 1977; Dasgupta and Heal 1979). They have also, however, directly considered the implications of the Brundtland approach to consumption. *Our Common Future* implied that there were two parts to the problem: overconsumption by the rich and underconsumption by the poor. Given this, Arrow *et al.* (2004) considered the problem of overconsumption, and asked when consumption might be described as excessive. They noted that the sustainability criterion does not imply a unique consumption path; and that a sustainable consumption path is not necessarily an efficient consumption path. They then showed that current consumption is most likely to be excessive where environmental resources are either not priced at all, or prices are distorted (Arrow *et al.* 2004). The implication of this is that consumption patterns are most likely to be unsustainable when people lack reliable indicators of changes in the value of environmental resources. People are likely to consume too much (or invest too little) when they ignore the impacts of current consumption on the future value of natural capital.

Many ecologists, on the other hand, have focused on the conditions that are necessary for systems to retain functionality and so continue to provide goods and services over time. Much of this research builds on the work of C. S. Holling (Holling 1973, 1986). Sustainability in this case is measured by the resilience of the system, or its capacity to function over a range of conditions. A necessary condition for the sustainability of a coupled social-ecological system is that economic activities that stress the ecological component of the system should not be destabilizing (Common and Perrings 1992). The appropriate measure of resilience in such systems is related to the magnitude of shock that the system can absorb and continue to provide desired goods and services. More resilient systems are able to absorb larger shocks than less resilient systems. More resilient systems also contain more of the components needed for adaptation and reorganization if they are disrupted than less resilient systems. In other words, they can cope, adapt, or reorganize without losing functionality.

Resilience is frequently argued to be increasing in the diversity of system components – since greater diversity implies a greater range of options for coping with shock or stress. The evidence on this is, however, ambiguous. There has been a long-standing debate in ecology about the relationship between species diversity and the stability of ecosystems. For example, a review of more than fifty empirical studies of the relationship between diversity and stability found that most studies reported a positive relationship between diversity and stability, depending on the measure of stability used (Ives and Carpenter 2007). However, the same paper also found that most of the positive findings involved studies of grassland or herbaceous communities, focused on a single trophic level only, and used a small subset of stability measures. Indeed, a number of the studies referred to in Chapter 3 fall into this category (Tilman and Downing 1994; Hooper and Vitousek 1997; Hector *et al.* 1999; Tilman *et al.* 2001). Ives and Carpenter were accordingly reluctant to draw general conclusions. It turns out, however, that there good reasons for the ambiguity. While resilience is often positively related to the diversity of system components, it is also often negatively related to the tightness of the connections between those components.

This chapter considers the relationship between changes in biodiversity and the stability and hence sustainability of coupled social-ecological systems. The relation between stability and the regulating services has already been touched on in Chapter 3. Here I delve a little deeper into this problem, focusing on the portfolio effect. This effect deals with the impact of biodiversity change on the variability with which particular ecosystem services are supplied. To approach the problem I first discuss the measures of biodiversity conventionally employed in ecology, and introduce a simple theoretical construct that will be used to aid discussion of several aspects of the problem of biodiversity change here and in later chapters. I then consider the mechanisms at work in the portfolio effects, and discuss their implications for the problem of directed biodiversity change.

4.2 Measures and models of biodiversity

Ecologists ordinarily measure biodiversity in one of four ways – all of which relate to the diversity of taxonomically distinct species. Alpha diversity is a measure of the taxonomic diversity (the species richness) within a particular community or ecosystem, often approximated by the diversity in a particular tract of land. The most common indices of alpha diversity are due to Shannon (1948) and Simpson (1949).[2] Both indices measure a combination of the number of species present in some location, and their abundance. By both measures, communities with many species, but where one accounts for 95 percent of all organisms, would not be considered diverse. Beta diversity is a measure of the difference in species diversity between ecosystems or along environmental gradients. More particularly, it measures the number of taxa that are unique to each of the ecosystems being compared.[3] Gamma diversity is a measure of taxonomic diversity in the whole area being evaluated. For the case of two communities with s_1 and s_2 species, c species of which occur in both communities, it is simply: $\gamma = s_1 + s_2 - c$. In other words it is a simple count of the number of distinct species in the whole area (Whittaker 1972). A fourth approach to biodiversity commonly encountered in ecology focuses on phylogenetic diversity, sometimes referred to as omega diversity, and is measured by the taxonomic difference between species. A number of indices have been proposed for phylogenetic

---

[2] The Shannon index takes the form $H' = -\sum_{i=1}^{S} p_i \ln p_i$ where s is the number of species in the reference location (the species richness) and p_i is the proportion of the number of individuals of the ith species to the total number of organisms in that location (the relative abundance of the ith species). The index is higher the greater the species richness in a location and the more even the relative abundance of species. Simpson's index, by comparison, has the form $D = \sum_{i=1}^{S} p_i^2$ where s is defined as before, but p_i is now the fraction of all organisms accounted for by the ith species. The value of the index varies between 1 (zero diversity) and 0 (infinite diversity). Other measures of alpha diversity exist, but like these focus on some combination of richness and abundance (Magurran 2004).

[3] One index of beta diversity, developed by Sørensen (1948), takes the following form in the case of two communities: $\beta = \frac{2c}{s_1 + s_2}$ where s_i is species richness in the ith community and c is the number of species common to both communities. Like the Simpson's index, it takes a value of 0 when there is no species overlap between the communities, and a value of 1 when exactly the same species are found in both communities.

diversity (Schweiger *et al.* 2008), most falling into one of two classes: one using a minimum spanning path approach, the other using a pair-wise distance approach.[4]

All indices are designed to provide statistical measures of taxonomic diversity at a particular time and place. The area covered by indices of alpha, beta, and gamma diversity will necessarily differ, but for any index there is some temporal and spatial reference point. All indices also weight species in some way, either explicitly or implicitly. The simple measure of gamma diversity, for example, implicitly weights all species at unity. That is, every species counts as much as every other species. The most commonly applied measures of alpha diversity weight each species by its relative abundance, the most common measures of omega diversity weight species by their phylogenetic distance from other species, and so on. The weight is a measure of the importance of that characteristic to the user.

Consider the gamma diversity of a region comprising both cropland and wildland. If all species are weighted at unity, the gamma diversity is simply the union of the set of taxonomically distinct species in each zone. But from the perspective of the farmer, a measure of the desired gamma diversity of the region is the union of taxonomically distinct species weighted by the value the farmer attaches to each species. Species that contribute directly or indirectly to the farmer's wellbeing would be positively weighted. If we wish to understand and project future trends in ecosystems that are impacted by human behavior, it is the weights that matter. More generally, if species are thought of in instrumental terms, then what will generally matter is not the diversity of taxonomically distinct species, but the diversity within and between functional groups of desirable or undesirable species (Naeem and Wright 2003). In other words, what generally matters is the set of all species capable of supporting production of those goods and services over the range of conditions expected to occur (Perrings *et al.* 2011).

---

[4] One example of this, due to Faith (1992), is $PD_{NODE} = \sum_i n_i$ where n_i is the number of i nodes within the minimum spanning path. The second approach, using pairwise distances, includes indices based on the entropy, taxonomic distinctiveness, and the distance of any given species to its nearest neighbor. The last, known as a pure diversity index, due to Solow *et al.* (1993) and Weitzman (1992), takes the form: $D_D = \sum_i d_{i\min}$ where $d_{i\min}$ is the nearest neighbor distance of species i to all other species.

What this means for the measurement of biodiversity in human dominated landscapes is that species will be weighted by their contribution to
the things that people care about. We need to think of ecosystems not
as *in situ* species museums, but as factories harnessing the energies of
current and reserve armies of species. We then need to understand which
services are important, and which are not, and what consequences are
associated with changes in the diversity within and between the functional groups of species supporting each service.

The point was made in Chapter 2 that ecological studies of the
relationship between biodiversity, traits, and ecological functioning
have led to the evolution of more appropriate measures of biodiversity
than traditionally employed, focusing on functional diversity (see, for
example, Díaz and Cabido 2001; Loreau, Naeem and Inchausti 2002;
Naeem 2002; Petchey and Gaston 2002; Petchey, O'Gorman and
Flynn 2009). They have also captured at least some of the importance
of trophic complexity in ecosystem functions, including the role of
microbes, and have explored the mechanisms involved in the relationship between biodiversity and stability (Pimm 1984; Kinzig, Pacala and
Tilman 2002; Loreau *et al.* 2002; Naeem *et al.* 2009). This work makes
it possible to begin constructing the production functions that connect
species to the production of goods and services.

To illustrate, consider a landscape of gamma diversity $\gamma = s_1 + s_2$ (i.e.
comprising two ecosystems or patches with no overlapping species).
Suppose that when these species are combined with other inputs,
summarized by x, they yield a service, $y = y\,(x, s_1, s_2)$. This function
describes the ecological processes involved, and the way that they
interface with the technology used by the human decision-makers.
Now suppose that the human decision-makers aim to maximize
some index of net benefit through choice of the combination of species
and other inputs:

$$Max_{x, s_i} V(p, y, w, x, c_i, s_i) = \sum_i py - wx - c_i s_i; \ i \in \{1, 2\}$$

in which p is a measure of the value of the service, c_i is a measure of the
cost of maintaining the ith set of species, and w is a measure of the cost
of other inputs. We can ask what conditions would need to be satisfied
for the combination of s_1 and s_2 to be optimal. This is a simple optimi-
zation problem, equivalent to asking where on the landscape the
decision-maker would choose to produce the service, and how intensively

they would exploit each set of species. The first-order necessary conditions for net benefits to be at a maximum are found by setting the partial derivatives of the maximand with respect to the choice variables equal to zero. That is:

$$\frac{\partial V}{\partial x} = p\frac{\partial y}{\partial x} - w_i = 0;$$

$$\frac{\partial V}{\partial s_i} = p\frac{\partial y}{\partial s_i} - c_i = 0; \quad i = 1, 2$$

These conditions imply two requirements on s_1 and s_2. The first is that employment of each set of species should increase up to the point at which the marginal value of an increment in that set of species should be equal to the marginal cost of their maintenance:

$$p\frac{\partial y}{\partial s_i} = c_i; \quad i = 1, 2$$

The second is that the rate at which s_1 and s_2 are substituted in the production of the service will depend on the ratios of their marginal maintenance cost and their marginal contributions to production of the service:

$$\frac{\partial y/\partial s_i}{\partial y/\partial s_j} = \frac{c_i}{c_j}; \quad i, j = 1, 2$$

The first requirement implies that the decision-maker will carry the cost of maintaining species richness up to the point at which it ceases to makes a positive net contribution to the production of the service. It follows that if $\partial y/\partial s_i = 0$ for one set of species (meaning that the species are irrelevant to the production of the service), then the decision-maker will expend nothing to maintain that set of species. Moreover, if $\partial y_i/\partial s_j < 0$ for one service or for one set of species (meaning that the species are harmful to the production of the service, i.e. are pests or pathogens) then the decision-maker will expend resources on reducing that set of species.

The second requirement implies that the rate at which the two sets of species will be traded off in the production of the service depends both on what they give to it, and what they cost. If both sets of species make an equal marginal contribution to the production of the service, for example, then the rate at which the decision-maker will trade those

species off against each other is just the ratio of the marginal maintenance cost of each. If two sets of species are equally valuable (have the
same net conservation value at some level of conservation, for example),
then the decision-maker will be indifferent between them. If they are not
equally valuable, then the effort committed to maintaining one over the
other will depend both on the marginal costs and benefits of doing so.
Where there are multiple services, and where different sets of services
are associated with different sets of species, these conditions imply that
sets of species will be traded off against each other up to the point at
which their marginal contribution to wellbeing will be equalized.

In general it will be possible to identify a socially optimal value for the
index of choice. Whether diversity at the optimal level of service provision is above or below initial diversity depends on technology broadly
defined to include not only the anthropogenic production technology,
but also the ecological functions and the ecosystem processes involved.
It also depends on the conditions in which decision-makers operate – the
legal environment and the structure of property rights. Decision-makers
may not, for instance, have the latitude to alter species abundance.

As we will see in later chapters, much of the problem of biodiversity
change is a direct result of just this. In many cases, people are not just
authorized to neglect the consequences of their actions that affect others
distant in either time or space, but are positively encouraged to do so.
Nonetheless, even if all the consequences of every action were taken
into account, we would still not expect the optimal combination of
species to be identical to the initial combination of species. This is the
sense in which the question of biodiversity measures is raised. In a world
of choice, the issue is not whether biodiversity is being altered at all – it
is – but whether it is being altered in ways that compromise the wider
and deeper interests of humanity.

4.3 The portfolio effect

To get a sense of the issues involved in finding the socially optimal level
of biodiversity, consider the portfolio effect (sometimes called the insurance effect in ecology (Loreau, Mouquet and Gonzalez 2003)). This effect
is analogous to the risk-spreading function of financial portfolios. If
environmental conditions vary, then some species in a community may
perform well when others are performing poorly. As was noted in
Chapter 3, there is a substantial body of experimental evidence that an

increase in the diversity within functional groups reduces variability in system functioning (Hooper and Vitousek 1997; Tilman *et al.* 2001, 2005; Griffin *et al.* 2009). The principal mechanism is straightforward. In heterogeneous environments, greater diversity within functional groups allows the group to be more productive via a niche differentiation effect (Tilman, Wedin and Knops 1996). If the conditions within which species secure a niche include the range of environmental conditions experienced over time, niche differentiation should lead to the emergence of species specialized in terms of environmental as well as geophysical conditions.

Portfolio effects depend on the correlation between responses to some environmental change. To see the intuition behind this, consider a variation of the simple model just described and suppose that the portfolio within a functional group, grasses say, consisted of just two species, s_1 and s_2, associated with yields of services $y_1 = y_1(s_1)$ and $y_2 = y_2(s_2)$. The expected yield of the portfolio would then be:

$$E(y) = \sum_i \rho_i E(y_i); \quad i = 1, 2$$

in which ρ_i is the share of total biomass accounted for by the ith species. The variance in the yield of the portfolio would be:

$$\sigma_p^2 = \sum_i \sum_j \rho_i \rho_j \sigma_i \sigma_j r_{ij}; \quad i, j = 1, 2$$

in which σ_i is the standard deviation of the yield associated with s_i, and r_{ij} is the correlation coefficient between yields from species s_i and s_j. For the two species case this takes the form:

$$\sigma_p^2 = \rho_1^2 \sigma_1^2 + \rho_2^2 \sigma_2^2 + 2\rho_1^2 \rho_2^2 \sigma_1 \sigma_2 r_{12}$$

Note that this is less than the weighted sum of the variance in yields associated with each species. If the correlation coefficient is positive, $r_{12} > 0$, both species respond to environmental perturbations in similar ways. If the correlation coefficient is negative, $r_{12} < 0$, the species respond in opposite ways (see, for example, Doak *et al.* 1998; Tilman, Lehman and Bristow 1998; Lhomme and Winkel 2002). The impact on stability of an increase in the size of the portfolio (the addition of more species) depends on the correlation coefficients between existing species and the new species. Negative correlation coefficients unambiguously enhance stability, but the portfolio effect can operate even if the responses to perturbations of different species are positively correlated. Yachi and Loreau, for example, showed that unless species' responses to environmental perturbations were perfectly correlated ($r_{ij} = 1$), increasing the number of species in a system would at once increase average productivity and reduce temporal variance in productivity (Yachi and Loreau 1999).

Many ecological studies of the relationship between diversity and stability have assumed a constant correlation coefficient for all species' responses to environmental change. In reality these are likely to vary both in magnitude and sign. Indeed, the theory of niche differentiation suggests that responses should be different. Natural selection typically reduces competition by forcing co-existing species to adopt different patterns of resource use or environmental response – different niches. Distinct species that are too similar in response or resource use cannot co-exist. One will competitively exclude the other (Schoener 1974). We have already noted that grassland experiments have shown that biomass and stability both increase with the number of different species through niche differentiation. A similar effect has also been shown in field research in grassland systems. The fact that functionally similar species have evolved dissimilar responses to stresses and shocks such as grazing pressure or fire increases mean productivity and reduces the variance in productivity (Walker, Kinzig and Langridge 1999). Others have suggested that response diversity of this sort is a quite general feature of ecological systems (Elmqvist *et al.* 2003).

The portfolio effect in ecological systems is closely related to the notion of redundancy. The idea is that at a given time and place there will be species that are functionally redundant in the sense that their deletion would have little if any effect on ecosystem functioning at that time and place. For "time" read "environmental conditions." For "place" read "biogeophysical properties of the system." This is a statement (1) that the contribution of individual species to ecosystem functioning is dependent on both environmental and biogeophysical properties of the system, (2) that the correlation coefficient between species is negative – that they respond to environmental conditions in opposite ways, and therefore (3) that seemingly redundant species have a role in maintaining ecosystem function as environmental conditions vary.

Two types of redundancy have been identified in the literature. One stems from the existence of spatially distinct but similar subsystems. The other is the redundancy created by functional overlap between distinct species. This is the kind of redundancy identified by Walker *et al.* (1999), and is the one most frequently encountered in the literature (see, for example, Naeem 1998; Wohl, Arora and Gladstone 2004). The existence of this kind of redundancy implies that a decline in one species may be functionally compensated by an increase in another (Low *et al.* 2002). If this occurs as a result of fluctuating environmental conditions, then it implies a classic portfolio effect.

To illustrate, suppose that the two species of our example generate different yields in different environmental conditions (precipitation), and let these be as follows:

Rainfall	π	y_1	y_2
h(high)	0.2	1.2	2
a(average)	0.6	1.3	1.4
l(low)	0.2	1.4	0.6

where π_j, $j \in \{h, a, l\}$ denotes the probability of rainfall condition j occurring, y_{ij}, $i \in \{1, 2\}$ denotes the yield associated with species j in conditions i. In this case the two species respond in opposite ways to changes in rainfall. Species s_1 has relatively constant yields over all conditions, but does better when rainfall is low. Species s_2 has much more variable yield. It does significantly better when rainfall is high, but significantly worse when rainfall is low. The expected yields from each of the two species in this case are:

$$E(y_i) = \pi_h y_{hi} + \pi_a y_{ai} + \pi_l y_{li}$$

which results in $E(y_1) = 1.3$ and $E(y_2) = 1.36$.

To see what effect the combination of species has on the stability of yields we need to return to the correlation coefficient between y_1 and y_2, referred to earlier. Note that the correlation coefficient is just the covariance between y_1 and y_2 normalized to lie between -1 and -1 (by dividing by the product of the standard deviation in the yields of both species). That is

$$r_{12} = \frac{\text{cov}(y_1, y_2)}{\sigma(y_1)\sigma(y_1)}$$
$$= \frac{\pi_h(y_{h1} - \bar{y}_1)(y_{h2} - \bar{y}_2) + \pi_a(y_{a1} - \bar{y}_1)(y_{a2} - \bar{y}_2) + \pi_l(y_{l1} - \bar{y}_1)(y_{l2} - \bar{y}_2)}{\sigma(y_1)\sigma(y_1)}$$

Calculating both for the numerical values in this example gives $\text{cov}(y_1, y_2) = -0.028$ and $r_{12} = -0.994$. The negative sign on these indicates that they are substitutes in the production of y. We would therefore expect a combination of s_1 and s_2 to result in more stable yields than would be possible if either were the only species in the system. This is easily verified for our numerical example. Varying the share of each species in total biomass between zero and one, and noting that the variance of the portfolio is $\sigma_p^2 = w_1^2\sigma_1^2 + w_2^2\sigma_2^2 + 2w_1^2w_2^2\sigma_1\sigma_2\text{cov}(y_1, y_2)$ it is possible to calculate both the expected yield from each combination of species, and the associated risk (approximated by the standard deviation in yields for each combination of species). The results are illustrated in Figure 4.1. If the only species in the system is s_2 then the expected yield is high, but so is the variance in yield. If the only species in the system is s_1 then expected yields and the variance in yields are much lower. However,

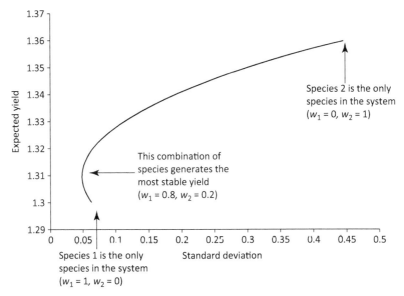

Figure 4.1 The portfolio effect, showing the impact of species diversity on the trade-off between expected yield and variance in yields. The curve in the figure describes the relation between mean (expected) yields, and the variation (standard deviation) in yields, as a function of the combination of two species. The highest mean yields are associated with lowest species diversity (the most high-yielding species only) but also the greatest variability in yields. The lowest variability in yields is associated with a combination of both species.

there exist combinations of s_1 and s_2 that are associated with both higher expected yields than occur with is s_1 alone, and with lower variance in yields. In financial markets this is referred to as the diversification effect. In ecological systems it is described as the insurance effect.

The significance of the portfolio effect for the optimal level of diversity is considered in Chapter 10. There are three things that are important to note at this point. The first is that the differences in yield associated with each species and each set of environmental conditions implies that this is an example of functional redundancy. Species 1 is functionally redundant in periods of high rainfall in the sense that it contributes little to yield in those conditions. Species 2 is functionally redundant in periods of low rainfall. However, taken over all expected environmental conditions, neither species is redundant. A frequently cited concern of conservation groups is that species that are functionally redundant in current conditions are taken to be functionally redundant in all conditions. In agricultural systems, for example, where plant breeding programs have narrowed the range of species exploited for the production of food to the point where 90 percent of global food supply derives from only eleven species, there has been widespread neglect of landraces and wild crop relatives that may be valuable in fundamentally different climatic conditions than we now experience. One result of this is that there has been significant genetic erosion in remnant landraces and wild crop relatives (Loskutov and Rines 2011). Protecting germplasm that may be valuable in conditions that are fundamentally different from those experienced in the Holocene is difficult, if only because agriculture did not exist prior to the Holocene. But in principle, the evaluation of the redundancy of such species should take into account the fact that on longer timescales the stable climate of the Holocene is highly unusual.

A second point is that portfolio effects exist because of response diversity among species within functional groups. While individual species do play a large role in the provision of some ecosystem services, changes in functional diversity generally matter more for ecosystem service provision than changes in species richness. Ecosystem services depend on ecosystem functions, and these in turn depend on functional traits rather than taxonomic differences. For this reason the role of biodiversity in the provision of ecosystem services has most frequently been explored through the linkages between diversity and functional traits (Solan *et al.* 2004; Bunker *et al.* 2005; McIntyre *et al.* 2007; Bracken *et al.* 2008; Kattge *et al.* 2011).

How much diversity is needed within a portfolio depends on the range of environmental and biogeophysical conditions expected, on the covariance in the response of distinct species to differences in those conditions, and on the risk tolerance of the decision-maker. The greater the expected variation in conditions, and the less the covariance in species responses, the greater will be the required diversity within functional groups (Elmqvist *et al.* 2003). While niche differentiation should lead to differences in species responses to environmental change, there are clearly some functional groups characterized by a high degree of substitutability between species over a wide range of environmental conditions, such as the marine phytoplankton involved in the production of oxygen. There are others, such as food grains, where substitutability between species is much more limited. The test in all cases is whether a change in the diversity within functional groups affects the riskiness of the function. Once again, the concern is that the simplification of many ecosystems has led to a reduction in the diversity of important functional groups.

I return to the question of decision-making under risk and uncertainty in Chapter 10. Here it is enough to say that risk is the product of both the probability attaching to some outcome and the value of that outcome. So outcomes that have trivial consequences for human wellbeing and almost never occur involve low risk, whereas outcomes that have either serious consequences for wellbeing, or are highly likely to occur, may both involve high risk. If some action equally increases the probability that two species are driven to extinction, for example, the associated risk will be greater for the species whose loss would have the greater impact on human wellbeing.

4.4 The portfolio effect and sustainability

So what does the portfolio effect tell us about the consequences of biodiversity change for the sustainability of an ever more closely integrated global system? It tells us that changes in the diversity of the functional groups of species responsible for the provisioning services can be expected to alter the risks we face in areas that matter. One particularly worrying area is the effect of change in crop genetic diversity on food production and food security. This effect is of most concern when it directly affects human wellbeing. Food security in low-income countries is sensitive to variations in both the volume and price of food supplies. Widespread hunger, riots, and political dissension have frequently followed either food shortages or food price rises. The rural poor in many countries still experience famine either when food supplies fail or when food prices rise. The proportion of the population that depends on the direct production of food is much higher in low-income countries than elsewhere.

In fact the vast majority of people in the least developed countries still live in rural areas, and still make a living from farming. On average, 68 percent of the population in low-income countries live and work in rural areas, relative to 43 percent in middle-income countries and 21 percent in high-income countries.[5] Even in urban areas, people in low-income countries are more vulnerable to food shortages than those elsewhere. In many low-income countries up to three-quarters of household income is spent on basic foodstuffs. This makes people more vulnerable to food price rises than elsewhere. Nor is the burden equally shared. The effects of both famine and food price rises are typically felt more strongly by women and children, often with lasting effects. Insufficient nourishment in pregnancy or infancy can have lifelong consequences (Food and Agriculture Organization *et al.* 2011).

As I write, the international community is extremely concerned about the effects of rising food price volatility. Food price riots in 2011 were a significant factor in the Arab Spring uprisings, and there is growing concern about the political implications of food insecurity in North Korea, Iran, and Somalia. Although food price volatility has been increasing in the last two decades (Figure 4.2) it is not a new phenomenon. There are many well-understood reasons why the price of agricultural commodities should be volatile. Among these are the impact of widespread adverse weather conditions, outbreaks of pests and pathogens, and the fact that both demand and supply elasticities for basic foods are low. Because supply of new crops typically takes time, it is argued that farmers are unable to respond to price increases in a timely way, and when they do the resulting oversupply can depress prices (Food and Agriculture Organization *et al.* 2011). Changes in crop genetic diversity

---

[5] Countries in which 75 percent or more of the population live in rural areas include Afghanistan, Bhutan, Burkina Faso, Burundi, Cambodia, Eritrea, Ethiopia, Kenya, Lao People's Democratic Republic, Lesotho, Malawi, Micronesia, Federated States of Micronesia, Nepal, Niger, Papua New Guinea, Rwanda, Samoa, Solomon Islands, Sri Lanka, Tajikistan, Trinidad and Tobago, and Uganda.

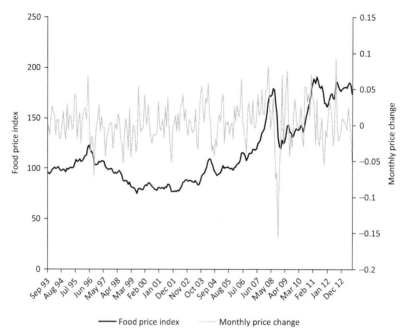

Figure 4.2 Commodity food price index, 2005 = 100, includes price indices of cereals, vegetable oils, meat, seafood, sugar, bananas, and oranges. The variability in the index is recorded in the monthly food price change reported on axis 2.

Source: data from www.indexmundi.com/commodities.

associated with the Green Revolution (the portfolio of crops), and the associated changes in production technologies, have had differential effects on volatility in food supply.

Figure 4.3 indicates annual gross production of cereals and the associated yearly changes in the last fifty years. Although this is a period of rising yields, and although many of the cultivars introduced in the period have been bred for drought tolerance or disease resistance, average variability in production has been increasing – particularly in developing countries.

The initial response to the Green Revolution was an increase in yield instability (Anderson, Hazell and Evans 1987). Subsequently, rice and wheat yields became more stable in Asia in the 1990s, but this was not generally true for maize and coarse grains (Hazell 2009). Specifically, adoption of crops with a narrow genetic base has increased average

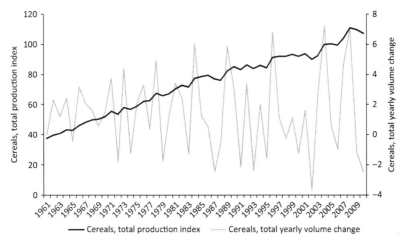

Figure 4.3 World cereal production index, 2004–2006 = 100. The increasing variability of cereal production is recorded in the total yearly volume change reported on axis 2.
Source: data from http://faostat.fao.org.

yields but, in the absence of additional controls, has also increased the variance of yields (Smale *et al.* 1998; Widawsky and Rozelle 1998; Carew, Smith and Grant 2009). At the same time, the widespread adoption of the same high-yielding varieties has affected the spatial correlation of changes in the variance of yields by making production in different locations vulnerable to the same stresses and shocks (Jones and Thornton 2002; Piesse and Thirtle 2010). The issue has not so much been yield stability at the plot level, but the fact that variation in yields has become more highly correlated across space as farmers have adopted the same varieties. All farmers have bumper crops or extremely low yields simultaneously.

The portfolio effect may be especially pronounced in crop production, but that is not the only area of activity in which it has been observed. Declining diversity among tropical bird species, for example, has been correlated with decreasing resilience of tropical ecosystems to shocks and stresses, and with increasing variability in pollination and pest predation functions. A study of a 2,880 bird census conducted over a decade along a land-use gradient in Costa Rica found that bird abundance, species richness, and diversity were 15 percent lower in land subject to low-intensity land use and 50 percent lower in land subject to high-intensity land use than in forested areas. Moreover, the difference was positively correlated with response diversity (Karp *et al.* 2011). There are also implications for the rate at which the system recovers from shocks. A number of studies have investigated the link between biodiversity and the stability or resilience of coupled systems. Examples include coral reefs (Hughes *et al.* 2003; Pandolfi *et al.* 2003), kelps (Steneck, Vavrinec and Leland 2004), boreal, temperate, and tropical forests (Thompson *et al.* 2009). A general conclusion of this work is that resilience generally increases with biodiversity. Particular mechanisms for changes in the level of marine resilience have also been explored, especially the impact of changes in species diversity on the level of functional redundancy across a range of systems (Diaz *et al.* 2003; McLeod and Leslie 2009).

Of course other factors also affect the stability of ecosystems. As the complexity stability debate and numerical experiments have both shown, it is not the case that more biodiversity will always and everywhere increase stability. Indeed, May's conclusion was that large and highly interconnected systems are generally unstable (May 1973; Pimm 1984). In fact the covariance in returns to distinct species strongly depends on the nature of the interactions between them. These determine whether a change in the relative abundance of a particular species is stabilizing or destabilizing. Recently, Allesina and Tang have analyzed the impact of different relationships between species and have identified substantial differences between predator–prey interactions that tend to be stabilizing, and mutualistic and competitive interactions that tend to be destabilizing (Allesina and Tang 2012). They show that predator–prey networks can be arbitrarily large and complex and still stable, provided only that predator–prey pairs are tightly coupled. However, they also find that the same is not true of competitive or mutualistic interactions. The stability of predator–prey networks can be increased by strengthening predator–prey interactions. The only way to increase stability in competitive or mutualistic networks, on the other hand, is to decrease average interaction strength. This is equivalent to decreasing complexity or increasing modularity.

For predator–prey systems this has different implications depending on how ecosystem services respond to a change in predator or prey abundance. For forest systems that are subject to damage by pests or pathogens, for example, the stability of forest services is positively correlated with the diversity of the tree population. A meta-analysis of fifty-four studies of the relationship between tree diversity and pest damage found that tree species growing in mixed stands overall experienced less pest damage, and had lower pest populations, than monocultures. The mechanisms involved include the effect of tree diversity on the likelihood that pests can access their host, on the effectiveness of pest predators, and the diversion of polyphagous pests (insects that feed on a variety of species) to the most palatable secondary tree species (Jactel, Brockerhoff and Duelli 2005). The same study also found, however, that overall damage from polyphagous pests was greater the greater the diversity of tree species. As an example of this, cottonwoods under box elder have been found to suffer significantly greater damage from cankerworm than cottonwoods under other cottonwoods (White and Whitham 2000).

Overall, this is consistent with Allesina and Tang's findings that weak interactions have no effect on random networks, are stabilizing for mutualistic and competitive networks, but are destabilizing for food webs (Allesina and Tang 2012). By contrast, strong interactions between pairs of species in food webs have the effect of stabilizing the whole web (Allesina and Pascual 2008). The stronger the negative feedback provided by these relationships, the more stable the food web. By the same token the disruption of strong feedback mechanisms in food webs has the potential to destabilize whole communities. One of the most common effects of demographic and economic growth has been the removal of top predators from many terrestrial and aquatic systems. The resulting impacts on the rest of the food web are generally known as trophic cascades. They include changes in the abundance and composition of all trophic levels, including autotrophic species – the producers in ecosystems. This has frequently led to the loss of ecosystem stability, and sometimes to a complete regime shift (Pace *et al.* 1999; Estes *et al.* 2011). Top predators whose removal by people has fundamentally restructured ecosystems include killer whales, great sharks, and sea otters in marine systems, and lions, leopards, cougars, and wolves in terrestrial systems. In East Africa, for example, a reduction in top predators has had a significant effect on the abundance of smaller herbivores (megaherbivores such as elephant, hippopotamus, and rhinoceros were less affected), and when combined with the elimination of rinderpest or cattle plague in the 1960s, this has had dramatic consequences for vegetation. Increased grazing pressure has reduced fuel loads, and with it the incidence of fire. Since fire is the primary regulator of tree growth, the result has been a change from grassland to woody savanna (Holdo *et al.* 2009).

Now consider the implications of the portfolio and network effects for the sustainability of real social-ecological systems. The link between the stability and sustainability of systems is, in some ways, a rather trivial one. The stability of a system in some state, subject to some disturbance regime, is sufficient to assure its sustainability. That is, the system will be able to persist in that state as long as it remains stable. It follows that if there is a preferred state – a state that is desirable to sustain – then assuring its stability will assure its sustainability. The insights that come from our understanding of risk portfolios can then help us design sustainability strategy for that system. But this also means locking the system into a particular state and a particular stability domain, and that is not consistent with the way the global system has evolved since Neolithic times.

It is a truism, as Heraclitus of Ephesus argued in the fourth century BC, that the only constant in our history is change. Change may occur at different rates in different times and different places, but no human society has had the will to remain in the same state for millennia. The language of change also differs in different times and different places. Now it is cast in terms of economic growth and development. The Millennium Development Goals are, for example, statements of intent to eliminate poverty and hunger, to assure universal access to education, to protect the health and rights of women, to combat emergent zoonotic diseases, to avoid irreparable harm to the environment, and to do this through cooperation at the global scale. The goals imply change not only in the efficiency with which we use resources and the equity with which they are distributed among people, but also in the way we collectively regulate our impact on the biophysical world. Development of global governance systems for environmental resources that lie beyond national jurisdiction implies change that is every bit as great as that involved in eliminating poverty, combating new and resurgent diseases, or reducing the rate at which other species are being driven to extinction.

Assuring the stability of the world's social-ecological systems in their current state would not be desirable, even if it were feasible. The sustainability problem requires that we secure more for a growing human population at less environmental cost. The Brundtland definition of sustainable development – development that meets the needs of the present without compromising the ability of future generations to meet their own needs (World Commission on Environment and Development 1987) – is a statement about the management of change. It requires that each generation passes to the next a set of global assets, the biophysical environment included, that is no less valuable than the set it itself inherited. Since we are currently in the midst of an extinction event, and since our best efforts to slow the rate of biodiversity loss have so far been woefully unsuccessful, this is a daunting prospect.

4.5 The biodiversity portfolio

What does this mean for the biodiversity portfolio? I have argued that the current portfolio reflects the ways in which people have altered their environment – by converting habitat to promote agriculture, by driving out pests and predators, by controlling harmful microorganisms, by promoting domesticates and their symbionts, and by protecting landscapes of special appeal. The current portfolio reflects both the intentional and unintentional consequences of the historic growth of agriculture, forestry, fisheries, mining and industry, the development of cities, the management of pests and pathogens, and the construction of transport, energy, and water infrastructures. But it also reflects the fact that societies have become locked into ways of doing things – technologies, institutions, structures of property rights, social norms of behavior – that have continuing consequences for biodiversity, even though the current cost of biodiversity loss is such that we would not now choose to do things the same way. It is the inefficiency of patterns of resource allocation produced through this form of path dependence that exercises environmentalists, political scientists, and economists alike. A particular example from the American southwest, where I now live, is the fact we have become locked into a set of water institutions and water rights established in the nineteenth century when climatic, economic, political, and demographic conditions were very different. These make it almost impossible to achieve an efficient allocation of water resources in the conditions of the twenty-first century (Reisner 1993; Libecap 2011).

There are many similar instances of path-dependent processes affecting biodiversity. Some derive from the structure and distribution of land ownership. Current patterns of biodiversity change in the Peruvian Amazon, for example, reflect the past distribution of land across households. Initial landholdings determined whether or not households became locked into the shifting cultivation technologies that drive change in forest cover, and hence the richness and abundance of forest species (Coomes, Takasaki and Rhemtulla 2011). Others derive from increasing returns to the adoption of modern agricultural technologies. In the 1990s Timothy Swanson argued that the species composition of agriculture in the developing countries was determined by prior choices made in developed countries. From the point of view of the adopters of new technologies this simply looked like best practice, but globally he argued that it reflected the same pattern of increasing returns that was responsible for path-dependent technologies in many other industries (Swanson 1994, 1995). The potential inefficiency in the process lies in the fact that the range of species initially selected for in the technologically leading countries may not be the most efficient everywhere. Initial selection of such species would have been driven by local conditions obtaining at a particular point in time, and not from long-term, global conditions. Yet the genetic erosion of crop wild relatives or traditional breeds that occurs alongside the diffusion of the results of plant or animal breeding programs means that such stocks are not available to future farmers (Tisdell 2003).

More important still are the large-scale processes that drive the whole system. Anthropogenic climate change and the closer integration of the global economic system both have implications for the richness and abundance of species that are destined to play out over the long future: the one by changing the natural range of species, the other by changing the rate at which they are dispersed. Both have consequences for ecological functioning, ecosystem services, and human wellbeing. Because they are the consequence of technologies, institutions, and systems of rights that are difficult to change, we are unable to avoid those consequences on any reasonable timescale. This poses a special challenge for policy. While it is important to address the symptoms – the obvious manifestations – of undesirable biodiversity change, that is not enough. Policy must at the same time address the less tractable underlying factors that have locked us in to patterns of change that are far from sustainable.

References

Allesina, S. and Pascual, M. (2008) Network structure, predator–prey modules, and stability in large food webs. *Theoretical Ecology*, 1, 55–64.

Allesina, S. and Tang, S. (2012) Stability criteria for complex ecosystems. *Nature*, 483, 205–208.

Anderson, J. R., Hazell, P. B. R. and Evans, L. T. (1987) Variability of cereal yields: sources of change and implications for agricultural research and policy. *Food Policy*, 12, 199–212.

Arrow, K., Dasgupta, P., Goulder, L., Daily, G., Ehrlich, P., Heal, G., Levin, S., Mäler, K.-G., Schneider, S., Starrett, D. and Walker, B. (2004) Are we consuming too much? *Journal of Economic Perspectives*, 18, 147–172.

Bracken, M. E., Friberg, S. E., Gonzales-Dorantes, C. A. & Williams, S. L. (2008) Functional consequences of realistic biodiversity changes in a marine ecosystem. *Proceedings of the National Academy of Sciences*, 105, 924–928.

Bunker, D. E., DeClerck, F., Bradford, J. C., Colwell, R. K., Perfecto, I., Phillips, O. L., Sankaran, M. and Naeem, S. (2005) Species loss and aboveground carbon storage in a tropical forest. *Science*, 310, 1029–1031.

Carew, R., Smith, E. G. and Grant, C. (2009) Factors influencing wheat yield and variability: evidence from Manitoba, Canada. *Journal of Agricultural and Applied Economics*, 41, 625–639.

Common, M. S. and Perrings, C. (1992) Towards an ecological economics of sustainability. *Ecological Economics*, 6, 7–34.

Coomes, O. T., Takasaki, Y. and Rhemtulla, J. M. (2011) Land-use poverty traps identified in shifting cultivation systems shape long-term tropical forest cover. *Proceedings of the National Academy of Sciences*, 108, 13925–13930.

Daly, H. E. (1973) *Towards a Steady State Economy*. W. H. Freeman, New York.

Dasgupta, P. and Heal, G. M. (1979) *Economic Theory and Exhaustible Resources*. Cambridge University Press.

Diaz, S. and Cabido, M. (2001) Vive la différence: plant functional diversity matters to ecosystem processes. *Trends in Ecology and Evolution*, 16, 646–655.

Diaz, S., Symstad, A. J., Chapin, F. S. I., Wardle, D. A. and Huenneke, L. F. (2003) Functional diversity revealed by removal experiments. *Trends in Ecology and Evolution*, 18, 140–146.

Doak, D. F., Bigger, D., Harding, E. K., Marvier, M. A., O'Malley, R. E. and Thomson, D. (1998) The statistical inevitability of stability-diversity relationships in community ecology. *The American Naturalist*, 151, 264–276.

Elmqvist, T., Folke, C., Nystrom, M., Peterson, G., Bengtsson, J., Walker, B. and Norberg, J. (2003) Response diversity, ecosystem change, and resilience. *Frontiers in Ecology and the Environment*, 1, 488–494.

Estes, J. A., Terborgh, J., Brashares, J. S., Power, M. E., Berger, J., Bond, W. J., Carpenter, S. R., Essington, T. E., Holt, R. D., Jackson, J. B. C., Marquis, R. J., Oksanen, L., Oksanen, T., Paine, R. T., Pikitch, E. K., Ripple, W. J., Sandin, S. A., Scheffer, M., Schoener, T. W., Shurin, J. B., Sinclair, A. R. E., Soulé, M. E., Virtanen, R. and Wardle, D. A. (2011) Trophic downgrading of planet Earth. *Science*, 333, 301–306.

Faith, D. P. (1992) Conservation evaluation and phylogenetic diversity. *Biological Conservation*, 61, 1–10.

Food and Agriculture Organization, International Fund for Agricultural Development, International Monetary Fund, Organization for Economic Cooperation and Development, United Nations Conference on Trade and Development, World Food Program, World Bank, World Trade Organization, International Food Policy Research Institute and United Nations High-Level Task Force on the Global Food Security (2011) *Price Volatility in Food and Agricultural Markets: Policy Responses*. FAO, Rome.

Griffin, J. N., O'Gorman, E. J., Emmerson, M. C., Jenkins, S. R., Klein, A.-M., Loreau, M. and Symstad, A. (2009) Biodiversity and the stability of ecosystem functioning. *Biodiversity, Ecosystem Functioning, and Human Wellbeing: An Ecological and Economic Perspective* (ed. D. B. S. Naeem, A. Hector, M. Loreau and C. Perrings), pp. 78–93. Oxford University Press.

Hartwick, J. (1977) Intergenerational equity and the investing of rents from exhaustible resources. *American Economic Review*, 66, 972–974.

Hazell, P. B. R. (2009) *The Asian Green Revolution*. IFPRI Discussion Paper, 00911.

Hector, A., Schmid, B., Beierkuhnlein, C., Caldeira, M. C., Diemer, M., Dimi-trakopoulos, P. G., Finn, J. A., Freitas, H., Giller, P. S., Good, J., Harris, R., Högberg, P., Huss-Danell, K., Joshi, J., Jumpponen, A., Körner, C., Leadley, P. W., Loreau, M., Minns, A., Mulder, C. P. H., O'Donovan, G., Otway, S. J., Pereira, J. S., Prinz, A., Read, D. J., Scherer-Lorenzen, M., Schulze, E.-D., Siamantziouras, A.-S. D., Spehn, E. M., Terry, A. C., Troumbis, A. Y., Woodward, F. I., Yachi, S. and Lawton, J. H. (1999) Plant diversity and productivity experiments in European grasslands. *Science*, 286, 1123–1127.

Holdo, R. M., Sinclair, A. R. E., Dobson, A. P., Metzger, K. L., Bolker, B. M., Ritchie, M. E. and Holt, R. D. (2009) A disease-mediated trophic cascade in the Serengeti and its implications for ecosystem C. *PLoS Biology*, 7, e1000210.

Holling, C. (1973) Resilience and stability of ecological systems. *Annual Review Ecology and Systematics*, 4, 1–23.

(1986) The resilience of terrestrial ecosystems: local surprise and global change. *Sustainable Development of the Biosphere* (ed. W. C. Clark and R. E. Munn). Cambridge University Press.

Hooper, D. U. and Vitousek, P. M. (1997) The effects of plant composition and diversity on ecosystem processes. *Science*, 277, 1302–1305.

Hotelling, H. (1931) The economics of exhaustible resources. *Journal of Political Economy*, 39, 137–175.

Hughes, T. P., Baird, A. H., Bellwood, D. R., Card, M., Connolly, S. R., Folke, C., Grosberg, R., Hoegh-Guldberg, O., Jackson, J. B. C., Kleypas, J., Lough, J. M., Marshall, P., Nystrom, M., Palumbi, S. R., Pandolfi, J. M., Rosen, B. and Roughgarden, J. (2003) Climate change, human impacts, and the resilience of coral reefs. *Science*, 301, 929–933.

Ives, A. and Carpenter, S. (2007) Stability and diversity of ecosystems. *Science*, 317, 58–62.

Jactel, H., Brockerhoff, E. and Duelli, P. (2005) A test of the biodiversity-stability theory: meta-analysis of tree species diversity effects on insect pest infestations, and re-examination of responsible factors. *Forest Diversity and Function* (ed. M. Scherer-Lorenzen, C. Körner and E.-D. Schulze), pp. 235–262. Springer, Berlin and Heidelberg.

Jones, P. G. and Thornton, P. K. (2002) Spatial modeling of risk in natural resource management. *Conservation Ecology*, 5, 27.

Karp, D. S., Ziv, G., Zook, J., Ehrlich, P. R. and Daily, G. C. (2011) Resilience and stability in bird guilds across tropical countryside. *Proceedings of the National Academy of Sciences*, 108, 21134–21139.

Kattge, J., Diaz, S., Lavorel, S., Prentice, I. C., Leadley, P., Bönisch, G., Garnier, E., Westoby, M., Reich, P. B., Wright, I. J., Cornelissen, J. H. C., Violle, C., Harrison, S. P., van Bodegom, P. M., Reichstein, M., Enquist, B. J., Soudzilovskaia, N. A., Ackerly, D. D., Anand, M., Atkin, O., Bahn, M., Baker, T. R., Baldocchi, D., Bekker, R., Blanco, C. C., Blonder, B., Bond, W. J., Bradstock, R., Bunker, D. E., Casanoves, F., Cavender-Bares, J., Chambers, J. Q., Chapin, F. S., Chave, J., Coomes, D., Cornwell, W. K., Craine, J. M., Dobrin, B. H., Duarte, L., Durka, W., Elser, J., Esser, G., Estiarte, M., Fagan, W. F., Fang, J., Fernández-Méndez, F., Fidelis, A., Finegan, B., Flores, O., Ford, H., Frank, D., Freschet, G. T., Fyllas, N. M., Gallagher, R. V., Green, W. A., Gutierrez, A. G., Hickler, T., Higgins, S., Hodgson, J. G., Jalili, A., Jansen, S., Joly, C., Kerkhoff, A. J., Kirkup, D. O. N., Kitajima, K., Kleyer, M., Klotz, S., Knops, J. M. H., Kramer, K., Kühn, I., Kurokawa, H., Laughlin, D., Lee, T. D., Leishman, M., Lens, F., Lenz, T., Lewis, S. L., Lloyd, J. O. N., Llusiá, J., Louault, F., Ma, S., Mahecha, M. D., Manning, P., Massad, T., Medlyn, B., Messier, J., Moles, A. T., Müller, S. C., Nadrowski, K., Naeem, S., Niinemets, Ü., Nöllert, S.,

Nüske, A., Ogaya, R., Oleksyn, J., Onipchenko, V.G., Onoda, Y., Ordoñez, J., Overbeck, G., Ozinga, W.A., Patiño, S., Paula, S., Pausas, J.G., Peñuelas, J., Phillips, O.L., Pillar, V., Poorter, H., Poorter, L., Poschlod, P., Prinzing, A., Proulx, R., Rammig, A., Reinsch, S., Reu, B., Sack, L., Salgado-Negret, B., Sardans, J., Shiodera, S., Shipley, B., Siefert, A., Sosinski, E., Soussana, J.-F., Swaine, E., Swenson, N., Thompson, K.E.N., Thornton, P., Waldram, M., Weiher, E., White, M., White, S., Wright, S.J., Yguel, B., Zaehle, S., Zanne, A.E. and Wirth, C. (2011) TRY – a global database of plant traits. *Global Change Biology*, 17, 2905–2935.

Kinzig, A.P., Pacala, S. and Tilman, D. (eds.) (2002) *Functional Consequences of Biodiversity: Empirical Progess and Theoretical Extensions*. Princeton University Press.

Lhomme, J.P. and Winkel, T. (2002) Diversity–stability relationships in community ecology: re-examination of the portfolio effect. *Theoretical Population Biology*, 62, 271–279.

Libecap, G.D. (2011) Institutional path dependence in climate adaptation: Coman's "Some Unsettled Problems of Irrigation." *American Economic Review*, 101, 64–80.

Loreau, M., Naeem, S. and Inchausti, P. (2002) *Biodiversity and Ecosystem Functioning: Synthesis and Perspectives*. Oxford University Press.

Loreau, M., Mouquet, N. and Gonzalez, A. (2003) Biodiversity as spatial insurance in heterogenous landscapes. *Proceedings of the National Academy of Sciences*, 22, 12765–12770.

Loskutov, I.G. & Rines, H.R. (2011) *Avena. Wild Crop Relatives: Genomic and Breeding Resources (Cereals)* (ed. C. Kole), pp. 109–184. Springer, Berlin.

Low, B., Ostrom, E., Simon, C. and Wilson, J. (2002) Redundancy and diversity: do they influence optimal management? *Navigating Social-Ecological Systems: Building Resilience for Complexity and Change* (ed. F. Berkes, J. Colding and C. Folke), pp. 83–114. Cambridge University Press.

Magurran, A.E. (2004) *Measuring Biological Diversity*. Blackwell, Oxford.

Malthus, T.R. (1999[1798]) *An Essay on the Principle of Population*. Oxford University Press.

May, R.M. (1973) *Stability and Complexity in Model Ecosystems*. Princeton University Press.

McIntyre, P.B., Jones, L.E., Flecker, A.S. and Vanni, M.J. (2007) Fish extinctions alter nutrient recycling in tropical freshwaters. *PNAS*, 104, 4461–4466.

McLeod, K.L. and Leslie, H.M. (eds.) (2009) *Ecosystem-Based Management for the Oceans*. Island Press, Washington, DC.

Mill, J. S. (1909) *Principles of Political Economy with some of their Applications to Social Philosophy*, 7th edn. Longmans, Green and Co., London.

Naeem, S. (1998) Species redundancy and ecosystem reliability. *Conservation Biology*, 12, 39–45.

  (2002) Disentangling the impacts of diversity on ecosystem functioning in combinatorial experiments. *Ecology*, 83, 2925–2935.

Naeem, S. and Wright, J. P. (2003) Disentangling biodiversity effects on ecosystem functioning: deriving solutions to a seemingly insurmountable problem. *Ecology Letters*, 6, 567–579.

Naeem, S., Bunker, D., Hector, A., Loreau, M. and Perrings, C. (eds.) (2009) *Biodiversity, Ecosystem Functioning, and Human Wellbeing: An Ecological and Economic Perspective*. Oxford University Press.

Pace, M. L., Cole, J. J., Carpenter, S. and Kitchell, J. (1999) Trophic cascades revealed in diverse ecosystems. *Trends in Ecology & Evolution* 14, 483–488.

Pandolfi, J. M., Bradbury, R. H., Sala, E., Hughes, T. P., Bjorndal, K. A., Cooke, R. G., McArdle, D., McClenachan, L., Newman, M. J. H., Paredes, G., Warner, R. R. and Jackson, J. B. C. (2003) Global trajectories of the long-term decline of coral reef ecosystems. *Science*, 301, 955–958.

Perrings, C., Naeem, S., Ahrestani, F., Bunker, D. E., Burkill, P., Canziani, G., Elmqvist, T., Ferrati, R., Fuhrman, J., Jaksic, F., Kawabata, Z. I., Kinzig, A., Mace, G. M., Milano, F., Mooney, H., Prieur-Richard, A.-H., Tschirhart, J. and Weisser, W. (2011) Ecosystem services, targets, and indicators for the conservation and sustainable use of biodiversity. *Frontiers in Ecology and the Environment*, 9, 512–520.

Petchey, O. L. and Gaston, K. (2002) Functional diversity (FD), species richness and community composition. *Ecology Letters*, 5, 402–411.

Petchey, O. L., O'Gorman, E. J. and Flynn, D. F. B. (2009) A functional guide to functional diversity measures. *Biodiversity, Ecosystem Functioning, and Human Wellbeing: An Ecological and Economic Perspective* (ed. S. Naeem, D. Bunker, A. Hector, M. Loreau and C. Perrings), pp. 49–59. Oxford University Press.

Piesse, J. and Thirtle, C. (2010) Agricultural R&D, technology and productivity. *Philosophical Transactions of the Royal Society B: Biological Sciences*, 365, 3035–3047.

Pimm, S. L. (1984) The complexity and stability of ecosystems. *Nature*, 307, 321–326.

Reisner, M. (1993) *Cadillac Desert: The American West and Its Disappearing Water*. Penguin, New York.

Schoener, T. W. (1974) Resource partitioning in ecological communities. *Science*, 185, 27–39.

Schweiger, O., Klotz, S., Durka, W. and Kuhn, I. (2008) A comparative test of phylogenetic diversity indices. *Oecologia*, 157, 485–495.

Shannon, C. E. (1948) A mathematical theory of communication. *Bell System Technical Journal*, 27, 379–423.

Simpson, E. H. (1949) Measurement of diversity. *Nature*, 163, 688.

Smale, M., Hartell, J., Heisey, P. W. and Senauer, B. (1998) The contribution of genetic resources and diversity to wheat production in the Punjab of Pakistan. *American Journal of Agricultural Economics*, 80, 482–493.

Solan, M., Cardinale, B. J., Downing, A. L., Engelhardt, K. A. M., Ruesink, J. L. and Srivastava, D. S. (2004) Extinction and ecosystem function in the marine benthos. *Science*, 306, 1177–1180.

Solow, A., Polasky, S. and Broadus, J. (1993) On the measurement of biological diversity. *Journal of Environmental Economics and Management*, 24, 60–68.

Sørensen, T. A. (1948) A method of establishing groups of equal amplitude in plant sociology based on similarity of species content, and its application to analyses of the vegetation on Danish commons. *Kongelige Danske Videnskabernes Selskabs Biologiske Skrifter*, 5, 1–34.

Steneck, R. S., Vavrinec, J. and Leland, A. V. (2004) Accelerating trophic-level dysfunction in kelp forest ecosystems of the Western North Atlantic. *Ecosystems*, 7, 323–332.

Swanson, T. M. (1994) *The International Regulation of Extinction*. New York University Press.

  (1995) Why does biodiversity decline? The analysis of forces for global change. *The Economics and Ecology of Biodiversity Decline: The Forces Driving Global Change* (ed. T. M. Swanson), pp. 1–9. Cambridge University Press.

Thompson, I., Mackey, B., McNulty, S. and Mosseler, A. (2009) *Forest Resilience, Biodiversity, and Climate Change: A Synthesis of the Biodiversity/Resilience/Stability Relationship in Forest Ecosystems*. CBD, Montreal.

Tilman, D. and Downing, J. A. (1994) Biodiversity and stability in grasslands. *Nature*, 367, 363–365.

Tilman, D., Wedin, D. and Knops, J. (1996) Productivity and sustainability influenced by biodiversity in grassland ecosystems. *Nature*, 379, 718–720.

Tilman, D., Lehman, C. L. and Bristow, C. E. (1998) Diversity–stability relationships: statistical inevitability or ecological consequence? *The American Naturalist*, 151, 277–282.

Tilman, D., May, R. M., Polasky, S. and Lehman, C. L. (2005) Diversity, productivity and temporal stability in the economies of humans and nature. *Journal of Environmental Economics and Management*, 49, 405–426.

Tilman, D., Reich, P., Knops, J., Wedin, D., Mielke, T. and Lehman, C. (2001) Diversity and productivity in a long-term grassland experiment. *Science*, 294, 843–845.

Tisdell, C. (2003) Socioeconomic causes of loss of animal genetic diversity: analysis and assessment. *Ecological Economics*, 45, 365–376.

Walker, B. H., Kinzig, A. P. and Langridge, J. (1999) Plant attribute diversity, resilience, and ecosystem function: the nature and significance of dominant and minor species. *Ecosystems*, 2, 95–113.

Weitzman, M. L. (1992) On diversity. *Quarterly Journal of Economics*, 107, 363–405.

White, J. A. and Whitham, T. G. (2000) Associational susceptibility of cottonwood to a box elder herbivore. *Ecology*, 81, 1795–1803.

Whittaker, R. H. (1972) Evolution and measurement of species diversity. *Taxon*, 21, 213–251.

Widawsky, D. and Rozelle, S. (1998) Varietal diversity and yield variability in Chinese rice production. *Farmers, Gene Banks, and Crop Breeding* (ed. M. Smale), pp. 159–172. Kluwer, Norwell, MA.

Wohl, D. L., Arora, S. and Gladstone, J. R. (2004) Functional redundancy supports biodiversity and ecosystem function in a closed and constant environment. *Ecology*, 85, 1534–1540.

World Commission on Environment and Development (1987) *Our Common Future*. Island Press, Washington, DC.

Yachi, S. and Loreau, M. (1999) Biodiversity and ecosystem productivity in a fluctuating environment: the insurance hypothesis. *Proceedings of the National Academy of Sciences*, 96, 1463–1468.

5 | *Biodiversity externalities and public goods*

5.1 Market failures and biodiversity externalities

The MA found that 60 percent of the ecosystem services evaluated had declined in the second half of the twentieth century (Millennium Ecosystem Assessment 2005). As Kinzig *et al.* have remarked, this should not have been at all surprising. The same 60 percent of services are unpriced in the market. We do not pay for them, and they generate no return to the landholders whose actions affect their supply. Since we get what we pay for, we should expect such services to be neglected (Kinzig *et al.* 2011). Indeed, this is only a problem if it imposes social costs we would prefer to avoid. The conclusion of the MA was that the physical changes it recorded were the socially undesirable consequences of the growth of markets for fuels, foods, and fibers. The external effects of market transactions, externalities for short, are the unintended or incidental consequences of the production or consumption of marketed goods and services. They may be positive or negative. The changes recorded by the MA would have been described by Crocker and Tschirhart as ecosystem externalities: market-driven actions that impact the wellbeing of either consumers or producers by altering the ecological functioning on which consumption or production depends, but where the welfare effects of those actions are ignored (Crocker and Tschirhart 1992). In what follows I refer to them as biodiversity externalities.

The drivers of the biodiversity loss recorded in the MA, and described in Chapter 2, define the most important of the biodiversity externalities. The expansion of land committed to agriculture or industry directly reduces habitat, and with it both species richness and abundance. The introduction of roads (and development along roads) leads to the fragmentation of habitat. While this may not immediately reduce species richness, the long-run effects are quite similar. The appropriation of water for human use in arid and semi-arid lands increases stress on other species, with direct effects on the abundance of those species. The accidental or deliberate introduction of invasive species through trade, transport, and travel frequently leads to the depletion of native species. Aside from these headline externalities, however, there are many more subtle stressors that also change biodiversity and the processes it supports.

Consider, for example, the effects of the application of nitrogen fertilizers. A well-recognized externality of the application of nitrogen to agricultural lands is nitrate pollution of ground and surface water. In the worst cases, runoff from agricultural lands affects estuarine and marine systems causing algae blooms, and leading to dead zones in which very few species can survive. At lower concentrations, nitrogen affects the abundance and richness of plant species. The Minnesota grasslands experiments described in earlier chapters showed that elevated nitrogen levels both decreased species richness (by up to 50 percent) and altered community composition (Tilman *et al.* 2001). It follows that the resulting impacts on the capacity of the system to function over a range of environmental conditions can be interpreted as an externality of nitrogen use. The externality is a decline in the capacity of an ecosystem to accommodate shocks without losing functionality, or an increased risk that services provided by ecosystems might fail if there were a change in environmental conditions.

There are two reasons why markets fail to signal the scarcity of ecosystem services. The first is that the structure of property rights authorizes landholders to ignore the effects they have on others. People who hold the right to cultivate land in the upper reaches of a watershed, for example, have no matching obligation to minimize the harm done to people lower down the watershed. Conversely those downstream have no rights in relation to the damage caused by changes in land use and land cover upstream. The second is that the ecosystem services in question are public goods. The non-exclusive and non-rival nature of public goods means that markets will not emerge naturally. Since no one is able capture the benefits of climate regulation through carbon sequestration, for example, no one has had an incentive to sequester carbon.

I have suggested that there are in fact very good reasons why people behave in ways that cause a loss of biodiversity, whether or not there are externalities and whether or not there is an incentive to free-ride on the conservation efforts of others. The need to produce food, to generate a safe living environment, or to combat disease all help to explain why people might choose to reduce biodiversity. The problem created by externalities and the public good nature of many ecosystem services is that the best choices people make may still be biased. Lacking good measures of the true scarcity of many ecosystem services, people may act in ways that underweight the effects of biodiversity change.

In this chapter I consider these two sources of market failure, and the way they play out at different scales. The problems posed by market failure turn out to be very different at the national and international scales. At the national scale the failure of markets to supply public goods may be compensated by the actions of local or national governments. There are national agencies with responsibilities for the provision of environmental public goods such as habitat for rare and endangered species, clean water, environmental health protection, and so on. There are also national strategies for encouraging landholders to conserve biodiversity, largely focused on the allocation of property rights and the extension of legal protections to private lands but also including incentive schemes such as the US biodiversity offset and banking programs (Madsen, Carroll and Moore Brands 2010). At the international scale, however, the absence of any supranational authority to take responsibility means that the failure of markets to deliver environmental public goods is more difficult to address. Externalities are harder to internalize and cooperation in the provision of public goods is harder to obtain (Sandler 1997, 2004; Barrett 2003a).

Several aspects of the public good problem are discussed. First, I consider the essential features of public goods in general, and what these features imply for their provision. Next I consider the characteristics of environmental public goods supported by biodiversity, noting that many are jointly produced with other services, and that their provision frequently involves landholders who are quite widely distributed in space. Similarly, I note that the benefits offered by distinct ecosystem services frequently accrue to people on quite different spatial and temporal scales. Since different actors are involved both in the production and consumption of environmental public goods, this also raises the question of how those different actors interact. I therefore consider the strategic options open to the providers of environmental public goods and how this relates to the technology of public good supply. In doing so I begin to disentangle the factors that make management of biodiversity change so challenging at the international level, and to distinguish between cases that are more or less tractable. While some aspects of the problem have no ready solution, others may be tackled effectively at one or more scales. In some cases, for example, it may be possible to secure one ecosystem service through interventions designed to support provision of another. Indeed, the exploitation of the co-benefits of biodiversity conservation has become a central plank of international environmental policy.

5.2 Identifying the social cost of externalities and public goods

Before examining the nature of the public good at risk from biodiversity loss it may be helpful to identify, conceptually, what the social costs of biodiversity externalities and public goods are. Once again, it is convenient to use a stylized description of the problem of the sort introduced in Chapter 4. Recall that we supposed that a landscape holds two non-overlapping communities of species of gamma diversity $\gamma = s_1 + s_2$. We also supposed that when combined with other inputs, denoted x, these generated a single service, y. To describe the problem of externality let us now suppose that each set of species is associated with a distinct service, and a distinct bundle of other inputs, and that the services are produced by distinct individuals (later we will think of these as communities of individuals). In addition, suppose that the two services are not independent. Specifically, suppose that the second set of species is affected by inputs to the first process. To fix ideas we could think of this as the set of species lying downstream of some activity, being affected by emissions generated by that activity. We can therefore describe the production functions for each service as:

$$y_1 = y_1(x_1, s_1)$$
$$y_2 = y_2(x_2, s_2(x_1))$$

in which $\partial y_1/\partial x_1, \partial y_1/\partial s_1, \partial y_2/\partial x_2, \partial y_2/\partial s_2 > 0$, but $\partial s_2/\partial x_1 < 0$. The marginal physical product of all inputs is positive, but an increase in employment of x_1 has a negative effect on s_2 and hence on y_2. Suppose that production of the two services is in the hands of two distinct sets of decision-makers, and each maximizes a net benefit function of the form

$$\pi_1 = p_1 y_1 - w_1 x_1 - c_1 s_1$$
$$\pi_2 = p_2 y_2 - w_2 x_2 - c_2 s_2$$

where p_i, w_i, c_i denote the "prices" – the social opportunity costs – of ecosystem services, material inputs, and species respectively. Maximization of net benefits, given the production functions, requires that employment of material inputs in each process be increased up to the point where the value of its marginal physical product is equal to its marginal cost.[1] The biodiversity index of each location will also be increased up to the point where the value obtained by increasing the index by one more unit is equal to the cost of so doing. If these conditions are satisfied each set of decision-makers will be maximizing their net benefits, taking no account of interactions between the processes. That is, the effect that employment of x_1 has on s_2, and hence on y_2, will be an externality of production of y_1.

To see what the cost of that externality is we need to identify the conditions that would have to hold if the objective was to maximize not the net benefits accruing to each set of decision-makers independently, but of all decision-makers taken together.[2] That is, we need to maximize $\pi_1 + \pi_2$ by choosing the levels of x_1, x_2, s_1, s_2. The new problem has the form:

---

[1] The first-order necessary conditions for profits to be at a maximum include, for $i \in \{1, 2\}$:

$$\frac{\partial \pi_i}{\partial y_i} \frac{\partial y_i}{\partial x_i} = p_i \frac{\partial y_i}{\partial x_i} = w_i$$

$$\frac{\partial \pi_i}{\partial y_i} \frac{\partial y_i}{\partial s_i} = p_i \frac{\partial y_i}{\partial s_i} = c_i$$

[2] The first-order necessary conditions required for maximization of the new objective function are:

$$\frac{\partial \pi_1}{\partial y_1} \frac{\partial y_1}{\partial x_1} + \frac{\partial \pi_2}{\partial y_2} \frac{\partial y_2}{\partial s_2} \frac{\partial s_2}{\partial x_1} = p_1 \frac{\partial y_1}{\partial x_1} + p_2 \frac{\partial y_2}{\partial s_2} \frac{\partial s_2}{\partial x_1} = w_1$$

$$\frac{\partial \pi_2}{\partial y_2} \frac{\partial y_2}{\partial x_2} = p_2 \frac{\partial y_2}{\partial x_2} = w_2$$

$$\frac{\partial \pi_1}{\partial y_1} \frac{\partial y_1}{\partial s_1} = p_1 \frac{\partial y_1}{\partial s_1} = c_1$$

$$\frac{\partial \pi_2}{\partial y_2} \frac{\partial y_2}{\partial s_2} = p_2 \frac{\partial y_2}{\partial s_2} = c_2$$

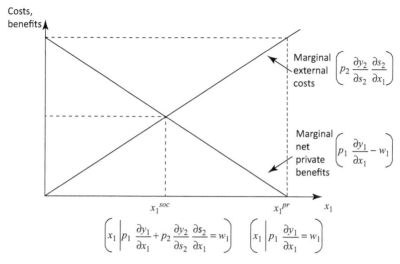

Figure 5.1 Socially and privately optimal level of employment of an input with negative externalities. Marginal net private benefit is the difference between the benefit of an additional unit of the resource, x, and its cost to the user, w. If no account is taken of the external effects of the resource it will be employed up to x_1^{pr} where the marginal benefit of an additional unit of x just offsets its cost. Marginal external cost is the impact of an additional unit of the resource, x, on the wellbeing of others. Society is best served if x is employed only up to the point where marginal net private benefits equal the marginal external cost, x_1^{soc}.

$$\underset{x_1,x_2,s_1,s_2}{Max} \quad V = p_1 y_1 + p_2 y_2 - w_1 x_1 - w_2 x_2 - c_1 s_1 - c_2 s_2$$

The difference between the first-order necessary conditions for maximizing this objective function, relative to those required for the earlier function, defines the value of the associated externality: $p_2 \frac{\partial y_2}{\partial s_2} \frac{\partial s_2}{\partial x_1} < 0$. It is negative because $\frac{\partial s_2}{\partial x_1} < 0$. That is, employment of additional units of x_1 causes a reduction in s_2. It follows that the use made of x_1 would be lower if the externality were taken into account than if not. This is shown in Figure 5.1, which illustrates the optimal level of employment of x_1 with and without the external effect on s_2.

The privately optimal employment of x_1, x_1^{pr} is at the point where the marginal net private benefits of employment are equal to zero. This is the point at which the marginal private costs of employment are just offset by the marginal private benefits of employment. The socially optimal employment of x_1, x_1^{soc} is at the intersection of the marginal external cost and marginal net private benefits curves associated with employment of x_1. At this point the external cost of an additional unit of x_1 is just offset by the gains from doing so. The figure also includes the formal definition of each point, and the marginal external cost and benefits functions, for the simple model described here.

Now consider the public good problem. It will be helpful to think of the decision-makers in this case being not individual agents, but communities of agents. Communities can imply local bodies, regional associations, or nation states. To identify the social cost of the under-supply of the public good, we may suppose that there are two communities contributing to global biodiversity, measured by gamma diversity. That is, $B = B(\gamma) = B(s_1 + s_2)$ and s_i is the set of distinct species occurring at the location of the ith community. We may also suppose that the ith community gains from their contribution to global biodiversity both directly, through the production of output, y_i and indirectly through the contribution they make to the global pool of species, a global public good. That is, we may suppose that each community maximizes a social utility function of the form $U_i = U_i(\pi_i, B)$. Suppose that this is additive separable, implying that the wellbeing of the ith set of decision-makers is the sum of the net benefits of producing y_i, on the one side, and of global biodiversity on the other. If $U_i(\pi_i) = p_i y_i(s_i) - w_i x_i - c_i s_i$, this implies that each set of decision-makers solve the following problem:

$$\underset{x_i, s_i}{Max}\, U_i = (p_i y_i(s_i) - w_i x_i - c_i s_i) + U_i\left(B\left(\sum_j s_j\right)\right)$$

taking the decisions of all others as given. The first set of bracketed terms on the right hand side are simply the profits accruing to the production of y_i. The second set of terms are the public benefits accruing to all from the global biodiversity stock. How does this change the conditions required for the private and social optima? If we consider only the ith community, the (first-order necessary) conditions for choice of s_i to maximize their social utility include the requirement that: $p_i \frac{\partial y_i}{\partial s_i} + \frac{\partial U_i}{\partial B} \frac{\partial B}{\partial s_i} = c_i$. In words, the ith community will increase s_i up to the point where the cost of doing so is just balanced by the value of the marginal physical product of s_i in production of y_i, together with the marginal utility to that community of the increment in global biodiversity due to s_i. So the effect of their actions on the global public good matters, but only to the extent that they themselves benefit from enhanced global biodiversity.

What is not being taken into account in this problem is the benefit of an increment in s_i to other communities. If the problem were to choose s_i to maximize social utility across all communities, i.e. if it were:

$$\underset{x_i, s_i}{Max}\ U = \sum_i \left[(p_i y_i(s_i) - w_i x_i - c_i s_i) + U_i \left(B \left(\sum_j s_j \right) \right) \right]$$

where $U = \sum_i U_i$, then the first-order necessary conditions for choice of s_i to maximize the utility of all communities would include the requirement that: $p_i \frac{\partial y_i}{\partial s_i} + \sum_j \frac{\partial U_j}{\partial B} \frac{\partial B}{\partial s_i} = c_i$. In words, again, the ith community would have to increase s_i up to the point where the cost of doing so was just balanced by the value of the marginal physical product of s_i in production of y_i, together with the marginal utility to the *global community* of the increment in global biodiversity due to s_i. So long as other communities derived positive benefit from global biodiversity, this would lead the ith community to choose a higher value of s_i than in the first case. That is, it would conserve more biodiversity.

This is illustrated in Figure 5.2, which shows the effect of benefits to the rest of the world on the socially optimal choice of s_1. Since $B(s_1 + s_2)$ is a global public good, if there are no mechanisms to compensate the first community for benefits provided to others, it would have no incentive to conserve at the socially optimal level. The loss to the global community is the difference between the net benefits to all communities of conservation at the socially optimal level of s_1^{soc} and conservation at the privately optimal level of s_1^{pr}. This is just the difference between the grey and hatched areas in Figure 5.2.

While this model is extremely simple, it helps to clarify why market failure and the public good nature of biodiversity and many ecosystem services are especially problematic at the international level. Externalities arise because of interdependencies in either production or consumption. If one consumption or production activity affects another and those effects are not registered in any market transaction

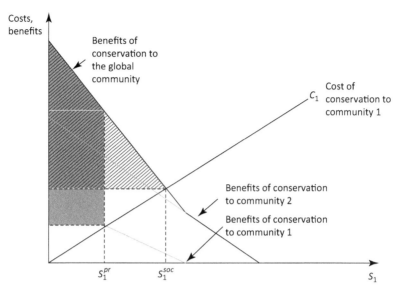

Figure 5.2 Socially and privately optimal conservation, where conservation is a public good. Showing the optimal level of conservation by the 1st community if the benefits to both communities of global biodiversity are taken into account, s_1^{Soc}, relative to the case where the wider benefits of local conservation are not taken into account, s_1^{Pr}.

between the parties, then they are said to be externalities of the activity. We will consider the range of solutions to the problem in more detail later, but the most common solutions since the 1960s have been direct regulation of the effect, internalization of the externality through the tax system, or the assignment of property rights (Tietenberg 1990; Stavins 2003). Each one of these solutions implies the existence of a sovereign authority with the power to assign rights. If there is no sovereign authority with that power, as is the case with international or transboundary externalities, this solution is not available. It may still be possible to reach bilateral or multilateral agreement on the rights and obligations of the parties, but the process is considerably more difficult.

A second aspect of the problem is reflected in the assumption that wellbeing is the sum of some quantifiable net benefit from the production of well-defined services and the utility offered by a global public good, biodiversity. Many environmental decisions require that the monetized net benefits of the production of private goods and services be weighed against the non-monetized net benefits of contributions towards public goods. In the international arena the incentive to free-ride on others – a problem with public goods of all kinds – is compounded by the lack of clear signals about the importance those goods have to different countries. In fact, each country has an incentive not to reveal its true interest in the public good. This makes it hard to identify the true value of the non-monetized public good.

A third aspect of the problem that is nicely illustrated by a basic model of this kind is that even if the global benefits of biodiversity conservation are understood, achieving higher levels of conservation in any one country than it would itself be willing to pay for requires a mechanism to cover the extra cost. In the absence of functioning markets, this means either a market-like mechanism such as the currently popular payment for ecosystem services schemes, or cooperative agreements between countries to invest in conservation in particular locations. Solutions of this sort are discussed in Chapter 11. At this point it is enough to note that moving from s_1^{pr} to s_1^{soc} in Figure 5.2 raises the cost of conservation as well. This will not happen without the second community compensating the first community.

The description of the problem in Figure 5.2 can be thought of as a metaphor for the conservation problem currently facing the global community, the first set of decision-makers being the Global South, the second set of decision-makers being the Global North. Meeting the cost of moving from s_1^{pr} to s_1^{soc} is, in fact, exactly the problem that the GEF was established to address. Discussion of that institution, as with other potential solutions to the problem, is deferred. At this point I want to explore the nature of the problems that such institutions have to solve if they are to achieve their goals.

5.3 Biodiversity as a "layered" public good

There are two characteristics of biodiversity (and other international environmental public goods) that have to be taken into account in designing solutions. First, biodiversity supports services that are public goods at many different spatial and temporal scales (Perrings and Gadgil 2003). Second, different services have different technologies of supply that affect the incentives both to providers and beneficiaries (Arriagada and Perrings 2011; Touza and Perrings 2011). In what follows I draw on these papers to identify the properties of environmental public goods that either help or hinder their supply.

Of the ecosystem services identified by the MA, only the provisioning services consistently generate benefits that are both rival and exclusive. The other services yield benefits that are generally non-exclusive and are sometimes non-rival. Many are both public and international. These are services that cover more than one group of countries, that benefit not only a broad spectrum of countries but also a broad spectrum of the global population, and that meet the needs of both present and future generations (Kaul, Grunberg and stern 1999; Anand 2004). Because they are international they must therefore generate spillover effects beyond a nation's boundaries (Morrissey, te Velde and Hewitt 2002).

In the most extreme case, if the marginal local benefits of public good provision are less than the marginal local costs, there will be no incentive to provide the public good at all. More generally, if the marginal local benefits of public good provision exceed the marginal local costs of provision, but benefits also accrue to other countries, there will be an incentive to produce the public good in some measure. However, unless the country is a best-shot provider, as we will see, it will not be at the socially optimal level (Kanbur 2003, 2004). The conservation of endangered species and the protection of tropical moist forests are classic examples. Efficiency requires that marginal benefit equals marginal cost where the relevant measure of marginal benefits is social marginal benefit – the sum of all countries' marginal benefits (as was illustrated in Figure 5.2). In general, therefore, private provision of public goods will be below the socially optimal level, and this will almost always be true where markets fail to signal the global benefit of public goods.

Many international environmental public goods are strictly global in scale. The conservation of the genetic diversity on which all future evolution depends, for example, is a public good at the global scale. So too is the control of emerging infectious diseases that have the potential to become globally pandemic. But the conservation of species that have totemic, cultural, or spiritual significance to particular groups of people is a public good at the scale of those groups of people. Ecosystem services that provide non-exclusive, non-rival benefits to people typically do so at many different scales. Pollination services, for example, tend to be quite localized. Watershed protection, on the other hand, can extend from extremely small scales to regions involving several countries. In all cases, the benefits of the service are non-exclusive in the sense that once the good is provided, none can be excluded from the benefits it confers. Some are also non-rival or indivisible, in the sense that consumption by one country or one group does not diminish the amount available for others. The protection against storm damage offered by mangrove systems, for example, extends to all those who live in low-lying coastal areas behind the mangroves. The protection offered to any one village does not reduce the protection offered to other villages.

If an ecosystem service is both non-exclusive and non-rival in consumption, it is said to be a pure public good. There is a clear and obvious link between the purity of a public good and the scale at which it provides benefits. Public goods are said to be impure if they are either partially excludable or partially rival. So local common pool resources of the kind analyzed by Elinor Ostrom would be impure public goods, since people outside the area may generally be excluded from accessing the benefits they offer (Ostrom 1990). Public goods that suffer from congestion, such as national parks, would also be impure since consumption by one group does restrict the benefits available to others (Sandler 1997, 2004). It follows that impure public goods have at least some of the characteristics of private goods in that they offer some privately capturable benefits. If the utility of the ith set of decision-makers can be described by a function such as $U_i = U_i(\pi_i(y_i, x_i, s_i), B(s_i, s_j)), j \neq i$, s_i would be an impure public good. The ith set of decision-makers gain directly from the biodiversity used to support production of y_i, but also from the contribution it makes to the global public good, $B(s_i, s_j), j \neq 1$.[3] The purity of public goods matters – as we will see later – because it affects the incentives that individuals or communities have to provide them.

Public goods can also be classified according to what Sandler termed their "technology of supply" (Sandler 2004). The technology of supply describes the relation between the benefits offered by a public good supplied by many countries, and the contributions of each of those countries. Like the purity of public goods, supply technologies are

---

[3] If it were a pure public good the utility function would have the form
$U_i = U_i(\pi_i(y_i, x_i), B(s_i, s_j))$.

important because they affect both the incentives communities have to supply public goods, and the cost of free-riding behavior. Recall that we have defined the global public good to be the benefits offered by global gamma diversity, and the contributions of each community to the global public good to be the set of all conserved species that are unique to the area managed by the community. If the benefits offered by biodiversity depend on gamma diversity, as they do in our base model, then the technology of supply would be said to be additive. That is, for the two-country case, $B(s_1, s_2) = B(s_1 + s_2)$, and the benefits depend on the simple sum of the contributions of each country. Another example of an additive technology of supply would be climate regulation through carbon sequestration. Since the global carbon balance is the sum of net contributions from all countries, total sequestered carbon is the sum of sequestered carbon in all countries.

The social cost of free-riding is generally greatest for public goods produced using an additive supply technology. It is least for public goods with the other polar supply technologies: best-shot and weakest-link (Touza and Perrings 2011). For best-shot public goods the benefit to all communities is determined by the community that is most effective at providing the public good. The example usually given in this case is defense. However, there are a number of ecosystem services that have this characteristic. The form of the supply function for a best-shot public good is $B(s_1, s_2) = B(Max(s_1, s_2))$. If we think of the global gene pool, for example, the benefits of the conservation of species that are endemic to some country will tend to be best provided by that country. This is not always the case, though. There are certainly examples of endangered species whose survival has depended on conservation outside the country. Père David's deer is a case in point (Goodall, Maynard and Hudson 2009). For weakest-link public goods, the benefits to all countries are limited to the benefits offered by the least effective provider, $B(s_1, s_2) = B(Min(s_1, s_2))$. A good example of this is the control of infectious diseases or the control of disease vectors. For many infectious diseases the level of protection available to all countries is only as good as the level of protection exercised in the poorest, most densely populated, and/or least well-coordinated country (Perrings *et al.* 2002).

Intermediate cases include better-shot and weaker-link technologies, in which the contributions of different countries are weighted asymmetrically. That is, for our two-community base case the benefit function has the form $B(s_1, s_2) = B(a_1 s_1 + a_2 s_2), 0 \leq a_i \leq 1$. The weights in such a case reflect the relative importance of the two contributions. In the case of habitat protection, for example, the contribution of each community to some transboundary protected area might depend on the characteristics of the landscape, the effectiveness of protection measures, the compliance of local populations, and so on. Such intermediate cases are more frequently encountered in international environmental public good problems than either weakest-link or best-shot cases (Arce and Sandler 2001). An example that will appear later is the control of the movement of invasive pests and pathogens or endangered species along trade routes, where the probability of introduction depends on the inspection, sanitary, and phytosanitary efforts of countries.

Other classes of supply technology that turn out to be important for biodiversity and ecosystem services are those in which the benefits depend on some threshold level of supply. Public goods where the benefits depend on a certain level of provision, but do not increase beyond that level of provision, are referred to as step goods. A typical example of this would be the establishment of bio-corridors between the sub-populations or sub-communities of a meta-population or meta-community. Just as half a bridge is no bridge at all, the benefits of biocorridors are zero unless the corridor is complete (Touza and Perrings 2011). Once established, though, making it bigger will not necessarily make it better. Public goods that offer no benefits below a certain scale of provision, but where the benefits increase if provision is increased beyond that point are known as threshold goods. The control of infectious diseases falls into this category. The long-term control of infectious diseases requires that the basic reproduction ratio (R0) – the number of individuals infected by each infected individual – is brought below 1. The level of effort required to do this represents a threshold level of effort. Beyond that threshold, however, there will still be benefits to further reductions in R0.

In our base case, suppose that there was a level of diversity, $\underline{s}$, in the area controlled by community 1 below which the benefits of conservation might be zero. The function describing supply of the public good would have the general form $B(s_1, s_2) = B(b_1 s_1, s_2)$, the value of b_1 varying depending on whether the supply technology involved a threshold or a step function:

$$b_1 = \begin{cases} \frac{\underline{s}}{s_1} & s_1 \geq \underline{s} \\ 0 & s_1 < \underline{s} \end{cases} \text{(threshold public good)}$$

$$b_2 = \begin{cases} 1 & s_1 \geq \underline{s} \\ 0 & s_1 < \underline{s} \end{cases} \text{(step public good)}$$

Threshold public goods may exist for a number of reasons. One is that while ecosystems may exist in multiple stable states, they may provide benefits (or impose costs) only if they are in particular states. Crossing thresholds may be either beneficial or harmful. Actions that cause a system generating benefits in some state to flip into another undesirable state will be associated with a sudden decrease in net benefits. For example, the benefits that derive from a water body in an oligotrophic (well-oxygenated) state may be marginally reduced with increasing levels of organic pollution (biological oxygen demand), but will collapse completely at the point at which the system flips from an oligotrophic into a eutrophic (hypoxic or anoxic) state (Carpenter, Luduig and Brock 1999; Scheffer *et al.* 2001). Other reasons to expect threshold effects include critical minimum population sizes, or critical habitat sizes for endangered species (Shaffer 1981; Reed *et al.* 2003). Reversing the degradation of systems that have flipped through stress from one state into to another may well involve hysteresis – that the stressor has to be reduced well beyond the level at which the flip originally occurred – but will still be associated with threshold effects. Where a step or threshold change is irreversible, as in the case of species extinctions for example, the costs of exceeding the threshold may be extremely high.

What complicates the conservation of biodiversity is that the multiple ecosystem services generated by a management action at some scale can have quite different spatial and temporal impacts, and involve quite different supply technologies. International environmental public goods are frequently jointly produced with local public goods. For example, biodiversity in tropical forests yields a set of private benefits in the form of timber and other products including medicinal plants, hunting, fishing, recreation, and tourism. At the same time, it contributes to a range of public goods at multiple scales including the global gene pool, microclimatic regulation, and watershed protection – commonly described as co-benefits (Perrings and Gadgil 2003). The spatial extent of such public goods depends partly on the natural hydrological and atmospheric flows, and partly on the social linkages between countries – the flow of goods, people, and information.

At the largest scale, the irreversible loss of genetic information caused by the extinction of species threatens an intergenerational global public good: the global gene pool (Sandler 1997). This comprises the genetic information now contained in the set of species on the planet, as well as the information that may be provided in the future through the genotypic evolution of those species. It is a global public good. At smaller scales, the reduction in the abundance or even the extirpation of local populations affects ecosystem services that offer more localized benefits. These are typically local public goods. Biodiversity conservation is generally an impure public good offering both locally or nationally capturable benefits as well as a set of non-exclusive and non-rival benefits to a wider community. The important point is that in the absence of cooperation, the level of conservation effort will be determined by the privately or at least locally capturable value of conservation. The problem is that this level of conservation will generally be less than the optimal level from the perspective of the global community. Each community has an incentive to free-ride on the conservation efforts of others, and to neglect the benefit their own conservation efforts confer on others.

5.4 Strategic behavior and the provision of international environmental public goods

One of the main reasons for the under-provision of international environmental public goods is that communities behave strategically. They form expectations about the payoffs to alternative strategies, given the public good's supply technology and any locally capturable benefits, and select strategies to maximize local benefits. In what follows, we will think about a particular category of communities: nation states. We will think about the collective decision-makers as national governments, and strategic interactions between national governments as including both non-cooperative unilateral behavior, and notional cooperation through bilateral or multilateral agreement. Since all countries behave strategically, the payoffs to particular strategies by one country reflect that country's expectations about how other countries will respond to those strategies. The free-riding behavior that characterizes public goods of all kinds – letting others carry the cost of public goods from which all benefit – represents a non-cooperative approach to the provision of public goods.

While one's instinct may be that we have collectively lost by the fact that countries choose not to cooperate in the provision of biodiversity-related international public goods, the reality is that we lose in some cases, but not in others. For one thing, international cooperation is not necessarily signaled by the existence of international agreements. There are examples of MEAs that deliver outcomes very close to the non-cooperative outcome – the outcome that would occur in the absence of an agreement (Sandler 2004). Moreover, there are examples of non-cooperative action that deliver environmental public goods at levels close to the social optimum (Murdoch and Sandler 2009). Nor are non-cooperation and full cooperation the only options. Coalitions between some of the countries affected by the provision of some public good can frequently achieve an outcome that is better than the non-cooperative outcome (Carraro and Siniscalco 1996; Barrett 2003a, 2007b).

To understand the incentives to provide biodiversity-related international public goods, and in particular to provide some of the regulating ecosystem services, we need to understand the ways in which social conditions affect the scope for cooperation. Aside from the technology of supply and the relative costs and benefits of alternative strategies, these conditions include the number of countries of involved, the homogeneity or heterogeneity of those countries, and the scope for repeated interaction between them (Holzinger 2001, 2008).

In what follows I draw on the discussion of game structures corresponding to different supply technologies and different numbers of participants in Touza and Perrings (2011) to identify the social cost of non-cooperation in the case of particular kinds of biodiversity-related international environmental public goods. Game structures describe patterns of payoffs that yield particular kinds of strategies. The well known "prisoner's dilemma," for example, is the game structure most often associated with non-cooperative outcomes that impose a significant social cost. Other game structures that characterize the strategic problem posed by biodiversity-related international environmental public goods go by equally colorful names, including "chicken," "stag hunt," and "battle of the sexes." They are likely to be familiar to many. In the prisoner's dilemma, for example, each country would benefit most if all were to cooperate in the provision of a public good, but face individual incentives that lead them to supply nothing. In the chicken game, each country would prefer not to contribute towards an international environmental public good, but since the worst possible outcome is one in which no country contributes, countries will contribute if they believe that others will not (unless the cost of unilateral action is so high that the game becomes a prisoner's dilemma). In the stag hunt, if all countries cooperate in the provision of an international environmental public good they get the outcome that is best for each, but if even one decides not to cooperate the good will not be provided (and the effort of all others will be wasted). In the battle of the sexes, countries have different preferences about how to provide an international environmental public good. Each would rather adopt the method preferred by others than risk defection by insisting on their own method.

Typically, public goods delivered using an additive supply technology involve a prisoner's dilemma or chicken game structure, while the polar technologies – best-shot and weakest-link – involve chicken and stag hunt game structures respectively (Touza and Perrings 2011). The optimal strategy in all cases depends not only on the supply technology, but also on the number of participating countries. Problems involving a small number of countries will generally yield better outcomes than problems involving large numbers of countries. There are, however, many factors influencing the incentives facing individual countries aside from the number of countries involved and the technology of supply. Among these are the spatial and temporal scale of public good provision, the resources available to change the structure of payoffs, the scope for implementing penalties for defection, and the frequency with which the parties interact (Barrett 1994, 2003a; Kaul *et al.* 2003).

To see the effect of the supply technology (leaving the number of participating countries to one side for the moment) consider our base model with two communities contributing to a public good with benefits $B(s_1, s_2)$. To keep things simple, suppose that each country has only two options, to cooperate in the provision of the public good or to defect. The payoff structure for the joint behavior of the two countries is characterized as $\begin{pmatrix} B_{cc} & B_{cd} \\ B_{dc} & B_{dd} \end{pmatrix}$ where B_{cc} is the payoff if both choose cooperation, B_{dd} is the payoff for mutual defection, B_{cd} is the payoff to the cooperating country if the other country defects, and B_{dc} is the payoff to the defecting country if the other cooperates. While a structure of this kind allows a large number of collective action problems depending on the relative payoffs to each country under each option (Holzinger 2008), only a few are commonly encountered.

Consider the conservation of a widely distributed but endangered species secured through the establishment of a protected area in all or part of its range. The impact of conservation efforts is likely to be the sum of the conservation efforts of each country within the species range: i.e. the supply technology is additive. Since the contribution of one country to the aggregate conservation effort can substitute for the contribution of the other country, however, there is also an incentive to each country to free-ride on the conservation efforts of the other. A game structure corresponding to this problem is the prisoner's dilemma, in which the payoffs to each country are such that $B_{dc} > B_{cc} > B_{dd} > B_{cd}$. That is, defection by one country (land conversion) pays more than cooperation (land protection) whether or not the other country cooperates. The dominant strategy in this case would be for each country to defect (to convert the land) because that yields the greatest payoff independently of the strategy pursued by the other country.

Suppose, however, that mutual defection was the worst outcome for each country. That is, suppose that the structure of payoffs was such that $B_{dc} > B_{cc} > B_{cd} > B_{dd}$. A payoff structure of this form implies that while land conversion by one country pays more than land protection as long as the other country protects its share of the species range, it does not pay more than protection if the other country chooses to convert its share of the species range. The strategic interactions in this case have the structure of a chicken game. Since the benefit from acting unilaterally is less than the cost of providing the public good, each country's preferred response would be to let the other country carry the cost of conservation. The next highest payoff is for the two countries each to protect the land, but since $B_{cd} > B_{dd}$ if one country persists in defecting, it is still in the best interests of the other to provide the public good. The technology of supply in this case is best-shot, and the problem has the structure of a chicken game. A good example of a best-shot public good of this kind is the US Centers for Disease Control (CDC), which track contagious diseases worldwide and provide all countries with information about current threats. The USA acts unilaterally to generate this information in order to avoid the threats to US citizens that would occur if no country acted. Other examples include the Pasteur Institute in Paris, or the Institute of Virology in Johannesburg (Sandler 2004).

The other polar case, weakest-link public goods, includes such public goods as the global eradication of infectious diseases. In our example, this requires contributions from both countries, but neither country can gain by providing more than the country making the least effective contribution. This results in a matching strategy from both countries. The game has the structure of a stag hunt, and the payoffs are such that $B_{cc} > B_{dc} > B_{dd} > B_{cd}$. This results in two Nash equilibria (where neither country can improve its payoff by unilaterally switching strategies once the other country has made its choice). They are full cooperation, B_{cc}, or full defection, B_{dd}. Only the cooperative equilibrium is optimal by the Pareto criterion (implying that it is not possible to make one country better off by changing the allocation of resources without making the other country worse off). In other words, it is best to cooperate if the other country cooperates, and it is best to defect if the other country defects. There is a benefit to cooperation, provided the other country does the same, but unilateral efforts will be wasted. In the infectious disease control problem, either all countries cooperate in the control of the disease or all will fail. Unilateral action by any one country cannot prevent the disease from spreading, although it may improve the prospects of a cooperative outcome if it encourages other countries to act (Sandler and Sargent 1995).

To see, now, how the number of participating countries affects the provision of international environmental public goods, consider the case where there are n countries, of which m ($m \leq n$) is the minimum number of contributors needed to provide the good. That is, there is some threshold number of countries needed before the good can be supplied. Under a best-shot supply technology it follows that $m = 1$, since a single country is sufficient to secure the public good. Under a weakest-link supply technology, on the other hand, $m = n$ since every country must at least match the contribution of every other in order to supply the public good (Holzinger 2008). Under a step or the threshold supply technology, m defines the minimum number of contributors needed to assure provision at the threshold level. One example of thresholds of this kind in MEAs would be the number of ratifying parties needed before the agreement comes into force (Sandler 2008). Another example would be the number of countries required to protect the habitat of migratory species.

If there is a minimum number m of contributors needed to generate the public good (with $m < n$), the strategic options open to individual countries will generally have the structure of a chicken game, since each country would prefer others to carry the cost of providing the public good. For example, suppose that in a three-country world conservation of a threatened species requires cooperation between at least two countries to secure the minimum viable protected area. The payoffs under alternative strategies can be described by $\begin{pmatrix} B_{c,cc} & B_{c,cd} & B_{c,dc} & B_{c,dd} \\ B_{d,cc} & B_{d,cd} & B_{d,dc} & B_{d,dd} \end{pmatrix}$ in which, for example, $B_{c,dd}$ describes the benefit of provision to the first country if it cooperates and both other countries defect. The best option from the perspective of the first country would be to free-ride on the efforts of the other two countries. A second-best option would be for all three to establish protected areas. A third-best option would be for the first country to share provision with one other country. A fourth-best option would be for all countries to defect. The worst possible option would be for the first country to commit land to protection, but for both other countries to defect so failing to reach the threshold level of provision.

To illustrate, consider the payoffs in Figure 5.4 which have the same structure as an example by Sollars (2003). There are three Nash equilibria in this case: the first where all countries cooperate, the second where two cooperate and one defects, and the third where all defect. The last is a coordination equilibrium, and is less preferred to either of the others.

Suppose that it was not possible for any two countries to cooperate because, say, conservation activities occurred in an area beyond national jurisdiction without any framework for agreement (see, for example, Hampton 1987). While each country might want conservation of the threatened species to occur, in the absence of coordination the public good would not be delivered at all. This problem has the structure of a battle of the sexes game.

		Countries 2, 3			
		c,c	c,d	d,c	d,d
Country 1	c	2,2,2	3,3,1	3,1,3	5,4,4
	d	1,3,3	4,5,4	4,4,5	**4,4,4**

Figure 5.3 The payoffs to conservation in a three-country world with a two-country threshold of provision. Strategic options are to cooperate, "c", or defect, "d". Each cell describes the payoff to the first, second, and third countries given the strategies indicated in the row and column heads. Nash equilibria are shaded grey, coordination equilibria are in bold type.

		Countries 2, 3			
		c,c	c,d	d,c	d,d
Country 1	c	3,3,3	**2,2,1**	**2,2,1**	3,3,3
	d	**1,2,2**	3,3,3	3,3,3	**3,3,3**

Figure 5.4 Payoffs to conservation in a three-country world with a two-country threshold of provision but no mechanism for coordination. Strategic options are to cooperate, "c", or defect, "d". Each cell describes the payoff to the first, second, and third countries given the strategies indicated in the row and column heads. Nash equilibria are shaded grey, coordination equilibria are in bold type.

For a third example, suppose that the threshold of provision was such that all countries had to cooperate for the public good to be supplied. This would be the case in, for example, public goods supplied using weakest-link technologies. Using a numerical example from the same source (Figure 5.5), we can see that each country would prefer cooperation to the case in which the group fails to form: i.e. $B_{c,cc}$ dominates $B_{d,dd}$ for all countries. Since defection by just one country will cause provision to fall short of the threshold, however, the worst outcome is for two cooperating countries to carry the cost of provision without achieving anything because the third country has failed to cooperate. There are just two equilibria: one in which all countries commit to meeting the threshold, the other where no country meets the threshold.

		Countries 2, 3			
		c,c	c,d	d,c	d,d
Country 1	c	**1,1,1**	3,3,2	3,2,3	3,2,2
	d	2,3,3	2,3,2	2,2,3	**2,2,2**

Figure 5.5 Payoffs to conservation in a three-country world with a three-country threshold of provision. Strategic options are to cooperate, "c", or defect, "d". Each cell describes the payoff to the first, second, and third countries given the strategies indicated in the row and column heads. Nash equilibria are shaded grey, coordination equilibria are in bold type.

Since all countries prefer cooperation, this induces the matching behavior associated with a stag hunt or assurance game.

Less extreme supply technologies, such as weaker-link or better-shot technologies, allow unilateral actions by one country to have a positive impact on supply of the public good, and hence imply weaker threshold conditions. In better-shot cases, for example, the greatest marginal gain from unilateral actions is derived from the country already making the highest overall level of contribution. But contributions by others can also have a measurable effect on the supply of the public good. The strategic interactions among countries involved in the supply of better-shot public goods still have the structure of a chicken game, and so an incentive to free-ride on the efforts of others (Arce and Sandler 2001).

So for public goods characterized by an additive supply technology, the strategic problem is characterized by the prisoner's dilemma game so long as the country-level benefits are lower than the country-level costs of provision. In such cases, the dominant strategy of countries is to free-ride on provision of the public good by others (Holzinger 2001; Sandler 2004). But for best-shot, better-shot, or weaker-link environmental public goods, there are no dominant strategies. The strategy that any one country will adopt will depend on the action taken by other countries. In most cases, countries will opt to take unilateral action rather than lose the environmental public good altogether, but they do face an incentive to defect if other countries commit to the provision of the public good.

For weakest-link or threshold public goods, countries will contribute to the public good only if they believe that enough other countries will contribute to meet the threshold. If not, it is in their best interests to defect. If there are enough co-contributors to meet the threshold, it is in their interest to cooperate. For threshold (or step) public goods there is no payoff to unilateral action if the threshold (step) cannot be met. Nor, in the case of step public goods, is there any benefit to contributing once other countries have provided the minimum amount. The strategic problem once again has the structure of a chicken game, although it is possible that a group of countries emerge that are able to sustain cooperation at the threshold (step) level, in which case defection of other countries will have no consequences for global provision of the public good.

5.5 Biodiversity-related international public goods

What, then, are the consequences of the public good nature of biodiversity and many of the ecosystem services it supports? While all public goods tend to be undersupplied, and while this is particularly problematic at the international scale, what this tells us is that the extent of the problem varies between public goods with different supply technologies, threshold levels of supply, and threshold numbers of contributing countries. To give a sense of which biodiversity-related international public goods are most at risk, it is worth characterizing the most important of them in these terms. Table 5.1 identifies a number of ecosystem services for which the functional diversity of supporting species is critical, and characterizes them in terms of the structure of payoffs and properties of public goods – whether they are pure or impure, local or global, what supply technology they have, and what the structure of strategic problem looks like. It also identifies the system of governance applying to their provision.

The table covers a wide range of public goods. Many are supplied as joint products, some being complements, others substitutes. Many offer distinct benefits at different scales. Some are subject to formal agreement, others are not. Moreover, while some are defined by the biophysical properties of the system, others are socially constructed. That is, they are non-exclusive not because of their biophysical properties but because of a set of socially constructed access rules.

The MA's provisioning services are typically private goods, but all depend on environmental resources that are collectively owned. Common pool resources can be thought of as part of the environmental

Table 5.1 *Ecosystem services that are international environmental public goods*

Environmental action	Ecosystem service and geographic scale	Pure, impure public good, supply technology	Current governance
Conservation of endangered species	Cultural, local to global	Pure public good Additive: e.g. endangered species census or the size of an ecosystem left aside for conservation Better shot: e.g. protection of a given endangered species; Weakest/weaker link: e.g. controlling illegal trade, or conservation of a meta-population Threshold: e.g. maintaining a minimum size habitat or corridors	Local-national regulation, PA, MEA
Conservation of genetic information	Provisioning or cultural, local to global	Pure public good Additive: e.g. *in situ* conservation policies Better shot: e.g. establishment of gene banks	Local-national regulation, PA, MEA
Conservation of harvested wild-living resources	Provisioning, regional to global	Common pool resource. Additive: e.g. establishing harvesting quotas in fisheries	Local-national regulation, PA, MEA

Table 5.1 (*cont.*)

Environmental action	Ecosystem service and geographic scale	Pure, impure public good, supply technology	Current governance
Protection of sites of special scientific interest, religious or cultural significance	Cultural, local to global	Joint product Best, better shot, weighted sum: e.g. establishment of World Heritage Sites	Local protection, PA, SPP
Management of infectious disease	Regulating, local to global	Impure public good Weaker, weakest link: e.g. monitoring/ controlling a disease outbreak Threshold: e.g. reducing basic reproduction ratio below one	Local-national regulation, MEA
Quarantine, port inspections	Regulating, local to global	Impure public good Weaker, weakest link	Local-national regulation, MEA
Pest and invasive species control	Regulating, local to global	Impure public good Weakest link: e.g. eradicating a pest species Weaker link: e.g. controlling invasive species	Local-national regulation, MEA
Vaccine development	Regulating, local to global	Pure public good Best, better shot: creation of centers for developing new vaccines for infectious diseases	Local-national regulation, MEA
Information about disease/pest/ invasive risks	Regulating, local to global	Pure public good Better shot: e.g. building pest databases	Local-national regulation, MEA

Table 5.1 (*cont.*)

Environmental action	Ecosystem service and geographic scale	Pure, impure public good, supply technology	Current governance
Storm and flood protection	Regulating, local to regional	Weakest link: e.g. reporting pest/ invasive species outbreaks Pure public good Weighted sum: e.g. maintenance of coastal barriers Weakest link: e.g. maintaining integrity of protective dykes	Local-national regulation
Coastal protection	Regulating, local to regional	Additive: e.g. maintenance of mangrove systems	Local-national regulation, MEA
Watershed or shared lake protection	Regulating, local to regional	Joint products Additive: e.g. reducing pollution to perfectly mixed lake Weighted sum: e.g. protecting watersheds that span jurisdictions Weakest link: e.g. setting pollution standards	Local-national regulation, MEA

Notes: Additive: prisoner's dilemma if benefits less than costs, chicken if inaction has very high cost; better shot: chicken game; weaker link: assurance game or chicken game if strong diminishing returns; threshold: assurance game if minimum size group known, otherwise chicken or battle of the sexes; SPP: state–private partnership; PA: protected area. For further details on international actions on human, animal and plant health, and air quality see Barrett (2003a); Sandler (2004); Barrett (2007b); on species conservation see Holzinger (2001, 2008); and on water management see Dombrowsky (2007).

Source: adapted from Touza and Perrings (2011).

infrastructure that supports the production of foods, fuels, and fibers. More of the MA's cultural services are public goods, and their supply – through conservation, preservation, or legal protection – frequently lies outside the market. World Heritage Sites, international wildlife parks or reserves, and *ex situ* global collections are examples. The regulating services are almost always supplied as public goods, even when they regulate the production of private goods. For example, the regulatory benefits offered by crop genetic diversity in agriculture operate all the way from the local to the global scale.

Equally important is the fact that many environmental public goods are jointly produced both with other public goods and with private goods and services, and that many of these public goods are produced at different spatial and temporal scales (Perrings and Gadgil 2003). For example, tropical forests are the source of a set of private benefits (e.g. timber, medicinal plants, hunting, fishing, recreation, and tourism), but they also yield a number of public goods. Some of these are global such as carbon sequestration and genetic information, and some are local such as the regulation of the hydrological cycle, or microclimatic regulation (Imai *et al.* 2009).

To summarize what we now know about incentives to provide international environmental public goods, the incentive to countries to free-ride on others is greatest in the case of additive supply technologies such as the conservation of endangered species, harvested wild-living species in areas beyond national jurisdiction, flood or coastal protection. It is least in the case of weakest-link technologies such as the management of infectious disease, quarantine and port inspections, pest control, or the eradication of invasive species. The incentive to individual countries to act unilaterally is greatest in the case of best-shot supply technologies such as vaccine development, or the provision of information about pest and pathogen risks. It is least in the case of additive technologies of the kind already described.

The likelihood that a country will seek to free-ride on others also depends on the net costs and benefits of public good provision. The joint production of public goods can significantly reduce the cost of their provision, as can their purity/impurity – whether they generate privately capturable benefits in addition to any non-capturable public benefit. Biodiversity conservation is an impure global public good since it yields both nationally capturable benefits, as well as a set of non-exclusive and non-rival benefits to the global community. The greater the nationally capturable benefits of environmental public good provision, and the greater the complementarity between these locally capturable benefits and the benefits to the wider community, the greater will be the incentive to provide the international environmental public good independent of the choices made by other countries. It follows that impure public goods such as the management of infectious disease, quarantine and port inspections, pest control, or the eradication of invasive species are likely to be provided not just because of the incentive to adopt matching strategies, but also because of the nationally capturable benefits secured by their provision.

Whether countries are able to capture the benefits of public good provision is, to a large degree, determined by the system of governance applied (Perrings 2012). Factors that are important to the efficiency of governance structure include the degree to which they permit exclusive use of environmental resources, the number of parties involved, the penalties for defection, the frequency of interaction between parties, and the symmetry between or homogeneity of parties. The point has already been made that many environmental resources are non-exclusive because of social rules of access rather than the properties of the resource itself. Environmental resources that are open access but also scarce are almost always overexploited: this is the tragedy of the commons although the reasons why it occurs are different from those noted in Hardin's original paper on the subject (Hardin 1968). By contrast, environmental public goods that are managed to deliver at least some capturable benefits by restricting access are frequently supplied at close to the socially optimal level.[4]

The number of parties involved in a system of governance is also important for its effectiveness. Barrett's analysis of the effectiveness of MEAs showed, for example, that the benefits they are able to deliver over and above the non-cooperative outcome are closely related to the number of parties to the agreement. For the case of biodiversity conservation, he showed the maximum number of countries that can sustain cooperation is determined by the ratio of the costs and benefits of the transfers needed to secure biodiversity conservation. Specifically, the larger the net benefits of cooperation, the smaller the number of countries that can sustain the cooperative outcome (Barrett 1994).

---

[4] For evidence of the effectiveness of local rules of management for common pool resources see the literature that builds on the seminal contribution by Ostrom (1990).

In addition, since governance structures at the international level need to be self-enforcing (there is no sovereign authority with an enforcement mandate), they need to contain disincentives to defect from an agreed course of action. Ordinarily this is achieved by penalties on (or payments to) non-contributors to offset the attraction of defection. In many cases, however, the adoption of cost sharing rules can achieve the same effect without incurring the costs involved in setting up and implementing transfer systems (Sandler 2004).

At the same time, the frequency with which parties interact affects the likelihood of cooperation. Repeated interactions allow experience of the effect of past interactions to inform future strategies – even in strategic problems as difficult as the prisoner's dilemma. This is because uncooperative behavior generally induces tit-for-tat behavior (Axelrod 1984). Indeed, many governance structures now institutionalize repeated interactions. At the international level the most effective multilateral agreements are those that involve a small number of signatories, repeated renegotiation, and that include effective penalties or disincentives to defect from a precisely defined set of objectives (Barrett 2003a, 2007b).

Finally, the asymmetry between countries is important. Differences in the value countries attach to different kinds of benefits, and differences in their capacity to provide public goods, both affect countries' willingness to commit to cooperative action. Indeed, differences of this kind are among the most frequently cited explanations for the failure of agreements like the UN Framework Convention on Climate Change (UNFCCC) to attract general support. Such differences require benefit sharing of the kind envisaged in the CBD (Perrings *et al.* 2011; Touza and Perrings 2011). Countries that benefit most from biodiversity conservation need to offer side payments to countries that benefit the least, providing an inducement to participate in an agreement that otherwise offers few advantages (Barrett 1994). Similar arrangements have been important in, for example, the global eradication of diseases (Barrett 2003b, 2007a).

5.6 Externalities and public goods in context

Returning to the ecosystem services described in Table 5.1, we can readily identify three vulnerable categories of ecosystem service. First, the international environmental public goods that are most vulnerable to free-riding behavior and that are most likely to be undersupplied are those for which the supply technology is additive, the cost of provision is high, and the number of countries involved is large: the *in situ* conservation of threatened species, the protection of the global gene pool, and the conservation of harvested wild-living resources from ecosystems beyond national jurisdiction. For this class of biodiversity-related international public goods, cooperation and unilateral action are least likely and defection most likely. The problem is lessened if public goods of this kind are jointly produced (reducing the national cost of provision) and yield nationally capturable benefits (increasing the national benefits of provision). Indeed, if the balance between nationally capturable costs and benefits changes enough, the structure of the strategic problem changes from that associated with the prisoner's dilemma to that associated with the harmony game, where it is in the best interests of individual countries to supply the global public good. For similar reasons, weighted sum public goods may be less problematic than one would expect. Examples include protection against storm damage and flood protection, in which the marginal impact of the contribution of each country varies with local environmental conditions. Weighted sum technologies are still additive, and so still contain an incentive to free-ride on the efforts of others, but local conditions affect the costs and benefits of local provision of the public good, and hence the payoffs to national action. If nationally capturable benefits are high enough, national provision will be encouraged.

A second vulnerable category involves public goods where benefits are limited by the capacity of the least effective country (in the weakest-link case) or group of countries (in the weaker-link case): i.e. the management of infectious disease, quarantine, port inspections, pest control, and the eradication of invasive species. While problems of this kind induce a matching strategy, the public good is still under-supplied relative to demand by either all but one, or a majority of countries. Of course, countries with the greatest capacity do have a positive incentive to invest in the capacity of the weakest or weaker links in the chain, and many multilateral agreements require this. Two examples we will come back to later are the SPS Agreement and the IHR. Both require high-income countries to invest in the capacity of low-income countries to comply with the terms of those agreements (Perrings *et al.* 2010a, 2010b).

The final category of international environmental public goods described in Table 5.1 is the least problematic of all. Best-shot, better-shot, and (some) threshold public goods, such as vaccine development, or the provision of information about potentially invasive pests and pathogens, will generally be supplied at close to the socially optimal level. Although each country would prefer others to carry the cost of provision, these public goods will generally be provided by unilateral action on the part of the countries that stand to gain the most from provision of the public good. The fact that other countries free-ride on their efforts in this case has no effect on the level of benefits enjoyed by all.

For at least the first two of these categories, the fundamental problem is that landholders lack effective signals about the wider effects of their own actions. More generally, the existence of biodiversity externalities is evidence that the signals guiding land-use decisions give little information about the impacts of those decisions on biodiversity, and the ecosystem services biodiversity supports. Most of the changes recorded by the MA were not signaled by market prices. Indeed, where market prices did signal the scarcity of resources, as in agriculture, aquaculture, and forestry, the MA recorded dramatic increases in the supply of services. The only exception was marine capture fisheries where markets signaled the scarcity of the service, but not the scarcity of the ecosystems that are the source of the service. In every case, however, there have been a myriad of environmental effects that have gone unnoticed by the market.

Part of the explanation for this lies in the lack of well-defined property rights for those effects. Since market transactions imply exchanges between property rights-holders, the development of markets implies the emergence of property rights. The fact that property rights have failed to emerge has many causes: among them the high cost of establishing new property rights, the existence of already entrenched rights that, in some sense, authorize the externality, and the public good nature of the external effects. Private actions that, for example, incrementally build pressure on wild-living species, that incrementally reduce crop genetic diversity, or that incrementally change the risks posed by emerging zoonotic diseases, all threaten public goods for which no markets exist. Biodiversity change is being directed by signals that are uninformed by its scarcity. How serious a problem that is depends in part on the nature of the public goods involved. Since countries behave strategically, the outcome in any particular case depends on the options open to it and other countries, and on the payoffs to the selection of different options by all countries. What we know about the structure of public good problems tells us that their choices are likely to impose much higher costs on global society for some problems than for others. Understanding this is critical to the development of solutions.

Externality and the public good nature of many ecosystem services may lie at the heart of the biodiversity change problem, but it is worth underlining the fact that they are not the only drivers of biodiversity change. Nor do they exist in a vacuum. They are the product of a set of feedbacks that at once reflects an evolving set of property rights, technological change, the homogenization of managed/impacted ecosystems, and the fact that the global economic and ecological systems are both becoming increasingly integrated. Moreover, their significance depends heavily on the distribution of income and assets. While we all carry the cost of a decline in the global gene pool, loss of the public benefits provided by common pool resources tends to weigh most heavily on poor people and poor countries. In the following chapters I consider both the relation between biodiversity change and poverty, and the effect of the closer integration of the global system.

References

Anand, P. (2004) Financing the provision of public goods. *The World Economy*, 27, 215–237.

Arce, D. G. and Sandler, T. (2001) Transnational public goods: strategies and institutions. *European Journal of Political Economy*, 17, 493–516.

Arriagada, R. and Perrings, C. (2011) Paying for international environmental public goods. *Ambio*, 1–9.

Axelrod, R. (1984) *The Evolution of Cooperation*. Basic Books, New York.

Barrett, S. (1994) The biodiversity supergame. *Environmental and Resource Economics*, 4, 111–122.

(2003a) Global disease eradication. *Journal of the European Economic Association*, 1, 591–600.

(2003b) *Environment and Statecraft: The Strategy of Environmental Treaty-Making*. Oxford University Press.

(2007a) *Why Cooperate? The Incentive to Supply Global Public Goods*. Oxford University Press.

(2007b) The smallpox eradication game. *Public Choice*, 130, 179–207.

Carpenter, S., Ludwig, D. and Brock, W. (1999) Management of eutrophication for lakes subject to potentially irreversible change. *Ecological Applications*, 9, 751–771.

Carraro, C. and Siniscalco, D. (1996) *Environmental Fiscal Reform and Unemployment*. Kluwer, Dordrecht.

Crocker, T. D. and Tschirhart, J. (1992) Ecosystems, externalities, and economics. *Environmental Resource Economics*, 2, 551–567.

Dombrowsky, I. (2007) *Conflict, Cooperation and Institutions in International Water Management: And Economic Analysis*. Edward Elgar, Cheltenham.

Goodall, J., Maynard, T. and Hudson, G. (2009) *Hope for Animals and Their World: How Endangered Species are Being Rescued from the Brink*. Grand Central Publishing, New York.

Hampton, J. (1987) Free-rider problems in the production of collective goods. *Economics and Philosophy*, 3, 245–273.

Hardin, G. (1968) The tragedy of the commons. *Science*, 162, 1243–1248.

Holling, C. S. (1973) Resilience and stability of ecological systems. *Annual Review Ecology and Systematics*, 4, 1–23.

Holzinger, K. (2001) Aggregation technology of common goods and its strategic consequences: global warming, biodiversity, and sitting conflicts. *European Journal of Political Research*, 40, 117–138.

(2008) Treaty formation and strategic constellations: a comment on treaties – strategic considerations. *University of Illinois Law Review*, 1, 187–200.

Imai, N., Samejima, H., Langner, A., Ong, R. C., Kita, S., Titin, J., Chung, A. Y. C., Lagan, P., Lee, Y. F. and Kitayama, K. (2009) Co-benefits of sustainable forest management in biodiversity conservation and carbon sequestration. *PLoS One*, 4, e8267.

Kanbur, R. (2003) IFIs and IPGs: operational implications for the World Bank. *Challenges to the World Bank and IMF: Developing Country Perspectives* (ed. A. Buira), pp. 251–266. Anthem Press, London.

(2004) Cross-border externalities, international public goods and their implications for aid agencies. *Global Tensions: Challenges and Opportunities in the World Economy* (ed. L. Beneria and S. Bisnath), pp. 65–75. Routledge, New York.

Kaul, I., Grunberg, I. and Stern, M. (1999) Defining global public goods. *Global Public Goods: International Cooperation in the 21st Century* (ed. I. Kaul, I. Grunberg and M. Stern). Oxford University Press.

Kaul, I., Conceição, P., Le Goulven, K. and Mendoza, R. (2003) How to improve the provision of global public goods. *Providing Global Public Goods: Managing Globalization* (ed. I. Kaul, P. Conceição, K. Le Goulven and R. Mendoza). Oxford University Press.

Kinzig, A. P., Perrings, C., Chapin, F. S., Polasky, S., Smith, V. K., Tilman, D. and Turner, B. L. (2011) Paying for ecosystem services: promise and peril. *Science*, 334, 603–604.

Madsen, B., Carroll, N. and Moore Brands, K. (2010) *Offset and Compensation Programs Worldwide*. Ecosystem Marketplace, Washington, DC.

Millennium Ecosystem Assessment (2005) *Ecosystems and Human Well-being: General Synthesis*. Island Press, Washington, DC.

Morrissey, O., te Velde, D. and Hewitt, A. (2002) Defining international public goods: conceptual issues. *International Public Goods: Incentives, Measurement, and Financing* (ed. M. Ferroni and A. Mody). Kluwer Academic Publishers, Dordrecht.

Murdoch, J. C. and Sandler, T. (2009) The voluntary provision of a pure public good and the Montreal Protocol: behavioral and data concerns. *Oxford Economic Papers*, 61, 197–200.

Ostrom, E. (1990) *Governing the Commons: The Evolution of Institutions for Collective Action*. Cambridge University Press.

Perrings, C. (2012) The governance of international environmental public goods. *Global Environmental Commons: Analytical and Political Challenges in Building Governance Mechanisms* (ed. E. Brousseau, T. Dedeurwaerdere, P.-A. Jouvet and M. Willinger), pp. 54–79. Oxford University Press.

Perrings, C. and Gadgil, M. (2003) Conserving biodiversity: reconciling local and global public benefits. *Providing Global Public Goods: Managing Globalization* (ed. I. Kaul, P. Conceicao, K. Le Goulven and R. L. Mendoza), pp. 532–555. Oxford University Press.

Perrings, C., Mooney, H., Lonsdale, M. and Burgeil, S. (2010a) Globalization and invasive species: policy and management options. *Bioinvasions and Globalization: Ecology, Economics, Management and Policy* (ed. C. Perrings, H. Mooney and M. Williamson), pp. 235–250. Oxford University Press.

Perrings, C., Burgiel, S., Lonsdale, W. M., Mooney, H. and Williamson, M. (2010b) International cooperation in the solution to trade-related invasive species risks. *Annals of the New York Academy of Sciences*, 1195, 198–212.

Perrings, C., Naeem, S., Ahrestani, F., Bunker, D. E., Burkill, P., Canziani, G., Elmqvist, T., Ferrati, R., Fuhrman, J., Jaksic, F., Kawabata, Z., Kinzig, A., Mace, G. M., Milano, F., Mooney, H., Prieur-Richard, A.-H., Tschirhart, J. and Weisser, W. (2011) Ecosystem services, targets, and indicators for the conservation and sustainable use of biodiversity. *Frontiers in Ecology and the Environment*, 9, 512–520.

Perrings, C., Williamson, M., Barbier, E. B., Delfino, D., Dalmazzone, S., Shogren, J., Simmons, P. and Watkinson, A. (2002) Biological invasion risks and the public good: an economic perspective. *Conservation Ecology*, 6, www.consecol.org/vol6/iss1/art1.

Reed, D. H., O'Grady, J. J., Brook, B. W., Ballou, J. D. and Frankham, R. (2003) Estimates of minimum viable population sizes for vertebrates and factors influencing those estimates. *Biological Conservation*, 113, 23–34.

Sandler, T. (1997) *Global Challenges*. Cambridge University Press.

(2004) *Global Collective Action*. Cambridge University Press.

(2008) Treaties: strategic considerations. *University of Illinois Law Review*, 1, 155–180.

Sandler, T. and Sargent, K. (1995) Management of transnational commons: coordination, publicness and treaty formation. *Land Economics*, 71, 145–162.

Scheffer, M., Carpenter, S., Foley, J. A., Folke, C. and Walker, B. (2001) Catastrophic shifts in ecosystems. *Nature*, 413, 591–596.

Shaffer, M. L. (1981) Minimum population sizes for species conservation. *BioScience*, 31, 131–134.

Sollars, G. (2003) Discussion: Hampton on free riding. *Economics and Philosophy*, 19, 311–320.

Stavins, R. N. (2003) Experience with market-based environmental policy instruments. *Handbook of Environmental Economics* (ed. K.-G. Mäler and J. R. Vincent), pp. 355–435. Elsevier, Amsterdam.

Tietenberg, T. (1990) Economic instruments for environmental regulation. *Oxford Review of Economic Policy*, 6, 17–33.

Tilman, D., Reich, P., Knops, J., Wedin, D., Mielke, T. and Lehman, C. (2001) Diversity and productivity in a long-term grassland experiment. *Science*, 294, 843–845.

Touza, J. and Perrings, C. (2011) Strategic behavior and the scope for unilateral provision of transboundary ecosystem services that are international environmental public goods. *Strategic Behavior and the Environment*, 1, 89–117.

6 Poverty alleviation and biodiversity change

6.1 Stating the problem

The Brundtland Report made a strong connection between environmental change and poverty. It argued that since poverty was both a cause and an effect of global environmental change it was "futile to attempt to deal with environmental problems without a broader perspective that encompasses the factors underlying world poverty and international inequality" (World Commission on Environment and Development 1987). The report asserted that there was a positive feedback between poverty and environmental degradation:

Many parts of the world are caught in a vicious downwards spiral: Poor people are forced to overuse environmental resources to survive from day to day, and their impoverishment of their environment further impoverishes them, making their survival ever more difficult and uncertain … the poor and hungry will often destroy their immediate environment in order to survive: They will cut down forests; their livestock will overgraze grasslands; they will overuse marginal land; and in growing numbers they will crowd into congested cities. The cumulative effect of these changes is so far-reaching as to make poverty itself a major global scourge. (World Commission on Environment and Development 1987)

It also noted the coincidence between poverty and species richness in the tropics, and identified the conversion of forest to agriculture in those regions as the primary cause of the loss of wild-living species. One implication of this is that by addressing the problem of poverty in the tropics, we can simultaneously address the problem of biodiversity loss.

Essentially the same arguments have since been made many times. Indeed, anyone with even a passing familiarity with the literature on biodiversity and poverty will have noticed a strongly held conviction among many scientists that poverty alleviation and biodiversity

184

conservation ought to be mutually consistent goals. A good example of this is an important paper by Jeffrey Sachs and others in which the authors argued for the integration of the poverty alleviation and biodiversity conservation agendas, claiming that policies addressing one objective could yield substantial benefits for the other (Sachs *et al.* 2009). In this, and many other cases, the primary link between poverty and biodiversity loss was argued to be population growth. Since fertility rates are typically increasing in poverty (Dasgupta 1995), a reduction in poverty is thought to lead to a reduction in population growth, and hence in demand for agricultural land. Others have focused on the fact that the poor are highly dependent on the resources provided by natural ecosystems to which they have access. More particularly, they have argued that the supply of wild foods obtained from such systems during times of famine, insecurity, or conflict are especially valuable to the poor (Ash and Jenkins 2007). Recent enthusiasm for the development of conservation incentives known as payments for ecosystem services is also fueled by a conviction that the instruments offer at least potential benefits for the poor (Ferraro and Simpson 2002; Pagiola 2002, 2008; Wunder, Engol and Pagiola 2008; Wunder and Wertz-Kanounnikoff 2009).

Yet evidence that poverty alleviation and biodiversity conservation in the poorest countries may be complementary – in the sense that an increase in one implies an increase in the other – is hard to come by. An evaluation of the linkages between poverty and deforestation at the end of the twentieth century found that rising poverty could either increase or slow forest loss, while rising income would generally stimulate forest loss by raising demand for agricultural land (Wunder 2001). There is also long-standing evidence for the persistent failure of integrated conservation and development or community-based natural resource management projects (Wells 1992; Adams *et al.* 2004). Similarly, the evidence for a win–win relation between poverty alleviation and biodiversity conservation through payments for ecosystem services schemes is very weak (Pattanayak, Wunder and Ferraro 2010; Kinzig *et al.* 2011). Indeed, a recent evaluation of the evidence concluded that while many payments for ecosystem services schemes have the potential to provide benefits to the poor, the amount is generally very small relative to governments' poverty alleviation goals. Moreover, government funded schemes in which poverty alleviation is the primary goal are less effective in securing conservation than user-funded schemes that focus on the delivery of specific ecosystem services (Pattanayak *et al.* 2010).

In this chapter I first consider the general relationship between environmental change and the persistence of poverty, and then focus on the specific linkages between threats to biodiversity and the factors behind income growth in poor countries. I ask what the data tell us about the specific relation between changes in income and threats to species. Drawing on collaborative work with George Halkos I show that while the results vary between taxonomic groups, the factors behind income growth in low-income countries are strongly and positively correlated with the number of threatened species in all taxonomic groups tested. The opposite relation holds in middle- and high-income countries. This suggests that if poverty alleviation means income growth through the usual channels, then poverty alleviation and biodiversity conservation are unlikely to be complementary strategies in low-income countries. Indeed, they involve some of the hardest trade-offs the global community has to make. The solution proposed in the Brundtland Report is essentially the same as the solution proposed by the international community today. It is the intensification of agriculture in the tropics. This solution is considered in greater detail in later chapters of this book. At this stage I seek only to show the nature and magnitude of the problem to be overcome.

6.2 Poverty and environmental change

The proximate causes of environmental change are described in detail in Chapters 1 and 2. They include the extensive and intensive growth of agriculture leading, respectively, to the conversion of habitat for agricultural production and the application of fertilizers, herbicides, and pesticides to eliminate crop and livestock pests, predators, and competitors. They also include an increasing pollution burden on ecosystems, the diversion of water and other resources from those systems, and the introduction of invasive species (Millennium Ecosystem Assessment 2005; World Bank 2006; Jones *et al.* 2008; Perrings, Mooney and Williamson 2010). These trends do reduce the income of those who depend on the exploitation of wild-living resources (Naidoo *et al.* 2008). However, they are also critical to the growth of agricultural income and employment – often the first steps to development in poor countries. In one of the more thoughtful reviews of the relation between poverty and environmental change, Anil Markandya suggested that to the question, "does poverty damage the environment?" the answer was "broadly no." To the question "does environmental degradation hurt the poor?" the answer was "broadly yes." Hence he concluded while poverty alleviation would not necessarily enhance environmental quality, and may in fact increase stress on the environment, environmental protection would generally benefit the poor (Markandya 2001).

The picture that comes out of the many case studies of environmental resource use in poor countries is, however, very mixed. For reasons that have long been understood, the scarcity of commodities that satisfy basic needs such as water and fuelwood affect the poor more than the rich (Kumar and Hotchkiss 1988). So it is not surprising that environmental change that reduces the supply of such things should hurt the poor. The relation between poverty alleviation and environmental change is, however, altogether less clear (Perrings 2007).

One issue is the measure of poverty itself. Of the many available poverty indices most involve some measure of income or consumption. This is sometimes combined with other indicators such as literacy, life expectancy, or vulnerability (see, for example, Duclos, Sahn and Younger 2006). However, the effect of including non-income variables is seldom significant, the outcome being similar to that observed when poverty is measured in terms of income only (Deutsch and Silber 2005). Of the indicators applied in intercountry comparisons, the most frequently used are the percentage of a country's population lying below a national or an international poverty line such as $1 per day or $2 per day (adjusted for purchasing power parity) (World Bank 2009), and two multidimensional indices – the Human Development Index (HDI) and Human Poverty Index (United Nations Development Programme 2007). All of these indicators turn out to be highly correlated with a conventional measure of average income, per capita GDP.[1]

The question is how do changes in income affect the environment? We have already seen that the connection is frequently argued to be via the impact of income change on population growth. There is, however, good reason to believe that there are two effects at work – each pointing in a different direction. One is the effect on fertility. Dasgupta's

[1] For low-income countries that may benefit from international development assistance and other international transfers a better measure may be per capita gross national income, but either way income is the most reliable measure to use.

investigation of the connection between poverty, fertility decisions, and environmental change concluded that both fertility decisions and the use made of environmental resources are strongly influenced by the long-term security of household income. Where poor households have low expectations of secure future income, they respond by increasing fertility rates. This, in turn, increases pressure on the environment. He found this to be particularly marked where access to environmental resources was unregulated. Moreover, since unregulated access to environmental resources itself increases uncertainty about future income, he argued that there is a positive feedback between poverty, fertility decisions, and environmental degradation (Dasgupta 1993, 2001).

The other is the effect on mortality. Declining mortality is often implicated as the main driver in the growth phases of the demographic transition. It is frequently associated with improving living standards – enhancements in sanitation, safety standards, and health care that are a concomitant of income growth. There is a close link between this and human migration. A study of deforestation in Belize in the late twentieth century, for example, found that in-migration accounted for around one-third of deforestation in that country (Lopez and Scoseria 1996). In-migration is frequently driven by at least the perception of greater opportunities in the destination area, and is usually a feature of either local or regional economic growth poles (Todaro 1969; Lall, Selod and Shalizi 2006; Mansoor and Quillin 2007).

Population growth from all sources has been implicated in environmental degradation in low-income countries for at least two decades (De Janvry and Garcia 1988; Lopez 1992; Cleaver and Schreiber 1994), but even there the evidence is mixed. Sub-Saharan Africa has provided some well-known counter examples, where population growth has stimulated productivity increases that have more than compensated for any reduction in environmental resources (Pingali, Bigot and Binswanger 1987; Tiffen, Mortimore and Gichuki 1994). Heath and Binswanger, using the cases of Kenya and Ethiopia, argued that whether or not population growth has had adverse effects on the environment in poor countries depends strongly on institutional conditions (Heath and Binswanger 1996).

Where the evidence does appear to support a positive relation between poverty and environmental change is in the depreciation of non-marketed environmental assets. There are no very good data on this, but the best current measures – the World Bank's adjusted net savings rate (World Bank 2010) and the inclusive wealth index (UNU–IHDP and UNEP 2012) – both indicate that in some poor countries the depreciation of environmental assets exceeds savings from income. Adjusted net savings modifies conventional measures of savings by subtracting the depreciation not only of produced capital, but also of human and natural or environmental capital.

Originally defined as genuine savings (Hamilton and Clemens 1999) or genuine investment (Dasgupta and Mäler 2000; Dasgupta 2001), adjusted net savings can be thought of as a measure of the change in a country's total wealth – both monetary and non-monetary. Estimates of adjusted net savings are generally lower than other savings measures, reflecting the depreciation or degradation of environmental assets. In fact, once population growth is taken into account many of the poorer regions of the world experienced negative changes in wealth per head during the last three decades of the twentieth century. In Sub-Saharan Africa, for example, annual per capita changes in wealth averaged –3.4 percent between 1965 and 1996. In other words, Africans lost almost half of their average wealth in that period (Dasgupta 2001).

The changes recorded in the adjusted net savings measures reflect the effect of both public and private investment strategies. Consider, for example, the contrasting cases of Botswana and Namibia. After independence in 1996 the government of Botswana chose to reinvest the profits (technically, the rents) from the mining sector to build both human and produced capital, by investing in education and infrastructure. Namibia did not. The result is that whereas Botswana tripled its per capita wealth in the last three decades of the twentieth century, Namibia's per capita wealth declined. In the 1980s Namibia's per capita wealth was 75 percent greater than Botswana's. By the end of the 1990s it was only 33 percent of Botswana's (Lange 2004). But changes in adjusted net savings also reflect the conversion of environmental assets by millions of independent rural households, and that is more directly influenced by poverty. In the same period, for example, there was concern that the rural poor were locked into unsustainable patterns of resource use, while a decline in agricultural extension services and marketing support were both depressing rural incomes and narrowing rural investment options (see, for example, Birdsall and Londono 1997). The effect was a widespread reduction in soil fertility, an increase in soil erosion, and the deterioration of infrastructure.

Table **6.1** *Regional and global poverty estimates*

	2005	2010	2015	2005	2010	2015
	Number of poor (millions)			Poverty rate (% population)		
East Asia	304.5	140.4	53.4	16.8	7.4	2.7
Europe and Central Asia	16.0	8.4	4.3	3.4	1.8	0.9
Latin America and Caribbean	45.0	35.0	27.3	8.4	6.2	4.5
Middle East and North Africa	9.4	6.7	5.4	3.8	2.5	1.9
South Asia	583.4	317.9	145.2	40.2	20.3	8.7
Sub-Saharan Africa	379.5	369.9	349.9	54.5	46.9	39.3
World	1,337.8	878.2	585.5	25.7	15.8	9.9

Source: Chandy and Gertz (2011).

Adjusted net savings rates since 2000 have been significantly higher than in the last three decades of the twentieth century. At the same time estimates of most measures of poverty have shown poverty to be declining. Indeed, before the recent recession the World Bank's ten-year projection of extreme poverty (the number of people living on less than $1.25 a day in 2005 prices) showed falling poverty rates in all regions except Sub-Saharan Africa (World Bank 2005). Nor has the recession had as large an effect as might have been expected. A recent Brookings Institution report, for example, argues that extreme poverty reduction has been much more rapid than expected in every region of the world. Even in Sub-Saharan Africa, they calculated that extreme poverty, which had stood at 55 percent in 2005, had already fallen below 50 percent by 2010, and was expected to be below 40 percent by 2015 (Table 6.1) (Chandy and Gertz 2011). These projections assume no change in the distribution of income across society, which is manifestly not the case, but the general picture is nevertheless clear. Poverty alleviation strategies have had an effect on the real incomes of people in almost all poor countries. The effect is very uneven. The large South and East Asian countries account for most poverty reduction, and Sub-Saharan Africa still experiences the consequences of the long decline in the last part of the twentieth century. But per capita incomes have generally been increasing.

What does this mean for environmental change? Recall that Markandya's answer to the question "does poverty damage the environment?" was "broadly no," and to the question "would poverty alleviation enhance environmental quality," "not necessarily" (Markandya 2001). Since poverty alleviation by definition enhances income, the implied question is whether the growth of income enhances biodiversity conservation. There is a school of thought that holds that all income growth is environmentally harmful and should be stopped (see, for example, Czech, Krausman and Devers 2000). While it would be unconscionable for anyone living in the affluent North to deny those in the South the opportunity to move out of poverty, it is at least worth posing the following questions: how is income growth related to biodiversity threats, and does the relationship between income growth and biodiversity change depend on the level of income?

6.3 Modeling the relation between income growth and biodiversity change

There is a very large literature, stimulated by Grossman and Krueger's assessment of the environmental implications of Mexico's inclusion in the NAFTA (Grossman and Krueger 1995), devoted to understanding the empirical relation between per capita income and environmental change. Grossman and Krueger showed that certain indicators of environmental quality might be expected first to deteriorate and then to improve as per capita incomes rose. Since this mirrored a relation between income and income inequality uncovered much earlier by Simon Kuznets (Kuznets 1966), this relation was dubbed "the environmental Kuznets curve." The relation between per capita income and various indicators of environmental change have since been studied, using a range of databases and econometric approaches.[2] An inverted U-shaped curve was found for the relation between per capita income and various atmospheric pollutants using both cross-sectional and panel data (Seldon and Song 1994; Shafik 1994; Cole, Rayner and Bates 1997; Stern and Common 2001); but the relation is by no means consistent. For some measures of environmental quality the relation with per capita income has been found to be monotonically increasing (for example, carbon dioxide or municipal waste) or decreasing (for example, fecal coliform in drinking water). Moreover,

---

[2] For a review of this literature see Stern (2004).

even where the best fit is given by a quadratic function – the inverted "U" – there are wide discrepancies in estimations of the turning point, or the level of per capita income at which the particular measure of environmental quality starts to improve as per capita incomes rise (Carson 2010).

The relation between biodiversity and income has been approached in three different ways in this literature, depending on the proxy for biodiversity loss (since there are no direct measures). The first takes deforestation to be a proxy for biodiversity loss. This approach appeals to the species–area relationship (MacArthur and Wilson 1967) to explain the link between changes in forest area and biodiversity loss. It also assumes that forests support more species than other biomes. The evidence for any well-defined relation between income and biodiversity loss using this metric is extremely weak (Dietz and Adger 2003; Mills and Waite 2009). A second approach uses the National Biodiversity Risk Assessment Index (Reyers *et al.* 1998) as the proxy for biodiversity loss. This combines indices of biodiversity pressure, state and response. Researchers using this proxy have also failed to find evidence for a statistically significant relation between the proxy and income per capita (Mozumder, Berrens and Bohara 2006). A third approach has focused on the direct measures of threat contained in the IUCN's Red List. Researchers using this approach find a statistically significant relation between threats to biodiversity and income, but it is not at all consistent across taxa. The relation between the natural log of per capita income and the number of threatened species is linear in the case of plants; "U"-shaped in the case of amphibians, reptiles, fishes, and invertebrates; and inverted "U"-shaped in the case of birds (Naidoo and Adamowicz 2001).

As we saw in Chapter 3, biodiversity generally supports an array of services that yield benefits at several different spatial scales. The local benefits of biodiversity conservation in the poorer regions of the world are likely to be less sensitive to species richness or endemism than the global benefits, and to be more tightly linked to the production of foods, fuels, and fibers (Perrings and Gadgil 2003). What is desirable to conserve if the goal is agricultural yield is not the same as what is desirable to conserve if the goal is protection of the global gene pool. Conservation in agricultural systems means protecting enough diversity to underwrite the productivity of the system, or to assure local flood control, water supply, waste assimilation, soil regeneration, and crop pollination. Since the proportion of the population that directly depends on agriculture, forestry, and fisheries is highest in poor countries, this is the kind of conservation that generally matters in such countries (Perrings 2007). Nor is agriculture unaffected by other species. Weeds, pests, pathogens, competitors, and predators all either increase costs or reduce yields. For the farmer, it is in fact desirable to remove them from the system. Of course farmers may also value biodiversity for aesthetic, spiritual, religious, or totemic reasons, but these two interests may pull in different directions.

The layered nature of the public good also means that there may be other constituencies sharing an interest in the biodiversity affected by agricultural activities. Some of these may be nearby, others at some distance. For many, the biodiversity it is desirable to conserve will be quite different from the diversity that best serves farmers or hunters and gatherers. If there are no mechanisms by which such constituencies can make their preferences known, then their interests will typically be neglected. The most common generic vehicles for conveying the preferences of distant communities are international development assistance and the conservation NGOs, both of which direct resources to local conservation activities in developing countries. The GEF administers a fund that supports local conservation activities that have a global payoff. The specific actions of such bodies are discussed in detail later in this book. Here it is sufficient to note that if we want to understand conservation in the poorest countries, we need to model the effects of international interventions of this kind.

To do this, consider once again the base model discussed in Chapter 4 in which the ith community/country derives utility from both income, y_i, and the non-market benefits of biodiversity as a global public good, $B = B(\gamma) = B\left(s_i, \tilde{S}\right)$, $\tilde{S}$ being the set of species in geographical areas occupied by other countries. The social utility function accordingly has the form $U_i = U_i(y_i, B)$. The question posed in this chapter concerns the relation between y_i and B. To be more specific, let us suppose that $U_i(y_i) = y_i^\alpha$, that $U_i(B_i) = s_i^\beta$, and that the social utility function of the ith country takes the Cobb-Douglas form:

$$U_i = y_i^\alpha s_i^\beta$$

in which y_i denotes per capita income. That is, social utility is assumed to be increasing in income but at a decreasing rate $(0 < \alpha < 1)$.

To address the problem of biodiversity loss, I take s_i to be a measure of biodiversity threat. More particularly I take it to be a measure of the number of species in the ith country at risk by the IUCN Red List, and assume that social utility is non-increasing in threats to biodiversity $(0 \geq \beta$ with β strictly less than zero if social utility declines as threats to biodiversity increase). In other words I suppose that although people may be indifferent to the loss of other species, they do not get satisfaction from species extinctions.

The IUCN Red List is the most commonly used measure of the biodiversity status of a country. It is not yet possible to use this data set to say how threat levels have changed over time at the country level, but the number of threatened species in a country at a moment in time can be taken as a proxy for the impact of land conversion on biodiversity. While something like a fifth of all vertebrate species are classified in the Red List as falling within the classifications critically endangered, endangered, and vulnerable, there is significant variation between taxa. Amphibians, for example, face more than twice the average extinction risk of other taxa.

Both income and the number of species at risk depend on land conversion, denoted A_i. I adopt the simplest functional form for income, summarizing the combined effects of technology, institutions, depreciation, and other factors of production in the exponent of A_i:

$$Y_i = P_i^{-1} A_i^{\gamma}$$

where P_i denotes population. I similarly exploit the basic insights of island biogeography in defining the number of threatened species in a country to be a function of the bioclimatic zone within which the ith country falls, denoted C_i, its total land area, denoted L_i, and the land area converted to alternative uses:

$$s_i = C_i L_i^{\eta} \left(\frac{A_i}{L_i} \right) = C_i L_i^{\eta-1} A_i$$

Other things being equal, large tropical countries have more species potentially at risk than small temperate countries. The number of species actually at risk, however, depends on the proportion of land area converted to alternative uses. So if all land is converted the number of species at risk is at a maximum. We can think about the maximum as the number of species in the country in its natural state, the bioclimatic zone determining the constant in a species–area relationship (MacArthur and Wilson 1967).

The optimal level of land conversion in the ith country is then found by maximizing social utility through choice of the land area converted to alternative uses. The first-order necessary conditions for land conversion to be socially optimal include the requirement that:

$$\frac{\partial U_i}{\partial A_i} = \alpha y_i^{\alpha-1} \frac{\partial y_i}{\partial A_i} s_i^{\beta} + y_i^{\alpha} \beta s_i^{\beta-1} \frac{\partial s_i}{\partial A_i} = 0$$

That is, an increase in the area of land converted for other uses – the area of land committed to development – will have two separate effects on social utility that should be balanced. First, it will increase income. This is the marginal benefit of land conversion. At the same time, however, it will increase the number of species at risk. This is the marginal cost of land conversion. Land conversion should be selected so as to balance the marginal utility of income and the marginal disutility of increasing threats to biodiversity.

Perrings and Halkos (2012) used conditions of this form to specify and estimate an implicit model of threats to biodiversity in which the benefits of conservation to country i included biodiversity-related development assistance, and the costs included forgone income from land conversion. Specifically, we estimated a regression model for each of three taxonomic groups – animals, plants, and birds:

$$\ln s_i^k = \beta_0 + \beta_1 \ln y_i + \beta_2 \ln y_i^2 + \beta_3 \ln W_i + \beta_4 \ln L_i + \beta_5 \ln P_i + \beta_6 C_i + \beta_7 \ln B_i + \varepsilon_i$$

where s_i^k is the number of threatened species of taxonomic group k, y_i is per capita gross national income in country i, W_i is the opportunity cost of land conversion, L_i is the area of land protected, P_i is population density, C_i is climate, and B_i is the change in international biodiversity-related development assistance. The data for GNI, population and protected areas derived from the World Resources Institute online database. Climate is a dummy variable capturing the Koppen–Geiger equatorial climates. Data on biodiversity-related development assistance derived from the OECD. Habitat conversion was measured by the change in forest area between 2000 and 2005, the data deriving from the Global Forest Resources Assessment 2010 (Food and Agriculture Organization 2010).

Table 6.2 *Estimated coefficients in models of the relation between threatened species (mammals, birds, and plants), income, population, area, and biodiversity aid*

	Log mammals	Log birds	Log plants
Constant	−12.782	−24.022	−35.150
	[0.0000]	[0.0000]	[0.0000]
Climate	0.447	0.609	1.780
	[0.0006]	[0.0003]	[0.0000]
Log protected areas	0.520	0.509	0.876
	[0.0000]	[0.0000]	[0.0000]
Log opportunity cost of protected areas	−0.443	−0.422	−0.405
	[0.0000]	[0.0000]	[0.0003]
Log population density	0.303	0.264	0.665
	[0.0004]	[0.0172]	[0.0028]
Log GNI per capita	2.514	5.137	8.015
	[0.0000]	[0.0000]	[0.0000]
Log GNI per capita squared	−0.129	−0.275	−0.454
	[0.0002]	[0.0000]	[0.0000]
Log biodiversity aid	0.047	−0.038	0.145
	[0.4959]	[0.6033]	[0.2067]
R^2-adj	0.61	0.49	0.45
Turning Point	17455	11388	6750

Note: P-values in brackets. Standard errors used are White heteroskedasticity consistent.
Source: Perrings and Halkos (2012).

We found that income increases among the poorest countries were positively correlated with stress on biodiversity. Although the effect was weaker for mammals than it was for birds or plants, it held for all taxonomic groups. We also found that the opportunity cost of protection was negatively related to the number of threatened species for all taxonomic groups. Interestingly, biodiversity aid was insignificant (Table 6.2).

Country characteristics – population, land area, and bioclimatic zone – all turned out to be significant sources of variation in the number of threatened species. The number of threatened mammal species was, for example, 50 percent higher in countries experiencing an equatorial climate relative to countries with other climates after correcting for other

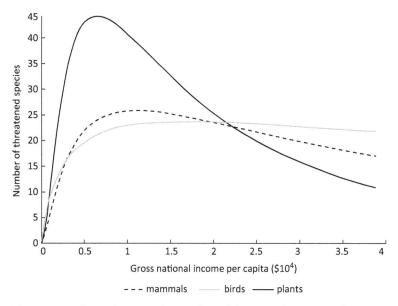

Figure 6.1 Relation between the number of threatened species and per capita income. For all species groups reported the number of threatened species first rises as per capita incomes increase, and then falls. However the turning point differs between species.
Source: Perrings and Halkos (2012).

factors. For birds and plants the corresponding increase in equatorial over other climates was even higher – 78 and 243 percent respectively. Population and land area were similarly associated with increasing threats to biodiversity. Large densely populated countries would be expected to have more threatened species than small sparsely populated countries.

The most striking finding was, however, the relation between the number of threatened species and per capita gross national income. In all cases the number of threatened species was found first to be increasing and then decreasing in income. In other words, while threats to biodiversity were negatively related to income growth in high- and middle-income countries, they were positively related to income growth in the poorest countries (Figure 6.1). While the inverted U-shaped relation was much more marked in the case of plants than in the case of either mammals or birds, it exists (and is significant) for all taxonomic groups. The turning points differ, however, as does the shape of the curve in each case.

The distribution of observations on threatened species is sufficiently skewed to raise concerns that the OLS estimates of the effect of income, climate, land area, and population on the conditional mean of the threatened species in each taxonomic group may not give a true impression of the effect of these variables at either very low or very high levels of threat. To test this we also estimated a set of conditional quantile regression models (Koenker and Basset 1978; Koenker 2005) for each taxonomic group. The results are indicated in Figure 6.2. To read the figure note that the OLS estimates are reflected in the dashed lines, while the quantile regression estimates are reflected in the solid line and band. The figure shows that while the sign and magnitude of effects did not change for most variables at their median values, the same was not necessarily true at either very low or very high levels of threat. Not all taxonomic groups are equally affected, though. The quantile regression estimates for mammals, for example, fall mainly within the 95 percent confidence intervals around the OLS estimates, and in only one case – the impact of habitat conversion on the 95th quantile of threatened species – does the sign on the estimate reverse. For bird species, the OLS estimates overstate the impact of climate, and understate the impact of income at low levels of threat. For plants, the problem again lies at low levels of threat. The OLS results significantly overstate the effect of climate, income, and habitat clearance at low levels of threat.

6.4 Biodiversity and poverty alleviation

There is no fixed relationship between income growth and biodiversity loss. We should expect continued growth in the production of goods and services to affect ecosystems. We should also expect some of the impacts of growth to be negative. Accelerating habitat conversion for the production of foods, fuels, and fibers, industrial and agricultural emissions, water resource depletion, species dispersal, and the homogenization of ecosystems, for example, all have negative implications for the structure and functioning of affected ecosystems. But there is no reason to believe that all growth is environmentally damaging. Nor, on the other hand, is there reason to believe that income growth will, in some sense, take care of the environment. As one of the earliest assessments of the first tranche of findings on the environmental Kuznets curve put it, the problem is not growth itself but the content of growth: the way that environmental resources are used, and the way that waste products are disposed of (Arrow *et al.* 1995).

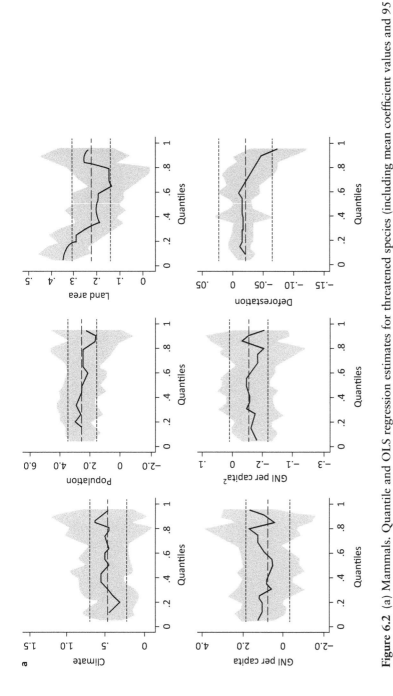

Figure 6.2 (a) Mammals. Quantile and OLS regression estimates for threatened species (including mean coefficient values and 95 percent confidence intervals). The black dashed lines indicate the mean estimates (the OLS estimate) and the dotted lines indicate the 95 percent confidence intervals around those estimates. The solid lines and grey areas indicate the quantile regression estimates, and 95 percent confidence intervals around those estimates.
Source: Author's calculations.

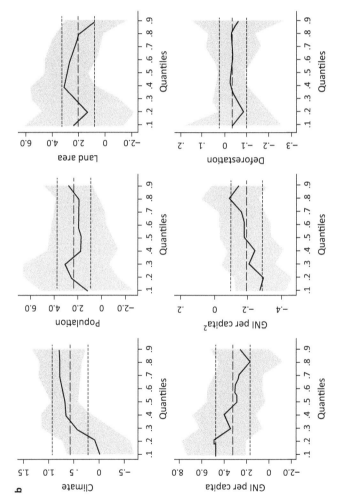

Figure 6.2 (b) Birds. Quantile and OLS regression estimates for threatened species (including mean coefficient values and 95 percent confidence intervals). The black dashed lines indicate the mean estimates (the OLS estimate) and the dotted lines indicate the 95 percent confidence intervals around those estimates. The solid lines and grey areas indicate the quantile regression estimates, and 95 percent confidence intervals around those estimates. *Source:* Author's calculations.

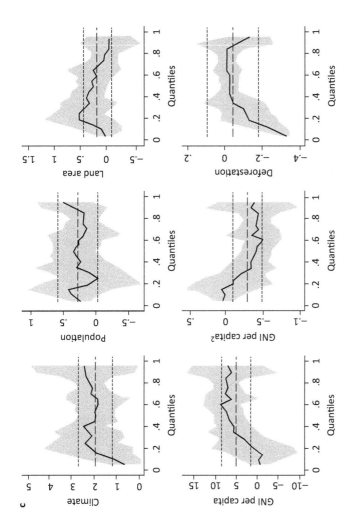

Figure 6.2 (c) Plants. Quantile and OLS regression estimates for threatened species (including mean coefficient values and 95 percent confidence intervals). The black dashed lines indicate the mean estimates (the OLS estimate) and the dotted lines indicate the 95 percent confidence intervals around those estimates. The solid lines and grey areas indicate the quantile regression estimates, and 95 percent confidence intervals around those estimates. *Source:* Author's calculations.

The Brundtland Commission had argued that economic growth could be sustainable provided that it respected environmental limits, restricted demand for energy and materials, and reduced the production and toxicity of waste (World Commission on Environment and Development 1987). In testing the evidence for a relation between biodiversity threats and growth, we found that the growth of agriculture provides a consistent explanation for the number of threatened species in three different taxonomic groups in low-income countries. But we also found that the relation changes as the level of income changes, mainly because the focus switches from extensive to intensive agricultural growth, and the value of remnant wildlands increases. This said, in low-income countries the relation between land conversion for development and threats to endangered species is clear. It is also consistent with what is known about the drivers of extinction risks.

There is broad consensus that habitat conversion for food and biofuel production is the most important factor in extinction risks. Conversion of land to agriculture is, for example, thought to have reduced habitat in affected areas by more than 50 percent (Green *et al.* 2005). It has also been implicated in 80 percent of globally threatened mammals, birds, and plants (Groombridge and Jenkins 2002). It is argued to be the most important threat to the world's 5,500 mammal species, and is a contributory factor in threats to 4,600 plant species. In Sub-Saharan Africa, 457 of the assessed plants and animals on the IUCN Red List that are threatened by agriculture: 65 being critically endangered and 182 endangered. In Latin America, 683 species are threatened by agriculture: 146 being critically endangered and 244 endangered (Vié, Hilton-Taylor and Stuart 2009).

But what are the circumstances in which the extensive growth of resource-based sectors characterizes economic growth? Extensive growth is generally indicative of a moving frontier. Historically, moving frontiers have been associated with the migration of people into new areas, with environmental or technological change that gives access to previously inaccessible resources, or with a combination of the two – the introduction of new technologies through conquest. Migration has many drivers, population growth and the resulting stress on resources among them. Migration is not, of course, the only response to population growth. Indeed, the work of Boserup (1965, 1981) and others (Pingali *et al.* 1987; Tiffen *et al.* 1994) suggests that innovation leading to the intensification of agriculture also occurs. Nevertheless, where scope exists to expand production by appropriating and converting new land, population growth is frequently associated with the extensive growth of food production systems. Indeed, much of the habitat loss identified in the MA is a direct result of the expansion of the area committed to agriculture (Millennium Ecosystem Assessment 2005).

The data show that the extensive growth of agriculture is positively correlated with growth in the number of threatened bird and mammal species, and that this process is observed primarily in low-income countries. There is evidence that the extensive growth of resource-based activities still occurs in middle- and high-income countries. One of the main causes of concern about the development of cellulosic ethanol technology, for example, is the scope it offers for converting remaining marginal lands in many middle- and high-income countries to biofuel production (Gutierrez and Ponti 2009). Nevertheless, the conversion of wildlands to food production is mainly a phenomenon of the low-income countries.

In places where large numbers of people are still in extreme poverty, the highest priorities are to expand the sectors that provide employment and income and to build the infrastructure needed to support market growth. In many such countries the vast majority of people still live in rural areas, and still depend primarily on agriculture. The point was made in chapter 4 that more than two thirds of the population of low income countries make their living in rural areas, mainly from agriculture. Indeed, there are still 23 countries in which more than three quarters of the population live in rural areas, and survive by exploiting natural resources. The main development options they face lie in the growth of agriculture, forestry, or fisheries. These are also the parts of the world where population growth remains highest. Figure 6.3 records population growth rates since the middle of the twentieth century for three groups of countries: more developed, less developed, and least developed. While population growth rates for the majority of developed and developing countries have been declining over this period, they remain persistently high in the least developed countries.

If we focus on the rural population alone, the difference between countries at either end of the income spectrum is even more striking (Figure 6.4). In both high- and middle-income countries, rural population

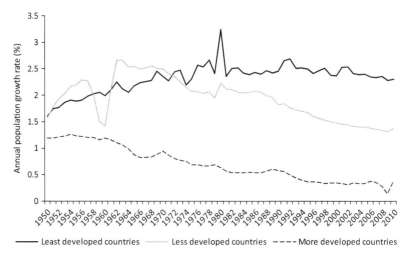

Figure 6.3 Annual population growth rates in more developed and less developed countries, 1950–2010.
Source: data from United States Census Bureau (2012).

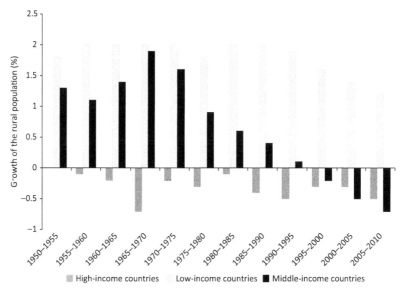

Figure 6.4 Rural population growth rates by income group, 1950–2010.
Source: data from World Resources Institute (2011).

growth rates are currently negative and falling. In the low-income countries, by contrast, they are still positive. Moreover, while average rural population growths rates in low-income countries have been falling since 1990, they are still increasing in a number of countries in Sub-Saharan Africa (specifically in Benin, Burkina Faso, Burundi, Eritrea, Guinea-Bissau, Mauritania, and Uganda). In such countries the extensive growth of agriculture at the expense of habitat for wild-living species is a natural response. It turns out that there is a close spatial correlation between income, engagement in agriculture, and the number of species at risk (Sachs *et al.* 2009). There are certainly differences between taxa. While habitat conversion is a primary threat to both mammal and bird species, for example, it is not as important a driver of threats to plant species. But in all cases, the greatest stress on wild-living species stems from the income-generating activities of people whose alternative investment options are still very limited.

The evidence for an inverted U-shaped relation between threatened species and levels of per capita income indicates that the relation between income growth and biodiversity stress changes as income rises. Although the size of the positive and negative coefficients on per capita income and per capita income squared – and the turning points – vary across taxa, the relation between threatened species and per capita income is quadratic and significant in almost all cases. The quantile regression models show that the relation does not hold for countries where there are currently very few threatened species. But for the rest, the marginal rate of substitution between income and biodiversity does appear to be highest at intermediate levels of income, and to decline at either end of the income scale.

It is important to be clear that there is no basis for assuming a win–win relationship between biodiversity conservation and income growth in biodiversity-rich, poor countries. Nor is it obvious that conservation is always the optimal strategy in low-income countries. Where the simplification of ecosystems to enable the poor to boost their income through the production of foods, fuels, and fibers is the best use of resources, taking all effects into account, that is what should happen. Although all effects are seldom taken into account, there is good reason to believe that in many low-income countries conversion is the locally optimal path.

It is also important to remember that there are two dimensions to agricultural growth. The extensive growth associated with the conversion of forests and grasslands to agriculture is one. Intensive growth deriving from productivity improvements is another. Over the last fifty years, all of the growth of agricultural output in developed countries has resulted from intensification. In fact, agricultural land in developed countries declined by 6 percent between 1961 and 2005. In developing countries, by contrast, increases in agricultural output have resulted largely from extensive growth, and land committed to agriculture increased by 20 percent (Fuglie 2008). While it has provided employment and income for many, the extensive growth of agriculture comes with an international price tag. It is the main source of stress on biodiversity in developing countries. It is also a major source of greenhouse gas emissions (Pachauri and Reisinger 2007), and of emergent zoonotic disease risks from the expanded contact zone between people and wildlife (Jones *et al.* 2008; Piesse and Thirtle 2010). The question to ask is how taking this price tag into account would change the rate at which habitat is converted, or the way in which agricultural growth is secured.

Nearly ten years ago, a review of the relation between biodiversity conservation and poverty eradication raised concerns that these two goals might be too much in conflict to achieve both. As the authors put it: "the co-listing of poverty elimination and environmental goals does not mean that integrated solutions are possible or that protected areas can contribute to growth and poverty reduction in poor countries." And they raised the concern that the elevation of the goal of poverty alleviation had "subsumed or supplanted" conservation goals (Adams *et al.* 2004). The evidence of decades of experiments with integrated conservation and development projects has in fact shown just how hard it is to marry conservation with the needs of a growing rural population looking for land to convert to the production of food. The establishment of protected areas has, for example, frequently dispossessed landholders while precluding future development options (Adams *et al.* 2004; Wells *et al.* 2004). There are certainly no easy wins.

6.5 Conclusions

The point was made in Chapter 5 that if there is underinvestment in conservation in biodiversity-rich, income-poor countries it may reflect the fact that conservation of biodiversity and the ecosystem services it supports is a layered public good: a public good at many different geographical scales. When conservation actions are additive, as they are for many widely distributed but endangered species, the incentive to free-ride on the efforts of others can be very strong. The evidence, at least to this point, is that there is no statistically significant relation between international biodiversity-related development assistance and the number of threatened species (Perrings and Halkos 2012). Yet there are mechanisms in place for channeling international support for national conservation efforts. There are two possible explanations for this. It is possible that current levels of biodiversity conservation in low-income countries are not optimal, but that the mechanisms set up to enable the global community to pay for local conservation efforts are ineffective. In other words, it is possible that the global community is simply unable to induce desirable levels of local conservation effort. It is also possible that increasingly levels of stress on biodiversity are, in some sense, globally optimal for very poor countries – that the most urgent and important objective in those countries is to address the many dimensions of poverty and not to protect biodiversity.

It has certainly been understood for some time that the inverted U-shaped relation between environmental quality and income often reflects the existence of legal, institutional, and social conditions need to internalize external effects and the provision of environmental public goods in higher-income countries (Arrow *et al.* 1995). Yet it is hard to believe that the rural poor in the least developed countries would support the conservation agenda of TNC, CI, or the WWF but for the lack of local public institutions. A more likely interpretation is that increasing stress on biodiversity is a concomitant of income growth in countries where most people live and work in rural areas, where rural population growth is persistently high, and where low incomes combined with the lack of credit markets make investment difficult. It also likely that the stresses placed on biodiversity reflect the fact that the rural poor are dependent on particular species. These include the species needed to support production of foods, fuels, and fibers; medicines (old and new); species that have totemic or cultural significance; and species that regulate water flows, microclimate, pests, and pathogens. The rural poor have a farmer's interest in predators, weeds, and diseases, a hunter's interest in ungulates, and a gatherer's interest in honey and fruits.

For the people occupying production landscapes the impact of changing technologies on the genetic diversity of crops and wild crop relatives, on pests and pest predators, and on human, animal, and plant diseases may be more important than the disappearance of wild species. I have not considered the relation between poverty alleviation and agro-biodiversity here. However, given that the intensification of agriculture is the primary strategy for poverty alleviation in the poorer countries of the world, and given that intensification is implicated in the genetic erosion of landraces and crop wild relatives, in the trans-formation of soil biodiversity, in the elimination of some pests and pest predators and the creation of others, one would expect it to have significant impacts. The relation between poverty and genetic resour-ces in production landscapes is considered in Chapter 14. What it is important to note now is that people facing declining resources do often increase the rate at which they exploit common pool forests, grasslands, rivers, and wetlands, as the Brundtland Report suggested. But poverty is not the only thing that prompts people to exploit natural ecosystems. The intensification of agriculture, forestry, or fisheries would be expected to increase the efficiency with which natural resour-ces can be used, and so the attractiveness of natural resource-based activities. Intensification may therefore make it feasible to bring ever more marginal land into cultivation.

References

Adams, W. M., Aveling, R., Brockington, D., Dickson, B., Elliott, J., Hutton, J., Roe, D., Vira, B. and Wolmer, W. (2004) Biodiversity con-servation and the eradication of poverty. *Science*, 306, 1146–1149.

Arrow, K., Bolin, B., Costanza, R., Dasgupta, P., Folke, C., Holling, C. H., Jansson, B.-O., Levin, S. A., Mäler, K.-G., Perrings, C. and Pimentel, D. (1995) Economic growth, carrying capacity, and the environment. *Science*, 268, 520–521.

Ash, N. and Jenkins, M. (2007) *Biodiversity and Poverty Reduction: The Importance of Biodiversity for Ecosystem Services*. UNEP-WCMC, Cambridge.

Birdsall, N. and Londono, J. L. (1997) Asset inequality matters: an assessment of the World Bank's approach to poverty reduction. *American Economic Association Papers and Proceedings*, 87, 32–37.

Boserup, E. (1965) *The Conditions of Agricultural Growth: The Economics of Agrarian Change under Population Pressure*. George Allen and Unwin, London.

(1981) *Population and Technological Change: A Study of Long Term Trends*. University of Chicago Press.

Carson, R. T. (2010) The environmental Kuznets curve: seeking empirical regularity and theoretical structure. *Review of Environmental Economics and Policy*, 4, 3–23.

Chandy, L. and Gertz, G. (2011) *Poverty in Numbers: The Changing State of Global Poverty from 2005 to 2015*. The Brookings Institution, Washington, DC.

Cleaver, K. M. and Schreiber, A. G. (1994) *Reversing the Spiral: The Population, Agriculture, and Environment Nexus in Sub-Saharan Africa*. World Bank, Washington, DC.

Cole, M. A., Rayner, A. J. and Bates, J. M. (1997) The environmental Kuznets curve: an empirical analysis. *Environment and Development Economics*, 2, 401–416.

Czech, B., Krausman, P. R. and Devers, P. K. (2000) Economic associations among causes of species endangerment in the United States. *Bioscience*, 50, 593–601.

Dasgupta, P. (1993) *An Inquiry into Well-Being and Destitution*. Clarendon Press, Oxford.
   (1995) Population, poverty, and the local environment. *Scientific American*, 272, 40–45.
   (2001) *Human Well-being and the Natural Environment*. Oxford University Press, New York.

Dasgupta, P. and Mäler, K.-G. (2000) Net national product, wealth, and social well-being. *Environment and Development Economics*, 5, 69–93.

De Janvry, A. and Garcia, R. (1988) *Rural Poverty and Environmental Degradation in Latin America: Causes, Effects and Alternative Solutions*. IFAD, Rome.

Deutsch, J. and Silber, J. G. (2005) Measuring multidimensional poverty: an empirical comparison of various approaches. *Review of Income and Wealth*, 51, 145–174.

Dietz, S. and Adger, N. (2003) Economic growth, biodiversity loss and conservation effort. *Journal of Environmental Management*, 68, 23–35.

Duclos, J.-Y., Sahn, D. E. and Younger, S. D. (2006) Robust multidimensional poverty comparisons. *Economic Journal*, 116, 943–968.

Ferraro, P. J. and Simpson, R. D. (2002) The cost-effectiveness of conservation payments. *Land Economics*, 78, 339–353.

Food and Agriculture Organization (2010) *Global Forest Resources Assessment 2010*, Main Report. FAO, Rome.

Fuglie, K. O. (2008) Is a slowdown in agricultural productivity growth contributing to the rise in commodity prices? *Agricultural Economics*, 39, 431–441.

Green, R. E., Cornell, S. J., Scharlemann, J. P. W. and Balmford, A. (2005) Farming and the fate of wild nature. *Science*, 307, 550–555.

Groombridge, B. and Jenkins, M. D. (eds.) (2002) *World Atlas of Biodiversity*. University of California Press for UNEP World Conservation Monitoring Centre, Berkeley, CA.

Grossman, G. and Krueger, A. (1995) Economic growth and the environment. *Quarterly Journal of Economics*, 110, 353–377.

Gutierrez, A. P. and Ponti, L. (2009) Bioeconomic sustainability of cellulosic biofuel production on marginal lands. *Bulletin of Science, Technology & Society*, 29, 213–225.

Hamilton, K. and Clemens, M. (1999) Genuine savings rates in developing countries. *World Bank Economic Review*, 13, 333–356.

Heath, J. and Binswanger, H. (1996) Natural resource degradation effects of poverty and population growth are largely policy induced: the case of Colombia. *Environment and Development Economics* 1, 65–84.

Jones, K. E., Patel, N. G., Levy, M. A., Storeygard, A., Balk, D., Gittleman, J. L. and Daszak, P. (2008) Global trends in emerging infectious diseases. *Nature*, 451, 990–993.

Kinzig, A. P., Perrings, C., Chapin, F. S., Polasky, S., Smith, V. K., Tilman, D. and Turner, B. L. (2011) Paying for ecosystem services: promise and peril. *Science*, 334, 603–604.

Koenker, R. (2005) *Quantile Regression*. Cambridge University Press.

Koenker, R. and Basset, G. (1978) Regression quantiles. *Econometrica*, 46, 33–50.

Kumar, S. K. and Hotchkiss, D. (1988) *Consequences of Deforestation for Women's Time Allocation, Agricultural Production and Nutrition in the Hills of Nepal*. IFPRI, Washington, DC.

Kuznets, S. (1966) *Modern Economic Growth: Rate, Structure and Spread*. Yale University Press, New Haven, CT.

Lall, S. V., Selod, H. and Shalizi, Z. (2006) *Rural-Urban Migration in Developing Countries: A Survey of Theoretical Predictions and Empirical Findings*. World Bank, Washington, DC.

Lange, G.-M. (2004) Wealth, natural capital, and sustainable development: contrasting examples from Botswana and Namibia. *Environmental and Resource Economics*, 29, 257–283.

Lopez, R. (1992) Environmental degradation and economic openness in LDCs: the poverty linkage. *American Journal of Agricultural Economics*, 74, 1138–1145.

Lopez, R. and Scoseria, C. (1996) Environmental sustainability and poverty in Belize: a policy paper. *Environment and Development Economics*, 1, 289–308.

MacArthur, R. H. and Wilson, E. O. (1967) *The Theory of Island Biogeography*. Princeton University Press.

Mansoor, A. and Quillin, B. (2007) *Migration and Remittances.* World Bank, Washington, DC.

Markandya, A. (2001) *Poverty Alleviation and Sustainable Development Implications for the Management of Natural Capital.* World Bank, Washington, DC.

Millennium Ecosystem Assessment (2005) *Ecosystems and Human Well-being: General Synthesis.* Island Press, Washington, DC.

Mills, J. H. and Waite, T. A. (2009) Economic prosperity, biodiversity conservation, and the environmental Kuznets curve. *Ecological Economics,* 68, 2087–2095.

Mozumder, P., Berrens, R. P. and Bohara, A. K. (2006) Is there an environmental Kuznets curve for the risk of biodiversity loss? *Journal of Developing Areas,* 39, 175–190.

Naidoo, R. and Adamowicz, W. L. (2001) Effects of economic prosperity on numbers of threatened species. *Conservation Biology,* 15, 1021–1029.

Naidoo, R., Balmford, A., Costanza, R., Fisher, B., Green, R. E., Lehner, B., Malcolm, T. R. and Ricketts, T. H. (2008) Global mapping of ecosystem services and conservation priorities. *Proceedings of the National Academy of Sciences,* 105, 9495–9500.

Pachauri, R. K. and Reisinger, A. (eds.) (2007) *Climate Change 2007: Synthesis Report – Contribution of Working Groups I, II and III to the Fourth Assessment Report of the Intergovernmental Panel on Climate Change.* IPCC, Geneva.

Pagiola, S. (2002) Paying for water services in Central America: learning from Costa Rica. *Selling Forest Environmental Services: Market-Based Mechanisms for Conservation and Development* (ed. S. S. Pagiola, J. Bishop and N. Landell-Mills), pp. 37–62. Earthscan, London.

(2008) Payments for environmental services Costa Rica. *Ecological Economics,* 65, 712–724.

Pattanayak, S. K., Wunder, S. and Ferraro, P. J. (2010) Show me the money: do payments supply environmental services in developing countries? *Review of Environmental Economics and Policy,* 4, 254–274.

Perrings, C. (2007) Pests, pathogens and poverty: biological invasions and agricultural dependence. *Biodiversity Economics: Principles, Methods, and Applications* (ed. A. Kontoleon, U. Pascual and T. Swanson), pp. 133–165. Cambridge University Press.

Perrings, C. and Gadgil, M. (2003) Conserving biodiversity: reconciling local and global public benefits. *Providing Global Public Goods: Managing Globalization* (ed. I. Kaul, P. Conceicao, K. Le Goulven and R. L. Mendoza), pp. 532–555. Oxford University Press.

Perrings, C. and Halkos, G. (2012) Who cares about biodiversity? Optimal conservation and transboundary biodiversity externalities. *Environmental and Resource Economics*, 52, 585–608.

Perrings, C., Mooney, H. A. and Williamson, M. H. (eds.) (2010) *Bioinvasions and Globalization: Ecology, Economics, Management, and Policy*. Oxford University Press.

Piesse, J. and Thirtle, C. (2010) Agricultural R&D, technology and productivity. *Philosophical Transactions of the Royal Society B: Biological Sciences*, 365, 3035–3047.

Pingali, P., Bigot, P. and Binswanger, H. (1987) *Agricultural Mechanization and the Evolution of Farming Systems in Sub-Saharan Africa*. Johns Hopkins University Press, Baltimore, MD.

Reyers, B., Van Jaarsveld, A. S., McGeoch, M. A. and James, A. N. (1998) National biodiversity risk assessment: a composite multivariate and index approach. *Biodiversity and Conservation*, 7, 945–965.

Sachs, J. D., Baillie, J. E. M., Sutherland, W. J., Armsworth, P. R., Ash, N., Beddington, J., Blackburn, T. M., Collen, B., Gardiner, B., Gaston, K. J., Godfray, H. C. J., Green, R. E., Harvey, P. H., House, B., Knapp, S., Kumpel, N. F., Macdonald, D. W., Mace, G. M., Mallet, J., Matthews, A., May, R. M., Petchey, O., Purvis, A., Roe, D., Safi, K., Turner, K., Walpole, M., Watson, R. and Jones, K. E. (2009) Biodiversity conservation and the Millennium Development Goals. *Science*, 325, 1502–1503.

Seldon, T. M. and Song, D. (1994) Environmental quality and development: is there a Kuznets curve for air pollution emissions? *Journal of Environmental Economics and Management*, 27, 147–162.

Shafik, N. (1994) Economic development and environmental quality: an econometric analysis. *Oxford Economic Papers*, 46, 757–773.

Stern, D. I. (2004) The rise and fall of the environmental Kuznets curve. *World Development*, 32, 1419–1439.

Stern, D. I. and Common, M. S. (2001) Is there an environmental Kuznets curve for sulphur? *Journal of Environmental Economics and Management*, 41, 162–178.

Tiffen, M., Mortimore, M. and Gichuki, F. (1994) *More People, Less Erosion: Environmental Recovery in Kenya*. John Wiley, New York.

Todaro, M. P. (1969) A model of labor migration and urban unemployment in less developed countries. *American Economic Review*, 59, 138–148.

United Nations Development Programme (UNDP) (2007) *Human Development Report*. Palgrave Macmillan, London.

United States Census Bureau (2012) *International Data Base*. Available at www.census.gov/population/international/data/idb/informationGateway.php (accessed 2012).

UNU-IHDP and UNEP (2012) *Inclusive Wealth Report 2012: Measuring Progress toward Sustainability.* Cambridge University Press.

Vié, J.-C., Hilton-Taylor, C. and Stuart, S.N. (eds.) (2009) *Wildlife in a Changing World: An Analysis of the 2008 IUCN Red List of Threatened Species.* IUCN, Gland.

Wells, M.P. (1992) Biodiversity conservation, affluence and poverty: mismatched costs and benefits and efforts to remedy them. *Ambio*, 21, 237–243.

Wells, M.P., McShane, T.O., Dublin, H.T., O'Connor, S. and Redford, K.H. (2004) The future of integrated conservation and development projects: building on what works. *Getting Biodiversity Projects to Work: Towards More Effective Conservation and Development* (ed. T.O. Mcshane and M.P. Wells), pp. 397–422. Columbia University Press, New York.

World Bank (2005) *Global Economic Prospects.* World Bank, Washington, DC.
(2006) *Where is the Wealth of Nations? Measuring Capital for the 21st Century.* World Bank, Washington, DC.
(2009) *World Development Report.* World Bank, Washington, DC.
(2010) *The Changing Wealth of Nations: Measuring Sustainable Development in the New Millennium.* World Bank, Washington, DC.

World Commission on Environment and Development (1987) *Our Common Future.* Island Press, Washington, DC.

World Resources Institute (2011) *Earthtrends Data Base.* Available at www.wri.org/project/earthtrends/ (accessed 2012).

Wunder, S. (2001) Poverty alleviation and tropical forests – what scope for synergies? *World Development*, 29, 1817–1833.

Wunder, S. and Wertz-Kanounnikoff, S. (2009) Payments for ecosystem services: a new way of conserving biodiversity in forests. *Journal for Sustainable Forestry*, 28, 576–596.

Wunder, S., Engel, S. and Pagiola, S. (2008) Taking stock: a comparative analysis of payments for environmental services programs in developed and developing countries. *Ecological Economics*, 65, 834–852.

7 | Globalization: trade, aid, and the dispersal of species

7.1 Globalization and biodiversity

Globalization is widely understood to mean the closer integration of the world's economies. But globalization also means the closer integration of the world's ecosystems, and this has important implications for the world's biodiversity, and the ecosystem services it supports. Globalization in the economic sense is reflected in the growth of international trade and travel. This has increased the rate at which species have dispersed across the world's ecosystems, with consequences for their functioning and the supply of ecosystem services. The opening of new markets or trade routes has resulted in the introduction of new species either as the object of trade or as the unintended consequence of trade. The growth in the volume of trade along existing routes has increased the frequency with which new introductions are repeated, and hence the probability that introduced species will establish and spread (Cassey *et al.* 2004; Semmens *et al.* 2004). Indeed, the more open economies are, the more likely they are to be both sources and sinks for the dispersal of species (Dalmazzone 2000; Vilà and Pujadas 2001), and the volume and direction of trade turn out to be good empirical predictors of the dispersal of harmful species (Levine *et al.* 2003; Costello *et al.* 2007).

The effects of trade-related species dispersal are both positive and negative. Trade in high-yielding crop varieties and the diffusion of biotechnologies, for example, have had strongly positive effects on productivity, output, employment, and health. They have also positively affected our capacity to maintain food supplies over a range of environmental conditions. At the same time, the trade-related dispersal of invasive pests and pathogens has had strongly negative effects on the same things. While particular attention has been paid to the harm done by emergent zoonotic diseases in humans (Hubalek 2003; Jones *et al.* 2008), these are merely the most publicized examples of a widespread and long-standing process of pest and pathogen redistribution (Williamson 1996, 1999; Daszak, Cunningham and Hyatt 2000; McNeely 2001; Daszak *et al.* 2007).

If the world is getting smaller, it is also getting faster. A second implication of globalization is that the time it takes for a perturbation in one part of the world to be felt everywhere is growing shorter and shorter. This partly reflects the fact that technological developments in transport have reduced the time it takes to move passengers or trade goods along particular routes. The first circumnavigation of the world, completed in September 1522 by the remnant crew of Ferdinand Magellan's ship *Victoria*, took more than three years. It is now possible to travel around the world by air in less than three days. There are also many more connections between the world's economic and ecological systems. The 2002–2003 outbreak of the SARS coronavirus in Hong Kong illustrates both things. As with many other emerging infectious diseases, its origins lay in a disease of wild animals, and its transmission to humans occurred through a close interaction between humans and infected animals. In this case a disease of civet cats was transmitted to humans who had eaten infected animals in Guangdong province, China (Jones *et al.* 2008). It was then spread through air travel to infect people in thirty-seven countries in a matter of days (Chowell *et al.* 2009). The establishment of pathways between wildlife and humans, combined with the ever-tighter connections between human societies, created a pathogen that was rapidly dispersed around the world.

Species dispersal often poses a Jekyll and Hyde problem. The same species can have good and bad sides. From a purely ecological perspective, any species introduced to an ecosystem beyond its home range that establishes, naturalizes, and spreads is an alien. Most alien species have either little impact on their host systems, or are beneficial. But some are not. From a policy perspective only those alien species that cause appreciable harm are of concern. Article 8(h) of the CBD requires member states "to prevent the introduction of, control or eradicate those alien species which threaten ecosystems, habitats or species" (United Nations 1993). In fact the term "invasive species" is now reserved for those alien species that do cause harm. It is usually interpreted to refer to harmful species whose home range lies beyond the jurisdiction of the country concerned. This includes both species that are deliberately introduced as domesticated plants or animals, and those that are introduced as an unintended byproduct of the import of other goods and services – the so-called hitchhiker species (Williamson 1996).

The costs of alien species that do turn out to be harmful include both direct and indirect effects. Direct effects comprise the impacts of pests and diseases on valued species, whether native or exotic. While there are no very good estimates of these costs, it is clear that they disproportionately affect countries that are heavily dependent on the exploitation of natural resources. I later record estimates by Pimentel and colleagues, who concluded that at the close of the twentieth century invasive species caused annual damage equal to 53 percent of agricultural GDP in the USA, 31 percent in the UK, and 48 percent in Australia, but 96 percent, 78 percent, and 112 percent of agricultural GDP in South Africa, India, and Brazil respectively (Pimentel *et al.* 2001). Few of the indirect effects of harmful alien species have been evaluated in the same way. Introduced pathogens, predators, or competitors have, for example, been implicated in the loss of native species in a number of ecosystems (Daszak *et al.* 2000), but the monetary value of such losses has not been estimated. This does, however, affect the capacity of ecosystems to deliver the services that underpin much economic activity, and to absorb anthropogenic and environmental stresses and shocks without losing functionality (Kinzig, Pacala and Tilman 2002; Loreau, Naeem and Inchausti 2002; Naeem *et al.* 2009).

This chapter considers the effects of globalization on biodiversity, focusing on the increased dispersal of species. It asks how closer integration of the global economy affects biodiversity, ecosystem functioning, ecosystem services, and human wellbeing. Much is known about the negative effects of dispersal on host ecosystems – the invasive species problem (Simberloff and Rejmánek, 2011). Indeed, invasion biology is now recognized as a distinct field of study (Reichard and White 2003). Rather less is known about the more positive effects of dispersal. The standard policy response to the negative effects of species introductions, at least until now, has been to raise the defensive barriers and eradicate the intruders wherever possible. In most cases, however, the enemy is already within the gates. As McNeely has observed, this is a process that has been in train for thousands of years (McNeely 2001). It may have accelerated dramatically in the twentieth century, but the Black Death in the fourteenth to eighteenth centuries, the Columbian exchange in the sixteenth century, the phylloxera and rinderpest outbreaks in the nineteenth century are all just points along a much longer path.

In many cases the negative effects of species introductions have been the unanticipated consequences of the deliberate introduction of species thought to offer a variety of benefits. For example, kudzu (*Pueraria lobata*) was initially introduced to the United States in the 1880s as a forage crop, and was actively promoted by the US Department of Agriculture (USDA) extension service for many years until its invasiveness was understood. By the turn of this century it covered more than 7 million acres of land in Alabama, Georgia, Florida, and Mississippi (Blaustein 2001). It is now also reported to be invasive in Oregon, North Dakota, Texas, Missouri, Arkansas, Illinois, Indiana, Kentucky, Tennessee, Virginia, West Virginia, Maryland, Delaware, New Jersey, and Connecticut (University of Georgia Center for Invasive Species and Ecosystem Health and National Park Service 2013). Since only some introduced species are harmful while many are beneficial, however, the process continues. In New Zealand, for example, introduced non-native plants valued for ornamental or other traits now outnumber native plants (Allen and Lee 2006).

The chapter begins by reporting the evidence for the relation between the closer integration of markets, the growth of trade and travel, and the dispersal of species. This includes the dispersal of harmful alien species – invasive species – the species that demand most attention. However, I am also interested in the impacts of dispersal more generally. I therefore consider the ecological and economic effects of the dispersal of other introduced species. Along the way I consider the real differences between invasive and alien species. It is not, *a priori*, clear where the boundary between alien and invasive species should lie. If the dispersal of an alien species has negative implications for native species, but is also the source of significant benefits, it will currently be designated invasive and subject to the terms of Article 8(h) of the CBD. But is this what should happen? I suggest that the answer depends, as in so many other cases, on the balance between the location-specific costs and benefits of species introductions. What McNeely called "the great reshuffling" is a central feature of the closer integration of the global system. It is also a central feature of directed biodiversity change. Understanding its dynamic effects on both the economy and the ecosystems that support the economy is critical to the development of realistic and appropriate policy responses.

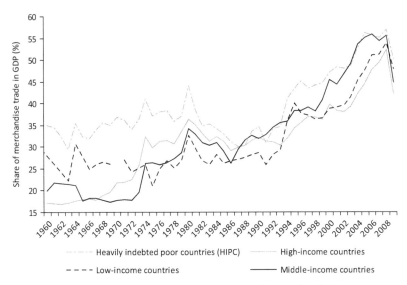

Figure 7.1 Merchandise trade as a percentage of GDP for different income groups.
Source: data from World Bank (2012b).

7.2 Globalization and the cost of biological invasions

There are many measures of globalization spanning economic, political, and social data (Andersen and Herbertsson 2005), but from a biodiversity perspective the most relevant relate to the growth of merchandise trade (trade excluding services) and passenger movements. The share of merchandise trade in GDP is a common indicator of globalization. It measures the proportion of value added in an economy that derives from the movement of trade goods. It is therefore an index of the openness of an economy, and hence its exposure to (and role in) the dispersal of species. As Figure 7.1 shows, while all countries have been becoming more open by such a measure, two groups of countries have been increasing their exposure more rapidly than others in the last three decades. These are the heavily indebted poor countries (largely through their dependence on food and manufactured imports) and the middle-income countries (largely through the growth of their raw material imports).

Over successive negotiating rounds of the GATT countries have progressively reduced tariffs on manufactured goods, facilitating a steady increase in trade in such goods. The same is not, however,

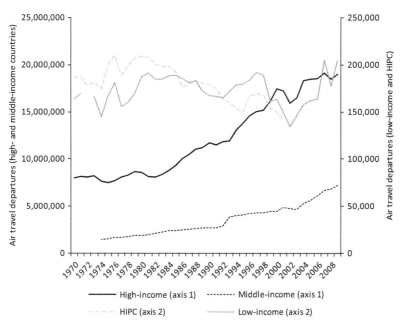

Figure 7.2 Air travel departures by income group, 1970–2009.
Source: data from World Bank (2012a).

true of agricultural products. The Uruguay Round of GATT negotiations (1986–1994) did bring agriculture into the multilateral trade rules, but tariffs on agricultural products are still much higher than tariffs on manufactured goods. The result is that while trade in all commodities has grown significantly, trade in agricultural products has grown less rapidly than trade in manufactures. Although all categories of trade are implicated in the dispersal of pests and pathogens, this has probably moderated the effect of trade growth on the dispersal of harmful species.

The dispersal of human diseases is affected more by travel (and especially air travel) than by trade, and there the pattern looks quite different. Air travel is a luxury that few people in the least developed countries can afford. Figure 7.2 shows air travel departures by income group between 1970 and 2009. At the bottom of the income scale there has been little growth in departures in the low-income countries, and departures have declined in the HIPC. At the top end of the income scale, however, there has been steady growth in departures in middle-income countries, and very substantial growth in departures in high-income countries. Given the importance of air travel in the spread of infectious diseases this is a growing source of concern.

What are the costs of dispersal? If we think only of the worst offenders it is clear that there are many ways of counting cost. For human pathogens cost is frequently counted in lives lost. The first global pandemic, the 1918–1920 Spanish influenza, was spread through the movement of troops and military supplies in the closing stages of the First World War. There is considerable uncertainty about the number of people who died, but it may have been as many as 100 million (McNeill 1977). More recently, HIV/AIDS, spread through the growth of air travel in the last quarter of the twentieth century, has killed some 30 million people worldwide. In both cases, however, the cost in lives was not independent of the conditions in which infected people found themselves. In the case of the Spanish influenza, four years of war had reduced the capacity of troops to resist the infection. In the case of HIV/AIDS, the disease has taken a greater toll in the countries of Sub-Saharan Africa where people's health is more frequently compromised by poverty than it is elsewhere (Dixon, McDonald and Roberts 2002; UNAIDS 2010).

Nor are the costs of human mortality independent of general conditions. For better or worse, the economic impact of mortality varies with the income and wealth of infected people. There is considerable uncertainty about estimates of the cost of HIV/AIDS, but they agree that in the worst affected countries the annual economic cost at the height of the pandemic was less than 5 percent of GDP, and the cost in terms of annual future growth rates of GDP was between 2 and 4 percent of GDP (Dixon *et al.* 2002; United Nations Department of Economic and Social Affairs Population Division 2004). That cost is high enough, but had the same prevalence rates been experienced in labor-scarce, high-skill economies, it would likely have been much higher.[1]

The first estimate of the economic costs of invasive species appeared in a report by the Office of Technology Assessment (OTA) of the US Congress (OTA 1993). The OTA considered the ecological and economic

---

[1] This is because productivity losses are the main costs of illness. An estimate of the cost of HIV/AIDS in the USA, for example, found that the cost of new HIV infections in 2002 was $36.4 billion, of which $6.7 billion was accounted for by direct medical costs and $29.7 billion by productivity losses (Hutchinson *et al.* 2006).

effects of harmful invasive species within the United States, and concluded that 59 percent of all species introduced to the USA during the twentieth century had at least some ecological impact, and that the seventy-nine most harmful species had caused damage of $97 billion over that period. As a reference point, nominal GDP in the year the report was published was $6,667 billion. Since that time a number of papers by Pimentel and colleagues have sought to update the OTA estimates, and to extend them beyond the USA (Pimentel *et al.* 2000, 2001; Pimentel, Zuniga and Morrison 2005). The second of the Pimentel papers included estimates for three developed and three developing countries. To date this remains the most comprehensive summary of the control costs and lost output associated with invasive species in agriculture, forestry, and fisheries in poor countries. The findings of Pimentel *et al.* (2001) are summarized in Tables 7.1 and 7.2. The numbers reported are the sum of annual damage costs in the countries concerned, averaged over the preceding decade.

Because of the way in which they were acquired, the estimates are not necessarily a very good approximation of the true costs of species

Table 7.1 *Economic losses to introduced pests in crops, pastures, and forests in the USA, UK, Australia, South Africa, India, and Brazil (billion dollars per year)*

Introduced pest	USA	UK	Australia	South Africa	India	Brazil	Total
Weeds							
Crops	27.9	1.4	1.8	1.5	37.8	17.0[a]	87.4
Pastures	6.0	–	0.6	–	0.92	–	7.52
Vertebrates							
Crops	1.0[b]	1.2[c]	0.2[d]	–e	–	–	2.4
Arthropods							
Crops	15.9	0.96	0.94	1.0	16.8	8.5	44.1
Forests	2.1	–	–	–	–	–	2.1
Plant pathogens							
Crops	23.5	2.0	2.7	1.8	35.5	17.1	82.6
Forests	2.1	–	–	–	–	–	2.1
Total	78.5	5.56	6.24	4.3	91.02	42.6	228.72

Notes: [a] Pasture losses included in crop losses. [b] Losses due to English starlings and English sparrows (Pimentel *et al.* 2000). [c] Calculated damage losses from the European rabbit. [d] Emmerson and McCulloch (1994).
Source: Pimentel *et al.* (2001).

Table 7.2 *Environmental losses to introduced pests in the USA, UK, Australia, South Africa, India, and Brazil (billion dollars per year)*

Introduced pest	USA	UK	Australia	South Africa	India	Brazil	Total
Plants	0.148	–	–	0.095	–	–	0.178
Mammals							
Rats	19.000	4.100	1.200	2.700	25.000	4.400	56.400
Other	18.106	1.200	4.655	–	–	–	23.961
Birds	1.100	0.270	–	–	–	–	1.370
Reptiles/ amphibians	0.006	–	–	–	–	–	0.006
Fishes	1.000	–	–	–	–	–	1.000
Arthropods	2.137	–	0.228	–	–	–	2.365
Mollusks	1.305	–	–	–	–	–	1.305
Livestock diseases	9.000	–	0.249	0.100	–	–	9.349
Human diseases	6.500	1.000	0.534	0.118	–	2.333	10.467
Total	58.299	6.570	6.866	3.013	25.000	6.733	106.481

Source: Pimentel *et al.* (2001).

introductions. They are based on a range of reports of damage costs in the literature that were not made in any consistent way, and were extremely patchy. There accordingly remains considerable uncertainty surrounding these estimates. But even if they were dramatically over-stated, which is unlikely, they would still indicate a problem. Public expenditure on invasive species control is not known in most countries, but where there are data it turns out to be very small relative to the Pimentel estimates. In the USA, for example, federal expenditure on invasive species in 2000 was just over $0.5 billion (United States General Accounting Office 2000), or around half of 1 percent of the estimated damage costs. We cannot tell from this how marginal control and marginal damage costs are related, but if control expenditures were efficient they would be equal – at the margin – to damage costs.

The Pimentel estimates show that the impact of invasive species on agriculture is proportionately greater in developing than in developed countries. Since agriculture accounts for a higher share of both GDP and employment in developing countries, this implies an even greater effect on human wellbeing. In India, for example, Pimentel's estimates imply that annual invasive species control and damage costs were as much as 20 percent of GDP in 1999, compared to less than 1 percent in the USA. Pimentel's 2005 update of the US estimates added an estimate of the cost of weeds in lawns (without attempting to isolate non-indigenous from indigenous weeds, or to separate weed control and fertilization), but otherwise reports similar figures (Pimentel *et al.* 2005).

The studies by Pimentel and colleagues aside, there are few attempts to aggregate the costs of invasive species. There are, on the other hand, a large number of case studies of the effects of particular invasive species (Stutzman, Jetter and Klonsky 2004). Examples of invasive plants in the USA for which there exist cost estimates inlcude leafy spurge (*Euphorbia esula*) (Leistritz, Bangsund and Hodur 2004), tansy ragwort (*Senecio jacobaea*) (Coombs *et al.* 1996), yellow starthistle (*Centaurea solstitialis*) (Jetter *et al.* 2003), and tamarisk (*Tamarix spp.*) (Zavaleta 2000). A number of case studies of the cost of aquatic species have also been carried out, of which the impact of the zebra mussel, *Dreissena polymorpha*, on power stations is the best known (O'Neill 1997). Others include the effect of the green crab, *Carcinus maenas*, on the north Pacific Ocean fisheries (Cohen, Carlton and Fountain 1995). Internationally, there have also been assessments of the role of the comb jelly, *Mnemiopsis leidii*, in changing the cost of fishing effort in the Black Sea (Knowler 2007).

There are fewer such case studies in developing countries, and those that do exist focus on the impact of invasive species on agriculture, forestry, and fisheries. Rice, maize, cassava, sorghum, and millet have all been affected by invasive species in various ways, including interference with crop growth through competition for light, water, and nutrients; allelopathy, or the production of toxins that inhibit the growth of other plants; contamination of harvested crops; and provision of vectors for pests, pathogens, nematodes, and insects. In the early 1990s, it was estimated that these effects cost up to 50 percent of the value of output (Oerke *et al.* 1994). Examples of pests and pathogens that have had particularly severe effects on crop yields in the world's poorest region, Sub-Saharan Africa, already mentioned, include witchweed, grey leaf spot, the large grain borer, cassava mealybug, and the cassava green mite (Rangi 2004).

Some of these species have been present for many decades. Others are new arrivals. The larger grain borer, for example, was apparently introduced from South and Central America during the 1970s. It was first detected in Tanzania in the late 1970s and is now established in east, central, south, and west Africa. It primarily affects grain in storage, causing losses of up to 30 percent within six months. Farrell and Schulten estimated that the income forgone as a result was in the order of $90 million for Tanzania alone (Farrell and Schulten 2002). The emergence of new agricultural pests has spurred the development of both new pesticides and alternative control measures, including biological control agents. For example, the cassava mealybug has been targeted by the parasitic wasp *Epidinocarsis lopezi*, the cassava green mite by the mite *Typhodromalus aripo*, and the large grain borer by the beetle *Teretrisoma negrescens* (Rangi 2004).

In some cases deliberate and accidental introductions have combined to have dramatic effects. Kasulo analyzed the ecological and socioeconomic impact of invasive species in African lakes (Victoria, Kyoga, Nabugabo, Kariba, Kivu, Itezhi-tezhi, and Malawi), focusing on the deliberately introduced Nile perch (*Lates niloticus*) and Tanganyika sardine (*Limnothrissa miodon*), and the accidentally introduced water hyacinth (*Eichhornia crassipes*) (Kasulo 2000). The introduction of Nile perch and Tanganyika sardine had major impacts on the structure and profitability of fisheries in these lakes, but completely transformed the trophic structure of lake fish communities. Taken in combination with the effects of water hyacinth it is believed to have caused the extinction of more than three hundred endemic cyclid species (Witte *et al.* 1992; Goldschmidt, Witte and Wanink 1993). The water hyacinth, on the other hand, has proliferated in most African lakes. It has obstructed water passages and displaced native aquatic plants, fish, and invertebrates by cutting out light and depleting dissolved oxygen (Masifwa, Twongo and Donny 2001). Kasulo's estimate of the annual cost of the hyacinth in terms of its impact on fisheries in this group of lakes during the latter part of the twentieth century was $71.4 million (Kasulo 2000).

The South African fynbos is affected by a number of invasive pinus, hakea, and acacia species. By 2000 two-thirds of the fynbos area in the Western Cape had been significantly impacted. Damage costs include a reduction in biodiversity and, in particular, of species important for the international flower trade. But they also include a change in ecosystem functioning and hydrology. A number of studies had argued that fynbos mountain catchments were extremely valuable in terms of their water yield, and that the cost of changes in water yields exceeded expected restoration costs (Turpie, Heydenrych and Hassan 2001; Le Maitre *et al.* 2002). The result was a major control program, the Working for Water Campaign, which had both restoration and poverty-alleviation goals. While the benefits of the program in terms of water, employment, and poverty alleviation are reasonably clear – the program employed some 24,000 people in 2000 – other environmental benefits are less easy to identify (Turpie, Marais and Blignaut 2008).

These studies of particular pests or pathogens show that the costs of infestation/infection and infestation/infection control can be extremely high. However, it is important not to ignore the benefits conferred by the alien species or the activities that support their introduction or spread. Most case studies of alien species involve estimates of damage and control costs and do not deal with the benefit side of the ledger. When such benefits are taken into account it is not always obvious that eradication or control is the optimal strategy. This may seem obvious in the case of alien species introduced and cultivated as a source of food, fuel, or fiber. But it also holds for accidental introductions. For example, siam weed (*Chromoleana odorata*) was introduced into Ghana in the 1960s and by the end of the century had spread to approximately 60 percent of the land area. A survey of users found, however, that few would support its eradication since it confers significant benefits as a source of fuel, building materials, and medicinal products (Rangi 2004). In semi-arid areas, mesquite (*Prosopis juliflora*) is a similar case. In South Africa, it has invaded the semi-arid Nama and succulent karoo biomes, but is nevertheless highly valued for its capacity to provide a more reliable source of fuel and fiber than many native species in dry conditions (Global Invasive Species Program 2004).

Species introductions are a frequently cited cause of extinctions, but the evidence is that they can in fact have both positive and negative effects on local taxonomic diversity (Wilcove *et al.* 1998; Sax and Gaines 2003; Gurevitch and Padilla 2004). They can also have both positive and negative effects on ecological functions and the supply of ecosystem services. At local scales, for example, invasive plants have been found to have functional traits associated with more rapid resource acquisition and growth than natives, which positively affects services that are increasing in biomass. At global scales, on the other hand, the effects of native and introduced plants on ecosystem processes are relatively minor (Cardinale *et al.* 2012). A meta-analysis of papers

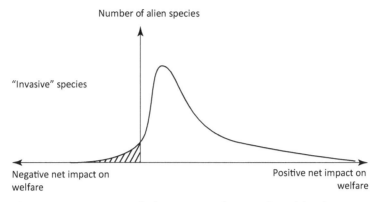

Figure 7.3 Proportion of alien species that are harmful. The majority of introduced alien species have little impact, positive or negative, on human wellbeing. The few that are harmful are termed "invasive" species. These are the species that attract most attention.

reporting over a thousand field studies of the effects of 135 alien plants on resident species, communities, and ecosystems found that alien plants had a significant effect in eleven of twenty-four impacts assessed, but that the magnitude and direction of the effect was not consistent. On average, abundance and diversity of the resident species decreased in invaded sites, whereas primary production and several ecosystem processes were enhanced. In particular, it was found that alien plants enhanced microbial activity by 32 percent, that they increased available nitrogen (53.7 percent), nitrogen, phosphorus, and carbon pools (22.1, 19.7, and 11.6 percent respectively), and that they reduced acidity pH (3 percent) (Vilà *et al.* 2011).

The important point is that while some alien species have imposed significant costs to host systems, most have not (Figure 7.3). Although the OTA found that a large proportion of alien species had some ecological impact, Williamson's tens rule is a better first approximation of the likelihood that an introduced species will cause significant harm. The tens rule holds that for certain classes of invasive species[2] one in ten of introduced species appears in the wild, one in ten of those appearing

---

[2] Originally claimed to hold for British angiosperms, *Pinaceae*, pasture plants in Australia's Northern Territory, and high-impact non-indigenous species in the USA, including terrestrial vertebrates, insects, fishes, mollusks, and plant pathogens.

in the wild establishes, and one in ten of established aliens becomes a pest (Williamson and Fitter 1996). The implication – that only 0.1 percent of introduced species is likely to cause significant damage – has not prevented widespread concern over non-native species in general. But it should give us pause. The dispersal of species through trade and travel has been the cause of disease outbreaks that have decimated human, animal, and plant populations, that have wiped out whole industries, and that have severely affected the production of foods, fuels, and fibers. But not all introduced species are culpable. Indeed, many have added much to the wellbeing of people in the host countries, or are the byproducts of highly beneficial activities. The CBD's strictures on alien species that threaten ecosystems, habitats, or species is what has led to the distinction between established alien and invasive species. Established alien species that are a source of harm and confer no benefits may attract control or eradication effort, but established alien species that both confer benefits and impose costs may not.

The growth of international trade has itself conferred substantial benefits on people everywhere. The dispersal of species is sometimes an intentional outcome of that, and sometimes an unintentional (external) effect. We would accordingly expect societies to accept at least some damage from species dispersal as the price of doing business. It may well be true that too little attention is paid to the cost of species dispersal, and that importers face none of the expected damage costs of introduced species. But there is no reason to believe that trade-related species dispersal is always and everywhere bad.

7.3 The invasive species risks of trade

We have already seen that the dispersal of species through the global trade system includes both the intentional shipment of species as objects of trade, and the unintentional shipment of species as passengers on trade goods. We have also seen that many of the best-known and most harmful invasive species have been intentional introductions. Such species were selected for their ability to survive in the environment where they are introduced (Smith, Lonsdale and Fortune 1999). Many other invasive species have been introduced as hitchhikers on trade vehicles or vessels. In the early 1990s the OTA estimated that four out of every five invasive terrestrial weeds in the USA were introduced as byproducts of trade (OTA 1993). Among aquatic pests the zebra mussel

(*Dreissena polymorpha*) and the Asian clam (*Corbicula fluminea*) were introduced to the Great Lakes in the ballast water of ships bringing trade goods from bioclimatically similar regions in eastern Europe – the Caspian, Black, and Azov seas (O'Neill 1997). The rapid global spread of SARS was supported by air travel (Tatem, Rogers and Hay 2006; Tatem 2009). The historic spread of tuberculosis, on the other hand, reflects quite complex interactions between the virulence of a disease, infected and susceptible populations, trade, settlement patterns and the level of development (Delfino and Simmons 2000).

It follows that the link between the growth in trade and invasive species risks is likely to be different for different species, different places, different times, and different trade patterns. Levine and D'Antonio considered merchandise trade as a predictor of invasions of insects, plant pathogens, and mollusks, and concluded that trade-induced invasions would increase by anywhere between 3 and 61 percent by 2020 depending on the taxonomic group (Levine and D'Antonio 2003). It is important to note that the invasive species risks of trade depend on several factors aside from the volume and composition of trade itself. Other important factors are the nature of the pathways (e.g. the time and conditions experienced by species during transit), the nature of the species themselves (e.g. traits, such as high plasticity, that make species invasive), and the invasibility of the ecosystems into which species are being introduced (e.g. the effects of fragmentation, biodiversity loss, or repeated exposure to alien species) (Williamson 1996). The probability that a species will be introduced may depend on the volume and composition of trade (Leung, Drake and Lodge 2004), and the characteristics of trade pathways (Costello *et al.* 2007; Hulme *et al.* 2008; Hulme 2009), but the probability that an introduced species will establish and spread depends on the bioclimatic similarities between source and sink countries, the traits of the species itself, the vulnerability of the host ecosystem to invasion, and the length of time the host country has been exposed to propagules (Lonsdale 1999; Rejmánek, Richardson and Pyšek 2004). The latter, in turn, depends on both biotic and abiotic factors (Lodge 1993; Moyle and Light 1996).

Small island states are frequently argued to be especially vulnerable from both an ecological and an economic perspective. Ecologically, small islands frequently lack the competitors and predators that control introduced species in their home range. In addition, they frequently have vacant ecological niches due to their distance from colonizing populations (MacArthur and Wilson 1967). Economically, small islands tend to be more dependent on imports than continental countries, and tend to depend on the exploitation of raw materials or natural ecosystems (tourism) for exports (Dalmazzone 2000).[3] It follows that trade potentially poses heightened risks in such economies.

Even in larger systems, though, land use can increase the vulnerability of host systems. Pyšek and colleagues observe that although some ecosystems are intrinsically more vulnerable to invasions than others, the vulnerability of all ecosystems increases with anthropogenic fragmentation, habitat disturbance, and the reduction in the number and abundance of native species (Polasky, Costello and McAusland 2004; Pyšek, Chytrý and Jarošik 2010). Fragmentation through road construction, the elimination of buffer zones, or an increasing pollution burden can also affect the vulnerability of ecosystems. Land uses that create habitat suited to particular species increase the likelihood that those species will establish and spread if introduced. One reason for the late twentieth-century resurgence of malaria, for example, was the elimination of public health programs designed to reduce habitat suitable for the vector *Anopheles spp.* (Mendis *et al.* 2009). More generally, interventions designed to select for one species may make the system more vulnerable to the competitors, predators, pathogens, symbionts, or commensals of that species. So, for example, the production of particular crops makes agricultural systems more vulnerable to weeds (competitors) and to crop pests and diseases (predators).

The fragmentation of habitats as a result of road, rail, and canal construction has mixed effects on the vulnerability of those habitats to invasive species. Road construction creates corridors for species able to exploit the conditions along roadsides (Christen and Matlack 2009), but also creates barriers against the spread of other species (Niemelä, Koivula and Kotze 2007). In Australia, for example, the cane toad (*Chaunus marinus*) spread at approximately 10 kilometers per year in the sugar cane fields of Queensland where it was inhibited by roads but much more rapidly in the natural landscapes of the Northern Territories (Phillips *et al.* 2006).

---

[3] For example, the average percentage of merchandise imports as a share of the GDP, in the sample considered in Dalmazzone (2000), is 43 percent for island countries, against an average 32 percent for the whole sample, and 26.8 percent for continental countries.

In naturally susceptible systems, such as small islands, the effects of land use on the structure of landscapes and the composition of native species can have especially pronounced effects on their vulnerability to invasion. Indeed, invasive pests and pathogens are commonly cited as the major driver of native biodiversity loss in such systems (Sax and Gaines 2008). Not all taxa are equally affected, but some are especially at risk. A number of species of frogs, toads, newts, salamanders, and caecilians, for example, either have already been driven to extinction or are at risk of extinction due to the effects of disease. An introduced parasitic fungus, amphibian chytrid (*Batrachochytrium dendrobatidis*), is currently one of the most severe threats to the survival of amphibians in both small and large systems. In Australia, for example, the disease has been implicated in four frog extinctions, and has put many more at risk (Daszak and Cunningham 1999).

Other vulnerable economies are those in which income and employment both depend heavily on agriculture, forestry, and fisheries. In most low-income countries the vast majority of people tend to live in rural areas, and to derive their income from agriculture. As a measure of this, the ratio of farm to non-farm income is around 1 percent in high-income countries, but ranges from 40 to 80 percent in low-income countries (Jaffee and Henson 2005). This makes the people in such countries vulnerable to the effects of introduced agricultural pests and pathogens (Perrings 2007). In the poorest countries an additional source of risk is international development assistance, and especially food aid. For example, grey leaf spot was first reported in South Africa in 1988 having been introduced in US food-aid shipments in the drought years of the 1980s. It subsequently spread northwards into all the main maize-growing areas of Africa, and has reduced maize yields everywhere between 30 and 60 percent (Ward *et al.* 1999; Rangi 2004). Parthenium weed from Mexico was also introduced to Ethiopia in food-aid shipments during the 1980s, with similarly negative effects on wheat yields (Global Invasive Species Program 2004). The fact that lower sanitary and phytosanitary standards are applied to emergency food aid makes this especially risky (Aksoy 2005).

So even though an increase in the volume of trade is likely to increase the probability of introductions, the risks involved depend on many other factors. The probability of establishment and spread depends as much on the traits of the introduced species and the invasibility of the host system as on the frequency and volume of introductions. The damage cost if an

introduced species does establish and spread depends on the value at risk –
the value of the assets or activities it threatens – and not on the volume or
value of trade. Nevertheless, the introduction of potentially invasive species
is an externality of international trade, and its management depends on the
institutions set up to regulate international trade.

7.4 The regulation of trade-related biological invasions

The multilateral agreement governing international trade is the General
Agreement on Tariffs and Trade (GATT). The environmental impacts of
trade are one of the few acceptable justifications for imposing trade
restrictions under the GATT. Article 20 of the GATT allows countries
to take action in restraint of trade to protect human, animal, or plant
health.[4] Implementation of these general exceptions is through the IHR
(2005), and the Sanitary and Phytosanitary (SPS) Agreement of the
World Trade Organization (WTO) (1994). The latter provides the rules
under which countries can interrupt trade to protect animal and plant
health. It encourages adoption of the standards set by the Codex
Alimentarius Commission for food safety, the International Office of
Epizootics for animal health, and the International Plant Protection
Convention (IPPC) for plant health, but allows countries to choose
their own level of protection (Jaffee and Henson 2005).

Liberalization of international trade through successive renegotiations of the GATT has done little to address many existing international
environmental market failures, and has created many more. The solution to the problem has been the development of MEAs to address
specific environmental issues. From a biodiversity perspective the most
important of these are the Convention on Biological Diversity (CBD)
and the Convention on International Trade in Endangered Species
(CITES), which deals specifically with international markets for biological resources. Beyond this there are a range of agreements dealing
with particular regional issues or with particular species. I discuss these
in later chapters. Here I consider how the institutional landscape affects
the ability of countries to deal with the invasive species externalities of
trade.

---

[4] Article 20(b) of the GATT: "nothing in this Agreement shall be construed to
prevent the adoption or enforcement by any contracting party of measures
necessary to protect human, animal or plant life or health."

A large number of institutions are directly or indirectly concerned with the impact of invasive species.[5] Several of these institutions have overlapping mandates, but while this should provide a basis for cooperation, or at least coordination, the reality is that individual bodies generally act non-cooperatively. The CBD has identified a number of gaps and areas of inconsistency induced by overlapping responsibility at the international level (Table 7.3). Animal invasive species, hull fouling, civil aviation, tourism, and development assistance are named as areas of special concern. For example, the World Animal Health Organization (OIE) focuses on diseases related to livestock and other commercially valuable animal species, but neglects interactions between domesticated and wild species. There is also no institution with responsibility for the international invasive species risks of some of the most important activities such as tourism, emergency aid and development assistance, military activity, and inter-basin water transfers (Perrings *et al.* 2010b).

In every case, however, the scope for strengthening the international response is compromised either by the lack of any well-defined responsibility for the problem, by the non-cooperation of bodies with overlapping mandates, or by the inability to connect related problems. The last issue is particularly important. The IPPC, for example, only deals with pests of plants. It can address invasive animals that impact upon agricultural crops or native plant species, but it has no remit to address invasive animals that may impact other animals or human health. The International Maritime Organization (IMO) is only authorized to address marine vessels of large tonnage, and so has nothing to say about hull fouling issues on smaller vessels (Perrings *et al.* 2010a).

---

[5] These include the "biodiversity conventions": the CBD and its Cartagena Protocol on Biosafety, the Ramsar Convention on Wetlands of International Importance, the CMS along with many other MEAs. They also include institutions that have some responsibility for the pathways (transport routes) along which species move. Examples of such institutions include the IMO, the International Civil Aviation Organization (ICAO), the International Air Transport Association (IATA), and the UNCLOS. Institutions concerned with trade along pathways include the CITES, but are dominated by the WTO and the GATT, along with supporting agreements such as the SPS Agreement and the Agreement on Technical Barriers to Trade (TBT). There are also institutions concerned with impacts of species movements on particular sectors such as agriculture, aquaculture, forestry, and fisheries. These include the OIE, IPPC, and the UN Food and Agriculture Organization (FAO) along with its Compliance Agreement and Code of Conduct for Responsible Fisheries. Last, but not least, there are institutions concerned with the impact of the spread of human diseases – principally the WHO and the IHR.

Table 7.3 *Areas of missing or overlapping responsibility for invasion pathways identified by the CBD*

CBD identified pathway gaps	Responsible organizations
Animals that are not plant pests, including pets, aquarium species, live bait, live food	OIE, FAO, WTO, SPS Agreement
Marine biofouling	IMO (only for ships of large tonnage – there is a gap for ships of low tonnage)
Civil air transport	ICAO, IATA
Aquaculture, mariculture	FAO
Conveyances, tourism, emergency aid and development assistance, military activities, and inter-basin water transfers and canals	None
Flowers, livestock, specific agricultural goods, timber and other raw materials	WTO, SPS, IPPC, OIE

Source: Convention on Biological Diversity (1993).

At present, the only international institutions with the capacity to take effective action on the invasive species risks of trade and trade pathways are those associated with the WTO. The actions available to these bodies are, however, limited by the WTO and the GATT. The IPPC and the OIE, for example, are authorized to develop international standards for trade involving pests and pathogens affecting animals and plants, and these standards are recognized as compatible with the SPS Agreement, and hence with the WTO's dispute settlement process. No other institutions have that status. While the CBD could, in principle, develop a protocol on invasive species, there is no evidence that it would be able to influence the WTO.

In the last two decades, the world trade system has seen the proliferation of bilateral and regional trade agreements, especially between developing countries (World Bank 2005). Such agreements now account for around 40 percent of world trade. A number cover environmental issues in recognition of the fact that specific trade links involve specific environmental risks, but their main purpose is to open up new trading opportunities between developing countries. Since this brings about closer linkages between ecosystems in which bioclimatic conditions are broadly similar, it increases the risk that species introduced through trade will be able to establish, naturalize, and spread. There is, for example, some evidence from the NAFTA that the agreement has facilitated the spread of introduced species within the NAFTA area (Perrault *et al.* 2003).

The promotion of agricultural trade between bioclimatically matching regions in which resources for the detection and control of potentially invasive species are weak increases the risk that damaging pests and pathogens will be dispersed through trade. A number of regional trade agreements do have mechanisms to address such risks. The Southern Common Market (MERCOSUR), for example, includes an environmental working group charged with eliminating the use of environmental barriers to trade, promoting upward harmonization of environmental management systems, and securing cooperation on shared ecosystems. Indeed, many of the main South–South regional trade agreements – MERCOSUR, the Andean Pact, the Common Market for Eastern and Southern Africa (COMESA), the Southern African Development Community (SADC), the ASEAN Free Trade Area, and the Caribbean Community (CARICOM) – include agreements on standards. But these are typically among the weakest aspects of regional trade agreements.

The general point to make is that the institutions regulating international trade do recognize that dispersal of species has potentially negative effects that are not part of the transactions between exporters and importers. Moreover, there do exist multilateral agreements that authorize action to limit the threat posed by invasive species. But the same agreements also limit the range of actions that can be taken, and specifically exclude the adoption of policies to internalize the cost of invasive species.

7.5 System-level effects of species dispersal

We now return to the wider impact of species dispersal. It is appropriate, from a policy perspective, to focus on the species most likely to do harm. But what of the rest: the species that appear in the non-negative orthant of Figure 7.3? The meta-analysis by Vilà *et al.* referred to earlier found that alien plants had a significant impact on nearly half the ecosystem processes assessed, and that the effect on many ecosystem processes was positive. Alien plants were found to have enhanced microbial activity, increased available nitrogen, along with nitrogen, phosphorus, and carbon pools (Vilà *et al.* 2011). They were also found to have adversely affected native species either directly through predation or competition, or indirectly through their effect on ecosystem processes. Reductions in the number of limiting nutrients, for example, would be expected to reduce diversity. Nonetheless, one implication of the findings of Vilà *et al.* is that ecosystem services that are increasing in nitrogen, phosphorus, and carbon pools might benefit from species dispersal. There is at least some support for this idea from within theoretical ecology although, interestingly, it turns out that the positive effects from the dispersal of species are sensitive to the rate at which it occurs.

Theoretical work on the effect of species dispersal on biodiversity, productivity, and resilience has shown that while intermediate dispersal rates can confer benefits in terms of species richness, productivity, and the capacity to accommodate environmental fluctuations, high rates of dispersal can have the opposite effect (Loreau, Mouquet and Gonzalez 2003). The study by Loreau and colleagues considers a spatially heterogeneous environment in which the sub-communities of a meta-community are linked by the movement of species between them. Environmental conditions are assumed to vary asynchronously across these sub-communities. Within each community, variation in species characteristics allows selection of the set of species best adapted to prevailing conditions. This in some sense optimizes the functioning of local ecosystems. The authors then argue that the performance of each local community may be covariant with the performance of other local communities in the meta-community, and that the mechanism is the dispersal of species between communities (Loreau *et al.* 2003).

The ecology behind the argument is the following. Different species are more or less adapted to different environmental conditions. Species dispersal regulates the set of species available to each community. At either very low or very high rates of dispersal, competitive exclusion leads to a reduction in the diversity of species in each community – alpha diversity. If species vary in their adaptation to particular environmental conditions and there is no dispersal (each community is closed with respect to all other communities), then the best-adapted species in each community will competitively exclude all other species. Alpha diversity will be low, but gamma diversity will be high. The biomass of the community will then change as environmental conditions change. At the other extreme, if the rate of dispersal is very high, then the meta-community will begin to behave as if it were a single community. This has the same effect. The species that is best adapted to average conditions across the meta-community will outcompete all other species. That is, competitive exclusion will cause the loss of biodiversity and increasing sensitivity to variation in environmental conditions. Alpha and gamma diversity will both be low. At intermediate rates of dispersal, on the other hand, the set of species available to exploit environmental changes in each community will be increased, making it better able to function over a range of environmental conditions, i.e. to be more resilient with respect to environmental shocks. The implication is that productivity in individual communities and the stability of productivity over time will be greatest at intermediate rates of dispersal, i.e. when the biodiversity enhancing effects of dispersal offset the biodiversity reducing effects of competitive exclusion.

In terms of the portfolio model described in Chapter 4, the value of a portfolio of species at the level of meta-community – at the largest scale – depends on the strength of the linkages between communities, and the differences in their response to fluctuating environmental conditions. The more highly correlated are the responses of distinct species, the lower the value of their inclusion in the portfolio. In the extreme case, if the risks attaching to two species are perfectly correlated, and the functions or services supported by species are the same, then the species with the lower mean yield is strictly redundant and may be dropped from the portfolio without loss. The variability of external environments, and the fact that the cyclical nature of succession allows local transients to persist, means that there may be redundancy at any one moment in time. But the redundancy of a species at a moment in time may mask the complementarity between species over space and time. A function best performed by one species under one set of environmental conditions may be best performed by another species under a different set of environmental conditions (Loreau *et al*. 2003; Gonzalez, Mouquet and Loreau 2009; Loreau 2010).

In the world described in this book, the dispersal of species between the sub-communities of a meta-community depends on market integration. The composition and volume of trade determines the dispersal rate of the species involved. In some cases this involves a direct trade in species. In others it involves the accidental dispersal of species as externalities of trade. The more closely integrated are world markets, and the higher the rate of economic growth, the higher will be the rate of dispersal. This potentially affects the level of biodiversity in each country. In the Loreau story, the impact on biodiversity in each community is assumed to work through competitive exclusion, and the higher the rate of dispersal, the greater the tendency for the species that does best in average conditions to competitively exclude others. A similar mechanism can be seen at work in today's managed ecosystems. The globalization of world agriculture, for example, has seen the disappearance of thousands of landraces and traditional livestock strains as a result of a very similar process. Where dispersal is an increasing function of market integration, trade growth in a spatially heterogeneous environment will first increase and later decrease biodiversity.

It follows that as the world comes to resemble a single community we might expect to see a reduction in the biodiversity of its component ecosystems. This may indeed relate to the traditional drivers of biodiversity loss – direct depletion and habitat conversion – but these are both expressions of anthropogenic competitive exclusion. If rangelands pay better than forests, and if there is a sufficient flow of livestock farmers into forested areas, forest habitat will be lost. If average yields on crops grown from genetically engineered seeds are higher than on landraces, and if the former are in sufficient supply, the landraces will be abandoned. The remaining species may be more productive, consistent with the findings of Vilà *et al.* (2011). But there will be fewer of them.

From a policy perspective the concern is that if the competitive exclusion of species is hastened by the fact that the costs of integration are not reflected in international commodity prices, there may be no way back. The local extirpation of a population may be reversible but, for all practical purposes, global extinction is not – de-extinction efforts notwithstanding. Moreover, even where a change is notionally reversible, it may still be characterized by hysteresis. Irreversibility and hysteresis mean that we should be especially concerned about the biodiversity consequences of globalization. Irrespective of the environmental stress posed by economic and demographic growth, the closer integration of the world economic system is putting a very particular strain on one of the main sources of resilience to environmental shocks. Moreover, this is occurring at the very moment when the general circulation models indicate that the extreme events and regime shifts are likely to occur with increasing frequency.

Like other species, introduced species are important for the effect they have on the functioning of ecosystems, and hence on the supply of ecosystem services. A potential cost of the reduction in diversity in homogenized ecosystems is a reduction in the range of environmental conditions over which the system can function effectively. A reduction in the diversity of some functional group, for example, affects the impact of environmental variability on the functions performed by that group. More particularly, it affects the capacity of the functional group to absorb anthropogenic and environmental stresses and shocks without losing resilience (Kinzig *et al.* 2006; Walker *et al.* 2006; Naeem *et al.* 2009). While the introduction of alien species may not immediately impact system performance, it can make it less able to cope with future variation in environmental conditions. In the language of the MA, this implies a reduction in the regulating services of ecosystems: i.e. in the security with which they are able to supply the things that people care about – the provisioning and cultural services.

7.6 Conclusions

The second part of this book considers what to do about the problems posed by directed biodiversity change in a globalizing world. The first part has been concerned with identifying the nature, the drivers, and the scale of those problems. Globalization means the closer integration of the world system. Its manifestations are everywhere, from the internet to the presence of Chinese manufactures in practically every household worldwide. Its impact on biodiversity derives from two related processes. The first is the dispersal of species beyond their "natural" range through trade and travel. The second is the homogenization of ecosystems. The two processes are related in several ways. The dispersal of species includes both the deliberate introduction of species that are valued for their role in the provision of foods, fuels, and fibers, and the accidental introduction of species that may outcompete or prey upon native species. Both things lead to a reduction in species richness: the first through the conversion of native species' habitat, the second through the competitive exclusion or predation of native species. Both things are also implicated in the homogenization of ecosystems.

Environmental heterogeneity, or variation of habitat within a landscape, means that one or a few species are not able to dominate. The conversion of many different habitats for the production of foods, fuels, and fibers reduces habitat heterogeneity directly, both by stripping out native species and by transforming hydrological flows, nutrient cycles, and so on. While the introduction of alien species in these systems has had many of the positive effects noted by Vilà *et al.* (2011), it has also had a range of other effects. As with many environmental impacts, the effect of either land conversion or species dispersal on the heterogeneity of landscapes is often ignored by those responsible. The forester who replaces old growth forest with a monoculture changes the heterogeneity of the landscape in the area under his control, and changes the heterogeneity of species over a much wider area. But the costs of these wider changes are seldom part of his calculus.

Among these costs is the fact that the converted system becomes more vulnerable to species introductions. For Elton this was because greater species richness confers biotic resistance – and the loss of species weakens that resistance (Elton 1958). If the argument is correct, we would expect simplified agro-ecosystems to be more vulnerable to invasions than other ecosystems. Although the evidence on biotic resistance in natural or at least less heavily impacted systems is ambiguous, and depends on the scale at which the analysis is undertaken (Levine and D'Antonio 1999), the evidence on agro-ecosystems is unambiguous. The simplification of agro-ecosystems is the source of most of the productivity gains they have made, but it comes at a cost. Simplified systems are significantly more susceptible to pests and pathogens than other ecosystems, and their susceptibility is greater the fewer the species in the system (Jackson *et al.* 2007). Indeed, the management of most simplified systems is largely about the exclusion of species that either compete with or predate on cultivated or protected species. Whether it is carried by public health officials, farmers, households, pest control agencies, conservation groups, or others, the cost of managing simplified systems is the control of potentially invasive species.

So to return to the question that motivates the chapter – how closer integration of the global economy affects biodiversity, ecosystem functioning, ecosystem services, and human wellbeing – it is clear that the dominant effect is to increase the rate at which species are dispersed across ecosystems. This, in turn, has a wide range of implications for human wellbeing depending on the traits of the species dispersed, the status of the host ecosystem, and the structure of the host economy. While most attention is paid to the dispersal of species whose traits make them pests or pathogens, it is important to bear in mind that species dispersal also includes the many plants and animals on which humans depend for essential foods, fuels, fibers, and pharmaceuticals.

It includes the distribution of the seeds and plant material that have revolutionized agriculture and freed an increasing share of the world's population to invest time, energy, and resources in all the other activities that contribute to human wellbeing. In more recent years it includes the deliberate movement of species at risk from climate change (McLachlan, Hellmann and Schwartz 2007; Schwartz *et al.* 2012). The process referred to variously as assisted migration, managed relocation, or assisted colonization is not uncontroversial, raising a number of ethical issues that worry conservation biologists (Minteer and Collins 2012), but it is still an example of deliberate species dispersal designed to enhance wellbeing – albeit by compensating for the effects of anthropogenic climate change.

The process is not cost free. Global production of foods, fuels, and fibers depends on the cultivation of a set of species that are generally non-native, and that generally confer benefits on humankind. At the same time, even though they might not establish or spread naturally, their cultivation has displaced native species everywhere. In so doing it has lowered biotic resistance to other introduced species – plant pests and pathogens – and created the need for mechanisms to control those pests and pathogens. The widespread use of herbicides, fungicides, insecticides, and other pesticides has in turn had wider impacts beyond the farm, setting in train other changes in species richness and abundance. It has also impacted the production of other ecosystem services. In all cases, though, it is the net effect that matters. The introduction of some species to support a particular ecosystem service, such as food production, may displace other species and may compromise other ecosystem services. But if the net benefits to society are still positive, the costs will be worth carrying. The problem is to ensure that the costs of species introductions that adversely affect other species and other ecosystem services are in fact taken into account. Since many such costs are external to the market they can frequently be displaced on to others and so ignored by the importer. The options for confronting importers with the true cost of their actions are addressed later in this book. Here it is important only to note that it is not enough to point to the adverse effects of introduced species. All introduced species that prey on or compete with others will have at least some adverse effects. What matters is the balance between the benefits their introduction confers on humankind, and the costs of the ecological changes they induce.

References

Aksoy, M. A. (2005) The evolution of agricultural trade flows. *Global Agricultural Trade and Developing Countries* (ed. M. A. Aksoy and J. C. Beghin), pp. 17–36. World Bank, Washington, DC.

Allen, R. B. and Lee, W. G. (2006) *Biological Invasions in New Zealand.* Springer, Berlin.

Andersen, T. M. and Herbertsson, T. T. (2005) Quantifying globalization. *Applied Economics*, 37, 1089–1098.

Blaustein, R. J. (2001) Kudzu's invasion into Southern United States life and culture. *The Great Reshuffling: Human Dimensions of Invasive Species* (ed. J. A. McNeeley), pp. 55–62. IUCN, Gland.

Cardinale, B. J., Duffy, J. E., Gonzalez, A., Hooper, D. U., Perrings, C., Venail, P., Narwani, A., Mace, G. M., Tilman, D., Wardle, D. A., Kinzig, A. P., Daily, G. C., Loreau, M., Grace, J. B., Larigauderie, A., Srivastava, D. S. and Naeem, S. (2012) Biodiversity loss and its impact on humanity. *Nature*, 486, 59–67.

Cassey, P., Blackburn, T. M., Russel, G. J., Jones, K. E. and Lockwood, J. L. (2004) Influences on the transport and establishment of exotic bird species: an analysis of the parrots (Psittaciformes) of the world. *Global Change Biology*, 10, 417–426.

Chowell, G., Bertozzi, S. M., Arantxa Colchero, M., Lopez-Gatell, H., Alpuche-Aranda, C., Hernandez, M. and Miller, M. A. (2009) Severe respiratory disease concurrent with H1N1 influenza circulation. *New England Journal of Medicine*, 361, 674–679.

Christen, D. C. and Matlack, G. R. (2009) The habitat and conduit function of roads in the spread of three invasive plant species. *Biological Invasions*, 11, 453–465.

Cohen, A. N., Carlton, J. T. and Fountain, M. C. (1995) Introduction, dispersal and potential impacts of the green crab carcinus-maenas in San-Francisco Bay, California. *Marine Biology*, 122, 225–237.

Coombs, E. M., Radtke, H., Isaacson, D. L. and Snyder, S. (1996) Economic and regional benefits from biological control of tansy ragwort, *senecio jacobaea*, in Oregon. *International Symposium on Biological Control of Weeds* (ed. V. C. Moran and J. H. Hoffmann), pp. 489–494. University of Cape Town, Stellenbosch.

Costello, C., Springborn, M., McAusland, C. and Solow, A. (2007) Unintended biological invasions: does risk vary by trading partner? *Journal of Environmental Economics and Management*, 54, 262–276.

Dalmazzone, S. (2000) Economic factors affecting vulnerability to biological invasions. *The Economics of Biological Invasions* (ed. C. Perrings,

M. Williamson and S. Dalmazzone), pp. 17–30. Edward Elgar, Cheltenham.

Daszak, P. and Cunningham, A. A. (1999) Extinction by infection. *Trends in Ecology and Evolution*, 14, 279.

Daszak, P., Cunningham, A. A. and Hyatt, A. D. (2000) Emerging infectious diseases of wildlife: threats to biodiversity and human health. *Science*, 287, 443–449.

Daszak, P., Jones, K., Levy, M., Gittleman, J., Patel, N., Mara, V., Nakielny, S. F., Chan, J. and Labo, M. N. (2007) Global trends in emerging infectious diseases. *American Journal of Tropical Medicine and Hygiene*, 77, 284–285.

Delfino, D. and Simmons, P. (2000) Infectious diseases as invasives in human populations. *The Economics of Biological Invasions* (ed. C. Perrings, M. Williamson and S. Dalmazzone), pp. 31–55. Edward Elgar, Cheltenham.

Dixon, S., McDonald, S. and Roberts, J. (2002) The impact of HIV and AIDS on Africa's economic development. *British Medical Journal*, 324, 232–234.

Elton, C. S. (1958) *The Ecology of Invasions by Animals and Plants*. Methuen, London.

Emmerson, G. and McCulloch, J. (1994) *Feral Peril: Queensland's Introduced Plants and Animals*. Queensland Parliamentary Library, Brisbane.

Farrell, G. and Schulten, G. M. M. (2002) Large grain borer in Africa: a history of efforts to limit its impact. *Integrated Pest Management Review*, 7, 67–84.

Global Invasive Species Program (2004) *Africa Invaded: The Growing Danger of Invasive Alien Species*. Global Invasive Species Program, Cape Town.

Goldschmidt, T., Witte, F. and Wanink, J. (1993) Cascading effects of the introduced Nile perch on the detritivorous/phytoplanktivorous species in the sublittoral areas of Lake Victoria. *Conservation Biology*, 7, 686–700.

Gonzalez, A., Mouquet, N. and Loreau, M. (2009) Biodiversity as spatial insurance: the effects of habitat fragmentation and dispersal on ecosystem functioning. *Biodiversity, Ecosystem Functioning, and Human Wellbeing: An Ecological and Economic Perspective* (ed. S. Naeem, D. E. Bunker, A. Hector, M. Loreau and C. Perrings), pp. 134–146. Oxford University Press.

Gurevitch, J. and Padilla, D. K. (2004) Are invasive species a major cause of extinctions? *Trends in Ecology and Evolution*, 19, 470–474.

Hubalek, Z. (2003) Emerging human infectious diseases: anthroponoses, zoonoses and sapronoses. *Emerging Infectious Diseases*, 9, 403–404.

Hulme, P. E. (2009) Trade, transport and trouble: managing invasive species pathways in an era of globalization. *Journal of Applied Ecology*, 46, 10–18.

Hulme, P. E., Bacher, S., Kenis, M., Klotz, S., Kuhn, I., Minchin, D., Nentwig, W., Olenin, S., Panov, V., Pergl, J., Pysek, P., Roques, A., Sol, D., Solarz, W. and Vilà, M. (2008) Grasping at the routes of biological invasions: a framework for integrating pathways into policy. *Journal of Applied Ecology*, 45, 403–414.

Hutchinson, A. B., Farnham, P. G., Dean, H. D., Ekwueme, D. U., del Rio, C., Kamimoto, L. and Kellerman, S. E. (2006) The economic burden of HIV in the United States in the era of highly active antiretroviral therapy: evidence of continuing racial and ethnic differences. *Journal of Acquired Immune Deficiency Syndrome*, 43, 451–457.

Jackson, L. E., Brussaard, L., de Ruiler, P. C., Pascual, U., Perrings, C. and Bawa, K. (2007) Agrobiodiversity. *Encyclopedia of Biodiversity* (ed. S. A. Lerin), pp. 1–13. Elsevier, New York.

Jaffee, S. M. and Henson, S. (2005) Agro-food exports from developing countries: the challenges posed by standards. *Global Agricultural Trade and Developing Countries* (ed. M. A. Aksoy and J. C. Beghin), pp. 91–114. World Bank, Washington, DC.

Jetter, K. M., DiTomaso, J. M., Drake, D. J., Klonsky, K. M., Pitcairn, M. J. and Sumner, D. A. (2003) Biological control of yellow starthistle. *Exotic Pests and Diseases: Biology and Economics for Biosecurity* (ed. D. A. Sumner), pp. 225–241. Iowa State University Press.

Jones, K. E., Patel, N., Levy, M., Storeygard, A., Balk, D., Gittleman, J. L. and Daszak, P. (2008) Global trends in emerging infectious diseases. *Nature*, 451, 990–993.

Kasulo, V. (2000) The impact of invasive species in African lakes. *The Economics of Biological Invasions* (ed. C. Perrings, M. Williamson and S. Dalmazzone), pp. 183–207. Edward Elgar, Cheltenham.

Kinzig, A. P., Pacala, S. and Tilman, D. (eds.) (2002) *Functional Consequences of Biodiversity: Empirical Progess and Theoretical Extensions*. Princeton University Press.

Kinzig, A. P., Ryan, P., Etienne, M., Elmqvist, T., Allison, H. and Walker, B. H. (2006) Resilience and regime shifts: assessing cascading effects. *Ecology and Society*, 11, 20.

Knowler, D. (2007) Estimation of a stock-recruitment relationship for Black Sea anchovy (*Engraulis encrasicolus*) under the influence of nutrient enrichment and the invasive comb-jelly, *Mnemiopsis leidyi*. *Fisheries Research*, 84, 275–281.

Le Maitre, D. C., van Wilgen, B. W., Gelderblom, C. M., Bailey, C., Chapman, R. A. and Nel, J. A. (2002) Invasive alien trees and water resources in South Africa: case studies of the costs and benefits of management. *Forest Ecology and Management*, 160, 143–159.

Leistritz, F. L., Bangsund, D. A. and Hodur, N. M. (2004) Assessing the economic impact of invasive weeds: the case of leafy spurge (*Euphorbia esula*). *Weed Technology*, 18, 1392–1395.

Leung, B., Drake, J. M. and Lodge, D. M. (2004) Predicting invasions: propagule pressure and the gravity of allee effects. *Ecology*, 85, 1651–1660.

Levine, J. M. and D'Antonio, C. M. (1999) Elton revisited: a review of evidence linking diversity and invisibility. *Oikas*, 87, 15–26.

(2003) Forecasting biological invasions with increasing international trade. *Conservation Biology*, 17, 322–326.

Levine, J. M. Vilà, M., D'Antonio, C. M., Dukes, J. S., Grigulis, K. and Lavorel, S. (2003) Mechanisms underlying the impacts of exotic plant invasions. *Proceedings of the Royal Society B: Biological Sciences*, 270, 775–781.

Lodge, D. M. (1993) Biological invasions: lessons for ecology. *Trends in Ecology and Evolution*, 8, 133–137.

Lonsdale, W. M. (1999) Global patterns of plant invasions and the concept of invasibility. *Ecology*, 80, 1522–1536.

Loreau, M. (2010) *The Challenges of Biodiversity Science*. International Ecology Institute, Oldendorf.

Loreau, M., Naeem, S. and Inchausti, P. (2002) *Biodiversity and Ecosystem Functioning: Synthesis and Perspectives*. Oxford University Press.

Loreau, M., Mouquet, N. and Gonzalez, A. (2003) Biodiversity as spatial insurance in heterogeneous landscapes. *Proceedings of the National Academy of Sciences*, 22, 12765–12770.

MacArthur, R. H. and Wilson, E. O. (1967) *The Theory of Island Biogeography*. Princeton University Press.

Masifwa, W., Twongo, T. and Denny, P. (2001) The impact of water hyacinth, *Eichhornia crassipes* (Mart) solms on the abundance and diversity of aquatic macroinvertebrates along the shores of northern Lake Victoria, Uganda. *Hydrobiologia*, 452, 79–88.

McLachlan, J. M., Hellmann, J. J. and Schwartz, M. W. (2007) A framework for debate of assisted migration in an era of climate change. *Conservation Biology*, 21, 297–302.

McNeely, J. A. (2001) An introduction to human dimensions of invasive alien species. *The Great Reshuffling: Human Dimensions of Invasive Alien Species* (ed. J. A. McNeely), pp. 5–20. IUCN, Gland.

McNeill, W. H. (1977) *Plagues and People*. Anchor Books, New York.

Mendis, K., Rietveld, A., Warsame, M., Bosman, A., Greenwood, B. and Wernsdorfer, W. H. (2009) From malaria control to eradication: the WHO perspective. *Tropical Medicine & International Health*, 14, 802–809.

Minteer, B. A. and Collins, J. P. (2012) Species conservation, rapid environmental change, and ecological ethics. *Nature Education Knowledge*, 3, 14.

Moyle, P. B. and Light, T. (1996) Fish invasions in California: do abiotic factors determine success? *Ecology*, 77, 1666–1670.

Naeem, S., Bunker, D., Hector, A., Loreau, M. and Perrings, C. (eds.) (2009) *Biodiversity, Ecosystem Functioning, and Human Wellbeing: An Ecological and Economic Perspective*. Oxford University Press.

Niemelä, J., Koivula, M. and Kotze, J. (2007) The effects of forestry on carabid beetles (*Coleoptera: Carabidae*) in boreal forests. *Journal of Insect Conservation*, 11, 5–18.

O'Neill, C. (1997) Economic impact of zebra mussels: results of the 1995 zebra mussel information clearinghouse study. *Great Lakes Research Review*, 3, 35–42.

Oerke, E.-C., Dehne, H.-W., Schönbeck, F. and Weber, A. (1994) *Crop Production and Crop Protection: Estimated Losses in Major Food and Cash Crops*. Elsevier, Amsterdam.

OTA (1993) *Harmful Non-indigenous Species in the United States*. Office of Technology Assessment, US Congress, Washington, DC.

Perrault, A., Bennett, M., Burgiel, S., Delach, A. and Muffett, C. (2003) *Invasive Species, Agriculture and Trade: Case Studies from the NAFTA Context*. North American Commission for Environmental Cooperation, Montreal.

Perrings, C. (2007) Pests, pathogens and poverty: biological invasions and agricultural dependence. *Biodiversity Economics: Principles, Methods, and Applications* (ed. A. Kontoleon, U. Pascual and T. Swanson), pp. 133–165. Cambridge University Press.

Perrings, C., Mooney, H., Lonsdale, M. and Burgeil, S. (2010a) Globalization and invasive species: policy and management options. *Bioinvasions and Globalization: Ecology, Economics, Management and Policy* (ed. C. Perrings, H. Mooney and M. Williamson), pp. 235–250. Oxford University Press.

Perrings, C., Burgiel, S., Lonsdale, W. M., Mooney, H. and Williamson, M. (2010b) International cooperation in the solution to trade-related invasive species risks. *Annals of the New York Academy of Sciences*, 1195, 198–212.

Phillips, B. L., Brown, G. P., Webb, J. K. and Shine, R. (2006) Invasion and the evolution of speeds in toads. *Nature*, 439, 803.

Pimentel, D., Zuniga, R. and Morrison, D. (2005) Update on the environmental and economic costs associated with alien-invasive species in the United States. *Ecological Economics*, 52, 273–288.

Pimentel, D., Lach, L., Zuniga, R. and Morrison, D. (2000) Environmental and economic costs of nonindigenous species in the United States. *Bioscience*, 50, 53–56.

Pimentel, D., McNair, S., Janecka, S., Wightman, J., Simmonds, C., O'Connell, C., Wong, E., Russel, L., Zern, C., Aquino, T. and Tsomondo, T. (2001) Economic and environmental threats of alien plant, animal and microbe invasions. *Agriculture, Ecosystems and Environment*, 84, 1–20.

Polasky, S., Costello, C. and McAusland, C. (2004) On trade, land-use, and biodiversity. *Journal of Environmental Economics and Management*, 48, 911–925.

Pyšek, P., Chytrý, M. and Jarošík, V. (2010) Habitats and land-use as determinants of plant invasions in the temperate zone of Europe. *Bioinvasions and Globalization: Ecology, Economics, Management and Policy* (ed. C. Perrings, H. A. Mooney and M. Williamson), pp. 66–82. Oxford University Press.

Rangi, D. K. (2004) *Invasive Alien Species: Agriculture and Development*. UNEP, Nairobi.

Reichard, S. H. and White, P. S. (2003) Invasion biology: an emerging field of study. *Annals of the Missouri Botanical Garden*, 90, 64–66.

Rejmánek, M., Richardson, D. M. and Pyšek, P. (2004) Plant invasions and invasibility of plant communities. *Vegetation Ecology* (ed. E. Van Der Maarel). Blackwell, Oxford.

Sax, D. F. and Gaines, S. D. (2003) Species diversity: from global decreases to local increases. *Trends in Ecology and Evolution*, 18, 561–568.

(2008) Species invasions and extinction: the future of native biodiversity on islands. *Proceedings of the National Academy of Sciences*, 105, 11490–11497.

Schwartz, M. W., Hellmann, J. J., McLachlan, J. M., Sax, D. F., Borevitz, J. O., Brennan, J., Camacho, A. E., Ceballos, G., Clark, J. R., Doremus, H., Early, R., Etterson, J. R., Fielder, D., Gill, J. L., Gonzalez, P., Green, N., Hannah, L. E. E., Jamieson, D. W., Javeline, D. and Minteer, B. A. (2012) Managed relocation: integrating the scientific, regulatory, and ethical challenges. *Bioscience*, 62, 732–743.

Semmens, B. X., Buhle, E. R., Salomon, A. K. and Pattengill-Semmens, C. V. (2004) A hotspot of non-native marine fishes: evidence for the aquarium trade as an invasion pathway. *Marine Ecology Progress Series*, 266, 239–244.

Simberloff, D. and Rejmánek, M. (eds.) (2011) *Encyclopedia of Biological Invasions*. University of California Press, Los Angeles.

Smith, C.-S., Lansdale, W. M. and Fortune, J. (1999) When to ignore advice: invasion predictions and decision theory. *Biological Invasions*, 1, 89–96.

Stutzman, S. K., Jetter, M. and Klonsky, K. M. (2004) *An Annotated Bibliography on the Economics of Invasive Plants.* University of California, Davis, Agricultural Issues Center.

Tatem, A. J. (2009) The worldwide airline network and the dispersal of exotic species: 2007–2010. *Ecography*, 34, 94–102.

Tatem, A. J., Rogers, D. J. and Hay, S. I. (2006) Global transport networks and infectious disease spread. *Advances in Parasitology*, 62, 293–343.

Turpie, J., Heydenrych, B. and Hassan, R. (2001) Accounting for fynbos: a preliminary assessment of the status and economic value of fynbos vegetation in the Western Cape. *Accounting for Stock and Flow Values of Wooded Land Resources: Methods and Results from South Africa, Pretoria, Centre for Environmental Economics and Policy in Africa.* CEEPA, University of Pretoria.

Turpie, J. K., Marais, C. and Blignaut, J. N. (2008) The Working for Water Programme: evolution of a payments for ecosystem services mechanism that addresses both poverty and ecosystem service delivery in South Africa. *Ecological Economics*, 65, 789–799.

UNAIDS (2010) *Global Report: UNAIDS Report on the Global AIDS Epidemic 2010.* United Nations, New York.

United Nations (1993) *Convention on Biological Diversity.* United Nations, New York.

United Nations Department of Economic and Social Affairs Population Division (2004) *The Impact of Aids.* United Nations, New York.

United States General Accounting Office (2000) *Invasive Species: Federal and Selected State Funding to Address Harmful, Nonnative Species.* General Accounting Office, Washington, DC.

University of Georgia Center for Invasive Species and Ecosystem Health & National Park Service (2013) *Invasive Plants Atlas of the United States.* Available at www.invasiveplantatlas.org/whereinvasive.html?sub=2425.

Vilà, M. and Pujadas, J. (2001) Land-use and socio-economic correlates of plant invasions in European and North African countries. *Biological Conservation*, 100, 397–401.

Vilà, M., Espinar, J. L., Hejda, M., Hulme, P. E., Jarošík, V., Maron, J. L., Pergl, J., Schaffner, U., Sun, Y. and Pyšek, P. (2011) Ecological impacts of invasive alien plants: a meta-analysis of their effects on species, communities and ecosystems. *Ecology Letters*, 14, 702–708.

Walker, B. H., Gunderson, L. H., Kinzig, A. P., Folke, C., Carpenter, S. R. and Schultz, L. (2006) A handful of heuristics and some propositions for understanding resilience in social-ecological systems. *Ecology and Society*, 11, 13.

Ward, J. M. J., Stromberg, E. L., Nowell, D. C. and Nutter, F. W. (1999) Grey leaf spot, a disease of global importance in maize production. *Plant Disease*, 83, 884–895.

Wilcove, D. S., Rothstein, D., Dubrow, J., Phillips, A. and Losos, E. (1998) Quantifying threats to imperiled species in the United States. *BioScience*, 48, 607–615.

Williamson, M. (1996) *Biological Invasions*. Chapman and Hall, London. (1999) Invasions. *Ecography*, 22, 5–12.

Williamson, M. and Fitter, A. D. (1996) The varying success of invaders. *Ecology*, 77, 1661–1666.

Witte, F., Goldschmidt, T., Wanink, J., Oijen, M., Goudswaard, K., Witte-Maas, E. and Bouton, N. (1992) The destruction of an endemic species flock: quantitative data on the decline of the haplochromine cichlids of Lake Victoria. *Environmental Biology of Fishes*, 34, 1–28.

World Bank (2005) *Global Economic Prospects*. World Bank, Washington, DC. (2012a) *Air Transport, Registered Carrier Departures Worldwide*. Available at http://data.worldbank.org/indicator/IS.AIR.DPRT (accessed 2012).

(2012b) *Merchandise Trade (% of GDP)*. Available at http://data.world bank.org/indicator/TG.VAL.TOTL.GD.ZS (accessed 2012).

Zavaleta, E. (2000) The economic value of controlling an invasive shrub. *Ambio*, 29, 462–467.

PART II

The search for solutions

States began to be established, and so two categories were made of the things which had been wrested away from early ownership in common. For some things were public, that is, were the property of the people (which is the real meaning of that expression), while other things were private, that is, were the property of individuals. Ownership, however, both public and private, arises in the same way ... Two conclusions may be drawn from what has thus far been said. The first is, that that which cannot be occupied, or which never has been occupied, cannot be the property of any one, because all property has arisen from occupation. The second is, that all that which has been so constituted by nature that although serving some one person it still suffices for the common use of all other persons, is today and ought in perpetuity to remain in the same condition as when it was first created by nature ... things which are called "public" are, according to the Laws of the law of nations, the common property of all, and the private property of none. The air belongs to this class of things for two reasons. First, it is not susceptible of occupation; and second its common use is destined for all men. For the same reasons the sea is common to all, because it is so limitless that it cannot become a possession of any one, and because it is adapted for the use of all.

(Grotius 1916)

8 | *Getting the prognosis right*

8.1 Understanding the "anthropogenic" in anthropogenic biodiversity change

The main elements of the biodiversity problem identified in Part I of this book are the following. The current extinction event is the outcome of human decisions to harvest some species, to domesticate others, to protect a few, to destroy those seen to be harmful, and to neglect those whose usefulness is unclear. It is the consequence of decisions to convert some ecosystems for use in agriculture, forestry, aquaculture, industry, commerce, and human habitation, and to impact others through the diversion of water, the extraction of minerals, the construction of road, rail, and energy infrastructures, and the emission of pollutants to soil, air, and water. Although there have been many unintended consequences of these decisions, none was taken blindly. The people who made them were behaving in a purposeful way, taking into account their goals, their resources, the social and environmental constraints within which they acted, and the information available about the likely consequences of alternative choices. Few decisions may have been completely informed, but none was completely uninformed. People's choices may have been more limited in some cases than others, but never have people had no choice at all. Understanding anthropogenic biodiversity change requires understanding of the goals people have when they make decisions that alter the richness or abundance of species. It requires understanding of the conditions within which they make decisions, and the information they have about the consequences of their actions. It requires understanding of the way those decisions change when conditions or information change.

Why do we need to know this? If people always made the same decisions regardless of conditions, prediction would be easy. Future anthropogenic impacts on the biophysical world would be found by simply scaling environmental impacts by the expected rate of growth of population. But people's decisions are sensitive to conditions. People make different decisions when they are old from when they are young, when they are rich from when they are poor, when they are well from when they are ill. Even in the simplest of all predictive models of environmental impact, the $I = PAT$ equation, it is recognized that the effect people might be expected to have on the environment depends not only on population, P, but also on the available resources, A, and the way those resources are used, T. Each variable is the product of choices that people make. The critical point in the paper that spawned the $I = PAT$ equation was that these elements operate on different timescales – that while population is a slowly changing variable, both the availability of resources and technology can be expected to change more rapidly (Ehrlich and Holdren 1971). Decisions about fertility are made less frequently than decisions about the balance between consumer goods or inputs in production (Dasgupta 1993). People select the technologies they apply, and change their selection as conditions change.

Despite this, human behaviors are persistently treated as exogenous drivers in most attempts to project future environmental impacts. Not only are human behaviors selected in a manner that largely ignores what we know about past decisions, but they are also assumed to be insensitive to the projected state of the system over long periods of time. Most projections of the future trajectories of biodiversity still ignore feedbacks between the social and ecological components of the coupled system (Pereira *et al.* 2010). This makes it difficult to incorporate human responses into projections of environmental change. Only by developing conditional predictive models of the system dynamics that include feedbacks between the social and environmental systems will it be possible to evaluate the future consequences of current decisions.

The famous report to the Club of Rome, *The Limits to Growth*, published in the year after Ehrlich and Holdren's paper (Meadows *et al.* 1972), considered a range of scenarios that led to the exhaustion of various natural resources. While the report argued that these outcomes reflected overshoot because of delayed decisions to adapt to increasing scarcity, the unresponsiveness of decision-makers had in fact been built into the models used to make the projections. Indeed, the report was strongly criticized for the fact that the various projections it made were insensitive to feedbacks in the coupled system that might be expected to change people's behaviors (see, for example, Beckerman 1992).

It is therefore ironic that most projections of anthropogenic environmental change are still made in the same way. The scenario approach adopted in *The Limits to Growth* has been enshrined as the dominant method for projecting global change in one environmental assessment after another. While people may be most familiar with the various emissions scenarios used by the IPCC to project climate change (IPCC 2000), the same device has been used in a number of other assessments. In all cases the human behaviors that drive each scenario are themselves insensitive to the changes they engender. Most relevant for this book is the fact that biodiversity scenarios with these same characteristics have been central to projections made in the MA (Millennium Ecosystem Assessment 2005b) and successive state of biodiversity reports issued by the CBD (Convention on Biological Diversity 2010a). The particular scenarios involved are considered later. At this point what is important to note is that an understanding of the feedbacks between the ecological and social components of the coupled system are critical to an understanding of its dynamics. These feedbacks determine people's responses to signals about environmental change. If we are to make environmental predictions conditional on the adoption of some policy, we need to model the way that people may be expected to change their behavior as the world around them changes. While some attempt has been made to incorporate socio-economic feedbacks in models of environmental change (Grubler, O'Neill and van Vuuren 2006; Moss *et al.* 2010), there is a long way to go.

Getting the prognosis for anthropogenic biodiversity change right does not mean making perfect predictions. It means making the best projections we can, conditional on our understanding of the system dynamics and the drivers of change. Whether the drivers of change are controllable or not is critical. If the drivers are not controllable, as is the case with non-anthropogenic climate change, plate tectonics, or seismic activity, the best we can do may be to model responses to the environmental changes induced by the range of values those drivers can take. If the drivers are controllable, as is the case with anthropogenic climate change, habitat conversion, or industrial emissions to air, land, and water, we may be able to direct environmental change to meet our goals, given resources, and constraints. Scenario planning is relevant to the first case. Its role is to make it possible to think through the best response to changes in conditions that are beyond the decision-maker's control. But where the drivers of environmental change lie in human

decisions that are amenable to policy we need a different approach. We
still need to understand the consequences of business as usual, but
beyond that we need to project the consequences of different policies
and the behavioral changes they induce in order to be able to select
between policies.

This chapter considers the challenges involved in projecting anthropogenic biodiversity change. Beginning with the scenarios adopted by
the MA and the CBD, it considers what has already been done and how
the conclusions reached might be expected to change if socio-economic
feedbacks were taken into account. This is not to assert that existing
feedback mechanisms are always effective. Indeed, the weakness of
existing feedback mechanisms has been a constant refrain of earlier
chapters. But feedback mechanisms do exist. Market prices provide
strong (albeit imperfect) indicators of the relative scarcity of resources
that are transacted between people. The political process provides
equally strong, though often less well directed, signals of the importance
to people of resources in the public domain. How would we expect
projections of future human behavior and environmental conditions to
change if these feedbacks were taken into account?

8.2 Biodiversity scenarios

At the turn of this century *Science* published one of the first attempts
to project biodiversity changes through to 2100 (Sala *et al.* 2000).
The study projected the consequence of five independent drivers of
biodiversity change for a set of ten terrestrial biomes. The drivers were
taken to be land use, atmospheric CO_2, nitrogen deposition, climate,
and biotic exchange, and the biomes considered were arctic tundra,
alpine tundra, boreal forest, grasslands, savannas, Mediterranean ecosystems, deserts, northern temperate forests, southern temperate forests, and tropical forests. The business-as-usual levels of all drivers were
calculated from global models of climate, vegetation, and land use.[1]
Land-use change largely meant habitat conversion, which was expected
to be greatest in tropical forests and in the temperate forests of South
America, and least in the arctic and alpine tundras and northern temperate forests. The independent effect of individual drivers was then

---

[1] Climate was modeled through the Hadley CM2 scenario, vegetation through
Biome3, and land use through the A1 scenario of IMAGE 2.

estimated, and two scenarios for interactions between drivers added – one in which all drivers were antagonistic and one in which all drivers were synergistic.

The approach shows just how strong the assumptions are that have informed such exercises. The assumption that all anthropogenic drivers have constant effects over a period of a hundred years is strong enough. But it pales by comparison with the assumption that people's behaviors will be unaffected by changes in the biophysical environment over a similar period. All of the evidence is that human responses to signals about the scarcity of resources change over time, that long-run responses are more elastic than short-run responses, and that social norms of behavior evolve to meet altered conditions (Kinzig *et al.* 2013). The capacity of societies to adapt to a changing environment is limited by a range of factors – including their understanding of the nature of environmental change, the rigidity of social institutions, and the availability of resources (Adger, Lorenzoni and O'Brien 2009a; Adger *et al.* 2009b) – but even Malthusian collapse is an adaptive response. In one historical case after another, adaptive responses to environmental change have included variation in activity levels, migration, institutional transformation, and the establishment of new laws, property rights, and customs (for case studies see, for example, Tiffen, Mortimore and Gichuki 1994; Dillehay and Kolata, 2004; for an overview see Brown and Westaway 2011).

Since publication of the paper by Sala *et al.*, biodiversity change scenarios for the twenty-first century have proliferated. They have been a feature of every major assessment, and all share essentially the same characteristics (Leadley *et al.* 2010). Consider, for example, the scenarios developed for the MA. It developed four scenarios of "plausible" futures based on different assumptions about driving forces and their possible interactions, calling its future worlds "global orchestration," "order from strength," "adapting mosaic," and "techno garden" (Millennium Ecosystem Assessment 2005b; Sala *et al.* 2005). Each assumed a different set of initial social, economic, political, and institutional conditions and a correspondingly different set of environmental strategies, none corresponding to current conditions. These were then held constant over the projection period – 2050, with some variables taken to 2100.

"Global orchestration" focused on the implications of failure to deal with large-scale processes, including abrupt, often catastrophic change. It suggested that the mean loss of ecosystem services might be relatively low but that the variance of loss would be high. The "order from strength" scenario focused on the implications of the patchy failure of ecosystem services, and the effect that had on poverty. It involved the most pessimistic outcomes for biodiversity. "Adapting mosaic" assumed local adaptation to changing conditions, and some scope for transferring best practice. It was the most optimistic of the scenarios. "Techno garden" focused on the capacity of technological change to address losses of ecosystem services, and questioned the ability of technological change to keep up. The proximate driver of biodiversity change in each case was the effect of human activities on habitat, summarized in Table 8.1.

Table 8.1 *Change in land cover in 2050 in four scenarios*

Category of land	2000	GO	OS	AM	TG	GO	OS	AM	TG
		Million hectares in 2050				Percentage of 2000 land cover			
Agricultural land	3,357	3,646	4,162	3,580	3,660	109	124	107	109
Extensive grassland	1,711	1,700	1,704	1,704	1,707	99	100	100	100
Regrowth forests	446	630	523	550	462	141	117	123	103
Ice	231	224	225	222	221	97	97	96	96
Tundra	768	727	727	726	724	95	95	95	94
Wooded tundra	106	84	83	86	89	79	78	81	83
Boreal forest	1,509	1,554	1,551	1,556	1,553	103	103	103	103
Cool conifer	168	196	188	192	194	117	112	114	116
Temperate mixed forest	201	262	236	250	287	130	117	124	143
Temperate deciduous forest	145	133	110	119	155	91	76	82	107
Warm mixed forest	95	79	62	76	109	83	65	80	115
Steppe	804	750	692	749	730	93	86	93	91
Desert	1,678	1,643	1,637	1,660	1,665	98	98	99	99
Scrubland	207	170	122	183	182	82	59	88	88
Savanna	705	404	316	511	450	57	45	73	64
Tropical woodland	483	517	426	524	503	107	88	109	104
Tropical forest	670	568	520	597	594	85	78	89	89

Note: GO global orchestration; OS order from strength; AM adapting mosaic; TG techno garden.
Source: Sala *et al.* (2005).

"Order from strength" recorded the largest loss of habitat (20 percent relative to 1970 levels) due to the impact of population growth on food demand and the slow increase in agricultural yields. "Techno garden" recorded the smallest loss (13 percent relative to 1970 levels) due to the rapid increase in crop yields assumed. "Adapting mosaic" and "global orchestration" were in between.

Since publication of the MA there has been increasing emphasis on strengthening the biophysical components of the models used to make projections of the impacts of global change on biodiversity. Efforts have been made to enhance both phenomenological and process-based models. The first involves improvements to the data sets used to estimate species–area, niche, or dose–response relationships to project biodiversity change. The second involves strengthening the treatment of ecological processes in models of biodiversity change (Leadley *et al.* 2010; Pereira *et al.* 2010). Pereira's summary of these various efforts is reported in Table 8.2.

While treatment of the biophysical feedbacks involved may have improved, however, treatment of the social dimension of the system remains as undeveloped as ever. Why is this a problem? Projections of this sort are intended to inform policy for future biodiversity and ecosystem conservation, to help decision-makers understand the consequences of strategic alternatives, and to identify priorities for action. Yet the information they offer cannot inform even the most basic choice between adaptation and mitigation.

Mitigation involves actions that change the likelihood of an event. Adaptation involves actions that change the impact of an event without changing the likelihood that it will occur. Mitigation accordingly implies action before the event. Adaptation may involve actions taken before, during, or after the event. It usually implies actions that reduce the expected damage, although it may also include actions that pool or transfer the risks. Whether mitigation or adaptation is appropriate depends on the degree to which the system is either observable or controllable. In the case of climate change, for example, mitigation alternatives involve reductions in carbon emissions or carbon sequestration. That is, it is assumed that the likelihood of climate change can be managed by managing greenhouse gas emissions. Adaptation alternatives, on the other hand, include defensive expenditures such as construction of coastal and estuarine defenses or the managed retreat of coastlines to adapt to sea-level rise. They also include the strengthening

Table 8.2 *Examples of biodiversity scenario studies highlighting methods used to calculate impacts of global change on several biodiversity metrics*

	Socio-economic scenarios	Direct drivers	Projections of direct drivers	Projections of impacts on biodiversity	Metric of biodiversity and ecosystem service	Year
Terrestrial	MA	LUC, CC	IMAGE	Species–area relationships	Species extinctions (plants) and habitat loss	2100
	IPCC SRES and others	CC	GCM (HadCM2)	Niche-based models; range changes converted to extinction risk using species-area curves or IUCN status	Species extinctions (plants and animals)	2050
	MA	LUC, CC	IMAGE	Habitat loss from current species ranges	Species extinctions (birds)	2100
	GBO2	LUC, CC, N	IMAGE	Dose–response model (GLOBIO)	Species abundance changes	2050
	IPCC SRES	CC	GCM (HadCM3)	Dynamic global vegetation models	Functional group range shifts (plants) and carbon sequestration	2100
Freshwater	MA	Water use and CC	Water-GAP	Phenomenological model relating river discharge to fish species richness	Species extinctions (fishes)	2100

Marine	GEO4, IAASTD	Fishing effort	Ecosim	Marine trophic model (Ecosim with Ecopath)	Functional group abundance changes and fish landings	2050
	IPCC SRES	CC	GCMs (HadCM3, PCM)	Phenomenological model relating sea surface temperature to bleaching frequencies	Habitat loss of tropical coral.	2100
	IPCC SRES	CC	GCMs (GFDL CM 2.1)	Niche based models	Species range shifts (vertebrate and invertebrates)	2050

Note: socio-economic scenarios: MA, GBO2, GEO4, IPCC Special Report on Emission Scenarios (IPCC SRES), International Assessment for Agricultural Science, Technology and Development (IAASTD). Direct drivers: land-use change (LUC), climate change (CC), nitrogen deposition (N), water use and fishing effort. Projections of direct drivers: indicates model that was used to simulate future changes in direct drivers (GCM = general circulation model with specific climate model indicated in parentheses).
Source: Pereira *et al.* (2010).

or relocation of infrastructure and industrial, commercial, or domestic constructions to adapt to the increased threat of storm damage, and other local features of global warming. Beyond this, they involve changes in land use, especially changes in crop and livestock mixes to adapt to changes in temperature and precipitation regimes. In all cases it is assumed that the consequences of climate change can be managed, even if the causes cannot. Choosing between these options requires information on the payoff to each.

Most strategies involve a combination of mitigation and adaptation. In principle, the optimal strategy is that which balances the marginal costs and benefits of alternative actions. The features of adaptation that influence the benefit–cost calculus are the following. First, adaptation represents a local response to global change, where global change is itself treated as exogenous to the problem. The benefits of adaptation expenditures are captured almost entirely by the decision-maker, or the community represented by the decision-maker in the case of public goods. This implies that private individuals or firms have a much stronger incentive to undertake private adaptation actions than they have to undertake private mitigation actions. Furthermore, public goods such as sea defenses or public health regimes allow free-riding by the local population, but do not in general offer significant benefits to the international community. No country has an incentive to free-ride on the adaptation expenditures by another country, and all countries are able to capture the benefits of adaptation.

Second, the timing of adaptation expenditures is less constrained by the dynamics of the circulation system than the timing of mitigation expenditures. Adaptation actions do not need to be undertaken so far in advance of climate change to deliver benefits. Indeed they may even take the form of reactions to climate change after the fact. It is not therefore surprising that adaptation is the best private response to climate change under most of the scenarios painted by the IPCC. Third, since adaptation is a local/national option, it is constrained by the same factors that constrain all local/national expenditures. International inequality in the distribution of income and assets is reflected in differences in the level of self-protection against the effects of climatic variability.

Among the MA scenarios, the "global orchestration" scenario came the closest to discussing the implications of the adoption of coordinated mitigation actions, and a comparison between "global orchestration" and "adapting mosaic" leaves the impression that projections based on adaptation rather than mitigation were thought to have a better outcome for a range of variables, including biodiversity. The "order from strength" scenario implied a failure of both adaptation and mitigation strategies, reflecting a positive feedback between poverty and environmental change. The "techno garden" scenario was another adaptation scenario, corresponding to a different set of initial conditions in the simulation model. No scenario combined mitigation and adaptation actions, or allowed for the evolution of human responses to changing environmental conditions.

The scenario methods chosen to represent uncertain futures by the IPCC, the MA, and the CBD derive from tools developed in the private sector to hone their adaptation skills. But while it made a lot of sense for Shell to use a scenario approach to develop the capacity to adapt to futures over which it had no control, this is not what the international community should be doing about anthropogenic global environmental change. Non-probabilistic scenarios may be an appropriate way to think about adaptation to exogenous changes in state, but they are not an appropriate way to think about mitigation actions in the face of endogenous changes in state. Wherever adaptation is not a feasible/desirable response, the scenario approach is not an appropriate scientific support to decision-making.

If we believe that biodiversity change is anthropogenically driven, and that we can affect the probability of different outcomes by choosing between policy options today, then the scenario approach is just not the right one to use. If we believe that there is nothing we can do to affect the probability distribution of outcomes, and that our best strategy is to ensure that we have a response to every possible outcome, then the scenario approach is appropriate. Note that the two strategies require different kinds of information and a different capacity to intervene in the system. Mitigation requires both an understanding of the probabilities attaching to different outcomes, and the capacity to influence those probabilities by taking action now. Adaptation does not require information about the probability of some outcome, but does require information about the cost if that outcome occurs. It also requires the capacity to take actions now or in the future that will alter that cost.

8.3 Current prognoses

The CBD's 2010 assessment of the future of biodiversity (Convention on Biological Diversity 2010a) summarizes the current state of our understanding of the consequences of existing trends in human activities for wild-living species. Consistent with Butchart *et al.* (2010) and Hoffmann *et al.* (2010), the CBD noted that the abundance of vertebrate species fell by around one-third between 1970 and 2006, and that it was projected to continue to fall, especially in the tropics and freshwater aquatic systems. It reached a number of conclusions about the most important factors involved. First, it concluded that none of the five principal pressures directly driving biodiversity loss – habitat change, overexploitation, pollution, invasive alien species, and climate change – is declining, and most are increasing in intensity. Second, because of this the majority of species whose risk of extinction has been assessed are moving closer to extinction. This includes nearly a quarter of all plant species, and a much higher proportion of amphibians and coral species. Third, even where species are not at risk of extinction, there have been significant and rapid changes in abundance. Fourth, natural habitats are projected to continue to decline in extent, to be increasingly fragmented, and to be altered through other stresses. Although the rate of conversion of some habitats, such as tropical forests and mangroves, has slowed, others face increasing pressure. These include freshwater wetlands, sea-ice habitats, salt marshes, coral reefs, sea-grass beds, and shellfish reefs.

As with early assessments, the CBD's recent efforts to project the consequences of these trends were informed by a set of scenarios drawn from prior assessments including the MA (Millennium Ecosystem Assessment 2005a), the Global Environmental Outlook (UNEP 2007), the CBD's own Global Biodiversity Outlooks (Convention on Biological Diversity 2006), and the IPCC (2000). These all imply that there will be continuing and often accelerating species extinctions, loss of natural habitat, and changes in the distribution and abundance of species, species groups, and biomes throughout the twenty-first century.

Model-based projections included three scenarios run through the IPCC's MiniCam model, of which the business-as-usual case comes the closest to being a projection of the consequences of current trends. The business-as-usual case projects changes in land either committed to the production of crops or remaining as habitat over the next hundred years. It concludes that the land area committed to crops, biofuels, managed pasture, and managed forest will all increase, while the area committed to unmanaged forest, unmanaged pasture, and (unmanaged) grassland will all decrease (Convention on Biological Diversity 2010a). The impact of changing land use on biodiversity in this approach depends primarily on the assumptions that actively managed forest and grassland systems have only limited capacity to support wild species.

In addition, however, the CBD concluded that ecosystems are likely to experience thresholds, positive feedbacks, and time-lagged effects leading to tipping points, as the system shifts from one stability domain to another (making the biodiversity effects of global change hard to predict). Effects of this kind were not demonstrated in any baseline models of biodiversity change, but were included as scenarios. That is, they were treated as plausible but unpredictable outcomes of either anthropogenic or other environmental stressors. They included the possibility that interactions between deforestation, fire, and climate change could induce rainforests to flip into a savanna or seasonal forest state; that overgrazing in areas of the Sahel could lead to desertification; or that biological invasions of islands could lead to the transformation of ecological communities. Events of this kind have potentially significant consequences for human wellbeing and so are worth considering. But since the drivers and mechanisms are both reasonably well understood in all three cases, and since we have at least some prior observations of such flips, it is not at all clear that they cannot be modeled to some degree. Of course there may well be other changes of state we have not seen before, and for which we have no possible control mechanism, that may be good candidates for scenarios of this kind. Such scenarios may have value in enabling us to improve our preparedness by identifying possible adaptive responses.

Where the drivers of some environmental change are understood it is possible to develop phenomenological models of the process, even if the mechanisms are not fully understood. The GLOBIO model is of this kind. It uses a dose–response framework to estimate changes in mean species abundance caused by land-use and land-cover change, land-use intensity, fragmentation, climate change, atmospheric nitrogen deposition, and infrastructural development (Alkemade *et al.* 2009). The model has been used to evaluate the biodiversity consequences of a number of quite specific strategies. These include climate-change mitigation through biofuels, the growth of plantation forestry, and the growth of protected areas. The outcomes are then compared to the outcomes of a reference scenario that the authors consider to be equivalent to the B2 scenario in IPCC (2000) or the "adapting mosaic" scenario in Sala *et al.* (2005). All model runs confirm that mean species abundance will continue to decline over the next five decades between 9 percent and 17 percent. However, the authors find that while plantation forestry may be expected to reduce the rate of loss, the growth of biofuels will have the opposite effect. Doubling the level of protection to 20 percent of all large ecosystems leads to only a small reduction in the rate at which mean species abundance is being lost (Alkemade *et al.* 2009; Pereira *et al.* 2010). The GLOBIO model is limited. It works with a very restrictive concept of biodiversity – remaining mean species abundance of original species, relative to their abundance in pristine or primary vegetation. It lacks the mechanisms needed to evaluate the effectiveness of policies aimed at the drivers. It is static not dynamic, and it is deterministic not stochastic. But it does at least identify outcomes as a consequence of present pressures.

8.4 The International Science-Policy Platform on Biodiversity and Ecosystem Services

In the coming years, projections of the implications of human behavior for biodiversity and ecosystem services will fall to the newly established IPBES. I noted at the beginning of this book that the notion of a standing assessment body for biodiversity along the lines of the IPCC was first proposed in 2005 by Jacques Chirac, then President of France. In 2010, the International Year of Biodiversity, the UN General Assembly effectively approved creation of IPBES by calling on UNEP to convene a meeting to finalize the form and functions of the new body. Two years later the body has been formally established, with a secretariat to be based in Bonn, and an agenda that was first agreed by an intergovernmental meeting held in Busan, Republic of Korea in 2009, and endorsed by the parties to the CBD in 2010.

The Busan agenda will doubtless be modified as IPBES evolves, but it provides a good indication of the things that the governments represented at the conference hope that the new body will do. It requires the new body:

- to identify and prioritize key scientific information needed for policy-makers at appropriate scales and catalyze efforts to generate new knowledge by engaging in dialogue with key scientific organizations, policy-makers, and funding organizations;
- to perform regular and timely assessments of knowledge on biodiversity and ecosystem services and their interlinkages, which should include comprehensive global, regional, and, as necessary, subregional assessments; thematic issues at appropriate scales; and new topics identified by science;
- to support policy formulation and implementation by identifying policy-relevant tools and methodologies, such as those arising from assessments, to enable decision-makers to gain access to those tools and methodologies, and, where necessary, to promote and catalyze their further development;
- to prioritize key capacity-building needs to improve the science–policy interface at appropriate levels and then provide and to catalyze financing for such capacity-building activities by providing a forum with conventional and potential sources of funding (Convention on Biological Diversity 2010b).

The charges were subject to a number of restrictions. The assessment body should not, for example, directly undertake new research; assessments should be scientifically credible, independent, and peer reviewed, and should identify uncertainties; there should be a clear and transparent process for sharing and incorporating relevant data; the new body should maintain a catalogue of relevant assessments, identify the need for regional and sub-regional assessments, and help to catalyze support for sub-regional and national assessments.

An evaluation of the differences between IPBES and the IPCC concluded that the emphasis on decision support in IPBES implied three things. First, in order to assure the policy relevance of assessments the governing body of IPBES should ask its working groups to assess the consequences of specific policies and programs. Second, assessments should be at a scale, frequency, and over a time horizon appropriate to the assessed processes, and projections should be based on these policies and programs. Third, the new body should catalyze resources to build capacity both in the underpinning science, in the meta-analytical and synthetic research on which all assessment is based, and in science-based policy development (Perrings *et al.* 2011).

The first of these implies that IPBES should structure its projection of trends in anthropogenic biosphere change around policies and programs specified by the plenary, and not around arbitrary non-probabilistic scenarios unconnected to particular human activities and policies. The rationale for this is straightforward. The notion of anthropogenic biodiversity change, like the notion of anthropogenic climate change, implies that the main drivers of change are to be found in the activities of people. Since human behaviors are causally related to the environmental changes recorded in assessments, it follows that projections of future environmental changes should be conditioned on variations in human behavior. To be relevant, the changes in behavior used to make projections should be attainable using the policy levers available to governments. There is still scope for developing projections based on alternative values for variables that are genuinely exogenous – beyond government influence – but the main options to be explored should be feasible alternatives to the existing set of policies.

While the science-based quantitative projections of biodiversity change included in, for example, the Global Environment Outlook 4 (GEO4) of UNEP, and the Global Biodiversity Outlook 3 (GBO3) of the CBD, are a significant improvement over simple storylines about plausible futures, there is still much to do. What are needed are integrated models of social and environmental change that are capable of providing conditional predictions of the outcomes of particular policy options. Such models should, for example, be able to provide member countries with guidance on the likely consequences of adopting measures different from the status quo (Perrings *et al.* 2011). As with projections of the consequences of business as usual, these alternative projections should indicate the probability distribution of outcomes associated with alternative policies and programs. Since potential policy options include alternatives being discussed within multilateral trade and/or environmental agreements, it follows that the new body could play an extremely valuable role in supporting the decision process within such bodies.

The role of MEAs is discussed in later chapters, but what is pertinent here is that IPBES has the potential to inform such agreements in ways that are much more relevant to negotiations between the parties than has been the case in either the IPCC or previous biodiversity assessments. Since IPBES assessments will address both the causes and consequences of biodiversity change they will provide information that is relevant to a large number of multilateral agreements in addition to the conservation agreements. The list of multilateral agreements that might be expected to benefit from IPBES in this way includes (but is not limited to): the Antarctic Treaty System – Convention for the Conservation of Antarctic Marine Living Resources and Madrid Protocol on the Protection of the Antarctic Environment; the IPPC; the Arctic Council for the Protection of the Arctic Marine Environment; the CMS; the CBD; the CITES; the Convention on Wetlands of International Importance (Ramsar); the IHR; the Marine Mammal Action Plan (MMAP); the SPS Agreement; the UNESCO WHC; the UNCLOS; the UN Convention to Combat Desertification (UNCCD); the UN Forum on Forests (UNFF); and the UNFCCC.

The second implication of the Busan agenda – that assessments should be at a scale, frequency, and over a time horizon appropriate to the assessed processes – follows from the fact that some impacts of biosphere change are purely local, while others are national, regional, or global; and that some processes of biosphere change may be extremely fast, while others operate on timescales more comparable with climate change. Perrings *et al.* (2011) identify a principle analogous to the subsidiarity principle of environmental governance. It is that biosphere change assessments should be undertaken at the lowest geographical and temporal scale consistent with capturing all relevant effects of change. The effect of vegetation shifts associated with land-use change within a catchment on water yield, for example, may not be felt outside the catchment. On the other hand, the geographical spread of the effects of trade-related species dispersal is limited only by the intersection of the trade area with areas of bioclimatic similarity. Some processes, such as the spread of infectious diseases, are extremely rapid. Others, such as the impact of habitat fragmentation on species extinction probabilities, are much slower. These differences mean two things for assessment.

One is that the spatial scale of IPBES assessments of anthropogenic biosphere change should match the spatial scale of its drivers and effects. Individual communities, provinces, states, or nations might wish to undertake assessments of change within their boundaries. The role of IPBES in such assessments would be limited to providing assistance with protocols to assure comparability of assessments across jurisdictions. IPBES assessments themselves should be concerned with biosphere change affecting multiple jurisdictions – so at the regional or global scale.

The other is that the temporal scale of IPBES assessments of anthropogenic biosphere change should match the temporal scale of their effects. This influences the timing and frequency of assessments. Changes occurring on longer timescales should be assessed less frequently than changes occurring on shorter timescales. Both causes and consequences of change are relevant here. If science shows that the diffusion of new technologies, or the spread of pests or pathogens as a result of changing trade patterns, have significant ecological consequences across jurisdictions, the phenomena can be assessed on relatively short timescales. This also has implications for the time horizon over which change is evaluated. Changes occurring on longer timescales should be assessed over correspondingly longer time horizons than changes occurring on shorter timescales.

It is worth repeating that the smaller the scale at which an assessment is done, the more likely it is that there will be factors that are exogenously determined. Since these are the circumstances in which it makes sense to plan adaptive responses using some sort of scenario-based approach, it is not surprising that scenario planning is a common way to deal with local environmental management (Kareiva *et al.* 2011). As the scale of assessment and management increases, however, and as an increasing proportion of the drivers of change are endogenously determined, scenario-based approaches become less and less appropriate and should give way to predictive modeling.

The third implication of the Busan agenda – that the new body should catalyze resources to build capacity both in the underpinning science, in the meta-analytical and synthetic research on which all assessment is based, and in science-based policy development – acknowledges the disparity in scientific capacity around the world, but also recognizes that we need to build capacity more generally both in science–policy interactions, and in the synthetic and meta-analytical research methods that are at the core of assessment. Differences in state of the science of biodiversity and ecosystem services in different countries are a consequence of differences in national research and research training efforts. Developing the funding base for the research on which assessments of biodiversity and ecosystem services are made and counteracting the effects of differences in North/South funding for research and research training are both required for the success of IPBES (Carpenter *et al.* 2009).

Given the restrictions placed on IPBES as an assessment body, it will not be able itself to fill any of the basic research gaps it identifies. IPBES will be able to do synthetic and meta-analytical research, but not the original research on which synthesis or meta-analysis is based. It follows that building capacity in the underlying science requires resources from elsewhere. This is most likely to be developed in consultation with research funding organizations.

The establishment of IPBES is an important step towards the international governance of biodiversity and ecosystem services. For the new body to fulfill its promise in this, however, it is important that it be informed by all of the relevant sciences: those dealing with human behavior, institutions, and government, as much as those dealing with the ecosystems affected by human behavior. Knowing when the effects of biodiversity change are contained within a decision-maker's jurisdiction, and when they are not, is critical to the development of coordinated or cooperative management of the problem across jurisdictions. Similarly, knowing the likely consequences of alternative policy options is critical to the choice of the best strategy. Earlier assessments provide useful evidence of what works and what does not. For IPBES to be an improvement over earlier assessments it needs to answer questions that are relevant to particular policy options. The IPBES plenary should specify the policy options to be evaluated and assessment should include quantitative conditional prediction of the consequences of those options (Perrings *et al.* 2011).

8.5 Social indicators of biodiversity change

Whatever the models developed to generate conditional projections of anthropogenic biodiversity change, their construction (if phenomenological) or calibration (if mechanistic) requires observations on both the biophysical and the social components of the system. Much attention has been paid to the development of effective earth observation systems. For example, the GEO Biodiversity Observation Network (GEO BON) is currently being designed as part of the Global Earth Observing System of Systems (GEOSS) (Andrefouet *et al.* 2008). GEO BON will collect, manage, analyze, and report data on the status of biodiversity and ecosystem services worldwide deriving from a network of biodiversity monitoring projects. It will provide countries with data at the national, regional, or global level as appropriate. GEO BON may develop and report indicators of the socio-economic importance of changes in ecosystem services, and provide these in an integrated, interoperable database (Perrings *et al.* 2011). Calls have also been made for a marine biodiversity observation network (Duffy *et al.* 2013).

What is needed for the development of effective predictive models, however, are data on the social precursors of environmental change, and on the feedbacks between changes in environmental conditions and human behavior. Since anthropogenic biosphere change is biosphere change forced by human behavior, projecting anthropogenic biosphere change requires both an understanding of the mechanisms that connect human behavior and the physical environment, and observations on the factors that drive human behavior (Carpenter *et al.* 2009). The capacity to make conditional predictions of ecosystem change makes it possible both to develop strategies for the sustainable management of complex systems that may fluctuate within bounds, and to undertake scenario planning to prepare responses to uncertain conditions within those bounds (Peterson, Cumming and Carpenter 2003; Bartholomew 2007; Nelson *et al.* 2009). Current projections of anthropogenic environmental change are, however, based almost exclusively on earth observations, human behavior being treated as a largely exogenous driver of environmental change. Neither the decision process, nor the way that decisions change in response to feedbacks from the physical system, is modeled. This is what needs to change.

An important goal of IPBES and the monitoring programs with which it engages should be to ensure that the socio-economic data needed to fit predictive models of anthropogenic environmental change are collected and integrated with data deriving from earth observations. People make decisions affecting the future state of the environment on the basis of a range of social indicators. These include, for example, prices and price trends, expected changes in the regulatory environment, changes in social norms and preferences. These are the social precursors of environmental change (President's Council of Advisors on Science and Technology 2011). Most existing environmental databases and new programs currently in development are based on earth observations, and do not include observations on the social precursors of environmental change (Andrefouet *et al.* 2008; Scholes *et al.* 2008). Yet many of the required social data currently exist in many countries (Table 8.3).

They include, for example, land and commodity prices, taxes, zoning restrictions, regulatory frameworks, social norms of behavior, and so on. Some of these are spatially explicit (e.g. land prices) or apply to well-

Table 8.3 *Indicators of some of the social precursors of environmental change*

Drivers	Socio-economic mechanisms	Ecosystem impacts	Precursors
Land-use change	Investment/ disinvestment in particular land uses, development of new infrastructure, technological change	Habitat conversion and fragmentation, water diversion, soil, water and air pollution, change in species abundance and richness impacting ecosystem functioning and ecosystem services	Commodity prices, input prices, land prices, interest rates, taxes and subsidies, investment grants, zoning restrictions, regulations, access rules and access fees
Trade, transport, travel	Dispersal of harmful pests and pathogens as items of trade or "passengers" on traded goods or transport vessels	Invasion by alien species leads to change in species abundance and richness (local extirpation), impacts on ecosystem functioning and services	International commodity prices, transport fuel costs, tariffs, trade restrictions, inspection and interception regimes
Overexploitation of wild-living species	Direct depletion through harvest	Change in species abundance due to harvest, bycatch, and food web effects, impacting ecosystem functioning and ecosystem services	Access rules and restrictions, commodity prices, environmental social norms on consumption of wild-living species

272

The search for solutions

Table 8.3 (*cont.*)

Drivers	Socio-economic mechanisms	Ecosystem impacts	Precursors
Climate change	Emissions of GHGs from industry, transport, and agriculture (including forest conversion), reduction in carbon sequestration from land-use change	Change in species distribution due to change in temperature and precipitation, changes in structure and function of terrestrial and marine ecosystems, changes in ecosystem services	Energy and commodity prices, land prices, access rules, international agreement, IPCC assessment reports

defined areas (e.g. zoning restrictions) and so may be integrated with spatially explicit earth observations. There is, however, currently little consistency across data sets. Most are neither integrated nor interoperable. They are subject to different access rules, are held in multiple locations for different periods and at different levels of disaggregation, and are characterized by numerous incompatible legacy systems and data formats. Their value lies in the fact that they anticipate ecosystem change through their effect on the decisions that lead to ecosystem change.

The responses to social indicators will ordinarily evolve over time. Consider a measure of the responsiveness of the quantity of land acquired to a change in its price – the price elasticity of demand. Demand for land will be more responsive to price, or more elastic, the greater the number of substitutes for land, the greater the price of land relative to their income, and the more essential land is. But it will also be more responsive the more time has elapsed since the initial price change. This is because there may be few substitutes for land initially – and other inputs may be in fixed supply. As options become available to intensify land use, the scope for substitution increases and demand becomes more responsive. For example, the long-run price elasticity of demand for oil, estimated over a twenty-one-year period, has been found to be anywhere between two and eight times the short-run elasticity (Cooper 2003). Of course demand for oil is still highly inelastic compared to the demand for many other inputs, and that is an important datum if change in the price of oil is used as a social precursor of environmental change.

8.6 Biodiversity change and social wellbeing

Getting the prognosis right means being able to make projections of anthropogenic changes in biodiversity conditional on the specification of a realistic set of initial human conditions. Some years ago I was asked to consider the greatest challenges to the development of sustainability science, and concluded that the most important of these was the improvement of our capacity to predict at least components of the coupled system as a precondition for mitigating the risks to future generations (Perrings 2007). Recall that the two options for dealing with the future consequences of human activities, mitigation and adaptation, have fundamentally different implications both for the distribution of the benefits of current decisions and for science. Mitigation implies action now to protect the interests of future generations everywhere (making it a public good). Adaptation provides benefits to those who adapt (making it a private good). Mitigation implies some capacity to predict the future consequences of present actions. Adaptation does not. Adaptation is well served by non-probabilistic scenarios. Mitigation is not.

I also noted that the task of informing the choice between mitigation and adaptation gets harder, not easier, the more rapidly systems evolve. Systems characterized by sensitivity to initial conditions, path dependence, non-linearities and discontinuities are less easy to predict than those that are well behaved. However, by understanding the dynamics of systems that may exist in multiple stable states, it is possible to identify actions that can trigger changes of state, even if the precise tipping point is unknown. By understanding social field effects, it is possible to identify levels of activity at which system momentum changes. For example, field effects in preference formation occur when people's beliefs or expectations are sensitive to the proportion of the population sharing those same beliefs or expectations. These have been shown to affect the transition rates between states (Aoki 1996). While the system may be more homogeneous, it is more sensitive to shocks. This is analogous to the point made by Holling that as terrestrial ecosystems approach carrying capacity they become less resilient and more brittle (Holling 1986).

Modeling complex systems is certainly more difficult than modeling simple systems, but at least there exist methods for selecting among competing models of system dynamics. There also exist methods for systematic learning about model error. Although there is still no way to anticipate surprises in an evolutionary system, there are methods for identifying early warnings of threshold effects that are signaled in the data. So, for example, wherever threshold effects are anticipated by changes in the volatility of particular system measures, analysis of the spectral properties of the data provides a potential early warning of impending change (Brock, Mäler and Perrings 2002; Brock and Carpenter 2006). Detection still depends on the existence of appropriate models of system dynamics, i.e. on an understanding of which measures matter and why. But the problem is less daunting than it seems.

Pereira *et al.* began their review of biodiversity scenarios with the optimistic observation that "Quantitative scenarios are coming of age as a tool for evaluating the impact of future socio-economic development pathways on biodiversity and ecosystem services" (Pereira *et al.* 2010). There is no doubt that our capacity to model the biophysical relationships involved in biodiversity change has substantially improved, but it is hard to see that these improvements form the basis for evaluating the environmental consequences of human behavior. Unless and until it is possible to model the feedbacks within the socio-economic system that drive human responses to changing environmental conditions, we will never be able to move beyond phenomenological models of the pressure-state-response kind. And that is what is needed if we are to get the prognosis right.

References

Adger, W. N., Lorenzoni, I. and O'Brien, K. L. (2009a) *Adapting to Climate Change Thresholds, Values, Governance*. Cambridge University Press.
Adger, W. N., Dessai, S., Goulden, M., Hulme, M., Lorenzoni, I., Nelson, D. R., Naess, L. O., Wolf, J. and Wreford, A. (2009b) Are

there social limits to adaptation to climate change? *Climate Change*, 93, 335–354.

Alkemade, R., van Oorschot, M., Miles, L., Nellemann, C., Bakkenes, M. and ten Brink, B. (2009) GLOBIO3: a framework to investigate options for reducing global terrestrial biodiversity loss. *Ecosystems*, 12, 374–390.

Andrefouet, S., Costello, M. J., Faith, D. P., Ferrier, S., Geller, G. N., Hoft, R., Jurgens, N., Lane, M. A., Larigauderie, A., Mace, G., Miazza, S., Muchoney, D., Parr, T., Pereira, H. M., Sayre, R., Scholes, R. J., Stiassny, M. L. J. and Turner, W. (2008) *The GEO Biodiversity Observation Network: GE0-V Document 20.* Group on Earth Observations/Biodiversity Observation Network.

Aoki, M. (1996) *New Approaches to Macroeconomic Modeling.* Cambridge University Press.

Bartholomew, K. (2007) Land use-transportation scenario planning: promise and reality. *Transportation*, 34, 397–412.

Beckerman, W. (1992) Economic growth and the environment: whose growth? Whose environment? *World Development*, 20, 481–496.

Brock, W. A. and Carpenter, S. (2006) Rising variance: a leading indicator of ecological transition. *Ecology Letters*, 9, 311–318.

Brock, W. A., Mäler, K. G. and Perrings, C. (2002) Resilience and sustainability: the economic analysis of non-linear dynamic systems. *Panarchy: Understanding Transformations in Systems of Humans and Nature* (ed. L. H. Gunderson and C. S. Holling), pp. 261–291. Island Press, Washington, DC.

Brown, K. and Westaway, E. (2011) Agency, capacity, and resilience to environmental change: lessons from human development, well-being, and disasters. *Annual Review of Environment and Resources*, 36, 321–342.

Butchart, S., Walpole, M., Collen, B., van Strien, A., Scharlemann, J. P. W., Almond, R. E. A., Baillie, J. E. M., Bomhard, B., Brown, C., Bruno, J., Carpenter, K. E., Carr, G. M., Chanson, J., Chenery, A. M., Csirke, J., Davidson, N. C., Dentener, F., Foster, M., Galli, A., Galloway, J. N., Genovesi, P., Gregory, R. D., Hockings, M., Kapos, V., Lamarque, J.-F., Leverington, F., Loh, J., McGeoch, M. A., McRae, L., Minasyan, A., Morcillo, M. H., Oldfield, T. E. E., Pauly, D., Quader, S., Revenga, C., Sauer, J. R., Skolnik, B., Spear, D., Stanwell-Smith, D., Stuart, S. N., Symes, A., Tierney, M., Tyrrell, T. D., Vie, J.-C. and Watson, R. (2010) Global biodiversity: indicators of recent declines. *Science*, 328, 1164–1168.

Carpenter, S. R., Mooney, H. A., Agard, J., Capistrano, D., DeFries, R. S., Díaz, S., Dietz, T., Duraiappah, A. K., Oteng-Yeboah, A., Pereira, H. M., Perrings, C., Reid, W. V., Sarukhanm, J., Scholes, R. J. and Whyte, A.

(2009) Science for managing ecosystem services: beyond the Millennium Ecosystem Assessment. *Proceedings of the National Academy of Sciences*, 106, 1305–1312.

Convention on Biological Diversity (2006) *Global Biodiversity Outlook 2*. Convention on Biological Diversity, Montreal.

(2010a) *Global Biodiversity Outlook 3*. Convention on Biological Diversity, Montreal.

(2010b) *Decision X/11. Science-Policy Interface on Biodiversity, Ecosystem Services and Human Well-being and Consideration of the Outcome of the Intergovernmental Meetings*. CBD Secretariat, Montreal.

Cooper, J. C. B. (2003) Price elasticity of demand for crude oil: estimates for 23 countries. *OPEC Review*, 27, 1–8.

Dasgupta, P. (1993) *An Inquiry into Well-Being and Destitution*. Clarendon Press, Oxford.

Dillehay, T. D. and Kolata, A. L. (2004) Long-term human response to uncertain environmental conditions in the Andes. *Proceedings of the National Academy of Sciences*, 101, 4325–4330.

Duffy, J. E., Amaral-Zettler, L. A., Fautin, D. G., Paulay, G., Rynearson, T. A., Sosik, H. M. and Stachowicz, J. J. (2013) Envisioning a marine biodiversity observation network. *Bioscience*, 63, 351–361.

Ehrlich, P. R. and Holdren, J. P. (1971) Impact of population growth. *Science*, 171, 1212–1217.

Grotius, H. (1916 [1608]) *The Freedom of the Seas, or the Right Which Belongs to the Dutch to take part in the East Indian Trade (Translated by Ralph Van Deman Magoffin)*. Oxford University Press.

Grubler, A., O'Neill, B. and van Vuuren, D. (2006) Avoiding hazards of best-guess climate scenarios. *Nature*, 440, 740.

Hoffmann, M., Hilton-Taylor, C., Angulo, A., Böhm, M., Brooks, T. M., Butchart, S. H. M., Carpenter, K. E., Chanson, J., Collen, B., Cox, N. A., Darwall, W. R. T., Dulvy, N. K., Harrison, L. R., Katariya, V., Pollock, C. M., Quader, S., Richman, N. I., Rodrigues, A. S. L., Tognelli, M. F., Vié, J.-C., Aguiar, J. M., Allen, D. J., Allen, G. R., Amori, G., Ananjeva, N. B., Andreone, F., Andrew, P., Ortiz, A. L. A., Baillie, J. E. M., Baldi, R., Bell, B. D., Biju, S. D., Bird, J. P., Black-Decima, P., Blanc, J. J., Bolaños, F., Bolivar-G., W., Burfield, I. J., Burton, J. A., Capper, D. R., Castro, F., Catullo, G., Cavanagh, R. D., Channing, A., Chao, N. L., Chenery, A. M., Chiozza, F., Clausnitzer, V., Collar, N. J., Collett, L. C., Collette, B. B., Fernandez, C. F. C., Craig, M. T., Crosby, M. J., Cumberlidge, N., Cuttelod, A., Derocher, A. E., Diesmos, A. C., Donaldson, J. S., Duckworth, J. W., Dutson, G., Dutta, S. K., Emslie, R. H., Farjon, A., Fowler, S.,

Freyhof, J., Garshelis, D. L., Gerlach, J., Gower, D. J., Grant, T. D., Hammerson, G. A., Harris, R. B., Heaney, L. R., Hedges, S. B., Hero, J.-M., Hughes, B., Hussain, S. A., Icochea M. J., Inger, R. F., Ishii, N., Iskandar, D. T., Jenkins, R. K. B., Kaneko, Y., Kottelat, M., Kovacs, K. M., Kuzmin, S. L., La Marca, E., Lamoreux, J. F., Lau, M. W. N., Lavilla, E. O., Leus, K., Lewison, R. L., Lichtenstein, G., Livingstone, S. R., Lukoschek, V., Mallon, D. P., McGowan, P. J. K., McIvor, A., Moehlman, P. D., Molur, S., Alonso, A. M., Musick, J. A., Nowell, K., Nussbaum, R. A., Olech, W., Orlov, N. L., Papenfuss, T. J., Parra-Olea, G., Perrin, W. F., Polidoro, B. A., Pourkazemi, M., Racey, P. A., Ragle, J. S., Ram, M., Rathbun, G., Reynolds, R. P., Rhodin, A. G. J., Richards, S. J., Rodriguez, L. O., Ron, S. R., Rondinini, C., Rylands, A. B., Sadovy de Mitcheson, Y., Sanciangco, J. C., Sanders, K. L., Santos-Barrera, G., Schipper, J., Self-Sullivan, C., Shi, Y., Shoemaker, A., Short, F. T., Sillero-Zubiri, C., Silvano, D. B. L., Smith, K. G., Smith, A. T., Snoeks, J., Stattersfield, A. J., Symes, A. J., Taber, A. B., Talukdar, B. K., Temple, H. J., Timmins, R., Tobias, J. A., Tsytsulina, K., Tweddle, D., Ubeda, C., Valenti, S. V., van Dijk, P., Veiga, L. M., Veloso, A., Wege, D. C., Wilkinson, M., Williamson, E. A., Xie, F., Young, B. E., Akçakaya, H. R., Bennun, L., Blackburn, T. M., Boitani, L., Dublin, H. T., da Fonseca, G. A. B., Gascon, C., Lacher, T. E., Mace, G. M., Mainka, S. A., McNeely, J. A., Mittermeier, R. A., Reid, G. M., Rodriguez, J. P., Rosenberg, A. A., Samways, M. J., Smart, J., Stein, B. A. and Stuart, S. N. (2010) The impact of conservation on the status of the world's vertebrates. *Science*, 330, 1503–1509.

Holling, C. (1986) The resilience of terrestrial ecosystems: local surprise and global change. *Sustainable Development of the Biosphere* (ed. W. C. Clark and R. E. Mann), pp. 292–317. Cambridge University Press.

IPCC (2000) *Emissions Scenarios: A Special Report of IPCC Working Group III*. IPCC, Geneva.

Kareiva, P., Tallis, H., Ricketts, T. H., Daily, G. C. and Polasky, S. (2011) *Natural Capital: Theory and Practice of Mapping Ecosystem Services*. Oxford University Press.

Kinzig, A. P., Ehrlich, P. R., Alston, L., Arrow, K., Barrett, S., Buchman, T., Daily, G., Levin, B., Levin, S., Oppenheimer, M., Ostrom, E. and Saari, D. (2013) Social norms and global environmental challenges: the complex interactions of behaviors, values, and policies. *Bioscience*, 63, 164–175.

Leadley, P., Pereira, H. M., Alkemade, R., Fernandez-Manjarrés, J. F., Proença, V., Scharlemann, J. P. W. and Walpole, M. J. (2010)

278   *The search for solutions*

Biodiversity scenarios: projections of 21st century change in biodiversity and associated ecosystem services. *Technical Series 50*, p. 132. Secretariat of the Convention on Biological Diversity, Montreal.

Meadows, D. H., Meadows, D. L., Randers, J. and Behrens, W. W. (1972) *The Limits to Growth*. Universe Books, New York.

Millennium Ecosystem Assessment (2005a) *Ecosystems and Human Well-Being: Biodiversity Synthesis*. World Resources Institute, Washington, DC.

  (2005b) *Ecosystems and Human Well-being: General Synthesis*. Island Press, Washington, DC.

Moss, R. H., Edmonds, J. A., Hibbard, K. A., Manning, M. R., Rose, S. K., van Vuuren, D. P., Carter, T. R., Emori, S., Kainuma, M., Kram, T., Meehl, G. A., Mitchell, J. F. B., Nakicenovic, N., Riahi, K., Smith, S. J., Stouffer, R. J., Thomson, A. M., Weyant, J. P. and Wilbanks, T. J. (2010) The next generation of scenarios for climate change research and assessment. *Nature*, 463, 747–756.

Nelson, E., Mendoza, G., Regetz, J., Polasky, S., Tallis, H., Cameron, D. R., Chan, K. M. A., Daily, G. C., Goldstein, J., Kareiva, P. M., Lonsdorf, E., Naidoo, R., Ricketts, T. H. and Shaw, M. R. (2009) Modeling multiple ecosystem services, biodiversity conservation, commodity production, and tradeoffs at landscape scales. *Frontiers in Ecology and the Environment*, 7, 4–11.

Pereira, H. M., Leadley, P. W., Proença, V., Alkemade, R., Scharlemann, J. P. W., Fernandez-Manjarrés, J. F., Araújo, M. B., Balvanera, P., Biggs, R., Cheung, W. W. L., Chini, L., Cooper, H. D., Gilman, E. L., Guénette, S., Hurtt, G. C., Huntington, H. P., Mace, G. M., Oberdorff, T., Revenga, C., Rodrigues, P., Scholes, R. J., Sumaila, U. R. and Walpole, M. (2010) Scenarios for global biodiversity in the 21st century. *Science*, 330, 1496–1501.

Perrings, C. (2007) Future challenges. *Proceedings of the National Academy of Sciences*, 104, 15179–15180.

Perrings, C., Duraiappah, A., Larigauderie, A. and Mooney, H. (2011) The biodiversity and ecosystem services science-policy interface. *Science* 331, 1139–1140.

Peterson, G. D., Cumming, G. S. and Carpenter, S. R. (2003) Scenario planning: a tool for conservation in an uncertain world. *Conservation Biology*, 17, 358–366.

President's Council of Advisors on Science and Technology (2011) *Sustaining Environmental Capital: Protecting Society and the Economy*. Executive Office of the President, Washington, DC.

Sala, O. E., Chapin, F. S., Armesto, J. J., Berlow, E., Bloomfield, J., Dirzo, R., Huber-Sanwald, E., Huenneke, L. F., Jackson, R. B., Kinzig, A.,

Leemans, R., Lodge, D. M., Mooney, H. A., Oesterheld, M., Poff, N. L., Sykes, M. T., Walker, B. H., Walker, M. and Wall, D. H. (2000) Global biodiversity scenarios for the year 2100. *Science*, 287, 1770–1774.

Sala, O. E., van Vuuren, D., Pereira, H. M., Lodge, D., Alder, J., Cumming, G., Dobson, A., Wolters, V., Xenopoulos, M. A., Zaitsev, A. S., Polo, M. G., Gomes, I., Queiroz, C. and Rusak, J. A. (2005) Biodiversity across scenarios. *Ecosystems and Human Well-Being: Scenarios (Findings of the Scenarios Working Group of the Millennium Ecosystem Assessment)* (ed. S. Carpenter, P. Pingali, L. E. Bennet and M. Zurek), pp. 375–408. Island Press, Washington, DC.

Scholes, R. J., Mace, G. M., Turner, W., Geller, G. N., Jürgens, N., Larigauderie, A., Muchoney, D., Walther, B. A. and Mooney, H. A. (2008) Toward a global biodiversity observing system. *Science*, 321, 1044–1045.

Tiffen, M., Mortimore, M. and Gichuki, F. (1994) *More People, Less Erosion: Environmental Recovery in Kenya.* John Wiley, New York.

UNEP (2007) *Global Environmental Outlook GEO4 Environment for Development.* UNEP, Nairobi.

9 | *Understanding what is lost*

9.1 Indicators of the importance of biodiversity change for human wellbeing

To understand what we lose from the extinction of some species and the genetic erosion of others requires that we understand how these species contribute to the wealth of nations. It is not enough to lament their disappearance. We need to be able to identify the consequences of their loss for human wellbeing. Just as it can be shown that the increasing abundance of cultivated and domesticated species enhances wellbeing, we need to be able show that the declining abundance of other species can have the opposite effect. There are currently few reliable indicators of the importance of biodiversity change for human wellbeing. Although we know quite a lot about the benefits that people obtain from exploiting particular groups of species, and about the ecosystem services that lie behind those benefits, we still do not have good measures of what society gains and loses from more general changes in species richness and abundance. The point was made in earlier chapters that while the MA was able to say whether the physical flows of ecosystem services had been enhanced or degraded in the last fifty years, it was unable to value the loss of cultural or regulating services relative to the gain in provisioning services. It was not able to say whether the trade-offs being made between ecosystem services were warranted, given the costs and benefits involved. Nor was it able to say whether the investments people have made in the conversion of ecosystems for the production of foods, fuels, and fibers has made us collectively richer or poorer.

Part of the problem lies in the fact that there are markets for some of the goods and services obtained from managed ecosystems, but not for others. Efforts by economists to value individual non-marketed services have generated measures of the local importance of ecosystems, but we are so far unable to make use of this information to monitor the effect of environmental change on the wealth of nations. Governments need metrics of the social importance of environmental change if they are to know whether the wellbeing of the people they represent is improving. The measures conventionally used as proxies for wellbeing – such as per capita GDP – provide useful information about particular dimensions of the problem, but because they are based on market transactions they necessarily exclude goods and services that lie outside the market. Only if environmental changes directly affect current private income will they be captured in such measures.

It has been understood for many years that if we are interested in knowing whether wellbeing is increasing or decreasing over time we should track changes in wealth – the assets that are the source of the goods and services people consume day to day (Samuelson 1961). It was only after the Brundtland Report defined sustainable development in terms of intergenerational changes in wealth (World Commission on Environment and Development 1987) that serious attention was paid to the construction of wealth accounts that reflect changes in the value of environmental assets (Hartwick 1990, 1994, 2000; Pearce and Atkinson 1993; Hamilton 1994; Pearce, Hamilton and Atkinson 1996; Hamilton and Clemens 1999). The starting point for this program of research was the notion that current consumption is sustainable only if it does not reduce the consumption possibilities available to future generations. The idea was originally introduced in Lindahl (1933). It was embedded in the definition of income as the maximum amount that could be consumed without reducing the value of the assets available to future generations. The same idea was later elaborated in Hicks (1939). Since income in the Lindahl sense is equivalent to the system of national accounts (SNA) concepts of net national product (NNP) or net national income (NNI), Hartwick and others considered what was needed for net national product or NNI to respect the Lindahl criterion taking all forms of wealth into account.

The SNA (or the national income and product accounts in the USA) that generate measures such as GDP were established to enable governments to track the performance of the national economy, and to measure the impact of economic policies. Since the environmental impacts of economic activities often feed back into the performance of the national economy we need to find ways of capturing this in the national income accounts. The capital accounts in the existing national income accounts do a poor job of tracking changes in wealth. This is partly because they focus on tangible assets and hence neglect human and other forms of capital, and partly because of the way they treat environmental assets. The weaknesses of the approach to environmental assets in the SNA have been recognized for more than twenty years (Repetto, Magrath and Wells 1989; Pearce and Warford 1993).

This chapter addresses the challenges in trying to do better: to construct accounts that capture the value of changes in biodiversity. Sustainable income is the portion of value added in production that is not required to maintain the assets available to future generations. While it is always possible for the present generation to increase its consumption by eating into the assets it leaves to future generations, such consumption is not sustainable, and such consumption expenditures are strictly greater than income in the sense of Lindahl or Hicks. What is needed are national accounts that include true measures of sustainable income, and that make it clear when society is choosing to make such intergenerational trade-offs. At present we cannot tell whether the per capita NNP reported by countries bears any relationship to average sustainable income. We need to be able to do this. This chapter considers what is involved in constructing a system of accounts that reports both consumption expenditures and sustainable income. It draws on a recent contribution to a volume on wealth accounting (Perrings 2012), while focusing more directly on the value of biodiversity as the pool of biotic assets from which ecosystem services derive. It also draws on work by Dasgupta and others to use shadow prices as weights to construct an aggregate index of the national stock of capital assets (Dasgupta and Mäler 2000; Dasgupta 2001, 2009; Arrow, Dasgupta and Mäler 2003; Arrow *et al.* 2012; UNU-IHDP and UNEP 2012).

9.2 The value of environmental assets

In Dasgupta's approach, output at a moment in time, $Y(t)$, is a measure of the goods and services produced from three main types of asset: produced capital, $K(t)$, human capital $L(t)$, and a stock of natural resources which may be thought about as an area of land or sea, along with the biodiversity that area contains, $N(t)$, together with the technology, institutions, and environmental conditions that collectively determine total factor productivity, $A(t)$. As indicated earlier, total factor productivity measures the proportion of output not explained by these measured factors of production. It therefore reflects the effect of technical progress, the efficiency with which inputs are used, institutional conditions, and the impact of environmental factors. Output can therefore be described by the function:

$$Y(t) = A(t)f(K(t)L(t)N(t))$$

If the depreciation corresponding to a particular capital stock is denoted $\delta_i, i \in \{K, L, N\}$, investment $I_i, i \in \{K, L, N\}$, and if natural resources regenerate through the function $g \ (N \ (t), \ I_N \ (t))$, then the growth rate for each type of asset is:

$$\frac{dK}{dt} = A(t)f(K(t)L(t)R(t)) - C(t) - I_L(t) - I_N(t) - \delta_K K(t)$$

$$\frac{dL}{dt} = I_L(t) - \delta_L L(t)$$

$$\frac{dN}{dt} = g(N(t)) - \delta_N N(t)$$

In words, the growth of produced capital is the difference between output and the sum of consumption, investment in human and natural capital, and the depreciation of produced capital. The growth of human capital is simply the difference between investment and depreciation, and the growth of natural capital is the difference between natural regeneration and depreciation of natural capital.

Denoting aggregate consumption at time t by $C(t)$ and intergenerational wellbeing by $V(t)$, it is assumed that wellbeing depends on consumption via the relation:

$$V(t) = \int_t^\infty U(C(t))e^{-r(t-\tau)}d\tau$$

in which $U(C(t))$ is instantaneous wellbeing measured at time t. No assumption is made about the optimality of $V(t), C(t)$, or the time paths of the various capital stocks. The wealth of a country at a moment in time can be described by the set of assets available to its people at that time:

$$W(t) = \{K(t), L(t), N(t)\}$$

Dasgupta defines an economic program to be a consumption and investment path from t onwards, $\{E(\tau)\}_t^\infty = \{C(\tau), K(\tau), L(\tau), N(\tau), I_L(\tau), R(\tau)\}_t^\infty$, and a resource allocation mechanism to be a mapping from wealth to an economic program: $\alpha : \{W(t),t\} \rightarrow \{E(\tau)\}_t^\infty$ (Dasgupta 2009). The intergenerational measure of wellbeing corresponding to a particular economic program is therefore:

$$V(W(t),t) = \int_t^\infty U(C(t))e^{-r(t-\tau)}d\tau$$

and the "shadow value" of each asset type is the partial derivative of this function with respect to that asset type. For assets for which there are well-functioning markets and few externalities, shadow value and market prices should be reasonably closely aligned. For assets for which there are no markets, or for which there are significant externalities, shadow prices would be expected to deviate substantially from market prices. Three things follow:

1 If total factor productivity is constant, $A(t)=A$, then the rate at which wellbeing changes is determined by the rate at which each of the capital stocks (evaluated at its shadow price) changes.[1] Since the growth of produced and human capital stocks is a measure of net investment, and the growth of natural capital is a measure of natural regeneration less depreciation, the sum of the two (aggregate net investment) determines the rate at which intergenerational wellbeing changes over time.
2 An economic program is sustainable if and only if aggregate net investment is positive, and aggregate wealth is non-declining.
3 Wellbeing can increase over time if and only if the Lindahl criterion is satisfied, i.e. if consumption is less than the difference between output and depreciation of assets.

These conditions imply that if we wish to understand changes in intergenerational wellbeing, we need to understand changes in wealth, and to do this we need to track changes in aggregate net investment.

Of course total factor productivity may not be constant. Since it is sensitive to changes in the efficiency of the allocation mechanism or environmental conditions, it may be expected to change as the set of species, $S(t)$, changes. Suppose that $S(t)$ is the sum of ubiquitous species

---

[1] This implies that

$$\frac{dV(W(t))}{dt} = \frac{\partial V(W(t))}{\partial K(t)}\frac{dK(t)}{dt} + \frac{\partial V(W(t))}{\partial L(t)}\frac{dL(t)}{dt} + \frac{\partial V(W(t))}{\partial N(t)}\frac{dN(t)}{dt}$$

wherever they are found, $S_0(t)$, and of endemic species in each of n countries, $S_i(t), i=1,\ldots,n$. That is

$$S(t) = \sum_{i=0}^{n} S_i(t)$$

If total factor productivity in country i is $A_i(t) = A_i(S(t), t), i = 1, \ldots, n$ and if

$$\frac{dV_i(W(t))}{dS_i(t)} = \frac{\partial V_i(W_i(t))}{\partial A_i(t)} \frac{\partial A_i(t)}{\partial S_i(t)}$$

the ith county is able to enhance its wellbeing through conservation of its own endemic species, $S_i(t)$. It will take account of this benefit, but it will ignore any effects it has on total factor productivity in other countries.

Specifically, if intergenerational wellbeing in the ith country depends on its capital assets and the global public good, $V_i(t) = V_i(\alpha_i, W_i(t), S(t), t)$, then a change in wellbeing in that country will depend on the change in its assets induced by investment in produced and human capital and the growth of natural capital $\frac{dW_i(t)}{dt} = I_{iK}(t) + I_{iL}(t) + \frac{dN_i(t)}{dt}$, and the change in the global public good secured by the set of all species. This depends both on its efforts, and the efforts of all other countries. That is:

$$\frac{dV_i(t)}{dt} = \frac{\partial V_i(t)}{\partial W(t)_i} \frac{dW_i(t)}{dt} + \frac{\partial V_i(t)}{\partial S(t)} \left(\frac{dS_i(t)}{dt} + \sum_{j \neq i} \frac{dS_j(t)}{dt} \right)$$

In words, the change in wellbeing in the ith country depends both on the change in capital stocks in that country, and the change in the assets underpinning the global public good in all countries – the set of all species in this story. Note, though, that only the quantity

$$\frac{\partial V_i(t)}{\partial S(t)} \frac{dS_i(t)}{dt}$$

is part of the ith country's decision. The contribution of all other countries to the wellbeing of country i,

$$\frac{\partial V_i(t)}{\partial S(t)} \sum_{j \neq i} \frac{dS_j(t)}{dt}$$

is taken as given, and the contribution of country i to all other countries,

$$\sum_{j \neq i}^{n} \frac{\partial V_j(t)}{\partial S(t)} \frac{dS_i(t)}{dt}$$

is ignored. Indeed, this is the essence of the public good problem discussed in Chapter 4.

Total factor productivity growth depends on a number of different elements, an understanding of which is extremely important for economic development. Most studies identify public sector research and development, and the efficiency of resource allocation as the key drivers of total factor productivity growth. The efficiency of resource allocation depends on the effectiveness of markets and regulatory institutions, the rule of law, and the trust that people have in the rule of law – or social capital. That is why these are paid so much attention by bodies like the World Bank and by national and international aid organizations. Environmental factors are also an important element of total factor productivity growth, however. The connection is intuitive for renewable resource-based sectors such as agriculture, forestry, fisheries, conservation, ecotourism, water supply, and so on, but it also applies to sectors in which productivity may be related to human, animal, or plant health. For renewable resource-based sectors improvements in ambient animal and plant health, water quality, soil loss, and the like would be expected to lead to productivity growth. But it is also the case that improvements in ambient human health are likely to have positive effects on productivity growth in many other sectors. Moreover, there are likely to be interactions between the drivers of total factor productivity growth.

There is also a connection between public-sector research and development and environmental factors that has received little attention, not because it is unimportant but because there is no way of accounting for it in the SNA. The historically high rates of productivity growth achieved in agriculture directly depend on research and development. The rate of return on agricultural research and development investment has been estimated to lie between 45 percent and 55 percent (Alston, Beddow and Pardey 2009; Alston *et al.* 2010). This reflects the rate at which new technologies become available and are diffused (Piesse and Thirtle 2010). In agriculture, those technologies depend on the genetic resources available to plant and animal breeders, and to genetic engineers. The availability of landraces and wild crop relatives to plant breeders, for example, has been critical to their effectiveness for thousands of years. That is what is captured by an expression such as:

$$\frac{\partial V_i(t)}{\partial S(t)}\left(\frac{dS_i(t)}{dt} + \sum_{j\neq i}\frac{dS_j(t)}{dt}\right)$$

There is empirical evidence that unaccounted contributions of the environment are an important driver of total factor productivity growth, and that explicitly accounting for environmental contributions can reduce estimates of total factor productivity growth by a significant margin – potentially driving it into the negative range effect (Vouvaki and Xepapadeas 2009) (Table 9.1). Explicitly accounting for such impacts is likely to be an important step towards the development of productivity-driven conservation strategies.

9.3 Adjusted net savings and wealth estimates

One problem with using GDP as a proxy for human wellbeing is that it neglects both transboundary flows and the depreciation of assets. Another of the standard SNA indicators, NNI, deals with both issues. However, the exclusion of most non-marketed production and consumption, externalities, environmental deterioration, and public lands and the inclusion of defensive or remedial expenditures (repairing depreciation) mean that this measure is also flawed. In addition, it is not possible to tell whether NNI is sustainable in the sense of Lindahl (1933), and hence whether it is consistent with maintaining national wealth. While a large number of alternative indices have been proposed in the literature[2] (Goossens *et al.* 2007), I consider only those that address these specific weaknesses of NNI.

Consider, first, what additional information is needed. Provisioning and cultural ecosystem services that are supplied through well-functioning markets are already recorded in the SNA through the product accounts for agriculture, industry, and services (European Communities *et al.*

---

[2] These include Nordhaus and Tobin's measure of economic welfare, the index of sustainable economic welfare, the genuine progress indicator, the UNDP's HDI, the gender-related development index, the ecological footprint, the environmental sustainability index, and the environmental performance index (Goossens *et al.* 2007).

Table 9.1 *Standard and externality-adjusted total factor productivity (TFPG)*

Countries	Standard TFPG	Externality-adjusted TFPG
Canada	0.670	−1.979
USA	0.275	−2.206
Austria	0.635	−0.779
Belgium	1.079	−1.039
Denmark	0.321	−1.289
Finland	1.144	−1.107
France	0.705	−0.778
Greece	0.831	−0.479
Italy	1.537	0.387
Luxembourg	1.699	−2.580
Portugal	1.690	0.649
Spain	0.415	−0.695
Sweden	−0.040	−2.028
Switzerland	−0.059	−1.122
UK	0.859	−0.896
Japan	1.646	0.235
Iceland	0.473	−2.533
Ireland	1.638	−0.172
Netherlands	0.489	−1.414
Norway	1.564	−0.247
Australia	0.567	−1.226
Mexico	0.330	−0.814
Turkey	1.420	0.214
Average	0.865	−0.952

Source: Vouvaki and Xepapadeas (2009).

2009). The prices of these may be distorted, but they are at least directly registered in the national income accounts. The problem lies with services that are not supplied through the market and so not currently captured in the national income accounts. The production of food, for example, depends on other ecosystem services including the regulation of soil and water flows, pest and disease regulation, pollination, nutrient cycling, and so on. Because these services are not marketed they are not explicitly accounted for. Insofar as such services are reflected in the price of the land, they will be indirectly measured in the system of national accounts.

Indeed, if all such services are contained within the boundaries of the property, they will be fully accounted for. Off-site flows of nutrients, pests and pesticides, siltation of rivers, and the like are externalities of land management and will ordinarily be missing from the accounts except where they impact the value of private land. The task is not therefore to account for all ecosystem services. It is to account for ecosystem services that have a significant impact on wellbeing, and that are not already priced.

Since the value of assets derives from the discounted stream of services they produce, we need to know the value of ecosystem services in order to understand the value of the underlying assets. We then need to know whether the value of those assets is increasing or decreasing. The most effective attempt to address this problem to this point has been the calculation of adjusted net savings as a measure of change in wealth. The concept of adjusted net savings grew out of the work of Pearce, Hamilton and Atkinson in the 1990s (Pearce and Atkinson 1993; Pearce, Hamilton and Atkinson 1996; Hamilton and Clemens 1999; Ferreira, Hamilton and Vincent 2008), and is a direct attempt to measure the net change in the value of a country's capital stocks, where that includes produced, human, and at least some stocks of natural capital (Hamilton and Clemens 1999). If wealth is the value of the stock of all assets plus net investment, then a necessary and sufficient condition for wealth to be increasing over time is that net investment be positive. Adjusted net savings is intended, following the arguments of section 9.2, to be a measure of the rate of change of wellbeing: $dV(t)/dt$.

In practice, adjusted net savings estimates are based on a partial correction of the figures in the SNA. The adjustments to gross savings reported in the national income accounts involve: (1) subtraction of the depreciation of produced capital, (2) addition of expenditure on education as a proxy for investment in human capital, (3) subtraction of the rents (surplus after deducting costs and normal returns) on depleted resource stocks, and (4) subtraction of specific pollution damages. The resource stocks currently included comprise energy (oil, gas, and coal), minerals (non-renewable mineral resources), and forest (rent being calculated on timber extraction in excess of the "natural" increment in wood volume). Pollution damages currently recorded include carbon dioxide and particulate (PM10) damages.

Although the correction is only partial, and although it includes only some natural resources, and some off-site external environmental effects, its impact on wealth is substantial. This is readily seen in Figure 9.1, which shows the World Bank's latest estimates of gross national saving and adjusted net saving rates, using the method. In almost every case, the gross national savings recorded in the SNA are greater than the adjusted net savings calculated by the Bank, and in many cases positive gross national savings rates are associated with strongly negative adjusted net savings rates. This implies that the value of aggregate capital stocks is decreasing, not increasing.

Of course it is possible that adjusted net savings could be negative in one year, but otherwise positive. To see whether an economic program is sustainable requires that adjusted net savings be calculated over a longer period of time. Figure 9.2 reports adjusted net savings rates for four groups of countries over the period 1970–2005. The groups of countries are high-, middle-, and low-income countries, together the subset of low-income countries in the IMF's Heavily Indebted Poor Country Program. Within that period all except the high-income countries had periods during which their adjusted net savings were negative, implying that they had periods during which they were depleting aggregate capital.

For most years, however, the adjusted net savings rates of most countries were positive. The exception is the heavily indebted poor countries, largely in Sub-Saharan Africa. This group of countries had negative adjusted net savings rates for most of the period. Since these countries are also characterized by high rates of population growth, the implication is that per capita wealth declined at an even faster rate.

In the adjusted net savings there are two core stocks of capital, produced and natural capital, and a balancing stock, intangible capital. Produced capital is machinery, equipment, and built structures. Whether it includes land depends on the degree to which land is modified. Natural capital is non-renewable resources such as oil, natural gas, coal, and minerals, together with arable lands, grazing lands, forested areas, and protected areas. It is valued by calculating the present value of resource rents over twenty-five years at a discount rate of 4 percent. The balancing stock, intangible capital, is determined as a residual. It is the difference between total wealth and the sum of produced and natural capital. It includes human capital (the knowledge, technical skills, cognitive capacities, and the physical attributes of the human population), together with the institutions of a country (sometimes referred to as social capital), net foreign financial assets, and any

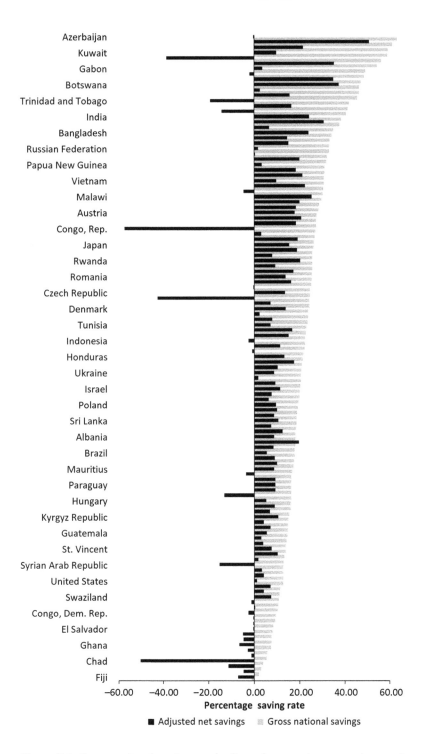

Figure 9.1 Gross national savings and adjusted net savings rates (percent), 2008. Note that a only a sub-set of countries are named on the figure.
Source: data from World Bank (2010).

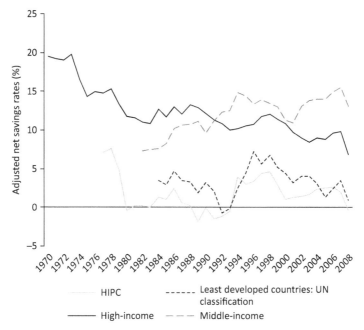

Figure 9.2 Adjusted net savings rates: high-, middle-, and low-income countries plus HIPC, 1970–2008.
Source: data from World Bank (2010).

produced or natural capital not explicitly accounted for in the produced and natural capital accounts (such as groundwater or fish stocks). The critical calculation in the adjusted net savings is the one that yields total wealth. Total wealth at time t is calculated from consumption at time t and the discount rate. Starting from the proposition that efficient (and sustainable) consumption is the return on wealth, the wealth of a country is estimated from consumption in that country by appealing to the relation: $C(t) = rW(t)$. The discount rate, r, used in the World Bank's calculations derives from the Ramsey formula $r = \rho + \eta g$, where ρ is the pure rate of time preference, η is the elasticity of the marginal utility of consumption, and g is the rate of growth in consumption. The World Bank assumed a pure rate of time preference of 1.5, an elasticity of the marginal utility of consumption of 1, and a rate of growth in consumption of 2.5 percent, yielding a discount rate of 4 percent (World Bank 2006, 2010).

Given this approach it is not surprising that intangible capital becomes increasingly significant as incomes rise. It accounts for 81 percent of aggregate capital in high-income countries, 69 percent in middle-income countries, and 57 percent in low-income countries (World Bank 2010). This is partly explained by the concentration of skill-intensive services in high-income countries, but it also reflects the greater importance of the service sector in high-income countries and the fact that many more services fall within the market economy in those countries. To tease out the relative importance of different factors in intangible capital, the World Bank (2006) modeled the residual in low- and middle-income countries as a function of domestic human capital (measured by per capita years of schooling of the working population), human capital abroad (measured by remittances from other countries), and governance/social capital (measured by the rule of law index). It found that most variation was explained by the rule of law, but that years of schooling were also important. This implies that human and social capital stocks are both important components of intangible capital, and that both also increase with per capita income.

Since intangible capital also includes environmental assets not recorded under natural capital this is not the whole story. Natural capital stocks account for a greater share of per capita wealth in low-income countries than in high-income countries. At the same time, however, natural wealth per capita rises with income, and in some cases rises very substantially. Per capita subsoil assets, for example, were found to be an order of magnitude greater in high-income than in low-income countries. Since there is no correlation between the size of proven mineral reserves and the value of subsoil assets, the implication is that a ton of iron or tin is simply more valuable in high-income countries than in low-income countries. The approach hinges on the assumption that total wealth can be estimated from current consumption in the manner described. Yet away from an efficient (and sustainable) equilibrium this assumption is highly problematic. If total wealth is to be estimated by adding up the stocks, however, then we need to be able to identify and value those stocks reliably. Among the challenges yet to be addressed in building wealth accounts are (1) the identification of net changes in physical stocks, (2) estimation of the value of ecosystem service flows that are external to the market, and (3) accounting for the environmental drivers of total factor productivity growth.

9.4 Assets in the system of national accounts

Addressing the first of these challenges requires correct identification of physical stocks, along with additions to and subtractions from those stocks. One difficulty here is that the distinction between produced and natural assets in the SNA is both ill defined and shifting. Another is that many environmental assets are currently excluded from the accounts. Only assets that are subject to well-defined property rights are included, leaving out human capital, social capital, and many natural resources.[3] Natural resources need both to be owned and capable of generating economic benefits for their owners, under "available technology, scientific knowledge, economic infrastructure, available resources and set of relative prices prevailing on the dates to which the balance sheet relates or expected to do so in the near future" (European Communities *et al.* 2009). This admits natural resources in collective ownership, but not resources where there are no defined property rights. In practice, therefore, natural resources comprise land, water, uncultivated forests, and mineral deposits that are subject to well-defined property rights – and hence private claims (see Table 9.2).

Gains and losses to biological resources are treated as either natural (not produced) or produced, depending on the control exercised by the resource manager. Where a change in biological resources is produced, it is valued separately from the land on which it occurs. Where it is natural is defined as an economic appearance, and is recorded under the category "other changes" in the volume of assets.[4] What this means is that ecosystems that span many parcels of land are not assets in the SNA. Nor can they be recorded as assets. If a change in the ecosystem changes the productivity of the land, it should appear in the accounts – at least in principle.

---

[3] "The coverage of assets is limited to those assets used in economic activity and that are subject to ownership rights; thus for example, consumer durables and human capital, as well as natural resources that are not owned, are excluded" (European Communities *et al.* 2009).

[4] So the value of land excludes "any buildings or other structures situated on it or running through it; cultivated crops, trees and animals; mineral and energy resources; non-cultivated biological resources and water resources below the ground. The associated surface water includes any inland waters (reservoirs, lakes, rivers, etc.) over which ownership rights can be exercised and that can, therefore, be the subject of transactions between institutional units" (European Communities *et al.* 2009).

Table 9.2 *SNA environmental assets*

AN.1 Produced assets
  AN.11 Fixed assets
    AN.111 Tangible fixed assets
      AN.1114 Cultivated assets
      AN.11141 Livestock for breeding, dairy, draught, etc.
      AN.11142 Vineyards, orchards and other plantations
    AN.112 Intangible fixed assets
    AN.1121 Mineral exploration
  AN.12 Inventories
    AN.122 Work in progress
      AN.1221 Work in progress on cultivated assets
AN.2 Non-produced assets
  AN.21 Tangible non-produced assets
    AN.211 Land
      AN.2111 Land underlying buildings and structures
      AN.2112 Land under cultivation
      AN.2113 Recreational land and associated surface water
      AN.2119 Other land and associated surface water
    AN.212 Subsoil assets
      AN.2121 Coal, oil and natural gas reserves
      AN.2122 Metallic mineral reserves
      AN.2123 Non-metallic mineral reserves
    AN.213 Non-cultivated biological resources
    AN.214 Water resources
  AN.22 Intangible non-produced assets
    AN.222 Leases and other transferable contracts

Source: SEEA (2003).

In practice, if ecosystem flows across property boundaries are external to the market, they will not be recorded. Since calculation of the shadow value of capital stocks requires that the rents on assets be calculated net of externalities, this is a problem. And the problem is least tractable for activities that generate public externalities. Private externalities that affect a small number of landholders are less of an issue, and can often be priced through parallel markets.

Externalities may be partially reflected in the accounts. If, for example, pollution damage inflicted by one activity on another increases the costs faced by the second activity, it will be reflected in the value added in that second activity and hence recorded in the accounts. There is still an advantage in explicitly measuring and accounting for such externalities (since it can result in a more efficient allocation of resources), but their effect will show up in the accounts. The more difficult case is where externalities cross the boundary between market and non-market activity. In this case they are not already reflected in the accounts, and estimating them would change the estimate of value added in the accounts (Nordhaus 2006).

Many ecosystem services (benefits) and disservices (costs) are off-site externalities of land uses intended to provide marketed goods and services such as foods, fuels, fibers, water, or recreation. These are the ecosystem services we need to measure and account for. In the absence of off-site costs or benefits, the rents to some land use should capture the net effect of the full set of ecosystem services generated by that use. If there are off-site costs or benefits of land use, however, these will not be captured in the rents to the landholder. Since it is simply not possible to estimate the value of every off-site effect of some land use, only those that significantly affect wellbeing are worth addressing explicitly in the accounts.

9.5 Satellite accounts and the capital accounts in the system of national accounts

To this point, amendments to the SNA to account for environmental assets have taken the form of the establishment of satellite environmental accounts. The satellite system of environmental-economic accounts (SEEA) is still under development by the UN, the European Community, the OECD, the IMF, and the World Bank. It is designed to address both changes in environmental stocks and environmental externalities. The SEEA (2003) includes measures of the effect of environmental change on capital stocks, and since it has a capital focus is, at least in principle, consistent with the inclusive wealth approach described above. Under the SEEA, development based on the exploitation of natural resources is regarded as unsustainable if those resources are degraded to the point where they are no longer provide what the SEEA refers to as "resource," "service," or "sink" functions. These functions correspond, very loosely, to the MA provisioning, cultural, and regulating/supporting services.

There are four sets of accounts in the SEEA. The first is a set of flow accounts for pollution, energy, and materials. These record industrial use of energy and materials as inputs to production, and the generation of pollutants and solid waste. The second set of accounts is the environmental protection and resource management expenditure accounts. These accounts record expenditures incurred by industry, government and households to protect the environment or to manage natural resources. This set of accounts reports data that are already recorded in the SNA. The third is a set of natural resource asset accounts. These report changes in traditional natural resource stocks, including land, fish, forest, water, and minerals. The final set reports the value of non-market environmental flows, and adjusts aggregates for natural resource depletion and degradation, and for environmentally defensive expenditures.

By contrast with the definition of natural resources in the SNA, environmental assets in the SEEA are defined as in Table 9.3. Two aspects of this definition of assets are worth noting. One is that aside from the intangible assets they are all place-based. That is, they involve the conversion and management of, or impact on, ecosystem services associated with a particular place. *In situ* subsoil resources are not generally associated with biological activity, but their extraction involves production, processing, and waste disposal on the surface that frequently has extensive direct and indirect off-site impacts on ecosystem services. Surface "land" and "land-based" or "water" resources are more immediately used to enhance the flow of particular ecosystem services, though this may be at a cost to other services.

The second thing to note is that there may be a much wider range of property rights applying to environmental assets in the SEEA than in the SNA. The SEEA admits assets that are subject to private ownership (freehold), time limited use rights (leasehold), common property (common pool resources and public lands), or undefined rights (open access). Within the SNA, by contrast, only assets subject to well-defined property rights are included, and most changes in environmental assets recorded in the SNA occur as "other changes in the volume of assets."

As a result the SEEA includes a wider and less well-defined range of environmental assets, comprising not just all land and natural resources, but also ecosystems. The inclusion of ecosystems turns out to be quite problematic, since it deliberately introduces an element of double counting in the interests of recording each of a number of distinct ecosystem services. Three types of ecosystem are reported – terrestrial, aquatic, and atmospheric – each being associated with multiple services. So an asset identified as EA1 or EA2 in Table 9.3 can also appear in EA3

Table 9.3 *SEEA environmental assets*

EA.1 Natural resources
    EA.11 Mineral and energy resources (cubic meters, tons, tons of oil equivalents, joules)
    EA.12 Soil resources (cubic meters, tons)
    EA.13 Water resources (cubic meters)
    EA.14 Biological resources
        EA.141 Timber resources (cubic meters)
        EA.142 Crop and plant resources, other than timber (cubic meters, tons, number)
        EA.143 Aquatic resources (tons, number)
        EA.144 Animal resources, other than aquatic (number)
EA.2 Land and surface water (hectares)
    EA.21 Land underlying buildings and structures
    EA.22 Agricultural land and associated surface water
    EA.23 Wooded land and associated surface water
    EA.24 Major water bodies
    EA.25 Other land
EA.3 Ecosystems
    EA.31 Terrestrial ecosystems
    EA.32 Aquatic ecosystems
    EA.33 Atmospheric systems
Memorandum items – intangible assets related to environmental issues (extended SNA codes)
    AN.1121 Mineral exploration
    AN.2221 Transferable licenses and concessions for the exploitation of natural resources
    AN.2222 Tradable permits allowing the emission of residuals
    AN.2223 Other intangible non-produced environmental assets

Source: SEEA (2003).

if it is associated with any of the services of EA3. With the exception of natural resources that provide direct use benefits, individual species are not classified as assets in the SEEA. This is because the SEEA assumes that it is not the components of ecosystems that benefit humans, but the systems as a whole. However, because natural resources are classified as specific assets, this means that elements of the environment can appear twice in the SEEA asset classification, once as natural assets and again as components of ecosystems. For example, forests that are used as a source of timber are classified as natural resource assets, but when they also provide services such as carbon sequestration or habitat provision they are classified as ecosystem assets. As natural resources, they provide direct use benefits, while as components of ecosystems they provide indirect use benefits. From the perspective of the SEEA it is necessary to recognize both roles of forests if a complete picture of the benefits provided to humans by the environment is to be captured in the accounts. As long as ecosystem services are only reported in physical terms the double counting of such assets is not an issue, but when the assets are valued, this is much more problematic.

The decision to include ecosystems as assets in the SEEA was well motivated. It was seen as a way of capturing valuable ecosystem services in the national income accounts. However, this may not be the best option for capturing non-marketed ecosystem services in the accounts. As we have seen, any piece of land will jointly produce a number of goods and services, some of which may have off-site effects. The social value of the land as an asset is the discounted flow of all the services it yields, whether marketed or not and whether on-site or not. The on-site benefits should be captured in land prices (where these exist), so the task of the SEEA is to identify the offsite services.

The SEEA approach to estimating asset values is summarized in Table 9.4. As in the SNA, multiple methods are used including both perpetual inventory methods and direct estimation of resource rents. For most environmental assets, the resource rent is derived by deducting costs from the market price received for marketed products, the value of the stock being calculated as the net present value of rents. The SEEA suggests that non-market valuation techniques be used for services that do not have a market price.

What is needed to correct the wealth accounts in the SNA (or the national income and product accounts in the USA) is both the extension of the set of stocks measured to comprise all relevant sources of wealth, and the inclusion of the non-marketed impacts of asset use on third parties. It is probably true that the most important single addition to make to the set of capital stocks measured is human capital. The findings of the World Bank (2006), along with numerous studies of total factor productivity growth, indicate that the most important driver of wealth creation is the skills and know-how of the population. This is excluded from both the SNA and US national income and product accounts (Jorgenson and Landefeld 2006; European Communities *et al.*

Table 9.4 *Methods used to estimate asset values in the SEEA*

Data needs for estimating stock values:
  Resource rent
  Stock of the resource
  Life length or rate of extraction of the resource
  Decision on how to record renewals/discoveries
  Discount rate for future income
Data for estimating resource rent
1. Appropriation method
    direct observation
2. Perpetual inventory based method
    stock of produced capital (estimated from price decline)
    net operating surplus
    rate of return to produced capital
3. Capital service based method
    stock of produced capital (estimated from efficiency decline)
    gross operating surplus
    capital services rendered by produced capital

Source: SEEA (2003).

2009). The most important environmental stocks to add are those that are currently excluded on grounds that they lack sufficiently well-defined property rights. These are not ecosystems as such, but the many public lands, open access resources, or sea areas within the exclusive economic zone (EEZ) currently excluded from the accounts.

The most important non-marketed impacts of asset use on third parties are off-site ecosystem service flows: environmental externalities. These include, for example, hydrologically mediated flows, including water pollution, siltation, soil loss, flooding, and so on; atmospherically mediated flows such as emissions with local (particulates (PM10), photochemical smog), regional (sulfur dioxide), and global (carbon dioxide, nitrous oxide, methane) consequences; the effects of human travel and transport (the transmission of pests and pathogens through local, regional, and global goods transport and travel networks); and access mediated flows (changes in on-site benefits of, for example, biodiversity conservation, accessed by people elsewhere).

Some of these flows might fit Nordhaus's category of external effects whose impact on asset values are already included in the accounts

(Nordhaus 2006). However, many regional and all global flows are international, and are not currently recorded in the accounts of any country. Since many of these flows are public goods and so are non-exclusive and non-rival in their effects, whether they are significant enough to be measured and recorded depends on the extent of the public interest affected. A simple test of this would be size of the affected population. The general point to make is that capturing important off-site ecosystem service flows is critical to the correct estimation of the value of the assets involved.

9.6 Towards the construction of inclusive wealth accounts

The World Bank's adjusted net savings measure is one attempt to estimate the errors involved in the existing measures of change in the value of capital stocks (World Bank 2006, 2010). Its greatest strength (and greatest weakness) lies in the fact that it adopts a theoretically consistent approach to the estimation of total wealth. Its strength is that it makes it possible to use observations on current and projected future consumption to derive plausible estimates of the wealth. Its weakness is that the conditions under which consumption can be used in this way do not hold if future consumption is not sustainable. The alternative is to obtain total wealth as the sum of all stocks of different types of wealth. The SEEA (2003) is an attempt to generate the environmental data needed to measure one of these stocks – environmental wealth. It does not, however, resolve the questions of what environmental stocks should be included, how they should be measured, and how they should be valued.

A recently issued report by the United Nations University (UNU), the International Human Dimensions Program, and UNEP offers preliminary estimates of changes in inclusive wealth for a selected set of countries, based largely on market prices (UNU-IHDP and UNEP 2012). Using environmental wealth estimates that are broadly consistent with the SNA, the report shows that many countries were running down their natural capital in that period (Table 9.5). Since the measure of environmental wealth in the report includes only assets for which there exist market prices, it does not correct for externalities. Nor does it have anything to say about the implications of biodiversity change. What it does do, however, is to construct a total wealth estimate by summing the different components of total wealth, rather than by projecting consumption rates.

Table 9.5 *Changes in natural capital: average annual growth rates,*
1990–2008

	Natural capital growth (decline) (%)	Population growth (%)	Natural capital per capita (%)	Inclusive wealth index per capita (%)
Australia	–0.49	1.29	–1.78	0.12
Brazil	–0.26	1.38	–1.64	0.91
Canada	–0.21	1.03	–1.24	0.37
Chile	–0.36	1.35	–1.71	1.19
China	–0.24	0.83	–1.07	2.07
Colombia	–0.39	1.70	–2.09	–0.08
Ecuador	–0.50	1.76	–2.26	0.37
France	0.48	0.51	–0.03	1.44
Germany	–0.47	0.23	–0.70	1.83
India	–0.34	1.74	–2.08	0.91
Japan	0.63	0.19	0.44	0.91
Kenya	0.05	2.79	–2.74	0.06
Nigeria	–0.07	2.44	–2.51	–1.87
Norway	–0.96	0.67	–1.63	0.66
Russia	–0.34	–0.19	–0.15	–0.31
Saudi Arabia	–0.08	2.72	–2.80	–1.12
South Africa	–0.60	1.64	–2.24	–0.07
UK	–2.50	0.38	–2.88	0.88
USA	–0.21	1.04	–1.25	0.69
Venezuela	–0.14	1.99	–2.13	–0.29

Source: UNU–IHDP and UNEP (2012).

A second (and related) attempt to estimate comprehensive wealth uses World Bank data for stocks of produced and natural capital, but separately estimates stocks of human capital (Arrow *et al.* 2012). Specifically, investments in human capital are calculated from projected changes in the labor force and labor productivity associated with different levels of education, and from changes in human health. Estimates of investment in natural capital were more similar to the estimates made by the World Bank, but included the assumption that exhaustible resource prices would rise at the rate of interest – after Hotelling (1931). Changes in selected resource stocks are weighted by their shadow price: the impact of a marginal change in those stocks on wellbeing. For non-renewable resources, the change in resource stock is the amount extracted and, ignoring externalities, the shadow value is taken to be the resource rent. For renewable resources, the change in stocks is the difference between the natural rate of regeneration and harvest, and the shadow value is calculated in the same way.

The results of this second approach for a sample of five economies (the USA, China, India, Brazil, and Venezuela) are reported in Table 9.6. The table shows estimates of investment in the last five years of the last century in the three main capital stocks – produced, natural, and human – as well as changes in the size of two significant environmental stocks, oil and carbon. Unlike the estimates reported in Table 9.5, it shows that natural capital declined in all countries except for the USA. Like the World Bank estimates it shows that the increase in total (comprehensive) wealth is due primarily to investment in human capital.

The natural capital stocks in this approach are still largely abiotic. They include, for example, oil, natural gas, bauxite, copper, iron, gold, lead, nickel, phosphate, and zinc. Indeed, the only biotic resource included is forests, the benefits being divided into timber production and other forest benefits. So few of the environmental changes discussed in this book are directly recorded in such attempts to generate wealth estimates. Some may be indirectly recorded in estimates of at least the health dimension of human capital, or in the environmental determinants of total factor productivity. But by and large they are not yet there.

A large part of the problem still to be addressed lies in the exclusions implied by the SNA's focus only on assets that are subject to well-defined property rights, and that give rise to well-defined private claims. The list of excluded resources includes most that are in public ownership and all that lie beyond national jurisdiction. Yet these resources matter. The stocks of environmental assets that need to be recorded include all lands that generate off-site benefits or costs as a result of environmental flows, noting that the word "land" in this context means any surficial area generating on- and off-site costs and benefits. It accordingly includes both terrestrial and aquatic systems. Nor should lands be restricted to the natural resource categories of either the SNA or the SEEA. Built environments – urban and industrial areas – create ecosystems that generate benefits and costs to people that are sometimes similar and sometimes different from other ecosystems. They also involve off-site flows that affect wellbeing. For example, industrial environments are a major source of pollution, imposing costs at a range of scales from local

Table 9.6 *Components of comprehensive investment (in 2000 US$ billion)*

	Natural capital	Human capital	Reproducible capital	Oil capital gains	Carbon damages	Total
USA						
1995 capital stock	5,694.73	60,086.93	13,430.66			79,212.320
2000 capital stock	5,702.41	64,802.68	15,923.83			84,889.968
Change 1995–2000	7.68	4,715.75	2,493.17	–1,367.38	–171.572	5,677.648
Percentage change	0.13	7.85	18.56			7.17
Growth rate (%)	0.03	1.52	3.46			1.39
China						
1995 capital stock	3,854.52	8,492.93	3,706.23		16,053.680	
2000 capital stock	3,847.62	9,394.69	6,471.69			19,398.916
Change 1995–2000	–6.90	901.76	2,765.46	–305.80	–9.284	3,345.236
Percentage change	–0.18	10.62	74.62			20.84
Growth rate (%)	–0.04	2.04	11.79			3.86
Brazil						
1995 capital stock	2,688.40	7,157.81	1,728.80			11,575.010
2000 capital stock	2,619.42	8,248.34	1,756.91			12,463.094
Change 1995–2000	–68.98	1,090.53	28.11	–119.05	–42.526	888.084
Percentage change	–2.57	15.24	1.63			7.67
Growth rate (%)	–0.52	2.88	0.32			1.49
India						
1995 capital stock	2,139.38	5,983.36	1,429.82			9,552.560
2000 capital stock	2,121.83	6,934.61	2,035.00			10,861.898

Change 1995–2000	−17.56	951.25	605.18	−141.50	−88.042	1,309.338
Percentage change	−0.82	15.90	42.33			13.71
Growth rate (%)	−0.16	2.99	7.31			2.60
Venezuela						
1995 capital stock	3,704.417	526.61	201.21			4,432.237
2000 capital stock	3,591.29	587.62	204.71			4,383.615
Change 1995–2000	−113.131	61.01	3.51	322.04	−11.552	261.866
Percentage change	−3.05	11.59	1.74			5.91
Growth rate (%)	−0.62	2.22	0.35			1.15

Source: Arrow et al. (2012).

to global. Urban environments also play a critical role in the transmission of infectious diseases.

It is worth repeating that the task is not to invent another class of assets – ecosystems – and to account for those assets. It is to understand how ecosystems mediate the off-site external effects of land use. The core problem to address is externality. From this perspective, ecosystems are important only to the extent that ecological flows are a vehicle for off-site costs and benefits. Assets of all kinds are embedded in a series of overlapping systems, and their value to society reflects their role in those systems. The weakness of the existing accounts is that they take no notice of off-site flows that do not give rise to well-defined claims. So uncompensated external benefits or costs have no place in the SNA. They are, however, relevant to the wellbeing of the people affected, and they do change the value of the generating assets. The creation of inclusive wealth accounts requires that existing uncompensated external benefits or costs be factored into the value of the generating assets.

There is certainly a case for extending the coverage of land in the SNA or the US national income and product accounts to include resources now excluded because they are subject to ill-defined property rights, or are in the public domain. But this is not the same as valuing ecosystems. The species inhabiting such lands, like the species inhabiting lands already reported in the accounts, are among the attributes of the land that confer value. They are also among the attributes that give rise to off-site costs or benefits. All else being equal, land that supports pest species would be expected to have a lower shadow price than land that supports species of high conservation value. In both cases, a measure of the costs or benefits conferred by those species would be the offsite ecosystem services/disservices they provide. In some cases – such as wild relatives of wheat, rice, or corn, or rare endemic species – their effects would be global. In others – such as crop pests or pest predators – they would be strictly local. Since a change in the abundance of such species affects the value of the land itself through its impact on ecosystem services, it also affects the wealth of the country in which that land is located. That is what inclusive wealth accounts should address.

References

Alston, J. M., Beddow, J. M. and Pardey, P. G. (2009) Agricultural research, productivity, and food prices in the long run. *Science*, 325, 1209–1210.

Alston, J. M., Andersen, M. A., James, J. J. and Pardey, P. G. (2010) *Persistence Pays: US Agricultural Productivity Growth and the Benefits from Public R&D Spending*. Springer, Dordrecht.

Arrow, K. J., Dasgupta, P. and Mäler, K.-G. (2003) The genuine savings criterion and the value of population. *Economic Theory*, 21, 217–225.

Arrow, K. J., Dasgupta, P., Goulder, L. H., Mumford, K. J. and Oleson, K. (2012) Sustainability and the measurement of wealth. *Environment and Development Economics*, 17, 317–353.

Dasgupta, P. (2001) *Human Well-being and the Natural Environment*. Oxford University Press, New York.

(2009) The welfare economic theory of green national accounts. *Environmental and Resource Economics*, 42, 3–38.

Dasgupta, P. and Mäler, K.-G. (2000) Net national product, wealth, and social well-being. *Environment and Development Economics*, 5, 69–93.

European Communities, International Monetary Fund, Organization for Economic Co-operation and Development, United Nations and World Bank (2009) *System of National Accounts 2008*. United Nations, New York.

Ferreira, S., Hamilton, K. and Vincent, J. R. (2008) Comprehensive wealth and future consumption: accounting for population growth. *The World Bank Economic Review*, 22, 233–248.

Goossens, Y., Mäkipää, A., Schepelmann, P., van de Sand, I., Kuhndtand, M. and Herrndorf, M. (2007) *Alternative Progress Indicators to Gross Domestic Product (GDP) as a Means towards Sustainable Development*. European Parliament: Policy Department, Economic and Scientific Policy, Brussels.

Hamilton, K. (1994) Green adjustments to GDP. *Resources Policy*, 20, 155–168.

Hamilton, K. and Clemens, M. (1999) Genuine savings rates in developing countries. *World Bank Economic Review*, 13, 333–356.

Hartwick, J. (1990) Natural resources, national accounting, and economic depreciation. *Journal of Public Economics*, 43, 291–304.

(1994) National wealth and net national product. *Scandinavian Journal of Economics*, 96, 253–256.

(2000) *National Accounting and Capital*. Edward Elgar, Cheltenham.

Hicks, J. R. (1939) *Value and Capital*. Clarendon Press, Oxford.

Hotelling, H. (1931) The economics of exhaustible resources. *Journal of Political Economy*, 39, 137–175.

Jorgenson, D. W. and Landefeld, J. S. (2006) Blueprint for expanded and integrated US accounts: review, assessment and next steps. *A New Architecture for the US National Accounts* (ed. D. W. Jorgenson, J. S. Landefeld and W. D. Nordhaus), pp. 13–112. Chicago University Press.

Lindahl, E. (1933) The concept of income. *Economic Essays in Honor of Gustav Cassel* (ed. G. Bagge), pp. 399–407. Allen and Unwin, London.

Nordhaus, W. D. (2006) Principles of national accounting for non-market accounts. *A New Architecture for the US National Accounts* (ed. D. W. Jorgenson, J. S. Landefield and W. D. Nordhaus), pp. 143–160. University of Chicago Press.

Pearce, D. and Atkinson, G. (1993) Capital theory and the measurement of sustainable development: an indicator of weak sustainability. *Ecological Economics*, 8, 103–108.

Pearce, D., Hamilton, K. and Atkinson, G. (1996) Measuring sustainable development: progress on indicators. *Environment and Development Economics*, 1, 85–101.

Pearce, D. W. and Warford, J. J. (1993) *World Without End: Economics, Environment, and Sustainable Development*. Oxford University Press.

Perrings, C. (2012) The road to wealth accounting. *Inclusive Wealth Report 2012. Measuring Progress toward Sustainability* (ed. UNU-IHDP and UNEP), pp. 143–164. Cambridge University Press.

Piesse, J. and Thirtle, C. (2010) Agricultural R&D, technology and productivity. *Philosophical Transactions of the Royal Society B: Biological Sciences*, 365, 3035–3047.

Repetto, R., Magrath, W. B. and Wells, M. (1989) *Wasting Assets: Natural Resources in the National Income Accounts*. World Resources Institute, Washington, DC.

Samuelson, P. A. (1961) The evaluation of social income: capital formation and wealth. *The Theory of Capital* (ed. F. A. Lutz and D. C. Hague), pp. 32–57. St. Martins Press, New York.

SEEA (2003) *Handbook of National Accounting Integrated Environmental and Economic Accounting 2003*. United Nations, European Commission, International Monetary Fund, OECD, and World Bank, New York.

UNU-IHDP and UNEP (2012) *Inclusive Wealth Report 2012: Measuring Progress toward Sustainability*. Cambridge University Press.

Vouvaki, D. and Xepapadeas, A. (2009) Total factor productivity growth when factors of production generate environmental externalities. *Fondazione Eni Enrico Mattei Working Papers*, 281.

World Bank (2006) *Where is the Wealth of Nations? Measuring Capital for the 21st Century*. World Bank, Washington, DC.

 (2010) *The Changing Wealth of Nations: Measuring Sustainable Development in the New Millennium*. World Bank, Washington, DC.

World Commission on Environment and Development (1987) *Our Common Future*. Island Press, Washington, DC.

10 Managing risk, uncertainty, and irreversibility in biodiversity change

10.1 The unknowns in the problem of biodiversity change

In summarizing the state of knowledge on biodiversity change in both natural and managed systems the major assessments (the Global Biodiversity Assessment, the MA, the IAASTD, and the Global Biodiversity Outlook) usefully clarified the limits of our current understanding of biodiversity change. They showed that our knowledge is still extremely patchy. We know much about changes in species richness and abundance for birds, for example, but little about many invertebrates. We have many data on the ecological consequences of biodiversity change in temperate grasslands, but relatively few on tropical forests. At the same time none of the assessments offers much insight into the value of one type of biodiversity change relative to another. In the opening chapters of Part II of this book I have considered what this means for the information needed to underpin management of biodiversity change. Chapter 8 considers the information requirements of the main management options, adaptation and mitigation, and what this means for the way we project the causes, consequences, and character of biodiversity change. In Chapter 9, I address the issue of valuation, and the challenges involved in generating information that can inform macro-economic policy.

In the best of all worlds, however, we will still be called on to make decisions on the basis of incomplete information. There are two dimensions to the problem of biodiversity change that complicate both calculation of what it costs society and development of options for its management: the irreversibility of some aspects of biodiversity change and the fundamental uncertainty that induces. For all practical purposes the extinction of species is forever. Its effects are unknown and unknowable at the moment it occurs. People undertaking activities that change either the survival prospects of a species or its range cannot imagine all possible consequences of their actions. Nor are they able to assign probabilities to the consequences they can imagine. Similarly, it is not possible to reverse the changes wrought by many invasive species, or to assess the potential costs and benefits of actions that irreversibly affect the future evolution of the system.

In such cases people typically take one of two approaches. Either they completely discount the uncertainty involved or they focus their attention on the worst-case losses. They either ignore fundamentally uncertain future costs and benefits, or they assume the worst. Neither response protects the public interest. This chapter considers the problem of decision-making where the consequences of decisions are irreversible and fundamentally uncertain. Not every change in species richness or abundance has these characteristics, but enough do that it is worth considering what it means for the way we make decisions.

The term uncertainty is used here to mean something different from the uncertainty involved in, say, rolling dice. In that case, assuming that the dice are true, it is known that each can take only one of six values, and that value is known. That is, the payoffs associated with all possible outcomes of the action are known with certainty. In addition, the probability of each outcome is also known. The value of an outcome multiplied by the probability that it will occur is referred to as risk. By contrast, uncertainty is used here to refer to a situation where either the set of all possible outcomes of an action is unknown, or the associated probability distribution is unknown.[1]

While relatively little attention has been paid to the problem of decision-making under uncertainty in this sense, the theory of decision-making under risk is very well developed. Indeed, Chapter 4 discussed the implications of risk for the selection of a portfolio of species. The theory of decision-making under risk and its application to biodiversity is summarized in the next section, as are the implications of the concepts discussed in Chapter 4. However, the main focus of this chapter is on the implications for decision-making of fundamental uncertainty about the irreversible consequences of biodiversity change. It is approached first through a discussion of how decisions are made under fundamental uncertainty, second through a review of how this is affected by irreversibility, and third through an assessment of the implications of both uncertainty and irreversibility for precaution in the social management of biodiversity change.

[1] This accordingly subsumes both "ambiguity" and "ignorance."

Part I of this book identified externalities and public goods as the key issues to be addressed if the biodiversity change problem is to be solved. At this point I am concerned with a challenge that spans both. For example, the loss of genetic information caused by the extinction of any species affects the information contained in the global gene pool (a global public good). By contrast, the introduction of an invasive pest to some ecosystem as a byproduct of the trade between two countries can affect both individual resource users who have to deal with the pest (a private externality of trade) and all members of society affected by any resulting change in biodiversity (a public externality of trade). The loss of genetic information is certainly irreversible. The introduction of an invasive pest may be. What should this mean for the decisions taken by conservation authorities, by border protection agencies, or by international bodies with responsibility for the biodiversity effects of trade: the WTO, the WHO, the OIE, the SPS Agreement, the IPPC, and so on?

The modern precautionary principle is thought to have originated in a German concept, *Vorsorgeprinzip*, which refers to the avoidance of potentially damaging actions even where there is fundamental uncertainty about the consequences of those actions (Harremoës *et al.* 2001). While a number of countries have formally adopted the principle, it has been applied in quite different ways. A frequently cited statement of the principle holds that where the costs of an activity are (1) uncertain but potentially both high and irreversible, and (2) *may* exceed the costs of preventative or anticipatory action, then society should take such preventative or anticipatory action before the uncertainty is resolved (Taylor 1991). In other words, it is seen as a way of dealing with fundamentally uncertain benefit and cost streams.

The principle has been widely adopted. At the national level it appears in regulatory statutes for health and the environment in Australia, Canada, New Zealand, and the UK. In the USA it is applied in the Food, Drug, and Cosmetic Act, the Clean Air Act, and the Endangered Species Act (Ashford 2007). At the international level, it is included in the 1992 Maastricht Treaty that frames all European-level legislation. It is also an element in a number of MEAs, including the Biodiversity Convention's Cartagena Protocol on Biosafety and the SPS (Cooney and Dickson 2005; Sadeleer 2007). The evidence for its application is, however, mixed. In cases where preliminary research on novel stressors identified outcomes involving high and possibly irreversible cost, there has frequently been no policy response at all. In some instances the problem lies in the quality of preliminary evidence. For decision-makers to take action in such instances they would have to apply a weaker test than that required by standard scientific proof. Examples of weaker tests include "scientifically based suspicion," "reasonable grounds for concern," and the "balance of evidence." In other instances, however, the problem lies more in the inertia of regulatory agencies. Indeed, many early experiments that indicated the potential for widespread, significant, and irreversible consequences of environmentally harmful activities did not trigger a policy response (Harremoës *et al.* 2001).

Most such cases involved novelty. They include emissions of halocarbons, polychlorinated biphenyls (PCBs), and methyl tert-butyl ether. The results of animal tests of PCBs were, for example, available in 1937 but were not acted upon for decades. The UK's Swann Committee had identified the problem of antibiotic resistance in humans in the 1960s, but research to test the conclusions of the Swann Committee was not undertaken until the 1990s. In some cases the problem was compounded by the same turf issues that dog decision-makers today. Among zoonoses, for example, bovine spongiform encephalopathy (BSE) in the UK fell within the remit of veterinary officials who regarded the risk of transmission to humans as acceptably slight, and hence neglected that outcome. In the USA, where the human health implications of transmission of scrapie and Creutzfeldt-Jacob Disease meant that human health officials made the decisions, there was a ban on infected animals being admitted to the human food chain as soon as it was recognized in the 1970s (Harremoës *et al.* 2001).

This chapter considers how an understanding of decision-making under uncertainty helps us both to interpret such past cases, and to identify the appropriate response to the problem of managing future biodiversity change. Since the future outcomes that most concern conservationists – species extinctions – are irreversible, it is worth asking what irreversibility means for the way that conservation decisions should be taken. Extreme, unique, rare, and irreversible events share the characteristics that they have either no or only a few historical precedents, and that their effects may be quite novel. They involve losses or gains that are qualitatively different from what has gone before. In such cases it is seldom possible to predict a probability distribution of outcomes with confidence. Nevertheless, decision-makers need to be able to act on the basis of non-probabilistic information concerning the outcomes of their actions. It follows that identification of non-probabilistic information on which to found decisions involving novel or unfamiliar effects is an essential element of a precautionary approach.

10.2 Decision-making under risk

The dominant theory of decision-making under risk is the expected utility approach. People are assumed to evaluate a risky prospect in terms of the expected utility – think of this as the expected net benefits – of the prospect. It implies that the attractiveness of a gamble, a roll of the dice, or turn of the roulette wheel, for example, that offers a set of payoffs $(x_1, \ldots, x_n)$, with probabilities $(p_1, \ldots, p_n)$, is evaluated by the expected utility of those payoffs. Economists typically represent this by a utility function suggested by John von Neumann and Oskar Morgenstern:

$$U(p, x) = \sum_{i=1}^{n} p_i u(x_i)$$

The von Neumann-Morgenstern utility function has a number of useful properties.[2] Among these is the fact that the shape of the function itself reflects the decision-maker's attitude to the risk involved in the gamble. If decision-makers are risk averse – if they prefer certain outcomes to risky outcomes – their utility function will be concave. If they are risk avid or risk seeking it will be convex, and if they are risk neutral it will be linear.

Consider the portfolio of species discussed in Chapter 4, and assume that the decision-maker is risk averse. Figure 4.1 describes the expected yield from each combination of species, and the associated risk

[2] It assumes that preferences are transitive, continuous, and independent. Transitivity implies that for three alternatives, A, B, and C, if decision-makers prefer A to B and B to C, then they will prefer A to C. Continuity implies that if A is preferred to B and B is preferred to C, then there exists some probability p, $0 < p < 1$, such that the decision-maker will be indifferent between outcome B with certainty and a compound $(A, p; C, 1 - p)$: i.e. a prospect in which A occurs with probability p and C occurs with probability $1 - p$. Independence implies that if A is preferred to B, and C is some other outcome, then if two compound prospects offer (i) A and C and (ii) B and C with the same probabilities, the decision-maker will prefer (i).

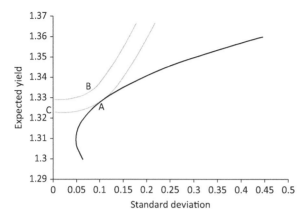

Figure 10.1 The optimal balance between mean and variance in the return on a portfolio of species.

(approximated by the standard deviation in yields for each combination of species). If the only species in the system is S_2 then the expected yield is high, but so is the variance in yield. If the only species in the system is S_1 then both the expected yield and the variance in yield is much lower. To see what combination of species would be best from the decision-maker's perspective, we need to understand how the decision-maker would balance certain gains against risky gains. Each of the grey curves in Figure 10.1 describes the combinations of mean and variance in yields that leave decision-makers indifferent. Since their utility is assumed to increase with their wealth, they prefer a higher rather than a lower expected yield. But since they are also assumed to be risk averse they would prefer lower to higher variance in yield. So while they would unambiguously prefer combination B to combination A (it has a higher mean and lower variance), they would be indifferent between combination C and combination A. Combination C (the vertical intercept of the curve) involves no variance at all, so this is an absolutely certain return. Combination A delivers a higher expected yield, but also involves more risk. They would be equally content with either.

Recall that the black line in the figure describes the expected yield from each combination of species, and the associated risk (approximated by the standard deviation in yields for each combination of species). We can call this the efficient species frontier. Not all combinations of species along the frontier are equally preferred. The optimal

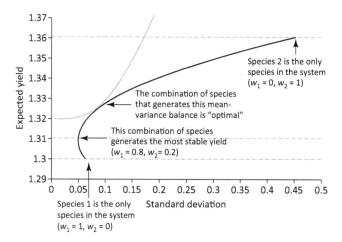

Figure 10.2 The optimal portfolio of species does not necessarily result in the most stable (least risky) yield.

portfolio of species is that which enables the decision-maker to be on the highest attainable indifference curve, i.e. the indifference curve that is tangential to the curve. This yields the species portfolio that delivers the mean-variance yield combination, A. Note that this is not the combination that gives the lowest variance in yields, since the decision-maker is content to accept some risk if this secures a higher mean yield.

Although expected utility provides a logical, internally consistent theory of decision-making, von Neumann-Morgenstern utilities are insensitive to low probability events and hence to catastrophic risk (Chichilnisky and Heal 1998). As a result, expected utility theory fails to predict people's decisions when faced with risks of this kind. More generally, people confronted with choices of a certain type systematically choose in a way that is inconsistent with the theory. There is, for example, systematic and long-standing evidence that people treat probabilities close to either zero or one in a quite distinctive way. The probability of an almost certain outcome is frequently assumed by decision-makers to be equal to one. On the other hand, the probability of a very unlikely outcome tends either to be overestimated, or to be assumed equal to zero depending on the value of the outcome. Indeed, this appears to happen even in well-functioning liability insurance markets (Katzman 1988). People tend to underestimate the probability of death from common causes, but to overestimate the probability of death from uncommon causes (Pigeon *et al.* 1992). In much the same way they overestimate the risks of high dread events, such as nuclear or toxic waste accidents, and to underestimate the risks of low dread events such as car accidents (McDaniels, Kamlet and Fischer 1992). For some people species extinctions are high dread events, for others they are low dread.

Empirical research has also shown that decision-makers have different attitudes to gains and losses. Individual decisions are frequently based on a reference point, often the status quo. The disutility people get from a loss of some magnitude relative to the reference point often outweighs the utility from a gain of the same magnitude relative to the same reference point (Kahneman and Tversky 1979). This implies that the utility function may be steeper for losses than for gains. The rhetoric around species extinctions (which emphasizes the costs of species extinctions or extirpations over the gains of species introductions) fits well with this observation. It also fits with experiments about the effect of framing. Whether risks are portrayed in terms of losses or gains has been shown to produce quite different estimates of willingness to pay for a reduction in risk (Loomis and du Vair 1993).

10.3 Decision-making under uncertainty

In contrast to decision-making under risk, there is no consensus about how decision-makers could (or should) proceed when faced with a decision under fundamental uncertainty. The most widely used approach has been to assume that people have subjective opinions about the likelihood of the future consequences of their decisions. That is, they have a set of prior beliefs about the likelihood attaching to the possible outcomes of their actions, and they maximize expected utility subject to those prior beliefs (Savage 1954). Many alternatives are variations on this theme. One of these, originally due to Shackle (1955) but later developed by Katzner, assumes that decision-makers do not form estimates of the probability distribution of all outcomes, only of those that have occurred with sufficient frequency to be routine (Katzner 1998). In the case of routine decisions the evaluation of options might well match the expected utility approach. But in the case of crucial or unique decisions, decision-makers are assumed to form opinions about the occurrence of all possible states of the world. Their opinion reflects the degree of disbelief or potential surprise associated with each state. In Katzner's work, a potential surprise density function maps the incomplete list of states of nature into a closed interval between zero and one, as with a probability distribution.[3] The intuition behind the approach is straightforward. Routine events, such as the harvest of crops, have occurred often enough in the past that the decision-maker is able to judge the likelihood that they will occur again. Crucial events, such as the loss of species, have not. In such cases the decision-maker ranks outcomes not by the likelihood that they will occur, but by the surprise that will result if they do.

An alternative way of capturing the process by which decision-makers approximate the probability of events that they believe to be fundamentally uncertain is through a set of weights. As with the subjective probability approach, decision-makers take whatever indication exists of the likelihood of some outcome, and weight it depending on their confidence in the existing estimate (Fishburn 1988). Such weighted preferences over outcomes can be represented by the function:

$$U(\rho, g, x) = \frac{\sum_i \rho_i g(x_i) u(x_i)}{\sum_i \rho_i g(x_i)}$$

where the ρ's represent best guess probabilities and $g(x_i)$ is the weighting function. Given that an underlying probability distribution is known this has the same structure as the expected utility problem. Provided that the weights attaching to all outcomes are identical it reduces to expected utility. The weights attaching to the different outcomes can be interpreted as measures of the decision-maker's confidence in the underlying probability distribution.

The related notion of rank dependent expected utility allows the weights attached to outcomes with the same probability to vary according to how good or bad the outcome is. Under this approach, extreme but low probability outcomes receive additional weight, consistent with the empirical evidence on how decision-makers respond to catastrophic risk (Quiggin 1982). Others have suggested that the probability weights will typically vary around some reference point, and that the weighting function is concave for gains and convex for losses (Tversky and Kahneman 1992; Starmer 2000).

---

[3] This is clearly similar to an inverted subjective probability density function, but does not imply anything about the frequency with which outcomes have been observed historically.

More recently, Klibanoff *et al.* have sought to distinguish between the aversion that decision-makers might have to risk in the von Neumann-Morgenstern sense, and to ambiguity in the information that informs their prior beliefs about the probabilities attaching to different outcomes (Klibanoff, Marinacci and Mukerji 2005, 2009). The approach reflects the fact that uncertainty stems not only from variation in environmental conditions, but also from the incompleteness of the decision-maker's model of the world. To distinguish between ambiguity and risk aversion they construct a utility function that, if we express it in the same manner, takes the form:

$$U(\mu, \rho, x) = \sum_{i=1}^{n} \mu_i \phi \left(\sum_{i=1}^{n} \rho_i u(x_i) \right)$$

ρ_i is defined as the probability that outcome x_i occurs, whereas μ_i is the decision-maker's subjective prior belief about which of all possible ρ_i's is the right one. The function $\phi(\cdot)$ captures the decision-maker's aversion to ambiguity in the data. As with the von Neumann-Morgenstern utility, if $\phi(\cdot)$ is concave decision-makers are ambiguity averse, if it is convex they are ambiguity avid or ambiguity loving, and if it is linear they are ambiguity-neutral.

In all cases the problem to be addressed is the way that decision-makers deal with the part of the information set that they perceive to be statistically incomplete. A common feature of many decision models is that the decision-maker has a special set of procedural rules to deal with that are part of the information set. The bounded rationality approach due to Simon applies procedural rules to decisions where the value of outcomes is such that it is not worth the decision-maker's effort to acquire the full information set (Simon 1957). But the weighting attached to the probability of rare but important events also involves a procedural rule. Similarly, prospect theory supposes that people first identify prospects using some procedure, and only then apply a set of weights that treat losses and gains asymmetrically (Kahneman and Tversky 1979). The rules that have most relevance to the problem of biodiversity change are those that govern the way we learn about uncertain outcomes.

It is the statistical incompleteness of information that differentiates the problems of decision-making under risk and decision-making under uncertainty. Repetition of the actions being considered will build up a historical record of the outcomes of those actions over time, so changing the boundary between known and unknown outcomes. As a result, the decision-making process itself evolves in response to the changing information available to the decision-maker, and to the decision-maker's changing perceptions of that information. Experimental research has consistently shown that people's risk choices evolve with learning. Where the underlying probability distribution of outcomes is known, but decision-makers are unfamiliar with that probability distribution, they initially decide in ways that are inconsistent with the expected utility hypothesis, but as they gain experience they tend to conform to the standard model (Plott 1996). In particular, Plott noted that inexperienced people often appear at first to make excessively conservative choices, but that when the same choices are repeated in market-like settings they tend to converge on the predictions of expected utility theory. In other words decision-makers engage in a learning process.

For this to happen, though, the experiment needs to be repeated often enough that the decision-maker is confident of the probabilities attaching to different outcomes. The characteristics of biodiversity change that get in the way of this are irreversibility and the evolutionary nature of biodiversity change. People may learn from repeated stock market transactions, for example, or from routine consumer choices, but there is no opportunity to repeat experiments in the extinction of a particular species. The important point here is that decisions made under fundamental uncertainty tend to contain both a procedural element (to deal with initial or residual uncertainty) and a deliberative element based on expected utility (to deal with risk). The balance between the two elements can change over time. The weights attaching to different outcomes are a function of the state of knowledge. They are not independent of time.

People form expectations about the utility to be gained from different outcomes conditional on the state of knowledge available to them. Their expectations would be expected to change over time as the state of knowledge changes through some sort of Bayesian learning process.[4] New observations on the state of the system will induce decision-makers to change their perception of quality of the data. If new observations on the system are not surprising, they will lead decision-makers to have

---

[4] Bayesian learning is a method of updating prior probability estimates by incorporating new information. The result, a posterior probability, depends both on the decision-maker's prior probability, and a likelihood function. That is, if the prior probability of an outcome is $P(H)$, and the likelihood of observing a new outcome, E, is, $P(E|H)$ then the posterior probability is $P(H|E) = [P(E|H)\,P(H)]/\,P(E)$.

more confidence in their understanding of the system. If new observations on the state of the system are surprising, they will have the opposite effect. Decision-makers will become less confident of their understanding of the system. The acquisition of new knowledge can work in both directions.

A feature of the uncertainty created by biodiversity change is that it may be irreducible if the action whose consequences are uncertain is irreversible. If a species that goes extinct is lost forever, learning about the opportunity cost of extinction after the fact cannot change the decisions that led to extinction. From an economic perspective, an irreversible action is one that is infinitely costly to reverse (Arrow and Fisher 1974). Actions that are not strictly irreversible by this definition, but are costly to reverse, have a similar effect on the decision-making. A somewhat looser definition holds that an action is irreversible if it significantly reduces the variety of choices that would be possible in the long term (Henry 1974). In practice, most economic studies of irreversibility have been concerned with actions that are difficult to reverse over relatively short periods. For example, Arrow and Fisher argued that although the logging of an old growth redwood forest was technically reversible, given the length of time required for regeneration it was effectively irreversible (Arrow and Fisher 1974). Dam construction in wilderness areas has been treated in much the same way (Fisher, Krutilla and Cicchetti 1972).

The economic problem of irreversibility stems from its effect on decisions made under uncertainty. The main conclusion from the theory of decision-making under uncertainty is that people will be more cautious about taking decisions whose consequences are irreversible if it may be desirable to reverse the effects of that action in the future (Perrings and Brock 2009). To fix ideas, suppose that the action under consideration was the conversion of habitat to industrial uses, and that additional information on the consequences of this for endemic species could be had from waiting. Because the information acquired by waiting has value (a quasi-option value in the sense of Hanemann 1989), the net benefits from conversion would be reduced. More generally, if it is possible to get better information about future benefits or costs of irreversible investment, this will reduce investment relative to the case where there is no possibility of getting better information (Ulph and Ulph 1997). The value of the options lost by undertaking an irreversible investment is equivalent to the expected value of the information that could have been acquired had the action not been undertaken (Conrad 1980; Pindyck 1991, 2000; Dixit 1992). But this, too, is an area in which procedural rules have been applied to the uncertainty associated with irreversibility. The rules often have the same effect – to secure a waiting period that will allow the acquisition of valuable information – but they do not assume that it is possible to form a prior expectation about the value of yet-to-be-acquired information.

10.4 The precautionary principle and decision-making under uncertainty

The procedural rules I wish to consider in more detail are those associated with the precautionary principle. As indicated in the introduction to the chapter, the central element in the precautionary principle is a desire to err on the side of avoiding potentially damaging actions even if there is fundamental uncertainty about the extent of the damage or the probability of its occurrence (Harremoës *et al.* 2001). It is a principle that is employed when two conditions are met. The first is that the currently available information is statistically incomplete. There is fundamental uncertainty. The second is that the possible outcomes of a decision include some that are extremely damaging. The procedural rules associated with any precautionary policy accordingly have these elements: a reference point, a test for the admissibility of information that modifies or substitutes for the probabilities attaching to different outcomes, and a mechanism for learning, or for updating the information on which decisions are taken (since expectations about the payoff to different outcomes are conditional on the state of knowledge, and are therefore revised as the state of knowledge changes).

The reference point defines the risks to be avoided by precautionary action. It may reflect an outcome that is, for whatever reason, regarded as dreadful (McDaniels *et al.* 1992). It may reflect the loss of some currently respected right, or the decision-maker's current asset position (the status quo) (Kahneman and Tversky 1979). It may reflect an irreversible change that affects the wellbeing of all people in the future. There is a close link between the reference points of precautionary policies and the safe minimum standards approach proposed by Ciriacy-Wantrup and Bishop (Ciriacy-Wantrup 1952; Bishop 1978) or the planetary boundaries identified by Rockstrom *et al.* (2009). The safe minimum standards approach, for example, involves setting quantitative and qualitative minimum (or maximum) limits on activities that are upheld unless the social opportunity costs of doing so are unacceptably high. The approach has been described as a means of minimizing maximum possible losses to society in the face of uncertainty and irreversibility.

The irreversibility of potentially harmful actions is, in practice, an important trigger of precautionary action. When it was adopted at the 1992 Rio conference, for example, the principle was described in the following terms: "where there are threats of serious or irreversible damage, lack of full scientific certainty shall not be used as a reason for postponing cost-effective measures to prevent environmental degradation" (United Nations Conference on Environment and Development 1992). Subsequent attempts to model decision processes that embed the precautionary principle have concluded that the irreversibility of the future consequences of current actions is the only thing that ensures the efficiency of precautionary responses. While other characteristics of the decision-problem may lead to conservatism in the face of potentially severe harm in particular circumstances, irreversibility always induces this response (Gollier, Jullien and Treich 2000; Gollier and Treich 2003).

Conservatism in the face of potentially severe harm is most clearly implied by maximin: a decision criterion that maximizes welfare under the worst-case outcome. By design, maximin strategies protect against catastrophic risk, but this protection comes at a cost. If the actual outcome of a decision turns out to be less dire than the worst possible outcome, resources will have been wasted. In practice, when maximin is applied, it is typically the first step in a strategy that evolves over time, moving toward an approach that looks more like expected utility maximization as decision-makers gain confidence in forecasts. For example, the IHR and the SPS Agreement both authorize trade interdictions as a first response to new information on infectious human, animal, or plant diseases. However, they also require such interdictions to be removed within a relatively short time unless there is statistically robust evidence of the risk posed by the commodities in question (World Trade Organization 1995; IHR 2005). In the same way, drug recalls by the US Food and Drug Administration (a maximin strategy) are followed by hazard assessments to re-estimate the risks associated with the drug (Food and Drug Administration 2010).

Nevertheless, because the potential costs of maximin strategies are so large, many agencies that implement precautionary policies require the cost of precautionary actions to be proportional to the value of the protection they provide. The expected utility approach balances the expected costs and benefits of an action. If it is not possible to calculate the expected net benefits of an action, however, an alternative procedure is needed to assure the proportionality of the costs of precaution. A decision criterion that directly addresses the proportionality of the costs of precaution is minimax regret (Iverson 2008, 2012; Iverson and Perrings 2012). This criterion minimizes the error or regret involved in precautionary actions. In particular, it minimizes the difference between the outcome after the fact, and the outcome that would have occurred if the decision-maker had known the true (but originally uncertain) model or state in advance.

To see the sense in which minimax regret implements a proportional response, note that regret can be decomposed into additive components that correspond to the two types of mistake that decision-makers make when taking precautionary action: false negatives and false positives. False negatives occur when concerns about the potential damage of an action are initially ignored but turn out to be valid. False positives, on the other hand, occur when concerns about the potential damage of an action are heeded, but turn out to have been unnecessary. Minimax regret guards against the two types of mistakes equally. While proportionality of costs is an important ingredient of a precautionary response, most statements of the precautionary principle also suggest a preference for erring on the side of caution in avoiding false negative mistakes. To balance these competing commitments, Iverson and Perrings (2012) present a procedure for choosing a precautionary policy that builds on a decision framework developed in Iverson (2012). The approach attaches a weight to the false negative mistake. When the weight equals one, the criterion reduces to minimax regret. In this case, it implements a strictly proportional response. If the weight is greater than one, the approach defines a continuum of policies between minimax regret and maximin. The maximin policy corresponds to the case in which the weight on the false negative mistake is very large. Intermediate weights give greater emphasis to the false negative mistake while still preserving proportionality.

The aim of proportional precaution, as a strategy, is to reduce exposure to the incidence of both false negatives and false positives. Iverson and Perrings's measure of false negatives is the harm caused by neglecting (weak) evidence of the damage that could be done by an action. The measure of false positives is the resources that turn out to have been wasted on unnecessary protective measures. Both errors relate to a policy chosen *ex ante* and a scientific model that turns out to be true *ex post*. There is a trade-off between the two types of error stemming from the fact that the more resources the decision-maker commits to reducing the incidence of false negatives, the greater is the likelihood of false positives. A strictly proportional policy would weight both objectives equally. That is, it would protect against false negatives and false positives symmetrically. On the other hand a strictly precautionary policy would guard exclusively against false negatives. A strictly proportional approach may be secured by applying minimax regret strategy, while a strictly precautionary approach may be secured by applying a maximin strategy.

More formally, it is assumed that there is a set of M distinct models describing the future consequences associated with an action or strategy. A distinct model within the set M is indicated by m. Decision-makers choose a strategy, a, without knowing which model is true. The optimal strategy for a given model m is denoted a^{*m}. Social utility is defined by the function $U(a, m)$, which depends both on the decision-maker's strategy and on the actual outcomes of the strategy (i.e. the model that turns out to be true). Regret – the utility loss caused by error – similarly depends on a and m. It is equal to the difference between the best the decision-makers could have done had they known the true model in advance and how well they actually do. So it depends on a strategy chosen *ex ante* and the model m that turns out to be true *ex post*:

$$R(a, m) = U(a^{*m}, m) - U(a, m)$$

Regret decomposes into components that align with the false-negative and false-positive mistakes. In particular,

$$R(a, m) = R_1(a, m) + R_2(a, m)$$

where $R_1(a, m) > 0$ means that the actual outcome is worse than the outcome that would have been optimal with hindsight – the false-negative mistake – and $R_2(a, m) > 0$ means that resources were wasted on unnecessary protective measures – the false-positive mistake. Applying the minimax regret criterion leads the decision-maker to select a in the following problem:

$$\min_{a} \max_{m\in M} R(a,m)$$

Because regret is an equally weighted sum of the two components, $R = R_1 + R_2$, the criterion guards equally against false negatives and false positives, and so implies a strictly proportional response. Applying the maximin criterion, on the other hand, leads the decision-maker to solve:

$$\max_{a} \min_{m\in M} U(a,m)$$

This maximizes utility assuming that the model predicting the worst outcome is correct. In this approach, the false-negative mistake is always avoided, i.e. $R_1 \geq 0$ for all $m \in M$, while the false-positive mistake will always be made, i.e. $R_2 > 0$ for all $m \in M$. The only exception to this is the borderline case where the worst-case model turns out to be true. In this case $R_2 = 0$. Because maximin guards exclusively against the false-negative mistake, it can be viewed as implementing a strictly precautionary response.

Minimax regret and maximin are therefore the extreme options among candidates for precautionary strategies. It is possible to construct a continuum of alternatives that guard against false negatives while still preserving proportionality. To implement this idea Iverson (2012) employs a decision criterion that includes a parameter to control the relative weight on the contrasting objectives of reducing exposure to each type of mistake. The crierion is an asymmetric version of minimax regret. It solves

$$\min_{a} \max_{m\in M} R^A(a,m)$$

in which $R^A(a,m) = \kappa_E R_1(a,m) + R_2(a,m)$ if $R_1 > 0$ and $R^A(a,m) = R_1(a,m) + R_2(a,m)$ if $R_1 > 0$. That is, the parameter κ_E weights $R_1 < 0$. This strategy spans the minimax regret and maximin strategies, and so reduces each to a special case, while also identifying a continuum of intermediate alternatives. If decision-maker sets $\kappa_E = 1$ the strategy is minimax regret, and for κ_E sufficiently large the strategy coincides with the maximin strategy.

10.5 Learning

This representation of the problem is essentially static. In most cases, however, precautionary responses are dynamic, and this is because they embed learning over time. The most common examples of precaution in the protection of public health – product recalls – can be interpreted as decisions in which a novel outcome (e.g. product failure or health response) triggers a reaction that is initially highly precautionary, but is relaxed as decision-makers learn about the true likelihood of the outcome. Other examples of temporary maximin responses authorized by the IHR are the closure of Toronto in response to SARS and the movement restrictions in response to swine flu, in both cases pending learning about the characteristics of the disease.

The arguments for precautionary approaches are strongest when strategies are seen as temporary measures that allow learning to occur without risking the worst possible outcomes. Without learning, maximin strategies are hard to justify since they ensure that resources will turn out to be wasted unless the worst case turns out to be true. However, where there is scope for learning and there is risk of severe and irreversible harm, maximin can provide a useful time-limited response. Learning is the third and most important element of any precautionary strategy. In fact the defining characteristic of a precautionary approach is that it enables learning without risking the most severe (but uncertain) consequences of an action. Since precautionary action is triggered by the potentially severe costs of novel policies, activities, or events, it should allow the decision-maker to establish whether or not an action does in fact involve such costs. That is, for example, the role of the research triggered by drug recalls, or proposals to introduce biocontrol agents.

To demonstrate the effect of learning when envisioning a precautionary response, consider the following application in Iverson and Perrings (2012). In this paper we use the methodology to motivate selection of a precautionary response to global climate change. In the simplest version, we identify scientific disagreement with the IPCC plausible range (IPCC 2007) for climate sensitivity, the equilibrium global-mean temperature change that would result from a doubled concentration of carbon dioxide relative to its preindustrial level. The IPCC plausible range spans 2.0 to 4.5 degrees Celsius. The analysis uses Nordhaus's 2007 DICE model to estimate exposure to false-positive and false-negative mistakes under a range of policy options. Figure 10.3 shows the implied trade-offs under maximin, minimax regret, and two intermediate (asymmetric-minimax-regret) alternatives. The magnitudes reflect a scenario of no learning. In particular, the full future trajectory of climate policies is chosen in the initial period and assumed to remain in place forever.

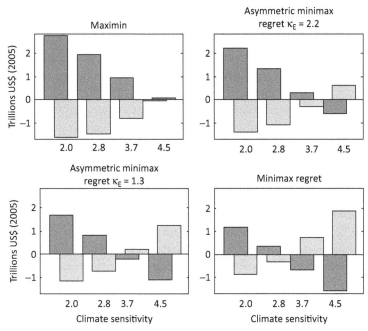

Figure 10.3 False negative and false positive errors under maximin, minimax regret, and asymmetric-minimax-regret strategies *with no learning*. Errors on the vertical axes are trillions of 2005 US dollars. Light grey bars denote false negatives (environmental damage); dark grey bars denote false positives (wasted resources). The term κ_E is the weight given to the false-negative mistake (that the actual outcome is worse than the outcome that would have been optimal with hindsight). Each panel displays the incidence of the two mistakes across a representative sample of models from the plausible range.
Source: Iverson and Perrings (2012).

To interpret the information in these figures, note that if the value of the environmental error, false negative (white bars), is greater than zero, the chosen action provides less protection against environmental damage than would have been optimal in hindsight. If it is less than zero, the chosen action overcompensates. It provides more protection against environmental damage than would have been optimal in hindsight. Symmetrically, if the value of the wasted resources error, false positive (black bars), is greater than zero, the chosen action wastes resources by overprotecting against environmental damage. If less than zero, the chosen action provides less protection than would have been optimal in hindsight. A comparison between the magnitudes of the two types of error shows the relative proportionality of each strategy for different levels of climate sensitivity. A maximin strategy clearly dominates if the worst-case climate sensitivity eventuates, and a minimax regret strategy dominates for the lowest plausible climate sensitivity. Asymmetric minimax regret strategies dominate for intermediate climate sensitivities. The first panel in both figures shows the two errors when a maximin strategy is pursued. Since the white bars are never positive this strategy always avoids the environmental error (false negative). However, since the black bars are never negative, it also always makes the wasted resources error (false positive) – unless the worst case eventuates. Figure 10.4 shows the same trade-offs, but under a scenario of learning, where learning means that the true model will be understood perfectly at a future date, and where the actions chosen will be optimal from that date.

The magnitude of each mistake in Figure 10.3 reflects the extreme scenario in which policy for all time is made on the basis of information available in the initial period. More plausibly, policy would be expected to adjust over time as new information becomes available. Figure 10.4 assumes instead that the true climate sensitivity becomes known in 2075. Since policy can adjust in response, the magnitude of the implied mistakes is necessarily smaller. The reduction in the cost of error is about 50 percent in the reported exercise relative to the case without learning.

10.6 Decision-making under uncertainty and biodiversity change

Consider what this means for the way we should collectively approach the management of biodiversity change. If there is statistically complete information about the potential yield of species in terms of the services they support, and the sensitivity of those services to variation in environmental conditions, then it is possible to identify both the mean yield of different combinations of species, and the associated risks. Moreover, if society's risk preferences are known, it is possible to identify the optimal portfolio of species. Put another way, in the absence of fundamental uncertainty, if our social tolerance for risk is known we can choose the mix of species that best serves our collective interests. This is effectively what people have sought to do since Neolithic times. They have intervened to increase the abundance of species whose traits make them desirable, and to decrease

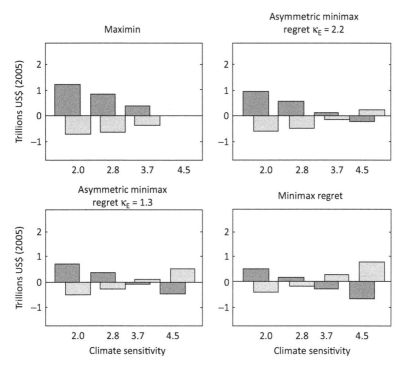

Figure 10.4 False negative and false positive errors under maximin, minimax regret, and asymmetric-minimax-regret strategies *with learning*. Errors on the vertical axes are trillions of 2005 US dollars. Light grey bars denote false negatives (environmental damage); dark grey bars denote false positives (wasted resources). The term κ_E is the weight given to the false-negative mistake (that the actual outcome is worse than the outcome that would have been optimal with hindsight). Each panel displays the incidence of the two mistakes across a representative sample of models from the plausible range.
Source: Iverson and Perrings (2012).

the abundance of species whose traits make them undesirable. The establishment of access rights, the development of agriculture and aquaculture, the introduction of public health programs, and so on are all designed to build a portfolio of species that satisfies human wants. Of course, many things that have got in the way, such as the difficulty of establishing access rights in areas beyond national jurisdiction. Nevertheless, the changes recorded by the MA reveal a broad consensus about the mix of traits reflected in species portfolios in different regions of the world.

If the information about yields and the variance in yields is not statistically complete, in the sense that either the set of outcomes associated with a given portfolio or the probabilities attaching to those outcomes is unknown, then the portfolio choice problem is more complicated. There are two reasons why selection for species with immediately desirable traits has increased uncertainty. One is that the action transforms the evolutionary potential of the system, inducing path-dependent changes of state that are hard to predict. Another is that it increases the rate at which species go extinct, and the irreversible consequences of species loss cannot be foreseen. For both reasons, it is hard to identify the efficient species frontier of Figures 10.1 and 10.2, or to identify the optimal portfolio of species.

Different societies have developed different procedural rules for dealing with statistically incomplete information about the consequences of biodiversity change, but all have opted for instruments that are more or less precautionary. That is, all have implemented conservation strategies that limit development options to those that are (at least in principle) consistent with the survival of endemic species. This has generally meant the establishment of protected areas. Indeed, protected areas covering landscapes of special significance, wildlife reserves, or sites of special scientific interest remain the primary mechanism for conserving biological resources, and use of the mechanism is growing. Since 1992 when the Caracas Action Plan of the World Parks Congress set a goal of protecting at least 10 percent of the world's major biomes, the proportion of the area protected has increased by around 44 percent (Figure 10.5).

There remain very substantial differences in the effectiveness of protected areas and in the degree to which the overall conservation strategy they support is precautionary. Of all conservation legislation, the USA's Endangered Species Act comes closest to being a pure minimax strategy. It is designed to protect (in a one-sided way) against false negative mistakes, which here imply inadequate response to a demonstrated risk of immanent species extinction. This is consistent with the safe minimum standards approach developed by Ciriacy-Wantrup (Ciriacy-Wantrup 1952), but makes the Act vulnerable to all the criticisms leveled at minimax strategies (Bishop 1978; Gollier and Treich 2003). In particular, as shown above, a maximin approach neglects the contrasting error of wasting resources – spending more on protection of a particular species than would turn out to have been justified in hindsight. This could imply excess spending on species

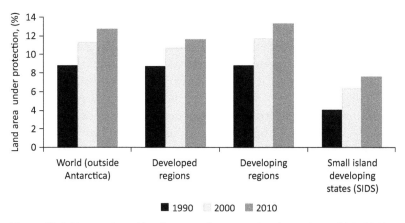

Figure 10.5 Proportion of land area under protection by region, 1990–2010. *Source:* UNEP-WCMC and the IUCN World Commission on Protected Areas (2012).

protection overall, though more likely in a situation where the overall expenditure on endangered species protection is capped, it would imply an inefficient commitment of scarce conservation resources among a portfolio of available conservation projects.

Other conservation legislation tends to be more sensitive to the opportunity cost of protected areas, and in many cases is designed more to support tourism development than to slow the rate of habitat conversion. Nevertheless, the establishment of protected areas, as with the earlier establishment of botanical gardens and other *ex situ* collections, creates at least some space to learn about the properties both of individual species and of functional groups of species.

By contrast, the treatment given to the more than 90 percent of the world's surface not under any form of protection is far from precautionary. It is implicitly assumed that the information available on the consequences of biodiversity change in this area is sufficiently complete, statistically, that it is possible to identify an efficient species frontier. Furthermore, it is implicitly assumed that the distribution of outcomes is sufficiently normal that it is possible to use expected utility to select the optimal portfolio of species. Both assumptions are problematic. In reality, novel threats occur more in exploited systems than in protected areas. All major emerging zoonoses of the last fifty years, for example, have their origins either in agricultural systems or in wildlands that are in the process of conversion to some economic use – agriculture, forestry or the exploitation of forest products (Jones *et al.* 2008). The existence of such emergent phenomena is also incompatible with the assumption that the outcomes of biodiversity change can be characterized by a normal or other thin-tailed distribution. As has been shown in the case of financial assets, treating the distribution of returns as normal when it is fat-tailed severely underestimates the risk involved.[5] The "yields" associated with different portfolios of species outside of protected areas depend on a range of ecosystem services that respond to changes in the relative abundance of species in different ways. They also reflect the uncertainty that springs from novelty, and the irreversibility that may follow extirpation of species. One would expect to see the use of procedural rules for the treatment of incomplete information in these areas, just as one would in protected areas.

Aside from the data needed to trigger a precautionary response, there needs to be a legal or institutional framework that allows precautionary action to be taken. The best examples of precaution are typically drawn from national health and safety legislation. There are fewer examples at the international level where, even if the scientific community is persuaded that hypothesized global change outcomes are realistic, there is frequently no responsible authority to take precautionary action pending the research needed to confirm them. Exceptions include the actions allowable under the IHR and the SPS Measures Agreement to protect human, animal, and plant health, but there is as yet nothing equivalent for climate, biodiversity, or sea areas beyond national jurisdiction.

We will return to the problem of collective action at the global scale in Chapter 13. What is important here is that the existence of uncertainty and irreversibility means that standard decision-procedures based on the expected utility hypothesis will not be sufficient to protect the public good. Some procedural rule to handle decision-making on the basis of statistically incomplete information will be required. Although rules of this kind are well developed for particular

---

[5] Fat-tailed distributions are much more likely to include extreme values – catastrophic outcomes – and so much higher variances than are found in the normal distribution. They typically exhibit large skewness or kurtosis. In extreme cases (such as the Cauchy distribution) the variance does not, technically, exist.

aspects of the biodiversity change issue, especially for the threats posed to human, animal, and plant health by emergent diseases, they have not been developed for many other pressing changes in biodiversity. While the traditional focus on conservation through protected areas is important, and while it does provide some security against the worst-case effects of species extinctions, it is not an adequate response to the uncertainty generated by irreversible changes in the richness and abundance of species.

References

Arrow, K. J. and Fisher, A. C. (1974) Environmental preservation, uncertainty and irreversibility. *Quarterly Journal of Economics*, 88, 312–319.

Ashford, N. A. (2007) The legacy of the precautionary principle in US law: the rise of cost-benefit analysis and risk assessment as undermining factors in health, safety and environmental protection. *Implementing the Precautionary Principle: Approaches from the Nordic Countries, the EU and the USA* (ed. N. D. Sadeleer), pp. 352–378. Earthscan, London.

Bishop, R. C. (1978) Endangered species and uncertainty: the economics of a safe minimum standard. *American Journal of Agricultural Economics*, 60, 10–18.

Chichilnisky, G. and Heal, G. M. (1998) Economic returns from the biosphere. *Nature*, 391, 629–630.

Ciriacy-Wantrup, S. V. (1952) *Resources Conservation*. University of California Press, Berkeley, CA.

Conrad, J. M. (1980) Quasi-option value and the expected value of information. *Quarterly Journal of Economics*, 94, 813–820.

Cooney, R. and Dickson, B. (eds.) (2005) *Biodiversity and the Precautionary Principle: Risk and Uncertainty in Conservation and Sustainable Use*. Earthscan, London.

Dixit, A. K. (1992) Invesment and hysteresis. *Journal of Economic Perspectives*, 6, 107–132.

Fishburn, P. (1988) *Non-Linear Preference and Utility Theory*. Wheatsheaf, Brighton.

Fisher, A. C., Krutilla, J. V. and Cicchetti, C. J. (1972) The economics of environmental preservation: a theoretical and empirical analysis. *American Economic Review*, 62, 605–619.

Food and Drug Administration (2010) *Regulatory Procedures Manual*. US Food and Drug Administration, Silver Spring, MD.

Gollier, C. and Treich, N. (2003) Decision-making under scientific uncertainty: the economics of the precautionary principle. *Journal of Risk and Uncertainty*, 27, 77–103.

Gollier, C., Jullien, B. and Treich, N. (2000) Scientific progress and irreversibility: an economic interpretation of the "precautionary principle." *Journal of Public Economics*, 75, 229–253.

Hanemann, W. M. (1989) Information and the concept of option value. *Journal of Environmental Economics and Management*, 16, 23–37.

Harremoës, P., Gee, D., MacGarvin, M., Stirling, A., Keys, J., Wynne, B. and Guedes, V. S. (2001) Late lessons from early warnings: the precautionary principle. *Environment Issue Report* No. 22. European Environment Agency, Copenhagen.

Henry, C. (1974) Investment decisions under uncertainty: the irreversibility effect. *American Economic Review*, 64, 1006–1012.

IHR (2005) *International Health Regulations*. World Health Organization, Geneva.

IPCC (2007) *Climate Change 2007: Synthesis Report*. Intergovernmental Panel on Climate Change, Geneva.

Iverson, T. (2008) *Cooperation amid Controversy: Decision Support for Climate Change Policy*. University of Wisconsin at Madison, Department of Economics.

  (2012) Communicating trade-offs amid controversial science: decision support for climate policy. *Ecological Economics*, 77, 74–90.

Iverson, T. and Perrings, C. (2012) Precaution and proportionality in the management of global environmental change. *Global Environmental Change*, 22, 161–177.

Jones, K. E., Patel, N., Levy, M., Storeygard, A., Balk, D., Gittleman, J. L. and Daszak, P. (2008) Global trends in emerging infectious diseases. *Nature*, 451, 990–993.

Kahneman, D. and Tversky, A. (1979) Prospect theory: an analysis of decision making under risk. *Econometrica*, 47, 263–291.

Katzman, M. T. (1988) Pollution liability insurance and catastrophic environmental risk. *Journal of Risk and Insurance*, 55, 75–100.

Katzner, D. W. (1998) *Time, Ignorance and Uncertainty in Economic Models*. University of Michigan Press, Ann Arbor, MI.

Klibanoff, P., Marinacci, M. and Mukerji, S. (2005) A smooth model of decision making under ambiguity. *Econometrica*, 73, 1849–1892.

  (2009) Recursive smooth ambiguity preferences. *Journal of Economic Theory*, 144, 930–976.

Loomis, J. and du Vair, P. (1993) Evaluating the effect of alternative risk communication devices. *Land Economics*, 69, 287–298.

McDaniels, T., Kamlet, M. and Fischer, G. (1992) Risk perception and the value of safety. *Risk Analysis*, 12, 495–503.

Perrings, C. and Brock, W. (2009) Irreversibility in economics. *Annual Review of Resource Economics*, 1, 219–238.

Pigeon, N., Hood, C., Jones, D., Turner, B. and Gibson, R. (1992) Risk perception. *Risk: Analysis, Perceptions and Management*. Report of a Royal Society Study Group. Royal Society, London.

Pindyck, R. S. (1991) Irreversibility, uncertainty and investment. *Journal of Economic Literature*, 29, 1110–1148.

  (2000) Irreversibilities and the timing of environmental policy. *Resource and Energy Economics*, 22, 223–259.

Plott, C. (1996) Rational individual behaviour in markets and social choice processes: the discovered preference hypothesis. *The Rational Foundations of Economic Behaviour* (ed. K. Arrow, E. Colombatto, M. Perleman and C. Schmidt), pp. 225–250. Macmillan, London.

Quiggin, J. (1982) A theory of anticipated utility. *Journal of Economic Behaviour and Organisation*, 3, 323–343.

Rockstrom, J., Steffen, W., Noone, K., Persson, Å., Chapin, F. S., Lambin, E. F., Lenton, T. M., Scheffer, M., Folke, C., Schellnhuber, H. J., Nykvist, B., de Wit, C. A., Hughes, T., van der Leeuw, S., Rodhe, H., Sörlin, S., Snyder, P. K., Costanza, R., Svedin, U., Falkenmark, M., Karlberg, L., Corell, R. W., Fabry, V. J., Hansen, J., Walker, B., Liverman, D., Richardson, K., Crutzen, P. and Foley, J. A. (2009) A safe operating space for humanity. *Nature*, 461, 472–475.

Sadeleer, N. (ed.) (2007) *Implementing the Precautionary Principle: Approaches from the Nordic Countries, the EU and the USA*. Earthscan, London.

Savage, L. J. (1954) *The Foundations of Statistics*. Wiley, New York.

Shackle, G. L. S. (1955) *Uncertainty in Economics*. Cambridge University Press.

Simon, H. A. (1957) *Administrative Behaviour*. Macmillan, New York.

Starmer, C. (2000) Development in non-expected utility theory: the hunt for a descriptive theory of choice under risk. *Journal of Economic Literature*, 38, 332–382.

Taylor, P. (1991) The precautionary principle and the prevention of pollution. *ECOS*, 124, 41–46.

Tversky, A. and Kahneman, D. (1992) Advances in prospect theory: cumulative representation of uncertainty. *Journal of Risk and Uncertainty*, 5, 297–323.

Ulph, A. and Ulph, D. (1997) Global warming, irreversibility and learning. *Economic Journal*, 107, 636–650.

UNEP-WCMC and the IUCN World Commission on Protected Areas (2012) *World Database on Protected Areas*, available at www.wdpa.org/ (accessed 2012).

United Nations Conference on Environment and Development (1992) *Rio Declaration on Environment and Development*. UNEP, Nairobi.

World Trade Organization (1995) *The WTO Agreement on the Application of Sanitary and Phytosanitary Measures (SPS Agreement)*. World Trade Organization, Geneva.

11 | Conservation incentives and payments for ecosystem services

11.1 Externalities and public goods revisited

The causes of the market failures behind the decline in ecosystem services reported by the MA have already been identified. Chapter 5 paid special attention to the differences in the problem of externality at the national and international scales. At the national scale it was noted that the failure of market prices to signal the scarcity of environmental resources, and the failure of markets to supply public goods, are both problems that can be resolved by government action. The fact that national governments have sovereign power makes it possible to address market failures directly by allocating property rights and by extending the legal protection of species or habitats on private lands. It also makes it possible to develop nationally funded incentive schemes such as the US biodiversity offset and banking programs considered in some detail later in this chapter (Madsen, Carroll and Moore Brands 2010). It makes it possible to establish national agencies with responsibilities for the provision of environmental public goods such as habitat for rare and endangered species, clean water, environmental health protection, and so on. The fact that national governments have sovereign authority over the land and people within national jurisdiction means that they are able to cut the Gordian knot of open or ill-defined access. At the international level, however, both externalities and the supply of environmental public goods are altogether more difficult to address. There is no supranational sovereign authority capable of assigning property rights or levying the taxes needed to fund the provision of public goods.

Recall that there are two reasons why markets fail to signal the scarcity of ecosystem services. One is that the structure of property rights authorizes landholders to ignore the effects they have on others. The example used to illustrate this in Chapter 5 was that people who have the right to cultivate land in the upper reaches of a watershed have no matching obligation to minimize the harm they do to people lower down the watershed through the effect of land clearance on flood risks or the siltation of rivers. Similarly, people whose actions in some place threaten the survival of species endemic to that place have no responsibility for the effect they have on the wellbeing of people all over the world. The second reason why markets fail to signal the scarcity of ecosystem services is that many such services are public goods: they are non-exclusive and/or non-rival in consumption. Because of this everyone has an incentive to free-ride on the efforts of others. If one landholder retains enough land in natural habitat to assure survival of local populations of pollinators, others have no incentive to do likewise. If one country establishes a protected area that assures the survival of a particular set of species, other countries that share in the natural range of those species have no incentive to do the same. Symmetrically, if one country fails to control the spread of an infectious disease, other countries face the fact that any efforts they make are likely to be ineffective.

While Chapter 5 considered what lies behind biodiversity externalities and the public good nature of many ecosystem services, this chapter considers at least some of the potential solutions to both problems. It focuses on the incentives of open or unregulated access, and of missing markets at the national scale. These are the effects of access rights on the incentives resource users have to take account of the consequences of their actions. I review the options for addressing these incentive effects, and consider how well the options transfer from the national to the international scale. I also consider what additional factors need to be addressed at that scale. The options considered include some, such as the establishment of exclusive access rights in fisheries, which have a relatively long history. But they also include others, such as payments for ecosystem services (PES), which are of more recent vintage.

Of course there are many well-functioning markets for the goods and services deriving from the exploitation of species. The point has been made repeatedly that foods, fuels, and fibers are well served by increasingly integrated markets that mediate not only current supply and demand for these products but also expected future supply and demand. There are also well-developed markets in many parts of the world for the control of pests and pathogens that threaten wellbeing either directly, through human disease, or indirectly through their effects on desirable species. An associated set of markets has developed in the supply of medicinal products. Bioprospecting rights for genetic material from plant or animal species that may lead to the development of pharmaceuticals are bought and sold in an emerging set of markets. The products of such services – pharmacologically active compounds – may yield drugs based either on the natural compound itself (such as the cancer treatments vincristine and vinblastine obtained from the rosy periwinkle, *Vinca rosea*), or on a synthetic compound developed from the natural compound.

The amenity value of biodiversity has also stimulated the development of markets for tourism and recreation. The point was made in Chapter 2 that ecotourism is one of the fastest growing segments of the tourism industry which itself accounts for nearly 10 percent of global GDP. The growth of ecotourism is especially important to the world's poorest countries, accounting for more than 20 percent of export receipts in Ethiopia, Mexico, Nepal, Mali, Kenya, Egypt, El Salvador, Thailand, and Costa Rica. Since these are also among the most species-rich countries this is significant both for the opportunities it offers, but also for the threats it poses (Roe *et al.* 2004). Tourist arrivals in a majority of the biodiversity hotspots grew at more than twice the global average for tourism in the ten years before the global recession (Hall 2006), and continued to grow during the recession in the region where tourism is most directly biodiversity based, Sub-Saharan Africa (World Tourism Organization 2011).

The fact that markets exist for these goods and services does not, however, imply that the prices they generate reflect all the consequences of every transaction. There are externalities in agricultural, health, and tourism markets just as in other markets, and these affect the incentives faced by decision-makers in those sectors. Markets for the products of agriculture, aquaculture, and forestry, for example, provide clear guidance to producers about consumer demand and the state of supply. At the same time, they provide producers with almost no guidance on the benefits of watershed protection (Heal 2000b), habitat provision (Bulte and Horan 2003; Barbier, Burgess and Grainger 2010), pest and disease regulation (Ostfeld, Keesing and Eviner 2008), micro- and macro-climatic regulation (Canadell and Raupach 2008), and hazard protection (Barbier 2008). Farmers have a strong incentive to increase production wherever they can capture the gains from doing so, but little incentive to reduce emissions to air or water wherever they are exempt from carrying the resulting costs (Hanley 1990). The result is that market prices for foods, fuels, and fibers seldom reflect the true social cost of their production, while market prices for many other ecosystem services simply do not exist.

11.2 Internalizing biodiversity externalities

Since external benefits and costs are uncompensated within the market, they are ignored in normal market transactions. That is, they do not inform the decisions made by any of the parties to a transaction. The internalization of externalities brings such benefits and costs into the decision process. It ensures that the parties to a transaction take account of those benefits and costs. There are various market and market-like mechanisms available to internalize externalities. These are discussed below. First, however, consider what it is that such mechanisms are designed to achieve in two cases: external benefits and external costs. Take the stylized description of external benefits described in Figure 4.2. The essential features of that case are summarized in Figure 11.1.

The figure describes conservation efforts of a local group that generate external benefits for the broader community within which the group is embedded. We can think of the local group as either a community within a nation, or one country within the international community. The level of

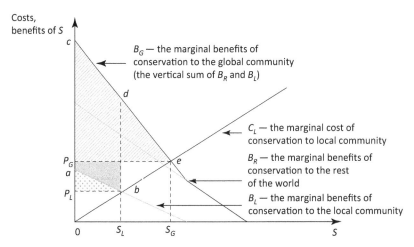

Figure 11.1 Internalization of the external benefits of local conservation effort. Local conservation without internalization of external benefits is at S_L (at which local producer surplus is given by the area $0bP_L$, local consumer surplus is at abP_L, and global consumer surplus is at $cdbP_L$). Local conservation effort with internalization of external benefits is at S_G (at which local producer surplus is $0eP_G$, and global consumer surplus is at ceP_G).

local conservation is denoted S_L. The marginal cost of conservation to that community is denoted C_L, and the marginal benefits B_L. From the equimarginal principle, the optimal level of conservation from the perspective of the local group will be S_G. At that level of provision, if the members of the community pay the marginal cost of conservation, P_L, then they would secure a consumer surplus (the difference between what they would be willing to pay for that level of conservation and what they actually have to pay) equal to the area abP_L, and the providers would secure a producer surplus (the difference between what they would be willing to accept for providing that level of conservation and what they actually receive) equal to the area $0bP_L$. Since conservation at that level also generates external benefits to the wider community, the local consumer surplus is strictly less than the global consumer surplus, equal to the area $bdcP_L$. These can be thought of as first approximations of the effects of this level of provision on human wellbeing.

If it is possible for those who are willing to pay for greater conservation efforts to do so – the mechanisms that might allow this to happen will be considered later – then the optimal level of local provision would be S_G: the intersection of the marginal benefit curve, the outer envelope of B_R and B_G, and the marginal cost curve, C_L. At this level of provision, the marginal cost of local provision would be equal to the marginal willingness of the global community to pay. Looking at our first approximations of the welfare effects of this level of conservation, local producer surplus would be $0eCP_G$, and global consumer surplus would be ecP_G. Even though there would be no local consumer surplus at the supply price associated with S_G, producer surplus would exceed the sum of both producer and consumer surplus at S_L. Since global consumer surplus at S_G would also exceed global consumer surplus at S_L, human wellbeing would be enhanced.

Now consider the case where the external effects of conservation are negative: i.e. where local conservation generates external costs for members of the local population. These could, for example, take the form of reduced access to resources within protected areas, increased wildlife damage to crops, or the increased risk of zoonotic diseases. This case is described in Figure 11.2, which summarizes the information in Figure 5.1. Once again, the level of local conservation is S_L. Line B now describes the marginal net benefit of conservation, implying that the optimal level of conservation in the absence of any external effects would be S_L, since this is the level at which the marginal benefits and

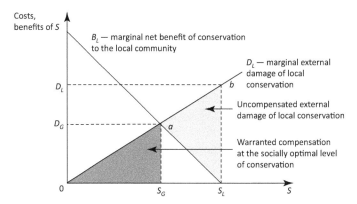

Figure 11.2 Internalization of the external costs of local conservation effort. Local conservation without internalization of external costs is at S_L (marginal external damage is D_L and uncompensated damage is abS_L). Local conservation with internalization of external costs is at S_G (marginal external damage is D_G, which could be fully compensated).

costs of conservation are equal. Line D describes the marginal external costs of local conservation activities. In the absence of any mechanism to internalize the externality, marginal external damage would be at the level D_L. Of total damages at this level, the area $0bS_L$, abS_L could not be compensated. If a mechanism to internalize the externality existed, the optimal level of conservation would be S_G, at which the marginal external damage, D_G, would be equal to marginal social benefit. The total damages at this level of conservation, $0aS_G$, could be compensated.

The most common way of managing activities that generate external costs in the past has been through what are commonly called command and control instruments. These are regulatory instruments – quantitative restrictions on the level of output in activities that generate external costs. The restrictions are generally intended to assure that external costs could, at least in principle, be fully compensated. So in Figure 11.2, a quantitative restriction could be placed on conservation effort that limits it to no more than S_G. Command and control instruments are often contrasted with economic instruments that work by changing the relative costs and benefits of alternative levels of effort, and so the incentives faced by the decision-maker. Of course command and control instruments still generate incentives. Enforcement of any quantitative restriction requires a penalty for non-compliance, and the existence of a penalty changes the cost of effort levels in excess of the regulated level by the amount of the penalty. Indeed, decision-makers are still free to adopt effort levels in excess of the regulated level as long as they are willing to pay the penalty.

The instruments generally used to address negative biodiversity externalities – external costs – comprise taxes, user-fees, access charges, environmental bonds, deposit-refund systems, and penalties for non-compliance with regulatory restrictions. The instruments generally used to address positive biodiversity externalities – external benefits – comprise subsidies, tax concessions, grants, and some forms of payments for ecosystem services. Instruments that apply both to positive and negative externalities are those that assign property rights, and then allow market transactions to determine the optimal level of effort. They include instruments that assign rights to the victims of negative externalities, and hence make those who are the source of damage responsible for that damage (e.g. the European Commission's Environmental Liability Directive). They also include instruments that do the opposite, assigning rights to those who are the source of damage (e.g. the REDD scheme).

For external costs, taxes that are set equal to the marginal external damage at the socially optimal level of effort, known as Pigovian taxes (Pigou 1920), should induce a reduction in effort to that level. In Figure 11.2, a unit tax levied at the rate D_G should lead effort to be reduced from S_L to S_G. Instruments of this kind are applied most frequently at the national level, since they exploit the powers and responsibilities of sovereign states. Indeed, governments have been strongly encouraged to build such instruments into their armory. The OECD, for example, has exhorted governments to:

make greater and more consistent use of domestic economic instruments in the application of their biodiversity policy frameworks, while attempting to reach further agreement at the international level on the use of economic-based policy instruments with respect to biodiversity conservation and management; (and to) integrate market and non-market (i.e. non-price) instruments – taking account of the respective advantages of each in lowering information and transactions costs, and in addressing the "public" values of biodiversity – into an effective and efficient mix of policies. (OECD 2004)

The effectiveness and efficiency of instruments developed to address external costs are in fact quite well understood (Stavins 2003). They have the capacity to meet environmental targets at least cost, to induce investment in environmentally beneficial technology, and to encourage an efficient commitment of resources to environmental enhancement.

The effectiveness of instruments developed to deal with external benefits is less well understood. Since subsidies have long had a bad press, most effort has gone to the development of markets for specific environmental benefits (Heal 2000a; Daily and Ellison 2002; OECD 2004). The inspiration for market creation as a solution to positive biodiversity externalities stems from Ronald Coase, who was the first to observe that externalities might be internalized by allocating rights to either the originator or the person impacted by an external effect, and that as long as transaction costs and wealth effects were low enough, bargaining between the two parties would lead to an efficient outcome (Coase 1960). The simple but powerful idea behind the proposition is that the assignment of rights to an effect would create a market in which the two parties would each have an incentive to reveal their willingness to accept compensation/willingness to pay for the effect. Moreover, the same level of the effect would be achieved irrespective of who received the rights. While the externality problems for which the Coase theorem offers a good solution are relatively rare because of the pervasiveness of transactions costs and wealth effects, the idea is still at the heart of efforts to create markets for the effects of biodiversity change.

In what follows I consider two sets of markets. The first are markets that have been created to encourage conservation effort directly. These are primarily markets for the protection of species or habitats. The second are markets that have been created to assure the supply of ecosystem services. These secure conservation of the species required to produce the service.

11.3 Markets for habitat conservation

One of the earliest market mechanisms used to promote biodiversity conservation is an analogue to the cap and trade schemes developed to manage SO_2 and other industrial emissions. Transferable development rights (TDR) are designed to minimize the environmental cost of meeting development targets, such targets being defined in terms of the area of land to be made available for development (Mills 1980). Development rights are allocated through some process, and a market in those rights is then allowed to operate. TDR schemes should, at least in principle, result in cost-effective conservation. The location specific characteristics of land, and the fact that each parcel is associated with multiple services, complicate identification of trades of equal value. But the mechanism offers a decentralized way of exploiting the specialized knowledge of resource users to establish best use. What TDRs add to long-established practices such as agro-ecological zoning (which concentrates agricultural development in areas of high productivity potential and restricts it in ecologically significant and sensitive areas) is a mechanism for eliciting people's willingness to accept compensation for forgoing development options (Chomitz 1999). Initially applied to development in urban areas (Field and Conrad 1975), TDRs have been applied to the conservation of habitat since the 1990s (Panayotou 1995; Merrifield 1996).

Two main types of biodiversity-related TDR program currently exist: single and dual zoning programs. Single zoning programs most closely match cap and trade systems for emissions control, or tradable quotas for the management of fish stocks. Once a quota of development permits for some land area has been issued, anyone with access to that land area can acquire permits. Dual zoning, on the other hand, separates the area into development (receiving) and conservation (sending) areas. It allows for more stringent controls to be placed on development in the conservation area (Chomitz 1999). In Brazil, for example, agricultural landholders not complying with the National Forest Code (Law no. 4771 approved on September 15, 1965) are required to buy forest reserves in other areas, usually close to their property (Pascual and Perrings 2007).

The driver of most biodiversity-related TDR schemes is some government-imposed restriction on development, some habitat conservation target, or some requirement that the biodiversity costs of development be minimized. The USA's Endangered Species Act, for example, aims to contain threats to listed endangered species requiring avoidance of damage where possible, minimization of damage where not, and mitigation of the impacts of land-use change on endangered species. This has led to the development of biodiversity-offset programs designed to compensate for the negative effects of development on biodiversity. Many such programs allow developers to engage third parties to meet their obligations. For example, private developers whose actions potentially threaten a listed species can satisfy their mitigation obligations by buying credits from biodiversity conservation or wetland and stream mitigation banks that maintain suitable habitat of different kinds (Madsen *et al.* 2010).

The market, in such cases, allows NGOs or private firms to supply the habitat at minimum cost. Those who provide conservation banks, for example, are able to sell credits to developers, thereby satisfying the developer's liability under the Endangered Species Act. A bank in this case is any site where habitat for endangered species is restored, enhanced or preserved, and where the aim is to provide compensatory mitigation of the biodiversity effects of development. The critical element in the viability of mitigation banks, as of TDR schemes more generally, is the substitutability of habitats.

A recent review of the state of biodiversity offset and compensation programs in North America reported fourteen active programs for wetland and species compensation (USA) or fish habitat compensation (Canada) and a number in development. It reported annual compensation payments between $1.5 and $2.5 billion, most in the form of offset credit banks (Madsen *et al.* 2010). The growth of wetland and stream mitigation and biodiversity conservation banks in the USA is shown in Figure 11.3.

Globally, the same review identified a total of thirty-nine programs, with another twenty-five in different stages of development, and an annual value of up to $2.9 billion (Madsen *et al.* 2010). So a majority of such offset programs and the bulk of the annual value of transactions occur within the USA. There are, however, a number of interesting variants on TDRs operating elsewhere. One is a system of auctioned conservation contracts (ACCs). These are designed to achieve a targeted level of protection within some landscape at least cost. In ACC schemes landholders are invited to bid to supply land for conservation, and in doing so reveal the cost of conservation to them. The conservation agency can then select the areas for conservation that meet minimum requirements in terms of their biological conservation value, but that also have the lowest opportunity cost. While conservation agencies might be expected to know more about the biological conservation value of land, landholders might be expected to know more about its development potential (the opportunity cost of conservation). ACC schemes enable both types of information to be exploited effectively, so minimizing the social cost of conservation.

An example of a system of auctioned biodiversity conservation contracts in Victoria, Australia, is known as BushTender. In this scheme

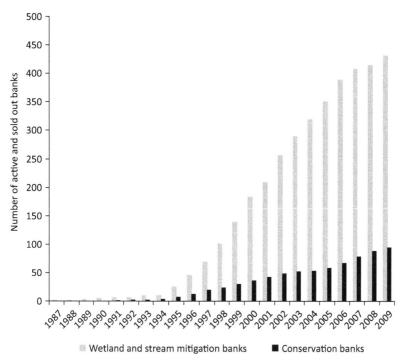

Figure 11.3 Growth of wetland and stream mitigation and conservation banks in the USA, 1987–2009. Grey columns measure the number of active and sold-out wetland and stream mitigation banks with known date of establishment (there are an additional seventy-seven active and sold-out banks without dates). Black columns measure the number of active and sold-out conservation banks. All except one conservation bank are located in California.
Source: Madsen *et al.* (2010).

farmers submit sealed bids associated with conservation action plans. The bids are evaluated in terms of the relative cost-effectiveness of these plans and their match to the state government's conservation objectives. It is estimated that BushTender has provided 75 percent more biodiversity conservation than comparable fixed-price payment schemes, and has offered the additional benefit of significantly lower enforcement costs (Stoneham *et al.* 2007). As of 2009 the scheme had secured some 17,000 hectares of habitat (Madsen *et al.* 2010).

As with any market, the effective functioning of TDR systems depends on the existence of supporting institutions, and especially property rights to the resources involved (Pascual and Perrings 2007). If markets for habitat are created without appropriate institutional and regulatory support, the costs can exceed the benefits from conservation (Barrett and Lybbert 2000; Tomich *et al.* 2001). Recall that Coase's suggested solution to the problem of externality was conditional on transactions costs being low enough to make development of a market feasible, and wealth effects being weak enough that people would be willing to participate in market transactions. It is not accidental that most markets of this kind have developed in middle- and high-income countries with well-developed institutions. The scope for development of such systems is less in low-income countries where people depend heavily on environmental resources but do not have secure rights to those resources (Dasgupta 2001).

Figure 11.1 represents the stylized facts about the relation between the global North and the global South in the conservation of threatened species. Income disparities between North and South, along with differences in preferences for conservation and the global distribution of species, create at least the preconditions for the development of markets or market-like mechanisms in biodiversity conservation. But the fact that few people in the global South are willing to pay for conservation at levels that equate marginal global costs and benefits is a source of tension. Local communities either unable to share in the producer surplus generated by conservation at globally optimal levels, or faced with financial losses from conservation such as wildlife damage to crops, frequently frustrate conservation activities. Trying to give local communities a stake in conservation has led to efforts to promote community-based conservation and integrated conservation-development projects (Wells 1992; Wells and Brandon 1992; Wells *et al.* 2004). Well-known examples of community-based conservation programs include the Communal Areas Management Program for Indigenous Resources (CAMPFIRE) in Zimbabwe. Such programs have, however, had very mixed success to date (Wells *et al.* 2004). In some communities with ecotourism potential or where ecosystems are a source of valuable services such as urban water supply, conservation and development may be consistent objectives. In many other cases, it has proved difficult to create incentives for the conservation of habitat that can be sustained.

A second set of options that potentially avoids these difficulties is direct conservation payments. The motivation for these is simple.

Changes in ecosystem services reported by the MA reflected the fact that market prices for some services had increased during the last fifty years – for foods, fuels, fibers, pharmacologically active compounds – but not for many of the regulating, supporting, and cultural services, which had declined in the same period – macro-climatic regulation, pollution buffering, water flow regulation, erosion control, and so on. We get what we pay for. If these other services are valuable, and if their supply is in the hands of local landholders, we should pay for that too.

The point has already been made that while markets tend to emerge when resources are recognized to be scarce (Demsetz 1967), markets have failed to emerge for many of the supporting, regulating, and cultural services despite their scarcity. The explanation for this lies partly in the public good nature of many ecosystem services (e.g. climatic regulation through carbon sequestration), partly in the lack of well-defined property rights to many environmental resources (e.g. sea areas beyond national jurisdiction), and partly in the cost of forming markets (e.g. the political cost of taking away historic rights of access). There is, however, a strong groundswell of opinion in favor of using payments to encourage landholders to increase the supply of environmental public goods (Chichilnisky and Heal 1998, 2000; Heal *et al.* 2005; Ferraro and Kiss 2007; Engel, Pagiola and Wunder 2008; Palmer and Filoso 2009).

The approach has been implemented for several decades in Europe and the USA (Food and Agriculture Organization 2007). Agri-environment schemes involving payments to farmers have been implemented since the 1980s. Conservation payments under a variety of agricultural land diversion programs were designed to compensate farmers for forgoing the financial benefits of profitable but environmentally damaging intensive farming practices (Ferraro and Simpson 2002). In the USA, for example, the Conservation Reserve Program was developed to counteract soil erosion in croplands. It offered annual payments of around $1.5 billion for ten- to fifteen-year contracts to farmers who established grass, shrub, and tree cover on some 12–15 million hectares of environmentally sensitive land (Wu 2000). In the United Kingdom, the Environmentally Sensitive Areas Scheme had a very similar aim, paying farmers in eligible areas for adopting less-intensive farming practices to protect wildlife values. By 2003 the scheme covered more than 570,000 hectares. Payments are set at a level to compensate farmers for the financial losses incurred. Schemes like the Environmentally Sensitive Areas Scheme (Wilson 1996) have since been established in Denmark, France, Italy, and Spain. They are also common in other developed countries (see Figure 11.4).

In like fashion, modern PES schemes aim to compensate those who provide ecosystem services for the cost of doing so. Payments are generally intended to do one of two things. One, like the UK's Environmentally Sensitive Areas Scheme, is to compensate landholders for the costs of adopting or avoiding particular land management practices (Grieg-Gran, Porras and Wunder 2005). Another is to purchase environmental services from local landholders who otherwise would not provide those services (Wunder 2007; Engel *et al.* 2008). In both cases it is widely accepted that transactions should be voluntary, should relate to a well-defined ecosystem service or a land use likely to secure that service, and should be conditional on the delivery of that service (Wunder 2007). Note, though, that those who implement PES schemes may well have multiple goals for doing so. As Chapter 6 made clear, they are frequently seen as pro-poor mechanisms. In cases where those making payments care more about poverty alleviation than the delivery of ecosystem services, the requirement that payments are conditional on delivery of the service may be relaxed. We will return to this issue later.

The declared aim of most PES schemes is to internalize the externalities of current land use, so inducing landholders to adopt land management practices or deliver services at the socially optimal level. In other words, the declared aim is to move from a position such as S_L to S_G in Figures 11.1 and 11.2. In practice, few PES schemes have turned out to be efficient. Among the main reasons for this are the lack of additionality – the actions paid for would have occurred anyway (Ferraro and Pattanayak 2006) – and leakage – the damage is simply displaced to other areas (Wunder 2007).

A large number of PES schemes are now being implemented, typically around four main ecosystem services: carbon sequestration, watershed services, landscape amenity, and habitat provision (biodiversity conservation). Many are quite localized, involve direct transactions between producers and consumers, and focus on ecotourism or the management of small watersheds (see Figure 11.5). Larger schemes tend to be government driven, working at the state and provincial level (e.g. in Australia, Brazil, China, and the USA), or at the national level (e.g. Colombia, Costa Rica, China, and Mexico) (Arriagada and

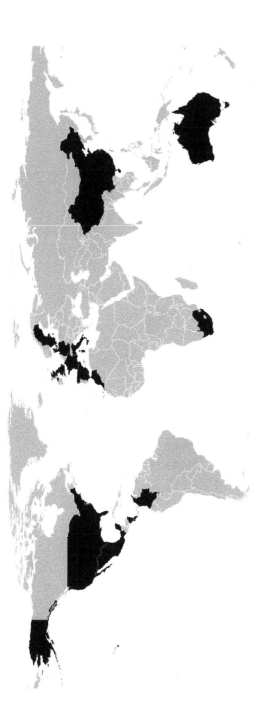

Figure 11.4 Countries implementing agro-biodiversity schemes involving payments to farmers (shaded black). Few PES programs have targeted farmers and agricultural lands in developing countries. There have also been relatively few examples of private payment mechanisms for agro-biodiversity.
Source: Arriagada and Perrings (2009).

Figure 11.5 Countries implementing PES schemes involving payments for the regulation of water supplies (shaded black). Unlike agro-biodiversity schemes, which tend to be found in developed countries, more watershed protection schemes are found in developing countries.

Source: Arriagada and Perrings (2009).

Perrings 2009). Aside from the US habitat protection schemes already referred to, examples include payments for carbon sequestration in China (Liu *et al.* 2008) and the UK (Dobbs and Pretty 2004), watershed protection in the USA (Claassen, Cattaned and Johansson 2008), Australia (Victoria Department of Sustainability and Environment 2008), South Africa (Turpie, Marais and Blignaut 2008), and Mexico (Múñoz-Piña *et al.* 2008), and biodiversity conservation in Sweden (Zabel and Holm-Müller 2008), Costa Rica, and Nicaragua (Pagiola *et al.* 2007; Pagiola 2008).

Whether such schemes are judged to be successful or not depends in part on the objectives of those establishing the schemes, and in part on their overall design. One evaluation of the efficiency of a sample of existing PES schemes found considerable variation in critical design features (see Table 11.1). Few of the examples considered had either effective monitoring programs to assure additionality, or penalties for non-compliance. A possible explanation for this is that the schemes had income redistribution or poverty alleviation goals in addition to those relating to the delivery of the listed ecosystem services.

A different dimension of the same problem is that payments intended to deliver a bundle of services may be more or less effective in delivering any one service within the bundle, depending on whether the services are complements or substitutes in production. If services are substitutes (implying that there are trade-offs between them) then the adoption of land management practices that will enhance one service will have the effect of reducing others. Only if services are perfect complements (are synergistic) can a single payment enhance the delivery of all services.

The challenge in many cases is that the relative value of services that trade-off against each other, at least to some degree, is not always clear. Consider, for instance, the relation between climate regulation through carbon sequestration, protection of genetic diversity, watershed protection, and the production of timber and non-timber forest products. The TEEB assessment used existing studies to estimate the value of the macro-climatic regulation offered by carbon sequestration relative to a range of other services offered by forest systems. As has already been noted, it found that the mean value of forest ecosystem services was dominated by regulatory functions. In fact the mean value of all provisioning services combined – timber and non-timber forest products, food, genetic information, pharmaceuticals – was less than the value of water flow regulation alone (TEEB 2009). Developing a

Table 11.1 *Factors behind the efficiency of selected PES schemes*

Case	Participants	Service	Additionality	Penalties for non-compliance	Cost of provision
Working for Water Program, South Africa (Turpie *et al.* 2008)	Small-scale contractors who perform restoration work on land under any type of ownership	Control of invasive alien plants to improve water delivery, biodiversity conservation and land productivity	Successful in restoring water supply in alien infested catchments	Self-supervised, does not include sanctions	Opportunity costs low: no land displaced and treated land becomes more productive. Labor costs low (few formal sector job opportunities)
Grain to Green Program, China	Farmers in Western China, cropland with slope > 25° and poverty	Reducing soil erosion and desertification, increasing forest cover	High for land retirement, lower for reforestation	Compliance is defined in terms of plant survival, subsidies withheld based on survival, no evidence of withholding	Future income from trees and grasses may offset forgone cropping income
Regional Integrated Silvopastoral Approaches to Ecosystem Management, Nicaragua (Pagiola, Rios and Arcenas 2008)	Lanholders in Matiguás-Río Blanco based on its location in a biological corridor	Biodiversity conservation and carbon sequestration	Program pays for additional services only	Any switch to land uses that reduce service provision reduces total payment	Payments based on the relative profitability of different practices, rate per unit increment in services fixed

Pimampiro, Ecuador (Wunder and Albán 2008)	Landholders in high-altitude zones with a minimum size of landholding	Drinking water for the municipality of Pimampiro	No evidence to assess additionality in water supply	Payment suspension, exclusion from project	PES schemes yield a higher NPV than incremental deforestation
PROFAFOR, Ecuador (Wunder and Albán 2008)	PROFAFOR, an Ecuadorian company extending the forests absorbing CO_2 emissions	Carbon emissions offset, financed by Dutch electricity companies	Additionality relative to a carbon baseline was built on vegetation and soil criteria	For individual owners a lien on their lands; for communal lands, reimbursement of payments received	Forgone revenues smaller than for Pimampiro
Scolel Té Project, Mexico (Tipper 2002)	Farmers from Tzeltal and Tojolobal communities in Chilón and Comitán	Carbon sequestration	Payments completed only when carbon is sequestered by account holder	Annual monitoring on all sites, 5% of the value of timber products ceded in the event of non-continuation	Discounted net benefits between $110 and $1,700 (excluding associated benefits)
Payments for Hydrological Environmental Services, Mexico (Múñoz-Piña et al. 2008)	Grading and regional balance of contract distribution	Hydrological services from forest ecosystems	Many payments in areas with low deforestation risk	Payments made after verifying that no land-use change, no payments yet canceled	Differentiated cash payments (higher for cloud forests)

Source: adapted from Arriagada and Perrings (2009).

payments scheme capable of inducing an efficient allocation of resources to the production of distinct ecosystem services requires information both on the marginal costs and benefits of the different services,
and on the interactions between them.

The dominant scheme for the management of climate regulation is the
REDD scheme. This is primarily designed to mitigate climate change by
reducing the carbon emissions associated with deforestation, but is
increasingly used to encourage adoption of a bundle of supposedly
complementary services: co-benefits. The primary motivation for the
scheme is the fact that forest conversion to cropland, pastureland, and
similar activities accounts for something like a fifth of all greenhouse gas
emissions. Only the energy sector accounts for more. Annual payments
under REDD are expected to be on the order of US$30 billion. The
intention is that REDD will both secure a reduction in carbon emissions
and a set of co-benefits in the form of enhanced biodiversity conservation
and the delivery of other ecosystem services. In addition, it is expected to
support pro-poor development (Arriagada and Perrings 2011).

The fact that REDD is expected to absorb some portion of existing
international development assistance and will not be conditional on the
level of carbon emission reductions indicates that its pro-poor stance
may dominate other goals, at least initially. It will, however, be implemented in three phases: the first focusing on strategy development and
core capacity building; the second providing support for national policies and compensation for proxy-based results for emission reductions;
the third being a compensation mechanism for emission reductions
from the forestry sector that will be conditional on results (Dutschke
and Angelsen 2008; Blom, Sunderland and Murdiyarso 2010).

Enthusiasm for REDD from those whose primary interest is the
conservation of wild-living species rests on the belief that incentives to
reduce the rate at which biodiversity-rich natural forests are being lost
or degraded offers benefits in terms of species conservation, but also on
the notion that biodiversity conservation supports the primary goal of
REDD (Brown, Seymour and Peskett 2008; Díaz, Hector and Wardle
2009; Long 2009). The evidence for the impacts of biodiversity on long-
term carbon storage (carbon stocks remaining in the system for ten
years or more) as opposed to sequestration is mixed, but the evidence
that biodiversity is positively correlated with biomass production and
therefore with the ecosystem services that depend on biomass is con-
clusive (Cardinale *et al.* 2012). Of all payment schemes REDD most

clearly demonstrates the need for careful design. The fact that it has multiple objectives and involves multiple services increases the likelihood that its implementation will have unanticipated consequences. Nonetheless, the same concerns affect all PES schemes. The history of environmentally motivated agricultural subsidies should give us pause. While many payments to farmers have ostensibly been motivated by an interest in reducing the environmental impact of intensive agriculture, agricultural subsidies have frequently had the opposite effect. Indeed, agricultural subsidies have everywhere been identified as among the most important drivers of environmental degradation (Myers and Kent 2001; Pearce 2003; Barde and Honkatukia 2004; Gottschalk *et al.* 2007; Schmid, Sinabell and Hofreither 2007).

11.4 Designing payments for ecosystem services

A recent review of PES schemes (Table 11.2) argued that while our collective failure to protect scarce ecosystem services provides an opportunity to build markets that reflect the new global patterns of scarcity, it also presents a challenge. Markets and market-like mechanisms are not a panacea. They need to be very carefully designed if they are to be effective, and in many cases they will simply be inappropriate (Kinzig *et al.* 2011). This makes calls on the science of both natural and social systems. The science of natural systems provides us with the needed understanding of the linkages between biodiversity, ecological functioning, and ecosystem services (Naeem *et al.* 2009). It is what allows us to "tinker intelligently" with ecosystems: to know which bits are essential to keep, and which can be altered. The science of social systems yields understanding both of what people value, and the institutions and policies needed to protect the public interest.

The great strength of markets is that they can rapidly transmit information about changes in relative scarcity. Their great weakness, at least as far as ecosystem services are concerned, is that they are not effective mechanisms for the allocation of public goods, and many ecosystem services are public goods. Absent intervention, markets will undersupply these types of services. There are currently five main institutional options for providing ecosystem services that are public goods (Stavins 2003):

1 regulation and penalty – regulations, such as zoning restrictions, harvest quota, open and close harvest seasons, or the informal rules

Table 11.2 *Effectiveness of different mechanisms for the provision of environmental public goods*

Ecosystem service	Public good type (A)				Verifiability (B)			Space (C)		Time (D)		Jurisdiction (E)				Mechanism (F)			
	Reflects the efforts of many	Reflects the efforts of a few	Depends on strongest provider	Depends on weakest provider	Local	National	International	Providers, beneficiaries co-located	Providers, beneficiaries not co-located	Benefits accrue now	Benefits accrue in the future	Local	National	International (sub-global)	International (global)	Regulation and penalty (type 1)	Cap and trade (type 3)	Direct payments (type 2)	Self-regulation (type 4)
Air quality regulation	✓				✓			✓		✓				✓					
Carbon sequestration		✓			✓		✓		✓		✓		✓		✓				
Disease control				✓	✓		✓		✓	✓					✓				
Freshwater provision		✓			✓	✓			✓	✓		✓	✓						
Habitat provision		✓	✓			✓		✓			✓		✓	✓					

Marine capture fisheries	✓		✓	✓	✓	✓
Storm protection		✓	✓	✓	✓	✓
Water quality regulation	✓	✓	✓	✓	✓	✓

Notes: Characteristics of ecosystem services and payment mechanisms. The table schematizes authors' impressions of the effectiveness of incentive mechanisms (column F) in providing environmental public goods. Column A classifies a sample of ecosystem services as public goods (Sandler 2004). Column B indicates the scale(s) at which delivery of a service can be verified (Wunder *et al.* 2008). Column C denotes the geographic location of providers relative to beneficiaries (Arriagada and Perrings 2011). Columns D and E indicate timing (Wunder *et al.* 2008) and the governance level(s) needed to achieve effective outcomes (Kaul and Le Goulven 2003). Darker shading in column F indicates mechanisms considered more effective for achieving the socially optimal level of provision, although effectiveness is context-dependent.

Source: Kinzig *et al.* (2011).

that govern the use of common-pool resources, are supported by penalties for non-compliance;

2 direct incentives – the payments for ecosystem services described here, plus an array of taxes, user charges, access fees, and the like;

3 mixed regulation and incentive systems – cap-and-trade schemes, tradable fisheries quotas, and tradable development rights;

4 self-regulation and voluntary agreements – voluntary agreements and social norms that enforce certain behaviors through informal penalties for non-compliance;

5 direct investment – public investment in the ecological and manufactured infrastructures needed for ecosystem service provision such as the protection of water supply, habitat for endangered species, or storm damage protection.

Which approach is the most appropriate in any given circumstances depends on the ecosystem services being managed in this way, as well as on prevailing socio-economic and political conditions. Kinzig *et al.* consider the conditions that are needed for the second and third of these mechanisms to be effective. They note that although PES schemes involve transactions between buyers and sellers of a service, they do not often have the characteristics of well-functioning markets. Few allow free exit and entry, or iteration towards a market-clearing price (a price at which supply and demand are balanced). The movement of prices in well-functioning markets offers an error-correction mechanism. Many of the prices used in PES schemes, by contrast, are insensitive to changing conditions (Kinzig *et al.* 2011).

Of greater concern is the fact that although PES schemes are generally designed to address an externality in existing markets, they may themselves be the source of external effects. Markets have the potential to allocate resources efficiently only if the prices they generate capture all relevant effects of the transactions between buyers and sellers. The point has already been made that the decline in many ecosystem services that motivates development of PES schemes has its origins in the external effects of existing markets for agricultural and industrial products. Market prices for foods, fuels, and fibers do not signal the scarcity of the other services generated by agro-ecosystems. Introducing payments for one service among a bundle of ancillary ecosystem services neglected by existing markets may make things worse, not better (Foley 2005; Millennium Ecosystem Assessment 2005).

Examples of the unanticipated consequences of a focus on a single service include incentives for biofuels production that lead to the conversion of wildlands (Hill *et al.* 2009), conversion of wetlands and stream corridors that reduces the water-purification capacity of ecosystems (Boyer and Polasky 2004), channel dredging that inhibits sediment delivery and reduces storm protection (Montague 2008), or homogenization of agricultural landscapes that reduces the capacity of ecosystems to contain pest or pathogen outbreaks (Hutchinson *et al.* 2009). Decisions that seem rational when only one service is considered are often inefficient when the full set of ecosystem services is taken into account (Kinzig *et al.* 2011). If PES schemes similarly single out an individual service for attention, then they risk similar unanticipated effects on others.

Another dimension of the problem considered by Kinzig *et al.* is the effect of multiple but incompatible social objectives. Much of the current enthusiasm for PES schemes in developing countries stems from the perception that they have a role in poverty alleviation. They argued that if PES schemes are indeed to signal the scarcity of ecosystem services, then they should not simultaneously be seen as vehicles for income transfers. PES schemes have their origins in the developed country agri-environment schemes. If, like some agri-environment schemes, their goal is primarily to transfer income to scheme participants, then monitoring and compliance may be expected to be low, prices may be expected to be insensitive to environmental conditions, and the impact on targeted services may be slight (Kinzig *et al.* 2011).

Correspondence around the paper (Corbera and Pascual 2012; Kinzig *et al.* 2012) helped clarify the points at issue. Corbera and Pascual considered that it was unethical to decouple the efficiency and equity dimensions of PES. They claimed that many existing PES schemes had exacerbated existing inequalities in income, access to resources, and decision-making, and that it was not possible to address this problem unless pro-poor management measures were included in the design of the mechanism. They further claimed that current schemes suffered from elite capture, implying that some participants in the scheme benefitted more than others.

In their reply Kinzig *et al.* agreed that PES schemes should be deployed only if they improve overall human wellbeing, and that their credibility and acceptability was likely to require participants see both process and outcomes to be fair. However, they also argued that if payments failed to signal the true scarcity of ecosystem services they would continue to be misused. Using payments to address social justice or poverty alleviation goals puts the first goal at risk. They also noted that there is already evidence on this point. Government-funded schemes with distributional goals have been shown to be significantly less effective than user-funded schemes in securing additional ecosystem service flows. Nor have PES schemes proved to be very effective at poverty alleviation. Although some schemes have been shown to help the poor, the benefits are typically very small (Pattanayak, Wunder and Ferraro 2010). So while poverty alleviation is an extremely important social objective, it should be addressed directly. Using PES schemes as the mechanism for alleviating poverty puts both efficiency and equity goals at risk.

11.5 The incentive effects of international payments for ecosystem services

Most market-based instruments developed to protect biodiversity and ecosystem services (most direct payment systems among them) are either local or national. Since conventional tax instruments require the existence of a body with the authority to levy taxes, such instruments are not an option at the international level. Direct payment systems, on the other hand, are an option at all levels. The majority of PES schemes may well be local or national, but there are some that operate across national boundaries, REDD among them. An important aspect of globalization is an increase not just in the degree to which the global market is integrated, but in the extent to which the external effects of activities in one part of the world impact the wellbeing of people in another. The globalization of environmental externalities is due to the closer connection between the ecosystems of the world that market integration brings. PES schemes potentially give the distant beneficiaries of ecosystem services generated in particular places the capacity to express their willingness to pay for those services. They have the capacity to internalize positive externalities that span national boundaries. The difficulty in implementing such schemes generally lies not with the international dimension of the scheme, but with the potentially conflicting goals of the buyers of ecosystem services, the rules governing monitoring and compliance, and the way these intersect with local institutions and laws (Phelps *et al.* 2010).

We will consider mechanisms for funding international public goods – the demand side of the problem – in the next chapter. The payment systems themselves are intended to provide landholders with the right incentives. This is the supply side of the problem. As Kinzig *et al.* note, however, PES schemes are not a panacea, and if poorly designed can do more harm than good (Kinzig *et al.* 2011). The most effective international PES systems are likely to be those where payments to landholders are direct, and are conditional on the delivery of well-specified services (or satisfaction of well-defined indicators) that do better than historic levels. For schemes on the scale of REDD, where payments take the form of country-to-country transfers, there are an additional and complicated set of principal–agent problems to be solved, in which the principals (at different levels) are likely to have different and potentially conflicting goals. But all such schemes do at least have the potential to provide landholders with clear signals about the relative social importance of alternative conservation strategies.

References

Arriagada, R. and Perrings, C. (2009) Making payments for ecosystem services work. *Ecosystem Services Economics Working Papers*. United Nations Environment Programme, Nairobi.

(2011) Paying for international environmental public goods. *Ambio*, 1–9.

Barbier, E. B. (2008) In the wake of tsunami: lessons learned from the household decision to replant mangroves in Thailand. *Resource and Energy Economics*, 30, 229–249.

Barbier, E. B., Burgess, J. C. and Grainger, A. (2010) The forest transition: towards a more comprehensive theoretical framework. *Land Use Policy*, 27, 98–107.

Barde, J.-P. and Honkatukia, O. (2004) Environmentally harmful subsidies. *The International Yearbook of Environmental and Resource Economics 2004/2005* (ed. T. Tietenberg and H. Folmer), pp. 254–288. Edward Elgar, Cheltenham.

Barrett, C. B. and Lybbert, T. J. (2000) Is bioprospecting a viable strategy for conserving tropical ecosystems? *Ecological Economics*, 34, 293–300.

Blom, B., Sunderland, T. and Murdiyarso, D. (2010) Getting REDD to work locally: lessons learned from integrated conservation and development projects. *Environmental Science & Policy*, 13, 164–172.

Boyer, T. and Polasky, S. (2004) Valuing urban wetlands: a review of non-market valuation studies. *Wetlands*, 24, 744–755.

Brown, D., Seymour, F. and Peskett, L. (2008) How do we achieve REDD co-benefits and avoid doing harm? *Moving Ahead with REDD: Issues, Options and Implications* (ed. A. Angelsen), pp. 107–118. CIFOR, Bogor.

Bulte, E. H. and Horan, R. D. (2003) Habitat conservation, wildlife extraction and agricultural expansion. *Journal of Environmental Economics and Management*, 45, 109–127.

Canadell, J. G. and Raupach, M. R. (2008) Managing forests for climate change mitigation. *Science*, 320, 1456–1457.

Cardinale, B. J., Duffy, J. E., Gonzalez, A., Hooper, D. U., Perrings, C., Venail, P., Narwani, A., Mace, G. M., Tilman, D., Wardle, D. A., Kinzig, A. P., Daily, G. C., Loreau, M., Grace, J. B., Larigauderie, A., Srivastava, D. S. and Naeem, S. (2012) Biodiversity loss and its impact on humanity. *Nature*, 486, 59–67.

Chichilnisky, G. and Heal, G. (1998) Economic returns from the biosphere. *Nature*, 391, 629–630.

　(2000) *Environmental Markets: Equity and Efficiency.* Columbia University Press, New York.

Chomitz, K. E. (1999) Transferable development rights and forest protection: an exploratory analysis. *Workshop on Market-Based Instruments for Environmental Protection.* Harvard University, John F. Kennedy School of Government.

Claassen, R., Cattaneo, R. and Johansson, R. (2008) Cost-effective design of agri-environmental payment programs: US experience in theory and practice.. *Ecological Economics*, 65, 738–753.

Coase, R. (1960) The problem of social cost. *Journal of Law and Economics*, 3, 1–44.

Corbera, E. and Pascual, U. (2012) Ecosystem services: heed social goals. *Science*, 335, 655–656.

Daily, G. and Ellison, K. (2002) *The New Economy of Nature.* Island Press, Washington, DC.

Dasgupta, P. (2001) *Human Well-being and the Natural Environment.* Oxford University Press, New York.

Demsetz, H. (1967) Toward a theory of property rights. *American Economic Review*, 57, 347–359.

Díaz, S., Hector, A. and Wardle, D. A. (2009) Biodiversity in forest carbon sequestration initiatives: not just a side benefit. *Current Opinion in Environmental Sustainability*, 1, 55–60.

Dobbs, T. L. and Pretty, J. N. (2004) Agri-environmental stewardship schemes and "multifunctionality." *Review of Agricultural Economics*, 26, 220–237.

Dutschke, M. and Angelsen, A. (2008) How do we ensure permanence and assign liability? *Moving Ahead with REDD* (ed. A. Angelsen). CIFOR, Bogor.

Engel, S., Pagiola, S. and Wunder, S. (2008) Designing payments for environmental services in theory and practice: an overview of the issues. *Ecological Economics*, 65, 663–674.

Ferraro, P. and Kiss, A. (2007) Direct payments to conserve biodiversity. *Science*, 298, 1718–1719.

Ferraro, P. and Pattanayak, S. K. (2006) Money for nothing? A call for empirical evaluation of biodiversity conservation investments. *PLoS Biology*, 4, 482–488.

Ferraro, P. J. and Simpson, R. D. (2002) The cost-effectiveness of conservation payments. *Land Economics*, 78, 339–353.

Field, B. C. and Conrad, J. M. (1975) Economics issues in programs of transferrable development rights. *Land Economics*, 4, 331–340.

Foley, J. A. (2005) Global consequences of land use. *Science*, 309, 570–574.

Food and Agriculture Organization (2007) The state of food and agriculture: paying farmers for environmental services. *FAO Agricultural Series*. FAO, Rome.

Gottschalk, T. K., Diekötter, T., Ekschmitt, K., Weinmann, B., Kuhlmann, F., Purtauf, T., Dauber, J. and Wolters, V. (2007) Impact of agricultural subsidies on biodiversity at the landscape level. *Landscape Ecology*, 22, 643–656.

Grieg-Gran, M., Porras, I. and Wunder, S. (2005) How can market mechanisms for forest environmental services help the poor? Preliminary lessons from Latin America. *World Development*, 33, 1511–1527.

Hall, C. M. (2006) Tourism, biodiversity and global environmental change. *Tourism and Global Environmental Change: Ecological, Social, Economic and Political Interrelationships* (ed. S. Gossling and C. M. Hall), pp. 211–228. Routledge, New York.

Hanley, N. (1990) The economics of nitrate pollution. *European Review of Agricultural Economics*, 17, 129–151.

Heal, G. (2000a) Biodiversity as a commodity. *Encyclopedia of Biodiversity* (ed. S. A. Levin), pp. 359–376. Academic Press, New York.

(2000b) Valuing ecosystem services. *Ecosystems*, 3, 24–30.

Heal, G. M., Barbier, E. B., Boyle, K. J., Covich, A. P., Gloss, S. P., Hershner, C. H., Hoehn, J. P., Pringle, C. M., Polasky, S., Segerson, K. and Shrader-Frechette, K. (2005) *Valuing Ecosystem Services: Toward Better Environmental Decision Making*. The National Academies Press, Washington, DC.

Hill, J., Polasky, S., Nelson, E., Tilman, D., Huo, H., Ludwig, L., Neumann, J., Zheng, H. C. and Bonta, D. (2009) Climate change and health costs of air emissions from biofuels and gasoline. *Proceedings of the National Academy of Sciences*, 106, 2077–2082.

Hutchinson, J. M. S., Margosian, M. L., With, K. A. and Garrett, K. A. (2009) Connectivity of the American agricultural landscape: assessing the national risk of crop pest and disease spread. *BioScience*, 59, 141–151.

Kaul, I. and Le Goulven, K. (2003) Institutional options for producing global public goods. *Providing Global Public Goods: Managing Globalization* (ed. I. Kaul, P. Conceição, K. Le Goulven and R. Mendoza). Oxford University Press.

Kinzig, A. P., Perrings, C., Chapin, F. S., Polasky, S., Smith, V. K., Tilman, D. and Turner, B. L. (2011) Paying for ecosystem services: promise and peril. *Science*, 334, 603–604.

(2012) Response – ecosystem services: free lunch no more. *Science*, 335, 656–657.

Liu, J., Li, S., Ouyang, Z., Tam, C. and Chen, X. (2008) Ecological and socioeconomic effects of China's policies for ecosystem services. *Proceedings of the National Academy of Sciences of the United States of America*, 105, 9477–9482.

Long, A. (2009) Taking adaptation value seriously: designing REDD to protect biodiversity. *Carbon and Climate Law Review*, 3, 314–323.

Madsen, B., Carroll, N. and Moore Brands, K. (2010) *Offset and Compensation Programs Worldwide*. Ecosystem Marketplace, Washington, DC.

Merrifield, J. (1996) A market approach to conserving biodiversity. *Ecological Economics*, 16, 217–226.

Millennium Ecosystem Assessment (2005) *Ecosystems and Human Well-being: General Synthesis*. Island Press, Washington, DC.

Mills, D. E. (1980) Transferable development rights markets. *Journal of Urban Economics*, 7, 63–74.

Montague, C. (2008) Recovering the sand deficit from a century of dredging and jetties along Florida's Atlantic coast: a reevaluation of beach nourishment as an essential tool for ecological conservation. *Journal of Coastal Research*, 24, 899–916.

Múñoz-Piña, C., Guevara, A., Torres, J. and Braña, J. (2008) Paying for the hydrological services of Mexico's forests: analysis, negotiations and results. *Ecological Economics*, 65.

Myers, N. and Kent, J. (2001) *Perverse Subsidies: How Tax Dollars Can Undercut the Environment and the Economy*. Island Press, Washington, DC.

Naeem, S., Bunker, D., Hector, A., Loreau, M. and Perrings, C. (eds.) (2009) *Biodiversity, Ecosystem Functioning, and Human Wellbeing: An Ecological and Economic Perspective*. Oxford University Press.

OECD (2004) *Recommendation of the Council on the Use of Economic Instruments in Promoting the Conservation and Sustainable Use of Biodiversity*. OECD, Paris.

Ostfeld, R. S., Keesing, F. and Eviner, V. T. (2008) *Infectious Disease Ecology: Effects of Ecosystems on Disease and of Disease on Ecosystems*. Princeton University Press.

Pagiola, S. (2008) Payments for environmental services in Costa Rica. *Ecological Economics*, 65, 712–724.

Pagiola, S., Rios, A. R. and Arcenas, A. (2008) Can the poor participate in payments for environmental services? Lessons from the Silvopastoral Project in Nicaragua. *Environment and Development Economics*, 13, 299–325.

Pagiola, S., Ramírez, E., Gobbi, J., de Haan, C., Ibrahim, M., Murgueitio, E. and Ruíz, J. P. (2007) Paying for the environmental services of Silvopastoral practices in Nicaragua. *Ecological Economics*, 64, 374–385.

Palmer, M. A. and Filoso, S. (2009) Restoration of ecosystem services for environmental markets. *Science*, 325, 575–576.

Panayotou, T. (1995) Economic instruments for environmental management and sustainable development. *Environmental Economics Series Paper no. 16*, United Nations Environment Programme Consultative Expert Group Meeting on the Use and Application of Economic Policy Instruments for Environmental Management and Sustainable Development, Nairobi.

Pascual, U. and Perrings, C. (2007) Developing incentives and economic mechanisms for in situ biodiversity conservation in agricultural landscapes. *Agriculture Ecosystems & Environment*, 121, 256–268.

Pattanayak, S. K., Wunder, S. and Ferraro, P. J. (2010) Show me the money: do payments supply environmental services in developing countries? *Review of Environmental Economics and Policy*, 4, 254–274.

Pearce, D. W. (2003) Environmentally harmful subsidies: barriers to sustainable development. *Environmentally Harmful Subsidies: Policy Issues and Challenges* (ed. OECD), pp. 9–30. OECD, Paris.

Phelps, J., Guerrero, M., Dalabajan, D., Young, B. and Webb, E. L. (2010) What makes a REDD country? *Global Environmental Change*, 20, 322–332.

Pigou, A. C. (1920) *The Economics of Welfare*. Macmillan, London.

Roe, D., Ashley, C., Page, S. and Meyer, D. (2004) *Tourism and the Poor: Analysing and Interpreting Tourism Statistics from a Poverty Perspective*. PPT Partnership, London.

Sandler, T. (2004) *Global Collective Action*. Cambridge University Press.

Schmid, E., Sinabell, F. and Hofreither, M. F. (2007) Phasing out of environmentally harmful subsidies: consequences of the 2003 CAP reform. *Ecological Economics*, 60, 596–604.

Stavins, R. N. (2003) Experience with market-based environmental policy instruments. *Handbook of Environmental Economics* (ed. K.-G. Mäler and J. R. Vincent), pp. 355–435. Elsevier, Amsterdam.

Stoneham, G., Chaudhri, V., Strappazon, L. and Ha, A. (2007) Auctioning biodiversity conservation contracts. *Biodiversity Economics: Principles, Methods, and Applications* (ed. A. Kontoleon, U. Pascual and T. Swanson), pp. 389–416. Cambridge University Press.

TEEB (2009) *TEEB Climate Issues Update*. UNEP, Nairobi.

Tipper, R. (2002) Helping indigenous farmers to participate in the international market for carbon services: the case of Scolel Té. *Selling Forest Environmental Services* (ed. S. Pagiola, J. Bishop and N. Landel-Mills), pp. 223–234. Earthscan, London.

Tomich, T. P., van Noordwijk, M., Budidarsono, S., Gillison, A., Murdiyarso, D., Stolle, F. and Fagi, A. M. (2001) Agricultural intensification, deforestation, and the environment: assessing tradeoffs in Sumatra, Indonesia. *Tradeoffs or Synergies? Agricultural Intensification, Economic Development and the Environment* (ed. D. R. Lee and C. B. Barrett), pp. 221–244. CAB International, Wallingford.

Turpie, J. K., Marais, C. and Blignaut, J. N. (2008) The Working for Water Programme: evolution of a payments for ecosystem services mechanism that addresses both poverty and ecosystem service delivery in South Africa. *Ecological Economics*, 65, 789–799.

Victoria Department of Sustainability and Environment (2008) *BushTender: Rethinking Investment for Native Vegetation Outcomes: The Application of Auctions for Securing Private Land Management Agreements*. State of Victoria, Department of Sustainability and Environment, Melbourne.

Wells, M. (1992) Biodiversity conservation, affluence and poverty: mismatched costs and benefits and efforts to remedy them. *Ambio*, 21, 237–243.

Wells, M. P. and Brandon, K. (1992) *People and Parks: Linking Protected Areas with Local Communities*. World Bank, Washington, DC.

Wells, M. P., McShane, T. O., Dublin, H. T., O'Connor, S. and Redford, K. H. (2004) The future of integrated conservation and development projects: building on what works. *Getting Biodiversity Projects to Work: Towards more Effective Conservation and Development* (ed. T. O. Mcshane and M. P. Wells), pp. 397–422. Columbia University Press, New York.

Wilson, G. (1996) Factors influencing farmer participation in the Environmentally Sensitive Areas Scheme. *Journal of Environmental Management*, 50, 67–93.

World Tourism Organization (2011) *World Tourism Highlights*. UNWTO, Madrid.

Wu, J. (2000) Slippage effects of the conservation reserve program. *American Journal of Agricultural Economics*, 82, 979–992.

(2007) The efficiency of payments for environmental services in tropical conservation. *Conservation Biology*, 21, 48–58.

Wunder, S. and Albán, M. (2008) Decentralized payments for environmental services: the cases of Pimampiro and PROFAFOR in Ecuador. *Ecological Economics*, 65, 685–698.

Wunder, S., Engel, S. and Pagiola, S. (2008) Taking stock: a comparative analysis of payments for environmental services programs in developed and developing countries. *Ecological Economics, 65*, 834–852.

Zabel, A. and Holm-Müller, K. (2008) Conservation performance payments for carnivore conservation in Sweden. *Conservation Biology*, 22, 247–251.

12 | *Paying for international environmental public goods*

12.1 International environmental public goods

Many of the externalities of biodiversity change stem from the fact that the ecosystem services supported by biodiversity are public goods. This encourages free-riding. Because people cannot be excluded from the benefits of environmental public goods once they are provided, they have an incentive to free-ride on the efforts of others. It also encourages undersupply. Because people cannot capture the benefits of provision, they have an incentive to supply less than is socially desirable. Both problems are especially acute for environmental public goods that span national boundaries. They do, however, vary from one environmental public good to another, depending on supply technologies and the existence of thresholds in the level of supply, or the number of contributing countries. The incentive for countries to free-ride on the efforts of others is greatest in the case of public goods with additive supply technologies such as the conservation of widespread but endangered species or climate regulation from carbon sequestration. The incentive to free-ride is least in the case of weakest-link technologies such as the management of infectious disease, pest control, or the eradication of invasive species. Conversely, the incentive for countries to act unilaterally is greatest in the case of best-shot supply technologies such as vaccine development, or the provision of information about pest and pathogen risks, and least in the case of additive technologies. Free-riding also depends on the costs and benefits of public good provision. It was noted, for example, that free-riding was likely to be less of a problem for (impure) public goods that also deliver a private benefit, such as quarantine and port inspections, than it is for (pure) public goods that do not.

Where the incentive to act unilaterally is weak, the institutional arrangements under which the good is provided are critically important. Access rights, the number of parties involved, the penalties for

370

defection, the frequency of interaction between parties, and the differences between parties all turn out to matter. Environmental resources that are non-exclusive because of social rules of access rather than the properties of the resource should be comparatively easy to address. The tragedy of the commons is a tragedy only if is not possible to agree rules of access (Ostrom 1990). Whether or not it is possible to reach agreement on the regulation of common pool resources depends on the incentives people have to defect. Paradoxically, the number of parties able to reach agreement, and to stick by it, tends to be inversely related to the benefits it delivers (Barrett 1994). The enforcement of agreements usually requires penalties for non-compliance with the agreed course of action, or at least clear cost-sharing rules (Sandler 2004). Since repeated interactions also allow past interactions to inform future strategies, the requirement for repeated interactions is often institutionalized. In sum, the most effective arrangements for the delivery of international environmental public goods tend to involve a small number of signatories, require repeated renegotiation, and include disincentives to defect from a precisely defined set of objectives (Barrett 2003a, 2007b).

It follows that ecosystem services that are most likely to be undersupplied are those for which the supply technology is additive, the cost of provision is high, the number of countries involved is large, and enforcement mechanisms are weak (Touza and Perrings 2011). Among the services put at risk by directed biodiversity change, this includes the protection of the global gene pool through *in situ* conservation of threatened species and the provision of harvested wild-living resources from ecosystems beyond national jurisdiction. Similarly, services where the benefits to all are limited by the capacity of the least effective country (the weakest link) or countries (weaker links), such as the management of infectious disease or invasive species, will be undersupplied from the perspective of most countries (Perrings *et al.* 2010a, 2010b).

Beyond these things, wealth and income differences turn out to be of fundamental importance. This is recognized in the benefit sharing provisions of agreements like the CBD (Perrings *et al.* 2011; Touza and Perrings 2011). Where the poor have less to gain from the provision of some environmental public good than the rich, their cooperation in any arrangement to secure collective provision of environmental public goods may require transfers – what are known as side payments in the theory of games (Barrett 1994, 2003b, 2007a). Indeed, many of the PES schemes discussed in Chapter 11 are designed to do just this.

This chapter addresses the other side of the problem: the generation of the resources needed to pay the providers of biodiversity-related international public goods, or to undertake collective investments in their provision. Mobilizing the resources needed to induce the socially optimal supply of international environmental public goods generally remains one of the greatest challenges confronting the global community. Although some progress has been made in securing the resources needed to make progress in climate change mitigation, and although collective action to counter particular aspects of biodiversity change – infectious diseases – has historically been adequately funded at the international level, most of the international public goods put at risk by biodiversity change have not.

The general issues involved in funding collective international bodies, such as the UN, have been well illustrated by Scott Barrett (2007b). This chapter considers the funding of international public goods at three levels: international cooperation between national governments (GEF), national funding of international environmental public goods, and the role of international NGOs. The first of these represents the ideal (first-best) solution to the problem of funding global public goods. The GEF is a common fund dedicated, at least in principle, to generating global public goods by supporting national actions that would not otherwise take place. The second and third represent adaptive responses by national governments and civil society to the global failure to generate resources on the scale needed to make a difference.

These are not the only sources of funding for international environmental public goods, but they are the most important. They also illustrate the nature of the problem in particularly stark form. They show that depending upon the size and distribution of the benefits of public good provision, individual countries will have a stronger or weaker incentive to commit resources unilaterally, and that securing more than that depends either upon agreement between nation states, or upon the actions of NGOs that increasingly span national boundaries.

The point was made earlier that the scale of biodiversity-related public goods that span national boundaries is highly variable. The conservation of the genetic diversity on which all future evolution depends, the control of emerging infectious diseases, and the management of sea areas beyond national jurisdiction are all global in scale. Others are regional, such as the regulation of international watersheds, the management of straddling fish stocks, or the protection of endemic species' habitat that spans jurisdiction. In all cases, the benefits of public good provision extend to people in multiple countries. The defining characteristics of these public goods, aside from the fact that they are non-rival and non-exclusive, is that they benefit not only a broad spectrum of countries but also a broad spectrum of the global population; and they benefit both present and future generations (Kaul, Grunberg and Stern 1999). International public goods generated in any one country will necessarily produce spillover effects beyond a nation's boundary (Morrissey, te Velde and Hewitt 2002). What matters for their funding is that they will also have different implications for national governments, transnational corporations, and NGOs – each of which have different constituencies. The emergence of a global environmental public interested in asserting new rights and responsibilities to the resources of the planet, and in developing new forms of governance of the biosphere, potentially affects all three (Arriagada and Perrings 2011).

12.2 The Global Environment Facility

The GEF was initially established in 1991 as a pilot program within the World Bank to finance the protection of the global environment. It was designed to fund the incremental cost of national projects offering global environmental benefits. In 1994 the GEF was restructured as a permanent independent financial mechanism for the UN CBD and the UNFCCC, with the involvement of both the UNEP and the United Nations Development Programme (UNDP). It has subsequently become the financial mechanism for two more international conventions: the Stockholm Convention on Persistent Organic Pollutants (2001) and the UNCCD (2003). Its remit accordingly covers several different international environmental public goods: biological diversity; climate change; international waters; land degradation, primarily desertification and deforestation; ozone layer depletion; and persistent organic pollutants (Global Environment Facility 2011).

The GEF operates a trust fund from which grants are made to nation states. Any country eligible to borrow from the World Bank or to receive UNDP technical assistance is also eligible to receive grants from the fund. In the fifth replenishment of the fund, covering financing commitments for July 2010 to June 2014, the member states approved the contributions described in Table 12.1. Taking account of

Table 12.1 *GEF Trust Fund, fifth replenishment of resources: table of contributions, in special drawing rights (million SDRs)*

Contributing participants	GEF5 shares and basic contributions[a]		Supplemental contributions (SDR)	Adjustment toward full funding (SDR)	GEF5 actual shares (%)	Total contributions	
	(%)	SDR				SDR	USD[b]
Australia	1.46	41.92	10.96	–	2.29	52.88	81.03
Austria	1.21	34.66[b]	5.50	–	1.74	40.15	61.53
Belgium	1.55	44.51	32.55[c]	–	3.33	77.05	118.07
Brazil	0.00	4.00[c]	4.00	–	0.35	8.00	12.26
Canada	4.28	122.89	12.28	–	5.85	135.17	207.13
China	0.00	4.00[c]	5.79	–	0.42	9.79	15.00
Czech Republic	0.00	4.00[c]	0.60[c]	–	0.20	4.60	7.05
Denmark	1.30	37.33	11.07	–	2.09	48.40	74.17
Finland	1.00	28.71	27.48[b]	–	2.43	56.20	86.12
France	6.76	194.16	–	–	8.40	194.16	297.53
Germany	10.89	312.64	–	–	13.53	312.64	479.09
Greece	0.05	1.44	2.92[b]	–	0.19	4.35	6.67
India	0.00	4.00[c]	2.39[b]	–	0.28	6.39	9.00
Ireland	0.11	3.16	2.46[b]	–	0.24	5.62	8.61
Italy	2.89	82.89	–	–	3.59	82.89	127.02
Japan	11.48	329.55	–	–	14.26	329.55	505.00
Korea	0.17	4.89	0.43[b]	–	0.23	5.33	7.50
Luxembourg	0.05	1.44	2.56	–	0.17	4.00	6.13
Mexico	0.00	4.00[c]	2.53[b]	–	0.28	6.53	10.01

Netherlands	2.60	74.69	—	—	3.23	74.69	114.45
New Zealand	0.12	3.45	0.55	—	0.17	4.00	6.13
Nigeria	0.00	4.00^c	—	—	0.17	4.00	6.13
Norway	1.34	38.47	—	—	1.66	38.47	58.95
Pakistan	0.00	4.00^c	—	—	0.17	4.00	6.13
Portugal	0.12	3.45	0.55	—	0.17	4.00	6.13
Russian Federation	0.00	6.53	0.58^b	—	0.31	7.10	10.88
Slovenia	0.03	0.86	3.85^b	—	0.20	4.71	7.22
South Africa	0.00	4.00^c	0.35^c	—	0.19	4.35	6.66
Spain	0.97	27.76	—	—	1.20	27.76	42.54
Sweden	2.29	65.65	19.78	—	3.70	85.43	130.91
Switzerland	2.10	60.30	1.10^b	14.01	3.26	75.41	115.55
Turkey	0.00	4.00^c	—	—	0.17	4.00	6.13
United Kingdom	6.93	199.12	15.32	—	9.28	214.43	328.59
United States	13.07	375.23	—	—	16.23	375.23	575.00

Notes: [a] The GEF5 basic shares reflect those of the GEF4 except for Austria, France, Germany, Italy, Japan, Korea, the Netherlands, Norway, Spain, Sweden, Switzerland, the United Kingdom, and the United States.
[b] Contributing participants have the option of taking a discount or credit for accelerating their payment/encashment schedule and: (1) including such credit as part of their basic share; (2) counting such credit as a supplemental contribution; or (3) taking such discount against the national currency contribution. Austria has opted to include such credit as part of its basic share. Belgium, the Czech Republic, Finland, Greece, India, Ireland, Korea, Mexico, the Russian Federation, Slovenia, South Africa, and Switzerland have opted to take the credit for accelerated encashment as a supplemental contribution. Canada, China, France, and the Netherlands have opted to take a discount against the national currency contribution.
[c] For those contributing participants that do not have a basic share, this represents the agreed minimum contribution of SDR 4 million.
Source: Global Environment Facility (2011).

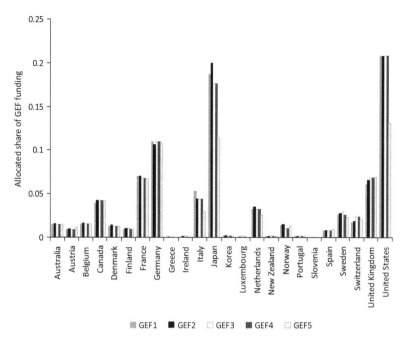

Figure 12.1 The basic allocation of shares in the GEF Trust Fund over the first five replenishments, by country.
Source: data from Global Environment Facility (2011).

investment income, carryover of GEF resources, paid-in but unallocated and deferred contributions, this implied resources of $4.34 billion for the full funding period (Global Environment Facility 2011). The evolution of the allocated share of GEF funding over the first five replenishments is indicated in Figure 12.1.

Initially the largest share of the cost was carried by Japan (18.7 percent) and the United States (20.9 percent), with the larger European countries, Germany (11 percent), France (7 percent), and the United Kingdom (6.2 percent) in a second group. The fifth replenishment differs from the previous four in the substantial reduction in the shares carried by the United States (13 percent) and Japan (11.5 percent). Since there has been no change in the allocated basic share to compensate for this, the proportion of expected costs covered by the basic allocation has fallen from around 90 percent to 72 percent. However, it is expected that supplemental contributions by other countries with an existing share of basic costs, and by countries that do not currently carry a share of basic costs – Brazil, China, the Czech Republic, India, the Russian Federation, and South Africa – will make up the difference (Global Environment Facility 2011).

As the financial mechanism of the CBD the proportion of GEF funds allocated to biodiversity necessarily focuses on CBD priorities. The CBD will be considered in more detail in later chapters, but its main remit is defined in Article 1 of the convention, which requires

the conservation of biological diversity, the sustainable use of its components and the fair and equitable sharing of the benefits arising out of the utilization of genetic resources, including by appropriate access to genetic resources and by appropriate transfer of relevant technologies, taking into account all rights over those resources and to technologies, *and by appropriate funding.* (Convention on Biological Diversity 1993, emphasis added)

In principle GEF funds are targeted at the incremental costs of local projects that offer global benefits. Incremental costs are the difference between the cost of a project that would be warranted taking into account only the national benefits it offers, and the cost that is warranted taking into account the global benefits it offers (Pearce 2003, 2005). Project costs that are warranted by national benefits are those at which the marginal cost of a project to some country are just balanced by the marginal benefits it offers to the same country. Project costs that are warranted by the global benefits it offers are those at which the marginal cost of a project to the country are just balanced by the marginal benefits it offers to global community – i.e. that country and the rest of the world. In Figure 12.2 this is the grey area. It includes both the extra cost of provision of the public good at S_G to country 1 *and* the extra producer surplus to that country. In Chapter 11 the same area in Figure 11.1 indicated the payments that it would be necessary to make to induce the country to increase its level of conservation to one that would be optimal from the perspective of the global community. By the incremental cost principle this is also the optimal level of project funding from the GEF.

Because the project generates a public good (conservation in this example), the rest of the world benefits from the level of provision that would be chosen by country 1 even if it received no support from the GEF. In Figure 12.2 the global consumer surplus is the area under the global benefit curve at S_L less the local cost of supply, $P_L S_L$. Expanding the level of conservation to S_G yields an increment in

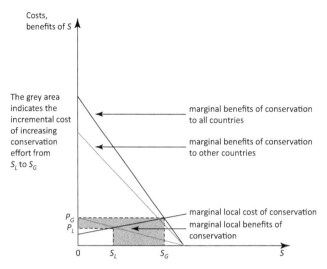

Figure 12.2 Incremental cost of increasing local conservation effort to assure the supply of the global public good.

global benefits equal to the area under the global benefit curve at supply S_G less the cost $P_G S_G$. If this increment in global benefits is greater than the incremental costs of the project then the rest of the world will have an incentive to cover the incremental costs.

What the incremental cost principle has in fact been interpreted to mean for biodiversity investments since the third replenishment, GEF3, is that GEF funding would be made available to cover most of the costs of projects in four areas: the sustainability of protected areas, mainstreaming biodiversity in production landscapes/seascapes, capacity building for the implementation of the UN CBD Cartagena Protocol on Biosafety, and the generation and dissemination of best practices for addressing current and emerging biodiversity issues (Zimsky *et al.* 2008). The first of these looks like the traditional conservationist's focus on protected areas, but the emphasis on sustainability brings the interaction with local landholders and resource users into play. The second focuses on conservation outside protected areas. The strategy has evolved under later replenishments, the basic principles established in GEF3 have remained.

During the pilot phase and the first four replenishments, the GEF had made $10.5 billion in grants and leveraged $51 billion in co-financing for some 2,700 projects in 165 countries. A little under one-third of GEF funding and a sixth of co-financing were targeted at biodiversity. Specifically, $3.1 billion in grants and $8.3 billion in co-financing were committed to projects addressing the loss of biodiversity in 155 countries. The bulk of these funds ($2.9 billion of GEF resources and $8.2 billion of co-financing) were committed to protected areas. This involved the establishment of conservation trust funds, revolving funds, private sector and village funds, and PES schemes (Zimsky *et al.* 2008, 2013).

In terms of biomes, the major part of GEF funding has focused on tropical forests. It has covered forest conservation (protected areas), sustainable use of forests (forest production landscapes), and sustainable forest management (interactions between forests and the wider landscape). This has drawn resources both from the biodiversity focal area and from the land degradation focal area. Since 2007 it has shifted its focus more towards sustainable forest management. At the same time, incorporation of land use, land-use change, and forestry into the GEF's climate change strategy has enabled the body to support projects that span climate change as well as biodiversity and land degradation. The biggest beneficiary of this shift has been the REDD+ program discussed in Chapter 11. In GEF5 the body will provide up to $1 billion for a joint Sustainable Forest Management/REDD+ program: $250 million directly as an incentive for developing countries to invest $750 million of the funds they could expect to receive for biodiversity, climate, and land degradation.

The first thing to note about the GEF as an institution and a mechanism for funding global environmental public goods is that while it may be the financial mechanism for the most important of the multilateral agreements concerned with global environmental public goods, the CBD, the UNCCD, and UNFCCC, the resources available to it are quite limited. Recall that funding for the whole of the GEF5 period is expected to be of the order of $4.3 billion, and that aggregate funding since the establishment of the GEF as an independent body in 1994 has been in the order of $10.5 billion. To put this in perspective, a single private foundation dedicated largely to the provision of global public goods and in existence for the same period as the GEF, the Gates Foundation, has committed $26.2 billion in the same period. The agency responsible for environmental protection in just one country, the United States Environmental Protection Agency (EPA), has an annual budget of $9.5 billion, nearly ten times the size of the GEF annual grants.

Of course the GEF is not the only source of international funding for international environmental public goods. While it operates as the financial mechanism for a number of conventions on behalf of the World Bank, the UNEP and the UNDP, there are also other UN agencies such as the WHO and the FAO with biodiversity-related remits. But even if the budgets of all these three are added together they are still only a little over a quarter of the annual budget of the EPA. Why?

One answer to this lies in the incentive to free-ride that dogs public goods of all kinds. The GEF program tends to fund international environmental public goods that are additive – the size of the global public good is a simple sum of the contributions of all nations. In such cases every decision to refrain from making a contribution or to reduce a contribution reduces the benefit to all. Moreover, the incentive to free-ride is even stronger in stringent financial conditions. Contributions to all of the UN programs and agencies declined substantially during the 2007–2009 recession as individual countries reduced their contributions. The GEF was not the only body affected. Both of the other agencies delivering biodiversity-related public goods mentioned earlier, the WHO and the FAO, were forced to implement significant budget cuts.

A second answer lies in the fact that there are options for addressing public goods that make it possible for countries to capture more or less of the benefit of their contributions. Of the two main options for addressing climate change, for example, mitigation expenditures by any one country generate benefit that accrue to all countries, but the benefits of adaptation expenditures accrue primarily to the country making those expenditures. The selection of an adaptation strategy over a mitigation strategy in that case will reduce national contributions to the provision of the global public good. At the same time, since climate change mitigation is an additive global public good, adoption of a mitigation strategy still allows countries the option of mitigating domestically or internationally. A ton of carbon sequestered in Brazil has the same effect on climate change as a ton of carbon sequestered in Switzerland.

A third answer is that countries behave strategically when they decide what to commit to the supply of an international public good. In addition to the nature of the public good (its supply technology) their decision depends on what they expect other countries to contribute, and whether their own contribution will affect the contributions of other countries (Holzinger 2001, 2008; Touza and Perrings 2011). Contributions to UN bodies are generally based on assessments that are sensitive to population and income. Assessments can and do change over time, but are quite sticky. History matters. They are also capped, at least in principle, at 22 percent of aggregate contributions. In the case of the GEF, while Brazil, the Russian Federation, India, China, and South Africa are still zero-assessed for base funding, they have started making positive contributions through supplemental funding. The introduction of the 22 percent cap had followed pressure from the USA that took the form of withholding of past dues (Barrett 2007b). Both the USA and Japan continue to pressure this group of countries to increase their contributions.

12.3 The national provision of biodiversity-related international public goods

The second source of funding for the provision of international environmental public goods I wish to consider is the internal expenditures of nation states. The main factors behind the incentives to individual countries to contribute to public goods that benefit other countries were discussed in Chapter 5. We saw that for additive public goods, where distinct contributions are perfectly substitutable, the strategic options facing individual countries are in the nature of a prisoner's dilemma. Although global wellbeing would be maximized if all countries were to contribute, the dominant strategy for each country is to free-ride on the efforts of others. If the cost to each country of contributing to the public good were less than the benefits to that country of its own contribution, none would contribute. But if individual contributions were not perfect substitutes, and had a different additive impact on the international public good, then the choice of each country would be determined by country-specific attributes (Sandler 2008; Touza and Perrings 2011). We also saw, however, that there are some types of international environmental public good where the incentives facing individual countries are quite different.

For international public goods characterized by best-shot supply technologies such as the provision of information on emerging threats, for example, the strategic options facing individual countries are those of the "chicken game." There are several possible outcomes to games of this sort. First, if the benefits of acting unilaterally exceed the cost of provision, countries will act independently to supply the public good. Second, if the benefits of acting unilaterally are less than the cost of provision, then the best response of each country will be to do nothing, allowing other countries to supply the public good. Third, if no other countries voluntarily supply the public good, then the next best response would be a cost-sharing arrangement with other countries. Finally, if no other country can be induced to supply the public good, then unilateral provision would still be better than no provision. The pursuit of self-interest, without regard to whether the other countries would cooperate or not, leads to joint international gains. At the same time, the outcome is seldom optimal from a global perspective (Holzinger 2001; Sandler 2004). Nevertheless, just because each country would prefer to free-ride on the contributions of others, there is some risk that no country would contribute.

One other type of international environmental public good is also relevant here: those characterized by weakest-link technologies, such as the global eradication of an infectious disease. Public goods of this kind require contributions from every country, but because of the nature of the problem little is gained by contributing any more than the country that is the weakest-link in the chain (Holzinger 2001). The strategic choices in this case correspond to a coordination assurance game, in which the best response is to match the provision of the weakest link. So in the case of emerging infectious disease control either all countries cooperate or all fail. Unilateral action by one country cannot protect that country, but can increase the likelihood of a cooperative outcome (Touza and Perrings 2011).

It follows that the minimum size of the group of countries that needs to cooperate to provide the public good is quite different for these different types of public good (Hampton 1987). For best-shot public goods one country is enough. For weakest-link public goods matching behavior by all is required. In intermediate cases there may be a threshold number of countries, as there is when the number of ratifying parties needed before the agreement comes into force is spelled out as part of the agreement (Sandler 2008). In this last case, although there exists a coordination equilibrium at which no country contributes, those benefitting the most will tend to cooperate to meet the threshold.

Bearing these remarks in mind, consider the investments made by nation states in international biodiversity-related public goods. Governments invest in biodiversity-related public goods in many different ways. For most people the first type of investment that springs to mind involves the establishment and maintenance of protected areas. In some countries at least, conservation activities of this kind are relatively easy to trace. In the USA, for example, conservation expenditures undertaken by the different branches of government are reported in the International Conservation Budget prepared by a set of non-governmental conservation organizations (Conservation International *et al.* 2010). In this chapter, however, I wish to consider two different types of international environmental public good that are both connected to the same problem: emerging infectious diseases. The first is the provision of information on emerging infectious diseases. The second is the control of emerging infectious diseases. The first has many of the characteristics of a best-shot public good. The second has many of the characteristics of a weakest-link public good. Both contrast with the public goods addressed by the GEF, most of which are additive.

Consider the work of the US CDC. The primary role of the CDC is to protect the United States from health threats, but in so doing it incidentally extends protection to all other countries. Its specific remits are to prevent and control infectious and chronic diseases; respond to international disasters; and build sustainable global public health capacity by training epidemiologists, laboratory scientists, and public health managers. The CDC has staff operating in more than fifty countries, many on assignment to bodies like the WHO. Three main sources of threat addressed by the CDC are changes in the range of tropical diseases and their vectors as a result of global warming, the emergence of zoonoses as a result of habitat conversion, and the dispersion of diseases as a result of the growth in world trade and travel. Changes in the natural range of diseases and their vectors mean that many tropical diseases, such as schistosomiasis, Chagas disease, and dengue are moving north. An outbreak of dengue fever in Florida in 2009, for example, was the first since 1934. The primary focus of the CDC is, however, on emerging disease threats. It aims to detect, identify, and contain emerging infectious disease, and its motivation for extending its reach internationally is that a "weakness in the surveillance system for infectious diseases in any one country – is a threat to all countries" (Centers for Disease Control 2012b).

The risks of trade and travel reflect three characteristics that have already been noted. The first is that as economies have become more open to trade in goods and services they have become more likely to experience the introduction of pests and pathogens. The second is that as the speed of transport increases the likelihood that passenger species will survive the journey increases. The third is that as the volume of trade between countries in bioclimatically similar zones increases the likelihood that introduced species will successfully establish increases (Perrings *et al.* 2010b). The CDC's goal in this case is to develop an international system to detect and respond to emerging, and re-emerging, infectious diseases, in part by developing the capacity of countries to discharge their responsibilities under the IHR (World Health Organization 2005). The IHR both imposes reporting obligations on countries, and requires that those countries develop the capacity to detect, assess, notify, and report events (World Health Organization 2005: Article 5(1)). At the same time, however, it imposes an obligation on the WHO to help member countries do this. Assisting the WHO in its capacity-building role is an explicit goal of the CDC.

To discharge its responsibilities the CDC had a budget in 2012 of $6.88 billion – more than three times that of the WHO, and more than six times that of the GEF. And while it is not immune from the cuts being applied in other parts of the US federal budget, it is significant that the only areas of expenditure that are expected to increase in the CDC's 2013 budget are the programs in HIV/AIDS, emerging zoonotic diseases, public health scientific services, and global health (see Figure 12.3) (Centers for Disease Control 2012a).

The CDC is, however, only part of the US commitment in this area. The Global Health Initiative launched in 2009 was originally planned as a six-year $63 billion commitment to global public health. While current commitments are below that (in 2012 it was funded at $8.8 billion) this is a substantial allocation of resources to enhance health protection around the world. The initiative amalgamates a number of separate global health programs, including those funded through the CDC, and now accounts for around 80 percent of the US global health funding. The programs incorporated in the Global Health Initiative include the Global Fund to Fight AIDS, Tuberculosis and Malaria (Global Fund); the President's Emergency Plan for AIDS Relief; the President's Malaria Initiative; the programs on neglected tropical diseases, maternal, newborn and child health, and family planning, and reproductive health and nutrition.

The motivation for the Global Health Initiative is clear. It is that protection of the health of US citizens requires intervention in the health of people in the rest of the world. In launching the initiative in 2009, the US President, Barack Obama, made the case as follows:

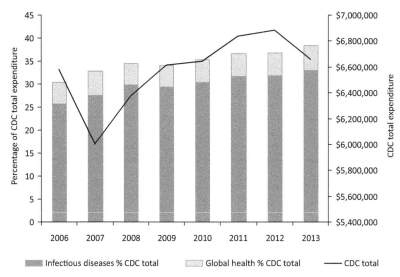

Figure 12.3 Total CDC budget ($ billion (axis 2)), and the percentage of the budget allocated to global health and infectious disease programs (axis 1). *Source*: CDC (2012b).

In the 21st century, disease flows freely across borders and oceans, and, in recent days, the 2009 H1N1 virus has reminded us of the urgent need for action. We cannot wall ourselves off from the world and hope for the best, nor ignore the public health challenges beyond our borders. An outbreak in Indonesia can reach Indiana within days, and public health crises abroad can cause widespread suffering, conflict, and economic contraction …We cannot simply confront individual preventable illnesses in isolation. The world is interconnected, and that demands an integrated approach to global health. (Obama 2009)

The initiative addresses both of the international environmental public goods considered here: information on emerging infectious diseases and the control of emerging infectious diseases. The CDC has often been cited as an example of a best-shot public good, funded by the USA but providing information on emerging diseases to the rest of the world (Sandler 2004). It is, however, clear that its interventions in support of the WHO and the IHR, and the specific campaigns on emerging zoonoses, HIV/AIDS, and tuberculosis are directed at our second problem: the control of infectious diseases. Although this is generally regarded as a weakest-link public good in which the dominant strategy is to match the performance of the countries with the least effective performance, these campaigns aim to raise the level of protection offered to all countries by the weakest links in the chain. They exploit the fact that in combating outbreaks the USA may have the skills and resources that make it a best-shot provider.

Of course not all countries are in a position to make similar investments in global health as a way of protecting their own populations, but all do face the fact that global health is a global public good that is impure – in the sense that one country's contribution to the public good yields two benefits. One is the direct benefit of enhanced protection of the nation's population. The other is the benefit accruing from improvements in the health of all others in the world. The direct benefit is what generally motivates national health expenditures, but the USA's Global Health Initiative is clearly targeted at the indirect benefits offered by improvements in the health of people elsewhere, and especially in the tropical countries most likely to be sources of emergent zoonoses (Jones *et al.* 2008). While the United States supports health programs in eighty countries, the Global Health Initiative will focus on the forty countries that are thought to offer the greatest benefits (see Figure 12.4).

12.4 The private provision of international environmental public goods

A third increasingly important source of funding for the provision of international environmental public goods is private foundations and NGOs. One of the best examples of this, the Gates Foundation, has already been mentioned, and will be discussed in more detail below. But there are many others. Most are quite small, and their spending is overwhelmingly biased towards Europe and North America. At the turn of the century, total world expenditure on protected areas was estimated to be just under $6 billion. The vast bulk of this, 88 percent, occurred in developed countries (see Table 12.2). In other regions, protected areas attracted much less funding. A recent review of expenditure by NGOs in Sub-Saharan Africa, for example, found that the total annual expenditure by 281 organizations active in 2006 was only $175 million (Brockington and Scholfield 2010).

There are, however, a few relatively large non-governmental conservation organizations that operate globally. The largest of these, the

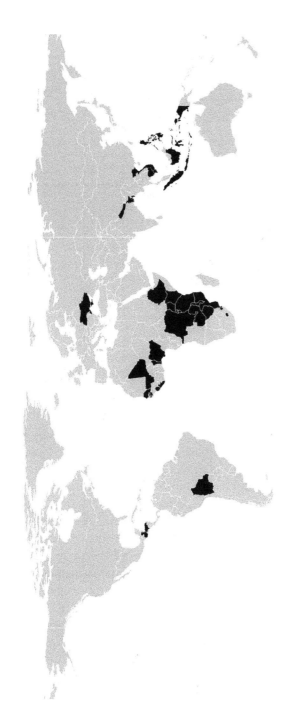

Figure 12.4 United States Global Health Initiative: focus countries (shaded black).
Source: US Global Health Initiative (2012).

Table 12.2 *Aggregate expenditure on protected areas by region* *($ million)*

		% total
North America	3,350	56.14
Europe	1,171	19.62
Australia/New Zealand	297	4.98
East Asia	453	7.59
Latin America	216	3.62
Russia and CIS	51	0.85
North Africa	43	0.72
Africa	245	4.11
Asia	105	1.76
Pacific	35	0.59
Developing regions total	695	11.65
Developed regions total	5,271	88.34
World total	5,967	100.00

Source: James *et al.* (2001); Berry (2007).

Nature Conservancy, has an annual budget of close to $1 billion, approximately the same as the GEF. Other large conservation organizations, the WWF and CI, are significantly smaller. WWF's 2011 budget was just under $240 million. CI, after being substantially funded by the Moore Foundation in its early years, is re-establishing its funding base to meet expenditures around half those of the World Wildlife Fund (WWF). All have a range of funding sources. In the case of WWF, for example, 35 percent of its revenue derives from individual contributions, 25 percent from in-kind revenue, and 18 percent from government contracts. The balance derives from foundations, corporations, and other sources (World Wildlife Fund 2012).

The commitments made by private foundations to the provision of biodiversity-related public goods outside the protected areas are significantly greater. The Gates Foundation, formed in 1994, has become a major force in two dimensions of biodiversity change: agricultural development and health. The motivation of the Foundation is similar in both cases – the failure of both national and international public agencies to address problems of health and nutrition in the poorest countries. The Foundation notes that following the success of the Green Revolution, agriculture in the poorest countries was largely taken off the agenda. From 1980 to 2004, the share of international development assistance devoted to agriculture declined from around 16 percent to less than 4 percent. Nor was the decline in development assistance compensated by an increase in local government expenditures. The result was a growing productivity gap between farmers in Africa, South Asia, East Asia, and North America. The proximate causes of this lie in the failure to manage agricultural pests and pathogens, nutrient flows, and the genetic diversity of crops and livestock strains. The underlying causes are many, but they include the reduction in public investment in agricultural research and development and in basic extension services. The Foundation has programs in both (Gates Foundation 2011).

Similarly, the Gates Foundation motivates its interventions in global health by reference to a long-established practice of private foundations intervening where governments and markets have both failed, citing the Rockefeller Foundation and the Wellcome Trust as examples. The specific problem the Gates Foundation seeks to address is the disparity in health outcomes between rich and poor countries induced by underinvestment by governmental and intergovernmental organizations alike in the health care needed to combat infectious diseases and the health of women and children, and its major programs focus on these two problems (Gates Foundation 2010).

In agriculture the primary problem addressed is the management of pests and pathogens, crop species, and livestock strains in ecosystems that have been simplified to enhance their value to people. The conversion of natural habitat to allow the expansion of agriculture is one of the main drivers of habitat loss, but the simplification of agro-ecosystems is also the source of productivity gains that have underpinned all other development. As was noted in Chapter 2, the biodiversity costs of land conversion, habitat fragmentation, nutrient and pesticide use, and invasive species are one part of the benefit–cost calculus of agricultural growth. The benefits from specializing ecosystems for the production of foods, fuels, fibers, pharmaceuticals, and other products are another. Farmers have increased the relative abundance of species with more desirable traits, and decreased the relative abundance of species with less desirable traits. They do not always make the best choice from the perspective of society. This may be because of market failures that encourage farmers to ignore the external effects of farming technologies, or preclude them from accessing the most effective technologies. Or it may be because of policies that discourage conservation of wild crop relatives, landraces, and traditional livestock strains. The Gates Foundation's investments in this area are designed to improve the options available to farmers in Sub-Saharan Africa and South Asia through plant and animal breeding and transgenic design, and through the development of what are effectively extension services (Gates Foundation 2011).

The second of the Gates Foundation's foci, health, addresses another dimension of biodiversity change – that associated with macroparasites (protozoa and helminthes) and microparasites (viruses and bacteria). The Foundation's major programs are focused on two areas: infectious diseases (enteric and diarrheal diseases, HIV/AIDS, malaria, neglected diseases, pneumonia, polio, and tuberculosis), and the health and nutrition of mothers and infants. The Foundation does not motivate the program in the way that the President motivated the Global Health Initiative – that the first line of defense in the health of Americans lies in the health of people in poor countries. Instead, it is motivated by reference to the differences in disability-adjusted life years lost in rich and poor countries to a range of common diseases including enteric and diarrheal diseases, HIV/AIDS, malaria, maternal/neonatal diseases, pneumonia, polio, tuberculosis, and a set of "neglected" diseases (Gates Foundation 2010). It is nevertheless consistent with the Global Health Initiative. Up to 2009 the Foundation had committed $13 billion to the program, distributed between these diseases as described in Table 12.3.

To date, the Gates Foundation has committed a total of $15.27 billion to health programs, $3.6 billion to global development (including the agricultural programs), and some $6.2 billion to programs within the USA. In 2010 the Foundation's assets were of the order of $34 billion deriving mainly from the Gates family and Warren Buffett who, since 2006, has annually transferred shares to the Gates Foundation with a value varying between $1.2 billion and $1.8 billion. The assets of the Foundation support annual grants of approximately $2 billion. This makes the Gates Foundation a source of funds for the provision of global public goods roughly equivalent to the WHO and roughly twice the size of the GEF.

Table 12.3 *Gates Foundation grant commitments (1994–2009) by global health program area*

Disease-specific program area	US$	% of total
HIV	2,200,275,199	17
Malaria	1,660,326,554	13
Neglected diseases	986,052,620	7
Tuberculosis	886,991,353	7
Diarrheal and enteric diseases	374,108,686	3
Pneumonia	474,450,398	4
Maternal, neonatal, and child health	830,793,255	6
Family planning	561,438,286	4
Nutrition	377,710,368	3
Tobacco	95,743,839	1
Advocacy	1,195,824,574	9
Delivery	1,863,483,538	14
Polio	815,622,746	6
Discovery	490,258,201	4
Special initiatives	303,029,362	2
Total	13,058,936,861	100

Source: Gates Foundation (2010).

12.5 Coordination

The first two sources of funding for the provision of international environmental public goods involve nation states, either operating individually or collectively through multilateral agreements. The third involves members of civil society. Nation states have undoubtedly made important contributions to the provision of a number of international environmental public goods. Indeed, for some there are few alternatives. In his evaluation of the incentives to cooperate in the provision of global public goods, Scott Barrett writes: "The supply of global public goods relies on the leadership of the big, rich and powerful states. When their efforts succeed, the poorest states benefit. Smallpox eradication benefitted every state, but . . . it benefitted the weakest and poorest states the most" (Barrett 2007b). But nation states have also shown that they are vulnerable to the curse of free-riding. Any contribution they may make to the provision of international public goods is determined by an assessment of the national interests at stake – weighed in terms of political cost. As Barrett observes, the failure of the big, rich, and powerful states to intervene to prevent genocide in Rwanda, or to provide vaccines for readily preventable diseases in other parts of Africa, rested on the perception that inaction carried no great political price and did not directly threaten their own citizens. Indeed, the political price may well have been higher with action. In tight financial conditions the constituents of many national governments have shown themselves only too willing to penalize government expenditures that are aimed at providing global benefits.

The lesson of the work of the Gates Foundation and the non-governmental conservation organizations is that global public goods need not only be in the hands of Barrett's "big, rich and powerful states." The problems that are being addressed by private foundations and NGOs are normally regarded as the *raison d'être* of government – market failure and the provision of public goods. Indeed, the Gates Foundation states clearly that it is addressing both things because governments have failed to do so. Moreover, even when the governments of richer countries have got together to establish bodies to undertake collective action on their behalf, they have then starved those bodies of resources. Of course the concentrated wealth behind the Gates Foundation is extremely unusual, and there are few other private foundations with the kind of resources it commands. But there are other players in the field whose resource base, though not quite as large, allows them to have a significant role in the provision of international environmental public goods. Collectively they command resources that, while much smaller than the resources available to national governments, are significantly greater than the resources granted by national governments to the intergovernmental bodies established to provide global environmental public goods.

Not surprisingly, the degree to which non-governmental and governmental efforts are coordinated is limited. The stated aims of organizations like the Gates Foundation are to complement both governmental and intergovernmental bodies. A number of conservation NGOs are dependent on government for at least part of their revenue, and if this involves a contractual obligation to provide services it ensures that their activities are complementary to those of governments. The scope for coordination is, however, more limited than it is in the case of governmental organizations.

There is often a tighter relation between governmental and inter-governmental bodies. The relationship between the CDC and the WHO, for example, is built around shared objectives in multiple campaigns to identify and manage disease outbreaks, along with shared personnel and a commitment on the part of the CDC to support the WHO's capacity-building role under the IHR. Nonetheless, the CDC is an agency of the US government, and the WHO is an agency of the UN and the 192 countries it represents, which means they will not always be pulling in the same direction.

Differences in institutional objectives and limitations in the scope for coordinated action in turn mean that we get only part way towards the globally optimum. In the stylized story of Figure 12.2 the full incremental cost of conservation is determined by the difference between the benefits to the global community and the benefits to the country making the investment in conservation. In practice, there are many interests embedded in the global community, and a calculation of the difference in incremental costs and benefits to each of these interests will not always yield the same end result. For some, the additional benefits gained from an additional unit of conservation will not outweigh the incremental cost, and they will prefer to free-ride. So in practice the aim is to get as close to the social optimum as possible, given the constraints within which all parties work. The world in which international environmental public goods are provided is very much a world of the second best.

Dasgupta distinguishes between utopia, a world characterized by a globally efficient allocation of resources, and kakotopia, a world characterized by myopia, corruption, and incompetence (Dasgupta 2001). In between is the world of good enough, a world in which a globally efficient allocation of resources may not be attainable, and social objectives require only that certain minimum criteria are satisfied. Those criteria may change over time as social aspirations and tolerances change. In some cases change is led by nation states, in others by civil society. The advent of private foundations and NGOs committed to the global public good reflects a change in civil society's tolerance for the degradation of environmental assets that are perceived as the birthright of all, and in the differential effects that has on the wellbeing of many. The Gates's own epiphany was apparently stimulated by a newspaper article on rotavirus, and the revelation that a disease as preventable as diarrhea was killing hundreds of thousands of children in the poorest countries, largely because of neglect (Gates Foundation 2010). Similar convictions are what motivate millions of others to support NGOs aimed at protecting global public goods wherever they can – often in the interstices between government indifference and private avarice.

Part II of this book has been about the options for managing biodiversity change, recognizing that the main driver of change is the interests that people have in the services provided by other species. It offers not a counsel of perfection, but an indication of where it is possible to do better: in projecting the future consequences of current actions, in estimating the value of environmental change, in using the best available information to make decisions where there is fundamental uncertainty, in changing the incentives to private resource users, and in funding international environmental public goods. Much is known, in abstract, about the optimal provision of public goods. But even though the GEF was founded on a principle, the incremental cost principle, that is wholly consistent with the theory of public good provision, we have seen that the reality is that it operates a different set of rules. The funding of international environmental public goods reflects the same strategic behavior that marks the funding of other international public goods. Nation states make funding decisions based on their own interests, and in most cases this means that international public goods are under-supplied. The effect differs from one public good to the next for the simple reason that the strategic interests of nation states differ from one public good to the next. In some cases – best-shot public goods such as the provision of information on global infectious disease threats – the difference between the non-cooperative Nash equilibrium outcome and the cooperative outcome may be very small. In others – additive public goods such as climate regulation through carbon sequestration – the difference can be very large.

The next chapter considers how the strategic interests of nation states affect the capacity of multilateral agreements to coordinate national provision of biodiversity-related international public goods. What I have sought to show in this chapter is that these are not the only options. At this point in world history, nation states are still the dominant decision bodies in the system of global governance, each representing a well-defined constituency of nationals. But there is emerging a constituency that spans national boundaries, and that does not approach the provision of international environmental public goods with the same strategic interests in mind. Judged in terms of the resources they bring to the problem, the combination of private foundations and international

NGOs is every bit as significant as the intergovernmental bodies created by nation states. While such bodies necessarily have to operate within the institutional framework created by nation states, they exist because nation states are unable to transcend the narrower interests of the majority of their constituents. In some cases, NGOs of this kind espouse an ecocentric or biocentric ethic that assigns primacy to the interests of wild-living species, in others they maintain an anthropocentric perspective but seek the wellbeing of humankind in general, rather than the wellbeing of particular national, tribal, racial, or cultural groups. Whatever their motivation, they are able to focus on the provision of public goods whose benefits cannot be captured by individual nation states. For many international environmental public goods "doing better" may mean relying more heavily on bodies of this kind.

References

Arriagada, R. and Perrings, C. (2011) Paying for international environmental public goods. *Ambio*, 1–9.

Barrett, S. (1994) The biodiversity supergame. *Environmental and Resource Economics*, 4, 111–122.

(2003a) *Environment and Statecraft: The Strategy of Environmental Treaty-Making*. Oxford University Press.

(2003b) Global disease eradication. *Journal of the European Economic Association*, 1, 591–600.

(2007a) *Why Cooperate? The Incentive to Supply Global Public Goods*. Oxford University Press.

(2007b) The smallpox eradication game. *Public Choice*, 130, 179–207.

Berry, P. M. (2007) *Adaptation Options on Natural Ecosystems: A Report to the UNFCCC Secretariat Financial and Technical Support Division*. Environmental Change Institute, University of Oxford.

Brockington, D. and Scholfield, K. (2010) Expenditure by conservation nongovernmental organizations in sub-Saharan Africa. *Conservation Letters*, 3, 106–113.

Centers for Disease Control (2012a) *Global Health – Global Disease Detection and Emergency Response*. Available at www.cdc.gov/globalhealth/gdder/gdd/ (accessed 2012).

(2012b) *Centers for Disease Control and Prevention (CDC) FY 2013 Budget Request Summary*. Available at www.cdc.gov/fmo/topic/Budget Information/index.html (accessed 2012).

Conservation International, Conservation International, Pew Trust, The Nature Conservancy, Wildlife Conservation Society and World Wildlife Fund (2010) *International Conservation Budget*. Conservation International, Pew Trust, The Nature Conservancy, Wildlife Conservation Society, World Wildlife Fund, Washington, DC.

Dasgupta, P. (2001) *Human Well-being and the Natural Environment*. Oxford University Press, New York.

Gates Foundation (2010) *Global Health Strategy Overview*. Gates Foundation, Seattle.

(2011) *Agricultural Development Strategy Overview*. Gates Foundation, Seattle.

Global Environment Facility (2011) *Instrument for the Establishment of the Restructured Global Environment Facility*. GEF, Washington, DC.

Hampton, J. (1987) Free-rider problems in the production of collective goods. *Economics and Philosophy*, 3, 245–273.

Holzinger, K. (2001) Aggregation technology of common goods and its strategic consequences: global warming, biodiversity, and sitting conflicts. *European Journal of Political Research*, 40, 117–138.

(2008) Treaty formation and strategic constellations. A comment on treaties: strategic considerations. *University of Illinois Law Review*, 1, 187–200.

James, A., Gaston, K. and Balmford, A. (2001) Can we afford to conserve biodiversity? *Bioscience*, 51, 43–52.

Jones, K. E., Patel, N., Levy, M., Storeygard, A., Balk, D., Gittleman, J. L. and Daszak, P. (2008) Global trends in emerging infectious diseases. *Nature*, 451, 990–993.

Kaul, I., Grunberg, I. and Stern, M. (1999) Defining global public goods. *Global Public Goods: International Cooperation in the 21st Century* (ed. I. Kaul, I. Grunberg and M. Stern). Oxford University Press.

Morrissey, O., te Velde, D. and Hewitt, A. (2002) Defining international public goods: conceptual issues. *International Public Goods: Incentives, Measurement, and Financing* (ed. M. Ferroni and A. Mody). Kluwer Academic Publishers, Dordrecht.

Obama, B. (2009) *Statement by the President on the Global Health Initiative*. Available at www.whitehouse.gov/the_press_office/Statement-by-the-President-on-Global-Health-Initiative (accessed 2012).

Ostrom, E. (1990) *Governing the Commons: The Evolution of Institutions for Collective Action*. Cambridge University Press.

Pearce, D. W. (2003) The social cost of carbon and its policy implications. *Oxford Review of Economic Policy*, 19, 362–384.

(2005) Paradoxes in biodiversity conservation. *World Economics*, 6, 57–69.

Perrings, C., Mooney, H., Lonsdale, M. and Burgeil, S. (2010a) Globalization and invasive species: policy and management options. *Bioinvasions and Globalization: Ecology, Economics, Management and Policy* (ed. C. Perrings, H. Mooney and M. Williamson), pp. 235–250. Oxford University Press.

Perrings, C., Burgiel, S., Lonsdale, W. M., Mooney, H. and Williamson, M. (2010b) International cooperation in the solution to trade-related invasive species risks. *Annals of the New York Academy of Sciences*, 1195, 198–212.

Perrings, C., Naeem, S., Ahrestani, F., Bunker, D. E., Burkill, P., Canziani, G., Elmqvist, T., Ferrati, R., Fuhrman, J., Jaksic, F., Kawabata, Z., Kinzig, A., Mace, G. M., Milano, F., Mooney, H., Prieur-Richard, A.-H., Tschirhart, J. and Weisser, W. (2011) Ecosystem services, targets, and indicators for the conservation and sustainable use of biodiversity. *Frontiers in Ecology and the Environment*, 9, 512–520.

Sandler, T. (2004) *Global Collective Action*. Cambridge University Press.

(2008) Treaties: strategic considerations. *University of Illinois Law Review*, 1, 155–180.

Touza, J. and Perrings, C. (2011) Strategic behavior and the scope for unilateral provision of transboundary ecosystem services that are international environmental public goods. *Strategic Behavior and the Environment*, 1, 89–117.

United Nations (1993) *Convention on Biological Diversity*. United Nations, New York.

US Global Health Initiative (2012) *Global Health Initiative, In Country*. Available at www.ghi.gov/country/ (accessed 2012).

World Health Organization (2005) *International Health Regulations*. World Health Organization, Geneva.

World Wildlife Fund (2012) *Funding and Financial Overview*. Available at www.worldwildlife.org/who/financialinfo/index.html (accessed 2012).

Zimsky, M., Fonseca, G., Cavelier, J., Gaul, D., Sinnassamy, J.-M., Watanabe, Y. and Yang, M. (2008) *Financing the Stewardship of Global Biodiversity*. Global Environment Facility, Washington, DC.

(2013) The Global Environment Facility: financing the stewardship of global biodiversity. *Encyclopedia of Biodiversity*, 2nd edn (ed. S. A. Levin), pp. 136–143. Academic Press, Waltham.

13 | *Strengthening the biodiversity-related multilateral agreements*

13.1 Identifying the biodiversity-related multilateral agreements

Nation states are not the only bodies capable of securing international environmental public goods, but they are still the most important. The standard approach to the provision of environmental public goods that span national boundaries is through multilateral agreements between nation states. The primary multilateral agreement for biodiversity change is the Convention on Biological Diversity (CBD). However, the CBD is only one among many multilateral agreements concerned with biodiversity change. There are several global agreements addressing different aspects of biodiversity conservation. Aside from the CBD these comprise the Convention on Migratory Species (CMS), the Convention on International Trade in Endangered Species (CITES), the International Treaty on Plant Genetic Resources (ITPGRFA), the Ramsar Convention on Wetlands, and the UNESCO World Heritage Convention (WHC). All are associated through the Biodiversity Liaison Group.

But these agreements too are just the tip of the iceberg. The international environmental agreements database project lists 522 MEAs (plus 412 amendments and 196 protocols) signed in the last one hundred and fifty years, the earliest among them addressing the regulation of fisheries in the Rhine (1877) and the North Sea (1882, 1884), and measures to combat the phylloxera outbreak that devastated the vineyards of Europe in the late nineteenth century (1881, 1882). The list includes 255 agreements for the management of particular species or groups of species, 157 concerned with the conservation of flora and fauna, and 30 concerned with the conservation of landscapes, seascapes, and habitat (Mitchell, 2002–2012). Most of these agreements have been signed within the last fifty years, and nearly a third of all agreements, amendments, and protocols were signed during the 1990s (see Figure 13.1).

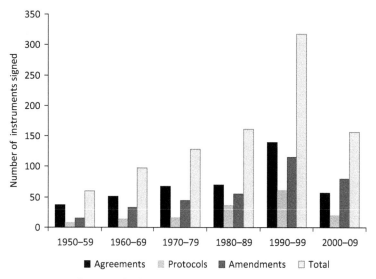

Figure 13.1 The growth of MEAs, 1950–2009.
Source: Mitchell (2002–2012).

While there are many conservation conventions, the bulk of MEAs relate to the production of goods and services, dealing either with the environmental effects of production or with the regulation of economically important natural resources. There are also a number of global agreements that, while not directly concerned with biodiversity change, nonetheless address important dimensions of the problem.[1]

This chapter considers the role of multilateral agreements in addressing the international environmental public goods affected by biodiversity change. It considers agreements of both sorts – the conservation conventions represented by the CBD, and those more directly concerned with the impact of biodiversity change on plant and animal health (e.g. the SPS Agreement) and the harvest of wild-living species (e.g. UNCLOS). There are two main points at issue. One is the relative effectiveness of different kinds of multilateral agreement, and the way that effectiveness evolves over time. A second is the relationship among agreements. The chapter first considers the generic problems of securing agreement on the provision

---

[1] Agreements of global significance in this category include the Law of the Sea; the Desertification and Climate Change Convention; the Convention for the Conservation of Antarctic Marine Living Resources; the Plant Protection Convention; the SPS Agreement; and the International Health Regulations.

of international environmental public goods, and then evaluates the particular challenges confronting agreements whose responsibilities intersect.

The point has already been made that several characteristics seem to be strongly correlated with the effectiveness of multilateral agreements – as measured by their capacity to deliver benefits over and above the non-cooperative outcome. One is the number of parties to the agreement. The greater the net benefits of cooperation, the smaller the number of countries that can sustain the cooperative outcome (Barrett 1994). This follows from the fact that the incentive to defect from an agreement is related to the losses that individual countries experience by complying. Agreements that deliver significant social benefits involve significant private costs. Another is the disincentives within the agreement for parties to defect from the terms of the agreement (Sandler 2004). A third is the frequency with which parties interact, since repeated interactions encourage cooperative behavior. So we have seen that the most effective multilateral agreements involve a small number of parties, repeated renegotiation, and effective penalties for defection from a precisely defined set of objectives (Barrett 2003, 2007).

The success of multilateral agreements in bringing about improvements in the supply of transboundary environmental public goods turns out to be highly variable across agreements and over time (Mitchell 2003). There are, however, a few commonalities to be found in the record of MEAs to this point (Touza and Perrings 2011). The first is that the agreement initially signed and submitted to governments for ratification is often quite close to the non-cooperative outcome. Moreover, this is true even of agreements that have later been perceived as highly effective. For example, the Montreal Protocol on Substances that Deplete the Ozone Layer initially required only the voluntary reductions on CFC levels that signatories were already undertaking prior to the treaty taking effect (Ringquist and Kostadinova 2005; Murdoch and Sandler 2009). Similarly, the 1985 Helsinki protocol to the Long Range Transboundary Air Pollution Convention required reductions in SO_2 emissions that signatories had largely already achieved by the time the treaty was signed (Murdoch, Sandler and Sargent 1997).

The aim in such cases was to get countries to commit to a process that, over time, could deliver benefits beyond the non-cooperative outcome. If the starting conditions are innocuous, countries are more willing to commit to the process than if they are not. Many such agreements have been strengthened through successive negotiations to the point where they now offer significantly greater benefits than the non-cooperative outcome. The key to success in such cases lies in the effect of repeated negotiation on the relative payoff to cooperation as countries compare the short-term gains from defection and the potential long-term losses that may result from retaliation (Barrett 2003; Sandler 2004; Dombrowsky 2007). The best examples of this are probably the Montreal Protocol, the London Dumping Convention on Radioactive Wastes, and the IHR (which will be discussed in more detail later in this chapter) (Touza and Perrings 2011).

A second commonality is that size always matters. Agreements involving fewer parties are initially more effective than agreements involving many parties, and typically remain more effective over successive renegotiations. There are several reasons why this occurs, but one that stands out is that agreements among fewer parties frequently have stronger enforcement mechanisms than agreements among many parties. The evidence also suggests that the advantages of size can be achieved by modularizing agreements involving many parties. The 1995 UN Fish Stocks Agreement, for example, allows straddling/highly mobile stocks to be managed on a region-by-region basis through Regional Fisheries Management Organizations (RFMOs). This has substantially improved outcomes for affected fish stocks, the Norwegian spring spawning herring stock being a good example (Munro 2000, 2008). The converse of this is that agreements involving many parties are frequently unable to achieve significant benefits over and above the non-cooperative outcome. The CBD and the UNCLOS are often cited examples. In such cases, since the gains from cooperation are small, so is the incentive to defect (Barrett 1994, 2003).

The relationship among agreements has not been considered in as much detail. We have seen that the interdependence between jointly produced ecosystem services has implications for their management, but have not considered what this might mean for their governance at the international scale. This is the problem addressed in the balance of the chapter. It considers the question of how multilateral agreements on distinct issues interact, and what this implies for their effectiveness. This is discussed in the context of the CBD's Aichi targets (the targets agreed in 2010 at the Tenth Conference of the Parties in Nagoya in the Prefecture of Aichi), and the vexed question of the relationship between trade and the dispersion of alien invasive species. It also considers multilateral agreements that cover all aspects of the use of a single ecosystem type, such as the UNCLOS.

13.2 The Convention on Biological Diversity's Aichi targets

In 1992, the global community entered into a commitment, through the CBD, for

> the conservation of biological diversity, the sustainable use of its components and the fair and equitable sharing of the benefits arising out of the utilization of genetic resources, including by appropriate access to genetic resources and by appropriate transfer of relevant technologies, taking into account all rights over those resources and to technologies, and by appropriate funding. (Convention on Biological Diversity 1993, Article 1)

The core obligations of the parties to the CBD are the conservation commitments entered into under Article 8 (see Table 13.1). Ten years later, the parties to the convention committed themselves to an ambitious target: "to achieve by 2010 a significant reduction of the current rate of biodiversity loss at the global, regional and national level as a contribution to poverty alleviation and to the benefit of all life on Earth." We now know that the global community comprehensively failed to achieve the CBD's 2010 target (Butchart *et al.* 2010).

To many this provides proof that the CBD is weak by design – unable to achieve significant benefits over and above the non-cooperative outcome. It was, for example, observed that the 2010 target itself was both vague and unrelated to any strategic plan of action for its achievement (Mooney and Mace 2009). The 2010 target was certainly consistent with the very "soft law" approach of the CBD, in which countries are obliged by the terms of the agreement only "as far as possible and as appropriate."[2] The fact that the convention is large (there are 193 parties), that it does not have disincentives to defect from its objectives, and that its objectives are far from precise has been taken as evidence of the difficulty of getting large numbers of countries to sign up to any agreement that offered anything very different from the non-cooperative outcome (Barrett 1994, 2003). It has been observed, for example, that even though governments have committed to many of the things needed to mainstream biodiversity and ecosystem services through the terms of the CBD, the agreement lacks the accountability and compliance mechanisms needed to turn these commitments into action (Kok *et al.* 2010).

---

[2] Soft law refers to instruments that are not legally binding. Most international agreements fall into this category.

Table 13.1 *CBD obligations under Article 8*

Article 8	Obligation
(a)	Establish a system of protected areas or areas where special measures need to be taken to conserve biological diversity
(b)	Develop, where necessary, guidelines for the selection, establishment and management of protected areas or areas where special measures need to be taken to conserve biological diversity
(c)	Regulate or manage biological resources important for the conservation of biological diversity whether within or outside protected areas, with a view to ensuring their conservation and sustainable use
(d)	Promote the protection of ecosystems, natural habitats, and the maintenance of viable populations of species in natural surroundings
(e)	Promote environmentally sound and sustainable development in areas adjacent to protected areas with a view to furthering protection of these areas
(f)	Rehabilitate and restore degraded ecosystems and promote the recovery of threatened species, *inter alia*, through the development and implementation of plans or other management strategies
(g)	Establish or maintain means to regulate, manage or control the risks associated with the use and release of living modified organisms resulting from biotechnology which are likely to have adverse environmental impacts that could affect the conservation and sustainable use of biological diversity, taking also into account the risks to human health
(h)	Prevent the introduction of, control, or eradicate those alien species which threaten ecosystems, habitats or species
(i)	Endeavour to provide the conditions needed for compatibility between present uses and the conservation of biological diversity and the sustainable use of its components
(j)	Subject to its national legislation, respect, preserve and maintain knowledge, innovations and practices of indigenous and local communities embodying traditional lifestyles relevant for the conservation and sustainable use of biological diversity and promote their wider application with the approval and involvement of the holders of such knowledge, innovations, and practices and encourage the equitable sharing of the benefits arising from the utilization of such knowledge, innovations and practices
(k)	Develop or maintain necessary legislation and/or other regulatory provisions for the protection of threatened species and populations
(l)	Where a significant adverse effect on biological diversity has been determined pursuant to Article 7, regulate or manage the relevant processes and categories of activities
(m)	Cooperate in providing financial and other support for *in situ* conservation outlined in subparagraphs (a) to (l) above, particularly to developing countries

Source: Convention on Biological Diversity (1993).

The reaction of the conference of the parties to the failure to meet the CBD's 2010 target was to establish a strategic plan of action, supported by a set of more precise goals and targets. At the tenth conference of the parties in Nagoya, a strategic plan for the next decade was adopted. The plan is built around a set of five broad goals supported by twenty SMART (specific, measurable, ambitious, realistic and time-bound) targets to be achieved by 2020. These are the Aichi targets (see Table 13.2). Can we expect the global community to be more successful

Table 13.2 *The CBD's Aichi targets*

Address the underlying causes of biodiversity loss by mainstreaming biodiversity across government and society	1 By 2020, at the latest, people are aware of the values of biodiversity and the steps they can take to conserve and use it sustainably.
	2 By 2020, at the latest, biodiversity values have been integrated into national and local development and poverty reduction strategies ...
	3 By 2020, at the latest, incentives, including subsidies, harmful to biodiversity are eliminated, phased out or reformed ...
	4 By 2020, at the latest, governments, business and stakeholders at all levels have taken steps to achieve or have implemented plans for sustainable production ...
Reduce the direct pressures on biodiversity and promote sustainable use	5 By 2020, the rate of loss of all natural habitats, including forests, is at least halved ... and degradation and fragmentation is significantly reduced.
	6 By 2020, all fish and invertebrate stocks and aquatic plants are managed and harvested sustainably ...
	7 By 2020, areas under agriculture, aquaculture and forestry are managed sustainably, ensuring conservation of biodiversity.
	8 By 2020, pollution, including from excess nutrients, has been brought to levels that are not detrimental to ecosystem function and biodiversity.
	9 By 2020, invasive alien species and pathways are identified and prioritized, priority species are controlled or eradicated, and measures are in place to manage pathways to prevent their introduction and establishment.

	10 By 2015 ... anthropogenic pressures on coral reefs, and other vulnerable ecosystems impacted by climate change or ocean acidification are minimized ...
Improve the status of biodiversity by safeguarding ecosystems, species, and genetic diversity	11 By 2020, at least 17 percent of terrestrial and inland water, and 10 percent of coastal and marine areas ... are conserved through ... systems of protected areas ...
	12 By 2020, the extinction of known threatened species has been prevented ...
	13 By 2020, the genetic diversity of cultivated plants and farmed and domesticated animals and of wild relatives ... is maintained ...
Enhance the benefits to all from biodiversity and ecosystem services	14 By 2020, ecosystems that provide essential services, including services related to water, and contribute to health, livelihoods and wellbeing, are restored ...
	15 By 2020, ecosystem resilience and the contribution of biodiversity to carbon stocks has been enhanced, through conservation and restoration ...
	16 By 2015, the Nagoya Protocol on Access to Genetic Resources and the Fair and Equitable Sharing of Benefits arising from their utilization is in force ...
Enhance implementation through participatory planning, knowledge management, and capacity building	17 By 2015, each party has developed, adopted as a policy instrument, and has commenced implementing an effective, participatory, and updated national biodiversity strategy and action plan.
	18 By 2020, the traditional knowledge, innovations and practices of indigenous and local communities relevant for the conservation and sustainable use of biodiversity ... are respected ...
	19 By 2020, the science base and technologies relating to biodiversity its values, functioning, status, and trends, and the consequences of its loss, are improved, widely shared and transferred, and applied.
	20 By 2020, at the latest, the mobilization of financial resources for effectively implementing the Strategic Plan 2011–2020 ... should increase substantially from the current levels ...

Source: Convention on Biological Diversity (2010).

in achieving the Aichi targets than they were in achieving the 2010 target? This is a question about the willingness of the parties to the Convention to undertake the actions needed to make progress towards the targets. Little has changed in terms of the structure of the convention or the incentives it offers to comply with its terms. There is, however, more evidence for the potential damage associated with particular kinds of biodiversity change, such as the genetic erosion of wild crop relatives or the rapid dispersal of emergent zoonotic diseases.

The Aichi targets are a set of specific objectives relating to each of five broad strategic goals. These goals respect the essence of the 2010 target: to improve the status of biodiversity by safeguarding ecosystems, species, and genetic diversity. However, they go beyond that to consider the proximate and underlying causes of biodiversity loss, and the benefits to humankind from conservation. There are goals to counter the underlying causes of biodiversity loss; to reduce the direct pressures on biodiversity and to promote sustainable use; to improve implementation of conservation through participatory planning, knowledge management, and capacity building; and to enhance the distribution of benefits from the sustainable use of biodiversity.

Two evaluations of the targets have considered the demands they make in terms of the timing of responses required, and the interdependence of those responses (Perrings *et al.* 2010c, 2011). Using the typology developed by Mace (Mace *et al.* 2010), the evaluations identified targets relating to: (1) imminent biosecurity threats due either to the collapse of ecosystems or populations, or to the rapid growth of pests or pathogens, (2) longer-term conservation goals, and (3) the scientific, socio-economic, and institutional conditions required to meet both shorter- and longer-term goals. Targets 5, 10, 11–13 in Table 13.2 are associated with longer-term conservation goals. Targets 1–4, 7, 14–20 are associated with supporting scientific or institutional conditions, and targets 6, 8, and 9 address imminent threats. The latter include, for example, targets for invasive pests and pathogens, excessive pollution, and destructive overfishing in sea areas beyond national jurisdiction.

The Aichi targets are clearly a significant step forward from the 2010 target. By asking what is needed beyond an increase in conservation effort, they encourage parties to the CBD to consider both the consequences of conservation for human wellbeing and the conditions that need to be satisfied if the targets are to be met. Conservation is now tied to a number of specific ecosystem services, though there is no clear correspondence between the Aichi targets and the non-marketed ecosystem services marked as declining by the MA. There are targets for carbon sequestration (target 15) and foods, fuels, and fibers (targets 6, 7, and 13), but not for many of the non-marketed cultural and regulating services.

The targets raise interesting and important questions about the governance of international environmental public goods. It is possible for some targets to be achieved by the sum of individual country efforts (such as targets 5 and 8). However, others require collaboration across international agreements and agencies (such as targets 4, 9, and 13). To take an example that will be considered in more detail in the next section, target 9 demands action to limit the effect of trade on alien invasive species. But this requires liaison between a number of MEAs as well as the GATT. Moreover, not all of the Aichi targets are complementary. Some targets trade off against each other, while others have conflicting conservation implications. The diversity that is needed in each case depends both on the set of desired services and on the range of environmental conditions expected. The species that support climate regulation, say, are not the same as the species that support services such as pest resistance or food production (Malhi *et al.* 2008). People have very divergent interests in ecosystem services, and hence in the diversity that supports those services.

One implication of these characteristics of the Aichi targets is that target development and implementation should include all agencies involved with the management of biodiversity and the ecosystem services they support. In most cases multiple agencies share responsibility for the system affected by biodiversity change, and this requires coordination or cooperation between agencies. In the invasive species case to be considered next, where the dispersal of pests or pathogens depends on the world trade network, management of the problem requires coordination with the WTO (and its instruments, the GATT, and the SPS Measures Agreement), the OIE, the IPPC, and the WHO (Perrings *et al.* 2010b). Because different agencies have different goals, however, targets will only be viable if those agencies are willing to compromise on their goals. If agencies set what turn out to be inconsistent targets independently, then those targets will not be met. And where multiple jurisdictions are involved, this could require interaction between multiple agencies – including firms, governmental organizations, and NGOs, intergovernmental organizations, and multilateral agreements (Perrings *et al.* 2011).

The CBD does have a close working relationship with the other conservation conventions: the CITES; the CMS, which supports conservation of terrestrial, marine, and avian migratory species; the ITPGRFA, which addresses the conservation and sustainable use of plant genetic resources for food and agriculture; the Ramsar Convention for the conservation of wetlands of international importance; and the WHC for the conservation of cultural and natural heritage. A liaison group between these conventions offers scope for coordination on conservation issues. However, this is not where the difficult trade-offs involved in meeting the CBD targets are likely to be found.

13.3 Negotiating the relationship between trade and biodiversity change

Consider Aichi target 9: "By 2020, invasive alien species and pathways are identified and prioritized, priority species are controlled or eradicated, and measures are in place to manage pathways to prevent their introduction and establishment." The problem this refers to has been described in some detail in Chapter 7 and elsewhere in this book. It is the dispersion of species as a byproduct of globalization. Not all species dispersed through trade are a problem, but the ones that are – pests and pathogens – have the potential to threaten human, animal, and plant health; to compromise the production of foods, fuels, and fibers; to contaminate water supplies; to disrupt the integrity of ecosystems; and, as is happening now with a number of amphibians, to drive native species to extinction.

In principle, CBD members are obligated to prevent dispersion of harmful organisms from their jurisdiction, and to notify others if it occurs. Article 3 of the CBD (1993), for example, asserts that "States have … the responsibility to ensure that activities within their jurisdiction or control do not cause damage to the environment of other States or of areas beyond the limits of national jurisdiction." Article 14 requires states to notify others of any action or event that is "likely to significantly affect adversely the biological diversity of other States or areas beyond the limits of national jurisdiction." Where damage to other states is imminent or grave, states are required to "initiate action to prevent or minimize such danger or damage" and to "encourage international cooperation to supplement such national efforts and, where appropriate and agreed by the States or regional economic integration organizations concerned, to establish joint contingency plans." Unfortunately, given the soft law nature of the CBD, these obligations have little force.

Chapter 7 gave some inkling of the institutional context within which the problem needs to be addressed. Many multilateral agreements are involved. Aside from the conservation conventions, there are those agreements concerned with the impacts of invasive species in particular sectors, such as agriculture, forestry, aquaculture, fisheries, and health: the OIE, the IPPC, the UN FAO, along with its Compliance Agreement and Code of Conduct for Responsible Fisheries, and the WHO and the IHR. Beyond these are all the agreements dealing with invasion pathways. The most important of these is the GATT administered by the WTO and supporting agreements such as the SPS Agreement and the Agreement on Technical Barriers to Trade. However, they also include a range of institutions dealing with transport and travel: the International Maritime Organization, the International Civil Aviation Organization, the International Air Transport Association and the Law of the Sea.

Since most of these bodies neither coordinate their actions nor cooperate with each other, their sectoral foci and their overlapping responsibilities are both problems. For example, the OIE was set up to address diseases related to livestock and other commercially valuable animal species. The IPPC only deals with pests and diseases of plants. The IHR deal with diseases affecting humans. None is concerned with interactions between the species involved in all three. Nor is there any institution to address the invasive species risks of tourism, emergency aid, and development assistance, military activity, or interbasin water transfers (Perrings *et al.* 2010b).

The effects of invasive species are an externality of international trade – probably the most important externality of trade. This means that the first-best solution to the problems they pose lies in the internalization of that externality. However, national intervention in international trade is constrained by the terms of the multilateral agreement governing trade, the GATT. The GATT does allow temporary trade interdictions where there is a potential threat to human, animal, or plant health under its Article 20. That article is implemented by the SPS Agreement, which specifies the conditions under which individual countries can take action in restraint of trade to protect themselves against animal or plant health risks. The GATT is not, however, the only agreement authorizing trade restrictions. Around twenty of the many MEAs contain provisions that either limit trade in particular species or products, such as the CITES, or that authorize countries to implement trade or travel restrictions or interdictions in particular circumstances, such as the IHR.

In a number of cases, the terms of such agreements turn out to be inconsistent with WTO rules. Since 2001 the WTO's Trade and Environment Committee has been negotiating the relationship between WTO rules and MEAs that contain specific trade obligations, but this only applies to members of the WTO who are also members of the MEA being discussed. While the overlap in membership of the WTO and multilateral agreements that have specific trade obligations is high in some cases, it is not always so (see Table 13.3). So even if agreement is reached about the interpretation of specific trade obligations that is binding on WTO members, it may not apply to anything up to 40 percent of the members of the MEA. The same is true of the multilateral agreements with direct responsibility for trade-related pest and pathogen dispersal, although they may have observer status on the WTO's Environment Committee.[3]

The nature of specific trade obligations in different agreements varies widely. Consider the two agreements most directly concerned with pathogens dispersed through the movement of trade goods or through travel: the IHR (concerned with human diseases), and the SPS Agreement (concerned with non-human animal and plant diseases).

---

[3] Observer status: African, Caribbean and Pacific Group of States (ACP group); Bioversity International; CBD; CITES; European Free Trade Association; the FAO; International Commission for the Conservation of Atlantic Tunas; the IMF; the International Organization for Standardization; the International Trade Centre; the Islamic Development Bank; the Latin American Economic System; the OECD; the Pacific Islands Forum; the Southeast Asian Fisheries Development Center; the UN; the UN Commission for Sustainable Development; the UN Conference on Trade and Development; the UNDP; the UNEP; the UNFCCC; the UN Industrial Development Organization; the World Bank; the World Customs Organization; the World Intellectual Property Organization (WIPO). Requested Observer status: Basel Convention; Cooperation Council for the Arab States of the Gulf; Energy Charter Conference; Gulf Organization for Industrial Consulting; International Tropical Timber Organization; League of Arab States; Organization of Arab Petroleum Exporting Countries; Organization of the Eastern Caribbean States; Organization of the Islamic Conference; Organization of the Petroleum Exporting Countries (OPEC); Montreal Protocol on Substances that Deplete the Ozone Layer; Rotterdam Convention; the WHO.

Table 13.3 *Overlap in membership of WTO and MEAs containing specific trade obligations*

	Total number of non-WTO members party to the MEA	Total number of MEA members
IPCC	34	177
International Commission for the Conservation of Atlantic Tunas	7	48
CITES	31	175
CITES (Bonn Amendment)	26	141
CITES (Gaborone Amendment)	7	87
Commission for the Conservation of Antarctic Marine Living Resources	3	34
Vienna Convention	46	196
Montreal Protocol	46	196
Montreal Protocol (London Amendment)	47	195
Montreal Protocol (Copenhagen Amendment)	45	192
Montreal Protocol (Montreal Amendment)	43	182
Montreal Protocol (Beijing Amendment)	39	166
Basel Convention	36	175
Basel Convention	7	69
Basel Convention Protocol on Liability	4	10
CBD	42	193
Biosafety Protocol	30	160
UNFCCC	44	194
Kyoto Protocol	44	193
International Institute of Tropical Agriculture	2	60
UN Fish Stocks Agreement	15	77
Rotterdam Convention	19	140
Stockholm Convention	33	172

Source: World Trade Organization Committee on the Environment (2011) *Matrix on Trade-Related Measures Pursuant to Selected Multilateral Environmental Agreements.* WT/CTE/W/160/Rev. 5, TN/TE/S/5/Rev. 3. WTO, Geneva.

Although both deal with the effects of disease transmission, and although both allow short-term trade interdiction as a mechanism for controlling disease transmission, their core objectives differ. The aims of the IHR are to provide a public health response to the international spread of disease, albeit in ways that avoid "unnecessary interference with international traffic and trade" (World Health Organization 2005: Article 2). The aims of the SPS are to ensure that the defensive measures taken by members to protect their own animal and plant health do not constitute a barrier to trade (World Trade Organization 1995: Article 2). The agreement is about minimizing the risk posed to trade by national health protection measures allowed under Article 20 of the GATT.

More particularly, the SPS Measures Agreement states that: "sanitary and phytosanitary measures shall not be applied in a manner which would constitute a disguised restriction on international trade" (World Trade Organization 1995: Article 2(3)). It further adds a burden of proof requirement intended to limit the time that trade restrictions can be applied without proof. It requires, for example, that any sanitary or phytosanitary measures be based on scientific principles and that they should not persist in the absence of sufficient scientific evidence. Both agreements allow precautionary restraints on trade of the kind discussed in Chapter 10. However, the intent of the SPS Agreement is primarily to limit the time before the uncertainty over the effects of a pathogen are resolved, and the intent of the IHR is primarily to contain the health risks it poses. The IHR does impose a requirement that the costs of containment should be commensurate with the threat posed by the pathogen, but its primary focus is the damage posed by the disease rather than the damage posed by any disruption of trade or travel.

A second difference between the IHR and the SPS Agreement that is worth flagging lies in the scale of international cooperation each allows. Under the SPS Agreement the disease externalities of trade are dealt with on a bilateral basis. One country is authorized to restrict imports from another country if it suspects that those imports pose a risk to human, animal, or plant health within its own jurisdiction. But there is no scope for the kind of international campaign that the IHR authorizes if there is some risk of a pandemic. There have certainly been campaigns against particular animal diseases undertaken by the OIE. The campaign to eradicate rinderpest has already been mentioned as an example of this

(Normile 2008). But under the SPS Agreement, individual countries are authorized only to take defensive action against trade partners that are thought to pose an imminent threat.

A third difference lies in the emphasis that each agreement places on capacity building. The IHR both impose reporting obligations on countries, and require that they develop the capacity "to detect, assess, notify and report events in accordance with these Regulations" (World Health Organization 2005: Article 5(1)). At the same time, however, they impose an obligation on the WHO to "assist States Parties, upon request, to develop, strengthen and maintain the capacities referred to." Within the SPS Agreement, capacity building is handled on a bilateral basis. Article 9(1) of that agreement contains a requirement that members should "facilitate the provision of technical assistance to other Members, especially developing country Members, either bilaterally or through the appropriate international organizations." Article 9(2) states that

where substantial investments are required in order for an exporting developing country Member to fulfill the sanitary or phytosanitary requirements of an importing Member, the latter shall consider providing such technical assistance as will permit the developing country Member to maintain and expand its market access opportunities for the product involved. (Article 9(2))

A commitment to "consider" bilateral assistance, or to "facilitate" multilateral assistance is much weaker than the obligation on the WHO under the IHR (Perrings *et al.* 2010b).

Given that the SPS Agreement is an instrument of the WTO it is not surprising that its primary focus should be on limiting the effect of trade-related disease risks for international trade. Nor is it surprising that the WTO is anxious to reduce the threat that trade externalities pose to trade liberalization. The history of the GATT is the history of the struggle to liberalize world trade, and the countries that have been leading that struggle are reluctant to allow the existence of externalities to get in the way. The same countries might be willing to intervene in domestic markets to internalize the external costs of domestic trade, but they do not want to put international trade liberalization at risk. The evidence suggests that relatively few countries have been able to use the provisions of the SPS Agreement to protect themselves against the invasive species externalities of trade.

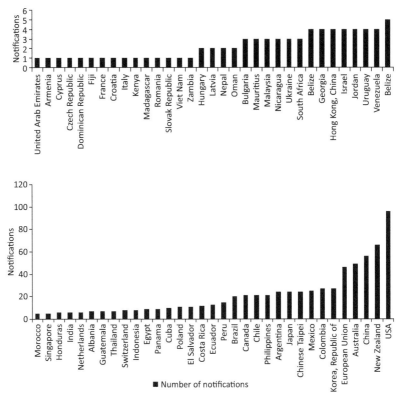

Figure 13.2 Notifications under the SPS Agreement citing animal diseases and zoonoses, 1994–2012.

Historically, developed countries have made much greater use of the provisions of the SPS Agreement than developing countries. Twenty-one of the thirty-eight disputes brought before the WTO (and citing the SPS Agreement) originated with either the USA or Canada. The situation has changed somewhat in recent years as the capacity of developing countries to meet the requirements of the system has developed, but there is still a marked income and regional bias. To illustrate, Figure 13.2 reports the results of a search of the SPS information system for notifications to the SPS Agreement citing either animal diseases or zoonoses, and naming animals and animal products. Of the 776 notifications made to the SPS Agreement for these search criteria since 1994, 47 percent originated with the USA, the EU, Canada, Australia, New Zealand, or Japan. And a further 26 percent originated with countries in Central or South America. There were only six notifications from Sub-Saharan Africa, less than 1 percent, and half of those originated from South Africa.

Because of the difficulty of internalizing international trade externalities of this kind, the emphasis has switched to strengthening national border protection and the monitoring and control of pathways – mainly shipping and air traffic routes. Much recent research has focused on identifying the characteristics of the network structures involved in an attempt to identify optimal intervention points (Tatem, Rogers and Hay 2006a; Tatem, Hay and Rogers 2006b; Kaluza *et al.* 2010). The fact that highly connected seaports and airports not only have many links, but are responsible for the bulk of trade, confirms their importance as potential control points for the management of invasive species (Williamson 1996; Mack *et al.* 2000).

The main vehicle for managing the invasive species risks of marine transport is ballast water control implemented by the IMO under the International Convention for the Control and Management of Ships' Ballast Water and Sediments (2004). But while the ballast water management practices required under the convention are expected to have some impact on the likelihood of the spread of marine organisms, they do not address the risks associated with marine cargoes. For that the only current option is defensive border protection measures and the trade interdictions allowed under the SPS Agreement. Since the latter are beyond the reach of most of the low-income countries, the dispersal of infectious agents through trade or travel remains a weakest-link public good.

To address this I have elsewhere suggested that two developments could be useful. The first would be to extend the range of responses allowable under the SPS Agreement beyond the bilateral defensive measures currently allowed to make it possible for coordinated campaigns against a range of pests and pathogens as allowed under the IHR. The second would be to consider a mechanism to generate and disseminate information on wider invasive species risks. This would enable the more effective use of defensive measures allowed under the SPS Agreement by developing countries, and would support cooperative international action on invasive species that may cause widespread harm to animals and plants (Perrings *et al.* 2010a).

13.4 The problem of resources beyond national jurisdiction

A third set of global environmental public goods that are particularly intractable lie in the (largely marine) ecosystems beyond national jurisdiction. Marine systems are a source of multiple benefits, the most obvious of which are wild harvested and farmed fish and fish products. Other rather less familiar services of marine systems include macroclimatic regulation through carbon sequestration, oxygen production, and the assimilation of waste. The relationship between marine biodiversity and fish production is well understood (Jackson *et al.* 2001; Worm *et al.* 2006). The importance of marine biogeochemical pathways for climate regulation (they are roughly equivalent to terrestrial systems) (Denman *et al.* 2007) and the production of O_2 (Behrenfeld *et al.* 2006) is less well understood. Nevertheless, the direct threat to fish stocks from harvesting is the most frequently cited source of stress in marine systems (Pauly *et al.* 2002; Myers and Worm 2003; Hughes *et al.* 2005; Worm *et al.* 2006). It is not the only stressor cited. Others include bycatch (Lewison *et al.* 2004), loss of habitat (Pyke 2004), and climate change (Hughes *et al.* 2003), and the spread of pathogens (Harvell *et al.* 2004). Nevertheless, marine biologists agree that overexploitation of fisheries is currently a more important driver of biodiversity change in the oceans (excluding coastal zones) than any other factor (Tittensor, Worm and Myers 2006).

The overexploitation of many marine wild capture fisheries tells us much about the global governance of resources beyond national jurisdiction. There is a widespread and long-standing recognition that the origins of the problem lie in the lack of effective regulatory institutions. In the 1950s H. Scott Gordon noted that "most of the problems associated with the words 'conservation' or 'depletion' or 'overexploitation' in the fishery are, in reality, manifestations of the fact that the natural resources of the sea yield no economic rent" (Gordon 1954). In other words they are not owned by anyone, and hence are free to all. Fifty years later, the problem looks much the same (Hilborn, Orensanz and Parma 2005). Yet these are resources that are subject to one of the longest standing multilateral agreements: the UN Convention on the Law of the Sea (UNCLOS) (1958).

The resources directly regulated by the UNCLOS are those in the Area: the seabed and ocean floor beyond the limits of national jurisdiction. These are defined to be the common heritage of mankind

(Article 136). The UNCLOS also asserts the freedom of the high seas to be a fundamental principle (Article 87). Specific freedoms include: freedom of navigation; freedom of overflight; freedom to lay submarine cables and pipelines; freedom to construct artificial islands and other installations permitted under international law; freedom of fishing; and freedom of scientific research. There is limited attention to the environmental consequences of exercising these freedoms, but Article 145 does require member states to ensure effective protection for the marine environment from harmful effects arising from activities in the Area, and commits to establishing rules, regulations, and procedures for

> the prevention, reduction and control of pollution and other hazards to the marine environment, including the coastline, and of interference with the ecological balance of the marine environment ... [and] ... the protection and conservation of the natural resources of the Area and the prevention of damage to the flora and fauna of the marine environment.

From the perspective of fisheries the important provisions of the UNCLOS are those relating to the use of resources within the exclusive economic zone. When the UNCLOS was first agreed the issue of the extent of territorial waters was already a matter of dispute. The United States had declared control of the natural resources of its continental shelf in 1945, and by 1950 Argentina, Chile, Peru, and Ecuador had claimed rights to the Humboldt Current fishing grounds (200 nautical miles). However, the treaty signed in 1958 sidestepped the issue. Over the next ten years most countries extended their territorial waters to 12 miles, and many had signaled their intention to claim 200 nautical miles. The issue was finally addressed in the third UNCLOS, which reached agreement on the 200 nautical mile exclusive economic zone in 1982. As of today, all coastal countries have claimed an EEZ (Table 13.4). In many cases, New Zealand for example, this has dramatically increased the resources under their control.

Under Article 56 of the treaty, the EEZ of a country effectively confers sovereign rights over all of the resources it contains. Specifically it gives countries

> sovereign rights for the purpose of exploring and exploiting, conserving and managing the natural resources, whether living or non-living, of the waters superjacent to the seabed and of the seabed and its subsoil, and with regard to

Table 13.4 *Areas acquired by coastal states as EEZs*

Country	EEZ km²	Country	EEZ km²	Country	EEZ km²
United States	11,351,000	Greece	505,572	Finland	87,171
France	11,035,000	Venezuela	470,666	Bangladesh	86,392
Australia	8,505,348	Vietnam	417,663	Taiwan	83,231
Russia	7,566,673	Ireland	410,310	Eritrea	77,728
United Kingdom	6,805,586	Libya	351,589	Trinidad and Tobago	74,199
New Zealand	6,682,503	Cuba	350,751	East Timor	70,326
Indonesia	6,159,032	Panama	335,646	Sudan	68,148
Canada	5,599,077	Malaysia	334,671	Cambodia	62,515
Japan	4,479,388	Nauru	308,480	Guinea	59,426
Portugal	3,877,408	Equatorial Guinea	303,509	Croatia	59,032
Chile	3,681,989	Republic of Korea	300,851	United Arab Emirates	58,218
Brazil	3,660,955	Thailand	299,397	Germany	57,485
Kiribati	3,441,810	Morocco	274,577	Malta	54,823
Mexico	3,177,593	Egypt	263,451	Estonia	36,992
Micronesia	2,996,419	Turkey	261,654	St.Vincent/ Grenadines	36,302
Denmark	2,551,238	Jamaica	258,137	Belize	35,351
Papua New Guinea	2,402,288	Dominican Republic	255,898	Bulgaria	34,307
Norway	2,385,178	Liberia	249,734	Benin	33,221
India	2,305,143	Honduras	249,542	Qatar	31,590
Marshall Islands	1,990,530	Tanzania	241,888	Congo, Republic	31,017
Philippines	1,590,780	Pakistan	235,999	Poland	29,797
Solomon Islands	1,589,477	Ghana	235,349	Dominica	28,985
South Africa	1,535,538	Saudi Arabia	228,633	Latvia	28,452
Seychelles	1,336,559	Nigeria	217,313	Grenada	27,426
Mauritius	1,284,997	Sierra Leone	215,611	Israel	26,352
Fiji	1,282,978	Gabon	202,790	Romania	23,627
Madagascar	1,225,259	Barbados	186,898	The Gambia	23,112
Argentina	1,159,063	Côte d'Ivoire	176,254	Georgia	21,946

Table 13.4 (*cont.*)

Country	EEZ km²	Country	EEZ km²	Country	EEZ km²
Ecuador	1,077,231	Iran	168,718	Lebanon	19,516
Spain	1,039,233	Mauritania	165,338	Cameroon	16,547
Maldives	923,322	Comoros	163,752	St. Lucia	15,617
China	879,666	Sweden	160,885	Albania	13,691
Somalia	825,052	Senegal	158,861	Togo	12,045
Peru	815,915	Netherlands	154,011	Kuwait	11,026
Colombia	808,158	Ukraine	147,318	Syria	10,503
Cape Verde	800,561	Uruguay	142,166	Bahrain	10,225
Iceland	751,345	Guyana	137,765	Brunei	10,090
Tuvalu	749,790	North Korea	132,826	St. Kitts and Nevis	9,974
Vanuatu	663,251	São Tomé-Príncipe	131,397	Montenegro	7,745
Tonga	659,558	Samoa	127,950	Djibouti	7,459
Bahamas	654,715	Suriname	127,772	Lithuania	7,031
Palau	603,978	Haiti	126,760	Belgium	3,447
Mozambique	578,986	Algeria	126,353	Democratic Republic of Congo	1,606
Costa Rica	574,725	Nicaragua	123,881	Singapore	1,067
Namibia	564,748	Guinea-Bissau	123,725	Iraq	771
Yemen	552,669	Kenya	116,942	Monaco	288
Italy	541,915	Guatemala	114,170	Palestine	256
Oman	533,180	Antigua and Barbuda	110,089	Slovenia	220
Myanmar	532,775	Tunisia	101,857	Jordan	166
Sri Lanka	532,619	Cyprus	98,707	Bosnia-Herzegovina	50
Angola	518,433	El Salvador	90,962		

other activities for the economic exploitation and exploration of the zone, such as the production of energy from the water, currents and winds.

It also confers an obligation to ensure that fisheries within the EEZ are managed efficiently, along with the right to establish the laws and regulations that govern those fisheries.

This includes the right to control fishing activities, to levy fees, to determine the species that may be caught, to fix catch quotas and the age and size of fish that can be caught, to regulate seasons and areas of fishing, the gear and vessels that can be used, and to monitor and enforce the regulation of fishing activity (Article 62). Whether or not the provisions of UNCLOS dealing with fisheries extend beyond the EEZ depends on whether those stocks are exploited. Three articles turn out to be especially important: Articles 63, 64, and 66. They address the conditions in which harvesting of fish stocks beyond the EEZ may be undertaken. First, for stocks occurring both within the EEZ and "beyond and adjacent" to the zone, the coastal state is authorized to fix "the measures necessary for the conservation of these stocks in the adjacent area" either directly or through a regional organization. Second, countries whose nationals fish for highly migratory species[4] are obliged to cooperate "directly or through appropriate international organizations with a view to ensuring conservation and promoting the objective of optimum utilization of such species throughout the region, both within and beyond the exclusive economic zone."

So the UNCLOS strategy has had two main parts to it. One is to legitimize the extension of coastal countries' claims to sovereignty over the resources of the open oceans – at present up to 200 nautical miles off shore – and to charge those countries with responsibility for the conservation and optimal use of those resources. The other is to give the same countries responsibility for negotiating agreements to manage fisheries beyond the current EEZ. To address this second problem the

---

[4] Highly migratory species comprise: albacore tuna: *Thunnus alalunga*; bluefin tuna: *Thunnus thynnus*; bigeye tuna: *Thunnus obesus*; skipjack tuna: *Katsuwonus pelamis*; yellowfin tuna: *Thunnus albacares*; blackfin tuna: *Thunnus atlanticus*; little tuna: *Euthynnus alletteratus*; *Euthynnus affinis*; southern bluefin tuna: *Thunnus maccoyii*; frigate mackerel: *Auxis thazard, Auxis rochei*; pomfrets: family *Bramidae*; marlins: *Tetrapturus angustirostris, Tetrapturus belone, Tetrapturus pfluegeri, Tetrapturus albidus, Tetrapturus audax, Tetrapturus georgei, Makaira mazara, Makaira indica, Makaira nigricans*; sail-fishes: *Istiophorus platypterus, Istiophorus albicans*; swordfish: *Xiphias gladius*; sauries: *Scomberesox saurus, Cololabis saira, Cololabis adocetus, Scomberesox saurus scombroides*; dolphin: *Coryphaena hippurus, Coryphaena equiselis*; oceanic sharks: *Hexanchus griseus, Cetorhinus maximus*, family *Alopiidae*; *Rhincodon typus*; family *Carcharhinidae*; family *Sphyrnidae*; family *Isurida*; cetaceans: family *Physeteridae*, family *Balaenopteridae*, family *Balaenidae*, family *Eschrichtiidae*, family *Monodontidae*, family *Ziphiidae*, family *Delphinidae*.

UNEP has establish a Regional Seas Program for the management of marine and coastal resources. The program now covers eighteen regions with fifty-seven large marine ecosystems (see Figure 13.3).[5]

Most regional seas are now managed through established action plans that are agreed and implemented by member governments, and fourteen have also added legally binding conventions that include protocols to deal with issues such as marine protected areas. A major objective of the Regional Seas Program is the use of regional agreements to achieve conservation goals, to strengthen national property rights, and to coordinate management of the resource (United Nations 2004). The most important manifestation of regional coordination is the RFMO (Table 13.5). There is certainly much to be said for management at a regional scale when the ecosystems being managed span EEZs. In the case of straddling or migratory stocks, for example, the appropriate regional grouping will cover the sea areas within which those stocks move. Matching political, economic, and environmental scales should promote efficiency. Yet, as the FAO has pointed out, the UNCLOS does not confer any management authority on regional fishery bodies. Indeed, in 2004 the FAO considered that many RFMOs were very little different from open access regimes (Food and Agriculture Organization 2004). Nevertheless, the RFMOs are still the preferred instrument for the regulation of fisheries in the high seas. The UN has urged states, through RFMOs, to prohibit destructive practices by vessels under their jurisdiction that have an adverse impact on marine ecosystems in areas beyond national jurisdiction, to address the impact of deep sea bottom trawling, to comply with existing obligations, and to implement the International Plan of Action to Prevent, Deter and Eliminate Illegal, Unreported and Unregulated Fishing adopted by the Committee on Fisheries of the FAO (UN 2004).

The FAO's own instruments include two that are less soft. The FAO Compliance Agreement (1993), and the UN Fish Stocks Agreement (1995) are notionally binding, and do affect some heavily stressed fisheries. The Fish Stocks Agreement, for example, now extends over the

[5] Antarctic, Arctic, Baltic, Black Sea, Caspian, Eastern Africa, East Asian Seas, Mediterranean, Northeast Atlantic, Northeast Pacific, Northwest Pacific, Pacific, Red Sea and Gulf of Aden, Regional Organization for the Protection of the Marine Environment (ROPME) sea area in the Persian Gulf, South Asian Seas, Southeast Pacific, Western Africa, and the Wider Caribbean.

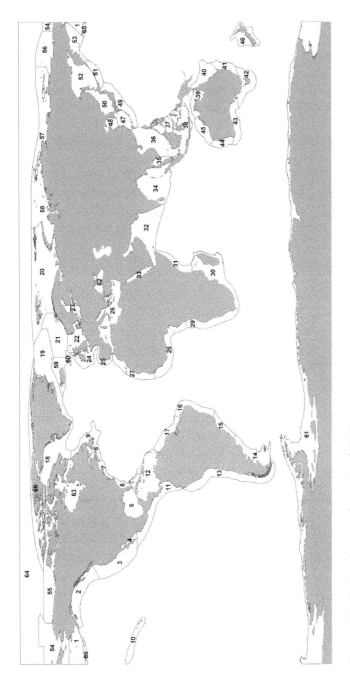

Figure 13.3 Regional seas and associated LMEs

I West and Central Africa
1 Benguela Current
2 Guinea Current
3 Canary Current
II Eastern Africa
4 Agulhas Current
5 Somali Current
III Red Sea and Gulf of Aden
6 Red Sea
IV Mediterranean
7 Mediterranean Sea
V Black Sea
8 Black Sea
VI ROPME Sea Area
9 Arabian Sea
VII South Asian Seas
10 Bay of Bengal
VIII East Asian Seas
11 Gulf of Thailand

12 Indonesian Sea
13 North Australia
14 Northwest Australia
15 South China Sea
16 Sulu Celebes Sea
17 West Central Australia
IX Pacific (SPREP)
18 East Central Australia
19 New Zealand Shelf
20 Northeast Australia
21 Southeast Australia
X Northwest Pacific
22 East China Sea
23 Kuroshio Current
24 Oyashio Current
25 Sea of Japan
26 Sea of Okhotsk
27 West Bering Sea
28 Yellow Sea

XI Arctic
29 Arctic Ocean
30 Beaufort Sea
31 Chukchi Sea
32 East Siberian Sea
33 Kara Sea
34 Laptev Sea
XII Baltic Sea
35 Baltic Sea
XIII North-East Atlantic
36 Barents Sea
37 Celtic-Biscay Shelf
38 Faroe Plateau
39 Greenland Sea
40 Iberian Coastal
41 Iceland-Shelf
42 North Sea
43 Norwegian Sea

XIV The North East Pacific
44 California Current
45 East Bering Sea
46 Gulf of Alaska
47 Gulf of California
48 Pacific Central-American
XV Wider Caribbean
49 Caribbean Sea
50 Gulf of Mexico
51 Southeast US
XVI Southwest Atlantic
52 North Brazil Shelf
53 East Brazil Shelf
54 Patagonian Shelf
55 South Brazil Shelf
XVII South-East Pacific
56 Humboldt Current
XVIII Antarctic
57 Antarctic

Source: Sherman and Hempel (2008).

Table 13.5 *RFMOs*

FAO bodies	
APFIC	Asia-Pacific Fisheries Commission
CECAF	Fishery Committee for the Eastern Central Atlantic
CWP	Coordinating Working Party on Fishery Statistics
GFCM	General Fisheries Commission for the Mediterranean
IOTC	Indian Ocean Tuna Commission
RECOFI	Regional Commission for Fisheries
WECAFC	Western Central Atlantic Fishery Commission

Non-FAO bodies	
AAFC	Atlantic Africa Fisheries Conference
CCAMLR	Commission for the Conservation of Antarctic Marine Living Resources
CCSBT	Commission for the Conservation of Southern Bluefin Tuna
COREP	Regional Fisheries Committee for the Gulf of Guinea (not yet in force)
CPPS	South Pacific Permanent Commission
CTMFM	Joint Technical Commission for the Argentina/Uruguay Maritime Front
FFA	South Pacific Forum Fisheries Agency
IATTC	Inter-American Tropical Tuna Commission
IBSFC	International Baltic Sea Fishery Commission
ICCAT	International Commission for the Conservation of Atlantic Tuna
ICES	International Council for the Exploration of the Sea
IPHC	International Pacific Halibut Commission
IWC	International Whaling Commission
NAFO	Northwest Atlantic Fisheries Organization
NAMMCO	North Atlantic Marine Mammal Commission
NASCO	North Atlantic Salmon Conservation Organization
NEAFC	Northeast Atlantic Fisheries Commission
NPAFC	North Pacific Anadromous Fish Commission
OLDEPESCA	Latin American Organization for the Development of Fisheries
PICES	North Pacific Marine Science Organization
PSC	Pacific Salmon Commission
SEAFO	Southeast Atlantic Fishery Organization
SPC	Secretariat of the Pacific Community
SRCF	Sub-regional Commission on Fisheries
WCPFC	Western and Central Pacific Fisheries Commission
WIOTO	Western Indian Ocean Tuna Organization

Source: Food and Agriculture Organization (2008–2012).

high-seas areas adjacent to the EEZs of fifty-one countries.[6] However, the FAO Code of Conduct for Responsible Fisheries (1995), which offers guidelines to fishing firms, sub-regional, regional, and global organizations, is also voluntary. Although there are four international plans of action agreed under the code, and although it embodies an "Agreement to promote compliance with international conservation and management measures by fishing vessels on the high seas," it does not impose any legally binding obligations.

How effective has this governance structure been? Until 2006 most scientists were reporting a clear decline in yields in many of the world's major fisheries. In that year, a study of catches from 1950 to 2003 within all sixty-four large marine ecosystems (LMEs) worldwide (the source of 83 percent of global catches) reported that the rate of fisheries collapses in these areas had been accelerating, and that 29 percent of fished species were in a state of collapse. The authors concluded that if one were to project these trends the collapse rate would reach 100 percent by 2048 (Worm *et al.* 2006).

Since 2006 a number of studies have appeared that take a more sanguine view of fisheries within the EEZs. A 2008 study of the relation between stocks that had collapsed by the criterion used by Worm *et al.* found a strong negative relationship between the rate at which stocks were collapsing and the use of tradable quota as the relevant management tool (Costello, Gaines and Lynham 2008). Specifically, the rates at which stocks collapsed declined as the proportion of the stock allocated through individual transferable quotas increased. The following year a review of fisheries in a number of LMEs announced that

> after a long history of overexploitation, increasing efforts to restore marine ecosystems and rebuild fisheries are under way... In 5 of 10 well-studied ecosystems, the average exploitation rate has recently declined and is now at or below the rate predicted to achieve maximum sustainable yield for seven systems. (Worm *et al.* 2009)

The year after that, the FAO's biennial review of the state of the world's fisheries observed that between 2005 and 2008 the world catch of fish was stable (Food and Agriculture Organization 2010).

---

[6] The Agreement covers straddling fish stocks and highly migratory fish stocks, and establishes principles for their conservation and management.

On the surface at least this indicates that the regional fishery management strategy devised in the 1970s is bearing fruit. National control of fisheries within the EEZs appears to have allowed harvest to be limited to sustainable levels. So, for example, the Magnuson–Stevens Fishery Conservation and Management Act in the USA (Public Law 94–265) both allows the use of transferable quota, and mandates action where fisheries are overfished. The establishment and extension of EEZs has frequently (but not always) led to a reduction in pressure on stressed resources in those sea areas.

At the same time, however, it has often increased pressure on remaining open access resources as effort has been diverted away from the EEZs. Indeed, the position in sea areas beyond national jurisdiction generally looks quite different. There, the record on epipelagic and deep-water species is full of examples of overexploitation followed by collapse. In its 2004 report on the state of the world's fisheries the FAO reported catches to be declining in twelve regions, in four very sharply. In the northwest Atlantic, for example, total catches had declined by 50 percent since 1968. In the southeast Atlantic, they had fallen by 47 percent since 1978, and in the southeast Pacific by 31 percent since 1994. This was ascribed to overfishing induced in part by rising demand for fish products, and in part by the ineffectiveness of mechanisms for the governance of the high seas (Food and Agriculture Organization 2004). Overfishing of deep-water species was flagged as a particular cause for concern, in large part because of the damage caused by bottom trawling on seamounts, cold-water corals, and deep-water corals. One reason for this trend is precisely the growing effectiveness of management within the EEZs. The tightening of regulations within national jurisdictions was displacing fishing effort on to the high seas where international law and management mechanisms were unable to operate nearly as effectively. The net effect is that the level of fishing effort committed to oceanic species, and to deep-water species in particular, had increased relative to the level of effort in other capture fisheries.

Nor has the position improved since that time. Worm *et al.* noted that although they had observed improvements in the performance of managed stocks, the position was very different in areas beyond national jurisdiction where there was still effectively no control over harvesting rates (Worm *et al.* 2009). The FAO's otherwise largely positive review of the state of the world's fisheries during the recession noted that of twenty-three tuna stocks, around 60 percent were fully exploited, and around 35 percent were overexploited. It also noted that because of substantial demand for tuna and overcapacity in the fleet, things were expected to get worse. It reported that concern about bluefin tuna stocks had reached the point that it was seriously proposed that the species be listed by the CITES (Food and Agriculture Organization 2010).

Since there is no sovereign authority with the right to assign property rights or to levy taxes in sea areas beyond national jurisdiction, it is not possible to use economic incentives of the kind used in the EEZs. Moreover, the problem is made significantly worse by the widespread practice of subsidizing national fleets that exploit the resources of the high seas. Subsidies are currently estimated to be around 20 percent of global fishery revenues. Japan, Russia, South Korea, Spain, and Australia are especially noted for the level of direct subsidies offered to the industry. In all cases the effect of subsidies is to exacerbate the overfishing induced by open access. It follows that even if it is not possible to address the problem of open access to the high seas directly, it would be possible to reduce pressure on the resource by the removal of subsidies to national fishing fleets. While removal of subsidies has been on the agenda for the Doha round of negotiations of the GATT for a decade, nothing has yet happened. A recent proposal to split the world's fisheries between domestic and international fisheries recognizes both that the scope for managing fisheries within the EEZs and in the high seas is very different, and that the incentive to eliminate overfishing subsidies is different in each location (Sumaila 2012).

Even if subsidies on fishing in the high seas were removed, however, there would still be a problem. The extension of national property rights over an increasing proportion of the sea area has led to an improvement in the management of fisheries in those areas. However, it has also increased pressure on the remaining sea areas. There are clearly no easy fixes to this problem. The clauses within the UNCLOS that oblige coastal states to search for solutions to the overexploitation of resources in sea areas beyond national jurisdiction, without providing any incentives to comply, remains a fundamental source of difficulty. Indeed in the absence of a body with the authority to police sea areas beyond national jurisdiction, it is hard to see a solution that does not involve the progressive appropriation of the high seas by coastal states.

13.5 The problem of scale revisited

The proliferation of multilateral agreements in the last two decades of the twentieth century was partly a response to the perception that efficiency in the governance of transboundary problems requires something like the European Union's subsidiarity principle (Golub 1996). Under this principle, authority is devolved to the lowest level consistent with the effectiveness of government. In the European context it implies that the European Union will only act where action by individual countries is ineffective. Since governance at the international level depends on cooperation or coordination between independent actors, formalized through multilateral agreement, the implication is that when management by individual nation states is ineffective, agreement should be sought between the minimum set of countries needed to be effective. It is possible to interpret the Regional Seas Programs and the RFMOs in this light.

The smaller number of parties to these agreements should, in principle, make them more effective than a global agreement such as the UNCLOS. But recall that the number of parties to an agreement is only one of several conditions that affect their ability to deliver benefits over and above the non-cooperative outcome. For agreements to be self-enforcing there need to be incentives discouraging non-compliance from a clear and well-defined set of objectives, along with a process allowing repeated interaction. In areas beyond national jurisdiction there is the additional challenge that members of the RFMOs do not have the capacity to exclude others (Munro 2008). Indeed, the FAO reports that illegal, unreported, and unregulated fishing that cannot be controlled by those organizations is the main challenge to management (Food and Agriculture Organization 2010).

Nonetheless, the establishment of regional bodies has created a structure of governance for the world's oceans that the global agreement, the UNCLOS, has at least until now been unable to provide. The question is whether the same principle can be applied in areas such as the impact of trade on the dispersion of pests and pathogens, and the answer is probably yes. The WTO has encouraged the formation of regional trade agreements. There are currently more than 400 of these. They have at least the potential to address the relation between trade and disease. The most important multilateral bodies for the problem of invasive species may be global agreements: the IHR, the SPS Agreement, and the three agencies that support the SPS Agreement (the Codex Alimentarius Commission for food safety, the International Office of Epizootics for animal health, and the International Plant Protection Convention for plant health). But not all invasive species problems are global. Indeed, since the number of host systems that particular species may successfully invade is generally quite limited, the level at which international cooperation is required may also be limited. Where species dispersal is between countries that are geographically co-located, regional trade agreements could provide a framework for addressing the problem. Where countries are not co-located a network of regional trade agreements may be needed.

To this point, the evidence on the role of regional trade agreements is mixed. In some cases regional trade agreements seem to have exacerbated the problem. There is, for example, reason to believe that the NAFTA has facilitated the spread of species within the free trade area (Perrault *et al.* 2003). At the same time, a number of regional trade agreements include environmental accords, and these can help encourage compliance with environmental laws and harmonize environmental standards between member states. The MERCOSUR, for example, includes an environmental working group charged with eliminating the use of environmental barriers to trade, promoting upward harmonization of environmental management systems, and securing cooperation on shared ecosystems. Many other South–South regional trade agreements, including the Andean Pact, the COMESA, the SADC, the ASEAN AFTA, and CARICOM, are actively seeking to harmonize environmental standards upwards (World Bank 2005).

There are also examples of regional strategies on invasive species.[7] Networks of this kind have a potentially important role in building capacity, and especially in enabling the weakest links in the chain to develop adequate biosecurity systems. More generally, there is scope for delivering benefits over and above the non-cooperative outcome by

---

[7] The European Strategy on Invasive Alien Species under the Bern Convention, and the regional Guidelines for Invasive Species Management in the Pacific and the Caribbean Regional Invasive Species Intervention Strategy. In the latter case, four different institutions are collaborating to support both national and region-wide efforts: the South Pacific Regional Environment Programme (SPREP), the Secretariat of the Pacific Community (SPC), the Pacific Invasives Initiative, and the Pacific Invasives Learning Network. SPREP is charged with helping the region's governments coordinate strategies on invasive species, and has used this to develop a regional strategy and funding program.

reaching agreement at a regional scale. The evidence indicates that the added value of international agreements does not scale with the number of countries involved. Inclusiveness is not always beneficial. Kaul has suggested that a principle of "the equivalence of publicness" be applied to international public goods (Kaul *et al.* 2003). She suggests that the set of stakeholders in a transboundary environmental public good should be matched with the set of participants involved in negotiation over its provision. This is much like the European Union's subsidiarity principle, and can be used to determine the minimum set of countries that need to be involved in the provision of public goods. It is possible to achieve better results with a relatively small group of countries than could be obtained from a global agreement partly because smaller agreements improve the options for using transfers to induce cooperation, and partly because they offer more scope for repeated negotiation. But the real strength of this approach is that it offers the potential for countries to capture more of the benefits of their actions. It does not solve the problem of environmental resources beyond national jurisdiction. Nor does it solve the problem of genuinely global public goods. But it does provide traction on at least some international environmental public goods.

It should not be surprising that the characteristics of MEAs reflect the nature of the public goods at issue. The features of public goods that make it difficult for countries to cooperate in their provision also compromise construction of multilateral agreements on the topic. Where the incentive to free-ride is greatest, as in the case of additive international public goods such as climate regulation or the protection of endangered but widely distributed species, the corresponding multilateral agreements are likely to be weakest. It is possible for multilateral agreements to grow teeth through repeated renegotiation. There is little doubt that the CBD, for example, is more effective now than when it first entered into force. But the limitations of the framework agreements – the CBD, the UNFCCC, and the UNCDD – are the limitations of global public goods characterized by an additive technology of supply.

The rescaling of agreements through modularization, or through the formation of coalitions of countries having shared interests in particular dimensions of public goods, is frequently a way of increasing the nationally capturable benefits of public good supply. This is the advantage offered by the RFMOs, for instance. It is also the advantage offered by regional trade agreements, and the many bilateral or multilateral agreements targeted at particular resources. The challenge for the framework conventions is to develop programs of action that create similar opportunities for collaboration between small numbers of states. It is possible to see the Aichi targets of the CBD in this light. There is greater scope for developing relatively small-scale programs of action around specific targets, or specific protocols, than around general objectives such as the 2010 target. The challenges facing the framework conventions are still orders of magnitude greater than those facing more focused multilateral agreements, but they are not insurmountable.

References

Barrett, S. (1994) The biodiversity supergame. *Environmental and Resource Economics*, 4, 111–122.

(2003) *Environment and Statecraft: The Strategy of Environmental Treaty-Making*. Oxford University Press.

(2007) *Why Cooperate? The Incentive to Supply Global Public Goods*. Oxford University Press.

Behrenfeld, M. J., O'Malley, R. T., Siegel, D. A., McClain, C. R., Sarmiento, J. L., Feldman, G. C., Milligan, A. J., Falkowski, P. G., Letelier, R. M. and Boss, E. S. (2006) Climate-driven trends in contemporary ocean productivity. *Nature*, 444, 752–755.

Butchart, S., Walpole, M., Collen, B., van Strien, A., Scharlemann, J. P. W., Almond, R. E. A., Baillie, J. E. M., Bomhard, B., Brown, C., Bruno, J., Carpenter, K. E., Carr, G. M., Chanson, J., Chenery, A. M., Csirke, J., Davidson, N. C., Dentener, F., Foster, M., Galli, A., Galloway, J. N., Genovesi, P., Gregory, R. D., Hockings, M., Kapos, V., Lamarque, J.-F., Leverington, F., Loh, J., McGeoch, M. A., McRae, L., Minasyan, A., Morcillo, M. H., Oldfield, T. E. E., Pauly, D., Quader, S., Revenga, C., Sauer, J. R., Skolnik, B., Spear, D., Stanwell-Smith, D., Stuart, S. N., Symes, A., Tierney, M., Tyrrell, T. D., Vie, J.-C. and Watson, R. (2010) Global biodiversity: indicators of recent declines. *Science*, 328, 1164–1168.

Convention on Biological Diversity (2010) Revised and updated strategic plan: technical rationale and suggested milestones and indicators. *Conference of the Parties to the Convention on Biological Diversity*, Tenth meeting, Nagoya, Japan, October 18–29. CBD, Montreal.

Costello, C., Gaines, S. D. and Lynham, J. (2008) Can catch shares prevent fisheries collapse? *Science*, 321, 1678–1681.

Denman, K. L., Brasseur, G., Chidthaisong, A., Ciais, P., Cox, P. M., Dickinson, R. E., Hauglustaine, D., Heinze, C., Holland, E., Jacob, D., Lohmann, U., Ramachandran, S., da Silva Dias, P. L., Wofsy, S. C. and

Zhang, X. (2007) Couplings between changes in the climate system and biogeochemistry. *Climate Change 2007: The Physical Science Basis*. Contribution of Working Group I to the Fourth Assessment Report of the Intergovernmental Panel on Climate Change (ed. S. Solomon, D. Qin, M. Manning, Z. Chen, M. Marquis, K. B. Averyt, M. Tignor and H. L. Miller). Cambridge University Press.

Dombrowsky, I. (2007) *Conflict, Cooperation and Institutions in International Water Management: An Economic Analysis*, Edward Elgar, Cheltenham.

Food and Agriculture Organization (2004) *The State of World Fisheries and Agiculture*. FAO, Rome.

(2008–2012) Regional Fishery Bodies (RFB). Available at www.fao.org/fishery/rfb/en (accessed 2012).

(2010) *The State of the World Fisheries and Aquaculture*. FAO, Rome.

Golub, J. (1996) Sovereignty and subsidiarity in EU environmental policy. *Political Studies*, 44, 683–703.

Gordon, H. S. (1954) The economic theory of common-property resources. *Journal of Political Economy*, 62, 124–142.

Harvell, D., Aronson, R., Baron, N., Connell, J., Dobson, A., Ellner, S., Gerber, L., McCallum, H., Lafferty, K., McKay, B., Porter, J., Pascual, M., Smith, G., Sutherland, K. and Ward, J. (2004) The rising tide of ocean diseases: unsolved problems and research priorities. *Frontiers in Ecology and the Environment*, 2, 375–382.

Hilborn, R., Orensanz, J. M. and Parma, A. M. (2005) Institutions, incentives and the future of fisheries. *Philosophical Transactions Royal Society of the London B: Biological Sciences*, 360, 47–57.

Hughes, T., Bellwood, D. R., Folke, C., Steneck, R. S. and Wilson, J. (2005) New paradigms for supporting the resilience of marine ecosystems. *Trends in Ecology and Evolution*, 20, 380–386.

Hughes, T. P., Baird, A. H., Bellwood, D. R., Card, M., Connolly, S. R., Folke, C., Grosberg, R., Hoegh-Guldberg, O., Jackson, J. B. C., Kleypas, J., Lough, J. M., Marshall, P., Nystrom, M., Palumbi, S. R., Pandolfi, J. M., Rosen, B. and Roughgarden, J. (2003) Climate change, human impacts, and the resilience of coral reefs. *Science*, 301, 929–933.

Jackson, J. B. C., Kirby, M. X., Berger, W. H., Bjorndal, K. A., Botsford, L. W., Bourque, B. J., Bradbury, R. H., Cooke, R., Erlandson, J., Estes, J. A., Hughes, T. P., Kidwell, S., Lange, C. B., Lenihan, H. S., Pandolfi, J. M., Peterson, C. H., Steneck, R. S., Tegner, M. J. and Warner, R. R. (2001) Historical overfishing and the recent collapse of coastal ecosystems. *Science*, 293, 629–638.

Kaluza, P., Kölzsch, A., Gastner, M. T. and Blasius, B. (2010) The complex network of global cargo ship movements. *Journal of the Royal Society Interface*, 7, 1093–1103.

Kaul, I., Conceição, P., Le Goulven, K. and Mendoza, R. (2003) How to improve the provision of global public goods. *Providing Global Public Goods: Managing Globalization* (ed. I. Kaul, P. Conceição, K. Le Goulven and R. Mendoza). Oxford University Press.

Kok, M. T. J., Tyler, S. R., Prins, A. G., Pintér, L., Baumüller, H., Bernstein, J., Tsioumani, E., Venema, H. D. and Grosshans, R. (2010) *Prospects for Mainstreaming Ecosystem Goods and Services in International Policies.* Netherlands Environmental Assessment Agency, The Hague.

Lewison, R. L., Crowder, L. B., Read, A. J. and Freeman, S. A. (2004) Understanding impacts of fisheries bycatch on marine megafauna. *Trends in Ecology and Evolution*, 19, 598–604.

Mace, G. M., Cramer, W., Diaz, S., Faith, D. P., Larigauderie, A., Le Prestre, P., Palmer, M. R., Perrings, C., Scholes, R. J., Walpole, M., Walther, B. A., Watson, J. E. and Mooney, H. (2010) Biodiversity targets after 2010. *Current Opinion in Environmental Sustainability*, 2, 1–6.

Mack, R. N., Simberloff, D., Lonsdale, W. M., Evans, H., Clout, M. and Bazzaz, F. A. (2000) Biotic invasions: causes, epidemiology, global consequences, and control. *Ecological Applications*, 10, 689–710.

Malhi, Y., Roberts, J. T., Betts, R. A., Killeen, T. J., Li, W. and Nobre, C. A. (2008) Climate change, deforestation, and the fate of the Amazon. *Science*, 319, 169–172.

Mitchell, R. B. (2003) International environmental agreements: a survey of their features, formation and effects. *Annual Review of Environment and Resources*, 28, 429–462.

(2002–2012) *International Environmental Agreements Database Project* (Version 2012.1). Available at http://iea.uoregon.edu/ (accessed 2012).

Mooney, H. A. and Mace, G. M. (2009) Biodiversity policy challenges. *Science*, 325, 1474.

Munro, G. (2000) The UN Fish Stocks Agreement of 1995: history and problems of implementation. *Marine Resource Economics*, 15, 265–280.

(2008) Game theory and the development of resource management policy: the case of international fisheries. *Environment and Development Economics*, 14, 7–27.

Murdoch, J. C. and Sandler, T. (2009) The voluntary provision of a pure public good and the Montreal Protocol: behavioral and data concerns. *Oxford Economic Papers*, 61, 197–200.

Murdoch, J. C., Sandler, T. and Sargent, K. (1997) A tale of two collectives: sulphur versus nitrogen oxide emission reduction in Europe. *Economica*, 64, 281–301.

Myers, R. A. and Worm, B. (2003) Rapid worldwide depletion of predatory fish communities. *Nature*, 423, 280–283.

Normile, D. (2008) Rinderpest: driven to extinction. *Science*, 319, 1606–1609.

Pauly, D., Chirstensen, V., Guénette, S., Pitcher, T. J., Sumaila, U. R., Walters, C. J., Watson, R. and Zeller, D. (2002) Towards sustainability in world fisheries. *Nature*, 418, 689–695.

Perrault, A., Bennett, M., Burgiel, S., Delach, A. and Muffett, C. (2003) *Invasive Species, Agriculture and Trade: Case Studies from the NAFTA Context*. North American Commission for Environmental Cooperation, Montreal.

Perrings, C., Mooney, H., Lonsdale, M. and Burgeil, S. (2010a) Globalization and invasive species: policy and management options. *Bioinvasions and Globalization: Ecology, Economics, Management and Policy* (ed. C. Perrings, H. Mooney and M. Williamson), pp. 235–250. Oxford University Press.

Perrings, C., Burgiel, S., Lonsdale, W. M., Mooney, H. and Williamson, M. (2010b) International cooperation in the solution to trade-related invasive species risks. *Annals of the New York Academy of Sciences*, 1195, 198–212.

Perrings, C., Naeem, S., Ahrestani, F., Bunker, D. E., Burkill, P., Canziani, G., Elmqvist, T., Ferrati, R., Fuhrman, J., Jaksic, F., Kawabata, Z., Kinzig, A., Mace, G. M., Milano, F., Mooney, H., Prieur-Richard, A.-H., Tschirhart, J. and Weisser, W. (2010c) Ecosystem services for 2020. *Science*, 330, 323–324.

Perrings, C., Naeem, S., Ahrestani, F., Bunker, D. E., Burkill, P., Canziani, G., Elmqvist, T., Ferrati, R., Fuhrman, J., Jaksic, F., Kawabata, Z., Kinzig, A., Mace, G. M., Milano, F., Mooney, H., Prieur-Richard, A.-H., Tschirhart, J. and Weisser, W. (2011) Ecosystem services, targets, and indicators for the conservation and sustainable use of biodiversity. *Frontiers in Ecology and the Environment*, 9, 512–520.

Pyke, C. R. (2004) Habitat loss confounds climate change impacts. *Frontiers in Ecology and the Environment*, 2, 171–182.

Ringquist, E. J. and Kostadinova, T. (2005) Assessing the effectiveness of international environmental agreements: the case of the 1985 Helsinki Protocol. *American Journal of Political Science*, 49, 86–102.

Sandler, T. (2004) *Global Collective Action*. Cambridge University Press.

Sherman, K. and Hempel, G. (2008) The UNEP Large Marine Ecosystem Report: a perspective on changing conditions in LMEs of the world's Regional Seas. *UNEP Regional Seas Report and Studies No. 182*. UNEP, Nairobi.

Sumaila, U. R. (2012) Overfishing: call to split fisheries at home and abroad. *Nature*, 481, 265.

Tatem, A. J., Rogers, D. J. and Hay, S. I. (2006a) Global transport networks and infectious disease spread. *Advances in Parasitology*, 62, 293–343.

Tatem, A. J., Hay, S. S. and Rogers, D. J. (2006b) Global traffic and disease vector dispersal. *Proceedings of the National Academy of Sciences*, 103, 6242–6247.

Tittensor, D. P., Worm, B. and Myers, R. A. (2006) Macroecological changes in exploited marine systems. *Marine Macroecology* (ed. J. D. Witman and K. Roy). University of Chicago Press.

Touza, J. and Perrings, C. (2011) Strategic behavior and the scope for unilateral provision of transboundary ecosystem services that are international environmental public goods. *Strategic Behavior and the Environment*, 1, 89–117.

The Sea Around Us Project (2012) *Exclusive Economic Zones*. Available at www.seaaroundus.org/eez/ (accessed 2012).

United Nations (1993) *Convention on Biological Diversity*. United Nations, New York.

(2004) *Oceans and the Law of the Sea: Report of the Secretary-General*. Fifty-ninth session Item 51 a. United Nations, New York.

Williamson, M. (1996) *Biological Invasions*. Chapman and Hall, London.

World Bank (2005) *Global Economic Prospects*. World Bank, Washington, DC.

World Health Organization (1995) *The WTO Agreement on the Application of Sanitary and Phytosanitary Measures CSPS Agreement*. World Trade Organization, Geneva.

(2005) *International Health Regulations*. World Health Organization, Geneva.

(2012a) *SPS Information Management System*. Available at http://spsims. wto.org/web/pages/report/report13/Report13.aspx (accessed 2012).

(2012b) *Relationship between WTO and MEA Rules*. Available at www. wto.org/english/tratop_e/envir_e/envir_neg_mea_e.htm (accessed 2012).

World Trade Organization Committee on the Environment (2011) *Matrix on Trade-Related Measures Pursuant to Selected Multilateral Environment Agreements*. WT/CTE/W/160/Rev. 5, TN/TE/S/5/Rev. 3. WTO, Geneva.

Worm, B., Barbier, E. B., Beaumont, N., Duffy, J. E., Folke, C., Halpern, B. S., Jackson, J. B. C., Lotzke, H. K., Micehli, F., Palumbi, S. R., Sala, E., Selkoe, K. A., Stachowicz, J. J. and Watson, R. (2006) Impacts of biodiversity loss on ocean ecosystem services. *Science*, 314, 787–790.

Worm, B., Hilborn, R., Baum, J. K., Branch, T. A., Collie, J. S., Costello, C., Fogarty, M. J., Fulton, E. A., Hutchings, J. A., Jennings, S., Jensen, O. P., Lotzke, H. K., Mace, P. A., McClanahan, T. R., Minto, C., Palumbi, S. R., Parma, A. M., Ricard, D., Watson, R. and Zeller, D. (2009) Rebuilding global fisheries. *Science*, 325, 578–585.

14 | *Genetic resources and the poor*

14.1 Biodiversity loss and poverty revisited

My discussion of the areas in which we can, and should, collectively do better in the management of biodiversity change has so far focused on the gains we can make in efficiency rather than in equity. It has emphasized the quality of the information we generate on the nature and significance of biodiversity change, and the way we use that information to inform decisions in a world where we cannot know everything. It has distinguished between the kind of information needed to support mitigation and adaptation strategies, and the options for balancing the costs and benefits of precautionary action. It has also identified the instruments available to convert information on the effects of biodiversity change into signals to those who supply and those who demand non-marketed environmental public goods. It has not considered issues of fairness or justice. Yet our starting point – the report of the Brundtland Commission – placed issues of equity at the core of sustainable development. The Commission famously argued that: "Poverty is not only an evil in itself, but sustainable development requires meeting the basic needs of all and extending to all the opportunity to fulfil their aspirations for a better life. A world in which poverty is endemic will always be prone to ecological and other catastrophes." It noted that the concept of sustainability necessarily implied a concern for equity between generations, and argued that the same concern logically extended to equity within generations. Specifically, it claimed that meeting the needs of this generation implied an assurance that the poor would receive their fair share of the resources required to sustain growth (World Commission on Environment and Development 1987).

The same concern for equity and poverty alleviation is embedded in the main multilateral agreement on biodiversity: the CBD. The CBD has, as its primary objectives, the conservation of biological diversity, the sustainable use of its components, and *the fair and equitable sharing*

436

of the benefits arising out of the use of genetic resources (United Nations 1993). In this chapter I address the CBD's equity goal and what it means for biodiversity change. In so doing I reconsider the complex relation between biodiversity and the rights of landholders, and explore how and why the equity goal matters. This is not because of any complementarity between poverty alleviation and habitat conservation. It is because the incentive to conserve – like the incentive to innovate – lies in the rights people have to the benefits of conservation.

Chapter 6 considered the relation between biodiversity change and income, and made the point that the factors that lie behind income growth in poor countries are the same factors that lie behind increasing stress on terrestrial species. They include the conversion of habitat for agricultural production and the application of fertilizers, herbicides, and pesticides to eliminate crop and livestock pests, predators, and competitors. Indeed, the relation between income growth and biodiversity loss in low-income countries turns out to be positive everywhere. As incomes grow so do the sources of stress on biodiversity. This should not surprise us given that the mechanisms are so transparent, but it does. Unfortunately, wanting the conservation of wild-living species and poverty alleviation to be compatible goals does not make them so. While the coincidence between areas of high species richness and poverty has focused attention on the scope for developing win–win policies (Sachs *et al.* 2009), the evidence largely points in the opposite direction. There do certainly exist local examples of protected areas and integrated conservation and development projects that have both enhanced conservation and alleviated local poverty (Ferraro, Hanauer and Sims 2011), but these are few and far between. Most empirical research on the resettlement of people displaced from protected areas concludes that their wellbeing has been significantly compromised, and recommends some version of integrated conservation and development instead (Cernea and Schmidt-Soltau 2006). Yet the general experience of such integrated projects suggests that few have been able to meet both goals (Wells *et al.* 2004; Brandon and Bruner 2008).

We have also seen that while poverty has been declining in many regions, biodiversity loss has not. Chapter 6 made the point that most studies show that extreme poverty was declining prior to the recession in all regions except Sub-Saharan Africa (World Bank 2005), and that since the recession even Sub-Saharan Africa has shown an improvement. The proportion of the population in poverty in that region was

reported to be 55 percent in 2005. Using the percentage of the population earning less than US$1.25 a day as its measure, the International
Fund for Agricultural Development estimated that 52.5 percent of the
population were in poverty in 2008 (see Table 14.1). A more recent
estimate claims that the proportion had fallen below 50 percent by
2010, and that it is expected to fall below 40 percent by 2015
(Chandy and Gertz 2011). The evidence on biodiversity loss is not
nearly as optimistic, and despite the CBD's targets, most projections
still show the rate of species extinctions to be increasing (Butchart *et al.*
2010; Hoffmann *et al.* 2010; Pereira *et al.* 2010).

The question I wish to explore here is how biodiversity change relates
to rights of ownership in genetic resources in poor countries. More
particularly, I am interested in property rights to the genetic information in domesticated species and wild relatives. The IAASTD, though
less a review of the state of scientific knowledge than other biodiversity-
related assessments, offered some insight into the problem. Like the MA
it drew attention to the relation between environmental degradation
and access rights to common pool resources, land tenure systems,
property rights, and conservation incentives. But beyond these well-
recognized issues it also considered the biodiversity impacts of changing
rights to the genetic information contained in domesticated and wild
species. It commended policy reforms that included "progressive evolution and proactive engagement in intellectual property rights (IPR)
regimes and related instruments . . . that value farmer knowledge, agricultural and natural biodiversity; farmer-managed medicinal plants,
local seed systems and common pool resource management regimes"
(International Assessment of Agricultural Knowledge Science and
Technology for Development 2008).

The context to the question is an evolving set of intellectual property
rights that reflects two processes: the arrogation by nation states of
common heritage rights to the genetic resources contained in wild and
domesticated species, and the assignment of intellectual property rights
to individuals and corporations over the results of plant breeding and
the genetic modification of plants. The CBD and the ITPGRFA are
outcomes of the first process, the International Convention for
Protection on New Plant Varieties (the UPOV Convention) and the
WTO's Agreement on Trade-Related Aspects of Intellectual Property
Rights (TRIPS) are outcomes of the second. The CBD and ITPGRFA
assign nation states the ultimate rights to the genetic resources

contained in biodiversity in both production and wild landscapes within their jurisdiction. The UPOV Convention and TRIPS assign rights to the results of genetic manipulation. The biodiversity at issue here is therefore the genetic diversity contained in wild-living species, landraces, traditional livestock strains, crop wild relatives,[1] as well as in the varieties created through modern plant breeding and genetic engineering. The rights to this diversity constitute assets that are – at least potentially – an important part of the wealth of landholders.

The point has already been made that the conservation problem has essentially the same structure in natural and managed landscapes. In both cases it will be optimal to conserve the system in some state if and only if the value of the assets it contains in the conserved state is expected to grow more rapidly than the value of the assets it contains in the converted state. As we saw in Chapter 9, one of the main challenges in understanding global change is that we do not currently have good measures of the effect of environmental change on wealth. The World Bank's adjusted net savings rate is an attempt to create such a measure at the national scale (World Bank 2010), but it offers only a partial correction of the savings measures in the national income accounts. It does include proxies for human capital and some natural resources. However, it does not address one of the main limitations of the national income accounts, that they report only assets that are subject to well-defined property rights. Resources that are not owned by individuals or groups of individuals are not counted. This is particularly problematic if we wish to understand changes in the wealth of groups of people who rely on accessing resources to which they have few formal rights. In extreme cases poor people may own the clothes they wear, their traps and tools, but little else – surviving off the exploitation of assets in the public domain. In such cases their wealth has both private and public components, and their wellbeing is affected by change in either component. A decline in the abundance of a hunter's prey, for example, can be as damaging as the loss of either hunting tools or the capacity to use those tools.

The importance of public assets to the welfare of poor people is one reason it has been so frequently claimed that biodiversity conservation

[1] These are local varieties of domesticated animal or plant species developed through informal plant and animal breeding, and through adaptation to the local environment.

Table 14.1 *Rural poverty*

	Asia and the Pacific	East Asia	South Asia	Southeast Asia	Sub-Saharan Africa	Latin America and the Caribbean	Middle East and North Africa	Developing world
Total population (millions)								
1988	2673	1121	1128	419	458	421	238	3791
1998	3143	1264	1374	498	603	499	299	4544
2008	3543	1349	1616	569	777	567	361	5247
Rural population (millions)								
1988	1962	827	837	293	333	129	124	2548
1998	2129	828	984	311	412	128	143	2812
2008	2188	763	1112	307	497	122	161	2968
Incidence of poverty (percentage of people living on <US$2/day)								
1988	80.1	83.6	80.3	66.6	74.8	23.1	16.1	69.1
1998	67.9	61.4	76.2	60.7	77.2	21.3	25.3	61.2
2008	55.0	36.3	71.1	53.5	75.6	14.3	17.2	51.2
Incidence of extreme poverty (percentage of people living on <US$1.25/day)								
1988	52.5	54.0	52.2	47.8	52.3	13.6	4.6	45.1
1998	39.0	34.4	44.6	35.0	57.9	10.8	5.2	36.1
2008	26.8	15.9	38.5	18.5	52.5	7.2	4.0	27.0
Incidence of rural poverty (percentage of people living on <US$2/day)								
1988	90.5	98.4	85.2	76.5	75.2	42.4	32.7	83.2
1998	82.4	76.1	86.8	87.7	86.7	44.3	30.7	78.6
2008	60.5	34.8	80.4	62.0	87.2	19.9	11.7	60.9

Incidence of extreme rural poverty (percentage of people living on <US$1.25/day)

1988	59.1	63.6	55.9	52.2	51.7	25.7	9.5	54.0
1998	49.7	44.1	53.8	52.7	64.9	21.8	6.6	48.4
2008	31.4	15.3	45.2	25.6	61.6	8.8	3.6	34.2

Number of rural people in poverty (<US$2/day, in millions)

1988	1775	814	713	225	251	55	41	2121
1998	1754	630	854	273	357	57	44	2212
2008	1325	266	894	190	433	24	19	1801

Number of rural people in extreme poverty (<US$2/day, in millions)

1988	1160	526	468	153	172	33	12	1377
1998	1057	365	530	164	268	28	10	1362
2008	687	117	503	78	306	11	6	1010

Rural people as percentage of those living in extreme poverty (<US$1.25/day)

1988	82.6	86.8	79.4	76.6	71.8	57.6	99.0	80.5
1998	86.4	84.0	86.5	94.2	76.6	51.9	61.3	82.9
2008	72.5	54.3	80.7	74.5	75.0	26.5	40.1	71.6

Note: Asia and the Pacific comprises figures for East Asia, South Asia, and Southeast Asia, and also the Pacific for which there is no breakdown in the table.

Source: International Fund for Agricultural Development (2010).

and poverty alleviation should be linked. Consider the following statement:

More than 3 billion people depend on marine and coastal biodiversity, while over 1.6 billion people rely on forests and non-timber forest products for their livelihoods. Habitat degradation and the loss of biodiversity are threatening the livelihoods of more than 1 billion people living in dry and sub-humid lands. Biodiversity is the basis for achieving sustainable development. (Secretariat of the Convention on Biological Diversity 2009)

The implication is that more than half the people on the planet rely on open access to common pool resources to which they have few formal rights. This may be an exaggeration. Many common pool resources are accessed through traditional structures that notionally give the authority to exclude others. Many others have been converted to leasehold or freehold regimes that enjoy formal rights of exclusion. In fact the growth of conventionally measured income in poor countries is frequently accompanied by an increase in dependence on privately or communally owned assets and a decrease in dependence on public-domain assets. As of now, however, some genetic resources are owned privately. Others are in the public domain. Some are distributed locally. Others are distributed nationally or internationally. The problem addressed in this chapter is that rights to genetic resources in the public domain are evolving in ways that affect both the wealth of people with traditional rights of access to those resources, and the diversity of domesticated species and their wild relatives.

14.2 Rights to the genetic resources of wild-living species

My main concern is the evolution of rights to biodiversity in production landscapes where many of the world's poor live. It is, however, useful to think first about the rights to the biodiversity that most concerns conservation organizations, and that is the subject of the CBD – the diversity of wild-living species. The point has already been made that in the UNCLOS, all resources of sea areas beyond national jurisdiction were defined to be the common heritage of humankind. The earliest international agreement about the genetic diversity of terrestrial species, the International Undertaking on Plant Genetic Resources adopted in 1983, similarly declared that it was a "universally accepted principle that plant genetic resources are a heritage of mankind and consequently should be available without restriction" (Rose 2004). Ten years later, the CBD took a very different stand. While the conservation of bio-diversity was declared to be "a common *concern* of humankind," the convention also declared that "States have *sovereign rights* over their own biological resources" (Convention on Biological Diversity 1993). Just as the recognition of EEZs by the UNCLOS had given national governments the right to exclude others from accessing species found in marine ecosystems within those zones, so the CBD gave national governments the right to exclude others from accessing species within their jurisdiction. This not only contradicted the common heritage idea in the international undertaking, but effectively ended that agreement. The agreement that was to replace it, the International Treaty on Plant Genetic Resources for Food and Agriculture, came into force in 2004 and was explicitly written to be compatible with the CBD.

Sovereign rights are not, of course, property rights. But they are a prerequisite for the allocation of property rights. Article 15 of the CBD asserts that authority to determine access to genetic resources rests with national governments, and is subject to national legislation. The focus of the Convention is on the conservation and sustainable use of wild-living species and the fair and equitable sharing of the benefits of use of the genetic resources of wild-living species. For the most part this has been interpreted as access for purposes of research and development in fields not covered by the ITPGRFA. The CBD simultaneously confers the power to assign access rights and establishes a bilateral system for sharing the benefits of access with both local communities and the country of origin: the country of origin being the country where the species concerned are in their natural habitat or, if domesticated, where they have developed the distinctive properties sought by others (Santilli 2012).

This effectively created a market for access to genetic resources and the traditional local knowledge about those resources. The poor who potentially benefit from the creation of this market are the local com-munities in developing countries on whose land the resources are found, and who have traditional knowledge about their use (Ten Kate and Laird 1999). Subsequent agreements have established the conditions under which the market operates. The Bonn Guidelines on Access to Genetic Resources and Fair and Equitable Sharing of the Benefits Arising out of their Utilization (2002) established criteria for the licens-ing of access to genetic resources, including prior informed consent of both the national government of the country of origin of the resource for transmittal as well as indigenous and local communities. They also established the monetary and non-monetary benefits to be provided, and the conditions under which genetic resources could be transferred to another party. The Nagoya Protocol on Access and Benefit Sharing (2010) later formalized these criteria, and extended them to the case where genetic resources and associated traditional knowledge were accessed without the prior and informed consent of all the countries within a species' natural range (Joseph 2010).

The establishment of rights to species that span several jurisdictions has yet to be resolved. The Nagoya Protocol encourages cooperation between parties wherever genetic resources or traditional knowledge fall within more than one jurisdiction, but no mechanisms have been established to do this. Instead, the Protocol asks parties to consider a global multilateral benefit sharing mechanism to address the problem. It also recommends that such benefits be used to support the conservation of biological diversity and the sustainable use of its components (Nagoya Protocol on Access to Genetic Resources and the Fair and Equitable Sharing of Benefits Arising from their Utilization to the Convention on Biological Diversity 2010).

Reviews of the way that national access and benefit sharing agreements have developed across the world reveal striking similarities in approach, and in the implications for the flow of benefits to local landholders (Lewis-Lettington and Mwanyiki 2006). Benefits are generally provided in both monetary and non-monetary form. In Ethiopia, for example, foreign users of national genetic resources or traditional knowledge are required to provide 50 percent of all benefits in money in a variety of ways, including license fees, upfront payments, milestone payments, royalties, and research funding.[2] In India, payment options also include provision for joint ventures, product development, and venture capital funding.[3] In Australia, users who wish to conduct research and development on native species of genetic resources or their biochemical compounds are also required to pay license fees in case of commercialization, plus special fees paid to trust funds

[2] Under the Access to Genetic Resources and Community Knowledge and Community Rights Proclamation (No. 482/ 2006).
[3] Under the India Biological Diversity Act (2002) and Biological Diversity Rules (2004).

supporting conservation.[4] Non-monetary benefits tend to be more variable, and include sharing in research and development results, research collaboration and cooperation, technology and knowledge transfers, royalty-free access to technology for domestic institutions in case of endemic species access, science and technology capacity development of national universities, drugs at cost (tax exempted), equipment donations, and the like (Suneetha and Pisupati 2008).

In all cases, the implementation of access and benefit sharing rules to the wild-living species of a country recognizes the value of the genetic resources they contain, and so adds to the value of the aggregate capital stock of the country. The additional value is, however, limited to the value of genetic resources to pharmacology or biotechnology, and does not include the value of species in the provision of a range of other ecosystem services. Yet given that genetic material of this kind was previously subject to the same open access rules as sea areas beyond national jurisdiction, this is a significant step forward. It raises the opportunity cost of biodiversity loss to those with ownership rights, since the extinction or extirpation of a species eliminates the possibility that the genetic resources it offers have sufficient potential pharmacological or biotechnological value to attract bioprospectors.

It is not yet clear whether the advent of access and benefit sharing rules has had any impact on the rate of biodiversity loss, although the existence of benefit sharing rules for wild-living species does provide the local communities on whose land those species are found with some incentive for their conservation. Nor is it clear what impact access and benefit sharing rules have had on poverty rates. Since they focus only on the expected value of genetically based research and development activities, the benefits generated under access and benefit sharing rules understate the social value of the biodiversity concerned. Moreover, since many benefits accrue to the state as opposed to the landholders they do not give full value to the landholders. Where benefit sharing has been most effective, perhaps, is in financing local biological research. Indeed, one of the earliest examples of benefit sharing was the 1991 contract between Costa Rica's National Biodiversity Institute (INBio) and the pharmaceutical company, Merck. Under the agreement, INBio agreed to supply Merck with samples of the plants, insects, and microorganisms collected

---

[4] Under the Australia Environment Protection and Biodiversity Conservation Act (1999) and Regulations (2000).

from Costa Rica's protected forests, which Merck could then use to create new pharmaceutical products. Currently, benefits are shared under Costa Rica's Biodiversity Law (no. 7788), implemented by the National Commission for the Management of Biodiversity, but they still include payments equivalent to 10 percent of the research budget of the National System of Conservation Areas (Suneetha and Pisupati 2008).

14.3 Rights to the genetic resources in domesticated species

More important for the wealth of the poorest people are the rights they have to the genetic information contained in species in production landscapes – simplified ecosystems committed to the production of foods, fuels, and fibers. These include lands held under a number of tenure systems. At one extreme are public lands that are effectively open access. Sea areas beyond national jurisdiction – the common heritage of humankind – also fall into this category. At the other extreme are lands held by individuals or corporations under tenure systems that offer varying degrees of security, ranging from private ownership, through various forms of leasehold, to informal tenure with no legal security at all. In between are communally owned and managed lands that operate a wide range of individual access rules, but that all allow for the exclusion of those who do not belong to the community.

The rights that people have to natural resources under different tenure systems, including the species associated with land, can and often do intersect. The right to sell or use a piece of land or to regulate sale or use, for example, may all be held by different people. There are three broad classes of rights typically associated with a given tenure system: use rights (the right to use land for arable production, grazing, gathering forest products and so on), ownership rights (the right to sell or mortgage land, or to transfer title to others), and control rights (the right to determine who should have access to land and how it should be used). These, in turn, confer a set of entitlements (e.g. to derive income from the land, to be protected from illegal expropriation, or bequeath land), but also a set of obligations (e.g. to use land in ways that do not harm others, or to surrender land that is legally expro-priated). These entitlements and obligations are different for different tenure systems.

A point that has made repeatedly in this book is that the degree to which landholders take account of the effect they have on others depends on whether or not others have rights covering those effects. Indeed, the effectiveness of market creation and market incentives as instruments for the conservation of biodiversity depends on the capacity to assign rights – the essence of the Coase theorem. Open access tenure systems are characterized both by the fact that resource users cannot be excluded from access, and that they have no obligation to take account of the effect of their own actions on others. This makes them *de facto* public goods, albeit ones that can suffer the effects of congestion. The assignment of exclusive rights to previously open access resources is what introduces an incentive to use them efficiently. It turns out, though, that there is also a close correlation between the system of tenure under which land is held and the income of the landholder. The rural poor tend to access land in one of three ways: through open access to ecosystems that are either beyond national jurisdiction or that are in public ownership, through insecure informal tenure, or through some form of customary communal tenure established by ancestral occupation and use of the land.

Historically, the tenure system has also structured the way that people access biological resources generally, and crop genetic resources in particular. Traditionally, farmers have employed both selection and breeding to improve crop varieties. This has involved both breeding out undesirable traits and breeding in desirable traits such as drought or disease resistance, or improved yields. It has also involved the exchange of seeds among farmers to maintain the intraspecific genetic diversity needed to protect crops against environmental fluctuations and to increase the pool of traits available to breeders. The social, legal, political, and economic systems to which particular tenure systems belong have accordingly influenced the extent of the genetic resources available to traditional breeders. In social groups with relatively limited external contacts, the wild and domesticated species found within the area they control limits the available gene pool. In many cases, the relation between wild and domesticated species was socially regulated. Without any formal concept of introgression, rules were established that conserved wild relatives of cultivated species. In Ethiopia, for example, where the staple food of the Ari people is a banana relative (*Ensete ventricosum*), areas where wild relatives of the plant grow are protected (sacred), ensuring their availability for cross-pollination with cultivated plants (Kingsbury 2009).

Other things being equal, the smaller the group to which the farmer belongs, and the fewer the transactions with others, the smaller the gene pool available for breeding and the more specialized the trait requirements they seek to promote. In fact the multiplicity and relative isolation of social groups is what lies behind the historic development of landraces – plants that are morphologically distinct, have some genetic integrity but are also genetically variable and dynamic, and have distinctive properties in terms of yield, date of maturity, pest and disease resistance, and so on. Indeed, it is the genetic variability of landraces that made them valuable in fluctuating environmental conditions (Kingsbury 2009). A reduction in the isolation of communities, whether through the development of market exchanges, migration, war, or conquest has therefore had the effect both of increasing the gene pool available to breeders, and of reducing the specificity of the traits sought in crops.

Consider what this means for biodiversity rights in agro-ecosystems, and for the wealth of farmers and the wider community. A first point to make is that while some of the issues involved overlap with those raised by access to wild-living species, there are important differences. If we consider only landraces and their wild relatives, for example, then the link between domesticated and wild biodiversity is quite similar. It is possible to identify historic ranges that can be used to assign rights. Landraces correspond to particular places in the same way that endemic wild species do. If we also consider varieties that are the result of modern plant breeding processes, however, then the concept of country of origin is much less well defined for cultivated species. For example, a single spring wheat variety developed by the International Maize and Wheat Improvement Center (CIMMYT) that was widely planted during the 1980s, VEERY, was the product of 3,170 different crosses involving fifty-one parent varieties from twenty-six countries (Moore and Tymnowski 2005). Property rights in the genetic material of such varieties cannot be anchored to a particular country, or even to a particular Vavilov center of origin.

It is not surprising, therefore, that the property rights now evolving for landraces and their wild relatives, and for the products of modern plant breeding and genetic engineering, are more varied than those assigned to wild-living species under the CBD. Intellectual property rights for crop and livestock genetic resources now span patents, a wide range of *sui generis* systems (singular systems involving the creation of specific entitlements or obligations), and a range of farmers' and livestock-keepers' rights. The USA Plant Patents Act (1930), and the UPOV Convention (1961) both imply rights that are different from the rights assigned under the CBD. The farmers' rights referred to in the ITPGRFA are, however, more compatible with the CBD.

While both systems still persist, the trend over the last two decades has been for rights to converge on patents or *sui generis* systems modeled on the UPOV Convention. Since 1994, all intellectual property rights to plant and animal genetic resources in agriculture have been subject to the TRIPS. TRIPS obliges countries to grant patents to products or processes that involve an inventive element and have some identifiable industrial application. It also requires countries both to recognize and protect intellectual property, and to resolve disputes over intellectual property using the WTO disputes procedure. The result is that a majority of countries now implement and enforce a system of protection based either on patents, as occurs in the USA, Australia, New Zealand, and Japan, or on a *sui generis* system of plant breeders' rights based on UPOV, as occurs in most other countries. The difference between patents and plant breeders' rights is that while both offer exclusive temporary rights to inventions, the latter assign breeders the right to use freely any plant breeding material without the prior consent of the owner of that material (Santilli 2012).

Landraces and wild relatives have not benefitted from the same protection. Based on the number of countries reporting examples of genetic erosion to the FAO, the most affected crop groups are cereals and grasses, fruits and nuts, and food legumes and vegetables. The crop groups least affected are stimulants and spices, medicinal, and aromatic plants. While the overall picture on crop genetic diversity is unclear, genetic erosion is agreed to be a result of the change from traditional production systems depending on farmer varieties to modern production systems depending on released varieties (Food and Agriculture Organization 2010).

If we think of this in terms of the biological wealth of farming communities, it represents a reduction in the number of stocks in the portfolio of assets available to farmers. Whether it also represents a reduction in the value of the portfolio, and hence the wealth of farmers, depends on the factors discussed in Chapters 7 and 10. It is the conservation of these stocks that is the goal of the ITPGRFA. The Treaty is designed to protect a global public good, the genetic resources needed to maintain global capacity to maintain food supplies under fluctuating environmental conditions, by establishing a system of access and benefit sharing. Article 1 of the Treaty describes its objectives to be: "the conservation and sustainable use of plant genetic resources for food and agriculture and the fair and equitable sharing of the benefits arising out of their use, in harmony with the Convention on Biological Diversity, for sustainable agriculture and food security." Like the CBD, the Treaty asserts that states have sovereign rights over their own plant genetic resources, and hence the authority to determine access to those resources. Unlike the Convention, however, it promotes a multilateral rather than a bilateral approach to both access and benefit sharing (International Treaty on Plant Genetic Resources for Food and Agriculture 2009).

While the Treaty explicitly recognizes the rights of farmers to save, use, exchange, and sell farm-saved seed and other propagating material it also recognizes (Article 9) that responsibility for realizing farmers' rights rests with national governments. It identifies specific rights including the protection of relevant traditional knowledge, the right to share in the benefits arising, and the right to participate in decision-making on the conservation and sustainable use of plant genetic resources for food and agriculture. These are subject to the same caveats as appear in the Convention: that realization of farmers' rights should be in accordance with national needs and priorities and subject to national legislation.

The benefit-sharing system contained within the Treaty stipulates that benefits arising from the use of plant genetic resources for food and agriculture under the multilateral system shall be shared via exchange of information, access to, and transfer of technology, capacity-building, and the sharing of the benefits arising from commercialization. Article 13.3 requires that such benefits flow directly or indirectly to farmers (especially in developing countries) who conserve plant genetic resources for food and agriculture. A critical aspect of the implementation of the Treaty has been the creation of a fund to implement farmers' rights. The original intention was that a fund on plant genetic resources would support plant genetic conservation in developing countries (Moore and Tymnowski 2005). Since 2009 a benefit-sharing fund has been established with support from Italy, Spain, Norway, and Australia, and now the European Union, that aims to support poor farmers in conserving important food crops at risk from climate change. The resources involved are, however, extremely modest (in the order of $10 million – a vanishingly small proportion of the resources flowing to the agricultural sector as subsidies in one form or another).

There are a number of models for national legislation to protect farmers' rights (and through them landraces and wild crop relatives). Among these the "African model" legislation for the protection of the rights of local communities, farmers, and breeders, and for the regulation of access to biological resources, identifies objectives that perhaps map most closely to the interests of traditional agricultural communities. They are to:

(a) recognize, protect and support the inalienable rights of local communities including farming communities over their biological resources, knowledge and technologies;

(b) recognize and protect the rights of breeders;

(c) provide an appropriate system of access to biological resources, community knowledge and technologies subject to the prior informed consent of the State and the concerned local communities;

(d) promote appropriate mechanisms for a fair and equitable sharing of benefits arising from the use of biological resources, knowledge and technologies;

(e) ensure the effective participation of concerned communities, with a particular focus on women, in making decisions as regards the distribution of benefits which may derive from the use of their biological resources, knowledge and technologies;

(f) promote and encourage the building of national and grassroots scientific and technological capacity relevant to the conservation and sustainable use of biological resources;

(g) provide appropriate institutional mechanisms for the effective implementation and enforcement of the rights of local communities, including farming communities and breeders, and the conditions of access to biological resources, community knowledge and technologies;

(h) promote the conservation, evaluation and sustainable utilisation of biological resources with a particular focus on the major role women play;

(i) promote improvements in the productivity, profitability, stability and sustainability of major production systems through yield enhancement and maintenance of biological diversity;

(j) promote the supply of good quality seed/planting material to farmers; and

(k) ensure that biological resources are utilised in an effective and equitable manner in order to strengthen the food security of the nation. (Organization for African Unity 2000)

Objectives (a) and (g) may be the most critical for farmers' rights: the recognition that farming communities have inalienable rights to genetic material and the establishment of mechanisms for the protection of those rights. These are the areas where the erosion of traditional rights has had the most adverse effect on conservation of landraces and wild crop relatives. Within Africa only Ethiopia has legislation in place that reflects at least aspects of the African model. However, an example of *sui generis* legislation outside of Africa that identifies group rights is India's Protection of Plant Varieties and Farmers Rights Act (2001). This Act defines a breeder to be a "person or group of persons or a farmer or group of farmers or any institution which has bred, evolved or developed any plant variety," and gives farmers, as breeders, the same rights as are given to professional breeders. However most national law focuses on intellectual property rights attaching to the products of modern plant breeding and/or genetic modification of plants, and neglects the rights of the farming communities that account for the majority of the world's rural population and most of the remaining landraces and wild crop relatives.

A recent very thoughtful evaluation of the consequences of these trends concludes that the effective recognition of farmers' rights requires that seed laws should either regulate only formal seed systems, leaving local farmers' seed systems out of their scope or they should regulate formal and local farmers' seed systems differently. Furthermore, farmers' rights should be recognized as collective, not individual, and benefit-sharing mechanisms should be developed accordingly (Santilli 2012).

14.4 Rights, and the conservation of genetic resources in poor regions

There are two main reasons why the trends in the establishment of rights to genetic resources over the last two decades are important. One is that they have major implications for the wellbeing of the world's poor, the vast majority of whom live in rural areas and depend on the exploitation of agro-biodiversity for their survival. More than 70 per-cent of the people in extreme poverty live in rural areas and depend, to a greater or lesser extent, on agriculture (see Table 14.1). The genetic erosion of landraces and wild crop relatives is, at least in part, a direct result of the evolution of seed laws and intellectual property rights. It signifies a loss in the assets available to those people. Even if the loss of landraces and wild species (crop relatives and others) had no other implications for human wellbeing this would be a source for concern. But the loss of landraces and wild species does have other implications for human wellbeing. A second reason why the trends of the last two decades are important is that the loss of landraces and wild crop relatives compromises global ability to adapt food supply systems to climate change.

Both reasons stem from the fact that the assets at stake in the discussions about farmers' rights, the genetic resources contained in landraces and wild crop relatives, have historically been the most important elements in a portfolio aimed at managing environmental risk. Since the poor do not have significant reserves, their strategies for managing risk have centered on diversification both within and between crop species. That is the logic behind traditional planting strategies that involve an array of landraces of different species. It is also the logic behind breeding strategies that both retain crop wild relatives *in situ* and evolve multiple landraces of each cultivated species. The displacement of landraces by high-yielding varieties has enhanced average output in many cases, but has not been as effective in reducing local vulnerability to environmental shocks. It has also dramatically increased the spatial correlation of risk. If all farmers in all communities plant the same seed, the probability that they will simultaneously succeed or fail rises sharply.

The recent report of the International Fund for Agricultural Development (IFAD) on the state of rural poverty argues that risk management is the most important component of poverty alleviation in rural areas. It notes that rural households still manage risk through crop diversification along with non-farm activities designed both to complement and reduce the risks attached to farming. Moreover, while the accumulation of both natural and financial assets is critical to buffer shocks, it notes that the scope for accumulation by those in extreme poverty is limited (International Fund for Agricultural Development 2010).

Among the reasons advanced for its focus on risk, IFAD points to the emergence of many new sources of risk including climate change, insecurity of access to land, increasing pressure on common property resources and related institutions, and greater volatility of food prices (International Fund for Agricultural Development 2010). The displacement of landraces, the diminished effectiveness of traditional common

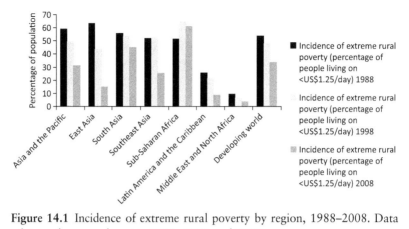

Figure 14.1 Incidence of extreme rural poverty by region, 1988–2008. Data relate to the years closest to 1988, 1998, and 2008.
Source: data from International Fund for Agricultural Development (2010).

property management regimes, and the erosion of traditional support networks have all contributed to the problem.

This is more of an issue in some places than others. As Table 14.1 shows, extreme poverty is still overwhelmingly a rural phenomenon, but the incidence of extreme rural poverty, and the change in that incidence over the last few decades differs substantially from region to region. Whereas the incidence of extreme rural poverty has declined quite dramatically in Latin America, East Asia, and Southeast Asia, it has been more resistant to change in South Asia and Sub-Saharan Africa (Figure 14.1). These are the regions in which the loss of collectively owned natural assets has had the greatest impact on wellbeing.

Global interest in these trends derives from the fact that declining agro-biodiversity in developing countries affects the rest of the world. Many of the modern plant breeding successes of the twentieth century took place under the regime that existed before the WTO's TRIPS in conditions that would be hard to replicate now. While the access and benefit sharing provisions of the ITPGRFA allow access to *in situ* agro-biodiversity, costs of access have increased sharply. As a result, the effort committed to establishing *ex situ* collections has increased. An international network of *ex situ* collections, all made under the open access regime, was originally initiated by the International Undertaking on Plant Genetic Resources. This network was charged with holding active collections of plant species for the benefit of the international community on the principle of unrestricted exchange, base or active collections of the plant genetic resources of particular plant. The FAO's Commission on Genetic Resources for Food and Agriculture subsequently took responsibility for the network, building on the collections developed by the (then) twelve centers of the CGIAR (Moore and Tymnowski 2005). Since the ITPGRFA came into force it has regulated access to the resources of the network. However, most of the effort to build *ex situ* collections is now undertaken by individual countries.

The FAO estimates that the total number of accessions conserved *ex situ* worldwide increased by approximately 1.4 million since 1996, the total now standing at around 7.4 million (of which some 2 million are distinct accessions) (Food and Agriculture Organization 2010). Most accessions are held by a relatively small number of countries (Table 14.2). The characteristics of national and CGIAR collections differ in important ways. The CGIAR centers hold only 12 percent of *ex situ* accessions globally, but are the most important repository of landraces and wild relatives, which account for 73 percent of all CGIAR accessions (landraces and wild relatives account for 16 percent of national collections).[5] Since the CGIAR *ex situ* collections are freely available to contributors, they have largely supplanted *in situ* collections as the primary source of genetic material from developing countries. At the same time, the incentive for individual countries to contribute material to the CGIAR system has been weakened. By the beginning of this century, the ratio of samples requested by developing countries to samples contributed by the same countries was more than 60 to 1 (Moore and Tymnowski 2005).

Why should this be of concern? The global interest in the conservation of landraces and crop wild relatives lies in their dynamic nature. In recent years international interest in the conservation of crop wild

---

[5] Eleven of the CGIAR centers currently manage germplasm collections for the global community: Bioversity International, International Center for Tropical Agriculture, CIMMYT, International Potato Center, International Center for Agricultural Research in the Dry Areas (ICARDA), the World Agroforestry Center, ICRISAT, International Institute for Tropical Agriculture, International Livestock Research Institute, International Network for the Improvement of Banana and Plaintain, International Rice Research Institute (IRRI), and AfricaRice. Four collections (CIMMYT, ICARDA, ICRISAT, and IRRI) hold more than 100,000 accessions. In total, the centers hold some 740,000 accessions of 3,446 species of 612 genera (Food and Agriculture Organization 2010).

Table 14.2 Ex situ *collections, 2008*

	2008 (number)			% change from 1995		
	Genera	Species	Accessions	Genera	Species	Accessions
Brazil	212	670	107246	56	115	165
Canada	257	1166	106280	8	13	6
China	–	–	391919	–	–	9
Czech Republic	30	175	15421	–12	82	6
Ecuador	272	662	17830	31	33	65
Ethiopia	151	324	67554	113	338	46
Germany	801	3049	148128	27	21	0
Hungary	294	915	45321	24	23	19
India	723	1495	366333	890	745	137
Japan	341	1409	243463	–	–	20
Kenya	855	2350	48777	511	708	39
Nordic countries	129	319	28007	47	70	16
Russian Federation	256	2025	322238	–2	10	–2
Netherlands	36	311	24076	20	112	39
Turkey	545	2692	54523	72	39	70
USA	2128	11815	508994	35	39	24
Average	**289**	**2098**	**178294**	**74**	**60**	**27**

Source: Data derive from Food and Agriculture Organization (2010).

relatives has been driven by the potential threats posed by climate change. It is argued that if *in situ* populations of landraces and crop wild relatives are able to evolve under climatic selection pressure, they may develop traits that are critical for future plant breeding (Food and Agriculture Organization 2010). *Ex situ* collections, such as those in the CGIAR system, provide valuable insurance against extinction in place, but they cannot substitute for this property. Yet *in situ* conservation of both landraces and wild crop relatives is compromised by trends in intellectual property rights.

Wild crop relatives are particularly problematic. There has been a tendency to think of this as a classic conservation problem to be addressed through protected areas, but while the land committed to protected areas generally has increased significantly over the last two decades, no protected areas have been selected with crop wild relatives in mind. All have been selected to protect rare and endangered wild species. Crop wild relatives have tended "to fall between the cracks of two different conservation approaches, ecological and agricultural; the former focusing mainly on rare or threatened wild species and ecosystems and the latter mainly on the *ex situ* conservation of domesticated crops" (Food and Agriculture Organization 2010).

The global risks posed by the genetic erosion of both landraces and crop wild relatives in a time of global environmental change have at least been recognized. A study for the FAO Commission on Genetic Resources for Food and Agriculture has, for example, identified *in situ* conservation priorities for the most important wild relatives of fourteen of the world's major food crops (Maxted and Kell 2009).[6] While pilot projects exist, however, this concern has not fed into the issue of farmers' rights in a systematic way. The problem is this. The Green Revolution was made possible by two things: an open access regime that gave plant breeders rights to use available genetic material wherever it was found, and an incentive system that gave landholders a reason to maintain landraces and wild crop relatives. Since the Green Revolution, rights of access to at least the CGIAR collections has been maintained, but farmer incentives to maintain landraces and wild crop relatives has been eroded.

14.5 Private affluence, public poverty

If there is a high road to affluence in the long history of humankind it lies in the private appropriation and conversion of environmental assets. The stocks of assets initially acquired in this way may have been transformed beyond all recognition in the process of development, but they share at least this characteristic – that they were initially appropriated from the environment in which people found themselves. The exploited environment has sometimes included other races or cultures (as in the

---

[6] These are, in Africa, finger millet (*Eleusine spp.*), pearl millet (*Pennisetum spp.*), garden pea (*Pisum spp.*), and cowpea (*Vigna spp.*); in the Americas, barley (*Hordeum spp.*), sweet potato (*Ipomoea spp.*), cassava (*Manihot spp.*), potato (*Solanum spp.*), and maize (*Zea spp.*); in Asia and the Pacific, wild rice (*Oryza spp.*) and the cultivated banana/plantain (*Musa spp.*); and in the Near East, the garden pea (*Pisum spp.*), wheat (*Triticum spp.* and *Aegilops spp.*), barley (*Hordeum spontaneum* and *H. bulbosum*), faba bean (*Vicia spp.*), chickpea (*Cicer spp.*), alfalfa (*Medicago spp.*), clover (*Trifolium spp.*), pistachio (*Pistacia spp.*), and stone fruits (*Prunus spp.*).

Americas in the fifteenth and sixteenth centuries, or in Sub-Saharan Africa in the eighteenth and nineteenth centuries) and sometimes been unoccupied by humankind (as in Antarctica or the high seas in the twenty-first century). But the appropriation of environmental assets, the most primitive form of asset accumulation, is still among the most common routes to wealth. It is a strategy that plays out at almost every scale, from the landless peasant squatting on a single acre to grow a few crops to the negotiated seizure of 140 million square kilometers of the oceans in national EEZs. It is a strategy that also covers almost every type of asset, from the minerals that underpinned the original development of tools and weapons to the genetic information at stake in the multilateral agreements discussed in this chapter.

There is, however, a balance to be struck. While the conversion of environmental assets adds to private wealth, it can also deplete public wealth. The point has been made repeatedly that the bundle of services yielded by ecosystems includes some that can be privately captured and some that cannot. Because people are unable to capture the benefits of services that are public goods, they tend to be undersupplied. But those benefits are also real, and they should be taken into account in the decisions people take about the appropriation and conversion of environmental assets in the public domain. It is one thing for an individual farmer or a traditional farming community to have to adopt a management strategy that puts the *in situ* conservation of both landraces and wild crop relatives at risk. It is another for the international community to treat this with indifference.

For the individual farmer or the traditional farming community the choice might be based on an evaluation of the balance between the mean and variance of yields associated with different current crop combinations, as we saw in Chapter 10. That choice would depend on the decision-makers' experience of weather fluctuations and their aversion to risk, among other things. For the global community, while the loss of landraces and crop wild relatives might mean little in the short term, it potentially permanently excludes the genetic resources they contain from future asset portfolios. That is, it creates a problem of the irreversible loss of genetic information. If that information has potential value under future uncertain conditions then, from a social perspective, decisions about crop combinations should preserve the option of learning. Indeed, this is the explicit motivation for promoting *ex situ* conservation of genetic material. However, as has already been noted, the characteristic feature of landraces and wild crop relatives that makes them valuable at a time of rapid environmental change is that they are genetically dynamic. But to realize the benefits this property confers, they have to be conserved *in situ*. This gives the global community an interest in encouraging local landholders to maintain landraces and wild crop relatives.

The access and benefit-sharing regimes of the international agreements are intended to meet this need. While all aim to give farmers an incentive to conserve these resources, they are divided on the critical question of who owns the genetic resources contained in landraces and wild crop relatives. Although the individual farming communities who developed landraces can claim prior right, the ITPGRFA, like the CBD, asserts that countries have sovereign rights to the genetic resources found in their borders. An increasing number of countries are in fact affirming state ownership of genetic resources. For example, the Andean Community has agreed (Decision 391) that genetic resources are the property or heritage of the state. Similarly, Ethiopia's Proclamation no. 482 (2006) asserts that genetic resources are the property of the Ethiopian state and the Ethiopian people (Food and Agriculture Organization 2010). As it happens, this is inconsistent with the African model, which proposed that *sui generis* legislation should include a commitment to "recognize, protect and support the inalienable rights of local communities" (Organization for African Unity 2000). But it is an indication of where countries are likely to go in the future.

Farmers' rights are certainly about much more than ownership of the genetic material in landraces and wild crop relatives. They include, for example, the right to save, exchange, sell, use, develop, and improve seeds of both local and commercial varieties, and protection of traditional farming knowledge (Santilli 2012). But ownership is fundamental: both of the basic resource and of innovations springing out of plant breeding activities. Ownership of the genetic resources in landraces and wild crop relatives is what gives farming communities the incentive to protect an asset of value both to themselves and to the global community. The alternative stewardship approach to farmers' rights (Andersen 2006) leaves open the option that farmers could be paid guardians of genetic material, but the incentive effects are likely to be significantly weaker and the outcome significantly less equitable.

Biodiversity loss affects human wealth and wellbeing at many different scales, and via its effects on many different services. The loss of landraces and wild crop relatives from production landscapes directly affects the wealth and wellbeing of farming communities by removing biological assets that help cope with fluctuating environmental conditions. But it also affects genetic resources available to the rest of the world that may be critical to development of the plants needed for the supply of foods, fuels, and fibers in the future. Since farming communities are unable to capture any of these benefits it is not surprising that they have failed to conserve these resources. The result is that we are collectively risking the irreversible loss of assets whose value can only be revealed as the selective pressures of global environmental change unfold.

References

Andersen, R. (2006) *Realising Farmers' Rights Under the International Treaty on Plant Genetic Resources for Food and Agriculture*. The Fridtjof Nansen Institute, Lysaker.

Brandon, K. and Bruner, A. (2008) Benefits of protected areas: perspectives and experiences of Conservation International. *Protected Areas in Today's World: Their Values and Benefits for the Welfare of the Planet* (ed. Secretariat of the Convention on Biological Diversity), pp. 29–36. Convention on Biological Diversity, Montreal.

Butchart, S., Walpole, M., Collen, B., van Strien, A., Scharlemann, J.P.W., Almond, R.E.A., Baillie, J.E.M., Bomhard, B., Brown, C., Bruno, J., Carpenter, K.E., Carr, G.M., Chanson, J., Chenery, A.M., Csirke, J., Davidson, N.C., Dentener, F., Foster, M., Galli, A., Galloway, J.N., Genovesi, P., Gregory, R.D., Hockings, M., Kapos, V., Lamarque, J.-F., Leverington, F., Loh, J., McGeoch, M.A., McRae, L., Minasyan, A., Morcillo, M.H., Oldfield, T.E.E., Pauly, D., Quader, S., Revenga, C., Sauer, J.R., Skolnik, B., Spear, D., Stanwell-Smith, D., Stuart, S.N., Symes, A., Tierney, M., Tyrrell, T.D., Vie, J.-C. and Watson, R. (2010) Global biodiversity: indicators of recent declines. *Science*, 328, 1164–1168.

Cernea, M.M. and Schmidt-Soltau, K. (2006) Poverty risks and national parks: policy issues in conservation and resettlement. *World Development*, 34, 1808–1830.

Chandy, L. and Gertz, G. (2011) *Poverty in Numbers: The Changing State of Global Poverty from 2005 to 2015*. The Brookings Institution, Washington, DC.

Convention on Biological Diversity (1993) *United Nations Treaty Series*, New York.

Food and Agriculture Organization (2010) *The Second Report on the State of the World's Plant Genetic Resources for Food and Agriculture*. Food and Agriculture Organization, Rome.

Ferraro, P. J., Hanauer, M. M. and Sims, K. R. E. (2011) Conditions associated with protected area success in conservation and poverty reduction. *Proceedings of the National Academy of Sciences*, 108, 13913–13918.

Hoffmann, M., Hilton-Taylor, C., Angulo, A., Böhm, M., Brooks, T. M., Butchart, S. H. M., Carpenter, K. E., Chanson, J., Collen, B., Cox, N. A., Darwall, W. R. T., Dulvy, N. K., Harrison, L. R., Katariya, V., Pollock, C. M., Quader, S., Richman, N. I., Rodrigues, A. S. L., Tognelli, M. F., Vié, J.-C., Aguiar, J. M., Allen, D. J., Allen, G. R., Amori, G., Ananjeva, N. B., Andreone, F., Andrew, P., Ortiz, A. L. A., Baillie, J. E. M., Baldi, R., Bell, B. D., Biju, S. D., Bird, J. P., Black-Decima, P., Blanc, J. J., Bolaños, F., Bolivar-G., W., Burfield, I. J., Burton, J. A., Capper, D. R., Castro, F., Catullo, G., Cavanagh, R. D., Channing, A., Chao, N. L., Chenery, A. M., Chiozza, F., Clausnitzer, V., Collar, N. J., Collett, L. C., Collette, B. B.,Fernandez, C. F. C., Craig, M. T., Crosby, M. J., Cumberlidge, N., Cuttelod, A., Derocher, A. E., Diesmos, A. C., Donaldson, J. S., Duckworth, J. W., Dutson, G., Dutta, S. K., Emslie, R. H., Farjon, A., Fowler, S., Freyhof, J., Garshelis, D. L., Gerlach, J., Gower, D. J., Grant, T. D., Hammerson, G. A., Harris, R. B., Heaney, L. R., Hedges, S. B., Hero, J.-M., Hughes, B., Hussain, S. A., Icochea M., Inger, R. F., Ishii, N., Iskandar, D. T., Jenkins, R. K. B., Kaneko, Y., Kottelat, M., Kovacs, K. M., Kuzmin, S. L., La Marca, E., Lamoreux, J. F., Lau, M. W. N., Lavilla, E. O., Leus, K., Lewison, R. L., Lichtenstein, G., Livingstone, S. R., Lukoschek, V., Mallon, D. P., McGowan, P. J. K., McIvor, A., Moehlman, P. D., Molur, S., Alonso, A. M., Musick, J. A., Nowell, K., Nussbaum, R. A., Olech, W., Orlov, N. L., Papenfuss, T. J., Parra-Olea, G., Perrin, W. F., Polidoro, B. A., Pourkazemi, M., Racey, P. A., Ragle, J. S., Ram, M., Rathbun, G., Reynolds, R. P., Rhodin, A. G. J., Richards, S. J., Rodriguez, L. O., Ron, S. R., Rondinini, C., Rylands, A. B., Sadovy de Mitcheson, Y., Sanciangco, J. C., Sanders, K. L., Santos-Barrera, G., Schipper, J., Self-Sullivan, C., Shi, Y., Shoemaker, A., Short, F. T., Sillero-Zubiri, C., Silvano, D. B. L., Smith, K. G., Smith, A. T., Snoeks, J., Stattersfield, A. J., Symes, A. J., Taber, A. B., Talukdar, B. K., Temple, H. J., Timmins, R., Tobias, J. A., Tsytsulina, K., Tweddle, D., Ubeda, C., Valenti, S. V., Paul van Dijk, P., Veiga, L. M., Veloso, A., Wege, D. C., Wilkinson, M.,

Williamson, E. A., Xie, F., Young, B. E., Akçakaya, H. R., Bennun, L., Blackburn, T. M., Boitani, L., Dublin, H. T., da Fonseca, G. A. B., Gascon, C., Lacher, T. E., Mace, G. M., Mainka, S. A., McNeely, J. A., Mittermeier, R. A., Reid, G. M., Rodriguez, J. P., Rosenberg, A. A., Samways, M. J., Smart, J., Stein, B. A. and Stuart, S. N. (2010) The impact of conservation on the status of the world's vertebrates. *Science*, 330, 1503–1509.

International Assessment of Agricultural Knowledge Science and Technology for Development (2008) *Agriculture at a Crossroads: Synthesis Report.* Island Press, Washington, DC.

International Fund for Agricultural Development (2010) *Rural Poverty Report 2011*. IFAD, Rome.

International Treaty on Plant Genetic Resources for Food and Agriculture (2009). Food and Agriculture Organization, Rome.

Joseph, R. K. (2010) International regime on access and beneft sharing: where are we now? *Asian Biotechnology and Development Review*, 12, 77–94.

Kingsbury, N. (2009) *Hybrid: The History and Science of Plant Breeding.* University of Chicago Press.

Lewis-Lettington, R. J. and Mwanyiki, S. (2006) *Case Studies on Access and Benefit-sharing.* International Plant Genetic Resources Institute, Rome.

Maxted, N. and Kell, S. P. (2009) *Establishment of a Global Network for the In Situ Conservation of Crop Wild Relatives: Status and Needs.* FAO Commission on Genetic Resources for Food and Agriculture, Rome.

Moore, G. and Tymnowski, W. (2005) *Explanatory Guide to the International Treaty on Plant Genetic Resources for Food and Agriculture.* IUCN, Gland.

Nagoya Protocol on Access to Genetic Resources and the Fair and Equitable Sharing of Benefits Arising from their Utilization to the Convention on Biological Diversity (2010) *Text and Annex.* Secretariat to the Convention on Biological Diversity, Montreal.

Organization for African Unity (2000) *African Model Legislation for the Protection of the Rights of Local Communities, Farmers and Breeders, and for the Regulation of Access to Biological Resources.* OAU, Addis Abbaba.

Pereira, H. M., Leadley, P. W., Proença, V., Alkemade, R., Scharlemann, J. P. W., Fernandez-Manjarrés, J. F., Araújo, M. B., Balvanera, P., Biggs, R., Cheung, W. W. L., Chini, L., Cooper, H. D., Gilman, E. L., Guénette, S., Hurtt, G. C., Huntington, H. P., Mace, G. M., Oberdorff, T., Revenga, C., Rodrigues, P., Scholes, R. J., Sumaila, U. R. and Walpole, M. (2010) Scenarios for global biodiversity in the 21st century. *Science*, 330, 1496–1501.

Rose, G. L. (2004) The International Undertaking on Plant Genetic Resources for Food and Agriculture: will the paper be worth the trees? *Accessing Biological Resources: Complying with the Convention on Biological Diversity* (ed. N. Stoianoff), pp. 55–90. Kluwer, Dordrecht.

Sachs, J. D., Baillie, J. E. M., Sutherland, W. J., Armsworth, P. R., Ash, N., Beddington, J., Blackburn, T. M., Collen, B., Gardiner, B., Gaston, K. J., Godfray, H. C. J., Green, R. E., Harvey, P. H., House, B., Knapp, S., Kumpel, N. F., Macdonald, D. W., Mace, G. M., Mallet, J., Matthews, A., May, R. M., Petchey, O., Purvis, A., Roe, D., Safi, K., Turner, K., Walpole, M., Watson, R. and Jones, K. E. (2009) Biodiversity conservation and the Millennium Development Goals. *Science*, 325, 1502–1503.

Santilli, J. (2012) *Agrobiodiversity and the Law*. Earthscan, London.

Secretariat of the Convention on Biological Diversity (2009) *Biodiversity for Poverty Alleviation and Development.* Convention on Biological Diversity, Montreal.

Suneetha, M. S. and Pisupati, B. (2008) *Benefit Sharing in ABS: Options and Elaborations*. UNU-IAS, Yokahama.

Ten Kate, K. and Laird, S. A. (1999) *The Commercial Use of Biodiversity: Access to Genetic Resources and Benefit-Sharing*. Earthscan, London.

United Nations (1993) *Convention on Biological Diversity*. United Nations, New York.

Wells, M. P., McShane, T. O., Dublin, H. T., O'Connor, S. and Redford, K. H. (2004) The future of integrated conservation and development projects: building on what works. *Getting Biodiversity Projects to Work: Towards more Effective Conservation and Development* (ed. T. O. Mcshane and M. P. Wells), pp. 397–422. Columbia University Press, New York.

World Bank (2005) *Global Economic Prospects*. World Bank, Washington, DC.

  (2010) *The Changing Wealth of Nations: Measuring Sustainable Development in the New Millennium*. World Bank, Washington, DC.

World Commission on Environment and Development (1987) *Our Common Future*. Island Press, Washington, DC.

15 | *Redirecting biodiversity change*

15.1 Assembling the pieces of the problem

I began writing this book in the small Galician town of Baiona where, on March 1, 1493, the arrival of the caravel *Pinta* from the Americas completed the initial stage of the Columbian exchange. It happens that I am back in Baiona as I write this final chapter – pulling together my conclusions about what it will take to redirect biodiversity change. I stated in the introduction to the book that this is by far the most significant environmental problem confronting humanity: that it dwarfs climate change; freshwater scarcity; soil, water, and air pollution; or any other of the environmental issues currently attracting attention. This is not due to any apocalyptic vision of the future, but to the observation that biodiversity change affects the quality of our lives in more ways, and more deeply, than any other environmental problem. The reason we are concerned about climate change, for example, is the effect it will have on life expectancy, health, and nutrition via its impacts on the species that determine these things. The reason we are concerned about freshwater lies in the importance of water for all of the species on which we depend. The reason we are concerned about pollution is the effect it has on the relative abundance of organisms in aquatic, terrestrial, and marine systems that directly support services we value.

Biodiversity change affects our ability to cope with the impact of changing environmental conditions. It may well be that our capacity to adapt to altered conditions is increased because of the scope for genetic engineering, but the scope for genetic engineering is itself constrained by the existing stock of genetic material in exactly the same way as traditional plant or animal breeding. Today's biodiversity is what provides the raw material for the evolution of all life on earth, whether inside or outside the production landscapes we have made for ourselves. Our short-term interest lies in the scope biodiversity offers for successful adaptation to changing environmental conditions in the space of a

464

generation or two. Given the fact that we happen to find ourselves at an unusually stable moment in the world's climatic history, however, we also have a longer-term interest in maintaining our capacity to accommodate much greater environmental change.

In this final chapter I both summarize the options available to us to do better than we have at managing the biotic resources of the planet, and indicate how things might be different if these options were selected. This is not an economist's description of the social optimum. The world we live in best fits Dasgupta's description of kakotopia: a world where ineptness, confusion, and corruption are commonplace. Utopia is beyond us. It is, instead, a description of the potential benefits of feasible reforms in a changing world. It is an opportune moment to be thinking about these things. The international community has recently embarked on a process to identify a set of sustainable development goals to replace the Millennium Development Goals (MDG) due to expire in 2015. Whereas the MDG were largely a blueprint for aid expenditures in a world dominated by the North–South divide, the sustainable development goals should capture collective preferences for managing global public goods in a world where the dividing lines between developed and underdeveloped, rich and poor, are not as clearly drawn.

The core of the problem addressed in the book is the fundamental difficulty we have in managing the supply of public goods at the international level. I have already remarked that the title of the book, *Our Uncommon Heritage*, at once reflects the diversity of life on earth and the changing structure of rights to both terrestrial and marine species. The collective perception of biodiversity as the common heritage of humankind held until quite recently. It represented a view most famously espoused by Grotius:

all that which has been so constituted by nature that although serving some one person it still suffices for the common use of all other persons, is today and ought in perpetuity to remain in the same condition as when it was first created by nature ... things which are called "public" are, according to the Laws of the law of nations, the common property of all, and the private property of none. (Grotius 1916)

That view has given way to a perception of biodiversity as an asset of nation states. The change in collective perception has yet to work its way into all of the legal structures and instruments affecting the management of biodiversity at national and international levels, and its implications for the conservation of biodiversity are accordingly far from clear. It has the potential to limit the stresses caused by open access, but it also has the potential to make it more difficult to reach agreement on the collective management of resources beyond national jurisdiction, or on the coordination of national efforts to manage resources that span jurisdictions.

I first summarize the main implications of the book for the task ahead of us. These are that we broaden our concept of conservation to embrace all of the species that are important to us; that we deepen our understanding both of the nature of biodiversity change and its significance for human wellbeing; that we better exploit the market mechanisms that guide individual decisions to use or abuse biodiversity; and that we directly confront the biodiversity change–poverty nexus. In some cases, incremental changes to existing policies have the potential to yield much. In others, what is needed is more far-reaching reform. To close I then ask what more far-reaching reforms of the rights and responsibilities of nations to the global public good might look like, and what they might deliver.

15.2 Refocusing conservation

I began by saying that while the book is not about conservation in the traditional sense of the preservation of wild-living species in protected areas and remnant wildlands, it is still about conservation. To determine whether or not we should conserve or convert any asset at all, we need to balance what is lost or gained in the process. For any asset, we should conserve that asset if and only if its value in the conserved state is expected to grow at least as fast as its value when converted to an alternative state. So we need to know the opportunity cost of conservation decisions. We need to know what has to be given up, and by whom. It follows that conservation decisions are not limited to protected areas or remnant wildlands. There are conservation decisions to be made about simplified or modified landscapes just as there are for natural landscapes. Indeed, that is exactly the problem addressed by those concerned with agro-biodiversity (Perrings *et al.* 2006; Jackson *et al.* 2007a, 2007b) and considered in Chapter 14.

The problem has traditionally been addressed in developing countries through projects that integrate conservation via protected areas and development in the surrounding land. But as was indicated in Chapter 6, the evidence on the performance of integrated conservation and development projects has in fact shown just how hard it is to marry protected area-based conservation with the needs of a growing rural population looking for land to convert to the production of foods, fuels, and fibers. Regardless of what opportunities are created in the neighborhood of protected areas, establishment of the latter generally dispossesses landholders and restricts development options (Wells and Brandon 1992; Adams *et al.* 2004; Wells *et al.* 2004). The approach to conservation in developed countries tends to be different, and is based not on the establishment of protected areas from which people are excluded, but on the introduction of zoning and other restrictions in selected areas, along with incentives for conservation or restoration in those areas. In Britain, for example, many of the fifteen national parks in England, Scotland, and Wales are on land in private ownership, and conservation takes the form of advice to land managers on wildlife and landscape conservation, on partnerships between landowners and conservation agencies, and on grants for conservation activities (Association of National Park Authorities 2012). Although a similar approach has been recommended for adoption in developing countries (Cernea and Schmidt-Soltau 2006), most conservation projects in such countries still rely on the establishment of exclusion areas. Recent evidence suggests that the exclusion approach can succeed in particular conditions: where the opportunity cost of establishing a protected area is low, and where demand for access to the protected area creates opportunities for people in surrounding areas (Ferraro, Hanauer and Sims 2011). This is clearly not an option, however, in production landscapes where many of the most acute conservation problems lie.

So one major implication of the book is that it is important to ensure that biodiversity conservation options are given appropriate weight everywhere – not only in areas under protection, or subject to integrated conservation and development projects. There are conservation questions to be addressed in agriculture, aquaculture, forestry, fisheries, and health just as there are in the protection of endangered species. Biodiversity matters in cities and production landscapes as much as it does in wild refugia. Of course the biodiversity to be conserved is likely to be specific not only to the ecosystem involved, but also to the use that is made of it. It makes little sense to have the same conservation objectives in agro-ecosystems, production forests, wildlands, and

EEZs. In a system simplified to produce foods, fuels, or fibers, the diversity of the functional groups involved in their production will be important. So too will the diversity of species supporting ancillary services from the same system – erosion control, pollution buffering, and so on. But this is quite different from the species conserved by a policy of protecting some proportion of each natural biome.

A point made repeatedly in the book is that the reason conservation organizations and bodies like the GEF are involved in traditional species preservation through protected areas is that if conservation were left to the market it would be undersupplied. Since the genetic benefits of species preservation are non-rival and non-exclusive, no one person and no one country has an incentive to preserve species at the globally optimal level. But similar market failures are evident in the oversimpli-fication of agricultural and other production landscapes, the overex-ploitation of marine ecosystems, the fragmentation of habitat through road, rail, and canal construction, or the establishment of *cordons sanitaires*.

The solutions to the conservation challenges in production land-scapes are necessarily different from those in wildlands. Within areas of national jurisdiction exclusion areas dedicated to the preservation of wild-living species are less appropriate than the kind of incentive-based approaches described in Chapter 11, or the public–private partnerships employed in some European national parks. Beyond areas of national jurisdiction there seems little alternative to a collective commitment to manage through the assignment of rights and responsibilities. These alternatives are discussed in more detail below. In both cases, though, what is needed to conservation beyond protected areas is the recogni-tion that there are generic conservation issues in any ecosystem that can and should be approached in a broadly consistent manner. These involve an assessment of the effects of interspecific and intraspecific diversity for the many services provided by those landscapes, and the development of strategies and instruments to ensure their conservation where warranted.

15.3 Knowing what is happening

Since we have few reliable indicators of the importance of biodiversity loss for human wellbeing, a precondition for making informed decisions about the conservation of resources is that we strengthen the indicators we do have. I have argued that enabling prices to do a better job of tracking social opportunity cost is an important part of this. So too is the extension of the system of national accounts to include changes in the value of the biological stocks that correspond to different forms of land use. The reason is straightforward. Most biodiversity change in terrestrial systems is the direct result of either land-use/land-cover change or the trade related dispersal of species. The simplification of systems to enhance the production of foods, fuels, and fibers represents a conscious choice to reduce the relative abundance of many species and to eliminate others. Most biodiversity change in aquatic systems, by contrast, is due to land-based pollution and overexploitation. The problem to be addressed is that many of the effects of land management are external to the market, and therefore ignored by resource users. The prices attaching to each resource are biased. To induce landholders to take due account of the effect they have on biodiversity they should be confronted by the real costs or compensated for the real benefits of their actions. This requires that we know what those costs and benefits are.

Given that many of the external costs of biodiversity change relate to the capacity of ecosystems to function in changed environmental conditions, the true social opportunity cost of resource use is typically uncertain. I have argued that this imposes additional requirements on assessments of biodiversity change at all scales. To project anthropogenic biodiversity change we need to improve our capacity to model interactions between human behavior and environmental change. To measure the importance of biodiversity conservation in the management of risk we need to improve our capacity to model system performance with different complements of species. In Chapter 9, I argued that the new IPBES could potentially play a significant role in this effort at multiple scales. Since it will have responsibility for projecting the consequences of strategic options both for nation states and for the international community, it will need to be able to model the feedbacks between the social and biophysical systems over the projection period. Establishing protocols for this that go beyond existing scenario planning exercises will help move us to the point where governments can evaluate the risks associated with policies that have differing impacts on biodiversity.

The two things we have yet to do effectively are (1) to develop indicators of biodiversity change that map into the set of indicators that inform governments' resource allocation decisions, and (2) to factor the risks associated with diversity change into those decisions. The development of the SEEA, the adjusted net savings measure and the inclusive wealth accounts described in Chapter 9 are useful steps along the way, but none yet addresses the biodiversity risks of land use or trade in an operational way. Without an indication of the consequences of biodiversity change in different sectors, governments have tended to treat those risks as negligible.

The one exception to this, as has been noted at several points, is the risks associated with changes in the relative abundance of specific pathogens. Because the impact of infectious human diseases (and at least some animal and plant diseases) can be both immediate and severe, governments have an incentive to mitigate risk. Internationally, since the public good at stake is the weakest link, governments have had an incentive to use development assistance to invest in mitigation in poor countries. The approach to the conservation of wild species has, by contrast, rested on the specification of protected areas in which the only risks at issue are those driving conservationists' recommendations on the proportion of each biome to put under protection. The access and benefit sharing provisions of the CBD notwithstanding, investment in conservation has not been driven by the risk of forgone opportunities in species extinction. In production landscapes, the introduction of projects to conserve landraces for their response to the selective pressures of climate change is evidence that at least some are concerned by the risks associated with the loss of landraces and crop wild relatives in production landscapes, but there is otherwise little evidence that governments are concerned about the risks associated with an exclusively *ex situ* approach to the conservation of crop genetic resources.

It follows that of all the functions of IPBES, the one that is likely to matter most as global change unfolds is the one that requires the assessment body to be forward looking. It is undoubtedly important to record current biodiversity status and trends, and to assess the consequences of this for human wellbeing. However, if the body is to serve the global community best it should be able to evaluate the future consequences of the policies affecting biodiversity change. Specifically, it should be able to evaluate the future risks of alternative policies. In the absence of risk projections, governments will have difficulty in making a rational choice between adaptation and mitigation strategies. Risk is also the way in which biodiversity and the sustainability of development strategies intersect. In production landscapes, the use of different crop species, and the use of genetically heterogeneous varieties within crop species, is one of the oldest of strategies for assuring the sustainability of agriculture. The value of the same strategy now lies in the potential it has for managing not just year on year environmental and market fluctuations, but the risks associated with future evolution of the bio-physical system. If sufficient biodiversity is conserved in production landscapes, selective pressure brought by global environmental change will induce genetic changes that offer traits fit not just for purpose but also for the changed conditions.

15.4 Enhancing the efficiency of biodiversity markets

The third general implication of this book is that better information on the costs and benefits of biodiversity change over a range of landscapes should translate into better signals to resource users. The abundance and richness of species around the world is determined by resource use decisions. Most are guided by market prices that fail to signal the opportunity cost of changes in either the relative abundance or richness of species. Wherever this occurs there is a case for interventions that change the incentives to resource users. The PES systems discussed in Chapter 11 are merely the latest in a long line of initiatives prompted by the same basic ideas. If market prices exist, but fail to signal the true scarcity of resources, they may be brought into line with social oppor-tunity cost through the application of corrective taxes or subsidies. If market prices for scarce resources do not exist, markets may be created. The first idea is due to A. C. Pigou (1920), the second to Ronald Coase (1960). Both are critical if the billions of independent decision-makers are to take account of the impact they have on others who share a common environment. It is not important that decision-makers know what impact they have on the environment. What is important is that they act *as if* they know. That is the role and the *raison d'être* of efficient pricing.

The theory and practice of the use of economic instruments for envi-ronmental management both have a long history (Tietenberg 1990; Pearce and Warford 1993; Panayotou 1995; Stavins 2003; OECD 2004). The options for inducing socially optimal levels of activity are well understood. Much is also known about the real impact of instru-ments of different kinds, and about what works and what does not. The case for corrective taxes, user fees, access charges, royalties, and the like is well established, and does not need to be made again. There are, however, three closely related sets of risks that have been re-examined in this book. The first is the risk associated with the use of subsidies to correct market failures. The second is the risk associated with the conflation of equity and efficiency goals in resource pricing. The third is the risk associated with the development of markets that are incomplete by design.

In principle, the mirror image of a Pigovian tax is a Pigovian subsidy. Just as a tax can ensure that negative environmental externalities are taken into account, so can a subsidy ensure that account is taken of positive environmental externalities. In practice, however, we have seen that few subsidies are designed to correct for market failures. Most are designed to support the expansion of particular industries for political purposes. Wherever industries supported in this way are themselves a source of negative environmental externalities, subsidies can make things worse. Economists and environmentalists alike have been drawing attention to the potentially negative impacts of subsidies on biodiversity for many years (Myers and Kent 2001; Pearce 2003; Anthoff and Hahn 2010). The scale of the problem is large. In 2004 it was estimated that OECD countries were providing subsidies to industries amounting to around $400 billion a year, with effects that include off-site pollution stemming from the overuse of pesticides and fertilizers in agriculture, the overexploitation of fish stocks, air pollution, and increased greenhouse gas emissions to the overconsumption of fossil fuels (Barde and Honkatukia 2004).

Whether subsidies reduce the marginal private cost of inputs below their marginal social cost, or increase the marginal private benefit of an activity above its marginal social benefit, they have the same effect: to increase the level of activity above the socially optimal level. In some cases subsidies have the effect of exaggerating other sources of inefficiency. In the case of high seas fisheries, for example, the open access rules that prevail encourage fishers to increase effort well beyond the level that would be optimal from a social perspective. Under open access fishers will increase effort up to the point at which total revenue and total cost are equated, which is generally well beyond the maximum sustainable yield of the resource. Subsidies that reduce total cost have the effect of increasing the privately optimal level of effort even further. It is estimated that subsidies for vessel construction, fuel costs, port and processing plant construction, and payments for foreign access agreements sum to around $16 billion annually (Sumaila *et al.* 2010). The result is overcapitalization of the world fleet and levels of fishing effort well above what would be socially optimal.

Of course not all subsidies are environmentally damaging. Indeed, subsidies pose a problem only if they widen the gap between private and social costs or benefits. There is evidence that many subsidies do exaggerate existing market failures, but there are also subsidies that have the opposite effect. In much the same way, if the effect of trade liberalization is to close the gap between private and social costs it should enhance the efficiency of resource allocation, but if it does not it can be equally damaging. Since trade liberalization generally increases activity levels, if it occurs without attention to environmental effects that are external to the market these effects will also be increased.

Globally, by far the largest subsidies – and the ones that have the most direct effect on biodiversity – are subsidies to agriculture. It has been estimated that $318 billion of the $400 billion in annual subsidies in OECD countries in the early years of this century were due to agriculture (Barde and Honkatukia 2004). Market price support accounts for the bulk of OECD agricultural subsidies (between 60 percent and 70 percent). The balance comprises payments for outputs, inputs, and transfers based on either area or historic entitlements. The environmental impacts of different kinds of subsidies depend on the way they affect land management. Market price support, for example, tends to increase levels of activity without particular implications for production technologies. Area payments and transfers based on historic entitlements are similar. However, payments for particular inputs and outputs directly affect both product and input mix. Wherever subsidies induce farmers to intensify production, or to reduce the area of land available to other than cultivated species, they are likely to affect both on-farm and off-farm biodiversity.

We have also seen that while some of the biodiversity impacts of agricultural subsidies in developed countries are local, others are regional or even global. A study of environmentally harmful subsidies in the Netherlands, for example, analyzed the impact of on-budget and off-budget subsidies on greenhouse gas emissions (global) and acidification (regional). Off-budget subsidies are tax deductions, exemptions, or special tariffs, provision of public goods and services below cost, capital subsidies such as loan guarantees or debt forgiveness, establishment of minimum prices, quantity restrictions, import quotas, and export credits.

It found that off-budget subsidies were largely responsible for emissions of carbon and sulfur (van Beers and van den Bergh 2009). Other studies suggest that important biodiversity externalities of agricultural subsidies include the international dispersal of plant pests and pathogens through the trade in agricultural products (Perrings *et al.* 2005). OECD agricultural subsidies are generally argued to affect developing countries through the impact they have on agricultural prices and hence agricultural incomes. This is also thought to impact the environment in developing countries through poverty–environment linkages of the kind discussed in Chapters 6 and 14.

The problem with subsidies is not that they are unable to correct market failures, but that they are seldom designed to do so. Agricultural price support schemes, for example, are generally aimed more at increasing the incomes of farmers than at compensating them for external benefits conferred on society. Similarly, many of the new payments for ecosystem services schemes are aimed more at poverty alleviation in developing countries than at compensating landholders for the external benefits of land management decisions. The pro-poor dimension of these schemes makes equity the primary goal, and economic efficiency a secondary goal of the schemes. There is nothing wrong with the intention behind pro-poor payment schemes, just as there is nothing wrong with the intention behind traditional agricultural subsidies. Governments have the right to identify and implement policies that change the distribution of assets and incomes to meet social equity goals. There is, however, something wrong with using payment schemes that are ostensibly designed to signal the true scarcity of resources to support incomes. If the inefficiency that stems from missing markets is to be dealt with, prices must be permitted to converge on the social opportunity cost of the resources involved. They should not be used to manipulate real incomes. There are other ways of dealing with social equity goals that are more effective.

The third set of risks – those associated with the creation of markets that are incomplete by design – is another manifestation of the same problem. Subsidies are problematic when they exaggerate the wedge between the private and social cost of environmental resources. The creation of markets for particular ecosystem services can be problematic for the same reason. The point has been made repeatedly that since we get what we pay for, we should pay for the things that matter to us collectively. The environmental costs of agriculture identified in the MA are external to the market precisely because farmers are not required to bear those costs. The dead zone in the Gulf of Mexico, for example, exists because no farmers in the Mississippi–Missouri basin bear any of the costs associated with fertilizer runoff from their land (Dodds 2006).

Externalities of agriculture of this kind have their origin in the fact that farmers' land-use decisions affect many things beyond the production of foods, fuels, or fibers. Since ecosystem services are jointly produced, raising the output of any particular service has implications for all other services. It increases the supply of services that are complements in production, and decreases the supply of services that are substitutes in production. It follows that while adding markets for specific non-marketed ecosystem services means that more account will be taken of the scarcity of those particular services, it will also have implications for the supply of other non-marketed services. In recent years the creation of markets for carbon sequestration has focused attention on this problem in a particularly acute way. Paying landholders for carbon sequestration is similar to paying them for the production of corn, timber, or the feedstock for biofuels. It will induce them to focus on the most effective methods for supplying carbon sequestration without regard for the production of other ecosystem services. Given that carbon sequestration is jointly supplied with a number of other services, however, this will have consequences for those services (Jackson *et al.* 2005; Díaz, Hector and Wardle 2009; Imai *et al.* 2009; Nelson *et al.* 2009). Indeed, this is the motivation for the expansion of the REDD program to take account of some of these ancillary services – or co-benefits (Brown, Seymour and Pesket 2008; Long 2009). But unless all the services in the bundle are priced, there will still be effects that are external to the transactions involved. As long as prices fail to signal the true social opportunity cost of the loss of biodiversity in production and wild landscapes, people will have an incentive to act in ways that drive too many species to extinction. Market mechanisms have the potential to improve the signals to resource users in many different ways, but not if they are burdened with distribu-tional goals and not if the prices they generate are distorted by tax structures that weaken their capacity to reflect social opportunity cost.

15.5 Reducing the biodiversity costs of poverty alleviation

The relation between biodiversity change and poverty is the focus of Chapters 7 and 14. The aim of poverty alleviation is enshrined in the

MDG, the mission of the World Bank, and many other intergovernmental organizations. It is hard to imagine a goal that has greater support from the international community. Yet the actions taken by people to escape poverty are among the main drivers of habitat loss and the attendant loss of biodiversity in natural landscapes. They are also among the main drivers of the loss of landraces and crop wild relatives in production landscapes. Other things being equal, the pursuit of poverty alleviation in countries where a majority of the population make a living from agriculture increases the rate of biodiversity loss. There are certainly examples of specific integrated conservation and development projects that have met both goals successfully, but they are quite rare.

In the poorest region of the world, Sub-Saharan Africa, the primary strategy for poverty alleviation is agricultural growth. For some individuals this is achieved by the conversion of forest or grassland – through extensive growth. For others it is achieved by increasing yields – through intensive growth. For the intergovernmental organizations with an agricultural remit the goal is to achieve the intensification of crop production. The conditions in which this has to occur are unusually difficult. Past attempts at intensification have left a legacy of degraded soil health, soil nutrient depletion, soil erosion, on-site and off-site damage from the inefficient use of fertilizers and pesticides in addition to the loss of important components of biodiversity. They have also adversely affected many ecosystem services important to agriculture, including pollination, pest control, and nutrient cycling. At the same time environmental conditions are changing more rapidly than at any time since agriculture began.

The impacts of the two strategies on wild biodiversity differ. The extensive growth of agriculture directly reduces the habitat available to other species, and brings humans into closer contact with wildlife. Intensive growth has effects both on farm and off farm, the off-farm effects being dominated by fertilizer and pesticide runoff. Nevertheless, I have argued that the conservation problems in both cases have a very similar structure. The main questions to ask about the extensive growth of agriculture are whether the value of conserved land is expected to grow at a faster rate than the value of converted land, taking into account externalities of conversion – such as the risk that closer contact between humans and wildlife leads to the emergence of zoonotic diseases. The main questions to ask about the intensive growth of agriculture are whether the value of land managed more intensively is expected to grow at a faster rate than the value of land managed less intensively taking into account any externalities of intensification. In both cases land is a proxy for the substrate and all of the biota associated with the use to which it is put. The focus of conservation may differ in each case – wild species in natural landscapes, landraces, and crop wild relatives in production landscapes – but the problem is essentially the same.

We have seen that the way in which the poverty of resource users affects the decisions they make about land use is also similar. People without private assets have little option but to exploit assets in the public domain. The landless exploit open access common pool resources through hunting, gathering, and fishing, grazing livestock on common land, or convert unused common land to plant crops. Those with access to land exploit its natural potential – its stocks of nutrients. However, those lacking title and security of tenure are unable to raise funds to invest in land improvement. They are also compelled to focus on current production rather than the future state of the resource. With few resources to combat pests and pathogens, they also rely heavily on naturally occurring pest predators. This is the sense in which poor people depend on biodiversity. Having few resources of their own, they exploit resources in the public domain.

The evidence suggests that the intensification of agriculture threatens biodiversity in several ways. Within production landscapes it encourages crop choices that favor modern high-yielding varieties, and discourages landraces and wild crop relatives. It also encourages the use of fertilizers and pesticides with effects on both on-farm pests and pest-predators. In wild landscapes it makes it possible to bring more and more marginal land under cultivation, leading both to the loss of habitats and their fragmentation. At the same time, fertilizer and pesticide runoff affects downstream biodiversity.

Evaluated in terms of the composition of their wealth, poor people have a portfolio that is skewed towards natural assets in the public domain. The goal and effect of poverty alleviation strategies is to increase the private asset holdings of the poor, and to reduce their reliance on open access common pool resources. The common pool species made redundant in the process are frequently displaced, or their conservation is neglected. From the perspective of the individual, poverty alleviation strategies are equivalent to an increase in the relative rate of return on intensive agriculture. Farmers benefitting from such strategies are encouraged to convert to intensive methods.

From a global perspective, the issue in this lies in the fact that the species displaced in the process have value that may not be recognized in farmers' decisions. Since farmers do not own the biological resources displaced in the process, they are unable to capture many of the benefits they generate. These benefits are accordingly external to the conversion decision. They include cultural, regulating, and supporting ecosystem services that frequently benefit people distant in both time and space. They also include the genetic resources contained within landraces and wild crop relatives that potentially benefit the global community for all time. It is possible that even if these assets were fully taken into account it would still be efficient to convert wildland to agriculture, or to adopt intensive agricultural techniques. The problem discussed in this book, however, lies in the fact that we have many reasons to believe that the opportunity cost of agricultural intensification is higher than previously thought: that the biodiversity effects of poverty alleviation may be important enough in many production landscapes that the decision would look different if they were to be taken into account.

Addressing the issue requires both that the nature of farmers' rights to the assets be clearly defined, and that farmers be able to capture the marginal benefit of conservation decisions made in the global interest. Payments for ecosystem services do offer a plausible mechanism, and there is certainly a groundswell of opinion in favor of this option and the potential it has for poverty alleviation. But I have argued that it would be a mistake to use the payments under a performance contract as the vehicle for poverty alleviation. It would be better to define farmers' rights well enough that their contribution to farmers' wealth was clear, and then to negotiate payments at the appropriate scale on the incremental cost principle. The appropriate scale may not always be obvious. Although sovereign rights to genetic diversity might rest with the nation state, there could be cases where it was appropriate to negotiate payments for the conservation of a class of landraces and wild relatives over an area that spanned several countries. There could also be cases where the appropriate scale was quite localized. Particular landraces might, for example, be more valuable at a national than a local scale, and again at an international than a national scale. The incremental cost between the local and national scale might generate one set of payments, and the incremental cost between the national and international scale might generate another.

The central point here is that the potential trade-off between poverty alleviation and conservation does have a solution. Finding the efficient level of conservation requires an understanding of the rate of growth in the value of conserved assets to all potential beneficiaries relative to their rate of growth if converted. Moreover, the calculation is the same whether we are interested in natural or production landscapes. This is a particular challenge for the access and benefit sharing provisions of the CBD and the ITPGRFA, but it applies in similar ways to the calculation of payments for many other ecosystem services. To this point, while poverty alleviation measures have delivered much to the individuals in poverty, they have also taken much from the global community. Resolving the problem requires recognition both of the rights of landholders and the interests of the global community. Recognition of landholders' rights is a prerequisite for defining their real assets. Recognition of the interests of the global community is a prerequisite for the calculation of the changes in the value of those assets.

15.6 The abrogation of common heritage rights

The leitmotiv of this book is that biodiversity change is driven by the purposeful behavior of billions of individuals. The biodiversity problem is to find a balance between the costs and benefits of actions that lead to the simplification of ecosystems, the dispersal of species between previously unconnected ecosystems, the extinction of some species, and the genetic erosion of others. What motivates the behavior of individuals are the private net gains to be had from alternative actions. These have a deserved place in the balance, but they are not the only things to be taken into account. The social costs of private actions also matter. Of the many reasons why the social costs of private actions are ignored, the one that recurs most frequently is the public good nature of many of the ecosystem services supported by biodiversity, and of the genetic information those species contain. It is this that lies behind the systematic tendency for the undersupply of services that confer net benefits on society, and for the oversupply of disservices that impose net costs. Some services are intrinsically public, in the sense that they are naturally non-rival in the consumption, and the technology does not exist that would allow exclusion from the benefits they offer. Others are public by social construction. Many open access common pool resources are in this category. Like Garrett Hardin's commons, the tragedy lies in the nature of access rights and not in the intrinsic properties of the resource.

For many such resources a solution to the problem has been found in the establishment of property rights that allow right-holders to exclude others. In some cases this simply means the formalization of traditional rights that were, in the past, enforced by distance. In others it means the re-establishment of rights that had been abrogated by national governments bent on asserting control. In other cases still, it means the establishment of new rights. Over the last three decades, the trend has been to the establishment of rights of exclusion to many open access common pool resources. The most dramatic moves in this direction have been the establishment of EEZs within the high seas under the UNCLOS (1982), the declaration that nation states have sovereign rights to wild biodiversity in the CBD (1993), and the declaration that this extends to all crop genetic resources in the ITPGRFA (2004). In all three cases the assertion of national sovereign rights was in direct conflict with the principles that had previously informed international agreement. Both the high seas and the genetic resources contained in biodiversity had previously been defined as the common heritage of humankind. Under these three treaties they became, in effect, state owned.

The establishment of national rights of exclusion to such resources may go some way to eliminating the worst effects of open access. There is at least some evidence that the establishment of more tightly regulated management regimes in the EEZs has reduced the overexploitation of fish stocks (Costello, Gaines and Lynham 2008; Worm *et al.* 2009). However, it does not guarantee either that nation states will take account of any effects of their actions on others or that there will be compensation for those who have lost assets in the process. Nor is the process at an end. As Shackleford has observed, all components of the international commons are either now being challenged or already shrinking and the only real question is whether the process will be directed by the international community through the establishment of considered multilateral legal and governance regimes, or will simply legitimate a sub-optimal status quo (Shackelford 2008).

Adam Smith published *The Wealth of Nations* in 1776. In the two centuries that followed the world has been transformed through the many processes he described. Among these, the appropriation of resources by the nation state through conquest or colonization may now be less important as a road to national wealth than it was in the eighteenth century, but it still continues. Access to natural resources is still a more likely cause of war between nations than anything else, and many countries are actively seeking to push out their frontiers. Seven countries have outstanding claims to large areas of Antarctica, and others – the USA, Russia, and Brazil – have reserved the right to lodge their own claims. Four countries have outstanding sector claims to the Arctic sea, and are poised to claim an extended continental shelf (with rights to resources on or below the seabed). Within areas of national jurisdiction governments have already signaled claims to sovereignty over the genetic resources, and we might expect these claims to be extended to the biodiversity in contested areas beyond national jurisdiction. While the national legal structures to support property rights in genetic resources have yet to be determined, the likelihood is that most will assert that these resources are state property. Some countries have already done so, and others have legislation in preparation that has the same intent.

What distinguishes the remaining territorial claims is that the resources at stake are part of the international commons. What distinguishes claims to genetic resources everywhere is the fact that they privatize a global public good. The wealth of individual nations is being built out of the wealth of all nations. The process offers some benefits. It strengthens the power of governments to regulate access to sovereign resources. It increases the incentive to innovate. But it also imposes costs. Since the strategic interests of individual nation states seldom align with the interests of the global community, we may be locking ourselves into a future that is increasingly constrained by a diminishing gene pool. Avoiding this is among the principal challenges of our time.

15.7 The uncommon heritage of humankind

To draw together the strands of this book that bear on that challenge let us first be clear that the problem to be solved is the provision of a multifaceted global public good: multifaceted because it encompasses the many opportunities offered by the genetic diversity of species, global because all of humankind reaps its benefits, public because, once provided, none can be excluded from those benefits. The current loss of biodiversity imposes costs on all future generations, everywhere. We do not know precisely what those costs are, but we know where they come from. The gene pool can be thought about as a portfolio of biological assets whose value lies in the capacity of different gene combinations to perform well in different conditions, under different technologies, and under different preferences. As we strip out species that compete with or prey upon the species that perform well in current conditions, we make ourselves more vulnerable to changing conditions. Aldo Leopold's famous dictum "to keep every cog and wheel is the first precaution of intelligent tinkering" is an assertion that while the balance between the components of the portfolio might change, components should not be needlessly dropped. Collectively, humankind invested some $300 million (nominal) between 1967 and 1980 in the eradication of smallpox, and some $5 billion (nominal) between 1994 and 2009 in the eradication of rinderpest. But these are the only deliberate extinctions. Every other species whose disappearance has been at human hands since Neolithic times has been a casualty of ignorance, carelessness, or neglect. They were needlessly dropped.

What further complicates the problem is that the portfolio is dynamic. Speciation takes place at different rates for different taxa, and extinctions occur for reasons other than human intervention. The growth of the *ex situ* seed collections, for instance, is a response to Leopold's dictum, but the *ex situ* collections alone cannot preserve the dynamic responses of landraces to changing conditions. The solution to this problem is clearly to promote *in situ* conservation, but then not everything can be conserved *in situ*. There are still choices to be made. So what would a system of global conservation look like that addresses the challenges identified in this book? How would it differ from the strategy that has dominated conservation efforts for the thirty years since the World Conservation Union's Third World Congress on National Parks and Protected Areas established a goal to create a worldwide network of national parks and protected areas to cover 10 percent of all terrestrial ecological regions? I close by sketching an answer to these questions.

First consider the abrogation of common heritage rights. Some who favored the change intended to give nation states an incentive to exercise stewardship over biodiversity within their jurisdictions. They wished to avoid the dangers that open access brings. Others intended to pave the way for private intellectual property rights in genetic material. They recognized the role of patents in encouraging research and development. Both saw the abrogation of common heritage rights as a way to increase the security of property in genetic resources, and hence to encourage their conservation. One unintended consequence of this process, however, was the progressive erosion of the interest of landholders in conserving the biodiversity in their immediate control. While all biodiversity is affected, the loss of the genetic resources of landraces, crop wild relatives, and traditional livestock strains has the most immediate and direct effect on human wellbeing. An implication of the arguments of Chapter 14 is that if we are to realize the conservation benefits of secure property rights, then systems of landholder rights in general, and farmers' rights in particular, need to be restructured to confer secure, time- and place-based rights to the genetic material in landraces and other biological resources. Another unintended consequence of the abrogation of common heritage rights is a reduction in the national incentive to contribute genetic material to the remaining open access pools (e.g. the CGIAR *ex situ* collections). While all retain an interest in exploiting such open access pools, none sees an advantage in adding to them. There seems little alternative, at this stage, to the establishment of time- and place-based rights to the accessions in *ex situ* collections if the incentive to contribute genetic material to those collections is not to be lost. Cooperation between nation states to contribute past vintages of the genetic material in landraces to common collections is likely to depend on royalty payments.

Beyond national jurisdiction the implications of the abrogation of common heritage rights remain highly uncertain. In principle, the UNCLOS still adheres to the Grotius view. In practice, it has presided over the extension of territorial claims through the EEZs. It is highly likely that this will continue. Areas beyond national jurisdiction still remain in the public domain, and are still effectively open access. It is the choice of national governments that these resources be regulated only weakly – through multilateral agreements that eschew enforcement. Yet the intergovernmental bodies already exist that could administer these areas on behalf of humankind. In the open oceans, for example, the same fishery management regimes now implemented in the EEZs could be operated by a UN body for the benefit of all countries. The same *ex situ* gene collections now operated for terrestrial systems by the CGIAR system could be operated by a UN body, again for the benefit of all countries. National governments that have not yet exhausted their territorial ambitions may well have little patience for the common heritage, but it can still be secured. There are many reasons why agreements at the global scale frequently fall short of what is possible, and both the CBD and the UNCLOS illustrate these quite clearly. Nor should the difficulties in strengthening such agreements be underestimated. But given that what is at stake is insurance for our collective survival in an uncertain world, it is worth the effort to try.

The main conclusion of the book is that provision of the many benefits offered by the world's ecosystems depends on the establishment of multiple governance mechanisms operating at many different spatial and temporal scales, all of which share one fundamental characteristic. No matter what the scale, no matter who the constituents, all seek to regulate the activities of people exploiting the common pool dimensions of ecosystems to meet the many objectives of those constituents. In some instances – the regulation of open ocean fisheries, for example – the activities are quite precisely defined. In others – the regulation of global nitrous oxide emissions, for example – they are not. At some scales – local conservation of specific landscapes, for example – there exists a well-defined authority with the power to enforce compliance with agreements on land use. At others – global protection of the gene pool, for example – there does not. By and large, the regulatory problem becomes more challenging the larger the spatial scale, but more manageable the larger the temporal scale. The larger the spatial scale the less likely there is to be a government with the power to impose compliance, and the greater the number and heterogeneity of constituents. The larger the temporal scale, the greater the opportunity there is for repeated interaction between constituents, for learning and for building trust.

Biodiversity change is the consequence of largely private actions that alter the diversity of genes, species, and ecosystems. Its regulation circumscribes private actions to protect against some outcomes and to promote others. If we take terrestrial systems as an example, then one conclusion of the book is that the regulation of land use to conserve biological resources should cover all the land surface of the earth. This is not nearly as far off current practice as it seems. The dominant approach to biodiversity conservation is through protected areas. These are, in effect, areas zoned for particular land uses. In some protected areas the only allowable land use is the preservation of pristine landscapes. In others it includes a wide range of economic activities, and very substantial modification of both the physical landscape and the species found there. I have argued that this is as it should be. Our collective interest in the conservation of species in different areas is likely to vary considerably, and the nature of the protection offered should also vary. In all landscapes, though, the effect of land use on species should be a factor in the zoning of activities. It is not enough to offer total protection to only 10 percent of the earth's land surface. The task should be to provide the appropriate level of protection to 100 percent of the land surface. The appropriate level of protection might be expected to vary significantly in different landscapes, both in terms of the targeted species and their relative abundance. Just as conservation biologists consider the optimal composition and structure of protected areas dedicated to the preservation of endangered species, so should agronomists, for example, consider the optimal composition and structure of zoning protected areas dedicated to the conservation of landraces and wild crop relatives.

The governance mechanisms required to achieve this would differ from one system to another since those with an interest in each system – the stakeholders – would vary, as would the spatial and temporal scale of the conservation problem. But the instrument that might be applied in all cases is already ubiquitous. The zoning of land uses is a near-universal phenomenon and its extension to consider the impact of land use on beneficial or harmful species is not as much of a change as might be thought. What is less familiar is the evaluation of interactions between zoned land uses in different locations. The separation of land uses across space is commonplace. Managing the interactions between land uses is not. Governance mechanisms to allow the coordination of zoning decisions may need to be developed along with the corresponding coordination instruments. Much has been made of the potential for the price system to coordinate behavior, for example, but the development of markets for scarce ecosystem services that are currently not priced requires governance mechanisms that address the rights and responsibilities that people have in the system, and that bound their actions so as to protect the public good.

The coordination of activities across space and time is one of the greatest challenges to be addressed in redirecting biodiversity change. Enough has been said to indicate that the challenge is qualitatively different at the national and international scales. At the international scale the lack of any supranational authority means that coordination of government interventions in ecosystems falling within national jurisdiction can only be achieved through bilateral or multilateral agreement between nation states. Each country then has an incentive to act strategically to protect its own best interests, and this encourages free-riding behavior. Moreover, the greater the differences among countries – in terms of the costs and benefits of coordination – the harder it is to reach agreement. There is, however, one good reason to be hopeful.

Increasing the number of parties to an international agreement makes it more difficult for countries to cooperate in taking collective action on any issue. This means that where international environmental problems require cooperation (are in the nature of a prisoner's dilemma) it is harder to sustain cooperation the more countries are involved. However, where the problem is to coordinate national action rather than to cooperate in taking international action, increasing the number of parties to an international agreement makes it more, not less, stable. The greater the number of parties, the greater is the scope for building a consensus (convergent strategies) within the agreement (Brousseau *et al.* 2012). So while framework agreements like the CBD have limited capacity to stimulate cooperative international action, they may be useful in coordinating national action.

Most terrestrial biodiversity change is place based. Most conservation options actions are therefore local. The appropriate governance structure is one that combines the devolution of responsibility for conservation to local levels and the establishment of mechanisms to coordinate conservation actions over space and over time. In a rapidly evolving global system it is also important that the coordination of local activities is sensitive to changes in both national and international conditions. That is, it is important that they are error correcting. Automatic error correction mechanisms, such as the market, have an advantage that negotiated changes in agreements lack. They can respond to changes in environmental conditions, in information, and in the preferences of those engaging in market transactions. Redirecting biodiversity change will involve the greater use of such mechanisms. But other things will be needed as well. The coordination of zoning rules, for example, requires both an information system that tracks the effects of interactions between land-uses, and a mechanism for feeding that information back into local land use planning systems. There are currently many different information systems, serving many different multilateral agreements. The problem of coordination accordingly spans both the development of standards for data and meta-data and the reconciliation of measures agreed in each of many different multilateral agreements.

Coordination of national conservation activities may be hard, but international cooperation in the management of ecosystems beyond national jurisdiction is harder still. Indeed, this is the greatest challenge we face in redirecting biodiversity change. I have suggested that the most likely outcome of current tensions is a scramble for the resources of the oceans and land areas beyond national jurisdiction. Action of this kind has happened many times in the past, and all of the signs suggest that countries are positioning themselves to enter the fray should it happen in the future. But the die is not yet cast. The option of developing governance mechanisms for the collective management of global common pool resources still exists. The many landlocked countries of the world, and the many members of civil society whose concerns transcend national boundaries, have a profound interest in protecting both their historic rights and their future options. Human history is littered with examples of actions that have locked societies into particular pathways, but there have also been moments at which societies have stepped back from the brink so as to keep their options open. The initial taking of the EEZs and seabed beyond provides a precedent for the progressive seizure of the open oceans by maritime states, but as of now resources beyond those limits are still regarded as the common heritage of humankind. As the international community reconsiders its collective objectives in the 2030 sustainable development goals, it is a good moment to reassess what we stand to lose from the abrogation of common heritage rights in areas beyond national jurisdiction. It is also a good moment to ask what governance mechanisms, short of national appropriation of common pool resources, can protect the biological resources of those areas.

References

Adams, W. M., Aveling, R., Brockington, D., Dickson, B., Elliott, J., Hutton, J., Roe, D., Vira, B. and Wolmer, W. (2004) Biodiversity conservation and the eradication of poverty. *Science*, 306, 1146–1149.

Anthoff, D. and Hahn, R. (2010) Government failure and market failure: on the inefficiency of environmental and energy policy. *Oxford Review of Economic Policy*, 26, 197–224.

Association of National Park Authorities (2012) *National Parks: Britain's Breathing Spaces*. Available at www.nationalparks.gov.uk (accessed 2012).

Barde, J.-P. and Honkatukia, O. (2004) Environmentally harmful subsidies. *The International Yearbook of Environmental and Resource Economics 2004/2005* (ed. T. Tietenberg and H. Folmer), pp. 254–288. Edward Elgar, Cheltenham.

Brousseau, E., Dedeurwaerdere, T., Jouvet, P.-A. and Willinger, M. (eds.) (2012) *Global Environmental Commons: Analytical and Political*

Challenges in Building Governance Mechanisms. Oxford University Press.

Brown, D., Seymour, F. and Peskett, L. (2008) How do we achieve REDD co-benefits and avoid doing harm? *Moving ahead with REDD: Issues, Options and Implications* (ed. A. Angelsen), pp. 107–118. CIFOR, Bogor.

Cernea, M. M. and Schmidt-Soltau, K. (2006) Poverty risks and national parks: policy issues in conservation and resettlement. *World Development*, 34, 1808–1830.

Coase, R. (1960) The problem of social cost. *Journal of Law and Economics*, 3, 1–44.

Costello, C., Gaines, S. D. and Lynham, J. (2008) Can catch shares prevent fisheries collapse? *Science*, 321, 1678–1681.

Díaz, S., Hector, A. and Wardle, D. A. (2009) Biodiversity in forest carbon sequestration initiatives: not just a side benefit. *Current Opinion in Environmental Sustainability*, 1, 55–60.

Dodds, W. K. (2006) Nutrients and the dead zone: the link between nutrient ratios and dissolved oxygen in the northern Gulf of Mexico. *Frontiers in Ecology and the Environment*, 4, 211–217.

Ferraro, P. J., Hanauer, M. M. and Sims, K. R. E. (2011) Conditions associated with protected area success in conservation and poverty reduction. *Proceedings of the National Academy of Sciences*, 108, 13913–13918.

Grotius, H. (1916 [1608]) *The Freedom of the Seas, or the Right Which Belongs to the Dutch to take part in the East Indian Trade* (trans. Ralph Van Deman Magoffin). Oxford University Press.

Imai, N., Samejima, H., Langner, A., Ong, R. C., Kita, S., Titin, J., Chung, A. Y., Lagan, P., Lee, Y. F. and Kitayama, K. (2009) Co-benefits of sustainable forest management in biodiversity conservation and carbon sequestration. *PLoS One*, 4, e8267.

Jackson, L. E., Pascual, U., Brussaard, L., de Ruiter, P. and Bawa, K. S. (2007a) Biodiversity in agricultural landscapes: investing without losing interest. *Agriculture, Ecosystems and Environment*, 121, 193–195.

Jackson, L. E., Brussaard, L., de Ruiter, P. C., Pascual, U., Perrings, C. and Bawa, K. (2007b) Agrobiodiversity. *Encyclopedia of Biodiversity* (ed. A. L. Simon), pp. 1–13. Elsevier, New York.

Jackson, R. B., Jobbagy, E. G., Avissar, R., Roy, S. B., Barrett, D. J., Cook, C. W., Farley, K. A., le Maitre, D. C., McCarl, B. A. and Murray, B. C. (2005) Trading water for carbon with biological carbon sequestration. *Science*, 310, 1944–1947.

Long, A. (2009) Taking adaptation value seriously: designing REDD to protect biodiversity. *Carbon and Climate Law Review*, 3, 314–323.

Myers, N. and Kent, J. (2001) *Perverse Subsidies: How Tax Dollars Can Undercut the Environment and the Economy*. Island Press, Washington, DC.

Nelson, E., Mendoza, G., Regetz, J., Polasky, S., Tallis, H., Cameron, D. R., Chan, K. M. A., Daily, G. C., Goldstein, J., Kareiva, P. M., Lonsdorf, E., Naidoo, R., Ricketts, T. H. and Shaw, M. R. (2009) Modeling multiple ecosystem services, biodiversity conservation, commodity production, and tradeoffs at landscape scales. *Frontiers in Ecology and the Environment*, 7, 4–11.

OECD (2004) *Recommendation of the Council on the Use of Economic Instruments in Promoting the Conservation and Sustainable Use of Biodiversity*. OECD, Paris.

Panayotou, T. (1995) Economic instruments for environmental management and sustainable development. *Environmental Economics Series Paper no. 16*. United Nations Environment Programme Consultative Expert Group Meeting on the Use and Application of Economic Policy Instruments for Environmental Management and Sustainable Development, Nairobi.

Pearce, D. W. (2003) Environmentally harmful subsidies: barriers to sustainable development. *Environmentally Harmful Subsidies: Policy Issues and Challenges* (ed. OECD), pp. 9–30. OECD, Paris.

Pearce, D. W. and Warford, J. J. (1993) *World Without End: Economics, Environment, and Sustainable Development*. Oxford University Press.

Perrings, C., Dehnen-Schmutz, K., Touza, J. and Williamson, M. (2005) How to manage biological invasions under globalization. *Trends in Ecology and Evolution*, 20, 212–215.

Perrings, C., Jackson, L., Bawa, K., Brussaard, L., Brush, S., Gavin, T., Papa, R., Pascual, U. and De Ruiter, P. (2006) Biodiversity in agricultural landscapes: saving natural capital without losing interest. *Conservation Biology*, 20, 263–264.

Pigou, A. C. (1920) *The Economics of Welfare*. Macmillan, London.

Shackelford, S. J. (2008) The tragedy of the common heritage of mankind. *Stanford Environmental Law Journal*, 27, 102–157.

Stavins, R. N. (2003) Experience with market-based environmental policy instruments. *Handbook of Environmental Economics* (ed. K.-G. Mäler and J. R. Vincent), pp. 355–435. Elsevier, Amsterdam.

Sumaila, U. R., Khan, A. J., Dyck, A., Watson, R., Munro, G., Tydemers, P. and Pauly, D. (2010) A bottom-up re-estimation of global fisheries subsidies. *Journal of Bioeconomics*, 12, 201–225.

Tietenberg, T. (1990) Economic instruments for environmental regulation. *Oxford Review of Economic Policy*, 6, 17–33.

van Beers, C. and van den Bergh, J. C. J. M. (2009) Environmental harm of hidden subsidies: global warming and acidification. *AMBIO: A Journal of the Human Environment*, 38, 339–341.

Wells, M. P. and Brandon, K. (1992) *People and Parks: Linking Protected Areas with Local Communities*. World Bank, Washington, DC.

Wells, M. P., McShane, T. O., Dublin, H. T., O'Connor, S. and Redford, K. H. (2004) The future of integrated conservation and development projects: building on what works. *Getting Biodiversity Projects to Work: Towards more Effective Conservation and Development* (ed. T. O. Mcshane and M. P. Wells), pp. 397–422. Columbia University Press, New York.

Worm, B., Hilborn, R., Baum, J. K., Branch, T. A., Collie, J. S., Costello, C., Fogarty, M. J., Fulton, E. A., Hutchings, J. A., Jennings, S., Jensen, O. P., Lotze, H. K., Mace, P. A., McClanahan, T. R., Minto, C., Palumbi, S. R., Parma, A. M., Ricard, D., Watson, R. and Zeller, D. (2009) Rebuilding global fisheries. *Science*, 325, 578–585.

Index

For EU product safety concerns, contact us at Calle de José Abascal, 56–1°,
28003 Madrid, Spain or eugpsr@cambridge.org.

www.ingramcontent.com/pod-product-compliance
Ingram Content Group UK Ltd.
Pitfield, Milton Keynes, MK11 3LW, UK
UKHW012155180425
457623UK00007B/51